# POWER, MEMORY, ARCHITECTURE

## CONTESTED SITES ON INDIA'S DECCAN PLATEAU, 1300–1600

RICHARD M. EATON
PHILLIP B. WAGONER

OXFORD
UNIVERSITY PRESS

OXFORD
UNIVERSITY PRESS

Oxford University Press is a department of the University of Oxford.
It furthers the University's objective of excellence in research, scholarship,
and education by publishing worldwide. Oxford is a registered trademark of
Oxford University Press in the UK and in certain other countries

Published in India by
Oxford University Press
2/11 Ground Floor, Ansari Road, Daryaganj, New Delhi 110 002, India



First Edition published in 2014
Oxford India Paperbacks 2017



ISBN-13: 978-0-19-947769-2
ISBN-10: 0-19-947769-8

Typeset in 11/13.5 Adobe Garamond Pro
by Excellent Laser Typesetters, Pitampura, Delhi 110 034
Printed and bound in India at Repro India Ltd., Mumbai

To the memory of my uncle, ever an inspiration,
Philip R. Adams,
Director, Cincinnati Art Museum, 1945–1973

—RME

In fond memory of
A.K. Narain (1925–2013),
skilful teacher of the virtue of looking closely

—PBW

# Contents

## SECTION IV THE RAICHUR DOAB IN THE AGE OF GUNPOWDER

# Figures and Tables

## FIGURES

**TABLES**

# Note on Translation, Transliteration, and Abbreviations

To produce a readable text that is accessible to the general reader, we have avoided using untranslated words from other languages. However, where straightforward equivalents were lacking we have retained untranslated terms, marking them in italics, and explaining their meaning on first occurrence. To satisfy specialist readers, we have in certain cases added technical terms in parentheses, and have excerpted passages in the original languages from texts we have quoted, placing them in the notes so that other readers may conveniently ignore them.

Diacritical marks have not been used for names of persons and places, and only appear in technical terms, titles of literary works, and short phrases and passages quoted from the original language. Elsewhere, a simplified system of transliteration has been used. For Sanskrit, Telugu, and Kannada, vowel length (short or long) and consonant class (in the case of retroflexes and dentals) are not indicated, and *ṛ* is represented by *ri*, *c* by *ch*, *v* by *v* or *w* depending on context, and *ś* and *ṣ* alike by *sh*. For Arabic and Persian, we follow the transliteration system used by the *Encyclopedia of Islam*, with the following changes: the letter *d̲j̲īm* is rendered as *j*, the Persian letter *che* as *ch*, the letter *dhāl* as *z*, and the letter *s̲h̲īn* as *sh*.

Abbreviations have been used for frequently cited sources, most of which are epigraphical series and archaeological reports. After the full title, our system of citation is indicated and an example is provided for each source. Detailed bibliographic information is provided for the following in the bibliography:

*ARADH* — *(Annual Reports of the Archaeological Department of Hyderabad) Annual Reports of the Archaeological Department of His Exalted Highness the Nizam's Dominions*, 1914–41. Cited by year of coverage (not year of publication) and page number, e.g., *ARADH 1929–30*, 17.

*ARIE* — *Annual Reports on Indian Epigraphy*, 1905–1978. Cited by year of coverage (not year of publication) and inscription number, e.g., *ARIE 1958*, D125.

| | |
|---|---|
| *ARMAD* | *Annual Reports of the Mysore Archaeological Department*, c.1885–c.1941. Cited by year of coverage (not year of publication) and inscription number, e.g., *ARMAD 1929*, inscription no. 90. |
| *CITD* | *Corpus of Inscriptions in the Telangana Districts*. Parts 1–4 (1940–73). Cited by part and inscription number, e.g., *CITD* 2: no. 40. |
| *EC* | *Epigraphia Carnatica.* Vols 1–16 (1889–1955). Cited by volume number, Taluk, and inscription number, e.g., *EC* 12: Tumkur Taluk, no. 1. |
| *EI* | *Epigraphia Indica.* Vols 1–43 (1892–2012). Cited by volume and inscription numbers, e.g., *EI* 12:32. |
| *EIAPS* | *Epigraphia Indica, Arabic and Persian Supplement*, 1951/52–77. Cited by year of coverage (not year of publication), page number(s) and plate number, e.g., *EIAPS 1962*, 56–8, pl. XVI(a). |
| *EIM* | *Epigraphia Indo-Moslemica*, 1907/08–49/50. Cited by year of coverage (not year of publication), page number(s) and plate number, e.g., *EIM 1907–08*, 4–5, pl. IV(a). |
| *EITA* | *Encyclopaedia of Indian Temple Architecture.* Cited by volume, part, and page/plate/or figure numbers. |
| *IAP—Warangal* | *Inscriptions of Andhra Pradesh—Warangal District.* 1974. Cited by inscription number, e.g., *IAP—Warangal*, no. 111. |
| *NDI* | *(Nellore District Inscriptions.) A Collection of the Copper-Plate and Stone Inscriptions in the Nellore District.* Vols 1–3 (1905). Cited by medium and inscription numbers, e.g., *NDI* 1: no. 14. |
| *SII* | *South Indian Inscriptions.* Vols 1–27 (1890–2001). Cited by volume and inscription numbers, e.g., *SII* 4: no. 260. |
| *TTDI* | *Tirumala Tirupati Devasthanam Inscriptions.* Vols 1–7 (1930). Cited by volume and inscription numbers, e.g., *TTDI* 6: no. 1. |

# Acknowledgements

Many institutions, colleagues, and friends supported the various phases of our work on this book, for which we are deeply grateful. First, we wish to thank the Getty Foundation (Los Angeles) for generously awarding us a Collaborative Research Grant, which facilitated two seasons of field research for this study, in 2005 and 2006. The Archaeological Survey of India (New Delhi) granted us permission to carry out the fieldwork and to photograph monuments under its protection, while the Department of Archaeology and Museums of the state of Karnataka graciously provided us with formal affiliation. We are especially grateful for the support of the Department's Director, K.R. Ramakrishna, and its Deputy Director, H.M. Siddanagoudar. For help with obtaining research clearance and affiliation, we thank Ralph Nicholas, Rick Asher, Pradeep Mehendiratta, and Purnima Mehta of the American Institute of Indian Studies.

In the course of our fieldwork, we were joined at several points by colleagues who made valued contributions to the project. John Friedrich and John Henry Rice assisted us with GPS survey, photographic documentation, and interpretation of features at Raichur, Yadgir, and Mudgal. At Kalyana, Gunjan Srivastava and Varalakshmi Bogale directed a team of volunteer architects and architecture students who helped prepare measured drawings of the Raj Mahal palace and the gateway complex: B. Sarath Chandra, Madhusudan Sahukar, Abhishek Singh Chauhan, Surya Phani Raj, K. Raghunath Reddy, Shailaja R., Shruti Bajaj, Vedika Mathur, and Vinay Shah. Without the good sense and initiative of our driver, Abid, we could not have visited all forty-eight sites included in our field explorations.

While in India, we received advice, assistance, and hospitality from many individuals, including Amit Akkihal, S.K. Aruni, the late Balasubramanya, V.K. and Shanti Bawa, K. Muhammad Ali Hashmi, Mahbub Jilani, Muhammad Kaleem, Baba Khan, Ghulam Ahmad Khan, Amar Kumar, the late T.M. Manjunathayya, Sheikh Muhammad, Ramayya and Lakshmi Mulukutla, S.S. Nayak, Aloka Parasher-Sen, Syed Ali Pasha, S.F. Patil, Fiyaz and Frauke Qadar, M. Panduranga Rao, Virabhadra Rao, Sankarappa, Habib Siddiqi, Samad Siddiqi, Kashi Visvanatha, Iftakar Wazir, and Mohammed Yousuf.

After returning from the field, we received helpful suggestions—and in some cases comments on drafts—from a host of colleagues, including Mark Brand, Yigal Bronner, Allison Busch,

Javier Castro-Ibaseta, Whitney Cox, Emma Flatt, Barry Flood, John Fritz, Sumit Guha, Deborah Hutton, Abdul Gani Imaratwale, Kumud Kanitkar, Katherine Kasdorf, Elizabeth Lambourn, Barry Lewis, George Michell, Sreenivas Paruchuri, Helen Philon, John Henry Rice, Klaus Rotzer, Marika Sardar, David Shulman, Robert Simpkins, Ajay Sinha, Robert D. Smith, Pushkar Sohoni, Cynthia Talbot, Laura Weinstein, and Mark Wyers. We also thank those who commented on oral presentations of our work in progress at the Centre for Deccan Studies (Hyderabad), Columbia University (New York), Yale University (New Haven), the British Association for South Asian Studies (London), the University of Pennsylvania (Philadelphia), and the Metropolitan Museum of Art (New York).

We thank Carl Ernst for providing us with an unpublished text of Rafi` al-Din Shirazi's *Tazkirat al-mulūk*, Lois Kain for preparing four of the maps in Chapter 1 and the two line drawings in Chapter 7, Ryu Hirahata for preparing the final architectural drawings in AutoCAD, and Elijah Huge for helping us solve some AutoCAD problems. We are also grateful to the following institutions and individuals for providing us with photographs and the permission to reproduce them: the American Institute of Indian Studies photo archive, the American Committee for Southern Asian Art, the British Library, Yigal Bronner, Katherine Kasdorf, John Henry Rice, and Uday Anand Shastry of the Archaeological Survey of India (Bijapur).

We record a special note of thanks to the University of Arizona (Tucson) and to Wesleyan University (Middletown) for their financial support of this project, and to the following colleagues at Wesleyan University, who cheerfully satisfied our seemingly endless requests for technical support and for more books, interlibrary loans, and images: Shawn Hill at Information Technology Services, Susanne Javorski and Mardi Hanson d'Alessandro at the Art Library, Kate Wolfe, Kathy Stefanowicz, and Lisa Pinette at the Interlibrary Loan office of Olin Library, and Susan Passman and Nara Giannella at the Visual Resource Center. Finally, we are grateful to the entire editorial team at Oxford University Press, India, with whom it has been a pleasure to work on this project.

# Introduction

This book examines the histories of three highly contested cities of the Deccan Plateau—Kalyana, Raichur, and Warangal—during the period 1300 to 1600, with special emphasis on the tumultuous sixteenth century. While focussing on these three cities, which provide the book's primary database, we bring several broad aims to the study, each directed at a different level of historical enquiry.

First, we seek a better understanding of how regional politics operated at the ground level. Most previous research on the Deccan has focussed on primary urban centres, meaning the capitals of the various Deccan states, for example, Bidar, Vijayanagara, Bijapur, Ahmadnagar, or Golconda. But this focus has meant ignoring the region's smaller but far more numerous secondary urban centres.[1] The plateau is covered with such sites, many of which lie on the plains. Many more are perched on hill tops, ringed by formidable defensive outworks that take advantage of the plateau's distinctively rocky terrain (see Figure 7.22). Ranging from less than a kilometre to more than 5 kilometres in circumference,[2] the walls of these forts consist of stone masonry of different fabrics and sizes, betraying distinct building traditions and different phases of construction over the centuries.[3] Most forts have several circuits of walls pierced by gateways with powerful bastions, crenellated parapets, guard houses, and inner courtyards. Gazing up at them from the plateau's floor, one marvels at the enormous investment of resources and the staggering number of man-hours required to build these imposing structures.

Throughout the period 1300–1600 such fortified secondary centres provided the key economic, social, and political links between the agricultural villages constituting their respective hinterlands and the courtly élites in the capital cities to which they were subordinate. They also mediated the culture of metropolitan courts to that of the agrarian countryside, and vice versa. Their strategic importance derived mainly from their ability to control the agrarian resources of their immediate hinterlands, since troops garrisoned at such sites could enforce the collection of state-imposed (or self-imposed) revenues in the form of grain and other foodstuffs. Above all, secondary centres converted the productive surplus of the land into political and military power, both for the city's governor and for the crown. Hence they were invariably well fortified, for their capture meant control of the resources of their surrounding districts. This also explains their pivotal role in state-formation, a fact well understood by contemporaries. For example, in narrating how the founder of the Sultanate of Bijapur rose to power in the 1490s, the chronicler Muhammad Qasim Firishta (fl. 1609) recorded that Yusuf `Adil Khan had 'wrested many forts from the governors of [the Bahmani sultan] Mahmud Shah, and subdued all the country from the river Bhima to Bijapur, the inhabitants of which territory submitted to his authority'.[4] In a very real sense, the political history of the Deccan revolved around struggles by primary centres for control of secondary centres.

Our first aim, then, is to examine such struggles, especially those over centres that were located on the frontiers between states and were, as a result, frequently contested. From the scores of such centres that could have been chosen for the purpose of this study, we focus on three, each of which straddled a contested frontier of a specific sort.[5] Kalyana was located on a frontier between three rival sultanates; moreover, as the one-time capital of the prestigious Chalukya empire, it was a much sought-after prize. Raichur was perennially contested between Vijayanagara and the Bahmani Sultanate (and later, its `Adil Shahi successor) on account of its rich agricultural hinterland. And Warangal lay on an ecological frontier that separated the eastern edge of the Deccan's dry, inland plateau from the wetter and more fertile coastal plain.

Second, a study of struggles over secondary centres illuminates the interrelations between this book's three principal themes—power, memory, and architecture. In tracking the projection of political power across the plateau, we of course follow military affairs, which are extensively covered in contemporary chronicles. But we also consider the kinds of power that can institutionalize or erase collective memory. We are especially interested in how power and memory combined to produce the Deccan's built landscape, as seen above all in monumental architecture. In recent years, scholars have sought to understand the relations between identity, memory, and landscape not just for peoples living in the present, but for those living in the past itself. Introducing a collection of archaeological and art historical essays tellingly entitled *Negotiating the Past in the Past*, Norman Yoffee notes that built landscapes can form the material of 'memory communities', and that people make choices about which part of their remembered past to accommodate and which to reject.[6] For us, then, the pertinent question is: in their struggles for control of secondary centres, how and why did peoples of the Deccan's past promote certain elements of their remembered past, while forgetting others? Inasmuch as artefacts have lives of their own after their creation, especially as sites of memory,[7] how can the study of the material evidence of the past, notably monumental architecture, shed light on this question?

Third, this book aims to rethink one of the basic categories by which South Asian history is conventionally studied, namely, the so-called Hindu–Muslim encounter. Since the Deccan was conquered by Muslims from north India in the period of our study, this book offers a case study of a part of the world often seen in terms of a binary, religiously defined 'clash of civilizations'.[8] Rather than viewing the Deccan's history in such narrowly religious terms, we ask whether it might more properly be framed in broadly literary–cultural terms. Specifically, we analyse this history in terms of an encounter between civilizations defined by Sanskrit or Persian literary traditions. Whereas north India from the eleventh century was the earliest arena of such an encounter, by the early fourteenth century the frontier of that arena had shifted south to the Deccan, following the conquest of the plateau by armies of the Delhi Sultanate (1206–1526).[9] Our study therefore seeks to understand how an initially military encounter was transformed over the course of the fourteenth, fifteenth, and sixteenth centuries, ultimately resolving in the mutual interpenetration of two civilizational traditions. We believe this to be a more nuanced, and more accurate, approach to India's pre-modern history than the conventional framework of an enduring and generally hostile confrontation between two allegedly homogeneous and unchanging religious communities. In this sense, the book is a case study of frontier dynamics at a macro-level, comparable in some respects with the Arab–Latinate encounter in the Mediterranean theatre between the seventh and fourteenth centuries.

Finally, at the level of methodology, the study seeks to bridge a wide chasm that, reinforced by decades of disciplinary apartheid, has long divided history from art history and archaeology. On most university campuses, practitioners of these disciplines are nested in different departments—often, different colleges—thereby inhibiting regular scholarly contact between them. In an attempt to overcome this divide, the authors of the present study—one trained in history, the other in art history and archaeology—not only combed through contemporary chronicles and literary, epigraphic, and numismatic evidence, but also spent two field seasons (in 2005 and 2006) in the Deccan directly examining material evidence.[10] The latter included, in particular, the rich architectural record found in some thirty-one secondary centres, most of them remote hill forts, scattered across the plateau. In addition to the types of structures that architectural historians traditionally study, for example, mosques, temples, tombs, and palaces, we also scrutinized less-studied features such as moats, fortifications, armouries, city gates, tanks, stepwells, roads, and granaries. And, while investigating such features from the standpoint of architectural history, that is, determining an object's patrons and builders, its intended use, the influences on its design and style, the conditions of its production, and so on, we also studied them from the standpoint of the discipline of buildings archaeology. That is, we wanted to learn what had happened to any given object *after* the moment of its initial creation, that is, how its fabric had changed over time, the different ways its purpose was re-conceived, changes in the different communities that used it, and so on. In short, being interested in how the Deccan's society and politics evolved and changed between the fourteenth and sixteenth centuries, we approached monuments and other material evidence as dynamic texts that could, after their creation, tell their own stories about how they related to different communities over time.

* * *

The book opens with two chapters that serve as background for the subsequent six, each of which focusses, though from a different angle, on the turbulent sixteenth century. Since the memory of earlier sovereign domains exerted such a profound influence on the Deccan's subsequent politics and architecture, Chapter 1 looks back at those earlier domains. One of them was the illustrious Chalukya empire, which flourished between the tenth and twelfth centuries, its capital at Kalyana in the middle of the plateau. The other was one of that empire's several successor states, the Kakatiya dynasty of Warangal, which flourished in the twelfth–fourteenth centuries. This chapter also traces and compares two civilizational traditions—the so-called Sanskrit cosmopolis and the Persian cosmopolis—that came to dominate political and cultural activities in the Deccan in the period of our study. Structured around Sanskrit and Persian literary traditions respectively, each cosmopolis was initially articulated by one of the two great empires that successively dominated the plateau between the tenth and fourteenth centuries, the aforesaid Chalukyas and the Delhi Sultanate. How the ideals of the two cosmopolises displaced, overlapped, or merged with each other in subsequent centuries is investigated in later chapters.

The violent conquest of the Deccan by armies of the Delhi Sultanate in the early fourteenth century forms the backdrop for Chapter 2. Here we investigate the complex interplay between power and architecture, tracing how officers of the Delhi Sultanate and its successor state in the region, the Bahmani Sultanate (1347–1510), responded to the Deccan's built landscape during and soon after the conquest. We focus specifically on how Muslim officials dealt with Hindu temples, which were the most durable, the most visually prominent, and the most culturally charged features of that landscape. Relying mainly on the architectural and epigraphic record, the chapter moves beyond crude stereotypes of a clash between Hindus and Muslims and attempts to identify—and also to explain—the wide range of ways that, at a critical point in the Deccan's cultural history, conquerors, administrators, and even local chieftains interacted with these key institutions.

Coming to the sixteenth century, Chapters 3 and 4 both analyse how and why rulers in two of the Deccan's primary centres—Vijayanagara in Chapter 3 and Bijapur in Chapter 4—asserted a direct association with the long-defunct Chalukya empire, which had reigned over the entire plateau from its capital at Kalyana more than four centuries earlier. Although the landscape had long been covered with that empire's physical remains—temples, water tanks, and sculptures in whole or in fragments—it was not until the sixteenth century that memories of the Chalukyas were publicly, even assertively, invoked. Rulers in either Vijayanagara or Bijapur, whether Hindu or Muslim, might incorporate ancient Chalukya temples into their palace complexes, display Chalukya columns or other structures in prominent sites in the heart of their capitals, claim direct descent from Chalukya emperors, or, especially, struggle for control of the Chalukyas' former capital of Kalyana.

In Chapters 5 and 6 the focus shifts from the central to the eastern plateau, and to Warangal, the former capital of one of the major Chalukya successor states, the Kakatiya kingdom (1163–1323). Chapter 5 follows the stormy career of Shitab Khan, a Telugu chieftain who, banished from service in the court of the Bahmani Sultanate in the mid-1400s, surfaced four decades later as an upstart 'king' on the eastern periphery of a declining Bahmani state. After capturing Warangal, a secondary centre far from any of the Deccan's primary centres, this vivid figure managed to carve out a new state, in part by strategically manipulating surviving material culture associated with the Kakatiya dynasty, still alive in collective memory several centuries after its collapse. The legacy of the Kakatiya state is further explored in Chapter 6, which argues that the design and layout of Hyderabad, founded by Sultan Muhammad Quli Qutb Shah of Golconda in 1591 and today one of India's premier cities, had been inspired by the layout of the former Kakatiya capital. The chapter seeks to explain that particular convergence of power, memory, and architecture.

The book's final chapters focus on Raichur, a town occupying the rich tract of land that separated the state of Vijayanagara to the south from the Bahmani Sultanate and its successor states to the north. These chapters investigate two dimensions of the intense and protracted rivalry between these states over the control of Raichur. Chapter 7 addresses the advent of gunpowder technology in the Deccan generally, and in Raichur in particular, since that city happened to witness the earliest recorded deployment of firearms anywhere in India's interior. Indeed, the surprising outcome of the Battle of Raichur (1520) led to not only revolutionary changes in cannon technology in the Deccan, but also innovations in regional military architecture, and indirectly to major shifts in the Deccan's geopolitics that culminated in the destruction of the great metropolis of Vijayanagara in 1565. The final chapter examines another dimension of the rivalry over control of Raichur—the use of city gateways to proclaim possession of the city. Occupying exceptionally prominent public spaces, such gates were understood as iconic tokens of the city, its public face, so to speak. As Raichur changed hands, victors would subject its entrance ways to extensive 'face-lift' operations—either remodelling earlier gates or building new ones—illustrating what Oleg Grabar called 'the symbolic appropriation of the land'.[11]

This book is written with several audiences in mind. For readers who perceive pre-modern South Asia as the story of the great dynasties of north India—those of the Delhi Sultanate or the Mughals—this study offers a glimpse of most of the lower half of the subcontinent, which, for the period 1300–1600, has been relatively neglected in scholarly literature. For those who see South Asia in this period as characterized by Hindu–Muslim issues, or even consumed by communal strife, this book offers an alternative analytical approach. In place of competing religions, we see a complex and often fruitful encounter between two literary–cultural systems, the Sanskrit and the Persian, each of which encompassed and transcended religious systems. For conventional historians, accustomed as they are to mining libraries, archives, or record rooms, this book sounds a clarion call to get out of their easy chairs and engage in true 'fieldwork', that is, to examine first-hand the rich body of material evidence left by past societies. And for art historians who might understand visual data as inhabiting a nearly autonomous realm of human experience, this book urges a more complete integration of the visual with the many other kinds of data available for study.

## NOTES

1. There are a handful of notable exceptions, including K. Paddayya's preliminary study of the important Shorapur Doab micro-region, and S.K. Aruni's study of the site of Sagar. See K. Paddayya, 'Towards the Archaeology of the Medieval Shorapur Doab, Deccan', *Islamic Culture* 64, nos 2–3 (1990), 75–112; and S.K. Aruni, 'Sagar: Provincial Headquarters of the Islamic Deccan', *Bulletin of the Deccan College* 56–57 (1996–97), 220–3.

2. The plains forts tend to be much smaller while the hill forts are generally larger. Considering the perimeter measurements in kilometres and the total enclosed area in hectares, the numbers for several representative examples are as follows: Udgir, 0.72/2.9; Ausa, 0.81/2.82; Kandhar 0.85/3.13; Parenda, 0.98/3.07; Kalyana, 0.99/5.92; Elgandal, 1.62/13.69; Balkonda, 1.62/13.05; Kaulas, 2.53/19.5; Mudgal, 3.44/62.74; Raichur, 4.29/99.87; Malliabad, 4.69/91.82; Naldurg, 5.56/41.63; Warangal, 8.36/471.21.

3. The earliest, dating from the thirteenth century, consist of enormous blocks of dressed granite, cut to fit perfectly together without the aid of mortar, while those of a later date are made of smaller, more irregular blocks of varying sizes, either dry or cemented with mortar.

4. John Briggs, trans., *History of the Rise of Mohamadan Power in India* (4 vols, London, 1829; repr. 4 vols, Calcutta: Editions Indian, 1966), 3:4–5. Spellings modernized.

5. Although these three sites were secondary centres during the period of this study, two of them—Kalyana and Warangal—had been primary centres prior to the fourteenth century.

6. Norman Yoffee, ed., *Negotiating the Past in the Past: Identity, Memory, and Landscape in Archaeological Research* (Tucson: University of Arizona Press, 2007), 3.

7. Ibid., 6.

8. Historiographically, the Hindu–Muslim encounter has roots deep in India's colonial and pre-colonial history. Its more recent trajectory may be understood as South Asia's manifestation of the controversial 'clash of civilizations' idea that Samuel Huntington popularized in the late 1990s. See Samuel P. Huntington, *The Clash of Civilizations and the Remaking of World Order* (New York: Simon & Schuster, 1996).

9. See the important work of Finbarr B. Flood, *Objects of Translation: Material Culture and Medieval 'Hindu–Muslim' Encounter* (Princeton: Princeton University Press, 2009), which addresses earlier phases of this encounter in northern India.

10. For an expanded discussion of our research methods, see 'Appendix 1: Notes on Method'.

11. Oleg Grabar, *The Formation of Islamic Art*, revised and enlarged edition (New Haven: Yale University Press, 1987), chapter 3, 'The Symbolic Appropriation of the Land'.

# SECTION ONE

# Orientations

CHAPTER 1

# Chalukya Emperors, Delhi Sultans, 1000–1350

Hail! While the victorious reign of His Majesty the fortunate [Vikramaditya VI], asylum of the whole world, favorite of Fortune and the Earth, paramount Emperor, Supreme Lord, Supreme Master, decoration of Satyasraya's race, ornament of the Chalukyas, is proceeding in its course of increasing success to last as long as the moon, sun, and stars, while He is reigning in His capital of Kalyana in the enjoyment of pleasant conversation … in the second year of the fortunate Chalukya-Vikrama-varsha [Vikrama Era]….

—Inscription of Vikramaditya VI, 1077[1]

The Sultan of the Sultans, the ruler of the surface of the earth, Shadow of Allah in the worlds, Second Alexander, the Dhu'l-Qarnain [Alexander the Great] of the Age, Qutb al-Dunya wa'l-Din Mubarak Shah, the Sultan, son of the Sultan, [joint-heir to the Caliph], may Allah perpetuate his kingdom and sovereignty and elevate his affairs and dignity, may he always be firmly fixed for limitless space of time in the foundation of kingship and administration of the affairs of sovereignty, and may the Friends of the State [i.e., officials] be victorious and the enemies of the court vanquished! …

—Inscription of Sultan Qutb al-Din Mubarak Shah Khalaji, 1318[2]

To contextualize our study of the fourteenth-through-sixteenth century Deccan, this chapter traces two prior developments, each of which deeply influenced the region's subsequent history. The first was the appearance of a major Indic polity, the Chalukya empire, which at its height between the late tenth and mid-twelfth centuries sprawled over nearly the entire plateau before fragmenting into several successor states. Although claiming ultimate origins in north India, the rulers of this dynasty were native Deccanis, their cultural homeland located in the Kannada-speaking, southwestern plateau between the Tungabhadra and Krishna Rivers. Despite their provincial origins, the Chalukyas established a model of not just aesthetic refinement and cosmopolitanism, but also universal, pan-Indian political dominion that long outlasted their several centuries of rule.

The second great development we explore is the conquest of the plateau by rulers of the Delhi Sultanate in the early fourteenth century. This constituted the first invasions of the plateau from north India in nearly two millennia.

Though brief, Delhi's rule in the Deccan was momentous. Significantly, it brought to the peninsula a Persianate vision of society, polity, and cosmic/moral order just as comprehensive and just as compelling as the Sanskrit-based vision of the Chalukyas. By a coincidence of some note, that Persianate vision had crystallized in Iran and Central Asia at the same time—between the late tenth and late twelfth centuries—that the Chalukya rulers and intellectuals formulated the ideals that underlay their Deccan empire. And, as with the Chalukyas, the ideals that informed the Delhi Sultanate's dominion in the Deccan persisted long after its own demise, and that of its political successors. We need, then, to pay close attention to what those respective visions were, and how they were articulated.

## THE HEIGHT OF CHALUKYA PRESTIGE: VIKRAMADITYA VI, 1076–1126

The dynasty that was established in 973 and for the next two centuries dominated the Deccan from its capital in Kalyana is usually called the Kalyana Chalukyas, distinguishing it from its distant forebears, the Badami Chalukyas (r. 543–753), whose capital had been Badami in the southwestern Deccan (Figure 1.1).[3] Its founder, Taila II, had been a feudatory chieftain of the Rashtrakutas, the dynasty that overthrew the Badami Chalukyas in the mid-eighth century. But in establishing his new dynasty, Taila II did not see himself as restoring the old Badami Chalukya line. Rather, his descendants appear to have 'discovered' that connection only in 1008, when they began deliberately grafting their own lineage on to the recorded genealogy of their long lost Badami 'ancestors'. Because the latter had claimed that their own ancestors had migrated to the Deccan from north India's sacred city of Ayodhya, the font of India's Rāmāyaṇa epic, the Kalyana Chalukyas could, by claiming descent from the Badami house, lay claim to the same illustrious origins.[4]

By the opening of the eleventh century, then, the dynasty had embarked on an ambitious ideological programme conferring on it both genealogical depth and geo-mythic reach. Initially, though, the extent of its effective authority hardly matched its grandiose claims. Only with the accession of the fifth dynast, Jayasimha II (r. 1015–43), and especially his son and successor, Someshvara I (r. 1043–68), did the Kalyana Chalukyas achieve imperial stature. To the north, both monarchs defeated armies of the Paramara rulers of Malwa, thereby extending their frontier to the Narmada River, the historic frontier between north India and the Deccan. And to the west, Jayasimha II consolidated Chalukya control over the rich coastal regions abutting the Arabian Sea. To the east, Someshvara I brought chieftains of the upland Telangana region of Andhra under his control. To the south and southeast, however, the Chalukyas confronted their biggest obstacle and rival for the status of peninsular superpower—the Cholas of the Tamil country. Someshvara I fought no fewer than five major battles against his Chola counterparts of the Kaveri delta, all of them destructive, and most of them over Vengi, the rich coastal strip between the Godavari and Krishna deltas. But in 1068 Someshvara I's 25-year-long career came to a tragic end. After suffering for several years from an incurable disease, he waded into the Tungabhadra River at the temple site of Kuruvatti and drowned himself.

The stage was now set for a dramatic contest for the Chalukya throne between the king's three sons. Thematically, the story of the fraternal struggle for the throne, and of the second son's challenge to the principle of primogeniture, recalls the work of Shakespeare. One thinks of Claudius, who murdered his

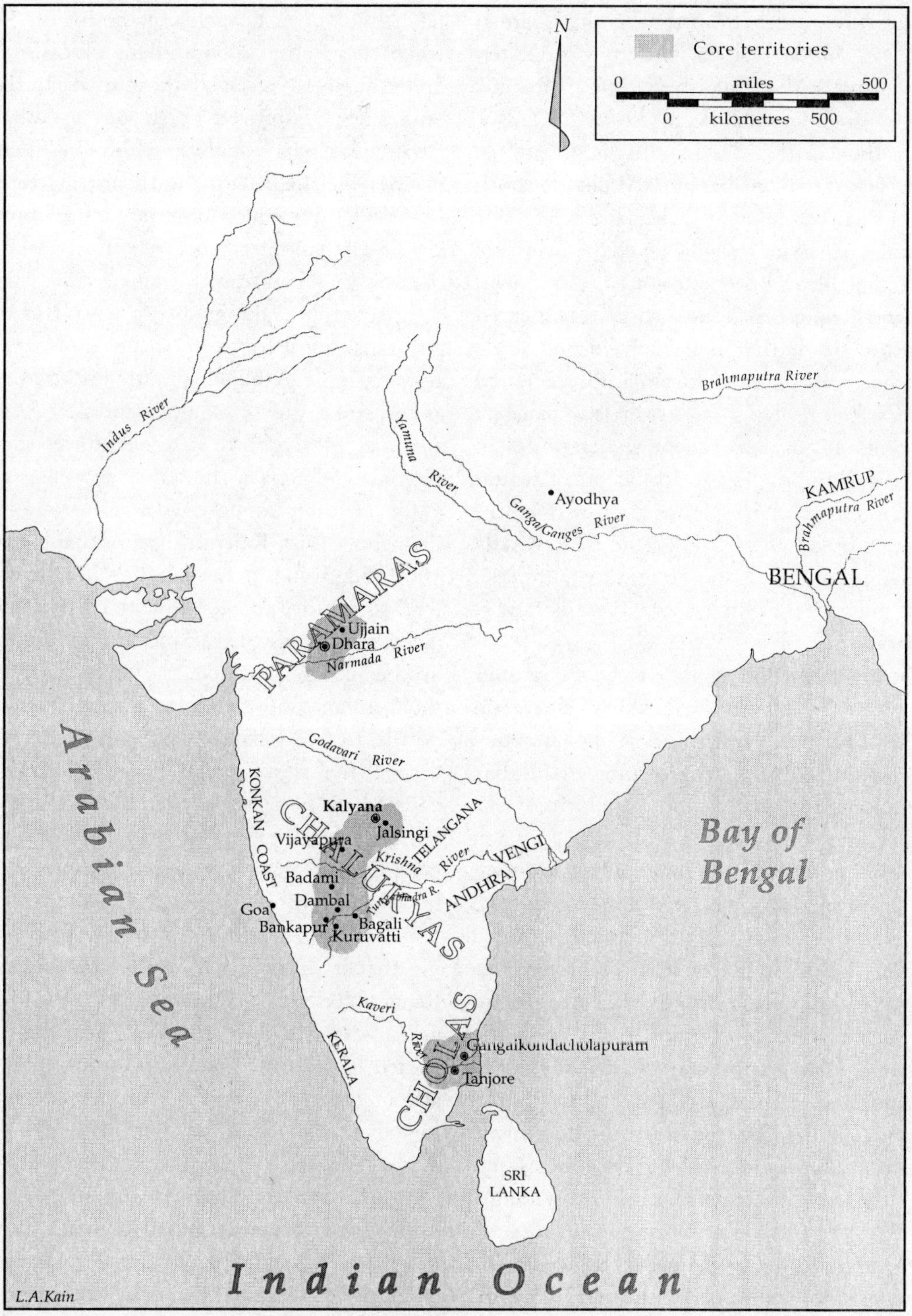


**Figure 1.1** India in the time of the Chalukya empire.

(presumably) older brother for the Danish throne in *Hamlet*; or Richard of Gloucester, who usurped the English throne from his older brother Edward IV in *Richard III*. But unlike the corrupt and conniving Claudius, or the deformed and paranoid Richard—both of them flawed characters who paid with their lives for their bloody challenge to the principle of primogeniture—Someshvara I's second son, Vikramaditya, usurped the throne and emerged unscathed. More than that, he went on to rule over the entire Deccan for an unprecedented 50 years before dying peacefully, so far as we know, in 1126. Subsequent generations, in particular those in the sixteenth century, would recall his long and prosperous reign with admiration and view the Chalukya house generally as having embodied the epitome of imperial glory and moral righteousness. Here is how it happened.

On 11 April 1068, less than two weeks after Someshvara I's suicide, the late king's eldest son and heir-apparent, Someshvara II, was crowned emperor in Kalyana, conforming to India's time-honoured principle of royal primogeniture.[5] Things began auspiciously enough when the newly crowned emperor repulsed an invasion by the Cholas, who had apparently tried to exploit the new regime's vulnerability. 'With the accession of Someshvara II,' records a contemporary inscription, 'victory was brought to *dharma*, religious associations to the good, the earth was made happy, and the *krita* [golden] age appeared to have dawned.'[6] But it soon became clear that the true threat to Someshvara II's young reign came not from the Cholas, but from the new monarch's ambitious younger brother, Vikramaditya. During their father's reign, the latter had already seen considerable military action and met with success on all frontiers of the realm. He had been especially active in the final years of their ailing father's reign, and in fact was campaigning in Vengi when their father died and his older brother, Someshvara II, received the crown. In 1070, Someshvara II moved north and invaded the Paramara king of Malwa, whom his younger brother had helped to the throne. This move was evidently aimed at removing a potential ally of his younger brother, whose ambitions the new king had reason to suspect.[7]

Meanwhile Vikramaditya, who had been posted far to the south along the Chola frontier, systematically gathered support for an attempt at usurping the Chalukya throne, forming alliances with subordinate feudatories such as Hoysala and Yadava chieftains, as well as those of Goa. Most treasonous were his intrigues with the Chola king Rajendra who by the end of 1069 had given him his daughter in marriage as well as territory to rule. But in 1071 Rajendra died and Vikramaditya failed to get his Tamil brother-in-law installed as successor. Instead, there emerged on the Chola throne a new king hostile to the Chalukya prince. Nonetheless, during the next several years Vikramaditya enlisted so many supporters to his cause that Someshvara II felt compelled to ally himself with the new Chola monarch, simply because he was his brother's enemy.[8] Now accusing Someshvara II with treason—notwithstanding that he himself had earlier intrigued with Rajendra Chola!—Vikramaditya cast himself as the savior of the Chalukya house and, supported by a formidable coalition of allies that also included their younger brother Jayasimha, forced a military showdown with the king. When the clash finally came, in late 1076, the outcome left Someshvara II defeated, imprisoned, and never heard from again, while the victorious younger brother was crowned emperor as Vikramaditya VI.[9] Six years later the new king's younger brother Jayasimha—the third son of Someshvara I—seeing how easily the principle of primogeniture could be overturned, intrigued with the Cholas in a bid to seize power for himself. But he, too, was defeated and imprisoned.

In view of his violent usurpation of power and his systematic elimination of his brothers, Vikramaditya's career path did indeed resemble that of Shakespeare's Richard III. But the new king possessed a literary asset nearly as formidable as the Bard himself. The job of rescuing Vikramaditya VI from public censure, or mere disapproval, fell to the emperor's brilliant court-poet, Bilhana, who composed his *Vikramāṅkadeva Caritam* in the 1080s, shortly after Jayasimha's failed rebellion.[10] The arguments that Bilhana advanced in defending his patron's bloody actions, astutely analysed by Yigal Bronner, were both masterly and audacious, that is, that Vikramaditya's succession had been decreed by destiny; that Vikramaditya had graciously acquiesced to his older brother's succession even though he himself had been favoured by their father; that the god Shiva had appeared in a dream ordering him to redeem the kingdom from his older brother's corrupt behaviour, and so forth.[11] This was more than a defence lawyer's brief; Bilhana shamelessly promoted his patron to the status of a mighty sovereign possessed of awesome power and a moral right to universal dominion. Thus the several military operations that Vikramaditya had undertaken while still a prince were, in this poet's skilled hands, transformed into a grand *digvijaya*, a 'conquest of the quarters', which in classical Indian thought properly preceded and legitimized the reign of a universal sovereign. According to Bilhana, the prince's conquests had included the shores of the Arabian Sea to the west, Malwa to the north, Vengi, Bengal, and even Kamrup in the east, and Kerala, the Chola country, and Sri Lanka to the south.[12]

The project of situating both Vikramaditya VI and his imperial capital at the centre of the broader pan-Indian cosmos was carried further by another luminary in the emperor's literary atelier—the famous jurist Vijnaneshvara, who wrote:

> There is not, was not, nor will ever be
> a city on this earth like Kalyana;
> Nor has there been seen, nor even heard of,
> a king to compare with Vikramaditya.
> And none can compare to the wise Vijnaneshvara:
> may these three remain for all time, like the celestial wishing-vine.[13]

One may excuse the arrogant note heard in the last line, in view of the enormous influence that this jurist exerted on subsequent generations, even down to modern times. Written as a commentary on a Hindu law code (*smṛti*) attributed to the sage Yajnavalkya, Vijnaveshvara's famous *Mitākṣarā* sought to provide 'a totalizing explanation of moral and legal knowledge', and to do so by 'citing masses of other works to amplify or modify Yajnavalkya's teachings'.[14] After analysing the sources of legal authority (Vedas, Purāṇas, Dharma-śāstras), the work offers a complete codification of Hindu law, giving detailed commentaries on ritual performances for the twice-born castes (brahman, kshatriya, vaisya), inter-caste relations, rites of passage, proscribed and prescribed duties, diet, purification procedures, penances, punishments for infractions, and so forth.[15]

Noting that Vijnaneshvara and Bilhana were both writing at Vikramaditya VI's court in Kalyana, possibly at the same time, Whitney Cox has drawn attention to the striking congruity between the creation of a self-aware body of codified treatises on dharma by the jurist, and the use of literary Sanskrit for purposes of political expression, as represented by the poet.[16] 'The creation of both *dharmaśāstra* and courtly poetry,' he writes,

> can thus be seen to be centrally concerned with the ideology of power in medieval India. The opinions of learned jurists and the imaginations of skilled poets both explored the moral underpinnings of power, especially that of kings, and in the process provided elaborate and compelling defences for why a certain family or a certain segment of the population had the ineluctable right to hold sway over others.[17]

Squarely at the centre of both the poet's biography and the jurist's codified law stood the emperor himself. For Bilhana, Vikramaditya VI was the conquering king (*cakravartin*) whose 'conquest of the quarters' had consolidated a righteous realm founded on peace and justice; for Vijnaneshvara, the emperor was the necessary agent without whom dharma, in the sense of cosmic and social order, could not be enforced.

The third member of the trio bolstering Vikramaditya VI's stature as an imperial and cosmic lynchpin was the king's own son and successor, Someshvara III (r. 1127–39), who contributed to his father's legend by composing a biography (now incomplete) of his own.[18] Attributed to the same royal author is a very different sort of text, the *Mānasollāsa*,[19] which was composed in 1131 in a mixed genre—part encyclopaedia, and part 'Mirror for Princes'.[20] It is a noteworthy work on both counts. As an encyclopaedia, the text attempts to catalogue, enumerate, and situate geographically all significant phenomena in the Chalukya world.[21] Resembling works in the contemporary Persian world's 'Mirror for Princes' genre, the *Mānasollāsa* offers concrete advice on how the prince should gain and hold a kingdom, including specific recommendations on matters such as military engineering and tactics, as well as the art of politics.

Taken together, Bilhana, Vijnaneshvara, and Someshvara III formulated the cognitive categories—historical/biographical, legal/cosmic, and encyclopaedic/princely practical—by which the Chalukyas theorized, and hence controlled, their lived world. It is perhaps for such reasons that the Chalukya era as a whole, and Vikramaditya VI's reign in particular, was viewed even in its own day as having constituted a fundamental break with the past. Indeed, the emperor himself perceived and articulated such a break immediately upon being crowned in late 1076. Just as French revolutionaries abandoned the Christian calendar and named 1792 Year One of a new era, so too did Vikramaditya VI abandon India's traditional Shaka Era, established in AD 78, and re-started time with the 'Chalukya-Vikrama Era' (see epigraph to this chapter), which commenced with his own accession.[22] In fact, given that he did this in year 999 of the conventional Shaka Era, one wonders whether the new king might have viewed his reign as heralding a new millennial age, as the Mughal emperor Akbar would later do in the year AH 1000 (AD 1591).

Notably, all three of the defining texts just cited—Bilhana's *Vikramāṅkadeva Carita*, Vijnaneshvara's *Mitākṣarā*, and the *Mānasollāsa*, attributed to Someshvara III—were composed in Sanskrit, the timeless, placeless 'language of the gods'. So, too, were all eight copper-plate donative charters known to have been issued by Chalukya sovereigns between 1009 and 1123. Significantly, the form of Nagari script that the imperial chancellery used in these Sanskrit plates would become the direct ancestor of the pan-Indian Devanagiri script of modern times—a development suggesting the extent to which subsequent Indian polities perceived the Chalukyas as embodying a template for pan-Indian imperial rule.[23]

On the other hand, the several hundred stone inscriptions found throughout the Deccan acknowledging Chalukya imperial authority—whether used for documentary or for expressive purposes—were composed mainly in Kannada, the vernacular language of the dynasty's historic homeland in southwestern Deccan.[24] Yet the use of Kannada by the Chalukyas or their subsidiaries did not necessarily indicate an exclusive appeal to regional sentiment. To the contrary, on the very eve of the rise of the Chalukyas, the literati were adapting Kannada—this 'language of region'—so as to accommodate, and even appropriate, the expansive world of what Sheldon Pollock has called the 'Sanskrit cosmopolis'. According to Pollock, the *Kavirājamārgam*, a text composed in 875 just 80 kilometres from Kalyana, was the first text in world culture to theorize vernacular poetics, its great achievement having been 'to graft the very discourse that made Sanskrit cosmopolitan onto the local world of Kannada'.[25] Then in 950, just several decades before Taila II launched the Kalyana Chalukya dynasty, the epic poet Pampa went further and wrote a Kannada text that localized for the Kannada-speaking regional world the great pan-Indian Sanskrit epic, the Mahābhārata.[26] As a result, by the time Vikramaditya VI launched his Vikrama Era, the literati writing in Kannada, the regional language of the Chalukyas' base territory, had already appropriated the ideals of the 'Sanskrit cosmopolis', that is, a pan-Indian, cosmopolitan discourse appropriate for aspirations of a universal empire. Whether composing inscriptions or texts, and whether in prose or poetry, writers under Chalukyan patronage could use Sanskrit and be exclusively cosmopolitan, or they could use Kannada and be simultaneously regional and cosmopolitan.

Paralleling this universalizing trend in the realm of language, we see a similar trend in the realm of religion. By the turn of the second millennium, kingdoms throughout India were patronizing institutionalized religions as a normal, if not necessary, state function. The Chalukyas were no exception in this respect, although most of the burst of temple-building activity that took place under their rule was sponsored by their many feudatories rather than directly by the court at Kalyana. Whereas most temples in the empire were dedicated to some form of Shiva, cults of other Hindu deities, or even other religious traditions, were also patronized. Local feudatory chieftains, generals, and especially merchants, patronized scores of Jain temples.[27] In 1095–96, Vikramaditya VI himself issued grants to several Buddhist monasteries in Dambal (in modern Haveri district).[28] Such an inclusive vision of religious patronage was stated explicitly in the *Mānasollāsa*,[29] which advised that the king should avoid abusing 'the gods of other religions and sects: he should worship and visit temples of other gods, too. The king who follows these instructions will be blessed by all gods'.[30]

Such an accommodating position is hardly surprising, since patronizing any and all religious communities is a normal function of most trans-regional, multicultural empires. What is crucial, though, is whether the ruling dynasty, while patronizing other Hindu or non-Hindu institutions, identified itself with a particular cult focussed around a principal royal temple in Kalyana. We do have literary evidence of such a structure in Kalyana. Towards the end of his *Vikramāṅkadeva Caritam*, Bilhana, Vikramaditya VI's 'poet-king', writes:

> The very lofty temple of the husband of Kamala (i.e., Vishnu), constructed by that king [Vikramaditya VI], appeared like the arm of righteousness (*dharma*) [having] emerged from the interior of the globe of the earth to destroy the Kali Age.

The poet then indulges in a rapturous description of this temple's awesome height, its dazzling spires, its statuary, its quadrangular layout, its adjacent tank, and its dancing girls.[31]

Given the preponderance of Shaiva temples throughout Chalukya domains, one might expect that had there been a royal temple at Kalyana at all, such a monument would have been Shaiva, not Vaishnava. But Bilhana's remark that Vikramaditya VI's great temple at Kalyana was dedicated to Vishnu points us in another direction. So, too, does the assertion in the *Mānasollāsa* that Someshvara III's praises to Vishnu were performed out of the king's devotion to that deity.[32] Moreover, we know that Vikramaditya VI cultivated a special affinity with Vishnu in the form of Rama. In his biography of his father, Someshvara III stated that Vikramaditya VI had been born under the same astronomical conditions as was the deity Rama, causing court astrologers to predict that the newborn son would be a ruler of the whole earth.[33] In his own biography of the emperor, Bilhana has Shiva predict that Vikramaditya VI, like Rama, would win Fortune from the other side of the ocean, referring to the rescue of Sita from captivity in Sri Lanka by the hero of the Rāmāyaṇa.[34]

In fact, the entire Rama narrative template was, in Bilhana's hands, superimposed on the story of Vikramaditya. Thus the poet notes that the Chalukyas' hereditary capital was originally Rama's city of Ayodhya. He also alludes to Rama in describing Prince Vikramaditya's indifference to power, and the brotherly love he displayed in the contest for the Chalukya throne. In this way, notes Bronner, Bilhana cleverly insinuates that it is precisely because Vikrama is such a devoted younger brother that he is the real Rama in the family. This trend intensifies later in the work, in the aftermath of Ahavamalla's (Someshvara I's) death. With his father dead, Vikrama is said to willfully embrace exile in a manner that is reminiscent of Rama's behavior after the death of his father.[35]

We see further evidence of this emperor's identification with Rama in a 1098 inscription sponsored by Someshvara Bhatta, Vikramaditya's superintendent of religious affairs (*dharmādhikārin*), and later his High Minister, who refers to the emperor as 'the Chalukyan Rama'.[36] Such evidence does not mean that the Vishnu temple in Kalyana mentioned by Bilhana and built by this 'Chalukyan Rama' was in fact dedicated to the god Rama. One can, however, reasonably conclude that from at least the time of Vikramaditya VI there was present in Kalyana a major, royal temple dedicated to some form of Vishnu, and that this temple was understood as housing the image of the dynasty's family deity (*kula-devatā*). But if this were so, where might it have been?

Several kilometres southeast of present-day Basavakalyan, the town believed to be the site of the former Chalukya capital, lies the village of Narayanpur, a name whose Vaishnava associations suggests a dim memory of a much earlier Vaishnava presence (Figure 1.2). In his recent survey of Chalukya architecture, Gerard Foekema characterizes a partly ruined temple in Narayanpur as the only impressive temple ruin surviving in and near the Chalukyas' imperial capital, with ornamentation more abundant and more sumptuous than that found on any other Nagara-type temple in northern Karnataka (Figure 1.3).[37]

There are no inscriptions associated with the temple, but Foekema dates it stylistically to the early twelfth century. Although the structure as we see it today is dedicated to Shiva, Foekema notes several iconographic details indicating that the shrine was originally dedicated to Vishnu. Specifically, the doorway guardians at the entrance to the shrine's sanctum carry

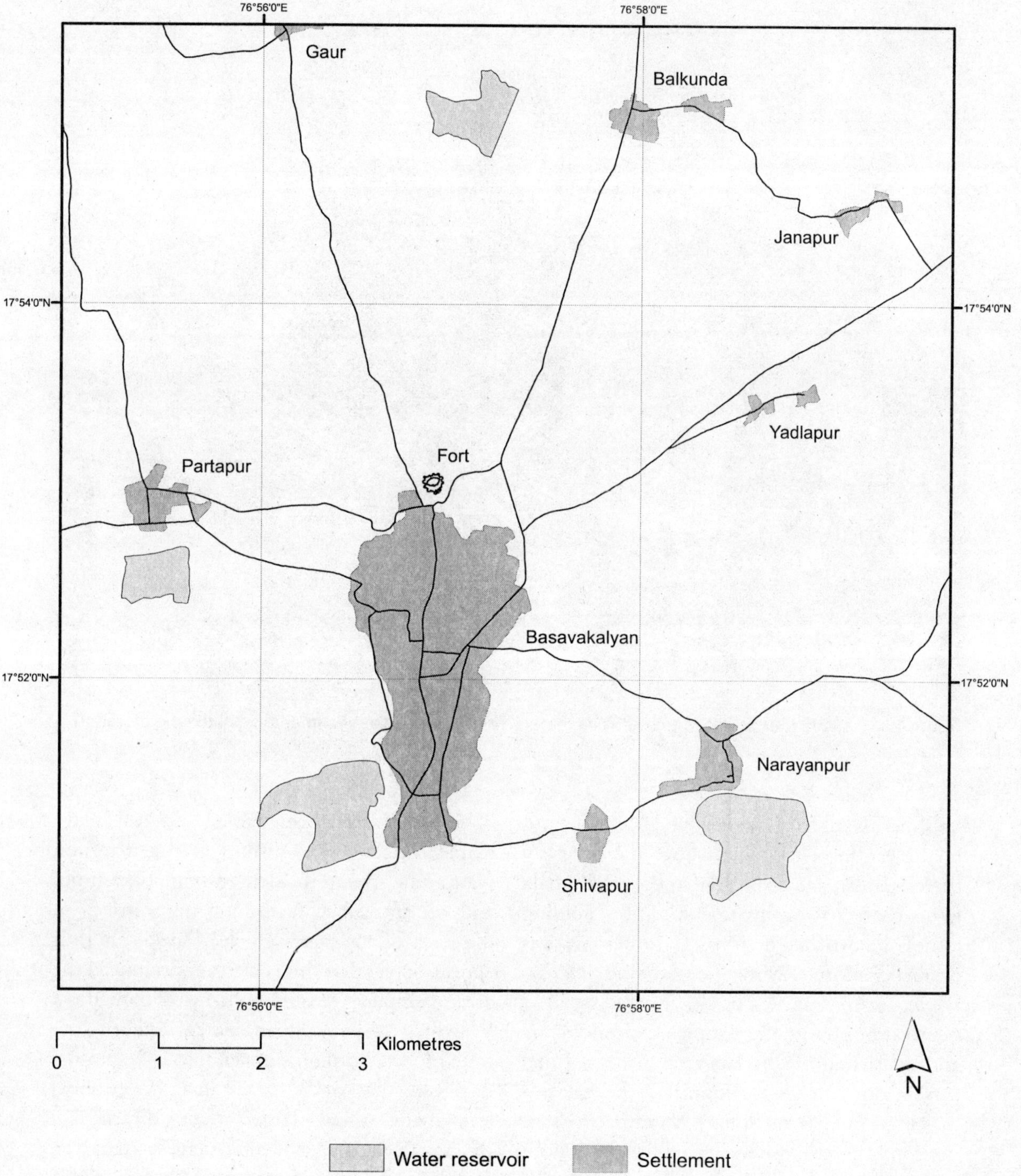


**Figure 1.2** Map of Basavakalyan and environs, showing Narayanpur.

**Figure 1.3** Narayanpur. Entrance to the 'Shiva temple', here identified as Vikramaditya VI's temple of Vishnu Kamalapati.

Vaishnava emblems (conch and discus), and in the centre of the lintel above the doorway there is an image of Vishnu's consort Kamala in her characteristically seated position, holding lotuses in two hands. Finally, the temple was originally adorned with a freestanding *makara-toraṇa* or entrance portal, situated in the courtyard opposite the temple's main doorway and consisting of an elaborately carved lintel carried on a pair of columns. Although this makara-toraṇa is no longer standing, a large portion of its exquisitely carved lintel has been preserved and serves today as a makeshift balustrade along the southern side of the stairway to the entrance porch (Figure 1.4). Both sides of this lintel have been carved with Vaishnava deities: on one side Vishnu as the man-lion Narasimha slaying the demon Hiranyakashipu, and on the other, Vishnu being carried on the back of his eagle-vehicle, Garuda. It thus appears likely that this structure was indeed the great Vaishnava temple built by Vikramaditya VI, which the poet Bilhana states had been dedicated to the Lord of Kamala, that is, Vishnu.[38]

Given that ancient Kalyana was doubtless many times larger than present-day Basavakalyan, the evidence suggests that the present village of Narayanpur occupies the core of the ancient city's sacred centre, focussed on this temple of the Chalukyas' family-deity,

Vishnu. In fact, as early as 1878 James Burgess, who made the earliest on-site archaeological inspection of Narayanpur, reached much the same conclusion. Noting that the shore of the lake next to the village 'is strewn for more than a mile with fragments of cut stones, the ruins of *ghat*s and temples, and here and there an image almost entire', Burgess concluded that this 'seems to have been the holy place of the Kalyana of early days'.[39]

The splendour of ancient Kalyana, as reflected in the exquisite stone carvings lying about both Narayanpur and present-day Basavakalyan, did not, however, survive the twelfth century. The empire's decline from the time of Someshvara III resulted in part from a paradox of so many large Indian states: the greater their pretensions to universal dominion, the more their emperors felt compelled to demonstrate their largesse by dispensing authority to their vassals—an ultimately self-defeating enterprise. Chalukya inscriptions are replete with references to feudatories bearing exalted titles like *mahāsāmanta* or *mahāmaṇḍaleśvara* and enjoying powers to grant land, dispose of local revenues, and administer civil and criminal justice within their domains. Some of Vikramaditya VI's generals were given all the insignia of royalty, such as the white umbrella, the great drum, and the fly-whisk. Although the emperor remained in theory the supreme bestower of honours, over time even this

**Figure 1.4** Narayanpur. Fragment of *makara-toraṇa* lintel at the 'Shiva temple', showing Vishnu's incarnation as the man-lion (right).

prerogative was increasingly delegated to feudal lords in his confidence.[40] Ultimately, the ceding of so much authority only encouraged larger feudatory lineages like the Hoysalas, the Yadavas, and the Kakatiyas to assert their autonomy from their imperial overlords, a process that accelerated soon after Vikramaditya VI's long reign.

The empire's disintegration, however, was not just political; it was also social, even ideological. As the state dispensed increasing authority to feudal lords, the latter in turn acquired rights to land, creating a wealthy class of local plutocrats. Much of this wealth was transferred to the building and maintenance of the monumental temples that, chartered and patronized by local lords, remain today the most visible evidence of the Chalukyas' refined aesthetic sense, not to mention their engineering abilities. But much of their wealth was also retained by those same plutocrats, creating a society sharply divided between the rich and the poor. The rigid social hierarchies codified by jurists like Vijnaneshvara and enforced by the Chalukya state set the stage for one of the most radical social revolutions in India's history—the Virashaiva movement. Originating in the 1160s as a religious reform movement among Shaiva worshippers who sought a personal and more direct relationship with Shiva, unmediated by brahman priests, the movement acquired a mass following by articulating the socio-economic grievances of the empire's large, disenfranchised underclass. The following verse, written by a principal leader of the movement, Basava (d. ca. 1167), reveals a deep resentment among the region's poor towards the wealthy. It also delivers a savage critique of conventional temple-worship:

The rich will make temples for Śiva,
What shall I, a poor man, do?
My legs are pillars, the body the shrine,
The head a cupola of gold.
Listen, O lord of the meeting rivers,
Things standing shall fall, but the moving ever shall stay.[41]

Herein one finds another paradox: the same dynasty that produced one of India's most refined traditions of temple architecture also produced a movement that challenged the religious efficacy of those same temples, together with the moral authority of the entire socio-ritual establishment that those temples represented—the plutocratic social order, the brahman-based religious structure, even the class system itself. It is true that the Chalukya imperial order had been declining from the mid-twelfth century on, and that the Virashaiva revolution occurred in the 1160s during an interregnum (1162–83) before the dynasty's final collapse. But that revolution not only spelled the end of Kalyana as a major political centre, it also led to the assassination of the ruling monarch and the destruction of much of the city itself.[42]

Yet despite the collapse of the state, the lustre of Chalukya authority lingered on. We see this in the attempts by some of the empire's largest feudatories—the Hoysalas in the south and the Yadavas in the north—to seize control of Kalyana, with the apparent aim of inheriting the mantle of Chalukya authority.[43] It is also seen in the manner in which the Chalukyas' successor states slavishly mimicked some of the epigraphic formulae of their former imperial masters—even if they stopped short of adopting full-blown imperial titles such as *mahārājādhirāja*.[44] Meanwhile, members of the ancient regime's ruling class dispersed throughout the Deccan, becoming petty chiefs. But even in their fallen state, some of them proudly flaunted their association with the former dynasty. In 1260, about a century after the de facto power of the regime had vanished, a copper-plate found in Ratnagiri district on the Konkan coast mentions a chief, one Kamvadeva, who bore the lofty title, 'the sun that blows open the lotus bud in the shape of the Chalukya race'. The chief was also called *Kalyāṇa-pura-varādhīśvara*, 'Lord of Kalyana, the best of cities'.[45] It is a phrase that would linger in memory for centuries to come. We shall encounter it again.

### A SUCCESSOR STATE OF THE CHALUKYAS: THE KAKATIYAS OF WARANGAL, 1163–1323

As a result of the break-up of the sprawling Chalukya empire and its succession by three major regional kingdoms, a trans-regional vision of polity based on ideals of the Sanskrit cosmopolis was replaced by a scaled-back vision of polity defined by regionally based vernacular languages. Mapping themselves over the Marathi-, Kannada-, and Telugu-speaking regions of the plateau respectively, the Yadava, Hoysala, and Kakatiya successors to the Chalukyas represented political manifestations of an ethno-regional consciousness that had already taken root across the Deccan (Figure 1.5). As early as 1053, the term *āndhra bhāṣa*, the 'language of Andhra', was used synonymously for Telugu. A century later, immediately upon throwing off their Chalukya overlords, political élites of the Andhra interior substituted Telugu for Kannada in their inscriptions.[46] This suggests that by the start of the second millennium the Kannada-speaking élites running the Chalukya empire might well have assimilated to their language the trans-regional, cosmopolitan vision formerly monopolized by Sanskrit. But Marathi or Telugu speakers nonetheless viewed Kannada as a geographically alien tongue deemed inappropriate for purposes of official documentation in their regions.

The easternmost successor state of the Chalukyas was the Kakatiya kingdom, its power base located in Telangana, the dry, upland eastern portion of the Deccan Plateau. Kakatiya chieftains first emerged as Chalukya feudatories in the mid-eleventh century and remained loyal to their overlords for over a hundred years, until 1163, when their ruling chief, Rudradeva (r. 1156–95), began omitting references to his family's former overlords in Kalyana. It was Rudradeva's nephew Ganapati (r. 1199–1262), however, who consolidated the kingdom by conquering coastal Andhra, bringing nearly all the Telugu-speaking eastern Deccan under his sway. Although Warangal is mentioned as the capital in Kakatiya inscriptions as early as Rudradeva's reign, Ganapati appears to have been responsible for rebuilding the city's inner wall, using enormous blocks of dressed granite.[47] Warangal remains today one of India's best-preserved pre-Turkic forts. Subsequent Kakatiya officials or feudatories built forts of similar construction across much of Telangana, such as the stone fort at Raichur (1294).[48]

Whereas the Kakatiyas had inherited much of their political culture from their former Chalukya overlords, the two houses differed profoundly in their social origins. The Chalukyas had proudly claimed warrior (kshatriya) status and adopted grandiose imperial titles like *mahārājādhirāja parameśvara* (see the epigraph to this chapter). The Kakatiyas, on the other hand, claimed neither kshatriya rank nor imperial status.[49] Instead, they and Telangana's other leading warrior families proudly claimed to belong to the lowest (sudra) section of India's traditional four-fold *varṇa* system of socio-ritual ranking.[50] This sudra dynasty with its network of sudra warrior families embraced a broadly egalitarian social outlook that was rooted in the frontier character of Telangana, a mixed dry zone where pastoralism co-existed with

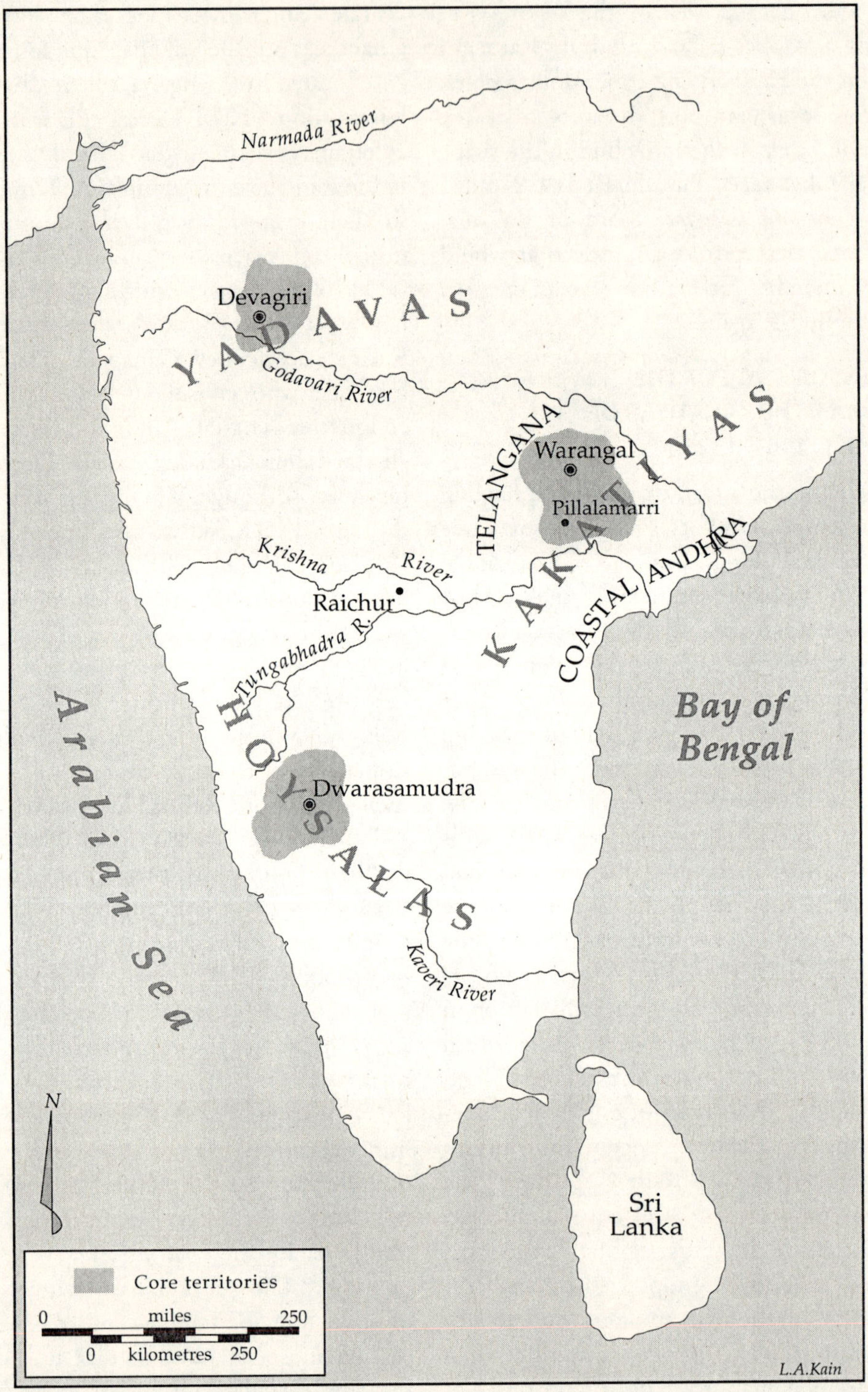


**Figure 1.5** Peninsular India under the Chalukya successor states.

tank-based wet agriculture, in marked contrast to the hierarchically organized society of the rich, rice-growing deltas of coastal Andhra.

Telangana's socially egalitarian society also structured how, at the highest level, religion and the Kakatiya state were mutually related. While still clients of Kalyana, the earliest Kakatiya rulers invariably opened their inscriptions by acknowledging the reigning Chalukya king with his full sequence of imperial titles, and only then introduced themselves with the humblest of titles, including 'a dependent on his lotus-feet' (*tat-pāda-padmopajīvi*), 'the great feudatory' (*mahā-maṇḍaleśvara*), and 'whose actions are always for the good of his master' (*pati-hita-carita*).[51] After the eclipse of the Chalukyas, Rudradeva continued to use the rhetoric of dependence, the difference, however, being that the new overlord was no longer a mortal Chalukya ruler, but the immortal 'Self-manifest Lord', Svayambhu Shiva.[52] The Kakatiyas now ruled at the behest of the god Shiva himself, in his form as self-manifest lord of the universe. What we see here, far more dramatically and decisively than with Vikramaditya's Vishnu cult at Kalyana, is the emergence of a full-blown state cult—that is, an institution in which a state's sovereign domain is understood as lying under the protection of a Cosmic Overlord, or state-deity (*rāṣtra-devatā*) manifested as a particular god whose image, housed in a richly ornamented temple complex in the heart of the capital, symbolized the security and prosperity of the state itself.

At Warangal, Shiva's status as an imperial entity akin to a cakravartin ('conquering emperor') was dramatically affirmed by the form of Svayambhu Shiva's temple and its place within the city. Of the original temple, nothing remains today except the four ceremonial gateways (*toraṇas*) that still stand at the boundary of the site, together with the temple foundations and hundreds of architectural fragments that were exposed through horizontal excavations of the site conducted early in the 1930s (Figure1.6). However, by examining the arrangement of the foundation stones and the distribution of the other excavated remains, we can reconstruct the general outlines of the complex with a high degree of certainty. First, it is clear that Svayambhu Shiva's temple was built according to a distinctive cruciform (*sarvatobhadra*) plan, in which the deity's central square sanctum was pierced by four doors aligned perfectly to the cardinal directions (Figure 1.7).[53] The linga of the deity would have been established at the very centre of this chamber, at the crossing of its two axes. Proceeding outward from the sanctum, each doorway was preceded by an identical pillared hall and, beyond that, by a smaller open-pillared pavilion connected to the central unit by a raised walkway. Finally, continuing outward along each of these cardinal axes, and just outside the stone enclosure wall (*prākāra*) defining the sacred precinct, was a monumental stone portal (*toraṇa*) standing over 9 metres high and 12 metres wide, precisely oriented towards one of the four quarters. The purpose of this unusual plan was to provide an ideal vantage point for Svayambhu Shiva's image, established at the very heart of the Kakatiya capital, to direct his gaze as he surveyed the four quarters of his earthly realm, like an emperor enthroned at the centre of his domain.

In short, what we have in Warangal, clearly evident even in the temple's presently ruined condition, is a visual, architectural expression of what Kakatiya inscriptions affirmed—namely, the presence of a state-deity that in a profound sense chartered and sustained the prosperity of the Kakatiya political enterprise. By contrast, the Chalukya state never defined itself in such servile terms as 'worshipping the

**Figure 1.6** Warangal Fort. Svayambhu Shiva temple site, eastern *toraṇa* viewed from inside the temple precinct.

divine lotus feet' of Vishnu, or of any other deity, even though we know that from at least the time of Vikramaditya VI, Chalukya rulers had a special connection with the Vishnu temple in present-day Narayanpur. Nor does the surviving architectural evidence suggest that the Narayanpur temple complex was as grandiose as Warangal's Svayambhu Shiva complex. And the Chalukyas' adoption of full-blown imperial, even quasi-divine, titles for themselves suggests a lesser degree of dependence on superhuman authority at Kalyana than was the case at Warangal. Indeed, we will see later that the Kakatiyas' conception of Shiva as a state-deity would have important consequences once Warangal fell to outside conquerors determined to overthrow the dynasty and uproot the most manifest signs of its former legitimacy.

## THE PERSIAN COSMOPOLIS AND THE DELHI SULTANATE, 1296–1347

In the early fourteenth century, each of the great successor states to the Chalukyas—the Yadavas, Kakatiyas, and Hoysalas—was in turn violently overthrown by armies of the Delhi Sultanate, a powerful new imperial formation emanating from north India. The conquest of the Deccan by these armies constitutes, after the rise of the Chalukya empire, the second great theme forming the backdrop to the events examined in this book. How should we understand the Delhi Sultanate and its presence in the Deccan?

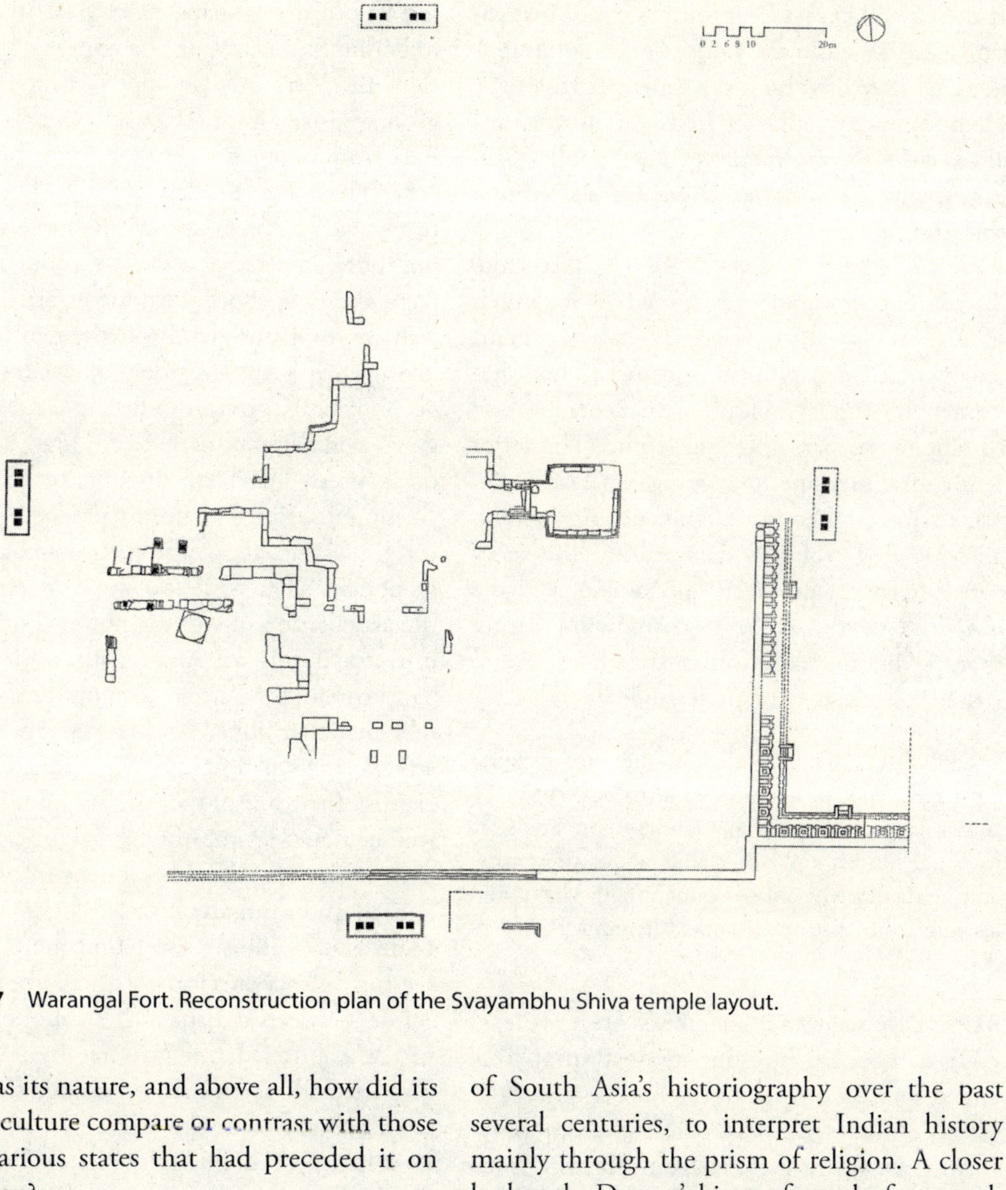

**Figure 1.7** Warangal Fort. Reconstruction plan of the Svayambhu Shiva temple layout.

What was its nature, and above all, how did its political culture compare or contrast with those of the various states that had preceded it on the plateau?

Because Delhi's conquest of the region was waged by a north Indian power whose ruling class was composed mainly of Muslims, this event has been conventionally understood as a 'Muslim' conquest, and even a rupture—if not, indeed, *the* fundamental rupture in the Deccan's history. Such an interpretation is rooted in the tendency, running through much of South Asia's historiography over the past several centuries, to interpret Indian history mainly through the prism of religion. A closer look at the Deccan's history from the fourteenth century on, however, reveals a more nuanced picture, one that would challenge the presumed primacy of religion as the fundamental category for analysing this region's history. Rather, what seems to be operating are two models of cosmopolitan culture which, while certainly in dialogue with religious systems, embraced a far wider spectrum of culture than religion alone.

If the Chalukyas had appropriated and institutionalized a Sanskritic model of cosmopolitanism that dated to about the fourth century, the Delhi Sultanate appropriated and institutionalized a Persianate model of cosmopolitanism that evolved somewhat later. Let us explore this idea.

What Sheldon Pollock has called the 'Sanskrit cosmopolis' expanded over much of Asia not by force of arms but by consent, and without any governing centre. This phenomenon contrasts sharply with a coercive sort of empire, such as imperial Rome. The latter required a metropolitan governing centre, an armed force, a complex bureaucratic system, and fortified frontiers demarcating the territorial extent of its sovereign domain. On the other hand, the Sanskrit cosmopolis, rather than relying on such Roman-style hard power, writes Pollock, may be understood as

> a symbolic network created in the first instance by the presence of a similar kind of discourse in a similar language deploying a similar idiom and style to make similar kinds of claims about the nature and aesthetics of polity—about kingly virtue and learning; the dharma of rule; the universality of dominion.[54]

As we have seen, the Chalukyas' great achievement had been to appropriate, institutionalize, and displace onto territory the discourse and ideals of that placeless Sanskrit cosmopolis. In their case, this meant accommodating such trans-regional ideals to the Kannada-speaking southwestern Deccan, the Chalukyas' ancestral homeland, while simultaneously using those ideals to underwrite a 'universality of dominion' across the Deccan Plateau. But the Sanskrit cosmopolis was only one such trans-regional ideology that took root in South Asia.

The diffusion of Sanskrit culture across great swaths of South and South East Asia after the fourth century anticipated by more than half a millennium the advent of a comparable formation, the 'Persian cosmopolis', which spanned great swaths of South, Central, and South West Asia from about the tenth century on (Figure 1.8). These two models of cosmopolitan culture—each of them deeply invested in preserving moral and social order—exhibited striking parallels. First, both expanded and flourished well beyond the land of their origination, giving each a trans-regional, 'placeless' quality. Second, both were grounded in a prestige language and a literature that conferred élite status on its users. Third, the discourse of the Persian cosmopolis, like its Sanskrit predecessor, made certain 'claims about the nature and aesthetics of polity'. That is, it too was concerned with the articulation of worldly power—specifically, universal dominion. And fourth, while both the Sanskrit and the Persian cosmopolises critiqued religious traditions, neither was grounded in any specific religion, but rather transcended the claims of any one of them. This point is crucial. Rather than viewing the history of early modern South Asia through the lens of two essentialized and mutually hostile religious systems, Islam and Hinduism, we might more fruitfully see this history in terms of the complex interaction between two parallel cosmopolises that first encountered one another in the twelfth century, and which then proceeded to relate to one another in complex ways.

What, then, defined the Persian cosmopolis, and how was it related to the Delhi Sultanate? This new, totalizing ideology began to evolve in the context of the Iranians' refusal to remain subject to Arab rule and Arab culture following the conquest of the Iranian Plateau in the seventh century. Accompanying this refusal was a self-conscious attempt to recover a rich but submerged pre-Islamic Persian civilization, a movement whose linguistic dimension saw the

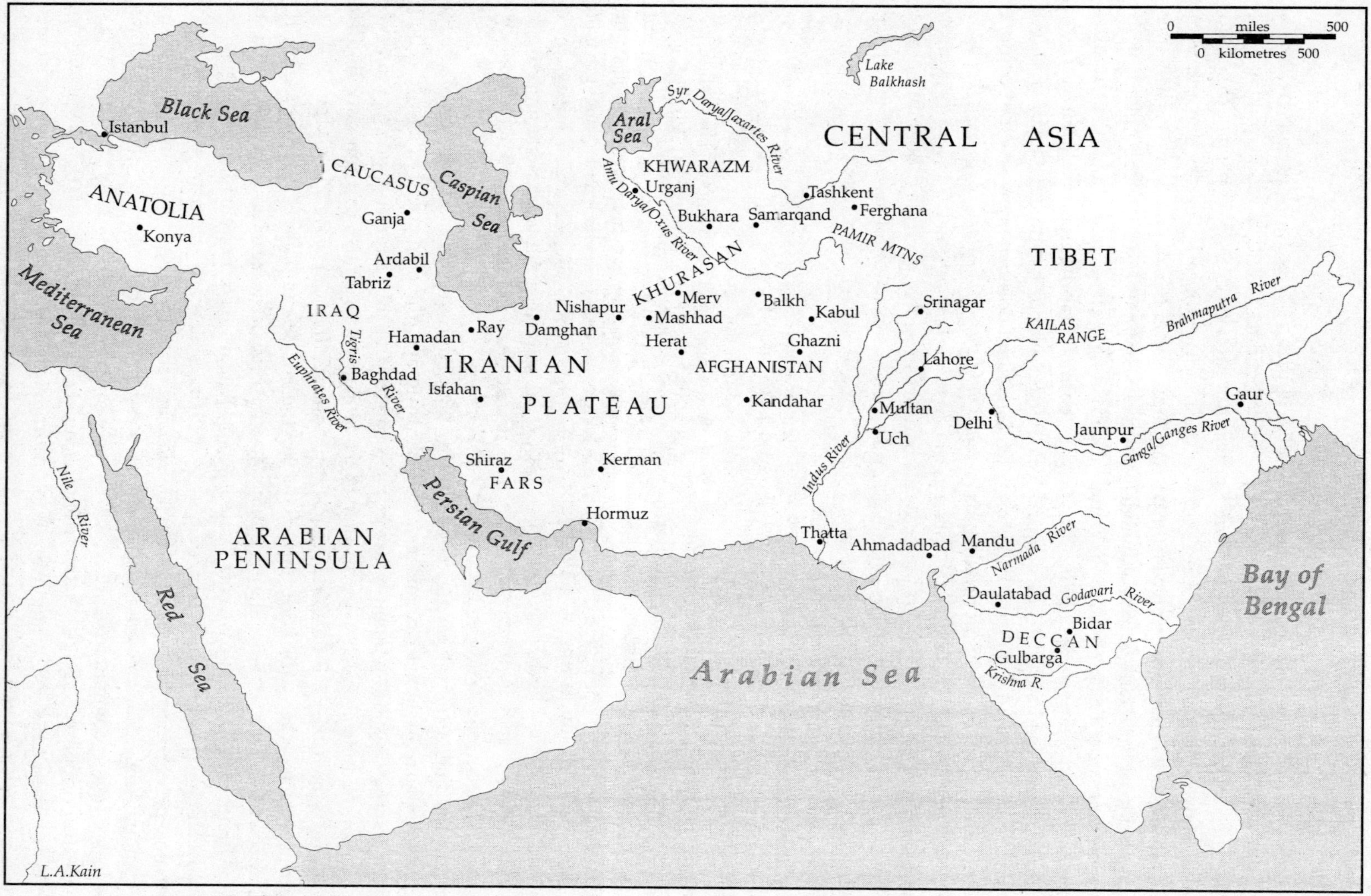


Figure 1.8 Major centres of the Persian Cosmopolis, 900–1500.

emergence of New Persian. Having assimilated considerable Arabic vocabulary in the centuries following the seventh, New Persian appeared first as a spoken lingua franca across the Iranian Plateau. Its written form evolved from a modified version of the Arabic script, although considerable time would elapse before the new language achieved literary respectability. That breakthrough came in the mid-tenth century, when writers in Khurasan (modern Turkistan and northeastern Iran) began appropriating for New Persian the heritage of both Arab Islam and pre-Islamic Iran.

Initially, at least, court patronage—namely, the court of the Samanid dynasty of kings (819–999)—played a decisive role in promoting the movement. Based in the Khurasani city of Bukhara (presently in Uzbekistan), the Samanid court straddled major trade routes connecting the Iranian Plateau with India to the south, Turkish Central Asia to the north, and, via the Silk Road, China to the east. Bukhara thus lay in a commercially vibrant zone that was also multi-lingual. Although Arabic and Turkish were both commonly used and Sogdian was still spoken in Khurasan in the ninth and tenth centuries, New Persian had just emerged as the lingua franca, having replaced the region's indigenous Iranian languages and dialects. Khurasan was also religiously diverse, with its communities of Jews, Christians, Manichaeans, Zoroastrians, Buddhists, pagans, and shamanists, together with both Shi`i and Sunni Muslims.[55] This extraordinarily plural social environment appears to have contributed to a particular conception of the sultan, then in its formative period of evolution, as a universal ruler standing above and beyond particular language or religious communities.

The Samanid court was also the first to adopt New Persian as its language of administration as well as a vehicle for both high literature and political theory. This, too, lent to New Persian a trans-regional vision. It was at Bukhara that the poet Rudaki (d. 940–1) penned thousands of verses that would later earn him the reputation as the father of (modern) Persian literature. In 963 the historian Bal`ami (d. 974), also writing at the Samanid court, naturalized the entire Arab-Islamic tradition for the Persianate world by producing an abridged Persian adaptation of the massive and comprehensive *Universal History* of Tabari (d. 923), who had earlier chronicled the early Muslim centuries in Arabic. In reality, Bal`ami's project was a *re*-appropriation of an earlier Iranian legacy. For as Michael Barry notes,

> The converted Persian scribes who served the first 'Abbasid caliphs in the eighth and ninth centuries believed that the ancient Sasanian Empire had been a holy, divinely sanctioned empire. They transcribed into Arabic the chronicles of the old Persian Empire, in order to convince the caliphs that the former Sasanian monarchy had been a polity willed into existence by God's secret design that sought to unify the earth under a wise rule and a just system of laws, and so prepare this lower world to receive the perfected message of the Prophet and the Koran.[56]

In 980, during the twilight years of the Samanid age, the epic poet Firdausi (d. 1020) began writing his great epic poem, the *Shāh-nāma*, a grand narrative that not only glorified pre-Islamic Iran, but gave Alexander the Great an Iranian descent, thereby appropriating for literary Persian the legacies of Greek imperialism and Hellenistic cosmopolitanism.[57]

In the eleventh century the writing of Persian history came into its own when, instead of merely translating from the Arabic or glorifying a real or imagined Persian past, scholars like Bayhaqi (d. 1077) began writing histories of their own days, with a special view to understanding how justice and morality were related to the rise and fall of past and present dynasties.[58] In the late eleventh century, the great Persian *vazīr* for the Seljuq Turks, Nizam al-Mulk (d. 1092), wrote the *Siyāsat-nāma* ('Book of Government'), the classic text in the genre of courtly advice literature known as the 'Mirror for Princes'.[59] This comprehensive manual addressed the practical business of running a universal empire, offering advice on subjects like maintaining spy systems, instituting state-supported schools (*madrasas*) to propagate a uniform, conservative religious education, and establishing an efficient revenue system.[60]

Although no writers of New Persian are known to have worked outside Iran before the eleventh century, the following centuries witnessed a widespread diffusion of Persian literati, driven in the eleventh and twelfth centuries partly by an agricultural decline in Iran, and in the early thirteenth century by the devastating onslaught of Mongol invasions.[61] It was thus in the south Caucasus region along the western shores of the Caspian Sea, a region where Persian was not the local vernacular, that the narrative poet Nizami Ganjavi (d. 1203) composed his *Khamsa* ('Quintet'). This work soon became, and would long remain, the most popular group of stories in the entire corpus of Persian literature, and among the most popular stories in world literature. Soon thereafter the great mystic poet Jalal al-Din Rumi (d. 1273) would settle in Anatolia, having been driven clear from northern Afghanistan by Mongol pressure. That same pressure would drive many more refugees into India. As a consequence of this cultural and demographic diaspora, New Persian, while never forgetting its misty ties to pre-Islamic Iran, had become a trans-regional, prestige language. Even while retaining their local languages, peoples from the Caucasus through South Asia would cultivate, and even produce, great works of Persian literature.[62] This portability of Persian letters across a vast geo-cultural space—and by the thirteenth century a corresponding absence of any geographic center of literary production—was an important aspect of an emerging 'Persian cosmopolis', analogous in this respect to its much older Sanskrit counterpart.

That said, even though the literati writing from within both the Sanskrit and Persian cosmopolises might have moved freely across vernacular regions and assumed that they inhabited a borderless universe, each cosmopolis was nonetheless informed by a distinctive mental map that was related to actual, finite territory. In the case of the Sanskrit cosmopolis, this map of cultural space was grander in scope and more cosmographic in nature than its Persian counterpart, featuring a vast scheme of seven concentric continents separated by seven seas.[63] At the centre of this vision stood the great cosmic mountain Meru, identifiable with the Pamir Mountains or with Mount Kailas in Tibet. The Indian subcontinent (*Bhārata-varṣa*) was therefore located to the south of this geographically specific *axis mundi*. Although one could not hope to reach Mount Meru directly, an aspiring conqueror could ritually reproduce it through architecture, as rulers of many dynasties did, by replicating its axial structure in the form of a towering temple situated at the center of his capital city. Through such practices, the centre of the larger mental map could be re-inscribed at any point within the larger ecumene.

In the Persian cosmopolis, the corresponding mental map of the 'Seven Climes' (*haft iqlīm*) was considerably more geographic in nature, but it still contained features that identify it as ultimately cosmographic in intent. The haft iqlīm model was originally derived from the *climata* of Ptolemy (second century AD), conceived as seven parallel bands of territory running around the globe, each sharing a common latitude and climate. Early Arab geographers had adopted this Ptolemaic scheme outright. But the great polymath al-Biruni (d. 1050), who lived in the eastern Iranian world (in Khwarazm, Bukhara, and Ghazni) at the very time that the Persian cosmopolis was crystallizing, modified the haft iqlīm by re-conceiving them in terms of the still older Persian notion of seven 'countries', or lands (*kishwar*).[64] Rejecting the parallel climatic zones of the Ptolemaic and Arab schemes, al-Biruni redrew the map along cultural lines, featuring six circular territories arrayed around the periphery of a seventh, central territory which, tellingly, corresponded with the Persianate heartland stretching from Iraq and Fars to Khurasan, where he himself was located. 'This partition,' he explained, 'has nothing to do with natural climatic conditions, nor with astronomical phenomena. It is made according to Kingdoms, which differ from one another for various reasons—different features of their peoples and different codes of morality and customs.'[65] These regions comprised the totality of the then known world, from Europe and north Africa in the west to India and China in the east, and from the Russian and Slavic lands in the far north to Ethiopia in the south.[66] In a process that became increasingly evident between the thirteenth and sixteenth centuries, the Persian cosmopolis—in the sense of a certain 'code of morality and customs' identified with al-Biruni's central circle—would ultimately embrace first northern India and then the Deccan, overlapping with the pre-existing Sanskrit cosmopolis.

Although the ideals of the Persian cosmopolis had first been patronized by the Samanid court in ninth- and tenth-century Khurasan, they, like the New Persian language that served as their carrier, quickly diffused beyond that state's frontiers. When the Ghaznavid sultans (962–1186) declared independence from their former Samanid overlords in the late tenth century, the production of a revived Persian language, literature, and culture gravitated eastwards with the Ghaznavids—first to Ghazni in eastern Afghanistan, home to Firdausi, Bayhaqi, and al-Biruni during the reign of Sultan Mahmud (d. 1030), and then to Lahore in the Punjab. In the verses of the Indo-Persian poet Mas`ud Sa`d Salman (d. 1121), himself a native of Lahore, we see an early encounter of the Sanskrit cosmopolis and its emerging Persian counterpart, in a region where neither Persian nor Sanskrit was the local vernacular.[67] In 1186 the Ghaznavids were overrun by another Persianized dynasty, the Ghurids, operating from their base in the mountains of central Afghanistan. Just six years later, in 1192, the Ghurids and their Turkish slave-clients burst out of their mountain strongholds in central Afghanistan and defeated several Rajput houses in north India, leading directly to the establishment of the Delhi Sultanate (1206–1526).

The successive dynastic houses of the Delhi Sultanate thus inherited from their Samanid, Ghaznavid, and Ghurid predecessors a legacy of Persian cosmopolitanism that had been elaborated between the tenth and thirteenth centuries. Politically, this legacy was realized in the idea of a trans-regional, sovereign state under the authority of a supreme ruler, the sultan. While from the Abbasid point of view such a figure governed a specific piece of territory as a deputy of the Islamic caliph in Baghdad, in fact a sultan wielded absolute authority over space that was, in his own mind at least, limitless. This was because the very idea of the Persian cosmopolis resisted geographical limits to claims of sovereign territory. The same, of course, was true of the Sanskrit cosmopolis. In the two inscriptions serving as epigraphs to this chapter, Vikramaditya VI is grandly depicted as the 'asylum of the whole world', while Sultan Qutb al-Din of Delhi claims to be the 'ruler of the surface of the earth'. Significantly, neither inscription mentions the territory over which the two sovereigns actually ruled, for doing so would have compromised their universalistic claims.

By the mid-eleventh century a major strand of political thought in the Persian-speaking world had decoupled Iranian conceptions of kingship and governance from Islam, or indeed from any religion.[68] Iranian ideologues had cast the figure of the sultan in the pre-Islamic Persian imperial role of the 'Shadow of God'—one of the titles claimed by Sultan Qutb al-Din Khalaji in the inscription mentioned earlier. From the eleventh century on, the caliph, though a sultan's theoretical master, was increasingly ignored as his effective political authority steadily diminished.[69] This de facto separation of Religion and State was made explicit by Ibn Balkhi in his *Fārs-nāma*, dedicated to the Seljuq sultan Muhammad bin Malikshah (1104–17). In this work Ibn Balkhi wrote that kingship in pre-Islamic Iran had been based on the supreme principle of justice, and that every king of that age taught his heir-apparent the following maxim:

> There is no kingdom without an army, no army without wealth, no wealth without material prosperity, and no material prosperity without justice.[70]

Several points are especially notable about this aphorism. First, it is to pre-Islamic Persian kings or their ministers, especially those of Iran's brilliant Sasanian dynasty (AD 224–651), that such aphorisms were usually attributed. Second, we note the scheme's totalizing, all-embracing character—that is, its ability to integrate economy, morality, might, and kingship all into a single coherent ideology. And third, we see the central place it gives to the idea of justice, and correspondingly, its omission of any reference to god or religion. As a ruling ideology, this formula became a stock theme throughout the Persian-speaking world, repeated with only slight variations by a host of writers of the 'Mirrors for Princes' genre of courtly advice literature, such as Kay Ka'us bin Iskandar (d. 1085), Nizam al-Mulk (d. 1092), and Abu Hamid Ghazali (d. 1111).[71]

Although the secular nature of the Persian cosmopolis—of a world upheld by a just sultan rather than a pious caliph—had been formulated well before the Mongol age, it was greatly reinforced in 1258 when pagan Mongols destroyed Abbasid Baghdad, executed the caliph, and effectively abolished the Islamic caliphate (although a remnant survived in Cairo).[72] Persian thinkers who served the Mongols, such as Nasir al-Din Tusi (d. 1274), then crafted political ideologies well suited for the Mongols' sprawling, multi-cultural state systems. 'The ideal ruler in the Nasirean tradition,' writes Muzaffar Alam, 'was the one who ensured the well being of the people of diverse religious groups, and not Muslims alone.'[73] Crucially, a Persianate ruling vision that accommodated cultural diversity and focussed on the principle of justice had become fully elaborated by the time the Delhi Sultanate's own ruling institutions were established in the early thirteenth century.[74] Moreover, the thirteenth and fourteenth centuries saw tens of thousands of Iranians and Persianized Turks, driven from their Central Asian homelands by invading Mongols, taking refuge in north Indian territories governed by the Delhi Sultanate. These refugees would contribute very significantly to the rooting of Persian cultural ideals in their adopted home.

What is perhaps most remarkable about the Persian cosmopolis, however, is how readily its ideals and values diffused into South Asian territories that lay *beyond* the realm of the Delhi

Sultanate. A distinctively Persianate ideology privileging the notion of justice and connecting economy, morality, and politics infiltrated the eastern Deccan Plateau even while that region was still under Kakatiya rule. At some point in the twelfth or thirteenth century, the Telugu poet Baddena, writing at the Kakatiya court, penned these striking lines:

> To acquire wealth: make the people prosper. To make the people prosper: justice is the means. O Kirti Narayana! They say that justice is the treasury of kings.[75]

Though more terse than the many formulations found in contemporary 'Mirror for Princes' literature, Baddena's lines clearly reveal the influence of the Persianate world in this corner of the Deccan, for the concept of justice as a central tenet of rulership was absent in the Sanskrit world of political thought. Like the Sanskrit cosmopolis, whose ideals were emulated or assimilated and not imposed, this Persianate formulation had apparently been borrowed by a Telugu court poet very far from the Delhi Sultanate. As we will see in this study, many other aspects of the Persian cosmopolis—architecture, dress, courtly comportment, cuisine, and, especially, language—would similarly diffuse among the Deccan's indigenous peoples and take root in the Deccan's cultural landscape.

In sum, it would be wrong to see the Sanskrit and Persian cosmopolises as mutually antagonistic, or even, in fundamental respects, as very different from each other. Although the former elaborated a vivid mythic reality, while the latter was more invested in the biographical, the historical, and the bureaucratic, both articulated coherent visions for maintaining moral and social order. Both were preoccupied with the universality of dominion; with codifying and explicating law, whether religious or administrative; and with proper etiquette and comportment, especially in the context of royal courts. And respecting all these matters, both produced similar discourses using similar idioms and styles. Curiously enough, the Persian cosmopolis crystallized at about the same time that the literati under Chalukya patronage were yoking the ideals of the Sanskrit cosmopolis to both Kannada vernacularism and Chalukya imperialism. Bal`ami's appropriation of Tabari and Arab Islam for New Persian, and Firdausi's appropriation of pre-Islamic Iran, appeared just decades after Pampa had translated the Mahābhārata from Sanskrit to Kannada (ca. 950). Bayhaqi's Persian historical account of living sovereigns appeared about a decade before Bilhana's Sanskrit narrative of the career of Vikramaditya VI. Similarly, Nizam al-Mulk wrote his *Siyāsat-nāma* between 1086 and 1091, synchronizing with Vijnaneswara's composition of the *Mitākṣarā*, which made available to Chalukya authorities a codified system of universal Hindu law. And the *Mānasollāsa*, which approximates the 'Mirror for Princes' genre as a work of courtly advice, was composed at the height of similar such writing in the Persianate world.[76]

The Delhi Sultanate's invasion and annexation of the Deccan Plateau, launched by the Khalaji dynasty in 1296 and completed in 1327 by Sultan Muhammad bin Tughluq (r. 1325–51), thus marked a momentous event in the region's history. Whereas the conquest completely re-configured the plateau's political geography—erasing forever the Yadava, Kakatiya, and Hoysala successors to the Chalukyas—its deeper significance should not be glossed, as it often is, in terms of an alien, aggressive 'Islam' colliding with, and suppressing, an indigenous 'Hinduism'. We can more profitably see Delhi's conquest and annexation of the Deccan as a catalyst for accelerating the diffusion of the ideals of the Persian cosmopolis in a region where those of the Sanskrit cosmopolis had already sunk deep roots.[77]

## THE DELHI SULTANATE'S SUCCESSOR STATES: THE BAHMANIS AND VIJAYANAGARA, 1347–1500

The first half of the fourteenth century saw the relatively brief moment of the Delhi Sultanate's rule over the Deccan Plateau. The conquest itself extended over a period of three decades, from 1296 to 1327, but Delhi's administration of this newest addition to its sprawling empire lasted only two more decades, until 1347—all of it under the turbulent reign of Sultan Muhammad bin Tughluq (r. 1325–51). During this period, the sultan used two different strategies for governing the Delhi Sultanate's new Deccan territories. He placed the northern half, lying between the Narmada and Krishna Rivers, under direct administration and systematically colonized it with north Indian immigrant-settlers. To this end, he ordered a road built between Delhi and the former Yadava capital of Devagiri, re-named 'Daulatabad', and he lined the road with shade trees and way-stations to serve weary travelers.[78] He placed governors in major urban centers and set up mints to issue imperial coinage. In the countryside, immigrant-colonists were garrisoned in forts or established on the land as rural landholders. Indigenous chieftains formerly in Yadava or Kakatiya service were assimilated into the Tughluq administration as *iqṭā`dār*s, or holders of revenue assignments. Applied across the northern plateau, such intensive administration—what we may call Direct Rule—allowed the regime to collect taxes at the grassroots level.

South of the Krishna River, however, Delhi exercised a far looser sort of authority. Here, Tughluq coins were neither minted nor circulated. There were no governors in provincial capitals, nor settler-colonists in the countryside. As the region lay too far from Daulatabad to be governed directly, authorities continued to collect annual tribute from Hoysala rulers, as they had been doing since 1311. But by the 1320s, the Hoysalas were losing control over their own subordinate chieftains, many of whom had taken to raising armies and roaming southern Karnataka as independent lords. In this politically fluid atmosphere, the sultan endeavoured to recruit such chieftains into Tughluq service as *amīr*s, or regional commanders, giving them honors and re-instating them in their former territories.[79] That is to say, the trans-Krishna southern Deccan was administered under a system of Indirect Rule, as native chieftains were brought into imperial service as tribute-paying amīrs.

Notwithstanding Sultan Muhammad bin Tughluq's rigorous efforts at governing the Delhi Sultanate's Deccan possessions, and despite his own extravagant commitment to the Persian ideal of justice,[80] by the 1330s Delhi's entire Deccan system—both to the north and to the south of the Krishna River—had begun to unravel. In the north, the sultan failed to calculate the effect that his colonization effort would have on the colonists themselves. As long as they were living in north India resisting attacks by Mongols from beyond the Khyber, India-born Muslims had seen themselves as Indians (*Hindiyān*), struggling to defend their homeland, Hindustan.[81] Within only several decades of living in the Deccan, however, northern immigrants and their offspring had acquired a distinctly Deccan-centric identity, now seeing the Deccan as their natural home, as opposed to the imperial heartland in north India, which they began to construe as a land of turbulence (*fitna*) and tyranny. In particular, they came to see their Tughluq overlords as alien oppressors, even condemning Sultan

Muhammad bin Tughluq, owing to his high-handed treatment of his Deccan colony, as a tyrant, even an infidel.[82]

As anti-Tughluq sentiment in the Deccan gathered through the 1330s and early 1340s, Delhi's presence in the plateau grew increasingly precarious. In 1345 Tughluq coins ceased being minted in Daulatabad, a sure sign of impending collapse. In the former Kakatiya capital of Warangal, which the Tughluqs had renamed 'Sultanpur', imperial control was even weaker. There, the minting of imperial coins, begun in 1324, had ceased altogether after just eight years. Across the northern plateau a self-aware class of people identifying themselves as 'Deccanis'—Muslim migrants from the north, or their offspring—had become progressively politicized, and by the 1340s they were rallying around one of their own, the charismatic Zafar Khan. In 1346 Deccani rebels besieged the imperial fort at Gulbarga, and when it fell after a four-month siege, they advanced directly to Daulatabad. Finally, in February 1347 Daulatabad fell to Deccani rebels, despite the 50,000 cavalry the sultan had hastily dispatched from Delhi to reinforce that city's garrison. The revolution had succeeded. Two months later Zafar Khan was crowned in Daulatabad's great congregational mosque as `Ala al-Din Hasan Bahman Shah (r. 1347–58), the first sultan of a new ruling house named after him, the Bahmani dynasty (1347–1510; Figure 1.9).

Meanwhile, the plateau south of the Krishna River had plunged into anarchy. By the 1330s chieftains who had thrown off allegiance to the Hoysalas and enrolled themselves as Tughluq amīrs were now throwing off their allegiance to the Tughluqs as well. Among these was Harihara Sangama, one of five brothers who had been gathering increasing power and authority in southern Karnataka.[83] By 1339 Harihara, ruling over parts of present-day Bijapur, Shimoga, and Chingleput districts, was grandly styling himself 'Lord of the Oceans of East and West'.[84] It was about this time that he and his brothers had begun asserting their independence from the Tughluqs, for in 1341 the world-traveller Ibn Battuta noted that Harihara controlled the port of Honavar in northern Malabar, without mentioning the chief's ties with imperial Delhi.[85] By 1344 most of Karnataka south of the Krishna had accepted the de facto authority of Harihara and his brothers. In February 1347 one of those brothers, Marappa, declared the Sangama family deity (*gotrādhidaiva*) to be Virupaksha, the god whose cult-shrine lay by the banks of the Tungabhadra River at a site later called Vijayanagara. Significantly, he also styled himself *hindu-rāya-suratālaḥ*, or 'sultan among Indian kings', reflecting the portability of the title 'sultan'.[86] What this really indicates, of course, is that by the mid-fourteenth century, the lexicon of the Persian cosmopolis had already begun to penetrate even the Deccan's deep south, far from the Delhi Sultanate's provincial capital of Daulatabad, and by a process of voluntary adoption.

In early 1347, then, new rulers on both sides of the Krishna River had successfully thrown off allegiance to Tughluq rule and, claiming the status of sultans, proclaimed new, independent states. To the north, a settler-colony had rebelled against a parent kingdom in distant Delhi, while to the south, five brothers, at least one of whom had been a Tughluq amīr, renounced Delhi's system of Indirect Rule and declared their own independence. As the two movements crystallized, they once again re-configured the Deccan's political space. In the north, Sultan `Ala al-Din Hasan Bahman Shah, seeking a more secure location in the Deccan interior, abandoned Daulatabad and established his capital in the more centrally located town of Gulbarga. In the south, another

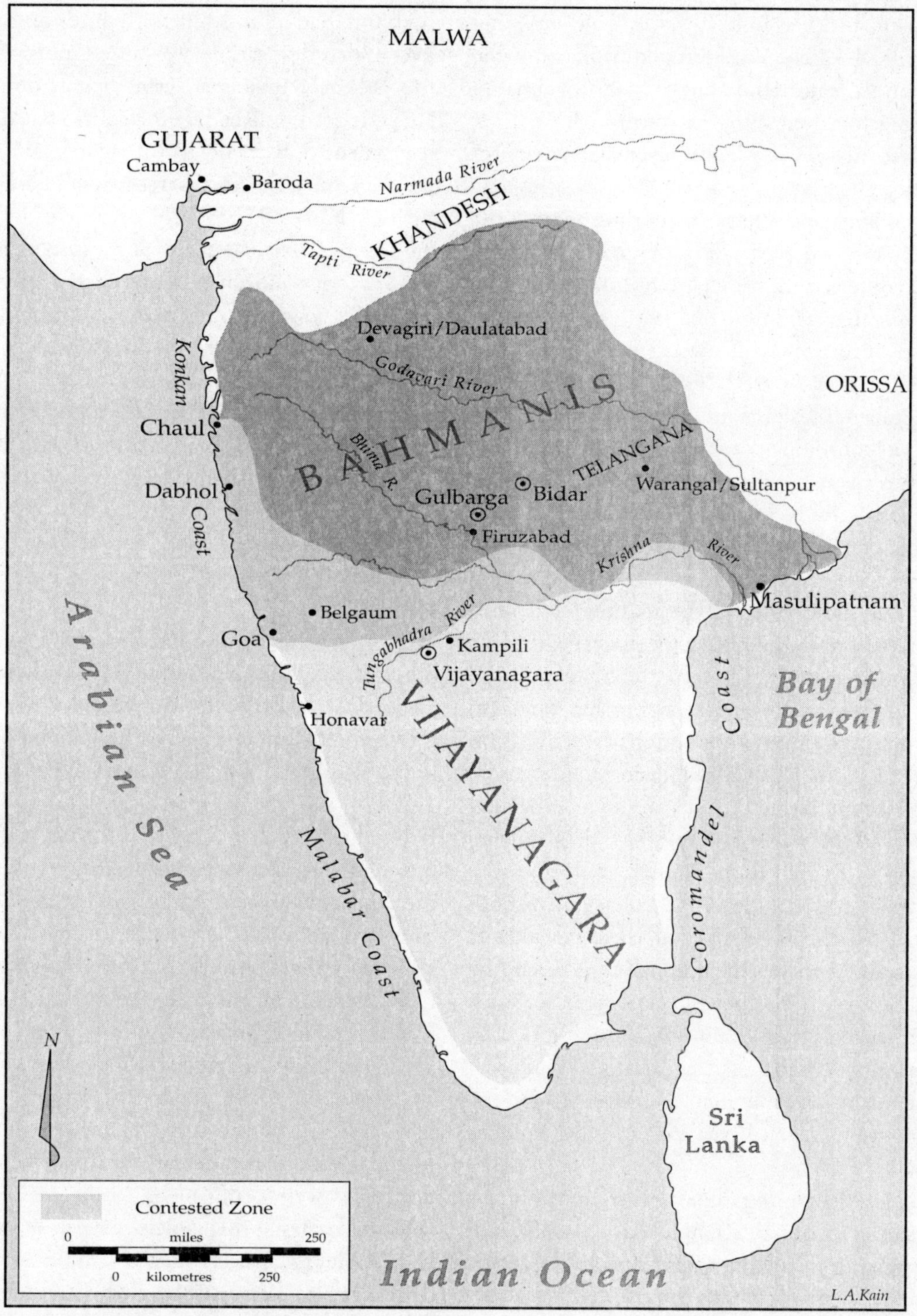


**Figure 1.9** The Bahmani and Vijayanagara kingdoms.

Sangama brother, Bukka, was by 1357 reigning over much of the southern peninsula from the city on the southern banks of the Tungabhadra River associated with the Virupaksha shrine, a place he now styled Vijayanagara, 'city of victory'.[87]

Gulbarga and Vijayanagara thus became the nuclei for two powerful states that, separated by a contested frontier zone running along the Krishna River, dominated the two halves of the plateau for nearly two centuries. In some respects, they were political twins, sharing remembered origins in Tughluq imperialism and a common experience of overthrowing Delhi's overlordship. Owing to those earlier Tughluq connections, they had also absorbed much of the political culture of the Persian cosmopolis, for example, the idea of the sultan as an absolute ruler in the manner of a reincarnated pre-Islamic Persian emperor, the place of justice as a central feature of their political ideologies, land revenue assignments based on the *iqṭā`* system, and a common aesthetic vision as seen in their royal architecture. Above all, neither state located its identity in a vernacular region in the way that the three Chalukya successor states had done. Rather, conforming to the trans-regional ideals of the Persian cosmopolis, both the Bahmani and the Vijayanagara states saw their sovereign domains as extending indefinitely over the Deccan terrain. With their shared vision of universal dominion, they frequently combatted one another, rendering perennially unstable their common borderland along the Krishna River, the so-called Raichur Doab.

Notwithstanding their underlying similarities, the two states employed very different means of legitimating their respective regimes. For their part the Bahmanis effected a conceptual transformation of the territory over which they claimed sovereign authority. Land that the Tughluqs had plundered with impunity only several decades earlier was now transformed into a legally inviolate, even sacred, domain. This was accomplished by the court's patronage of eminent Sufis, who in turn conferred their blessings on a sultan, thereby sanctifying the territory he ruled. In a Sufi discourse running counter to Persianate claims of a sultan's absolute sovereign authority, only charismatic and spiritually powerful Sufis exercised *true* authority over the affairs of the world, since they were felt to embody the blessings of God. Sultans accepted this view, since the same discourse also allowed Sufis to 'lease' their authority over worldly affairs to them. This is why it was a charismatic Sufi who symbolically crowned the first Bahmani sultan, `Ala al-Din Hasan Bahman Shah, when he came to power in 1347.[88]

To the south of the Krishna River, on the other hand, the new state of Vijayanagara asserted its claims to legitimate sovereignty by very different means. Although the state's political origins were rooted in the same anti-Tughluq movement that had produced the Bahmani state, its geo-cultural legitimacy grew upon a river goddess cult that had emerged on the southern banks of the Tungabhadra River as early as the seventh century.[89] At that time the site was known simply as Pampa's *tīrtha*—or the 'crossing' of the river goddess Pampa—where passing chieftains would halt and make votive offerings during military campaigns. By the ninth century the first stone temple had appeared at the site, dedicated evidently to this goddess. By the early eleventh century, donations were being made to the male deity Mahakala Deva, the violent aspect of Shiva. But by the twelfth century, a temple complex dedicated to Virupaksha, who represented Shiva's more universal and benign aspect, had emerged at the site. Unlike the earlier phase, when she was merely protected by Mahakala Deva to whom she was in no way subordinate, the river goddess Pampa was now reduced to a subordinate status as Shiva's consort. At the same time, south Indian texts had begun describing Pampa's marriage to Virupaksha in terms paralleling the all-Indian story of Shiva's marriage to Parvati.

In this way, over the course of 500 years a regional shrine had gradually become Sanskritized, as a local river goddess was pulled up into, and transformed by, the big world of pan-Indian Shaivism. At the same time, the site grew ever more important as a pilgrimage centre. From the thirteenth century on, politically ambitious or already-dominant rulers in the area had begun cultivating closer ties with the shrine and its deities, whereas earlier only passing chieftains had patronized the shrine. In the early fourteenth century, the short-lived kingdom of Kampili tried to reap the ritual and political benefits of an expanding goddess-cum-Shiva shrine by building a state on the site, until Sultan Muhammad bin Tughluq crushed the fledgling kingdom in 1327. Soon thereafter, though, the Sangama brothers proclaimed themselves to be the site's 'protectors'. And when those chieftains established their capital at the site, which they now called 'Vijayanagara', their family-deity Virupaksha was elevated to the status of state-deity.[90] All important state documents bore the 'signature' of this deity, and his temple complex by the banks of the Tungabhadra River became the object of lavish architectural patronage by the Sangamas.

* * *

Between 1000 and 1350 two powerful empires, each informed by a compelling model of societal coherence and universal dominion, swept over the Deccan Plateau. The first was the Chalukya empire, which had managed to appropriate, institutionalize, and displace onto territory the universalist ideals of the Sanskrit cosmopolis. It was mainly this achievement that would make the Chalukyas such a cherished object of memory long after the institutional shell of their empire had vanished. A similar dynamic operated when their successor states, basking to some extent in the Chalukyas' afterglow, in turn disappeared. But the memory of the Yadava, Hoysala, and Kakatiya successor states never extended beyond their own boundaries, since each kingdom had self-consciously expressed itself through regional, and not trans-regional, visual idioms, language, and literature.

All three Chalukya successor states met their demise, directly or indirectly, due to the second imperial wave to wash over the plateau. Much as the Chalukya emperors had appropriated, institutionalized, and displaced onto territory the universalistic ideals of the Sanskrit cosmopolis, rulers of the Delhi Sultanate appropriated, institutionalized, and displaced onto territory the universalistic ideas of the Persian cosmopolis. Having evolved in Central Asia and the Iranian Plateau between the late tenth and late twelfth centuries, just when the Chalukya imperium had reached its apogee, these ideals had been incarnated in the Delhi Sultanate in the thirteenth century and were carried into the Deccan a century later. Here they took root in the Bahmani Sultanate that revolted against its Delhi parent-state. As we shall see, they persisted in the several states that succeeded the Bahmanis around the turn of the sixteenth century. But aspects of the Persian cosmopolis would also merge with those of its Sanskrit counterpart, as happened in Vijayanagara, where Persianate ideals of courtly culture merged with Indic ideals of religious culture, or in cities like Bijapur and Golconda, where Persianate culture would prove receptive to Indic political and cosmological ideas.

In the chapters that follow we trace how political power and the memory of earlier Deccani states—both the Chalukyas of Kalyana and the Kakatiyas of Warangal—interacted with the most visually prominent expression of any society's culture: its monumental architecture. The interplay between power and architecture was especially intense during the initial conquest of the Deccan by the Delhi sultans and their Bahmani successors. In the course of these conquests, no monuments attracted more attention than did Hindu temples, largely because they stood as the most visible and durable emblems of pre-Persianate state authority.

## NOTES

1. *Epigraphia Indica* (*EI*) 12: 32 (lines 205ff.).

2. *Epigraphia Indica, Arabic and Persian Supplement* (*EIAPS*) *1972*, 12–19, pl. II(b), line 1.

3. Our earliest notice of the site as a capital of the Chalukyas dates to the dynasty's second monarch, Satyashraya (r. 997–1008), who was said to have been reigning in 'Kalyanapura', *Indian Antiquary* 14: 140ff., cited in Sheldon Pollock, *The Language of the Gods in the World of Men: Sanskrit, Culture, and Power in Premodern India* (Berkeley: University of California Press, 2006), 159. However, Kalyana did not become the sole, imperial capital of the Chalukyas until the reign of Someshvara I (r. 1043–68). Earlier in their reign, the dynasty's capitals changed frequently. See B.R. Gopal, *The Chālukyas of Kalyāṇa and the Kalachuris* (Dharwad: Karnatak University, 1981), 120–1.

4. Pollock, *Language of the Gods*, 155–9.

5. This is confirmed by one of Vikramaditya VI's own inscriptions issued in 1098: 'Now the elder of these two princes, Bhuvanaikamalla [Someshvara II], occupied the kingdom bestowed upon him by his father, (holding to) the course which inspired dread in hostile kings and gave delight to his own adherents.' *EI* 15 (1919–20), 257. See also S.C. Banerji and A.K. Gupta, trans., *Bilhaṇa's Vikramāṅkadeva Caritam: Glimpses of the History of the Cālukyas of Kalyāṇa* (Calcutta: Sambodhi Publications, 1965), Canto 3:39, 59; pp. 58, 61.

6. *Epigraphia Carnatica* 15 (part 1), 102. Cited in Vishwambhar Sharan Pathak, *Ancient Historians of India: A Study in Historical Biographies* (Bombay: Asia Publishing House, 1966), 67.

7. B.R. Gopal, *The Chalukyas of Kalyana and the Kalachuris* (Dharwad: Karnatak University, 1981), 227–8.

8. Pathak, *Ancient Historians of India*, 68. See also A.K. Warder, *An Introduction to Indian Historiography* (Bombay: Popular Prakashan, 1972), 47–8; and V. Venkataraya Sastry, 'Bilhana's Vikramankadeva Charitam', in *The Chalukyas of Kalyana (Seminar Papers)*, ed. M.S. Nagaraja Rao (Bangalore: The Mythic Society, 1983), 80–1.

9. In 1098, Vikramaditya VI's High Minister issued an inscription tersely stating the official version of events: 'Then, when [Someshvara II] had enjoyed the kingdom for some time and became neglectful of his subjects' burdens because of his being infatuated by pride, his younger brother, who was righteous of soul, putting him under restraint, making all hostile monarchs entirely to bow down because of his mighty prowess, Tribhuvanamalla, the Chalukya king Vikramaditya, became the darling of the earth.' *EI* 15: no. 24 (line 13 and verse 16).

10. See Banerji and Gupta, trans., *Bilhaṇa's Vikramāṅkadeva Caritam.*

11. Yigal Bronner, 'The Poetics of Ambivalence: Imagining and Unimagining the Political in Bilhana's *Vikramāṅkadevacarita*', *Journal of Indian Philosophy* 38, no. 5 (2010), 464–70.

12. Banerji and Gupta, trans., *Bilhaṇa's Vikramāṅkadeva Caritam*, 62–8. Even the king's marriage to his favorite queen, Chandralekha, is made into a grand political drama. Preceding the marriage, writes Bilhana, was a *svayamvara*, or 'self-choice', in which the princess selected a husband from amongst an assembled group that included, besides Vikramaditya himself, the Chola and Pandya kings of south India, the Paramara king of Malwa, the king of Gwalior, and the Chandella and Gurjara-Pratihara kings of north India. Her selection of Vikramaditya VI thus suggested a symbolic submission of India's ruling monarchs to the new Chalukya emperor. Banerji and Gupta, trans., *Bilhaṇa's Vikramāṅkadeva Caritam*, 153–6.

13. *Mitākṣarā* colophon, verse 4 (our translation). See Narayana Sastry Khiste Sahityacarya and Jagannatha Sastri Hosinga Sahityopadhyaya, eds, *The Yājñavalkya-smṛti, with Vīramitrodaya, the Commentary of Mitra Miśra, and Mitākṣarā, the Commentary of*

*Vijṇāneśvara* (Benares: Chowkhambha Sanskrit Series, 1930), 1106.

14. Whitney M. Cox, 'Law, Literature, and the Problem of Politics in Medieval India', in *Law and Hinduism: an Introduction*, eds Timothy Lubin, Donald R. Davis, Jr, and Jayanth K. Krishnan (Cambridge University Press, 2010), 169. See also K. Krishnamorrthy, 'Vijnaneshvara's Contribution to Hindu Law', in *Chalukyas of Kalyana*, ed. Nagaraja Rao, 131–6.

15. See Srisa Chandra Vidyarnava, trans., *Yajnavalkya Smriti, with the Commentary of Vijnaneshvara called Mitaksara and Notes from the Gloss of Balambhatta*, Book 1: *The Achara Adhyaya* (Allahabad: Panini Office, 1918); and S.N. Naraharayya, trans., *The Sacred Laws of the Aryas as Taught in the School of Yajnavalkya and Explained by Vijnaneshvara in His Well-Known Commentary Named the Mitaskara*, vol. 3: *The Prayaschitta Adhyaya* (Allahabad: Sudhindranatha Vasu, 1913).

16. Cox, 'Law, Literature', 169.

17. Ibid., 171.

18. See Chapter 4, 'The *Vikramāṅkābhyudaya* of Someshvara III, Bhulokamalla', in Pathak, *Ancient Historians of India*, 84–97.

19. P. Arundhati, *Royal Life in Manasollasa* (Delhi: Sundeep Prakashan, 1994).

20. Pollock, *Language of the Gods*, 184.

21. For example, in the fine arts it lists the five kinds of ragas, the fourteen types of metrical compositions, the five kinds of paintings, the three kinds of paint brushes, etc.; in courtly life: the five types of umbrellas, the seven types of beds, etc.; and in the natural world: the eight kinds of deer, the five kinds of buffalo, etc. In the latter respect, the *Mānasollāsa* resembles a gazetteer, inasmuch as types of animals are matched with regions as mapped by the Chalukyas' understandings of geographical and cultural space.

22. In an inscription dated 1098, Vikramaditya VI is described as 'the hero who put an end to the famous Śaka era and by setting up the Vikrama era made his own name illustrious on earth, a unique giver of bounty to the world, delighting in righteousness'. *EI* 15: no. 24 (verse 17). The Chalukya–Vikrama era is not to be confused with the older Vikrama era that begins in 58 BC. See D.C. Sircar, *Indian Epigraphy* (Delhi: Motilal Banarsidass, 1965), 251–8, 302–4.

23. Whitney M. Cox, 'Scribe and Script in the Calukya West Deccan', *Indian Economic and Social History Review* 47, no. 1 (2010), 21. Here Cox follows the work of Georg Buhler, *Indian Paleography*, appendix to *The Indian Antiquary* 33 (1904), trans. John Faithfull Fleet (Bombay, 1904), 51.

24. Cox, 'Scribe and Script', 18.

25. Pollock, *Language of the Gods*, 338, 347.

26. Ibid., 356–78. See also Sheldon Pollock, 'The Cosmopolitan Vernacular', *Journal of Asian Studies* 57, no. 1 (February 1998), 6–37.

27. M.A. Dhaky, *Encyclopaedia of Indian Temple Architecture*, vol. 1, part 3: *South India, Upper Dravidadesa, Later Phase, A.D. 973–1326* (New Delhi: AIIS, 1996), 129. For details of patronage of Jain institutions under the Chalukyas, see P.B. Desai, *Jainism in South India and Some Jain Epigraphs* (Sholapur: Jaina Samskrti Samrakshaka Sangha, 1957), 229–337 passim. See also A.V. Naik, 'Inscriptions of the Deccan: An Epigraphical Survey (*circa* 300 B.C.–1300 A.D.)', *Bulletin of the Deccan College Research Institute* 9, nos 1–2 (Poona, December 1948), 117–44 passim.

28. *Indian Antiquary* 10:185 and 273, cited in J. F. Fleet, *The Dynasties of the Kanarese Districts of the Bombay Presidency from the Earliest Historical Times to the Muhammadan Conquest of A.D. 1318* (Bombay: Govt. Central Press, 1882), 49. See also Naik, 'Inscriptions', 132.

29. 'Out of devotion to Bhagavan Vishnu, I have sung his praises in these compositions. But there is no invariant rule for these to be directed only to Vishnu. One can praise Vishnu or Shiva or Brahma or the Sun or Ganesa or Bhairava or Ksetrapala (Shiva), Devi or Sarasvati or Gauri or Laksmi or Candi or any other deity.' Cited in Pollock, *Language of the Gods*, 427.

30. Arundhati, *Royal Life in Manosollasa*, 9.

31. Banerji and Gupta, trans., *Bilhaṇa's Vikramāṅkadeva Caritam*, Canto 17:15–21, pp. 260–1.

32. See note 29.

33. Pathak, *Ancient Historians of India*, 87.

34. In Bilhana's estimation, the emperor symbolically followed Rama's steps by marrying a princess from a Maharashtrian house that styled itself kings of Sri Lanka. Warder, *Introduction to Indian Historiography*, 48.

35. Yigal Bronner, 'Poetics of Ambivalence', 408.

36. *EI* 15 (1919–20), 357.

37. Gerard Foekema, *Calukya Architecture: Medieval Temples of Northern Karnataka Built during the Rule of the Calukya of Kalyana and Thereafter, AD 1000–1300* (New Delhi: Munshiram Manoharlal, 2003), 589–90.

38. Foekema suggests that the half-lintel on the northern side of the stairway is the other portion of the temple's freestanding lintel. Based on our examination of the two pieces, however, we believe that they belong to two separate *makara-toraṇas*, and that the one on the northern side of the stairway belonged to a Shaiva shrine. This is indicated by the Shaiva attendant figures flanking the (missing) deities from the centre of the toraṇa. The two toraṇa fragments are also distinguished by significant stylistic differences. The stone matrix of the southern fragment has been completely cut away around some of the figures, while the northern fragment has not been cut through in this manner. Indeed, the greater refinement of the Vaishnava makara-toraṇa fragment currently used as the southern balustrade of the temple's porch suggests the work of a master sculptor commissioned by Vikramaditya himself for the temple of the family deity. Although we have not located the missing portion of the Vaishnava toraṇa, what would appear to be the other half of the Shaiva lintel is preserved a short distance from the main temple at Narayanpur, leaning up against the *maṇḍapa* of a badly ruined second temple. This second temple, described by Burgess, likewise appears to have been a Vaishnava dedication; given its proximity, it was perhaps cultically related to the main temple. There are two further fragments of what must be at least one additional makara toraṇa—one lying with some other architectural fragments on the edge of the tank bund, and the other cemented into the interior wall of a small Shiva temple still in worship nearby. See James Burgess, *Report on the Antiquities of the Bidar and Aurangabad Districts* (London: Wm. H. Allen, 1878), 40.

39. Ibid.

40. Y. Gopala Reddy, 'The Feudal Element in the Western Chalukyan Polity', in *Chalukyas of Kalyana*, ed. Nagaraja Rao, 115–20.

41. A.K. Ramanujan, trans., *Speaking of Śiva* (London: Penguin Books, 1973), 88.

42. R.G. Bhandarkar, *Early History of the Deccan and Miscellaneous Historical Essays* (1933; repr. Poona, Bhandarkar Oriental Research Institute, 1983), 129–31; Fleet, *Dynasties of the Kanarese Districts*, 60; Dhaky, *Encyclopaedia of Indian Temple Architecture*, 131; P.V. Narayana, 'Importance of Vachanas in the Study of Social Life in 12th Century Karnataka', in *Chalukyas of Kalyana*, ed. Nagaraja Rao, 19–65.

43. S.H. Ritti, 'Last Phase of the Chalukya rule', in *Chalukyas of Kalyana*, ed. Nagaraja Rao, 84–5.

44. Just as Chalukya inscriptions (such as the one in the epigraph heading this chapter) normally used the phrase 'while He is reigning in His capital of Kalyana in the enjoyment of pleasant conversation ...', rulers of the Yadava, Kakatiya, and Hoysala successor states used the same formula in their own inscriptions, the only change being to substitute their own capital city for Kalyana.

45. Bhandarkar, *Early History of the Deccan*, 126.

46. 'With the expansion of Telugu epigraphic use during the Kakatiya period,' writes Cynthia Talbot, 'the contours of the modern linguistic state were beginning to take shape.' Cynthia Talbot, *Precolonial India in Practice: Society, Region, and Identity in Medieval Andhra* (New York: Columbia University Press, 2001), 35–6.

47. Rudradeva is said in one inscription to have been ruling from Warangal as early as 1195 (*Inscriptions of Andhra Pradesh* [*IAP*]—*Warangal District*, no. 42), and in another inscription issued by Ganapati in 1231, he is credited with having built the city (*EI* 3: no. 15, verse 3). Ganapati is credited in a later historiographical text (the *Pratāparudra Caritramu*, datable to c. 1550) as having replaced the fort's original 'boundary wall' (*prahari-goḍa*, probably of brick or mud) with stone walls (*śilā-prākārambulu*). C.V. Ramachandra Rao, ed., *Ekāmranāthuni Pratāparudra Caritramu* (Hyderabad: Andhra Pradesh Sahitya Academy, 1984), 24 and 29.

48. In fact, the era of the Kakatiyas—and of their Yadava and Hoysala contemporaries in the northern and southwestern Deccan respectively—witnessed a proliferation of both plains-forts and hill-forts across the plateau. A recent study of the forts of Maharashtra argues that most forts in that part of the Deccan were built between the twelfth century, coinciding with the break-up of the Chalukyas, and the seventeenth century. To be sure, we hear from literary sources of the existence of Chalukya forts. As we have seen, the *Mānasollāsa* discusses managing and besieging forts of various kinds, and as early as 1006 Chalukya rulers or generals were styling themselves *durga-traya-malla* ('wrestler of three forts') or *durga-churekara* ('crusher of forts'), referring to the practice of capturing and burning enemy forts. But archaeological evidence does not permit the secure dating of existing Deccani forts to the Chalukya period. Indeed, it is notoriously difficult to date the original construction of most Deccani forts, which as a rule lack foundational inscriptions

and were in any event subject over time to continual rebuilding, repairs, and expansion. See M.S. Naravane, *Forts of Maharashtra* (New Delhi: APH Publishing Corporation, 1995), 14; N.S. Ramachandra Murthy, *Forts of Andhra Pradesh (from the Earliest Times upto 16th c. A.D.)* (Delhi: Bharatiya Kala Prakashan, 1996), 41.

49. Parabrahma Sastry, P.V. *The Kakatiyas of Warangal* (Hyderabad: Government of Andhra Pradesh, 1978), 175.

50. Talbot, *Precolonial India*, 51.

51. The typical full sequence of early Kakatiya titles is: '[Chalukya titles and emperor's name] tat-pāda-padmopajīvi samadhigata-paṃca-mahāśabda mahāmaṇḍaleśvara Anumakoṇḍa-pura-varādhīśvara parama Māhēśvara pati-hita-caritam vinaya-vibhūṣaṇam śrīman mahāmaṇḍaleśvara Kākatiya[name]'. See, for example, *Corpus of Inscriptions in the Telengana Districts* (*CITD*) 2: no. 5; and *IAP—Warangal*, nos 15, 22, 29, etc.

52. Rudradeva and his descendents would present themselves as 'worshipping the divine lotus feet of the god Svayambhunatha' ('śrī-svayambhū-nātha-deva-divya-pāda-padmārādhaka'). See, for example, *IAP—Warangal*, nos 37 and 63; *CITD* 2: no. 52; and *SII* 10: no. 241. Cynthia Talbot notes that this is one of the four most common royal Kakatiya titles. Talbot, *Precolonial India*, 145.

53. The most detailed account of the *sarvatobhadra* design is found in the *Viṣṇudharmottara Purāṇa*, a Sanskrit ritual manual for kings which, according to a recent analysis, was composed in Kashmir at the Karkota court of Lalitaditya Muktapida (c. 725–60). For a summary of the text's account of this temple type, see Stella Kramrisch, *The Hindu Temple* (Calcutta: University of Calcutta, 1946), 2: 418–21. Actual examples of sarvatobhadra planned temples can be found throughout India, from Himachal Pradesh in the north to the southwestern coast of Karnataka. See Ronald Inden, 'Imperial Puranas: Kashmir as Vaiṣṇava Center of the World', in *Querying the Medieval: Texts and the History of Practices in South Asia*, eds Ronald Inden, Jonathan Walters, and Daud Ali (New York: Oxford University Press, 2000), 29–98; Michael W. Meister, 'Mountain Temples and Temple-Mountains: Masrur', *Journal of the Society of Architectural Historians* 65 (2006), 26–49; John Henry Rice, 'The Chaturmukha Temples of Kanara: Architectural Assertions of Autonomy', in *South India under Vijayanagara: Art and Archaeology*, eds Anila Verghese and Anna Dallapiccola (New Delhi: Oxford University Press, 2011), 194–215.

54. Sheldon Pollock, 'The Sanskrit Cosmopolis, A.D. 300–1300: Transculturation, Vernacularization, and the Question of Ideology', in *Ideology and Status of Sanskrit: Contributions to the History of the Sanskrit Language*, ed. J.E.M. Houben (Leiden: Brill, 1996), 230.

55. Louise Marlow, 'A Samanid Work of Counsel and Commentary: the *Naṣīḥat al-mulūk* of Pseudo-Mawardi', *Iran: Journal of the British Institute of Persian Studies* 45 (2007), 182–3. For Khurasan's ethnic and religious diversity at this time, see also Elton L. Daniel, *The Political and Social History of Khurasan under Abbasid Rule* (Minneapolis: Biblioteca Islamica, 1979), 13–24; and Richard W. Bulliet, *The Patricians of Nishapur: A Study in Medieval Islamic Social History* (Cambridge, MA: Harvard University Press, 1972), 14–19.

56. Michael Barry, *Figurative Art in Medieval Islam and the Riddle of Bihzad of Herat (1465–1535)* (Paris: Flammarion, 2004), 57–8. See also Andrew Peacock, *Medieval Islamic Historiography and Political Legitimacy* (New York: Routledge, 2007).

57. Firdausi's *Shāh-nāma* was based on a Sasanian chronicle whose translation into New Persian had been commissioned by a Samanid governor in Khurasan. Said Amir Arjomand, 'Evolution of the Persianate Polity and Its Transmission to India', *Journal of Persianate Studies* 2 (2009), 117.

58. Julie Scott Meisami, *Persian Historiography to the End of the Twelfth Century* (Edinburgh: Edinburgh University Press, 1999), 282–3. See also Marilyn Robinson Waldman, *Toward a Theory of Historical Narrative: A Case Study in Perso-Islamicate Historiography* (Columbus: Ohio State University Press, 1980).

59. For the 'Mirror for Princes' genre, see Patricia Crone, *God's Rule: Government and Islam* (New York: Columbia University Press, 2004), 148–64.

60. Marshall Hodgson, *The Venture of Islam: Conscience and History in a World Civilization*, vol. 2: *The Expansion of Islam in the Middle Periods* (Chicago: University of Chicago Press, 1974), 44–7.

61. For a novel interpretation connecting the diffusion of New Persian with the collapse of cotton cultivation in Iran, which had resulted from a cooling trend in the region's climate, see Richard W. Bulliet, *Cotton,*

*Climate, and Camels in Early Islamic Iran: A Moment in World History* (New York: Columbia University Press, 2009). The important thing, notes Bulliet, is that master poets like Rumi 'rhapsodized for Persian-speaking audiences and had Persian-speaking colleagues and imitators in these foreign lands. So far as is known, the pre-Islamic dynasties never exported their languages to other lands. Not even to Mesopotamia, which was under Iranian rule for most of the millennium preceding the Arab conquests'. Bulliet, *Cotton*, 141.

62. Rebecca K. Gould, 'How Newness Enters the World: The Methodology of Sheldon Pollock', *Comparative Studies of South Asia, Africa, and the Middle East* 28, no. 3 (2008), 547.

63. Joseph E. Schwartzberg, 'Cosmographical Mapping', in *The History of Cartography*, vol. 2, book 1: *Cartography in the Traditional Islamic and South Asian Societies*, eds J.B. Harley and David Woodward (Chicago: University of Chicago Press, 1992), 332ff.

64. Ahmet T. Karamustafa, 'Cosmographical Diagrams', in ibid., 76–80.

65. Al-Biruni, *The Determination of the Coordinates of Positions for the Correction of Distances between Cities*, trans. Jamal Ali (Beirut: American University of Beirut, 1967),102, as quoted in Karamustafa, 'Cosmographical Diagrams', 77–80.

66. Gerald R. Tibbetts, 'The Beginnings of a Cartographic Tradition', in Harley and Woodward, *The History of Cartography*, 2, book 1, 93–4, and figure 4.2.

67. Though clearly situating himself in the Punjab, the land of his birth, Mas`ud Sa`d looked to Iranian lands to the west for cultural inspiration. 'In essence,' writes Sunil Sharma, 'Mas`ud Sa`d belonged to both worlds and to neither.' Sunil Sharma, *Persian Poetry at the Indian Frontier: Mas`ud Sa`d Salman of Lahore* (New Delhi: Permanent Black, 2000), 13.

68. Ann K.S. Lambton, '*Quis custodiet custodies*: Some Reflections on the Persian Theory of Government', *Studia Islamica* 5 (1956), 125–48.

69. Synthesizing Perso-Indian statecraft with Greek political science, the Shafi`i jurist and philosopher Fakhr al-Din Razi (d. 1209) established an absolute independence of royalty from the caliph, maintaining that world order is impossible without 'the king (*pādshāh*) who is God's Caliph'. As Amir Arjomand remarks, 'The `Abbasid Caliphate was thus made redundant even before its overthrow.' See Said Amir Arjomand, 'Evolution of the Persianate Polity and Its Transmission to India', *Journal of Persianate Studies* 2 (2009), 124.

70. Ann K.S. Lambton, 'Justice in the Medieval Persian Theory of Kingship', *Studia Islamica* 17 (1962), 100.

71. Ibid., 101–7.

72. Notwithstanding the abolition of the caliphate in Baghdad, the *idea* of the caliph as a legitimizing force continued to hold sway for Indian sultans. For nearly four decades following the execution of al-Musta`sim and the abolition of the Caliphate, sultans of Delhi continued to invoke al-Musta`sim's name on their coins. But the office of caliph soon became little more than an honorific title, adopted by several Indian sultans (in Delhi in 1317 and in Bengal in 1427). In 1341 the Delhi sultan, Muhammad bin Tughluq, invoked the name of an Abbasid 'caliph' that the Mamluk court in Egypt had established to promote its own legitimacy. Two years later he received a deputation from Cairo with a certificate of investiture and a robe of honor (*khil`at*) from the then Egyptian caliph, al-Hakim II. Yet by then, the barrier between the domain of an all-powerful sultan and that of a rather fictive caliph had become absolute. Stan Goron and J.P. Goenka, *The Coins of the Indian Sultanates* (New Delhi: Munshiram Manoharlal, 2001), 29–35, 40–1, 59–61.

73. Muzaffar Alam, *The Languages of Political Islam: India, 1200–1800* (Chicago: University of Chicago Press, 2004), 49.

74. On the Persian origins of the 'Circle of Justice' ideology and its transmission to India during the Delhi Sultanate and Mughal periods, see Linda T. Darling, '"Do Justice, Do Justice, for That Is Paradise": Middle Eastern Advice for Indian Muslim Rulers', *Comparative Studies of South Asia, Africa and the Middle East* 22, nos 1 and 2 (2002), 3–19.

75. Quoted from the Telugu *Niti* of Baddena, cited in Phillip B. Wagoner, *Tidings of the King: A Translation and Ethnohistorical Analysis of the* Rāyavācakamu (Honolulu: University of Hawaii Press, 1993), 95. The term for 'justice' used by Baddena is *nyāyam*, a Sanskrit term usually used in the sense of 'logic', 'reason', or 'principle'. It also carries the sense of 'justice' in *dharma-śāstra* literature where court cases and lawsuits are discussed. But this seems to be a secondary, more specialized meaning. Until Baddena, the term was never elevated to the status of *the* fundamental principle of statecraft.

76. The statement attributed to Someshvara III that the best horses come to the Deccan from 'Yavana' countries, that is, the Arab and Persian worlds, points to commercial contact between the Chalukya and Iranian worlds in the twelfth century. But such contact hardly furnishes evidence of mutual influences in the ideological realm. See Arundhati, *Royal Life in Manosollasa*, 36.

77. This was not the first time that Persian or Arabic speakers had come into contact with the Indian peninsula; there had been more or less continuous maritime contact between the Persian Gulf and the Konkan and Malabar coasts from at least Roman times. These contacts only intensified from the seventh century on, but they do not appear to have been informed by ideals of the Persian cosmopolis until the twelfth century.

78. Wrote the famous world traveler Ibn Battuta, who trod this road in 1342, 'The road between Delhi and Daulatabad is bordered with willow trees and others in such a manner that a man going along it imagines he is walking through a garden; and at every mile there are three postal stations.... At every station (dawa) is to be found all that a traveler needs.' Ibn Battuta, *The Rehla of Ibn Battuta*, trans., Mahdi Husain (Baroda: Oriental Institute, 1953), 44.

79. Among these were the eleven sons of the chieftain of Kampili, a small kingdom in modern Bellary district. After their father died resisting Tughluq authority, the sons signed up as Tughluq *amīr*s. Between 1337 and 1342 Ibn Battuta met three of these sons, commenting that Muhammad bin Tughluq had made them all imperial *amīr*s 'in consideration of their good descent and [the] noble conduct of their father'. Ibn Battuta, *Rehla*, 96.

80. Not only did he wish to be known as 'the Just' and even name his Delhi fortress 'Adilabad', or 'the Abode of Justice', Ibn Battuta records that on occasions when commoners brought accusations of the sultan's injustice before ordinary judges, he would appear before such judges, on foot and unarmed, and, if found guilty, he would insist that his accusers personally administer corporal punishment on himself. Tim Mackintosh-Smith, trans., *The Travels of Ibn Battutah* (London: Picador, 2002), 174–5.

81. `Abd al-Malik `Isami, *Futūḥu's Salāṭīn*, ed. and trans., Agha Mahdi Husain, 3 vols (London: Asia Publishing House, 1967) 2:613, 3:701. Text: *Futūḥus-salāṭīn*, ed. A.S. Usha (Madras: University of Madras, 1948), 405, 465.

82. These sentiments were recorded by `Abd al-Malik `Isami, the earliest Deccan-based Persian-writing historian, and a contemporary of the events that led to the uprising of the colonists against their Tughluq masters. `Isami, *Futūḥ*, trans., 1:15–16, 3:765.

83. In 1350, 'Isami referred to Harihara as a *murtadd*, literally 'one who turns away,' by extension, a 'turncoat' or 'renegade'. This refers to his subsequent renunciation of his former association with the Tughluqs.

84. Vasundhara Filliozat, *l'Épigraphie de Vijayanagara du début à 1377* (Paris: École Française d'Extrême-Orient, 1973), 2–4.

85. Ibn Battuta, *Rehla*, 180.

86. *Annual Reports of the Mysore Archaeological Department* (*ARMAD*) *1929*, inscription no. 90 (see lines 24–5 and 39).

87. Filliozat, *l'Épigraphie*, xxxii, 39–42.

88. The historian `Isami, himself patronized by `Ala al-Din, relates that on the latter's coronation in 1347, the kingdom's most eminent Sufi, Zain al-Din Shirazi, bestowed on the sultan the actual robe worn by the Prophet Muhammad on the night he ascended to Paradise, a robe that had been passed down through twenty-three generations of holy men. See `Isami, *Futūḥ*, trans., 1:13, 3:687. For a discussion of the role of Sufi biographies, or *tazkira*s, in sanctifying the soil of new land in South Asia, see Marcia Hermansen, 'Religious Literature and the Inscription of Identity: The Sufi Tazkira Tradition in Muslim South Asia', *The Muslim World* 87, nos 3–4 (1997), 315–29.

89. See Phillip B. Wagoner, 'From "Pampa's Crossing" to "The Place of Lord Virupaksa": Architecture, Cult, and Patronage at Hampi before the Founding of Vijayanagara', in *Vijayanagara: Progress of Research, 1988–1991*, eds D. Devaraj and C.S. Patil (Mysore: Directorate or Archaeology and Museums, 1996), 141–74.

90. By the late fourteenth century, inscriptions of the ruler Harihara II state that the king inherited not only the city, but also 'Virupaksha himself as the supreme deity of his family'. They go on to describe the king as 'a royal bee at the lotus feet of Virupaksha'. Similarly, the sixteenth-century ruler Krishna Raya referred to Virupaksa in the introduction to his Sanskrit

play *Jāmbavatī-kalyāṇam* as 'the protective jewel of the Karnata kingdom' (*karṇāṭa-rājya-rakṣā-maṇi*), 'Karnata' being the actual name used for what we now call the Vijayanagara state. The nature of this state cult is most clearly seen in a distinctive form of epigraphic practice documented in hundreds of Vijayanagara copper-plate inscriptions that record land grants. Anila Verghese has shown that these inscriptions invariably contain a phrase stating that the donation was carried out 'in the presence of Virupaksha on the banks of the Tungabhadra river' and conclude with a large 'signature' of the god 'Srī Virūpākṣa', written in Kannada script. These formulae and conventions suggest that whenever state land was alienated, the ritual act marking the transfer of property was performed in Virupaksha's temple, so that the god—as owner of all state land within his kingdom—could himself participate in the act and 'sign' the document to attest to the validity and finality of the transfer. One fifteenth-century inscription (*Epigraphia Carnatica* [*EC*] 12: Tumkur Taluk no. 11) even refers to a special 'dāna-maṇṭapa', or 'hall of prestation', located within the temple. See Anila Verghese, *Religious Traditions at Vijayanagara as Revealed through Its Monuments*, Vijayanagara Research Project Monograph Series, vol. 4 (New Delhi: Manohar and American Institute of Indian Studies, 1995), 19 and Appendix A. For *Jāmbavatī-kalyāṇam*, see S. Krishnaswami Ayyangar, *Sources of Vijayanagar History* (Madras: University of Madras, 1919), 142–3.

CHAPTER 2

# Temples and Conquest, 1296–1500

The enemy's capital city should be burned—the palace of the king, beautiful buildings, palaces of princes, ministers and high ranking officers, temples, streets with shops, horse and elephant stables.

—*Mānasollāsa*, a Chalukya text attributed to Someshvara III (r. 1127–39)[1]

Permission to build a temple (*kanīsa*) in a Muslim country can be accorded only to those who pay the *jizya* [poll-tax]. If you agree to pay it, permission for building the temple can be given.

—Sultan Muhammad bin Tughluq, in a letter to the emperor of China, 1342[2]

Surely one of the most contentious issues in the writing of India's pre-modern history centres on the fate of Hindu temples under the sway of Muslim conquerors or rulers. School textbooks, not to mention more popular forms of mass media, are replete with tales of scores, hundreds, even thousands of Hindu temples desecrated or destroyed by conquerors or rulers between about 1000 and 1757, India's so-called Muslim era. This notion has a long history. Driven by their own zealous piety, and seeing the world through the binary categories of righteous 'believers' and wicked 'infidels', some court chroniclers of the thirteenth and fourteenth centuries made exaggerated claims respecting the destructive deeds undertaken by their courtly patrons, while others enthusiastically urged their Indo-Turkish patrons to engage in temple demolition.[3] More recent generations, driven by particular ideological agendas, have accepted such assertions at face value. In the nineteenth and early twentieth centuries, British imperialists endeavoured to legitimize their conquest and occupation of India, in part, by demonizing their political predecessors there, who happened to be Muslims. More recently, Hindu nationalists have sought to promote the idea of India as a naturally Hindu realm, again by demonizing the Muslim presence in South Asia's pre-modern history. For both groups, the idea of temple-destroying Muslim fanatics seemed to provide convenient historical justifications for their respective agendas.

The question, however, should not be whether ruling élites of the Delhi Sultanate and their successors in the Deccan engaged in temple desecration, which they certainly did. The problem is that the question so framed is both too broad and too narrow. It is too broad in the sense that there was nothing distinctive about that activity. Ever since the seventh century, when royal temples were first perceived as objects of political contestation, states throughout India—including the Chalukyas of Kalyana (see the first epigraph to this chapter)—routinely engaged in desecrating the temples of their enemies as a matter of policy. But the question is also too narrow in that it isolates only one response—physical desecration or even destruction—out of a wide range of possible responses that conquering or ruling authorities might have had towards temples occupying a conquered landscape. A more responsible way of framing the question would consider a wider range of possible responses, and then seek to explain why any particular response occurred in a given circumstance.

One might then pose the question thus: in any given zone of armed conflict, what did victors do with the built landscape of defeated regimes, and why? In particular, how did they deal with architectural monuments most closely associated with such regimes? Framed in this way, one is not necessarily limited to considering the fate of temples alone; indeed, in principle one is not even limited to considering only pre-modern India. The church of Hagia Sophia in Istanbul, the Aztec Templo Mayor in Mexico City, Jerusalem's second temple, the Eiffel Tower in Paris—such monuments experienced very different treatment by Ottoman Turks, Spanish conquistadors, Rome's Tenth Legion, and Germany's Third Reich respectively. Yet even on such a broader canvas, scholars have not systematically examined the fates of monuments after their patrons had been swept away by outsiders. This is likely because the question, framed in this way, falls squarely in the shadowy space between art history and political history, two academic disciplines that have suffered too long from mutual isolation. As a result, the exploration of the intricate ways that architecture and power are mutually related is something of an orphan, neglected by both of those venerable academic disciplines.

The present chapter raises precisely the question of how invaders or rulers in the post-thirteenth-century Deccan dealt with the built landscape they conquered or governed and, more particularly, with the most culturally and politically significant structures encountered on that landscape—Hindu temples.[4] The aim is to move beyond the narrow issue of whether a given temple was or was not desecrated, and to flesh out the wider range of responses available to conquerors or rulers when confronted with that landscape. This is because the Deccan's terrain did not present an empty, pristine slate on which sultans or their agents could, by raising new monuments on politically prominent sites, simply inscribe themselves *de novo*. Victors usually had to deal with cluttered, built environments inherited from defeated rivals, as well as, in many cases, structures inherited from earlier, often much earlier, occupants of the land. Confronting such a complex situation, and wishing to assert their own claims to possessing the land and its people, the new rulers actually faced a range of options. They might continue to patronize pre-existing structures in the manner their defeated rivals had done. They might rebuild them. They might redefine them. They might imitate them. They might destroy them. Or, they might ignore them altogether.

Notwithstanding the widespread violence that accompanied the conquest of the Deccan by armies of the Delhi Sultanate, most Hindu temples were in fact left alone. These include, among hundreds of others, the magnificent Chalukya temples built in the metropolitan style of the northern Deccan, such as that of Jalsingi (Figures 3.1b and 3.2b, p. 80 and p. 81 respectively), or the famous 'Thousand Pillar' temple at Hanamkonda, the original royal temple of the Kakatiya kings (Figure 2.1).

Confronted with such spectacular monuments, not to mention thousands of humbler temples, the conquerors typically made no intervention whatsoever. Since their default response in such circumstances was to do nothing, the challenge for the historian is to account for the several temples that were *not* left alone, and to explore the different ways in which the conquerors—and later ruling administrators—engaged with them. Fortunately, we have considerable material and literary evidence with respect to the Delhi Sultanate's initial encounter with the Deccan's built landscape, the focus of this chapter.[5]

## PILLALAMARRI, 1309

The earliest known occasion when officers of the Delhi Sultanate did not leave a temple alone is revealed in a Telugu inscription in Pillalamarri, a town located some 115 kilometres east of modern Hyderabad (Figure 1.5, p. 16). Dated 1357, the inscription records that in that year the chieftain ruling over that town had performed the rituals appropriate for re-establishing regular worship in a temple dedicated to Erakeshvara, a form of Shiva. The reason such a ritual was necessary, so the inscription relates, was that the temple's cultic icon, a Shiva linga, had been struck (though not

**Figure 2.1** Hanamkonda. 'Thousand Pillar' temple, view southwards from the main temple showing the detached *maṇḍapa*.

completely broken) by armies of Sultan `Ala al-Din Khalaji 'during the troubles (*viḍvarālu*) of that time and place'.[6]

What were the 'troubles' to which the inscription refers? Although Sultan `Ala al-Din Khalaji himself had never ventured into this part of the Deccan, in 1309 he ordered his trusted general, Malik Kafur, to invade Kakatiya territory and reduce its king to tributary status. The historian Firishta relates that when Malik Kafur reached the Kakatiyas' western frontier, having marched south and eastwards from Devagiri, he issued orders 'to lay waste the country with fire and sword'.[7] Inasmuch as Pillalamarri is located about 100 kilometres south of the Kakatiya capital of Warangal, some of Malik Kafur's military units evidently ranged within a logistically feasible radius of that city in pursuit of the dynasty's most prominent supporters. And indeed, the Pillalamarri temple had been built and patronized by a powerful lineage of chiefs—the Recherlas, of the Reddi caste—who happened to be among the staunchest feudatory supporters of the Kakatiya regime.[8] It therefore seems reasonable to view the desecration of the Pillalamarri temple as the product of an army on the march under orders to plunder, and as collateral damage in Malik Kafur's larger military and political objective, namely, the siege of Warangal and the humbling of the Kakatiya sovereign.

## DEVAGIRI, 1313–18

The next known engagement of the Delhi Sultanate with a Deccan temple was of a very different nature, and would have far-reaching consequences. During the seventeen years following the very first invasion of the Deccan by an army of the Delhi Sultanate, `Ala al-Din Khalaji's 1296 raid on Devagiri (modern Daulatabad), the Yadava king, Ramachandra, was made to purchase Delhi's protection by paying an annual tribute. During this time the Delhi sultans are not known to have intervened in the city's landscape in any way. But after Ramachandra's death in 1311, the king's successors proved less compliant in paying their tribute, giving northern armies an excuse to re-invade the kingdom. So in 1313 `Ala al-Din's slave general, Malik Kafur, invaded Yadava territory then ruled by Ramachandra's recalcitrant son, Singhana II. After defeating and killing the latter, Malik Kafur remained in Devagiri until 1315, when the sultan, ill and consumed by a swirl of intrigues about him, recalled his trusted general from Devagiri. But early the next year the sultan died, and Kafur only inserted himself in those intrigues. His attempt to seize the throne for himself, however, was foiled when the late sultan's son, Mubarak, bribed the men Kafur had sent to blind him and induced them to slay Kafur instead. In April 1316 the prince ascended the throne of Delhi as Sultan Qutb al-Din Mubarak (r. 1316–20).

In Devagiri, meanwhile, a son-in-law of the late king Ramachandra had revived Yadava rule, giving Delhi yet another excuse to invade the Deccan. This time, in 1318, Sultan Qutb al-Din Mubarak himself determined to forcibly annex Yadava territories once and for all by leading an army down to Devagiri. The political relationship between Delhi and Devagiri now became permanently altered: a northern governor was placed in the former capital, garrisons were set up in the hinterland, and the revenue system of the newly annexed territory was aligned with that of Delhi.

As a result of these two invasions, some time between 1313 and 1318 Devagiri's physical landscape underwent considerable renovation. Delhi's most prominent architectural intervention was to construct in the city's centre a grand congregational mosque, the Deccan's earliest surviving Islamic monument (Figure 2.2).[9] It is not certain, however, whether the mosque was built during Malik Kafur's two-year occupation of Devagiri (1313–15) or soon after Qutb al-Din's invasion of 1318. According to `Isami, in 1313 Sultan `Ala al-Din Khalaji had ordered Malik Kafur not just to invade Devagiri, but 'to remain there, consolidate his position and administer properly that newly acquired territory, construct there a *Jāmi` Masjid*, demonstrate Islam, demand revenue from the peasants, and trample the estates of the rebels'.[10]

Firishta, on the other hand, writes that it was Sultan Qutb al-Din Mubarak who, having invaded Devagiri and executed the last Yadava ruler, 'now ordered a chain of posts to be established as far as Dwar Sumoodra, and built a mosque in Dewgur, which still stands'.[11] It thus seems that even if Malik Kafur had built the city's first congregational mosque, as `Isami reports, five years later Sultan Qutb al-Din Mubarak either replaced it or added to it, since it was the sultan's mosque that still stood in 1609, when Firishta completed his history.[12]

In any event, among Indian mosques of its day, Devagiri's Khalaji mosque ranked second only to Delhi's Qutb mosque in size.[13] Consisting of a great, enclosed square measuring 79 metres on a side externally, the structure contains 177 reused columns carved in distinctive Yadava style, 106 of which were placed in the central prayer hall.[14] These were evidently stripped from nearby Jain and Hindu temples, brought to the site, and then stacked end-on-end to give the prayer hall its great height. Writing in 1350, the chronicler `Isami states that temples had been replaced by mosques during Malik Kafur's two-year occupation of the city, thus confirming that standing temples

**Figure 2.2** Devagiri. Congregational mosque, c.1313–18.

had been dismantled for the purpose of building the mosque.[15] Historians M.S. Mate and T.V. Pathy estimate that between twelve and fourteen Hindu or Jain temples would have been necessary to furnish the requisite number of columns for the mosque. They further estimate that this number of temples would have occupied about seven of the fifty acres comprising 'Mahakot', the inhabited portion of Devagiri at the time of the conquest.[16] From the city's sheer density of temples thus calculated, they reason that the site had likely been an important Jain and Hindu pilgrimage centre even before the Yadavas made it their capital in 1196. This conclusion is supported by the presence of many rock-cut cave-temples that were hewn out of the city's most spectacular natural feature—a single, conical hill of rock that rises sharply from the surrounding plain. Measuring up to 20 metres in depth and 25 metres in width, these spacious Jain and Shaiva cave-temples definitely predate the Khalaji occupation; indeed, they suggest the origin of Devagiri's name: 'mountain of gods'.[17]

Both Malik Kafur and Sultan Qutb al-Din Mubarak understood the religious and political significance of the city they had conquered. By radically changing the context in which familiar Yadava material culture was displayed, the new mosque simultaneously liquidated and absorbed most if not all the religious monuments that had theretofore defined the city. Their mode of engagement with the built environment was thus highly destructive. Yet it also followed conventional Indian practice. For centuries, states in the Deccan—as in India generally—had desecrated royal temples of defeated enemies by way of delegitimizing the latter's authority. This they did on the premise that a royal temple contained the image of a ruling dynasty's state deity, who was considered responsible for protecting a king's sovereign territory.[18] Given the large number of columns in the Devagiri mosque, it is likely that the Khalajis invoked the idea behind the *Mānasollāsa* quote at the head of this chapter, namely, that Indian kings were expected to destroy the entire capital city of an enemy, including palaces, markets, and stables, in addition to temples.

But that would have constituted only one aspect of the Khalajis' radical renovation programme. The other was to build a monumental mosque that symbolically projected imperial Delhi's presence onto the Deccan landscape, publically announcing Delhi's sovereign claims over this newly annexed territory. Features of Devagiri's great Khalaji mosque nearly precisely replicated the metropolitan style of mosques that had been patronized by earlier Delhi sultans in Ajmer, Kaman, Khatu, and in Delhi's Qutb complex itself. These features include a spacious central courtyard encircled by pillared aisles on the north, south, and east sides, a monumental projecting entrance, a corbelled dome over the main *miḥrāb* bay, and trabeated beams borne by reused pillars stacked end-on-end.[19] In addition to these features, Devagiri's mosque also has engaged towers on its northwestern and southwestern corners that resemble miniaturized replicas of the most striking icon of contemporary imperial Delhi—the Qutb Minar. Visually speaking, Delhi had projected itself into the Deccan.[20]

## BIJAPUR, 1320

In 1320, just several years after the completion of Devagiri's mosque, the Khalaji government's provincial administration sought to consolidate its grip over its recently annexed Yadava territory by installing a governor in the important but distant provincial town of Bijapur. Located some 350 kilometres south of Devagiri, Bijapur—or 'Vijayapura' as it was then known—had been a major Chalukya urban centre.[21] Yadava kings, inheriting this territory after the fall of the Chalukyas in the late twelfth century, continued to patronize, and to make additions to, the city's Chalukya-period temples. These included the Narasimhadeva temple, whose earliest known endowment dates to 1033, and the Svayambhu Shiva temple, which the Chalukyas had established in 1074–5.[22]

Between 1318 and 1320, when the region was annexed to the Delhi Sultanate, Khalaji administrators constructed a number of new buildings using Yadava-period materials. Foremost among these is the Karim al-Din mosque, a congregational—and hence very public—house of prayer named after the city's first Khalaji governor, Karim al-Din, who patronized the building of the structure in 1320 (Figure 2.3). Nothing in the historical or the archaeological record indicates with certainty that Karim al-Din had ordered Yadava temples to be desecrated and dismantled to yield building materials for his mosque. But since these recent structures had most likely been associated with the city's displaced Yadava élite, it is quite likely that this was the case—much as had occurred at Devagiri just a few years earlier. With respect to its deployment of reused components, however, Khalaji operations at Bijapur clearly departed from what had happened at Devagiri. Whereas the final design of the Devagiri mosque was modelled on imperial precedents in metropolitan Delhi, the design of the Karim al-Din mosque clearly resulted from a productive engagement with local traditions of temple architecture. That is, at Bijapur—unlike at Devagiri—strategies of reuse served to establish points of continuity between mosque and temple.

One sees the nature of this engagement in the mosque's design, in its concepts of sacred space, and in its accompanying epigraphy. An inscription on the mosque's façade states that

**Figure 2.3** Bijapur. Mosque of Karim al-Din, 1320.

its founder, Karim al-Din, had entrusted its actual construction to Indian craftsmen under the supervision of a local builder (*sutaru*, from the Sanskrit *sutradhara*) named Revaiya.[23] The involvement of these local craftsmen, and the specific choices they made relating to the building's design and conception, gave the mosque a much more familiar and local feel than was the case with the Devagiri mosque. As Katherine Kasdorf has pointed out in an important article, the placement of the mosque's reused temple columns involved deliberate architectural planning and followed long-established principles of design local to the region.[24] For example, it had been customary to distinguish between different spatial zones within the pillared hall (*maṇḍapa*) in front of the temple sanctum by visually marking these zones with different types of columns. The most ornate pillars always defined the central bay of the maṇḍapa on axis with the sanctum (*garbha-gṛha*), while simplified and more slender columns occupied the peripheral spaces. What is remarkable is that Revaiya and his builders adapted this same design principle to their placement of the reused columns in the mosque's prayer hall, positioning the most ornate and monumental columns on either side of the central miḥrāb aisle, and the simpler columns with trimmer proportions in the spaces to either side. Kasdorf interprets this as an instance of 'translation', in which the underlying aim was 'to express one type of sacred space in terms of … [an]other, and in so doing to communicate a certain degree of commonality between the two.'[25] In effect Karim al-Din on the one side, and Revaiya and his masons on the other, appear to have deliberately identified points of commensurability between mosque and temple, between Islam and Hinduism, and ultimately, between the newly arrived Persian cultural order and the older, established Indic cultural order.

This search for commensurability is even more strikingly apparent in the mosque's most ritually important feature, the miḥrāb, in whose upper portion several verses from the Qur'an (2: 255–7) are inscribed in two bands (Figure 2.4). The outer band contains the famous 'Throne Verse', which proclaims God's majesty: 'His Throne comprises the heavens and earth.' Very significantly for a public monument on the cutting edge of an expanding Muslim state, the verse also prohibits religious coercion—'there is no compulsion in religion'—suggesting the mosque's overall intent as offering a non-coercive invitation to non-Muslims. What is more, the miḥrāb is composed of two separate sections clearly distinguished by colour. Its upper portion, which contains the Qur'anic passages, consists of a newly carved stone of light red hue that was cut exactly to fit with the miḥrāb's lower portion, which consists of recycled stone of grey hue. The latter can be recognized as having originally served as the jambs of a doorway leading to the sanctum of a temple. Indeed, the inner vertical moldings of the miḥrāb's lower register contain carved motifs that are identical to those on the doorframes from a nearby temple datable to the late twelfth century, the Sankarlinga temple at Nimbal, just 32 kilometres northeast of Bijapur.[26]

Placing the most important part of a Hindu temple in the analogous part of the mosque seems to have provided a conceptual overlap, translating the new ritual space of the miḥrāb into the familiar terms of the temple. After all, both a miḥrāb and a temple sanctum are sacred spaces that open up beyond a pillared hall, and both constitute the ultimate ritual focus of their respective edifices. Recycling the doorjambs from a temple sanctum to frame the opening of the miḥrāb's niche can therefore underscore the commensurability of the two types of space, while the decorative imagery carved on the

**Figure 2.4** Bijapur. *Miḥrāb* of Karim al-Din mosque (*courtesy of* Katherine Kasdorf).

doorframe—including auspicious motifs such as lotus scrolls and fierce forms of the lion-like *kīrtimukha* monster—lends to the mosque its powers to ward off evil and protect the sacred space of the miḥrāb. One notes, too, that the stone cutters who crafted the miḥrāb's upper, Arabic, portion continued the diamond motifs that appeared along the inner band of the doorframe below—an apparently deliberate effort to achieve an aesthetic continuity between old and new (Figure 2.5).

However, as much as the reuse of the temple doorjambs constitutes another form of 'translation', it stops short of proclaiming pure equivalence. A miḥrāb may be akin to a temple sanctum, but in the end it is fundamentally different, since unlike a sanctum, it is empty and contains no 'idol' or physical image of God. It is for this reason that the miḥrāb frame does not consist of an entire, recycled sanctum doorway. Instead, halfway up it suddenly yields to newly carved slabs of a different material exhibiting a different vocabulary of form. Here, the post and lintel forms of the doorway change to the convergent form of a pointed arch, and two of the decorated bands suddenly transform themselves into the Qur'anic calligraphy of the Throne Verse and its sequel (Figure 2.5). Although verse 2:256 begins by proclaiming that 'there is no compulsion in religion', it goes

**Figure 2.5** Bijapur. Karim al-Din mosque, detail of *miḥrāb* (*courtesy of* Katherine Kasdorf).

on to hold up an invitation to abandon old ways, adding,

> Rectitude has become clear from error. So whosoever disbelieves in idols and believes in God, has laid hold of the most firm handle, unbreaking.[27]

In short, whereas miḥrāb and sanctum certainly share points of continuity, they are not the same. The particular form of reuse employed here communicates quite clearly that the miḥrāb has superseded the sanctum.

## BODHAN, 1323

No sooner had Karim al-Din's mosque been built than a revolution took place in Delhi in the course of which a new dynasty of Turks, the Tughluqs, overthrew and replaced the Khalaji regime. Upon assuming power, the founder of the new dynasty, Ghiyath al-Din Tughluq (r. 1320–5), put in motion an aggressive drive to annex larger tracts of Deccan territory—especially the eastern plateau where Pratapa Rudra, the Kakatiya sovereign at Warangal, had withheld his annual tribute to Delhi during the confusion surrounding north India's dynastic revolution. Accordingly, in 1321 Ghiyath al-Din sent an army led by his eldest son and heir-apparent, Ulugh Khan, to Warangal with a view to destroying the Kakatiya dynasty and annexing its territory. The prince's three-year campaign in the Deccan would be among the most momentous military expeditions in Indian history. First, it demonstrated the clear superiority of north Indian weaponry and fighting techniques over those of the Deccan. Second, it showed the north's grim determination to overwhelm and dominate the peoples of the Deccan, which in turn sowed the seeds of a bitter resentment that would only grow over subsequent generations. And third, it led directly to the outright colonization of northern Deccan and to Delhi's indirect rule over much of the southern plateau.

Directing and towering over these operations was the larger-than-life figure of Ulugh Khan, whom we first meet as a Tughluq prince, and later as the Delhi sovereign himself—Sultan Muhammad bin Tughluq (r. 1325–51). Inasmuch as this extraordinary figure was involved in each of the next four architectural encounters to be considered—Bodhan, Warangal, Rajahmundry, and Kalyana—we shall follow him on his great southern campaign, taking care to trace the different ways in which, along the way, he engaged with the Deccan's built environment.

Departing Delhi in 1321 with much fanfare, Ulugh Khan unfurled the imperial standards and marched first south to Devagiri, headquarters of Delhi's new Deccan province. There, imperial officers and garrisoned cavalry joined the northern army as it moved east into the domains of Pratapa Rudra, the Kakatiya *raja*. Gauging the size of Ulugh Khan's advancing army, the raja prudently drew his own forces within the two concentric walls of Warangal's fort and prepared for a siege. Ulugh Khan's long, six-month siege nearly succeeded, but tensions between Khalaji and Tughluq factions in early 1322 rendered the northern army's operations so ineffective that the prince was forced to lift his siege and withdraw to Devagiri, his forces reduced to just 3,000 mounted archers.[28] However, when his father sent down substantial reinforcements and ordered him to renew the siege, the Tughluq prince regrouped and prepared for a second invasion of Andhra. In 1323, he left Devagiri at the head of a powerful army of 63,000 mounted archers[29] and marched south, camping at Sunari (near modern Barsi, in southern Maharashtra).[30] From there he proceeded to Kalyana, where he patronized the construction of a congregational mosque, a sure sign that a sizeable Muslim population had already settled in the former Chalukya capital.[31] Then for a second time he crossed the frontier into Kakatiya territory. First, he seized the fort of Bidar, a strategic site that a century later would become the Bahmani capital. After this, writes Firishta, the prince went on to seize 'some other forts along the way', leaving behind trustworthy men to guard the roads.[32]

Among these 'other forts' was Bodhan, the site of one of the most distinctive mosques in India (Figure 2.6). But the structure in question had not always been a mosque. Locally known as the 'Deval Masjid' in Urdu, or the 'Vandastambhala-gudi' (hundred-pillared temple) in Telugu, the structure had originally been a temple, built in the late twelfth or early thirteenth century in the Kakatiya style. On its western side was a single sanctum and vestibule, adjoined to an open-pillared hall (maṇḍapa) of nine bays (3 by 3), with single-bay porches projecting from the middle of the north, east, and south sides. It rested on a raised platform, accessible by stairs with balustrades on the north and south sides. When the temple was converted into a mosque, the walls and superstructure were removed from the shrine itself, and a prayer hall of forty-five bays (5 by 9) was constructed in its place. This prayer hall was of open-pillared construction along its north, east, and south sides, but was closed off on the west side—the direction of the *qibla*—by a solid wall. A miḥrāb niche was built into the middle of the qibla wall, a stone pulpit (*miṃbar*) placed immediately to its north (Figure 2.7). Although the temple's shrine had been dismantled, the uppermost course of its foundations was deliberately left intact, tracing the shrine's ghostly outlines as a perpetual visual reminder that the edifice had earlier been a temple.

In striking contrast to the treatment of the sanctum, the temple's pillared maṇḍapa was carefully preserved in almost its original form, now recast as a majestic entry pavilion into the adjoining prayer hall. The only significant alterations were iconographic: the figural sculptures on the four pillars of the central bay were chiseled off, and twelve semi-spheroid domes made of brick-and-mortar—the structure's most arresting feature as seen from afar—replaced the 'rotated squares' type of flat ceiling that had originally covered the temple's three porches and central maṇḍapa. One may reasonably wonder why the trabeate ceilings of the old maṇḍapa were replaced with domes, especially inasmuch as the newly built prayer hall featured flat ceilings throughout its structure, except in the bay containing the miṃbar.[33] The likely reason for this distinction is that since the maṇḍapa of the old temple was being redefined as part of a mosque, the builders were asked to supply some readily visible feature that the patron took to be emblematic of its new Islamic purpose.[34]

But how, in the end, might one explain this unusual structure? Who transformed it into a mosque, and why? One might suspect Ulugh Khan himself, since the prince had already patronized a congregational mosque (no longer traceable) in nearby Kalyana while on the same

**Figure 2.6** Bodhan. 'Deval Masjid' or 'Vanda-Stambhala-gudi'.

**Figure 2.7** Bodhan. Interior of 'Deval Masjid' showing *miḥrāb*.

campaign taking him towards Warangal. But no inscription or chronicle mentions Ulugh Khan's building activities in Bodhan. There are, to be sure, fragments of two stone inscriptions lying in the courtyard in front of the site, both of them patronized by Ulugh Khan *after* he became sultan several years later. But neither inscription records the dedication of a mosque.[35] Indeed, from a strictly architectural standpoint, it is difficult to associate this structure with Tughluq patronage at all. Not only does its miḥrāb-arch lack the pointed horseshoe profile so characteristic of Tughluq architecture, its makeshift composition is utterly anomalous when placed beside other Tughluq mosques in India. In particular, the profusion of domes that seem to sprout from atop the monument's eastern side contrasts with most mosques built in the Deccan in the Khalaji and Tughluq periods, which were either flat-roofed throughout or possessed only a single, iconic dome (of either arcuate or trabeate construction) located before the miḥrāb or miṃbar.[36]

A clue to the puzzle is found in the near-contemporary account of `Isami who, alone among chroniclers of the day, mentioned the Tughluq army's passing through Bodhan during its 1323 invasion of Andhra. 'When the Khan of auspicious stars arrived at Bodan [*sic*],' he wrote, referring to prince Ulugh Khan,

he laid siege to that fortress for three to four days. Then the garrison became so panicky that the Rai [chief] came out of his own accord, suing for

> amnesty. He made an offer of the whole of his dominion and wealth. When he was given amnesty, he embraced Islam, not alone but with all the members of his family and other dependants. Next day, the Khan started from there, and on the tenth day, he arrived at the foot of [Warangal].[37]

This suggests the possibility that Bodhan's chief himself, having negotiated an amnesty with Ulugh Khan and converted to Islam, supervised the building's reconfiguration. As Bodhan's principal political figure, after all, he would likely have been the temple's chief patron and hence in a position of authority to undertake the project. And as a new convert to Islam, he would have had the motive to do so, for at the time there would have been no mosques in the town.

Architecturally, what points us towards this interpretation is the multitude of prominent semi-spheroid domes that dominate the structure's eastern façade. Domes, of course, are ritually irrelevant for a mosque; yet, to Deccani eyes at the very outset of Delhi's conquest, they would have been strikingly unusual features—indeed, they might well have been viewed as distinctive, signature elements of the new class of buildings. If the structure had been redesigned by a local convert eager to make an unambiguous statement as to his new religious identity, the use of high domes—and not one, but twelve, no less—certainly would have served the purpose of declaring the former temple's new status, and its total break with its earlier identity.

## WARANGAL, 1323

As `Isami notes, from Bodhan it took Ulugh Khan ten days to reach Warangal, which the prince at once besieged and which, owing to his enormous cavalry and sophisticated siege equipment, ultimately capitulated to Delhi's will. Having defeated the Kakatiya army, captured the capital city, and dispatched its king, Pratapa Rudra, to Delhi, Ulugh Khan now faced the challenging question of how to integrate the former Kakatiya realm into the Delhi Sultanate's sovereign territory. Standing before the great temple to Svayambhu Shiva in the heart of Warangal's citadel, the Tughluq prince would immediately have understood the political significance of the monument, which communicated architecturally that the icon of the god was also the emblem of the state and the source of its authority. Consistent with his resolution to efface every remaining vestige of Kakatiya authority, he set about dismantling the edifice. Every structure standing within the complex was pulled down to its foundations, sparing only the four ritual gateways, or *toraṇa*s, that stood at the four cardinal directions just beyond the sacred precinct (Figure 1.6, p. 18). To the extent possible, the building's structural elements were carefully preserved, since Ulugh Khan had plans to recycle them in the new buildings he was planning for the city. This would play a crucial role in recasting Warangal, renamed 'Sultanpur', as a provincial capital of Delhi. But most importantly, Ulugh Khan had the Svayambhu Shiva linga uprooted from its pedestal and broken in two, thus rendering it ritually incapable of serving as a vehicle for the deity's manifestation (Figure 5.3, p. 174). This act of desecration decisively undermined the Kakatiyas' authority; it also removed a potential focus for a rebellion that might attempt to restore their state.

With the symbolic fount of Kakatiya authority uprooted, it still remained for Warangal's conquerors to establish their own authority as the city's new rulers. Following the Khalajis' example at Devagiri, Ulugh Khan constructed a great congregational mosque on the former site of Svayambhu Shiva's temple. After removing the recyclable building components yielded by dismantling the temple, all remaining fragments were buried where they lay, under soil nearly a metre deep.[38] The mosque was laid out upon this new, higher surface on the general site where the temple had stood, but with its centre of gravity shifted somewhat towards the southwest. Although precious little of this mosque remains standing today—five columns, five beams, and one ceiling slab, to be precise—we may reconstruct its location and appearance from the evidence of the fragments that still lie scattered about the surface of the site (Figure 2.8).[39] When intact, the mosque consisted of a covered prayer hall to the west that was most likely preceded by an enclosed courtyard to the east. It also contained, just north of the main domed miḥrāb bay, a stone miṃbar from which the *khuṭba* address would have been delivered each Friday in the name of the Tughluq sultan in Delhi. The limited evidence at hand thus suggests that Ulugh Khan's mosque at 'Sultanpur' stood in the same tradition of north India's imperial mosques as did the Khalaji mosque of Devagiri. Yet, even while the mosque projected Delhi's presence in the Andhra country, placing it on the site of the Svayambhu Shiva temple lent it a degree of continuity, as one politically charged religious building had been replaced by another.

But there was still more to Ulugh Khan's redesign of Warangal's citadel. Although the

**Figure 2.8** Warangal Fort. Remains of the Tughluq congregational mosque.

prince carefully retained the four spectacular toraṇas that had framed and centred the Svayambhu Shiva temple, he modified these structures in a way that made them far more than just visual delimiters of a sacred zone around the mosque. As part of the same levelling operation that had buried the rubble fragments of the dismantled temple, the carved stone bases of the Kakatiya toraṇas were likewise covered over by the soil infill, in effect removing them from the ritual pedestals that had underscored their purely symbolic significance in the Kakatiya period. Brought down to ground level, the toraṇas could now serve as functional portals, inviting and accommodating actual physical passage. Since the enclosure wall that had originally run continuously behind them was also removed, the toraṇa portals would have served as monumental markers indicating preferred points of entry into the newly defined plaza. The eastern portal would have marked an axial path of movement into the precinct, running due west towards what was evidently the mosque's principal entrance pavilion.

In addition to the mosque, the Tughluqs built a second major monument from materials salvaged from the demolished temple. This is the royal audience hall known today as the Khush Mahal, situated some 160 metres west of the westernmost toraṇa (Figure 2.9). Unlike the mosque, however, this building is still in excellent condition. In fact, it is among the

**Figure 2.9** Warangal Fort. Tughluq audience hall, known as the 'Khush Mahal'.

best preserved Tughluq audience halls in all of India, being in far better condition than its likely prototype, the hall of public audience (*diwān-i `ām*) of Tughluqabad-Delhi, which Ulugh Khan's father, Sultan Ghiyath al-Din Tughluq, completed about the same time his son took Warangal.[40] Everything about the Khush Mahal, from the pronounced batter of its heavy walls to its northern orientation and longitudinal focus, connects it conceptually to imperial Tughluqabad-Delhi. Like Devagiri's Khalaji mosque and the nearby mosque on the Svayambhu Shiva temple site, the structure presents a striking instance of how the metropolitan architectural style of contemporary Delhi was transplanted in nearly pure form in the new provincial outpost of Warangal.

Above all, the hall conveyed a sense of power (Figure 2.10). In its southern end is a slightly narrower chamber with an elevated platform that would have held the seat of the ruler. A rectangular water pool was placed in the main chamber, near the base of the ruler's elevated platform. Once inside the hall's northern entrance, the visitor's eye is pulled forcefully towards the throne platform opposite, thanks

**Figure 2.10** Warangal Fort. Tughluq audience hall, interior.

to the focussing effect of the six transverse arches that bear the Tughluqs' characteristic pointed horseshoe profile, and which articulate the main space of the hall. Here, Tughluq governors would have sat to grant formal audience to their assembled subordinates. We can well imagine how their image of might and glory would have been augmented by the strength and power of the hall's design.

The audience hall was also intended to be connected both visually and conceptually to the citadel's main plaza. This was accomplished by means of an arched niche in the outer wall of the Khush Mahal's east side that is perfectly aligned along an axis running eastward through the plaza's eastern and western toraṇas. The niche most likely marked the western end of a ceremonial avenue that would have run due east from the northern end of the audience hall, through the portal of the western toraṇa, and ending at a small doorway in the back wall of the mosque that led into the prayer hall adjacent to the miṃbar pulpit. The city's governor could have moved along this pathway between the audience hall and the mosque on the occasion of the Friday noonday prayers, when he would be present for the delivery of the khuṭba.[41] The elaborate measures that Ulugh Khan took in redesigning Warangal's central plaza suggest his grasp of the site's importance for the defeated Kakatiyas, as well as his determination to transform the place into a colonial outpost of a distant imperial order.

## RAJAHMUNDRY, 1324

After appointing officers to govern the eastern Deccan, Ulugh Khan left Warangal for his long return trip back to Delhi. But instead of retracing his steps via Devagiri, he turned eastwards toward the Andhra coast on a route that took him through Orissa.[42] It seems also to have taken him through the rich Godavari delta, where one of his appointees, an officer named Salar `Ulwi, commissioned the construction of a mosque in the town of Rajahmundry in 1324. Presently standing on that town's main road near the police station, this is the only Tughluq mosque in the Deccan for which both the building and its foundational inscription are intact.[43] Its prayer hall consists of twenty-one bays (3 by 7) divided by twelve starkly plain *citrakhaṇḍa* columns that appear to have been newly fashioned for this building by local masons. The structure is entered through a formal gateway that leads from the street into the mosque's enclosed courtyard. A Tughluq-style pointed arch with a horseshoe profile frames the outer doorway of this gateway, beyond which a corridor takes one to another such arched opening, which in turn leads to the courtyard.

Built into this second arched opening is the mosque's most notable feature—an elaborately carved doorway taken from the sanctum of a temple (Figure 2.11).[44] On the basis of its style, this finely carved doorway appears to date to the twelfth or thirteenth century, having originally been patronized by local feudatories of the Kakatiyas. Fixed directly above the lintel of the temple doorway is a tablet on which a Persian inscription declares the sovereignty of Sultan Ghiyath al-Din Tughluq and the 'ever-increasing prosperity' of Ulugh Khan. It also identifies Salar `Ulwi as the mosque's patron. Although the inscription makes no mention of a temple, whether at this site or elsewhere, by placing the entranceway to a temple's most sacred space in the entrance of the mosque, Salar `Ulwi seems to have appealed not only to a locally familiar aesthetic, but to the deeper purpose of a temple sanctum's doorway, namely, its function of demarcating a zone of purity within. Unlike a sanctum doorway, however, which is intended to protect the deity within

**Figure 2.11** Rajahmundry. Gateway to mosque, inner entrance.

and to restrict access to this sacred zone, the reused doorway in the mosque functions to invite all worshippers inside. In this respect, the doorway serves as a bridge, connecting a pre-conquest world with a new, Tughluq-sponsored world, in a manner not unlike the miḥrāb of Bijapur's Karim al-Din mosque, or indeed, the four Kakatiya toraṇas that framed Warangal's redesigned plaza.

## KALYANA, 1326

Having left Salar `Ulwi to govern the Godavari delta from Rajahmundry, Ulugh Khan continued on his return trip to Delhi, where in 1324 the victorious prince was greeted with a hero's welcome. But soon thereafter his father, Sultan Ghiyath al-Din, died, and in early 1325 Ulugh Khan rose to power as Sultan Muhammad bin Tughluq (r. 1325–51).[45] The very next year, the government of the new sultan implemented policies respecting an important monument in Kalyana, the former Chalukya capital, that departed radically from the policies the former prince had applied in Warangal. Whereas Ulugh Khan as a Tughluq prince and general had demolished Warangal's great Shiva temple, just three years later an inscription was recorded in the name of the same man, now sultan, to the effect that the Shiva temple at Kalyana was to be repaired, guaranteed imperial protection, and its worship reinstated. We shall address this seemingly contradictory behaviour presently, but first let us review the facts in the matter.

The earliest evidence of Delhi's presence in Kalyana comes from an inscription dated 1323 stating that 'in the large town of Kalyani' a congregational mosque was built in the reign of Ghiyath al-Din Tughluq. Since the inscription also mentions 'Ulugh', it seems likely that Ulugh Khan erected this mosque during his 1323 march from Devagiri en route to Warangal.[46] Although the site of that mosque cannot be traced, the fact that such a mosque existed points to the city's sizeable Muslim population at that time, mostly colonists who had settled in the region after the Khalaji conquest ten years earlier. But then in 1326, just three years after that mosque had been built, and one year after Ulugh Khan had become Delhi's new ruler, a public charter was issued in Kalyana in the sultan's name (Figure 2.12). It is an extraordinary record in several respects.[47] First, it was drafted by a certain Vijaditya not in Persian, the power-language of the Delhi Sultanate and of the Persian cosmopolis, but in Sanskrit—the language of that *other* cosmopolis— and in Nagari script. It was also dated in the Shaka, not the Islamic calendar, corresponding to 10 November 1326. Appearing at the top of the stone slab bearing the inscription is the image of the sun and a crescent moon, the same iconographic programme that Chalukya inscriptions would have borne. And finally, Sultan Muhammad bin Tughluq was given the Sanskrit title 'mahārājādhirāja śrī-suratāṇa'—'great king of kings and prosperous sultan'—while the governor of the Deccan, Qiyam al-Din Qutlugh, was called 'mahāpradhāna'—'great minister'—both of these (except *suratāṇa*, 'sultan') being terms that the Chalukyas and other pre-Turkic dynasties of the Deccan would have used in reference to their own public officials.

The inscription itself refers to the outbreak of a serious anti-Tughluq rebellion led by the sultan's cousin, Baha al-Din Gurshasp, who had earlier been put in charge of the frontier fort of Sagar, located 160 kilometres south of Kalyana near the Krishna River. At the time of the rebellion, which must have broken out not long before the date of this record, the Tughluq governor in charge of Kalyana, Khwaja Ahmad, together with his Hindu secretary, Jandamala, left the city in order to consult with other government officials, presumably about how to deal with the uprising. But in their absence, unidentified unruly elements disrupted worship in Kalyana's temple of Madhukeshvara and even damaged its Shiva linga. Some devotees of the deity planned to repair the image and for this purpose approached the temple trustees. When Khwaja Ahmad returned to Kalyana, the official in charge of managing the temple, one Thakkura Malla, appealed to him, as the governor of the region, to restore the structure and reinstate the deity's image. After first consulting Jandamala, his secretary, Khwaja Ahmad approved the request, reasoning that for the temple's petitioners, worship in the temple was a religious duty. Accordingly, the temple's Shiva linga was repaired and re-installed according to the prescribed rites for such procedures, including the nocturnal chanting of *mantras*.

One finds fascinating stories in this episode, not the least being the unhappy fate of the sultan's cousin, whose revolt seems to have triggered the chain of events that somehow led to the attack on the temple.[48] But what stands out most clearly is the extent to which

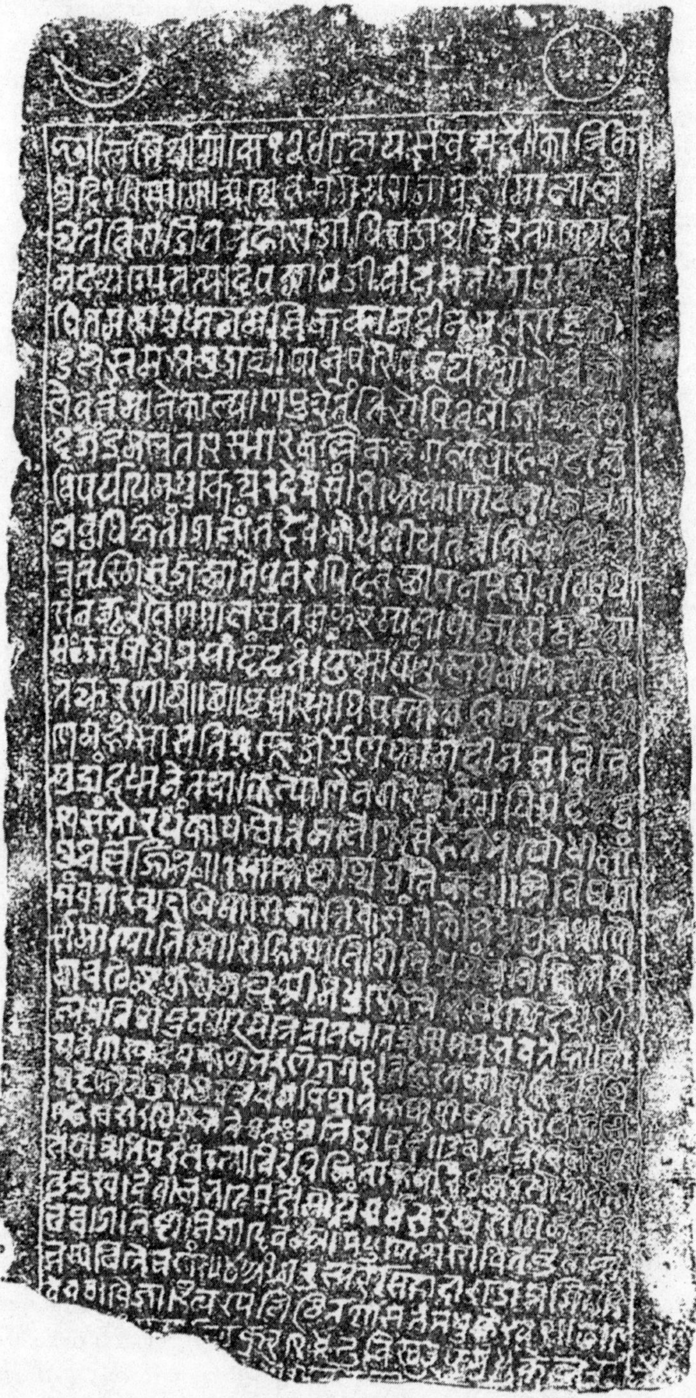

**Figure 2.12** Sanskrit inscription of Sultan Muhammad bin Tughluq respecting a Shiva temple at Kalyana, dated 10 November 1326 (*courtesy of* Archaeological Survey of India).

the Tughluq government had enmeshed itself in the religious and political affairs of Kalyana's local society, and correspondingly, the extent to which that society had assimilated the mahārājādhirāja śrī-suratāṇa in distant Delhi into their conceptual world. Sandwiched between Sultan Muhammad bin Tughluq and the devotees, trustees, and manager of the Madhukeshvara temple was Khwaja Ahmad, the local governor who had been charged with managing and sustaining the status quo in matters of local religious institutions. The Tughluq government's clear priority respecting this recent addition to its realm was to secure and maintain an institutional continuity with the past. This is conveyed as much in the inscription's media—its language, script, honorific titles, and iconography—as it is in its message.

Looking back over the extraordinary career of prince Ulugh Khan/Sultan Muhammad bin Tughluq, one is struck by the apparently contradictory behaviour he exhibited towards the built environment of the territory he conquered and ruled. As prince, he had demolished the Shiva temple of Warangal, whereas only several years later as sultan he preserved and protected another Shiva temple in Kalyana. How is one to explain what might seem a stunning reversal in official policy concerning the disposition of temples in conquered domains? One is tempted to explain his behaviour in terms of his famously bipolar personality, for stories of the sultan's wild vacillations between horrific cruelty and lavish generosity were legend even in his own day.[49] But regarding Hindu temples, his policies were actually consistent. Temples associated with enemy kings whose territories lay in the path of his advancing army were liable to be destroyed and their salvaged materials reused, as occurred at Warangal—or as had earlier occurred in Devagiri under the orders of Khalaji administrators. But by 1326, Kalyana had long since ceased being the capital of an enemy king. When the Chalukya empire broke up towards the end of the twelfth century, the city's status fell from imperial capital to a distant outpost on the Yadava frontier, with the Kakatiyas to the east and the Hoysalas to the south.[50] Although still important as a strategically situated fort, Kalyana and its temples played no role in underwriting the legitimacy of the Yadava state, in the way, for instance, that Warangal and its Svayambhu Shiva temple had done for the Kakatiya state. The temple thus posed no threat to the stability of the Tughluq regime. Indeed, since supporting local temples was what local populations expected legitimate rulers to do, the sultan had a natural incentive to follow suit.

There was yet another reason why Muhammad bin Tughluq patronized Kalyana's Shiva temple. In a pattern found throughout the history of Indo-Muslim polities, once enemy territory had been annexed to the state, immovable property already on that territory was regarded as state property and hence deserving of state protection and support. In the case of Kalyana, then, when a temple that had existed from before the conquest was somehow desecrated after the region was annexed to the sultanate, imperial officers were obliged to have the structure repaired. In Muhammad bin Tughluq's view, this was because any territory annexed to the sultanate automatically became subject to Islamic Law, under which non-Muslims and their property enjoyed protected status. By the same reasoning, if non-Muslims should wish to build a new temple on land *after* it had been annexed, permission would be granted so long as they paid the poll-tax (*jizya*) required of non-Muslims, as specified in Islamic Law. Based on his correspondence with the emperor of China, we know that the sultan, who was well versed in Islamic theology and jurisprudence, held precisely this view. In 1342, when the Chinese emperor petitioned the Delhi court to have a temple built somewhere in Tughluq India, Muhammad bin Tughluq replied that permission would be granted so long as the petitioner paid a poll-tax.[51] It follows that in the sultan's view, the Hindus of Kalyana, as tax-paying subjects of the Delhi Sultanate, were permitted not only to repair an existing temple, but also, should they wish, to build a new one.

## SHOLAPUR, c. 1323–47

This discussion on the legal status of the Deccan's temples during and after the conquest is pertinent to considering two buildings in the fort of Sholapur, a town in the central Maratha country dating at least to Yadava times. One structure is a small dilapidated temple of the Yadava period (twelfth or thirteenth century) located just inside the fort's north wall, and the other is a thirty-six bay (9 by 4) mosque located about 30 metres south of the temple (Figures 2.13 and 2.14). Although neither structure appears to be mentioned in chronicles or inscriptions, the archaeological evidence indisputably establishes that the mosque was assembled from columns and dressed masonry slabs taken, in part, from the temple nearby. The mosque's prayer hall is carried on thirty-one free-standing columns, divided into two

**Figure 2.13** Sholapur Fort. Dilapidated temple, from southeast.

**Figure 2.14** Sholapur Fort. Mosque, from southeast.

groups according to length.[52] Sixteen columns have full-length shafts (2.15 metres each), and fifteen have shorter shafts (1.89 metres each) that require separate blocks to attain their proper height. In morphology, style, material, and dimensions, the shorter columns of the mosque exactly match those still remaining in the temple, thus establishing that the mosque's fifteen shorter columns had been dismantled from the temple, whereas the sixteen full-length columns were taken from some other source, as yet unidentified.[53]

No textual sources indicate when the mosque might have been built, but several of its stylistic features suggest a date in the early fourteenth century, under either Khalaji or Tughluq patronage. These include, most notably, the pointed horseshoe profile and the doubled concentric placement of the arches framing its central miḥrāb (Figure 2.15). This suggests that the temple could have been disassembled, and the mosque built, during one of the sultanate's early expeditions into the interior Deccan. If a Hindu chief had resisted the expansion of state power, any temple patronized by that chief would have been liable for desecration—or as in the present case, demolition—since it would have been perceived as an architectural manifestation of that chief's authority. There are several possibilities for when this could have taken place. In 1313 Malik Kafur, upon executing the Yadava king of Devagiri, is reported to have laid waste the Maratha country as far south as Mudgal, some 175 kilometres beyond Sholapur.[54] In 1318, Sultan Qutb al-Din Mubarak established and garrisoned forts in Sagar, Gulbarga, and other centres of the region, Gulbarga being only 100 kilometres east of Sholapur.[55] And in 1347, just as the Bahmani state was being consolidated, the new officer posted to Maindargi—only 50 kilometres east of Sholapur—is reported to have captured three or four forts in the region by way of punishing local chiefs who had resisted state power.[56]

## MANVI, 1406

In the Sholapur case, we can infer only from architectural data that a temple had been pillaged for building a nearby mosque in the context of military action against refractory elements. But regarding the next recorded case in which a sultanate engaged architecturally with a temple, contemporary epigraphic data can be seen to confirm this pattern. The case involves the town of Manvi, located in the Raichur Doab, which the eighth sultan of the Bahmani dynasty, Firuz Shah (1397–1422), attacked and seized in 1406. As a consequence of the conflict, a temple inside the fort was dismantled and elements of it were reassembled to build a small mosque (Figure 2.16). The mosque's roof is supported by twelve reused citrakhaṇḍa columns, probably of Yadava provenance (twelfth–thirteenth centuries), eight of them

**Figure 2.15** Sholapur Fort. Mosque, prayer hall and central *miḥrāb*.

**Figure 2.16** Manvi. Interior of mosque, 1406.

engaged and four of them free-standing. Its entrance consists of an arched opening above a doorframe—two jambs and a lintel—that had been taken from a temple. A Persian inscription, located directly above the doorframe and currently whitewashed, reads:

A mosque has been converted out of a temple as a sign of religion, in the reign of the world-conquering emperor, the king who is the asylum of Faith and possessor of the crown, whose kingdom is young (i.e., flourishing), viz. Firuz Shah Bahmani, who is the cause of exuberant spring in the garden of religion, Abu'l-Fath [Firuz Shah Bahmani], the king, who conquered this fort by the firm determination of his mind in a single attack (lit. on horseback). After the victory of the emperor, the chief of chiefs, Safdar (lit. the valiant commander) of the age, received (the charge of) the fort. The builder of this noble place of prayer is Muhammad Zahir Aqchi, the pivot of the Faith. He constructed in the year … AH 809 = 1406–07 this Ka`ba-like memento.[57]

As always, context is everything. The fort of Manvi was located in the heart of the bitterly contested Raichur Doab, the rich sliver of land between the Tungabhadra and Krishna Rivers that had been the object of one of the most prolonged struggles in medieval Indian history. Between 1362 and 1406, when Manvi fell to Firuz Shah, the rajas of Vijayanagara and the Bahmani sultans had already fought five wars over control of the region. Between

1406 and 1512, the same contestants would wage six more wars over it.[58] The struggle with which we are concerned was initiated by Vijayanagara's Deva Raya I (r. 1406–22), who attacked the fort of Mudgal, then held by the Bahmanis. When the sultan learned of this unprovoked invasion in the summer of 1406, he assembled a large army at his palace city of Firuzabad and marched deep into the Doab. According to Firishta, he did not stop until he reached metropolitan Vijayanagara itself, in the environs of which the armies of the two kings skirmished for four months before reaching a truce.[59] Since Manvi is located directly between Vijayanagara and Raichur, the logical site from which Firuz would have staged his assault on Deva Raya I's capital, the evidence suggests that he attacked Manvi, which was then held by a refractory chieftain, while marching en route to Vijayanagara. He would then have dismantled the temple patronized by the defeated chief of the fort and used its elements to construct the mosque.

## KONDAPALLI, 1478

If Manvi lay on a contested frontier zone that saw repeated wars between powerful foes, our last instance of a sultanate's engagement with the built landscape took place in a very different political context. By the third quarter of the fifteenth century, the northern Deccan was no longer a frontier zone on the cutting edge of an expanding state. Rather, it was now firmly integrated into the stable administration of the Bahmani Sultanate, then guided by its sober and judicious minister, Mahmud Gawan (fl. 1453–81). By the 1470s many non-Muslims had been recruited into Bahmani service, including a chieftain named Bhimraj Orriya. Sometime in 1477, however, the garrison in the government fort at Kondapalli, in the lower Krishna delta, rose up in mutiny, murdered the commandant, and seized the fort. Mutiny was then followed by treason. When the rebels handed over control of the fort to Bhimraj Orriya—who may or may not have led the uprising—this former government servant invited the king of Orissa to invade Bahmani territory, proposing to assist the raja if the latter would allow him to retain Kondapalli and the surrounding countryside. The king of Orissa obliged, reaching the delta with 10,000 cavalry. Responding to these acts, the Bahmani king, Sultan Muhammad Bahmani III (r. 1463–82), personally marched to the delta region with 20,000 cavalry, forcing the king of Orissa to retreat and Bhimraj to take refuge in Kondapalli Fort. In early 1478, after first dealing with the king of Orissa, the sultan besieged the fort of Kondapalli, which Bhimraj finally surrendered after six months. Following the *Bahman-nāma*, a chronicle that is no longer extant, Firishta then writes:

> The sultan mounted his horse and, after inspecting the city and fort, demolished a large temple that was there and beheaded several Brahmans and temple servants. He then ordered that a mosque be built on the temple site. Builders diligently went to work laying its foundation. Having made a wooden *miṃbar*, Muhammad Shah ascended the pulpit and, calling the name of the Prophet, offered several prayers of thanks, distributed gold to the needy, and gave a sermon declaring that henceforth the *khuṭba* would be read in his name.[60]

Here, then, we have an unambiguous instance of a temple destroyed and a mosque built for manifestly political reasons. In the mind of the Bahmani sultan, since Bhimraj had earlier sworn loyalty to the Bahmani state, the fort's temple that he patronized was effectively state property, and hence at the disposal of the sultan. Therefore, when its patron committed an act of treason, both Bhimraj and the temple were subject to punishment.

* * *

Whenever territory is acquired by a new sovereign authority, the possible outcomes respecting the fate of the territory's built landscape are everywhere the same. Do the victors intervene in that landscape, or not? And if they do intervene, in what manner do they do so? In other words, how do they respond to the built environment they have acquired? The annexation of the Deccan Plateau by the Delhi Sultanate in the thirteenth century—and the consolidation of authority by its immediate successor, the Bahmani kingdom—confronted commanders, governors, or sovereigns with precisely these questions. A historian would further ask, what factors in a given situation might have shaped their response? The data presented in this chapter suggest a range, or a spectrum, of architectural outcomes of military conquest. We may distinguish these outcomes one from another according to the extent to which the conquering power intervened in the existing built landscape, especially respecting its most prominent feature—Hindu temples.

At one end of this spectrum is *non-intervention*, by far the most common response. As most temples and their patrons were politically irrelevant, they posed no threat to the stability of new ruling regimes, which consequently ignored them. Temples patronized by powerful chiefs, however—and especially those that underpinned the authority of ruling regimes of powerful states—were problematic. But even such temples would be ignored if their patron-rulers no longer held effective power. Like a light bulb whose power cord has been cut, such temples had lost their charge; politically, they were dead. This would explain why the Delhi sultans and their successors ignored a spectacular royal monument like the 'Thousand Pillar' temple of Hanamkonda near Warangal. Although it had been the Kakatiya dynasty's principal temple in the twelfth century, it no longer was so when the armies of Delhi first reached the area in 1309. The same is true for all the temples associated with the imperial Chalukyas, who of course had been long defunct by the early fourteenth century.

The least intrusive form of active intervention in a built environment was *patronage*, that is, a state's endorsement of the *status quo ante* by continuing to support a pre-conquest institution. The Shiva temple of Kalyana provides a dramatic example of this. Acting through his appointed governor of the city, Sultan Muhammad bin Tughluq in 1326 directly intervened to restore a temple to regular worship by overseeing physical repairs to it. But in truth, he was doing far more than repairing a temple. He was underwriting the entire social order in which the temple's institutional structure—its devotees, trustees, and manager—had traditionally functioned. In the case of this temple, we do not hear of any chieftain whose authority or legitimacy might have depended on the temple's well-being. Instead, governing authorities acted in such a manner that the sultan himself, having assumed proprietary rights over the institution, adopted the role of the temple's *de facto* if not *de jure* patron.

A greater degree of intervention in the built environment was *desecration*, which includes any action that would render a temple incapable of facilitating normal interactions between the public and the divine world. At Pillalamarri in 1309, a temple icon was struck, damaging it sufficiently to render the temple unusable until it was repaired and re-consecrated. The incident is known to have occurred during an invasion of Warangal by Malik Kafur, who had ordered his units to attack Kakatiya territory. Since the chiefs who patronized the Pillalamarri temple were also firm supporters of the Kakatiya ruling house, the attack on their principal temple would appear to have been politically driven.

A fourth and still more intrusive form of engagement was *redefinition*. Here, the structural integrity of a monument was maintained, but its function was transformed by adding and/or removing ritually critical components. The Mosque of Cordoba became a cathedral, and Istanbul's church of Hagia Sophia became a mosque, when new ruling authorities made strategic alterations to these monuments. The same can be said for the 'Deval Masjid' in Bodhan, where the ritually critical miḥrāb replaced the sanctum of a Kakatiya temple. What is exceptional about this structure, though, is that its redefinition appears to have been accomplished not by the governing Tughluqs but by the local chief, who was a convert to Islam. Also exceptional about the structure is the addition of semi-spheroid domes on its eastern side, replacing the 'rotated squares' roof system of the former temple. Given the prominence of domes in the contemporary mosques of Tughluq Delhi, the chief of Bodhan would appear to have used a profusion of high, prominent domes as iconic features declaring the building's—and his own—new Islamic identity.

The most drastic intervention in a built environment was *reassemblage*, which occurred whenever a structure was torn down and its disassembled elements recycled for constructing something new. The mosques at Devagiri, Bijapur, Warangal, Sholapur, and Manvi were all built, at least in part, from reused temple elements following military engagements. In two of these cases, we can precisely identify the origin of the reused temple elements. At Sholapur, the remains of one of the temples plundered for building the mosque are lying just 30 metres from the mosque. Similarly, the columns of the Warangal mosque had been taken from elements of the demolished Svayambhu Shiva temple, which had occupied the very same site. At Manvi, elements from the fort temple were evidently reassembled in the mosque following a known military engagement. And at Devagiri, we can infer that something of the same sort had happened, given the site's status as the former Yadava capital and given, as well, the Khalajis' determination to annihilate any visible evidence of the defeated dynasty's former legitimacy. At Bijapur, too, the oldest portion of the mosque of Karim al-Din appears to have been built from Yadava-period temples that were in active use just prior to the Khalaji invasion. On the other hand, at Rajahmundry it is not possible to identify the original sites from which recycled architectural elements had been taken.

Recent years have seen a dramatic growth in scholarly literature concerning the use and meaning of recycled architectural elements, both in the field of art history generally,[61] and in South Asia studies in particular.[62] At the outset we can distinguish between those elements that are merely put to a practical use and those that are put to meaningful, iconic use.[63] The former would include any locally available architectural members, including those salvaged from dilapidated or abandoned buildings that were reused for strictly utilitarian purposes, such as holding up a ceiling beam or framing a doorway. We can identify this kind of reuse at many sites, such as in the great gateway to the citadel at Sagar, an important Turkic fort dating to the Tughluq period, located 72 kilometres northwest of Raichur. Inside this gateway, built by Firuz Bahmani in 1407, interior doorways were flanked with reused doorjambs that had originally belonged to some pre-Turkic structure. But the presence of plaster over these recycled jambs, now partially peeled away, indicates that they were never intended to be seen, and that they were used for their structural functionality alone.

Such a usage contrasts with elements that, placed in visually prominent positions, functioned as meaningful icons that were definitely intended to be seen. Yet iconic reuse could serve opposing purposes—intended sometimes to emphasize continuity with the past, and at other times to proclaim a break with the past. In fact, most instances of iconic reuse would appear to do both simultaneously, as Alka Patel has recently argued, although emphasizing one or the other in varying degree.[64] Thus, as we have seen, the builders of the Karim al-Din mosque at Bijapur (1320) recycled columns from temple maṇḍapas to carry the roof of their mosque's prayer hall. There is admittedly a certain element of disjunction here, since the physical condition of the reused columns—and, in particular, the violation of certain rules of syntax governing the arrangement of their various parts—revealed that these columns were no longer in the structures for which they had been fabricated, but had been placed into service in a new and ritually distinct type of building. But at the same time, there are other factors, such as the builders' decision to concentrate the more ornate columns along the mosque's miḥrāb axis—much as they would have done in the central bay of a maṇḍapa—that served to emphasize the commensurability between mosque and temple and to suggest the continuities linking their respective conceptions of sacred space.

In the case of the Karim al-Din mosque, the suggestion of continuity appears to have taken the upper hand. But there are other cases where the primary message seems to have been one of rupture. For example, when the bastions of the fort at Kalyana were rebuilt in the 1570s, hundreds of temple sculptures were taken from nearby Chalukya temples and recycled into the bastions' outer walls. There are certain undeniable elements of continuity in the deployment of these sculptures. Placed in the fabric of outer walls where state enemies were likely to be confronted, some of these sculptures may well have been intended as protective images to ward off malevolent forces, in keeping with their original conception as deities of violent aspects. Such would seem to be the intention behind two images built into the wall of one bastion—icons of Karttikeya the war god and Narasimha slaying the demon Hiranyakashipu.[65] In other cases, however, the message of rupture is clearly paramount. On another bastion built at the same time, some of the divine images have purposefully been positioned so as to lie on their sides, while others have been fully inverted and stand upside down on their heads (Figure 4.13, p. 149).[66] Moreover, their placement on the walls not of a temple, but of a fort, means that they would have been exposed to heavy artillery fire. It would be difficult to find a more vivid example of a message of rupture proclaimed by iconic reuse.

To conclude, most discussions of public monuments and armed conflict in pre-modern South Asia are framed in binary terms: either a given structure was destroyed or it was not. The evidence from the Deccan in the fourteenth and fifteenth centuries, however, suggests a need to move the discussion beyond this crude opposition and to consider a wider range of possible architectural outcomes to interstate conflict. These outcomes, at least from the evidence encountered thus far, lie along a continuum from non-interference to reassemblage, with active patronage, desecration, and redefinition lying between those extremes. With the exception of practical reuse, which involved recycled elements that were not necessarily intended to be seen, all these responses betray spectacular instances of political theatre. That is to say, they occurred at the juncture where architecture and power meet.

Less prominent in these fourteenth- and fifteenth-century encounters was the role of memory. When we come to the sixteenth century, however, this third component of our study, memory, became increasingly important in Deccan history, interacting with both power and architecture in significant ways. In the next several chapters we explore how this happened.

## NOTES

1. P. Arundhati, *Royal Life in Manosollasa* (Delhi: Sundeep Prakashan, 1994), 66.

2. Ibn Battuta, *The Rehla of Ibn Battuta,* trans. Mahdi Husain (1953; Baroda: Oriental Institute, 1976), 150–1.

3. Writing between 1205 and 1217, during the earliest consolidation of the Delhi Sultanate, the historian Hasan Nizami claimed that in Benares alone, Qutb al-Din Aibek had 'destroyed nearly one thousand temples, and raised mosques on their foundations'. In 1350 the poet-chronicler `Isami advised his royal patron, `Ala al-Din Hasan Bahman Shah, the founder of the Bahmani Sultanate, to replace temples with mosques. See H.M. Elliot and John Dowson, eds, *History of India as Told by Its Own Historians* (Allahabad: Kitab Mahal, 1964), 2:223. `Isami, *Futūḥ*, trans., 1:66–7.

4. With very few exceptions, Hindu temples were also the only monumental structures in pre-Sultanate India that were built of stone.

5. Parts of this chapter draw on Richard M. Eaton, 'Muhammad bin Tughluq and Temples of the Deccan, 1321–26', in *Sultans of the South: Arts of India's Deccan Courts, 1323–1687*, eds Navina Najat Haidar and Marika Sardar (New York and New Haven: Metropolitan Museum of Art and Yale University Press, 2011), 178–87.

6. *Corpus of Inscriptions in the Telengana Districts* [*CITD*] 2: no. 40. Our translation.

7. John Briggs, trans., *History of the Rise of Mohamadan Power in India* (4 vols, London, 1829; repr. 3 vols, Calcutta: Editions Indian, 1966), 1:212. Text: Muhammad Qasim Firishta, *Tārīkh-i Firishta* (2 vols, Lucknow: Nawal Kishor, 1864–5), 1:119. 'Vaqtī ki pargana Indor ki sarḥad-i Tilang ast rasīd, ḥukm bi nahb va ghārat va qatl va asīr farmūda.'

8. P.V. Parabrahma Sastry, *The Kakatiyas of Warangal* (Hyderabad: Government of Andhra Pradesh, 1978), 1443–5.

9. Elizabeth Lambourn has published evidence that there was already a congregational mosque in Devagiri *before* the earliest Khalaji raids on the Deccan. Arabic documents preserved in Yemen indicate that the Rasulid sultans (1229–1454) maintained salaried *khaṭībs* and *qaḍis* at over forty urban centres in peninsular India, including Devagiri, as early as the early 1290s. These khaṭībs were expected to deliver the *khuṭba* in the name of the Rasulid sultan, which implies that each of these centres must have held a congregational mosque. These structures were likely constructed of wood and other perishable materials, as no remains of them have been found to date. See Elizabeth Lambourn, 'India from Aden: *Khuṭba* and Muslim Urban Networks in Late Thirteenth-Century India', in *Secondary Cities and Urban Networking in the Indian Ocean Realm, c. 1400–1800*, ed. Kenneth R. Hall (Lanham: Lexington Books, 2008), 55–97.

10. `Abd al-Malik `Isami, *Futūḥu's Salāṭīn*, ed. and trans., Agha Mahdi Husain (3 vols, London: Asia Publishing House, 1967), 2:514.

11. Briggs, trans., *History of the Rise*, 1:222.

12. One possibility is that Malik Kafur had the post-and-lintel hypostyle constructed, together with its domed *miḥrāb* bay, while Mubarak Shah was responsible for the four pairs of piers and arches that front the colonnade. The masonry of these piers is discontinuous from the stonework of the colonnade, which runs continuously behind the piers, suggesting that the latter may have been added subsequently.

13. Delhi's Qutb mosque (1192) measured approximately 135 by 230 metres after its expansion by `Ala al-Din Khalaji in 1311. Ajmer's Arhai-din-ka-Jhompra mosque (1199) measured 77 by 77 metres; the Kaman mosque (1206) was 31 by 23 metres; and the Khatu mosque (1203) was 25 by 25 metres.

14. See M.S. Mate and T.V. Pathy, eds, *Daulatabad (A Report on the Archaeological Investigations)* (Pune: Deccan College Post Graduate & Research Institute, 1992), 24. Yadava columns are directly descended from metropolitan Chalukya style antecedents, and are typically of the *citrakhaṇḍa* type (see definition in Chapter 3, in this chapter later, and in Figure 3.3).

15. `Isami, *Futūḥ*, trans., 2:515.

16. Mate and Pathy, *Daulatabad*, 10, 53.

17. Ibid., 24.

18. Richard M. Eaton, 'Temple Desecration and Indo-Muslim States', in David Gilmartin and Bruce B. Lawrence, eds *Beyond Turk and Hindu: Rethinking Religious Identities in Islamicate South Asia* (Gainesville: University Press of Florida, 2000), 254–7.

19. Finbarr B. Flood, *Objects of Translation: Material Culture and Medieval 'Hindu–Muslim' Encounter* (Princeton: Princeton University Press, 2009), 144.

20. It is remarkable how little was needed, from a structural standpoint, for transposing the idea of imperial Delhi to distant Devagiri. This phenomenon is hardly unique in the history of architecture. Richard Krautheimer notes that in the eleventh century

> Bishop Meinwerk of Paderborn [in northern Germany] wanted to build a church "ad similitudinem s. Jerosolimitane ecclesie" and dispatched Abbot Wino of Helmershausen to Jerusalem to bring from there the required measurements…. [T]he interior length of each side of [the Paderhborn church's] octagon is 5.80 m. and this corresponds roughly to the distance of 5.70 m., measured between the outer corners of the pairs of main piers in the east–west axis of the Anastasis [the rotunda of the Church of the Holy Sepulchre]. The eight piers at Jerusalem would seem to have suggested to Meinwerk's messenger an octagon and the measurements taken between two of those piers were used as a basis for the construction of the whole plan. This selective transfer of measurements finds its exact parallel in the way in which prototypes are generally copied in the Middle Ages. It has been pointed out before that the model is never imitated *in toto*.… Evidently the mediaeval beholder expected to find in a copy only some parts of the prototype but not by any means all of them. (Richard Krautheimer, 'Introduction to an Iconography of Mediaeval Architecture', *Journal of the Warburg and Courtauld Institutes* 5 [1942], 4, 13.)

For other instances of 'copying' the Qutb Minar, see Ebba Koch, 'The Copies of the Qutb Minar', in her *Mughal Art and Imperial Ideology: Collected Essays* (New Delhi: Oxford University Press, 2001), 269–81.

21. In 1074–75, just several years before he was overthrown by his younger brother Vikramaditya, the Chalukya emperor Someshvara II had patronized the construction of a major Shiva temple in the city. See J.F. Fleet, 'Sanskrit and Old-Canarese Inscriptions', *Indian Antiquary* 10 (May 1881), 129.

22. Judging from the number of preserved inscriptions that record gifts to Narasimhadeva of Vijayapura, and the diversity of social groups that were involved in this support, it appears likely that this deity was of major importance within the region, and that his temple served as the focus of a regional pilgrimage network. See *South Indian Inscriptions* [*SII*] 18: nos 51, 156, 158, 165, 198, 216, 260, 271, 350, and 377. See also Katherine E. Kasdorf, 'Translating Sacred Space in Bijapur: The Mosques of Karim al-Din and Khwaja Jahan', *Archives of Asian Art* 59 (2009), 66.

23. Muhammad Nazim, *Bijapur Inscriptions, Memoirs of the Archeological Survey of India*, No. 49 (Delhi: Manager of Publications, 1936), 25.

24. Kasdorf, 'Translating Sacred Space', 67–8.

25. Ibid., 68.

26. Ibid., 70.

27. A.J. Arberry, trans., *The Koran Interpreted* (New York: Macmillan, 1970), 65.

28. Briggs, trans., *History of the Rise*, 1:233.

29. Vilasa Inscription, dated 1330, cited in B.D. Chattopadhyaya, *Representing the Other? Sanskrit Sources and the Muslims* (New Delhi: Manohar, 1998), 58.

30. `Isami, *Futūḥ*, trans., 2:607.

31. *Epigraphia Indo-Moslemica* [*EIM*] *1935–36*, 1–3, pl. I. As Yazdani points out, several lacunae in this inscription make it unclear whether the mosque was built by Ulugh Khan or Qutlugh Khan.

32. Briggs, trans., *History of the Rise*, 1:233. Text: Firishta, *Tārīkh-i Firishta*, 1:131. 'Bā ba`ḍīḥiṣār-hāyi dīgar ki dar ithnā-yi rāh būd maskhar va maftūḥ sākhta, bi mu`tamadān-i khūd sipurd, va ḍabṭ-i rāh-hā bi `uhda-yi īshān numūda bi Warangal raft.'

33. This bay is covered with a three-tiered ceiling of rotated squares, capped by a flat slab with a carved lotus medallion.

34. There is at least one other such case in fourteenth-century southern India where a dome was used in a seemingly iconic manner, so as to announce the structure's 'Islamic' affiliation. This is the shrine of sultan `Ala al-Din Udauji in Madurai, built between 1356 and 1360, where the square-planned tomb chamber carries a monolithic dome measuring 5.9 metres in diameter. Mehrdad Shokoohy, *Muslim Architecture of South India: The Sultanate of Ma`bar and the Traditions of Maritime Settlers on the Malabar and Coromandel Coasts (Tamil Nadu, Kerala, and Goa)* (London: Routledge Curzon, 2003), 34–42, figure 2.7 and plate 2.13.

35. One mentions the construction of a watchtower, and the other refers vaguely to an 'auspicious building' (`*imārat al-maimūnat*), which cannot possibly refer to

this structure, since in Indian inscriptions mosques are normally identified as such. See *EIM 1919–20*, 16–17, pl. XVI (a) and XVI (b).

36. Examples of flat-roofed mosques, or those in which the ceilings are made up of 'rotated squares', include the Karim al-Din mosque at Bijapur (which, however, also features a trabeated cupola, added at some point after the mosque's initial construction), the mosque of Salar `Ulwi at Rajahmundry, and the Sholapur mosque as originally constructed (the latter two are discussed later). Mosques with flat roofs throughout but with a single iconic dome include the Daulatabad and Warangal mosques, and the Sholapur mosque as it was later rebuilt.

In Delhi, however, even mosques built in the early Tughluq period sometimes include multiple domes. An example is the poorly preserved Jami` Masjid in Tughluqabad, which seems originally to have had a prayer hall of fourteen domed bays (2 by 7). Especially intriguing is the later Khirki Masjid (1352–4), which was built from a series of nine-bayed (3 by 3) modules in a manner reminiscent of the Bodhan mosque. See Mehrdad Shokoohy and Natalie H. Shokoohy, *Tughluqabad: A Paradigm for Indo-Islamic Urban Planning and Its Architectural Components* (London, Araxus Books, 2007), 151ff. and figure 8.9; Anthony Welch and Howard Crane, 'The Tughluqs: Master Builders of the Delhi Sultanate', *Muqarnas* 1 (1983), 133ff. and figure 5.

37. `Isami, *Futūḥ*, trans., 2:607.

38. Three of the five columns that have not collapsed happen to be standing directly on a solid stone foundation, provided by preserved segments of temple basement (*adhisthana*), suggesting that the rest of the mosque may have collapsed due to the gradual compaction and subsiding of the soil infill under the weight of the structure.

39. For the reconstruction of the mosque, see Phillip B. Wagoner and John Henry Rice, 'From Delhi to the Deccan: Newly Discovered Tughluq Monuments at Warangal-Sultanpur and the Beginnings of Indo-Islamic Architecture in the Deccan', *Artibus Asiae* LXI, no.1 (2001), 84–106.

40. For the Khush Mahal, see ibid., 79–84. For the hall at Tughluqabad, see Shokoohy and Shokoohy, *Tughluqabad*, 113–22, figures 7.4 and 7.7, plates 7.31–39.

41. Formal pathways between palace and mosque have a long history in Islamic architecture, dating back to at least as early as Umayyad times. As Flood notes, in some cities 'elevated walkways, arcaded lanes and narrow streets served to connect the mosque with the palace behind it'. Indian examples include several Deccani cities that are more or less contemporary with Warangal, namely Daulatabad, Firuzabad, and Bidar. Finbarr Barry Flood, *The Great Mosque of Damascus: Studies on the Makings of an Umayyad Visual Culture* (Leiden: E.J. Brill, 2001), 153, and note 66; Wagoner and Rice, 'From Delhi', 112.

42. Zia al-Din Barani, 'Tarikh-i Firuz Shahi', in *History of India*, eds Elliot and Dowson, 3:234.

43. *Epigraphia Indica, Arabic and Persian Supplement* [*EIAPS*] *1923–24*, 13–14, pl. V.

44. Reused temple doorways are often found in Indian mosques, going all the way back to the entrance to the royal chamber (*mulūk khāna*) in Delhi's Qutb mosque, which dates to the late twelfth century. In the Deccan, reused temple doorframes are most commonly inserted at the entrance to the mosque's courtyard, as here at Rajahmundry, and also in Sultan Quli's Masjid al-Safa in Golconda. Other examples include the mosque in the fort at Manvi (see later) and the Karim al-Din mosque at Bijapur, where an entire Chalukya entrance pavilion was reconstructed. See Flood, *Objects of Translation*, 160–3 and figure 86; M.A. Nayeem, *The Heritage of the Qutb Shahis of Golconda and Hyderabad* (Hyderabad: Hyderabad Publishers, 2006), 146, and figure 1 on p.165; and Marika Sardar, *Golconda through Time: A Mirror of the Evolving Deccan* (PhD diss., New York University Institute of Fine Arts, 2007), 70 and plate 116.

45. Though officially recorded an 'accident', the sultan's death was soon enough rumoured to have been engineered by his ambitious son. If true, Ulugh Khan's behaviour would have echoed that of prince `Ala al-Din Khalaji. On his own return to Delhi after raiding and plundering the Yadava capital of Devagiri in 1296, the prince assassinated his uncle, Sultan Jalal al-Din Firuz (r. 1290–6), and ascended the throne.

46. *EIM 1935–36*, 1–3, pl. I. Due to several lacunae in the inscription, Yazdani was uncertain whether the mosque was built by Ulugh Khan or by the Tughluq governor of the Deccan at the time, Qutlugh Khan, whose name also appears in the inscription. When Yazdani published this report, the stone tablet bearing this inscription was fixed into the eastern wall of the *dargāh* of Hazrat Ya`qub, located outside Kalyana.

47. *EI* 32: no. 19.

48. In the course of his failed rebellion, Baha al-Din Gurshasp had joined forces with the raja of Kampila, an independent state in the Tungabhadra valley, east of modern Hampi. When captured, the raja, who had never sworn allegiance to Tughluq authority and therefore was not guilty of treason, received the relatively light punishment of a beheading. But the sultan's cousin, who was a high-ranking officer in the Tughluq administration, was spat upon by his female relatives and flayed alive; then his skin was stuffed with straw and paraded throughout the imperial provinces as a cautionary tale to the public, while his body was mixed with rice and fed to elephants. As a last touch to this gory tale, Ibn Battuta notes that the elephants—in one final indignity—refused to eat the meal that had been mixed with the rebel's body. `Isami, *Futūḥ*, trans., 3:658–9; Ibn Battuta, *Rehla*, 96.

49. Wrote the famous Arab traveller Ibn Battuta, who served in the sultan's court for many years:

Of all the people this king loves most to make presents and also to shed blood. His door is never free from an indigent person who is to be enriched and from a living person who is to be killed. Stories of his generosity and bravery as well as of his cruelty and severity towards the offenders have obtained great currency among the people. (Ibn Battuta, *Rehla*, 56)

50. G. Yazdani, ed., *The Early History of the Deccan,* Parts VII–XI (London: Oxford University Press, 1960), 524.

51. See the second epigraph to this chapter.

52. There would originally have been thirty-two columns, but one was removed when a dome was subsequently constructed to cover four of the original bays, namely, the miḥrāb and miṃbar bays, and the two adjacent bays on the east.

53. As one might expect, the columns taken from the temple were removed from the southern and western sides of the temple maṇḍapa—that is, the side closest to the mosque—while those still remaining are located along the temple's northern and eastern sides.

54. Briggs, trans., *History of the Rise*, 1:217.

55. Firishta, *Tārīkh-i Firishta* (text), 1:125.

56. `Isami, *Futūḥ*, trans., 3:836–7. `Isami refers to the post as 'Mahendri', which can be identified with Maindargi, since one of the other nearby sites he mentions is Akalkot, just 10 kilometres from Maindargi and 40 kilometres from Sholapur.

57. *EIAPS 1962*, 56–8, pl. XVI(a).

58. A.A. Kadiri, 'Bahmani Inscriptions from Raichur District', *EIAPS 1962*, 54–6.

59. Briggs, trans., *History of the Rise*, 3:236–7. P.M. Joshi and N. Venkataramanayya both doubted Firishta's claim that Firuz Shah penetrated deep into the Raichur Doab, let alone clear to the Vijayanagara capital, owing to a lack of corroborating evidence. But as A.A. Kadiri observes, Firuz Shah's inscription at Manvi vindicates Firishta's claims that the Bahmani army had driven far into the Doab, certainly as far as Manvi. See R.C. Majumdar, ed., *The Delhi Sultanate* (Bombay: Bharatiya Vidya Bhavan, 1960), 255, 285; Kadiri, 'Bahmani Inscriptions', 55. Firishta's account of the conflict is also spiced with romantic details, on the basis of which Adam Watson wrote his *The War of the Goldsmith's Daughter* (London: Chatto and Windus, 1964).

60. Firishta, *Tārīkh-i Firishta* (text), 1:354. Our translation. In his translation of this passage, Briggs has the sultan pardoning Bhimraj Orriya. But this is not in the Persian text, which only reports that Bhimraj had begged for mercy. See Briggs, trans., *History of the Rise*, 2:304–6.

61. See Anthony Cutler, 'Reuse or Use? Theoretical and Practical Attitudes toward Objects in the Early Middle Ages', *Settimane di Studi del Centro Italiano di Studi Sull'alto Medioevo* 46 (1999), 1055–79; Tim Eaton, *Plundering the Past: Roman Stonework in Medieval Britain* (Stroud, Gloucestershire: Tempus Publishing Ltd, 2000); Jas Elsner, 'Iconoclasm and the Preservation of Memory', in *Monuments and Memory, Made and Unmade*, eds Robert S. Nelson and Margaret Olin (Chicago: University of Chicago Press, 2003), 209–311; Maria F. Hansen, *The Eloquence of Appropriation: Prolegomena to an Understanding of Spolia in Early Christian Rome* (Rome: L'Erma di Bretschneider, 2003); Dale Kinney, 'Rape or Restitution of the Past? Interpreting Spolia', in *The Art of Interpreting*, ed. Susan C. Scott (University Park, PA: Department of Art History, Penn State University, 1995), 53–67; idem., 'Making Mute Stones Speak: Reading Columns in S. Nicola in Carcere and S. Maria in Aracoeli', in *Architectural Studies in Memory of Richard Krautheimer*, ed. Cecil L. Striker (Mainz: Verlag Phillipp von Zabern, 1996); idem., 'Spolia, Damnatio and Renovatio Memoriae', in *Memoirs of the American Academy in Rome* 43 (1997), 117–48; idem., 'Roman Architectural Spolia', in *Proceedings of the American Philosophical Society* 145, no. 2 (June 2001), 138–61;

Constantin A. Marinescu, 'Transformations: Classical Objects and Their Re-use during Late Antiquity', in *Shifting Frontiers in Late Antiquity*, eds Ralph W. Mathisen and Hagith S. Sivan (Brookfield VT: Variorum, 1996), 285–98; Helen Saradi, 'The Use of Ancient Spolia in Byzantine Monuments', *International Journal of the Classical Tradition* 3, no. 4 (Spring 1997), 395– 423; David Stocker, 'Rubbish Recycled: A Study of the Re-Use of Stone in Lincolnshire', in *Stone: Quarrying and Building in England, AD 43–1525*, ed. David Parsons (Chichester, Sussex: Phillimore & Co., 1990), 83– 101.

62. See Michael Meister, 'The "Two-and-a-Half-Day" Mosque', *Oriental Art* 18, no. 1 (1972), 57–63; Joanna Williams, 'A Recut Asokan Capital and the Gupta Attitude towards the Past', *Artibus Asiae* 33, no. 3 (1973), 225–40; Richard Davis, 'Indian Art Objects as Loot', *Journal of Asian Studies* 52, no. 1 (Feb. 1993), 22–48; idem., *Lives of Indian Images* (Princeton: Princeton University Press, 1997); Phillip B. Wagoner, 'Retrieving the Chalukyan Past: The Politics of Architectural Reuse in Sixteenth-Century Deccan', *South Asian Studies* 23 (2007), 1– 29; Flood, *Objects of Translation*; idem., 'Appropriation as Inscription: Making History in the First Friday Mosque of Delhi', in *Reuse Value:* Spolia *and Appropriation in Art and Architecture from Constantine to Sherrie Levine*, eds Richard Brilliant and Dale Kinney (Burlington, VT: Ashgate, 2011), 121–47; Alka Patel, *Building Communities in Gujarat: Architecture and Society during the Twelfth through Fourteenth Centuries* (Leiden: Brill, 2004); idem., 'Expanding the Ghurid Architectural Corpus East of the Indus: The Jagesvara Temple at Sadadi, Rajasthan', *Archives of Asian Art* 59 (2009), 33–56; Tamara I. Sears, 'Fortified Mathas and Fortress Mosques: The Transformation and Reuse of Hindu Monastic Sites in the Thirteenth and Fourteenth Centuries', *Archives of Asian Art* 59 (2009), 7–31; Kasdorf, 'Translating Sacred Space', 57–80.

63. This distinction mirrors that made by Tim Eaton, who uses the term 'practical re-use' to cover two of the three forms of reuse proposed by David Stocker: 'casual reuse', that is, utilitarian recycling without any consideration of the element's original structural function; and 'functional re-use', in which a structural element is employed in accordance with its original function but without any secondary significance. Eaton prefers 'meaningful re-use' to Stocker's 'iconic re-use'. Eaton, *Plundering the Past*, 134–6.

64. Alka Patel, 'Architectural Histories Entwined: The Rudra-Mahalaya/Congregational Mosque of Siddhpur, Gujarat', *The Journal of the Society of Architectural Historians* 63, no. 2 (June 2004), 144–63. Patel speaks of 'modified continuity' (159).

65. These images are found on bastion no. 4 of the lower circuit, dated to 1580 by a foundation inscription.

66. Such is the case with the profusion of images placed in a decorative band near the top of bastion no. 9 of the lower circuit, datable to the period 1573–80.

SECTION
TWO

# Kalyana and the Chalukya Legacy

CHAPTER 3

# Reviving the Chalukya Imperium at Sixteenth-Century Vijayanagara

That Rama attained Kalyana (i.e., marriage) on this earth by serving Visvamitra, the Friend of All;
This Rama attained Kalyana (i.e., the city) on this earth through the service of all his friends.

— References, respectively, to the hero of the Rāmāyaṇa, and to Rama Raya (d. 1565), the ruler of Vijayanagara[1]

'Lord of the Excellent City of Kalyana'
'The One who Captured the City of Kalyana'
'Chalukya Emperor'

—Titles assigned to Rama Raya[2]

One of the central arguments of this book is that new and unprecedented forms of architectural reuse arose in the sixteenth-century Deccan. Previously, as we have seen in Chapter 2, architectural reuse had been closely linked with the expansion of the Delhi Sultanate into the region, and the practice tended to be one-sided, focussing on components taken from temples to be reused in mosques. Moreover, most of the temples that provided these materials for reuse were still being patronized by political leaders at the time of conquest; indeed, their contemporary political relevance was typically a principal cause of their dismantlement.

In the sixteenth century, by contrast, a new pattern emerges. For the first time, reuse focussed on antique components taken from structures built as many as five centuries earlier. What is more, these elements were now reused not only in mosques, as had generally been the case in the fourteenth century, but also in other types of structures, including temples, royal palaces, and ceremonial buildings. This underscores another crucial point: namely, that in the sixteenth century the practice was being pursued by patrons in both Indic and Persianate contexts. And finally, whereas earlier forms of reuse had aimed primarily at displacing one contemporary political and religious order by another, the sixteenth century reuse of antique components reveals a practice of deliberate revival, utilizing the antique form to affirm links between the present and an idealized, remembered past.

The following chapters explore various aspects of this phenomenon. In this chapter and the next, we look at sixteenth-century reuse of Chalukya antiques—by the ruling élite of Vijayanagara in Chapter 3, and by their `Adil Shahi counterparts in the Bijapur Sultanate, including at Kalyana itself, in Chapter 4. The sixteenth-century preoccupation with the Chalukya past raises a host of questions. Just what explains the appeal of the Chalukyas to the ruling élites in this period? Why did the revival extend to both sides of the presumed Indic–Persianate cultural divide? And finally, what specific historical conditions led to such a revival in the sixteenth century, and not before? But first, in order to understand what it was that later patrons sought to revive, we must consider the nature of Chalukya architecture in its heyday, during the eleventh and twelfth centuries.[3]

## THE CHARACTER OF CHALUKYA ARCHITECTURE

From the beginnings of the scholarly study of India's architectural history in the nineteenth century, Chalukya architecture has been recognized as a distinct taxonomic entity.[4] But those who have used the term have rarely been clear about what they mean by it. Is 'Chalukya' architecture to be defined on the basis of patronage, in a restricted sense as architecture erected under the direct initiative of Chalukya dynasts? Or is it to be taken in a geographic sense, as the architecture that was built within the territories of the Chalukya empire, regardless of who was responsible for its construction? Or again, is it to be defined in terms of shared stylistic features that can be recognized even in the absence of any information about patronage?

Until very recently, most authors have tended to use the term in the last of these three senses, taking Chalukya architecture as primarily a stylistic category. They have used the term to designate a distinctive variety of temple architecture that first emerged in the last quarter of the tenth century, reached its zenith in the late eleventh and early twelfth centuries, and had as its epicentre the ancient Belvola region of Karnataka—roughly corresponding to today's Dharwar district and adjacent parts of neighbouring districts (Belgaum, Bagalkot, Gadag, Koppal, Haveri, and Bellary).[5] The style is sometimes called 'Later Chalukya' or 'Kalyana Chalukya', to distinguish it from the very different 'Early Western Chalukya' style of architecture that flourished on the northern edge of this same region in the seventh and eighth centuries.

Unfortunately, designating the style by a dynastic name tends to assume clear and direct links between this architectural style and the Chalukya rulers. With very few exceptions, however, the temples in this style were not patronized by members of the Chalukya family themselves, but by various subordinates and feudatories. Ultimately, it was neither the Chalukyas nor even their subordinates who defined this style—which we call simply the 'Dharwar style'. That was the work of well-organized guilds of architects and sculptors who designed and built the temples, and who left many inscriptions shedding light on their organization and practices.[6] But as compelling as this Dharwar-based style may be, buildings in this style occupy only a very limited portion of the larger Chalukya realm. Temples in this style are exceedingly rare to the north of the Krishna River, and they are totally absent in the vicinity of Kalyana itself, the imperial capital.[7] Here, buildings were constructed in a thoroughly different style—one whose northern, Nagara affinities are as clear as are the southern, Dravida affiliations of the Dharwar style.[8] We shall refer to this style of Kalyana and its environs as the 'Metropolitan style'.[9] This pattern of stylistic bifurcation within the territories of the Chalukyas is hardly surprising, given the intermediate position of the Deccan between north and south India, and the natural tendency of the lower Deccan to orient itself southwards towards the Tamil country, and of the upper Deccan to look north towards central India and the Indo-Gangetic plain. It is perfectly understandable that two great 'Chalukya' styles should have flourished; the only mystery is why the northern variant should have remained neglected for so long.

For their own part, sixteenth-century patrons understood the remains belonging to both the Dharwar and the Metropolitan Kalyana styles as products of the Chalukya past and actively sought them out for recycling in royal projects. But because the old Chalukya territories straddled two major states in the sixteenth century, Vijayanagara and Bijapur, and because the sovereign territories of these states roughly coincided with the two different stylistic regions of Chalukya architecture—the dividing line more or less following the course of the Malprabha and Krishna Rivers—Vijayanagara's projects tended to reuse components exhibiting the Dharwar style, while Bijapur's employed components belonging mainly to the Metropolitan Kalyana style. To understand the reuse of Chalukya elements in the sixteenth century, then, we must first become familiar with key characteristics of both styles of Chalukya architecture.

First, the two styles differ with respect to their preferred materials, the Dharwar style typically employing the locally available schists, and the Metropolitan style the basalts of the 'Deccan trap' formations.[10] Although both types of stone are dark in colour, the various schists tend towards cooler, bluish-greenish tints, while the Deccan basalt is usually a warmer, darker grey. Moreover, the schists of the south are fine-grained, metamorphic rocks containing an abundance of soft, platy minerals, including predominantly chlorite and talc. Because of the softness of these constituent minerals, schists are easily carved with flat chisels and can accommodate a high degree of fine detail and undercutting.[11] To the north, the Deccan basalt is similarly fine-grained. But being a harder, igneous stone, composed largely of well-bonded minerals,[12] it is more difficult to carve and less capable of supporting detail or undercutting.[13]

These two preferred materials greatly influenced the development of the two styles, especially their architectural ornament and applied figural sculpture (Figure 3.1). The Dharwar style exhibits a highly plastic quality, with a preference for sensuously modelled organic forms whose smoothly polished passages are often accentuated with contrasting areas of finely detailed jewellery and ornaments. In the Metropolitan style, on the other hand, the harder structure of the preferred basalt medium led to less plasticity, a simplification of forms, and a generally lower and less crisp level of detail. Especially in the area of architectural ornaments, the Metropolitan style prefers contrasting figure–ground relationships on two-dimensional surfaces, leading to the development of a whole family of highly abstract 'silhouette' designs that decorate various mouldings and parts of columns. While one cannot assert that the respective materials they employed determined the distinctive characteristics of the two Chalukya styles, the aesthetic qualities of each style closely correlate with the type of stone preferred by its builders. Notably, the geographical boundary between

a

b

**Figure 3.1** Chalukya sculptural styles compared: (a) Dharwar style: bracket figure from the Mallikarjuna temple at Kuruvatti and (b) 'Metropolitan' style: wall figures from the Mahadeva temple at Jalsingi.

the two styles falls along the Krishna River, which also happens to mark the approximate boundary between the Dharwar schist belts to the south and the overlaying Deccan basalts to the north.[14]

With respect to overall architectural morphology, the two styles adopted differing systems of articulating a building's exterior, in keeping with their different affiliations with the Dravida and Nagara traditions (Figure 3.2). In the Dharwar style—ultimately rooted in the Dravida tradition—the building stands on a southern-style plinth, and the walls rise directly from the top of this base. The plane of the wall is divided into corner units (*karṇas*) at each end, a projecting unit in the middle (*bhadra*), and intermediate projections in between (*pratibhadras*), with intervening recesses offsetting each unit from adjacent ones. The edges of the corner units, as well as of the central projection, are invariably articulated by means of slender, attenuated pilasters, while the intermediate projections are typically articulated as a single wall-column covering the full width of the projection. Recesses and faces of projecting units alike are commonly decorated with miniature shrine towers standing on columns (*kūṭa-stambhas*). The superstructure consists of a series of successively diminishing storeys, each girt by a 'necklace' of ornately carved miniature shrines.

In the Nagara-affiliated Metropolitan style, on the other hand, the building typically stands on an abbreviated northern-styled plinth, and nearly the entire lower half of the walls is articulated with a complex series of basal mouldings (*vedibandha*) that visually continues the horizontal lines of the plinth. The walls are divided into corners, intermediate, and central projections, just as in the Dharwar style, but here each of these units is articulated as a single wall-column covering its full width. Instead of the shrine-tower-on-column motif favoured in the Dharwar style, large-scale figures of women and deities provide the primary sculptural ornamentation for the recesses, and in some temples, also for the projections. Very few of these Metropolitan style temples have survived with their superstructures intact—most likely because brick, apparently the preferred medium above the walls, has not stood up to weathering as well as have the stone superstructures preferred in the Dharwar style. Nonetheless, fragmentary remains at several sites suggest that most of these superstructures were probably of the Bhumija type—a variant of the north Indian curvilinear superstructure in which the quadrants of the tower between the central vertical spines are ornamented with miniature Nagara towers on pillars, arranged in horizontally and vertically disposed tiers.

Although practically every aspect of a building reveals the distinctive character of each style, the forms and treatment of columns are especially important for us, since columns were some of the most frequently reused building components in the sixteenth century (Figure 3.3). Nothing represents the nature of the Dharwar Chalukya style better than its characteristic *śrīkāra* column type, with its double-flexed circular bell near the top of the shaft and its dense profusion of sharply carved circular mouldings both at the centre of the shaft and above the bell, appearing as if they had been turned on a lathe.[15] In fact, above the tall, square-sectioned shank at the base of the shaft, all parts of the śrīkāra column are circular in section, up to the square abacus atop the column's second, dish-shaped capital (*maṇḍi*). The third and final capital appears as a bracket-capital (*potika*), with the arms generally treated as spiralled scrolls.

In contrast, the Metropolitan Chalukya style knows nothing of this śrīkāra pillar type, employing instead a local variant of the *citra-khaṇḍa* type of column.[16] The shafts of these columns invariably consist of lower and upper blocks that are square in section, separated by an intervening portion (*paṭṭi*) that is divided vertically into five horizontal bands. The lower,

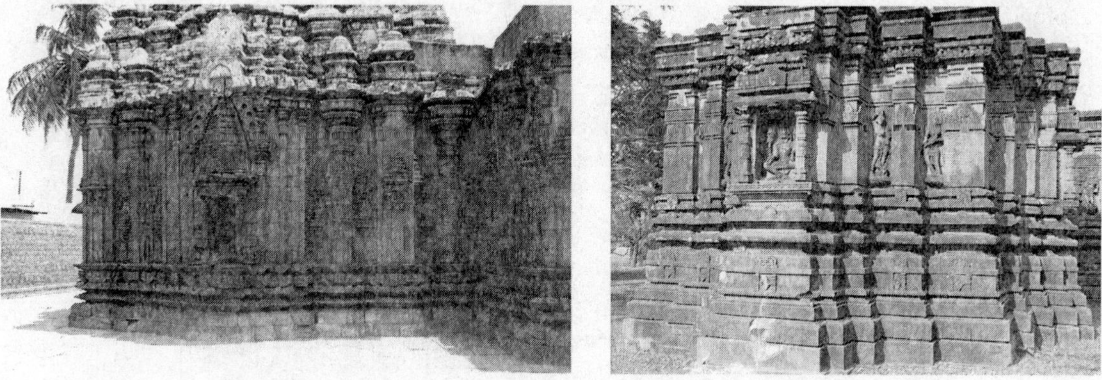

a b

**Figure 3.2** Chalukya temple styles compared: (a) Dharwar style: plinth and wall of Mallikarjuna temple, Kuruvatti, and (b) 'Metropolitan' style: plinth and wall of Mahadeva temple, Jalsingi.

a

b

**Figure 3.3** Chalukya column styles compared: (a) Dharwar style: *śrīkāra* type, from the Kalleshvara temple at Bagali and (b) 'Metropolitan' style: *citrakhaṇḍa* type, from the Mahadeva temple at Jalsingi.

the central, and the upper bands of the paṭṭi are all octagonal in section, while the two intervening bands are either circular or sixteen-sided. The sequence of capitals—cushion capital (*kumbha*), dish and abacus, and bracket-capital—is the same as in the śrīkāra columns of the Dharwar style, but the abacus is sometimes circular, following the shape of the dish that supports it, while the bracket arms are occasionally carved with figures of dwarfs. In addition to this basic structural syntax, these columns typically carry certain forms of linear and abstract ornaments, including a characteristic lotus-petal motif on the lowest octagonal band of the central section, and pendant leaf-patterns or vegetal scrollwork contained within a pair of festoons on the upper block (*caturasra*).

## SIXTEENTH-CENTURY GEO-POLITICS AND THE RENEWAL OF INTEREST IN KALYANA

In Chapter 1 we saw that by the end of the fifteenth-century Kalyana had devolved into a place of little cultural and political significance. Doubtless, many of the temples established during Vikramaditya VI's reign were still functioning, and some may still have served as a focus of religious, social, and economic life in the region. The Delhi Sultanate period had also seen the establishment of a sizeable Muslim presence in the town, and by the mid-fifteenth century Bahmani rulers had built a small but well-fortified stronghold on a small hillock several kilometres northwest of the heart of the old Chalukya city. The fort likely had little strategic importance, being just one among the

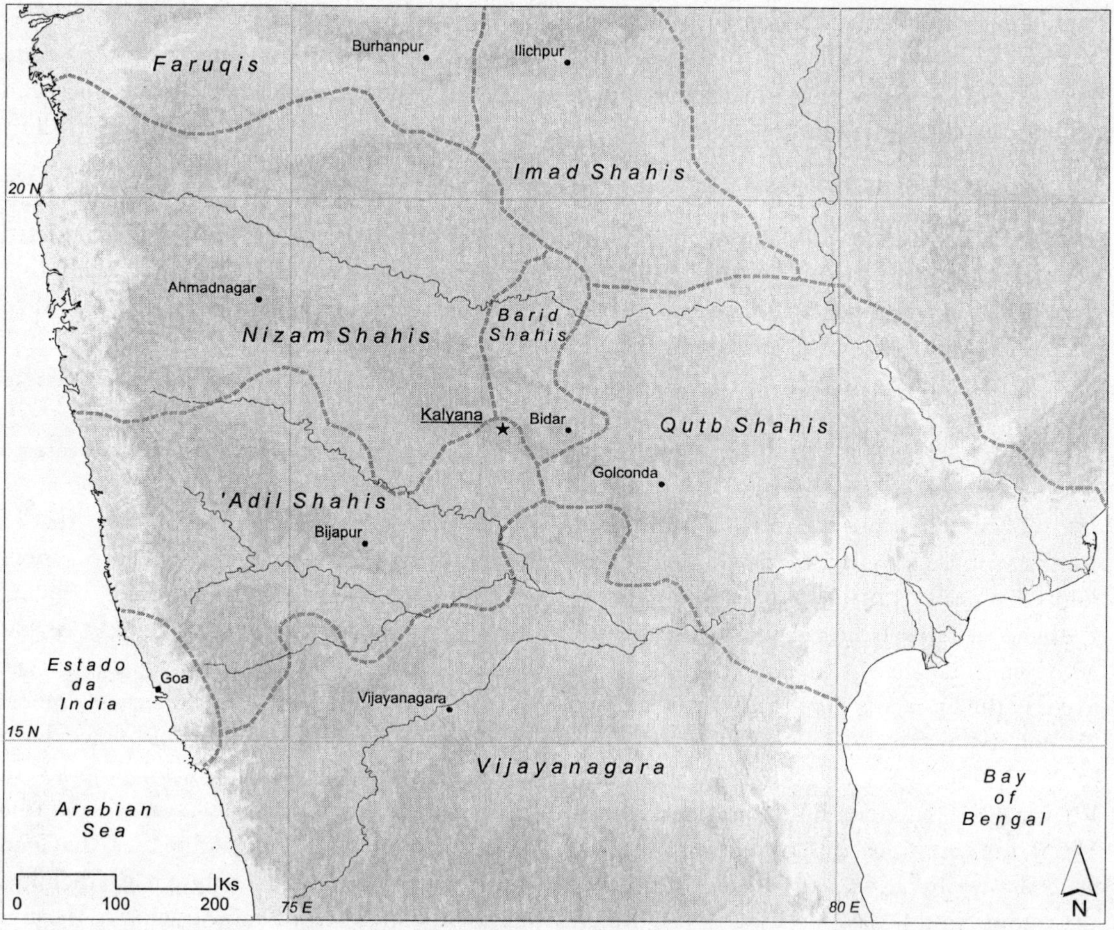


**Figure 3.4** Geopolitical configuration of the Deccan, c.1560, showing Kalyana, capital cities, and boundaries between states.

scores of Bahmani forts that dotted the region. In all likelihood, it played a far more important role in enabling the state to collect revenue from the surrounding countryside than it did in defending anyone from outside enemies. After all, Kalyana was located not on some distant frontier, but only a day or two's journey from Bidar, the Bahmani capital since 1424, which completely overshadowed it culturally and politically.

But already by the last decades of the fifteenth century, the Bahmani state was in crisis, as real power rapidly fell into the hands of its most influential *amīrs*, who, one by one, dispensed with the fiction of serving the sultan and proclaimed their independence. By the second decade of the sixteenth century, the former Bahmani territories had been carved up into five different successor states, whose rulers in all but one case were based in newly ascendant centres of power quite distant from Bidar. It so happened that Kalyana straddled the political frontier between three of these states—the `Adil Shahi kingdom of Bijapur, the Nizam

Shahi kingdom of Ahmadnagar, and the much smaller Barid Shahi kingdom, based in Bidar itself (Figure 3.4). Kalyana thus emerged as a major bone of contention between these three polities. In fact, during the course of the sixteenth century the city was three times ceded or promised in exchange for another city,[17] was besieged twice,[18] and was the specific goal of three different campaigns that aimed to recover it.[19] As a result of these various actions, the city changed hands three times in the thirty-year period from 1529 to 1559.[20]

Although Bijapur, Ahmadnagar, and Bidar were the main players in these struggles to control Kalyana, it was the intrusion into these conflicts of their powerful neighbour to the south that proved crucial to the development of a Chalukya revival. Successively aligning itself with one sultanate or another according to the needs of the moment, Vijayanagara participated in contests for the control of Kalyana in 1549, in 1559, and again in 1562.[21] At this time Vijayanagara was ruled by Rama Raya (1484–1565), the ambitious, unscrupulous, and gifted general who by 1542 had effectively usurped the throne from Sadashiva Raya, the legitimate ruler of Vijayanagara, and the last king of the Tuluva dynasty. It was Rama Raya's obsession with obtaining a kind of indirect sovereignty over the former Chalukya capital that dictated Vijayanagara's policies towards the northern sultanates. From at least 1549 on, Rama Raya ensured that whichever northern sultan he was at the moment allied with also controlled Kalyana, as though that sultan were an intermediary between himself and the old Chalukya capital. The most dramatic and explicit action by which Rama Raya articulated his claims to sovereignty over the Chalukya capital came in 1559, when he defeated and then humiliated Sultan Husain Nizam Shah of Ahmadnagar by demanding that, as the first of three conditions by which he would allow Husain to recover his own capital, the Ahmadnagar sultan would have to pay personal homage to Rama Raya and surrender to him the keys to Kalyana.[22] Rama Raya's brothers Tirumala and Venkatadri—both of them accomplished military commanders and provincial governors—also conducted military campaigns to Kalyana, as did other members of Rama Raya's clan, the extended Aravidu family, which came to dominate the increasingly patrimonial Vijayanagara state in this period.[23]

Taking part in these campaigns appears to have been a poignant experience for members of Vijayanagara's military aristocracy, thanks to the living memory of the Chalukya imperium among the state's courtly society. Owing to the continued vitality of Chalukya-period literary works—both in Sanskrit and in the Telugu and Kannada vernaculars—members of the Vijayanagara court would have been well-acquainted with the Chalukya past. In particular, Bilhana's *Vikramāṅkadevacarita*, the royal biography of Vikramaditya VI that had immortalized the reign of the great Chalukya emperor, continued to enjoy a wide readership in the Vijayanagara period, though composed more than three centuries earlier. Many of its individual verses were included in later anthologies owing to their poetic excellence, while the poem itself served as a model for the many new works in the genre of biographies (*carita*) that Vijayanagara patrons commissioned between the fourteenth and sixteenth centuries.[24] Further recollections of Chalukya greatness were preserved in non-poetic texts such as the *Mitākṣarā*, also composed at Kalyana under the patronage of Vikramaditya VI. A few lines following the *Mitākṣarā*'s colophon, which praised both Vikramaditya VI and his imperial capital,[25] appears a verse proclaiming the desire that Vikramaditya VI's rule may last forever and encompass the entirety of the imaginable world:

From northern Himalaya, Lord of Mountains to the southern bridge to Lanka built by the pride of Raghu's [i.e., Rama's] line
From the eastern ocean to the western sea rising with its whale-churned waves—
May his majesty Vikramaditya protect this entire earth
as long as moon and stars endure:
his feet aglow with rays of light from gems on the crowns of bowing kings.[26]

Kalyana also figured vividly in the vernacular literary imagination, as a number of Virashaiva poets writing in Kannada during the Vijayanagara era waxed eloquent praising the former Chalukya capital. Basava, the twelfth-century founder of the Virashaiva movement, had been an officer in the treasury of Bijjala, the Kalachuri usurper of the throne of Kalyana, and had accompanied him to the capital city when Bijjala declared his paramountcy in 1162.[27] As a result, Kalyana became a veritable stage for a whole host of Virashaiva saints and poets whose lives and actions in the city are celebrated in the *Basava-Purāṇa* and other hagiographical works in Telugu and Kannada.[28] Some two hundred years later, Vijayanagara itself emerged as an important centre of Virashaiva poetic and social activity, and a number of its residents penned Kannada hagiographies in which Kalyana figured as a key setting. These works include the *Basava Purāṇa* of Bhimakavi (c. 1369), based on the original Telugu version of Palkuriki Somanatha; *Prabhulingalīle* of Camarasa (c. 1430), a biography of the saint Allama Prabhu; *Śivatattva-cintāmaṇi* of the Vijayanagara minister Lakkana Dandesa (c. 1450);[29] and the *Cannabasava Purāṇa* of Virupaksha-pandita (c. 1585).[30] Through the continued copying and reading of Sanskrit and Kannada texts reflecting Kalyana's golden age, memories of the Chalukya imperium would have been preserved in Vijayanagara society right down to the sixteenth century.

Until the middle of the sixteenth century these memories remained largely latent. From the 1540s, however, all this quickly changed, as Kalyana rose in status as a coveted political prize, and as Vijayanagara's armies became regularly involved in campaigns that aimed at capturing the city. Thanks to these vigorous struggles over control of the former Chalukya capital, and also to the active exploration of the city's cultural landscape, the Vijayanagara imagination was stirred. Kalyana in its period of imperial magnificence became charged with a powerful new symbolic valence that led to the creation of new cultural products—both literary and architectural—and which capitalized on this newly intensified historical awareness.

## ARAVIDU APPROPRIATION OF CHALUKYA TITLES AND GENEALOGY

From about the 1540s on there began to appear a fascinating series of texts, written in both Telugu and in Sanskrit, that provide literary evidence for a new, active mode of responding to the Chalukya past. These texts include both works of court poetry (*kāvya*) and laudatory prologues (*praśastis*) introducing royal donative inscriptions. Together, they reveal a creative interest in asserting connections with the Chalukyas and Kalyana that had not been seen, so far as we are aware, in any earlier period of Vijayanagara's history.

Though diverse in nature, all these works shared a common context of production: all were patronized by members of the newly ascendant Aravidu clan of Rama Raya and his kinsmen. While the Aravidus held enormous political and military power, the naked truth revealed them as recent upstarts and usurpers who might easily be seen as lacking legitimate authority. Concern, even anxiety, about public perceptions of their legitimacy very likely contributed to their eagerness to invoke the Chalukya past, even to the point of asserting an outright genealogical connection with the ancient imperial line.

One sees the earliest evidence of an Aravidu attempt to link itself to the Chalukya past in the preface to Doneru Konerunatha-kavi's *Padya-Bālabhāgavatamu*, composed between 1543 and 1547. Patronized by Rama Raya's cousin Timma-Tirumala and dedicated to the latter's younger brother China-Timmaraja, who governed the province of Chandragiri, the *Padya-Bālabhāgavatamu* was a versified Telugu adaptation of the classic Vaishnava text *Bhāgavata-Purāṇa*.[31] In his preface, Konerunatha deploys a number of grand conceits to depict Tirumala as a latter-day Chalukya, including 'master in the maintenance of the Kalyana kingdom' (*kalyāṇa-rājya-sthāpanācāryuḍu*, 1.11) and 'friend of the Chalukya kingdom' (*cāḷukya-rājya-praṇayaṇuṃḍu*, 1.11). More explicitly, he is said to be 'born in the Chalukya lineage' (*cāḷukyānvaya-bhava*, 3.1), and in two places he is even accorded the grandiose title 'Chalukya emperor' (*cāḷukya-cakravarti*).[32]

Konerunatha surpassed his contemporaries in constructing a distinguished genealogy for his patron. Whereas contemporary inscriptions until as late as 1570 trace the Aravidu ancestry no further back than four generations,[33] Konerunatha provides his patron's family with a full-blown Puranic genealogy, tracing the line all the way back to the respected Lunar Dynasty of the warrior class (kshatriyas) through Puru, the progenitor of the heroes of the great epic Mahābhārata (Figure 3.5).[34] Doing so served to distinguish the Aravidus from Vijayanagara's previous ruling dynasties, which had traced their Lunar origins not through Puru himself but through one of his brothers, either Yadu or Turvasu. Significantly, such a genealogy also suggested an affinity with the Chalukyas, who had likewise claimed descent from Puru.[35]

It was another Tirumala—Rama Raya's younger brother and, as Tirumala Raya (r. 1570–2), the first *de jure* ruler of the Aravidu line—who took this interest in the Chalukyas and developed it to the next logical level. In Tirumala Raya's Tumkur plates inscription of 1571, we find the first recorded instance of an explicit, public claim to Chalukya descent for the Aravidus.[36] The genealogical portion of this inscription, composed by the court poet Kavisasana Svayambhu, traces the same Lunar pedigree that Konerunatha had earlier presented for Tirumala Raya's cousin. But now it fills in some of the gaps after the Mahābhārata heroes with a series of four 'Chalukya' kings, each separated from the previous one by a number of generations (Figure 3.6). The first of these rulers is named simply 'Chalukya' (literally, 'Chalikka', a variant form of the name), which most likely represents a generalized memory of the dynasty's eponymous founder. After several generations, Chalikka is followed by 'Rajanarendra', doubtless a representation of Rajarajanarendra, the famed eleventh-century ruler of the Eastern Chalukya dynasty of coastal Andhra. Rajanarendra is followed after several generations by 'Bijjalendra', and then by 'Vira Hemmadiraya'. These last two rulers can be recognized as the famous Kalachuri ruler Bijjala, who briefly usurped the Chalukya throne in the mid-twelfth century, and—in an intriguing chronological inversion—Bijjala's father, Hemmadiyarasa,[37] who had been a Chalukya feudatory under Someshvara III (r. 1127–39).

What seems especially relevant here is that, in the historical vision of Tirumala Raya and his court poet, several loosely related royal lines were being tightly woven together within the single pedigree of the Aravidus. Not only were

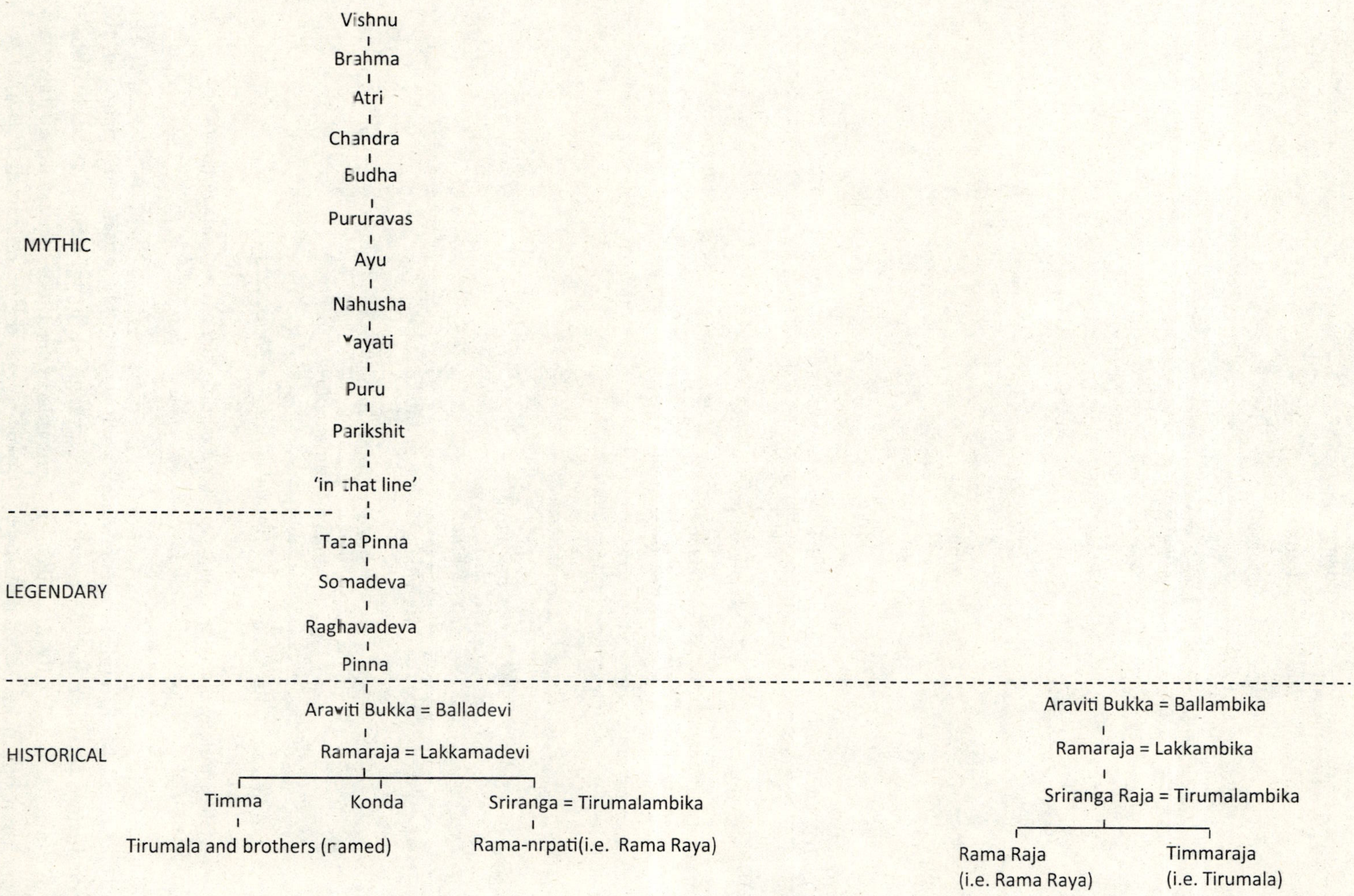


**Figure 3.5** Aravidu genealogy, according to (left) Konerunatha-kavi's *Padya Bāla-Bhāgavatamu*, written c. 1543–47, commissioned by Timma-Tirumala; and (right) contemporary inscriptions, c. 1548 through 1570.

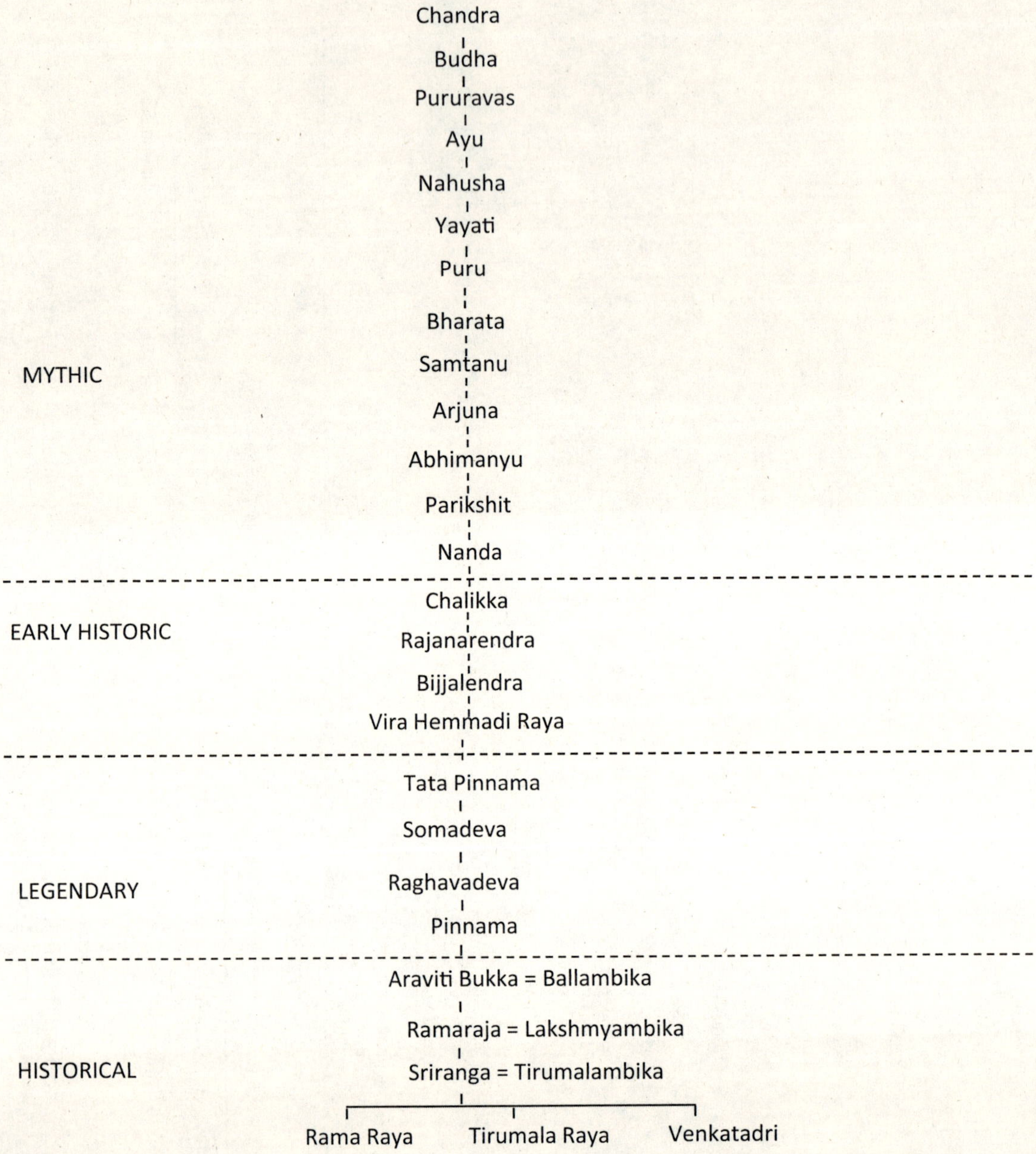


**Figure 3.6** Aravidu genealogy, official and public version, according to the Tumkur inscription of Tirumalaraya, dated 1571.

the Eastern Chalukyas, a collateral branch of the family, brought into the main line of descent, so too was the Kalachuri family of Bijjala, a maternal grandson of Chalukya Vikramaditya VI who had only a tenuous claim to the succession but nonetheless usurped the throne and ruled over the imperial city of Kalyana.[38] In his role as a distantly related usurper who maintained the continuity of rule from imperial Kalyana, Bijjala must have been particularly attractive to the Aravidus, in view of their own similar situation as matrimonially related usurpers of the Vijayanagara throne struggling to project an image of dynastic continuity.[39]

Once defined and publicized in Tirumala's Tumkur plates, this genealogy—with its explicit claim of a Chalukya pedigree—would remain the standard, official genealogy of the Aravidu rulers for the remainder of their rule. In practically identical wording, this genealogy is found in such records as the Vilapaka (1601–02) and Mangampudi (1602–03) plates of Venkata I,[40] and the Utsur plates of Ranga VI (1647–48).[41] It even appears at the very end of the dynasty, in the expanded and poetically embellished version of the *Narapati Vijayamu* written by Andugula Vengakavi in the last quarter of the seventeenth century. Though composed long after the height of the Chalukya revival, this work is especially interesting for the many titles, or *biruda*s, it records for the rulers of each generation. These biruda sections, however, begin only with Bijjala, who is called 'Kalyana-Bijjala', the text explains, 'because he ruled the city of Kalyana, which was a veritable support of the earth'.[42] Although Bijjala had usurped power from the Chalukyas in 1162, he is here neatly woven into a smooth Chalukya dynastic history. Similarly, Rama Raya, who had usurped power from Vijayanagara's Tuluva dynasty by 1542, is likewise neatly woven into both the Vijayanagara and the Chalukya dynastic genealogies. His career is thus represented as homologous with that of Bijjala; accordingly, his birudas reflect a similar obsession with Kalyana. Now he is called 'Radiant King of Kalyana' (*Kalyāṇa-mahīpāla-bhāswara*), 'Lord of the Excellent City of Kalyana' (*Kalyāṇa-puravarādhīśvara*), 'The One Who Captured the City of Kalyana' (*Kalyāṇa-nagara-sādhaka*)—and, of course, 'Chalukya Emperor' (*Cāḷukya-cakravarti*).[43]

Significantly, Aravidu claims to a special relationship with the Chalukya imperial line were acknowledged by contemporaries as far away as the city of Warangal, then deep within the Qutb Shahi kingdom. In the *Pratāparudra Caritramu*, a Telugu folk-history of the Kakatiya dynasty composed around 1550, two Chalukya emperors—Someshvara II and his brother Vikramaditya VI—figure prominently.[44] At one point in the text, the former emperor learns that the Vijayanagara king, Vira Narasimha Raya, has assumed the presumptuous titles 'Hero among all Mortals' (*sakala-martya-gaṇḍa*) and 'Best on Earth' (*dharaṇī-vara*). When Someshvara II challenges the impudent ruler by fearlessly approaching his palace gate, Narasimha Raya is so impressed that he invites the Chalukya emperor into his inner apartments and 'seats him upon the lion-throne of Vijayanagara', effectively constituting himself as Someshvara II's vassal.[45] Although the account is full of gross anachronisms, such as casting Someshvara II (r. 1068–76) and the sixteenth-century Vijayanagara king as contemporaries, one is struck by its central image of a Chalukya emperor sitting on the throne of Vijayanagara. The episode vividly reveals the broad geographical reach of the Aravidus' claim to the Chalukya imperium during Rama Raya's rule.[46]

## CHALUKYA REUSE IN SIXTEENTH-CENTURY VIJAYANAGARA ARCHITECTURE

It was not only through their creative manipulation of genealogies and titles, however, that rulers of the Aravidu house sought to associate themselves with the imperial Chalukyas. Even while making these titular and genealogical interventions, they went to great lengths to locate remnants of antique Chalukya buildings, dismantle them, transport them to Vijayanagara, and reuse them in new architectural settings.[47] Such architectural manipulations constitute dramatic instances of how power, memory, and architecture could—and did—converge in the sixteenth-century Deccan. Power enabled ruling élites to patronize vast enterprises; memory of a prestigious Chalukya past informed what projects they would patronize; and the architectural works themselves publicly displayed both that memory and their patrons' ability to project it.

In the four centuries since the decline of Chalukya power, architecture in the Deccan had undergone a number of profound changes. As a result, sixteenth-century architecture at Vijayanagara displays a distinctive style that cannot possibly be confused with either of the Chalukya styles of half a millennium earlier. For one thing, there had been a major influx of artisans from the Tamil country after Vijayanagara expanded into the south in the mid-fourteenth century. As a result, fifteenth- and sixteenth-century Vijayanagara temples manifest a decidedly more 'southern' feel.[48] Moreover, the primary building materials used at Vijayanagara and its environs differed drastically from those that had been used in either of the Chalukya styles. At Vijayanagara, the preferred materials included granite and a variety of metamorphic rocks of granitic origin, all of which were abundantly available in Vijayanagara and the lands to the east.[49] All of these materials are hard and relatively coarse-grained. Accordingly, Vijayanagara architecture tends to be much bolder and more architectonic in its effects, and certainly less sculpturally elaborated, than either of the Chalukya styles. As a result, a single Chalukya trophy carefully displayed within an otherwise Vijayanagara-style context could exert an aesthetic impact far beyond what might be expected simply on the basis of its limited scale. The effect is not unlike that produced by a handful of classical Roman marble columns, redeployed centuries later within the medieval fabric of a Carolingian palace.

Not only were these antique Chalukya building components visually distinct from everyday building materials at Vijayanagara, they were also difficult to procure. It is striking that not a single complete Chalukya style building—in either the Dharwar or the Metropolitan styles—stands *in situ* at Vijayanagara, or even, for that matter, anywhere in the immediate environs of the city. All Chalukya-style vestiges at the site show in one way or another clear signs of having been removed from their original locations and re-erected in a new, Vijayanagara context. Some authorities have assumed these to be the remains of Chalukya-style buildings that had been originally constructed at Hampi during the eleventh and twelfth centuries.[50] The facts of stylistic geography, however, argue forcibly against such a conclusion. As a glance at the map in Figure 3.7 shows, the easternmost limits of the distinctive Dharwar Chalukya style run along a line passing roughly north-northwest to south-southeast some 65 kilometres west of Vijayanagara, where not coincidentally, the Dharwar schist belts also abruptly end.[51] To the east of this line, in the region known as Ballakunde-nad (eastern Raichur and Bellary districts), temples had in fact been constructed during the Chalukya period, but their builders inevitably used the locally available granites, granulites, and gneisses. Preference for these hard and often coarse-grained stones went hand in glove with the conservative, archaizing style evinced by these temples, which differ so decidedly from the contemporary Chalukya style of the Dharwar region.[52]

Table 3.1 and the map in Figure 3.8 document the instances of reuse that we have

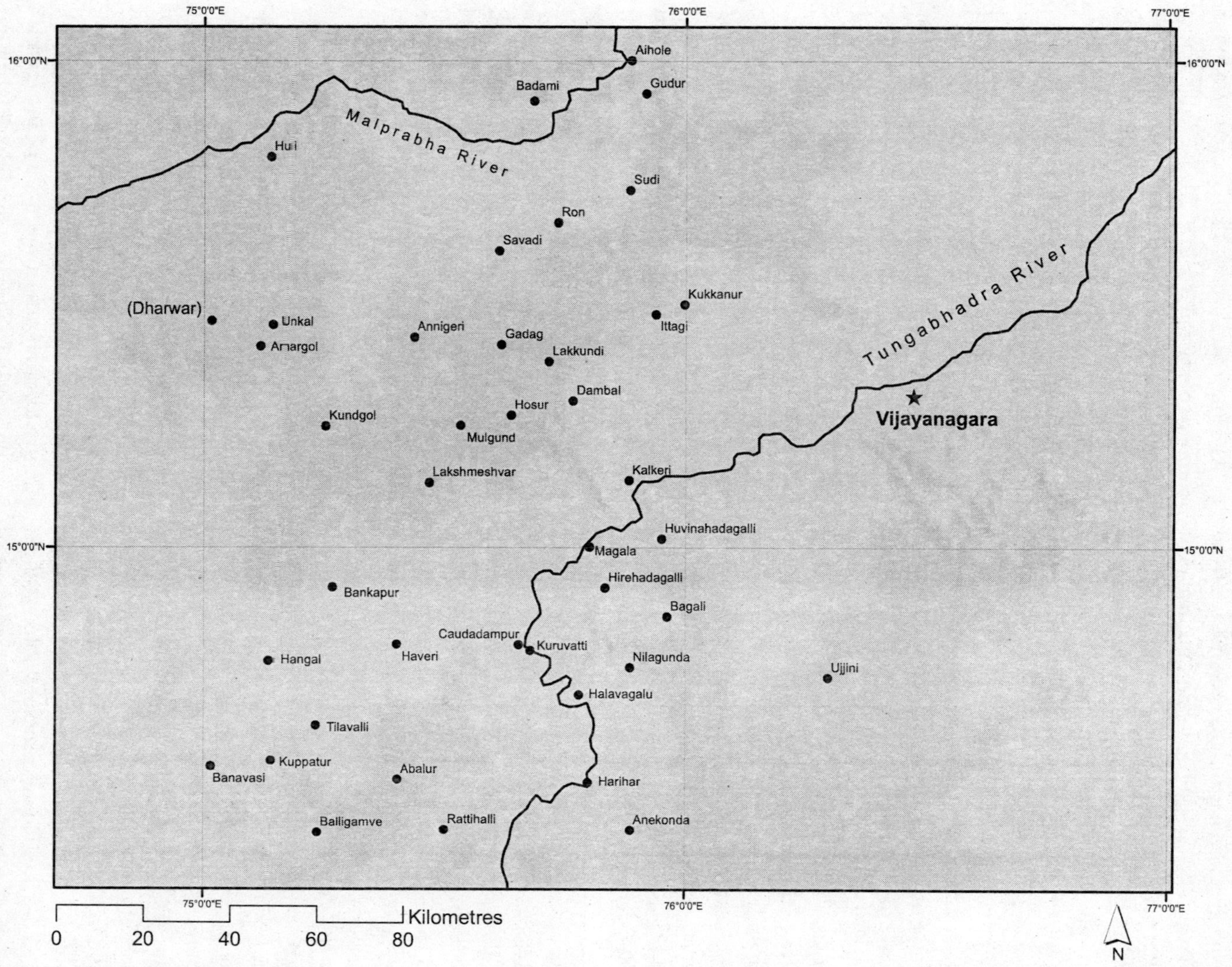


**Figure 3.7** Distribution of temples in Dharwar Chalukya style.

observed in our explorations of the site. To summarize this information, first, all the reused elements at Vijayanagara are specimens of the Chalukyas' Dharwar style; we find no instances of reuse of Metropolitan style components. This is not surprising, since most of the Dharwar region fell within the Vijayanagara kingdom, while all of the Metropolitan-style sites were located deep within the territories of Bijapur or the other sultanates. Second, with only one significant exception, all of the reused elements are interior components of temples. Doorframes, columns, ceiling beams, and carved ceiling panels make up the bulk of these reused materials.[53]

Given the external sculptural lavishness of Chalukya temples, it may seem surprising that the external elements were not recycled, but there are good reasons for this. Since the exterior walls and superstructures of Chalukya temples were generally constructed from many smaller and irregularly shaped stone blocks, a single exterior ornamental motif—such as a pilaster carrying a shrine model (*kūṭa-stambha*) or a blind entrance portal topped by fabulous crocodiles (*makara-toraṇa*)—in most cases extended over as many as ten or fifteen different blocks (Figure 3.9). Transporting such members would have posed significant problems, since the precise order of the irregular blocks needed to be carefully noted and accurately preserved in order to be properly reassembled in their new location. Using just one or two of the stones by themselves could not maintain the integrity of the applied sculptural motif. By contrast, in all of the types of interior elements actually reused, the extent of a decorative form is confined nearly perfectly within the boundaries of an individual structural block. Pillar shafts inevitably consist of just a single block of stone, and doorframes are typically composed of just three blocks—one for each of the jambs and a third for the crowning lintel—making re-assembly relatively uncomplicated.

The map also shows that reused Chalukya components are not distributed evenly across metropolitan Vijayanagara. Rather, they are restricted to three specific locations. One is in the public 'Zone of Royal Performance' in the city's 'Royal Centre' (following the nomenclature of Fritz, Michell, and Nagaraja Rao), where two structures—the 'underground chamber' (IVa/22) and the 'stepped tank' (IVc/6)—together account for the greatest numbers of reused materials anywhere at the site.[54] These two structures are both located in enclosure IV, near the centre of the thirty-one enclosures that make up the Royal Centre. Enclosure IV served as one of the primary arenas where Vijayanagara rulers presented themselves in audience and engaged in other forms of ritualized court activity. The second location of Chalukya reuse is in the Sacred Centre on the site's northern end, where four major temple complexes dominate the level lands along the south bank of the Tungabhadra, and literally hundreds of smaller temples and shrines seem to occupy every remaining parcel of land, however rocky.[55] Here in the Sacred Centre, reuse is restricted to the Virupaksha temple complex alone—a significant pattern given Virupaksha's position as Vijayanagara's state deity, a role this manifestation of Shiva continued to play even in the sixteenth century when most of Vijayanagara's rulers were themselves Vaishnavas. Here, three separate structures employ reused elements: the shrines of Virupaksha's two divine consorts, the goddesses Pampa and Bhuvaneshvari, and the two-storeyed pillared hall, or *maṇḍapa* (NMa/2), that marks the eastern terminus of the temple's chariot street.[56] The third location of Chalukya reuse is across the river in Anegondi, the 'royal village' that not only preceded Vijayanagara as

**Table 3.1** Instances of Chalukya reuse at Vijayanagara

| *Feature* | Map location | Doorframes | Columns | Pilasters and wall columns | Beams and ceiling slabs | Assorted components | Tank components |
|---|---|---|---|---|---|---|---|
| 1. Pampa shrine in Virupaksha temple | A | X | | | | | |
| 2. Bhuvaneshvari shrine in Virupaksha temple | A | X | X | X | X | X | |
| 3. Two-storeyed maṇḍapa (NMa/2) at end of Virupaksha bazaar | B | | X | | | | |
| 4. Underground chamber in Royal Centre (IVa/22) | C | | | X | X | X | |
| 5. Structures north of underground chamber (IVa/14, 20, 21) | C | | | | | X | |
| 6. Stepped tank in Royal Centre (IVc/6) | D | | | | | | X |
| 7. Unccappa matha, Anegondi | E | | X | | X | | |
| 8. Ranganatha temple in Anegondi | F | X | X | | | | |
| *NOT IN SITU* | | | | | | | |
| New Delhi, National Museum 59.159/3* | | X | | | | | |

*Source*: Authors.

*Notes*: Vijayanagara Research Project feature identification codes are given in parentheses.

* This is a Dharwar Chalukya-style *makara-toraṇa* lintel from a temple doorway, discovered by the Archaeological Survey of India 'amidst the ruins of a medieval temple at Hampi' (B.N. Sharma, 'A Western Chalukya Lintel from Hampi'). No further indication of the specific location of the findspot is given.

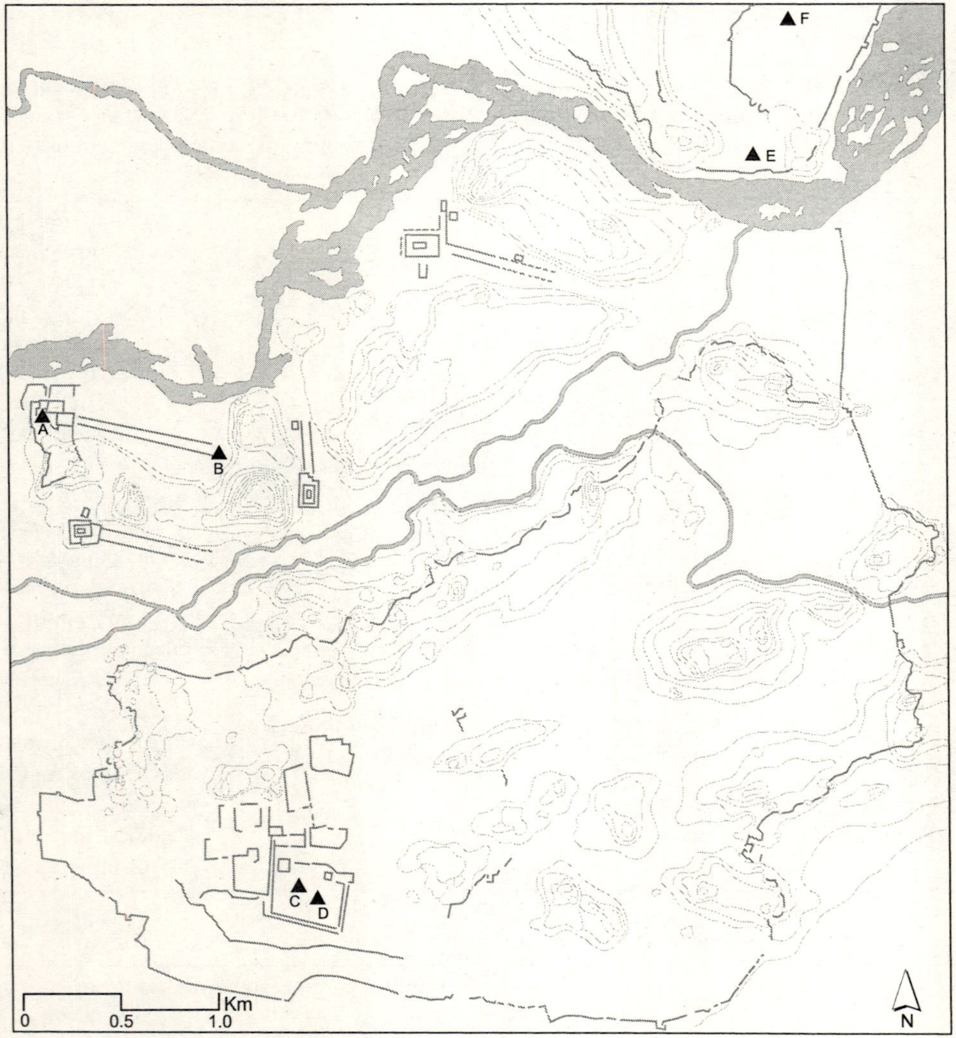


**Figure 3.8** Vijayanagara. Find spots of reused Chalukya components.

**Figure 3.9** Kuruvatti. Mallikarjuna temple, exterior wall detail showing extension of individual decorative motifs across many stone blocks.

the capital under the early Sangamas, but also remained a royal residence after the fall of the city in 1565. Here, Chalukya components have been recycled at two locations: in the Uneeappa Matha near the ferry gate and at the Ranganatha temple across from the market square.[57]

Had an abundance of this Chalukya material lain ready to use around the Vijayanagara site, and were it employed in a random fashion, one might reasonably conclude that the recycling was casual or functional, devoid of any specific significance. But the logistical complexities involved in procuring and transporting these materials from distant sites, as well as the care taken to display them in a manner that accentuated their stylistic difference from the surrounding Vijayanagara matrix, are both factors suggesting that we are dealing with meaningful, 'iconic' reuse (as defined in Chapter 2). In the two-storeyed maṇḍapa (NMa/2) located at the end of the Virupaksha bazaar, for example, the upper storey features nondescript Vijayanagara granite columns of a plain-shafted variety, while the twelve pillars of the lower storey are all reused Chalukya components of blue-green schist (Figure 3.10).[58] Not only are the two different types of columns juxtaposed by level, but even within the lower storey, the antique elements have been deliberately bracketed between bases and dish capitals manufactured from the typical Vijayanagara gray granite (Figure 3.11).[59] As a result, the reused columns are set off visually, as though they were prized gems being carefully fitted into a setting for display. Such a systematic approach to the aesthetics of reuse suggests that these elements were indeed being used iconically, and not just in a utilitarian fashion.

What, then, would have been the specific iconic charge carried by these recycled elements? We see these elements today and immediately think of the Chalukyas of Kalyana, but as we have explained at the outset of this chapter, that is largely due to the accidents of historiography and James Fergusson's decision to label the style of the Dharwar monuments as 'Chalukya'. We now know that there was nothing inherently 'Chalukya' about this style—that it was not patronized directly by Chalukya rulers, and that it was not even used in the core area of their empire around Kalyana. If we were then to assume that sixteenth-century viewers associated this style of construction with the Chalukya dynasty, would we not then be guilty of anachronistically projecting our own misconceptions back upon the past? To the contrary, the evidence overwhelmingly suggests that such a connection would certainly have been drawn in the sixteenth century, and that Vijayanagara's literate élite would have associated remains in this style not only with the Chalukyas but with the very idea of imperium that they embodied.

The best evidence for asserting these claims is that, well into the sixteenth century, the temples from which such elements were taken still retained legible tokens of Chalukya memory.

**Figure 3.10** Vijayanagara. Two-storeyed *maṇḍapa* (NMa/2) at end of Virupaksha bazaar.

**Figure 3.11** Close-up of reused Chalukya *śrīkāra* column in *maṇḍapa* shown in Figure 3.10.

Most of them possessed monumental stone steles recording donative inscriptions (Figure 3.12). Even when a given donation did not result from direct imperial patronage, epigraphic conventions dictated that these records should begin by reciting the standard string of imperial titles of the reigning Chalukya king. At Bagali, for example, some 80 kilometres southwest of the Vijayanagara capital, the Kalleshvara temple stood in the midst of a courtyard with as many as thirty-eight stone inscriptional stelae lined up along its periphery.[60] With each step through the courtyard, sixteenth-century visitors would have been reminded that this distinctive building belonged to the Chalukya past. They would also have known, as the inscriptions state, that the Chalukya emperor had reigned as

> The Asylum of all the Worlds, Beloved of the Goddesses Prosperity and Earth, the Great King of Kings, the Supreme Lord, the Supremely Venerable Lord, the Paragon of the Line of Satyasraya, the Ornament of the Chalukyas.[61]

**Figure 3.12** Hirehadagalli. Kalleshvara temple. Chalukya-period inscription stele, which opens with the standard list of imperial Chalukya titles.

Under such conditions, the distinctive architectural features of such a temple would have been seen as relics of the Chalukya imperium. Sixteenth-century rulers who saw themselves as latter-day 'Chalukya emperors' therefore eagerly sought such relics for reuse in their own monuments.

## THE CULT OF BHUVANESHVARI AND HER NEO-CHALUKYA SHRINE

Let us turn now to consider in detail two of the most striking instances of Chalukya reuse at Vijayanagara. The first is provided by the shrine of Bhuvaneshvari, one of the two consorts of Vijayanagara's state deity, Virupaksha (Figure 3.13). The earlier of these two consorts, the local river goddess, Pampa, had been present at the site since as far back as the seventh century.[62] On the other hand Virupaksha's other consort, Bhuvaneshvari, unlike Pampa is both a pan-Indic divinity and a much later arrival, as her cult is not attested at the site until the sixteenth century.[63] Belonging to a group of Tantric goddesses known as the Ten Mahavidyas, Bhuvaneshvari appears to have enjoyed a particular upsurge in popularity during the sixteenth and seventeenth centuries in various parts of India.[64] As her name, 'Mistress of the World', suggests, she personifies the idea of cosmic dominion, which is clearly reflected in her iconography. Thus, the *Tantrasāra* dictates that she should appear at the centre of a mandala encircled at the perimeter by the 'Eight Lords of the Directions', or *aṣṭa-dikpālas*, a device symbolically suggesting her dominion over the totality of space.[65]

Given Bhuvaneshvari's role as the divine ruler of the cosmos, it is not surprising that her cult should have been introduced at Vijayanagara in the mid-sixteenth century, just when the Aravidu dynasty was becoming preoccupied with its own imperial image. Nor is it surprising that Bhuvaneshvari's cosmocratic image is housed in a small shrine made from imperially charged Chalukya building components, all in the Dharwar style, including a number of beautiful śrīkāra columns carved from schist (Figure 3.14).[66] Although at first glance, the shrine recalls an authentic Chalukya-period structure, a number of features reveal it to be a later, Vijayanagara-period pastiche. First, the Chalukya-period components have clearly been inserted into the surrounding architectural matrix, which consists of a platform with a colonnaded cloister dating to the end of the fourteenth century (Figure 3.15).

Evidence of this insertion can be seen on the shrine's east side, where projecting portions

**Figure 3.13** Vijayanagara. The goddess Bhuvaneshvari in her shrine in the Virupaksha temple.

**Figure 3.14** Vijayanagara. Reused Chalukya column in the Bhuvaneshvari shrine.

**Figure 3.15** Vijayanagara. *Maṇḍapa* of the Bhuvaneshvari shrine, built in the sixteenth century from eleventh-century components inserted within a late fourteenth-century cloister. The shrine's doorway is to the left; the three larger columns and the pavement in the foreground belong to the cloister.

of an adjacent column have been hewn off in order to permit the shrine's eave to be hoisted up into place (Figure 3.16).

Similarly, on its south side, the two fourteenth-century columns flanking the shrine's main entrance stairway have been displaced about half a metre to the south in order to accommodate the shrine's pillared hall (Figure 3.17). Finally, and most tellingly, the typical sequence of ritual spaces in the shrine has been abbreviated due to the limited amount of space available on the platform. Whereas the adjacent shrine of goddess Pampa exhibits the standard sequence of spaces—pillared hall (maṇḍapa), entrance vestibule (*antarāla*), and enclosed sanctum (*garbha-gṛha*)—Bhuvaneshvari's shrine eliminates the intermediate vestibule, and simply articulates the pillared hall directly with the sanctum (Figure 3.18).

Careful inspection reveals that the Bhuvaneshvari shrine's components were selectively retrieved from at least two different temples, and that once brought to the Virupaksha complex they were ingeniously combined to compensate for unavailable pieces and differences of scale. A magnificent Chalukya

**Figure 3.16** Vijayanagara. Bhuvaneshvari shrine, southeastern corner of *maṇḍapa* as seen from the north. Portions of the square block (*phalaka*) atop the dish capital and one arm of the bracket capital (*potika*) of the pre-existing fourteenth-century column have been hewn off to allow the eave to be hoisted into place.

**Figure 3.17** Vijayanagara. Bhuvaneshvari shrine, southern side of *maṇḍapa* viewed from the east, revealing southward displacement of one of its two central columns (to left), and the trimming of its capitals as in Figure 3.16.

schist doorframe (*dvāra-bandha*, Figure 3.13) evidently served as the point of departure for the new design. Even though it was originally designed to frame the opening of an antarā-la-vestibule and not a shrine,[67] the designers decided to use this doorframe anyway, probably because of the exquisite sculptured frieze running across the upper part of its lintel. This frieze is divided into nine sections that alternately project and recede, following the articulation of the eave beneath it. The five projecting sections are carved (left to right) with frontally conceived icons of Ganapati, Brahma, Shiva, Vishnu, and Durga, while the four intervening sections, which portray the epic battle between Rama and Ravana, are conceived as a continuous narrative composition running behind these figures. The images of Rama and Ravana face off on either side of the central icon of Shiva, standing on their chariots with bows drawn, and surrounded by the teeming hordes of their respective monkey and demon armies (Figure 3.19). In the outer pair of recesses, these figures are backed up by their most prominent allies: Hanuman stands behind Rama, his arm raised and ready to strike, while Ravana is backed up by another demon on a chariot, possibly his son Indrajit or one of his brothers.

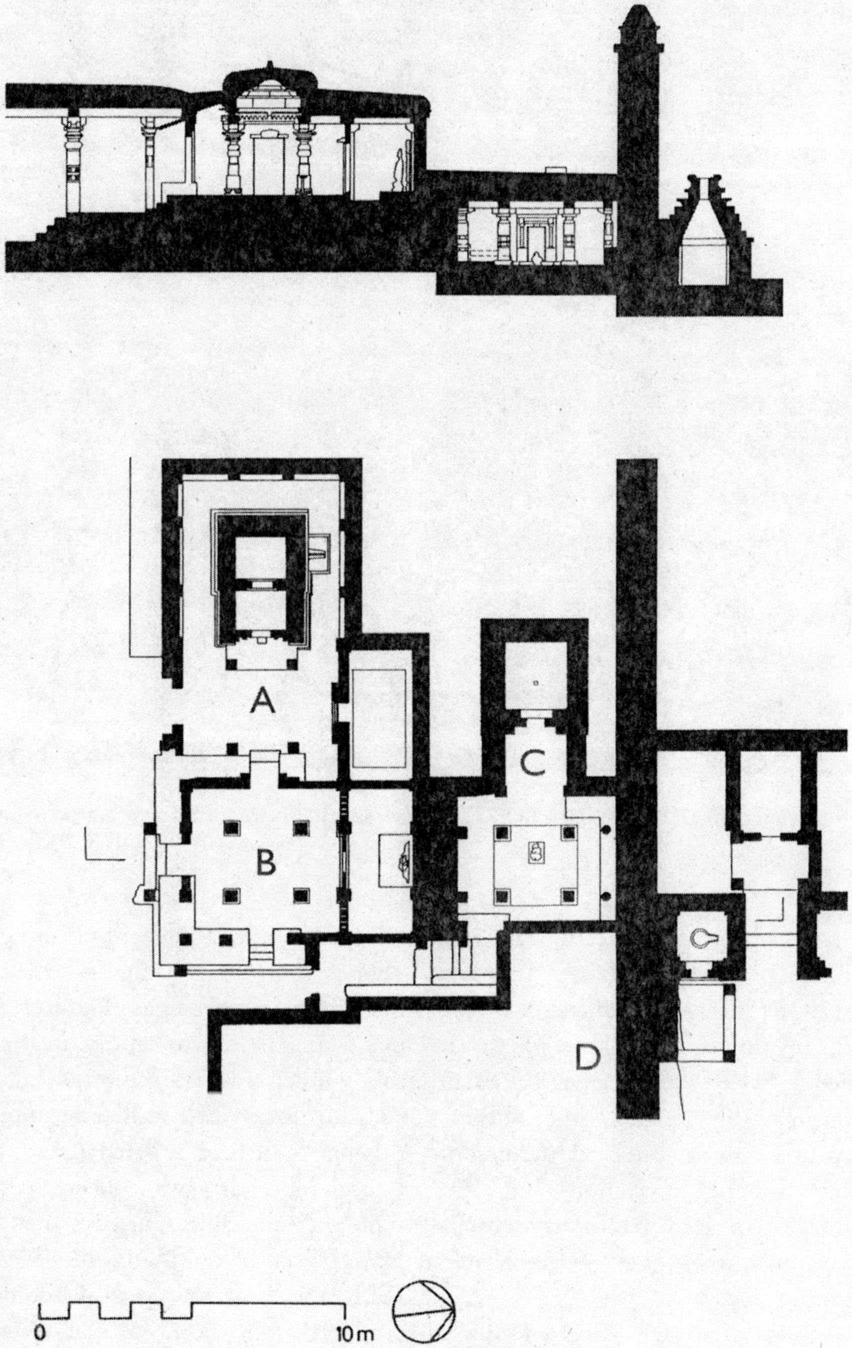


**Figure 3.18** Vijayanagara. Above: Cross section of Pampa shrine and Bhuvaneshvari shrine. Below: Plan of Pampa shrine (A) and Bhuvaneshvari shrine (B). An unrelated shrine (C), a portion of the outer wall of the Virupaksha temple (D), and two abutting shrines can be seen to the right.

**Figure 3.19** Vijayanagara. Lintel of reused Chalukya doorframe in Bhuvaneshvari shrine, showing combat of Rama and Ravana.

As a work of Chalukya-period sculpture, this impressive depiction of the battle between Rama and Ravana recalls the centrality of the Rama cult during the reign of Vikramaditya VI. Now recycled in its new context of imperial, sixteenth-century Vijayanagara, the shrine's iconography not only highlighted themes of kingship and imperial dominion, but also linked seamlessly with local traditions identifying Vijayanagara as the site of key events related in the Rāmāyaṇa epic.[68]

Because this doorway had originally belonged to a temple that was larger in scale than that from which the four central maṇḍapa columns were taken, the architects placed each shaft upon a separate rectangular block of salvaged schist, thus reduplicating the lower 'shank' (*jaṅghā*) section and making up for the difference in height (Figure 3.14).[69] They made similar improvisations in the exterior of the maṇḍapa, where the outer range of pillars rises up from a half-wall. The outer surface of this half-wall is articulated not in the manner typical for such a wall; rather, it features the standard moulding sequence met with in the *pīṭhika* type of temple plinth (Figure 3.15).[70] Evidently, because no wall-mouldings were available from either of the source temples, Vijayanagara's architects used these plinth segments as substitutes.

In addition to the doorway, another key element in the shrine's new design involved reusing two separate sculptural groups of the Eight Lords of the Directions (aṣṭa-dikpālas), just mentioned as part of Bhuvaneshvari's mandala (Figures 3.20 and 3.21). Representations of these eight divinities commonly appear in Chalukya-style temples, where they were often carved in the ceiling panels over the central bay of a pillared maṇḍapa. In the Bhuvaneshvari shrine, one set is recycled in that typical location, forming the vertical face of the lowermost tier of a corbelled lotus dome. But another set, carved as a flat panel with a nine-squared grid, is seen in the completely anomalous location of the sanctum, where it forms the ceiling over the central bay occupied by Bhuvaneshvari.[71] The unusual positioning of this slab within the sanctum suggests that the designers were less interested in issues of exact authenticity in presenting recycled elements than they were in stressing Bhuvaneshvari's cosmocratic functions, for her Vijayanagara patrons had placed her directly under a microcosmic representation of the totality of the world.

In short, what we see here is a perfect harmony between the imperial associations of the reused Chalukya components and the cultic functions of Bhuvaneshvari as a goddess of cosmic dominion. One might read still more

**Figure 3.20** Vijayanagara. Reused *aṣṭa-dikpāla* ceiling in *maṇḍapa* of Bhuvaneshvari shrine.

**Figure 3.21** Vijayanagara. Reused *aṣṭa-dikpāla* ceiling in sanctum of Bhuvaneshvari shrine.

into the iconography of the shrine, seeing the doorway—with its frieze of Rama's epic battle against Ravana—as expressing the goddess's empowerment of her new patron, the king of Vijayanagara. It would not be the first time that kings were symbolically equated with Rama at the City of Victory.

## MOVING A CHALUKYA STEPWELL TO THE VIJAYANAGARA CAPITAL

An even more arresting example of wholesale Chalukya reuse at Vijayanagara is provided by an elaborate stepwell located at the heart of the Royal Centre, in the southeastern quadrant of enclosure IV (feature IVc/6; Figure 3.22). This zone of the site was especially rich in tanks and related waterworks, with at least twelve having been excavated and documented. The tanks vary greatly in size, from the 'Great Tank'—measuring 67 by 22 metres—that dominates the southeastern quadrant of enclosure IV to the several small stone or brick tanks that measure just a few metres square. Most of these tanks appear to have been supplied with water from the Kamalapuram reservoir to the south of the urban centre, via an aqueduct entering the enclosure on its eastern side. How these various tanks and pools were used is not known with any certainty, but Dominic Davison-Jenkins, who has studied the irrigation and water supply systems of the city in detail, believes that the water supplied for domestic consumption in this part of the site served a dual purpose, including sanitary and culinary needs on the one hand, and ritual functions on the other. Water was an absolute necessity not only for bathing and cooking, but also for all Hindu ritual activities, ranging from individual purification rituals to the performance of the royal consecration, or *paṭṭābhiṣeka*.[72]

The specific tank in question was excavated by the Archaeological Survey of India in 1984 and is located between the Great Tank, which lies to its south, and the great Mahanavami platform, which lies to its northeast.[73] The tank is made of chloritic schist, according to a design completely foreign to the local, Vijayanagara tradition of tank architecture. While the other tanks in this enclosure are relatively shallow, and have stairways on only one or two sides providing access down to the water level, this tank is arranged in five descending and diminishing tiers, each with a broad terrace at the top and stairways arranged symmetrically along each of its four sides.[74] Although the tank seems to have no direct comparisons among documented Chalukya-period tanks in the Dharwar style, it nonetheless manifests a decidedly Chalukya character, due to its use of schist and its employment of compositional principles that resonate closely with those seen in the temple architecture of the Dharwar style.[75]

**Figure 3.22** Vijayanagara. Stepped tank of chloritic schist in the Royal Centre.

Our suspicion that the tank represents another instance of reuse of Chalukya components—this time an entire structure—was confirmed by the discovery that each stone is carved with a brief inscription indicating its exact location through a carefully coded system of letters, numbers, and symbols, first deciphered in an important contribution by Jagdish.[76] For example, the stone illustrated in Figure 3.23 is carved with a five-part coded address:

3 *u* 2 *kṣa* 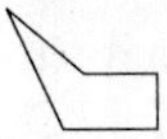

indicating that it belongs in the third projecting stairway from the left, on the north side ('*u*' being the abbreviation for the word '*uttara*', north), that it is the second stone from the left within this stairway, and that it occupies the thirty-fifth masonry course from the top of the tank (the conjunct consonant '*kṣa*' being the thirty-fifth letter of the alphabet, not counting the vowels and starting from the consonants). The fifth mark is a graphic symbol—an irregular, five-sided polygon—indicating that the block belongs to the second lowest tier of the tank on the north side (see Figure 3.24).[77] The almost obsessive detail of this notational system, combined with the redundancy of the information encoded within the fifth mark, suggests that it was concocted by the Vijayanagara masons responsible for

**Figure 3.23** Vijayanagara. Five-part locational inscription carved into one of the slabs of the stepped tank (photograph retouched to sharpen contrast).

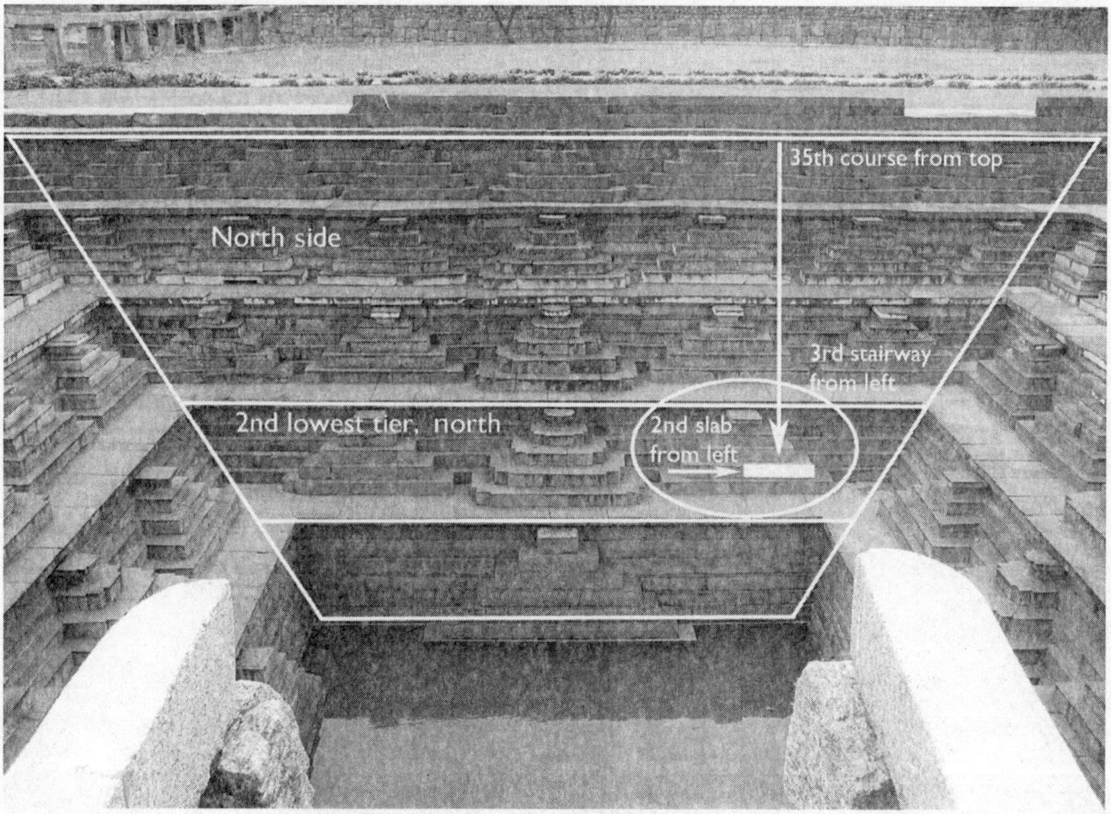


**Figure 3.24** Vijayanagara. Graphic representation of the content of the code illustrated in Figure 3.23, which is inscribed on the slab indicated in white.

dismantling the tank and transporting it to the capital for reassembly.[78] Given the intricacy of the tank's design, and the irregular dimensions of its individual stone blocks, such directions would have been absolutely essential for the tank to be reassembled correctly.

But how do we know that these inscriptions were not simply masons' marks from the time of the tank's original Chalukya construction? Might not the tank have been constructed *in situ*, making it the only known outlier of the Dharwar style to have been built in the Hampi region? The evidence argues forcibly against such a scenario. First, there is the testimony of paleography: the forms of the letters used in the coded inscriptions are those of the sixteenth century, not the eleventh or twelfth. Second, the language of the inscriptions is Telugu, not Kannada, and while Telugu was widely used at the Vijayanagara court in the sixteenth century, it was not used in the districts west of the site during the Chalukya era.[79] Third, the numbering system for vertical placement runs from top to bottom, rather than from bottom to top. Since the tank would necessarily have been disassembled from the top down, the numbering system suggests that the inscriptions were carved at the time of dismantlement and not at the time of original construction.

Fourth, and most intriguingly, there is a discrepancy between the actual vertical location of each course and its location as specified in

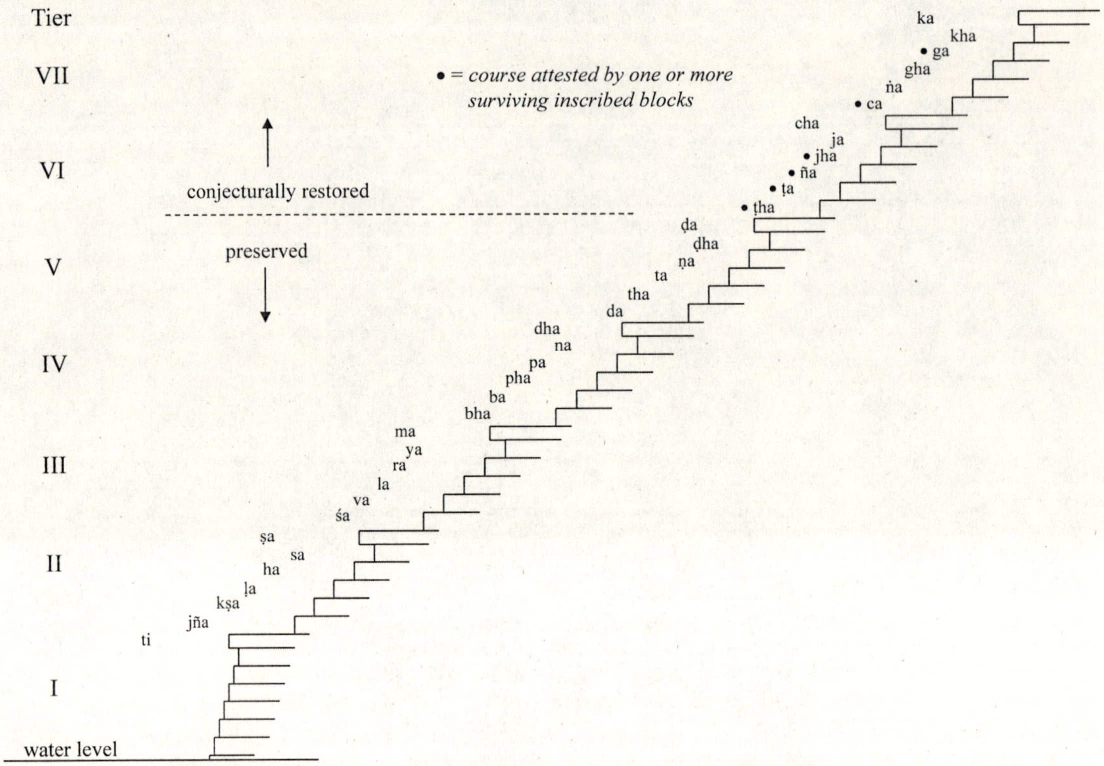


**Figure 3.25** Vijayanagara. Schematic elevation of stepped tank, showing inscriptional scheme for horizontal masonry courses. Bullets indicate courses in tiers VI and VII for which inscribed stones have been preserved.

the inscriptional address. For example, in the stone we have just considered, the inscription specifies that it should be placed in the thirty-fifth course from the top of the tank, whereas in fact it appears only twenty-three courses from the top. This implies that when the masons inscribed the locational positions before dismantling the structure, there would originally have been twelve more courses at the top of the tank—in two more tiers of six courses each, just as in the preserved tiers. For some reason, however, it proved impossible to use the two uppermost tiers of the original tank in its new location. Perhaps, upon transporting all the stones to Vijayanagara, the engineers discovered a pre-existing drainage system that prevented excavating sufficient earth to reassemble the entire tank. Or perhaps they hit bedrock in the course of excavation.[80]

In any event, because excavations at Vijayanagara could not accommodate reassembling the entire original tank, the tank's upper levels—comprising several hundred stones that bear inscriptions for levels 'ka' through 'ṭha'—could not be assembled, and its stones were never used (Figure 3.25).[81] Indeed, many of these unused stones can still be identified, scattered about at several locations near the tank. The stone illustrated in Figure 3.26, for example, is lying amidst a pile of discarded schist pieces just north of the tank. Had it been possible to install the tank in its entirety, this stone—according to its inscription, *ṭha 1 da* (Figure 3.27)—would

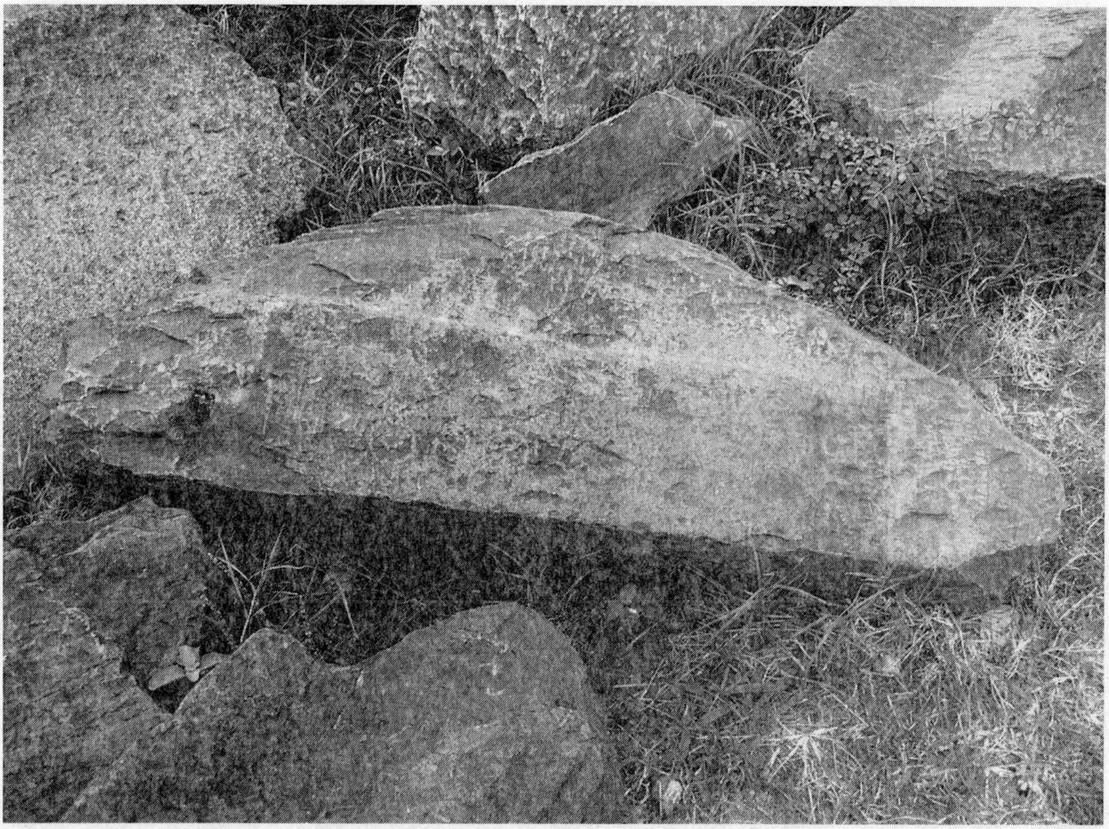

**Figure 3.26** Vijayanagara. Unused stone from the original Chalukya stepped tank, lying in a pile of discarded schist pieces to the north of the tank.

have been the first stone on the south side in the next course of masonry above the present top of the tank. This slab is of additional interest in that it contains material evidence attesting to its having actually been used, centuries before, in the original Chalukya-era tank. For on it are the remnants of a rusted iron clamp that would have bound it to the adjacent stone on the left, which was the last stone at the south end of the east side of this course. The stone in question also carries faint lines of white mineral deposits that had accumulated over many years, marking the front edge of the next higher course of masonry before it was removed in the sixteenth century. These mineral deposits silently testify that the stone had previously seen centuries of use near the top of the original tank.[82]

Taken together, then, this evidence strongly suggests that the tank was originally seven-tiered, and that it was built in the Chalukya period at some site—as yet unidentified—in the Dharwar region. At some point during the sixteenth century, a patron had ordered the tank dismantled and moved to the Vijayanagara capital to be reconstructed in the heart of the Royal Centre. To guide this reconstruction, the individual blocks were first labelled with locational inscriptions, but in the midst of the reconstruction it became impossible to utilize the two uppermost tiers. Accordingly, those

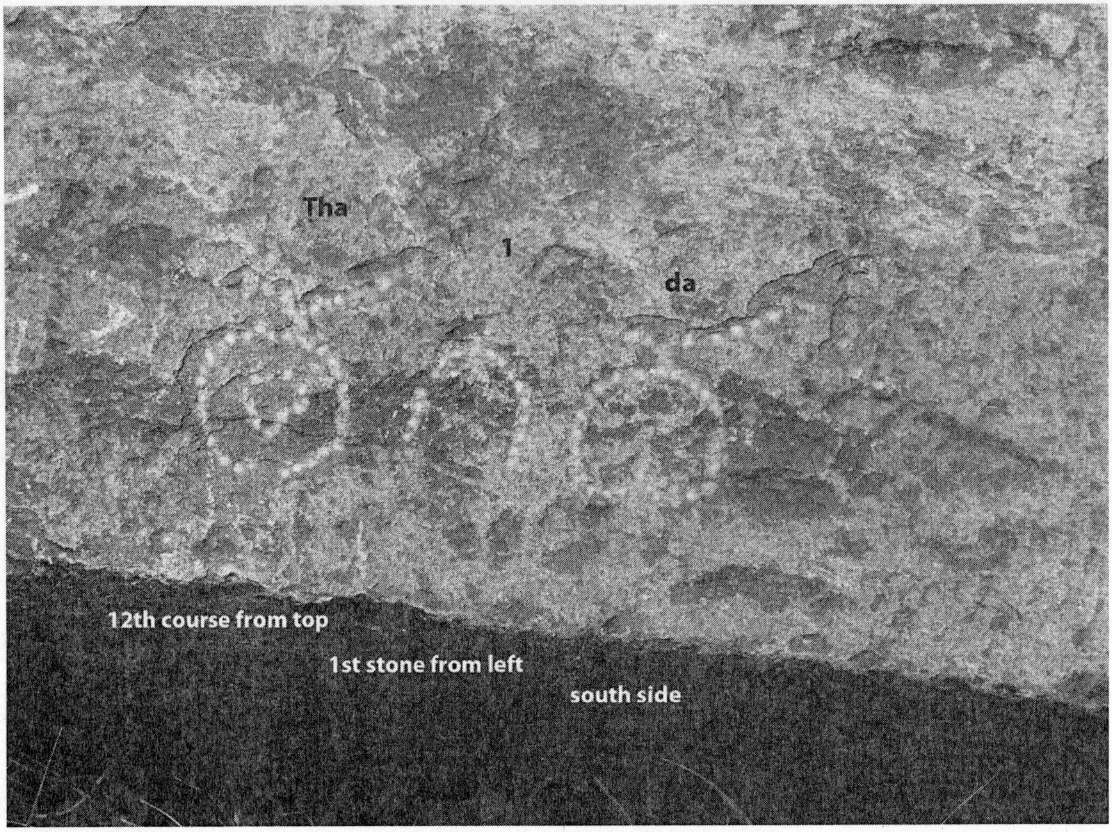


**Figure 3.27** Vijayanagara. Detail of stone from Figure 3.26, showing a three-part locational inscription.

stones were recycled in several different ways in other contexts.

Although it is not certain how this tank was used in the Vijayanagara period, it seems likely—given its prominent location in the 'Zone of Royal Performance'—that it would have served some ritual purpose in connection with the rites of kingship. Possibly, it was used in connection with the paṭṭābhiṣeka, the elaborate set of consecration rituals through which royal power was infused into the person of the king. According to the *Sāmrājyalakṣmī-pīṭhika*, a manual of royal rituals and statecraft produced at Vijayanagara during the reign of Krishna Raya (1509–29), the paṭṭābhiṣeka was to be performed not only when a prince ascended the throne, but also on various occasions thereafter, such as on the king's birthday, or in the face of plague, drought, and other calamities.[83] According to this text, a temporary thatched pavilion is to be erected for the performance of this ceremony, with a central altar to serve as the primary focus of the rituals. On the day before the consecration proper, the officiants are instructed to proceed to a river, fill five golden jars with water, and bring them back to the pavilion. The waters from these jars are then transferred into nine other jars, and the powers of the seven oceans and eleven sacred rivers are invoked with mantras into the jars, together with the deity Varuna, the lord of all water. The nine jars are arranged in the form of an aṣṭa-dikpāla-maṇḍala, that is, an image of Vishnu is placed on the central jar, and those of the Eight Lords of the Directions appear on the surrounding jars. After worshipping these deities, the officiating priests sprinkle the king with the waters from these nine jars, thus infusing him with the power of Vishnu and the Lords of the Directions.[84]

Although the text specifies that the water for this ritual should be brought from a river, elsewhere it suggests that rivers and tanks are interchangeable for ritual purposes.[85] If the water for the 'occasional consecration' ceremony (*naimittika-abhiṣeka*) had been brought from the stepped tank, then the king would have been infused not only with the power and authority of his divine archetypes, but also with the aura of his esteemed Chalukya 'ancestors'. Finally, one notes that the 'Eight Lords of the Directions', or aṣṭa-dikpālas, play a central role both in the iconography of the shrine to Bhuvaneshvari, just discussed, and in the rites that the *Sāmrājyalakṣmī-pīṭhika* prescribed for royal rituals associated with water. This link suggests that both the Chalukya artifacts discussed here—the shrine and the tank—could have been reassembled with a common ideological programme in mind, and perhaps at the same time.

## STAGES OF CHALUKYA REUSE AT VIJAYANAGARA

Throughout this chapter, we have spoken only in the most general terms about the authorship and chronology of Chalukya reuse at Vijayanagara, arguing that it is best understood in the light of the Aravidus' rise to power during the nearly thirty-year period between 1542, when Rama Raya launched his project of usurping the throne, and 1570, when Tirumala was finally crowned as king. Specifically, we have argued that Chalukya architectural reuse was part of a broader strategy of legitimation pursued by the usurping Aravidus, and that it served to stress their connections with the imperial Chalukyas, much as their assumption of Chalukya titles and genealogies did in the literary works they sponsored. If we have not yet addressed the question of the precise chronology of this reuse, and the attendant question of which of the various Aravidu personalities was primarily responsible for it, it is because the evidence is somewhat complex and far from conclusive. But now that we have finished our detailed examination of the material evidence, we may return to the historical record and attempt to arrive at some tentative answers to these questions.

Taking first the question of authorship, we believe it may be more productive to think in terms of multiple Aravidu patrons, rather than attempting to find a single figure to whom we can assign all of the diverse instances of reuse at Vijayanagara, both simple and complex. It seems quite plausible that some of the more limited and straightforward instances of reuse—such as the insertion of a single Dharwar-style Chalukya doorframe into the doorway of Pampa's shrine, or the recycling of śrīkāra columns in the two-storeyed maṇḍapa—were accomplished through the initiative of some of the junior members of the Aravidu clan. Rama Raya's cousins of the Avuku and Nandyala families could have undertaken such preliminary types of reuse as improvisatory exercises, much as the poet Doneru Konerunatha had undertaken the first tentative experiments in imagining Chalukya connections for the Aravidus before Tirumala Raya took them to their logical conclusion in the official Chalukya genealogy that he promulgated after his coronation.

It seems equally plausible that the two most ambitious and significant projects—the Bhuvaneshvari shrine and the stepped tank—were undertaken at the initiative of Rama Raya himself, doubtless in collaboration with other élite members of the ruling Aravidu clan. After all, ever since 1542, Rama Raya possessed the authority to command the resources necessary for undertaking these projects. He also had good motives for linking himself and his clan to the Chalukyas. For it was between 1543 and 1547, just as he was beginning to usurp power for himself and his family, that the poet Konerunatha began associating Rama Raya's Aravidu clan with the memory of Chalukya glory. Only *after* the collapse of metropolitan Vijayanagara, from 1571, did the Aravidu clan publicly assert an official genealogy connecting itself with the Chalukya emperors. Significantly, as this association grew in subsequent memory, the clan's remembered connection with the Chalukyas focussed more on Rama Raya than on other members of the Aravidu family. By the late 1600s, more than a century after the eclipse of the great capital city following Vijayanagara's catastrophic defeat at the Battle of Talikota (discussed later and in Chapter Seven), poets were styling Rama Raya himself not only as 'Chalukya emperor' (*cāḷukya-cakravarti*) and 'Radiant King of Kalyana' (*Kalyāṇa-mahīpāla-bhāswara*), but as 'The One Who Captured the City of Kalyana' (*Kalyāṇa-nagara-sādhaka*).

The last title doubtless signals a memory of Vijayanagara's 1559 capture of the Chalukya capital from the sultan of Ahmadnagar, when Rama Raya personally compelled Husain Nizam Shah to hand over the keys to Kalyana (discussed later and in Chapter Seven). That action, more than anything else he did in the area of war or diplomacy, proclaimed Rama Raya's bold claim to be the true heir to Chalukya sovereignty and glory. In Vijayanagara's architectural history, the most dramatic analogue to such a claim was the retrofitting of the Chalukyas' Bhuvaneshvari shrine into the heart of the city's Sacred Centre and the reassembling of a Chalukya stepped tank at the heart of its Royal Centre. It would seem logical that the same man who exerted himself to conquer the Chalukya capital would also have taken the lead in patronizing these two monumental projects.

When might Rama Raya have patronized the two projects? As long ago as 1927, Rev. Henry Heras detected three distinct stages in Rama Raya's relationship with the *de jure* Tuluva sovereign Sadashiva Raya. In the first stage, from 1542 to about 1550, Sadashiva Raya was still too young to rule and Rama Raya assumed the role of regent. At this time, Rama Raya presented himself in inscriptions variously as a *mahāmaṇḍalēśvara*, a minister, or an 'agent' of Sadashiva Raya—all titles that affirmed his subordinate status vis-à-vis his sovereign. The second stage began about 1550 when Sadashiva Raya had become old enough to rule, but was instead imprisoned by the domineering Rama Raya to prevent the king's interference in the affairs of the state. Yet the puppet ruler was still allowed to appear to his subjects once a year, thereby maintaining the fiction that Rama Raya was technically only an agent of the legitimate ruler's will. During this period Rama Raya presented himself as an equal to Sadashiva Raya, almost as a co-ruler sharing in the royal aura. Finally, after 1562 Rama Raya in his inscriptions altogether ceased making references to Sadashiva Raya and instead assumed full imperial titles for himself. A copper plate land grant issued in that year describes Rama Raya as 'the Great King of Kings, the Supreme Lord among Kings' (*śrīman-mahārājādhirāja-rājaparamēśvara*), while Sadashiva Raya's name is conspicuously absent.[86]

Had Rama Raya indeed patronized the retrofitting of the Bhuvaneshvari temple and the stepped tank, he would most likely have undertaken these projects during the final stage in his progression to power, between 1562 and his death in 1565, shortly after his capture of Kalyana. At that time, with Sadashiva Raya no longer in the picture, the usurper needed more than ever to prove in public the legitimacy of his rule. It is significant that both of these Chalukya-style monuments were associated with the ideas and rituals of imperium and royal empowerment: the goddess Bhuvaneshvari appeared as the divine manifestation of imperial, cosmic dominion, while the tank could serve in the rituals of royal consecration. Although no direct evidence confirms that Rama Raya ever underwent a formal ritual of royal consecration, patronizing these two ambitious projects involving Chalukya reuse could certainly have paved his way to the throne. But in 1565 fate intervened: Rama Raya was slain on the battlefield after the epochal Battle of Talikota.

Seen in this light, Tirumala's actions after that fateful battle make perfect sense. Learning of his brother's death on the battlefield and witnessing the routing of the Vijayanagara army, Tirumala quickly fled back to the capital, where he collected the captive Sadashiva Raya and repaired with him to a stronghold further south. His concern for the puppet emperor reveals his awareness of the precariousness of his own position, and his acknowledgment that as the brother of a usurper, he too needed a source of legitimation. But Tirumala was evidently vacillating, for his return to the city of Vijayanagara in early 1566 without Sadashiva Raya suggests that he was preparing to abandon the fiction of Aravidu servitude to the captive Tuluva king and openly to assume the throne. To this end he would use his brother's architectural projects to present himself as a latter-day Chalukya and a legitimate king in his own right. In fact, we learn from the eyewitness account of Cesare Federici, a Venetian merchant who was present at Vijayanagara during the first half of 1566, that Tirumala had reoccupied the city and had spent two years attempting to revive its economic infrastructure and rebuild its damaged fabric. Although Tirumala never succeeded in reviving the city's prosperity, and accordingly had to abandon the site in 1567 for Penugonda, he would soon succeed in establishing his own Aravidu line as Vijayanagara's fourth and final dynasty. This would happen only after Tirumala's son had put Sadashiva Raya to death, precipitating an outright crisis of authority among the nobles of the realm. Federici writes that 'the Barons and Noblemen in that kingdome would not acknowledge… [Tirumala] to be their king', thus plunging the kingdom into a state of anarchy.[87]

It was in this context, that, in 1569, Tirumala had his royal consecration performed. Within a year he was issuing donative inscriptions, assuming full imperial titles, and publicizing his descent from the Chalukyas, as we have seen earlier. Although we are nowhere told where Tirumala's consecration was performed, we cannot help but wonder whether the court might have returned briefly to the old capital to celebrate it, since it is recorded that Tirumala's queen was not present at the ceremony, as would have been ritually expected. These festivities are described in the Kuniyur Plates of Tirumala's successor, Venkata II:

> At the coronation of this moon among kings (*and*) foremost among the famous,
> this earth, being sprinkled with floods of water (*poured out*) at donations,
> occupied (*as it were*), the place of queen.[88]

We can well imagine Tirumala on the watery occasion, standing by the tank originally erected centuries before by his supposed Chalukya ancestors and moved to the City of Victory by his late brother, basking in the sovereignty to which he had just been anointed.

## NOTES

1. *Vasucaritramu* by the poet Bhattumurti (1570), verse I, 47. See Ravuri Dorasami Sharma, ed., *Rāmarājabhūṣaṇuni Vasucaritramu: Āndhra Pancakāvyamulalo Reṇḍavadi* (Vijayawada: Emesco Books, 1997), 14.

2. The seventeenth-century poet Vengakavi, *Rāmarājīyamu*, v. 288. See C.V. Ramachandra Rao, ed., *Andugala Vengakavi Rāmarājīyamu lēka narapati vijayamu mariyu Dōnēru Kōnērunāthakavi Padya Bālabhāgavatamu Dvipada Bālabhāgavatamu (Aravīṭi Rājula Praśamsa)* (Nellore: Manasa Publications, 1995), 38.

3. Parts of this chapter draw on Phillip B. Wagoner, 'Retrieving the Chalukyan Past: The Politics of Architectural Reuse in the Sixteenth-Century Deccan' *South Asian Studies* 23 (2007), 1–29; and idem., 'Retrieving the Chalukyan Past: The Stepped Tank in the Royal Centre', in *South India under Vijayanagara: Art and Archaeology*, eds Anila Verghese and Anna L. Dallapiccola (New Delhi: Oxford University Press, 2011), 118–35.

4. See, for example, James Fergusson, James Burgess, and Richard Phené Spiers, *History of Indian and Eastern Architecture* (Delhi: Munshiram Manoharlal, 1967 [rev. ed. of 1876]). Book IV deals with 'Chalukyan Style'.

5. On (Later) Chalukya architecture, see Alexander Rea, *Chalukyan Architecture: Including Examples from Bellary District, Madras Presidency*, Archaeological Survey of India, New Imperial Series, vol. 21 (Madras: Government Press, 1896); Henry Cousens, *The Chalukyan Architecture of the Kanarese Districts*, Archaeological Survey of India, New Imperial Series, vol. 42 (Calcutta: Government of India, 1926); M.A. Dhaky, *The Indian Temple Forms in Karnata Inscriptions and Architecture* (New Delhi: Abhinav Publications, 1977); idem., *Encyclopaedia of Indian Temple Architecture*, vol. I, part 3: *South India, Upper Dravidadesa, Later Phase, A.D. 973–1326* (New Delhi: American Institute for Indian Studies, 1996); Adam Hardy, *Indian Temple Architecture: Form and Transformation—The Karnata Dravida Tradition, Seventh to Thirteenth Centuries* (New Delhi: Indira Gandhi National Centre for the Arts and Abhinav Publications, 1995); Ajay Sinha, *Imagining Architects: Creativity in the Religious Monuments of India* (Newark, DE: University of Delaware Press, 2000); Gerard Foekema, *Calukya Architecture: Medieval Temples of Northern Karnataka Built during the Rule of the Calukya of Kalyana and Thereafter, AD 1000–1300*, 3 vols (New Delhi: Munshiram Manoharlal, 2003).

6. On Chalukya-era artists' inscriptions, see John Henry Rice, 'Image, Text, Monument: A Reexamination of the Philadelphia Brahma and "Later Cālukyan" Sculpture', *Artibus Asiae* 68, no. 2 (2008), 169–214, and the works cited therein. See also Shrinivas H. Ritti, 'Udega, the Chief Architect of the Saraswati Temple at Gadag', in *Indian Epigraphy: Its Bearing on the History of Art*, eds Frederick M. Asher and G.S. Gai (New Delhi: Oxford and AIIS, 1985), 213–14.

7. See, for example, Sinha, *Imagining Architects*, figure 1, 'Map of southern India showing Vesara [i.e. later Chalukya] sites in Karnataka', 20; and Hardy, *Indian Temple Architecture*, map 2, 'Karnata Dravida Temple Sites'. In both maps, the only site located north of the Krishna River is Sirval, a site with some important transitional Rashtrakuta–Chalukya style temples. Kalyana, though the capital of the dynasty, is not shown on either of these maps.

8. In signalling the Dravida character of the Dharwar style, we do not suggest that it is purely Dravida, as Hardy has argued in *Indian Temple Architecture* and elsewhere. Rather, we agree with the established view that the Dharwar style represents a hybridization or admixture, in which certain Nagara organizational principles were adopted within a primarily Dravida formal architectural vocabulary, as argued by Dhaky and more recently by Sinha (see the works cited in note 4).

9. This label should not be confused with the 'Metropolitan Style' (or 'Trend B') of M.A. Dhaky, *Encyclopaedia* I/3, 83–4. Dhaky uses 'Metropolitan Style' to refer to the stylistically more advanced trend within what we here term the 'Dharwar Style'. However, as John Henry Rice points out, Dhaky's use of the term is problematic, 'since its examples survive not at the "metropolises" of the Later Cālukyan period, but far south of them' ('Image, Text, Monument', 209, note 78). In contrast to monuments in the Dharwar style, temples in the Metropolitan style have been greatly neglected. Several examples are documented in James Burgess, *Report on the Antiquities in the Bidar*

*and Aurangabad Districts* (London: W.H. Allen and Co., 1878); for Nilaga, see especially 3:20–2, and for Narayanpur, see 3:40–1 and plates XXI–XXVI. See also Henry Cousens, *Mediaeval Temples of the Dakhan*, Archaeological Survey of India Reports, New Imperial Series, vol. 48 (Calcutta: Government of India, 1931). More recently, only Foekema, in his *Calukya Architecture*, has considered both the Dharwar and the Metropolitan styles together in an integrated fashion.

10. Dharwar is near the centre of an extensive series of schist belts dominating western central Karnataka. These belts yield weakly foliated schists of a wide variety, including metamorphics of both sedimentary origin (metasilt stones) and igneous origin (metabasalts and metaultramafics). For a discussion and map of the Dharwar schist belts and related geological formations, see Richard Newman, *The Stone Sculpture of India: A Study of the Materials Used by Indian Sculptors from ca. 2nd Century B.C. to the 16th Century* (Cambridge: Harvard University Art Museums, 1984), 25ff. and figure 23. For a more technical study, see J. Swami Nath and M. Ramakrishnan, eds, *Early Precambrian Supracrustals of Southern Karnataka*, Memoirs of the Geological Survey of India, vol. 112 (Calcutta: Geological Survey of India, 1981). For the Deccan Traps, see R. Bruce Foote, *The Geological Features of the South Mahratta Country and Adjacent Districts*, Memoirs of the Geological Survey of India (Calcutta: Geological Survey of India, 1876), 171–91; D.N. Wadia, *Geology of India*, 3rd edition (London: Macmillan and Co., 1953), 291–303; and *Geological and Mineral Map of Maharashtra* [Scale 1:2,250,000] (New Delhi: Government of India, 1969).

11. On the Mohs scale of mineral hardness (on which 1 is softest and 10 is hardest) chlorite has a hardness of 2.5, and talc 1. See Ole Johnsen, *Minerals of the World* (Princeton University Press, 2007).

12. According to Wadia, citing a chemical analysis of eleven specimens by H.S. Washington, these consist predominantly of the plagioclase feldspars anorthite (23.07%) and albite (22.01%), and the pyroxenes hypersthene (17.78%) and diopside (17.41%). All of these minerals have a hardness of 6 on the Mohs scale, except hypersthene, which ranges from 5 to 6. The Deccan basalts are unusual for their lack of olivine. Wadia, *Geology of India*, 296–7; Johnsen, *Minerals.*

13. For an insightful discussion of the properties of rocks as they affect the sculptor's art, see Newman, *The Stone Sculpture of India*, 8.

14. Rice has similarly stressed the aesthetic impact of available materials on the development of sculptural and architectural style in the Later Chalukya period. His comments, however, relate more to the historical shift from sandstones—favoured by artists of the Early Western Chalukya and Rashtrakuta periods—to the schist preferred by artists in the Later Chalukya period (in what we term the 'Dharwar Style'). See Rice, 'Image, Text, Monument', 178–9.

15. The name of the type is known from an inscription carved on the edge of the abacus of one of the columns at the Amriteshvara temple at Holal (Dhaky, *Indian Temple Forms*, 2–3). The name, which literally means 'the letter śrī', would appear to derive from the resemblance between the double-flexed curvature of the column's bell and the similarly curved graph for the syllable 'sri' as it is written in Kannada. Columns of the śrīkāra type are generally used for the four columns defining the central bay of the maṇḍapa, while other types are frequently employed for columns around the periphery of the maṇḍapa. Many of these peripheral types are variants of the śrīkāra type but are based on a square-sectioned plan, either with a single projecting face in the middle of each side (the *bhadraka* type) or with multiple proliferating projections (*vardhamāna*). There are also stellate variants.

16. *Citrakhaṇḍa* type columns are also employed in the Dharwar style, although usually in locations of secondary importance, and always with recognizable Dharwar-style proportions and ornamentation.

17. In 1529, Isma`il `Adil Khan yielded control of Kalyana to the Barid Shahi ruler Amir Barid, having taken the latter's base of power at the old Bahmani capital of Bidar. The next year, in 1530, Isma`il `Adil Khan promised to restore Bidar to Amir Barid provided that the latter return Kalyana to him—an exchange that never occurred. In 1554, Ibrahim `Adil Shah I agreed to support `Ali Nizam Shah in his (unsuccessful) contest with his brother Husain Nizam Shah for the throne of Ahmadnagar, in exchange for which Ali promised to return Kalyana (then under Nizam Shahi control) to Ibrahim `Adil Shah. Briggs, trans., *History of the Rise*, 3:40–1, 64.

18. In 1549, Burhan Nizam Shah successfully besieged the fort, taking it from the Barid Shahis, while in 1558, Husain Nizam Shah attempted to take Kalyana back from `Ali `Adil Shah, who then controlled it, but the siege was unsuccessful. Ibid., 3:62, 73.

19. These campaigns—in 1531, 1549, and 1559—were all undertaken by the `Adil Shahis, who tried unsuccessfully to recover Kalyana from the Barid Shahis in 1531, from the Nizam Shahis in 1549, and finally successfully from the Nizam Shahis in 1559. Ibid., 3:41, 62–3, 71, 145–6.

20. The city passed from `Adil Shahi to Barid Shahi hands in 1529 by cession in exchange for Bidar, from Barid Shahi to Nizam Shahi hands in 1549 by siege, and from Nizam Shahi to `Adil Shahi hands in 1559 by cession when Nizam Shahi core territories were threatened. Ibid., 3:40, 62–3, 141–3, 71, 145–6.

21. Richard M. Eaton, *Social History of the Deccan, 1300–1761: Eight Indian Lives* (Cambridge: Cambridge University Press, 2005), 95–9.

22. Briggs, trans., *History of the Rise*, 3:146–7.

23. In addition to Rama Raya's own Aravidu line—which would soon be established as Vijayanagara's fourth ruling dynasty after Tirumala's consecration as king in 1570—two other prominent lines of Aravidu warriors were closely related to Rama Raya's family. One was his immediate cousins, the sons of his father's brother Potlapati Timmaraja. They controlled the province of Chandragiri and the fort at Avuku; accordingly, their descendants came to be known as the Avuku chiefs. Then, there were Rama Raya's more distant cousins—progenitors of the line of Nandyala chiefs—who were descended from his grandfather's brother Singaraja, and who controlled a number of key forts including Nandyala, Udayagiri, and Gandikota. At least one of Rama Raya's cousins from the Avuku family appears to have participated in some of the Kalyana campaigns. Most of these warriors were probably involved in these contests at one point or another. For the Avuku and Nandyala lines and their relationship with the Aravidu house, see Krishna Sastri, 'The Second Vijayanagara Dynasty: Its Viceroys and Ministers', in *Archaeological Survey of India, Annual Report for the Years 1908–09* (Calcutta: Superintendant of Government Printing, 1910), 194ff., and especially the annotated genealogy on 201; and C. Hayavadana Rao, *Mysore Gazetteer, vol. 2, Historical, part 3 Medieval, from the Foundations of the Vijayanagara Kingdom to the Destruction of Vijayanagara byTipu Sultan in 1776* (Bangalore: Government Press, 1930), 2108–112.

24. B.N. Misra has shown that fifty-seven verses from the *Vikramāṅkadevacarita* are quoted by Jalhana in his anthology *Sūktimuktāvali*, written at the Yadava court in 1258. While this abundance of quoted verses might be attributed to the direct historical and geographic linkages between the Yadava and Chalukya polities, anthologies composed in distant Rajasthan and even Bengal also feature verses from the *Vikramāṅkadevacarita*. The *Śārṅgadharapaddhati*, produced in Rajasthan, contains twenty such verses, while the *Sadūktikarṇāmṛta* of Śrīdharadāsa, produced in Bengal, has seven. These anthologies also enjoyed currency throughout southern India, as witnessed by the provenance of surviving manuscripts. See B.N. Misra, *Studies on Bilhaṇa and His Vikramāṅkadevacarita* (New Delhi: K.B. Publications, 1976), 65–7; A.S. Altekar, 'The Yadavas of Seunadesa', in *The Early History of the Deccan*, ed. G. Yazdani (London: Oxford University Press, 1960), 570. For the Sanskrit carita genre of royal biography and its popularity at the Vijayanagara court, see D. Sridhara Babu, *Kingship, State, and Religion in South India According to South Indian Historical Biographies of Kings Madhurāvijaya, Acyutarāyābhyudaya, and Vemabhūpālacarita*, Inaugural Dissertation, Georg-August-Universitat, Gottingen, 1975.

25. Quoted in Chapter 1.

26. Verses 4 and 6 of the colophon, translation ours. See Narayana Sastry, Khiste Sahityacarya, and Jagannatha Sastri Hosinga Sahityopadhyaya, eds, *The Yājñavalkya-smṛti, with Vīramitrodaya, the Commentary of Mitra Miśra, and Mitākṣarā, the Commentary of Vijṇāneśvara* (Benares: Chowkhambha Sanskrit Series, 1930), 1106. Vijnaneshvara's allusion to the Rāmāyaṇa in this benediction—through his mention of the bridge to Lanka built by Rama, 'the pride of Raghu's line'—recalls the similar but more extensive appeals to the Rāmāyaṇa made by Vikramaditya VI's court poet, Bilhana, in relating his patron's biography.

27. K.A. Nilakanta Sastri, 'The Chāḷukyas of Kalyāṇi, Appendix C: The Kalachuris of Kalyāṇi', in *Early History of the Deccan*, ed. G. Yazdani (London: Oxford University Press, 1960), 1:456–68; K. Ishwaran, *Religion and Society among the Lingayats of South India* (Leiden: E.J. Brill, 1983), 20–3, 36–50.

28. For a translation of the Telugu *Basava-Purana*, see V. Narayana Rao and Gene H. Roghair, *Śiva's Warriors: The Basava Purāṇa of Pālkuriki Somanātha* (Princeton: Princeton University Press, 1990).

29. Lakkana Dandesa, a minister of the Vijayanagara ruler Deva Raya II, is remembered in Virashaiva history as the founder of the so-called 101 Virakta association, an alternate order of Virashaiva ascetics

(*jangamas*) opposed to the older Guru-jangama order. See Ishwaran, *Lingayats*, 82.

30. For details on these works, see C.T.M. Kotraiah and Anna L. Dallapiccola, *King, Court, and Capital: An Anthology of Kannada Literary Sources from the Vijayanagara Period*, Vijayanagara Research Project Monograph Series, vol. 9 (New Delhi: Manohar and American Institute of Indian Studies, 2003). Many other works produced beyond the Vijayanagara capital in this period no doubt enjoyed currency among Virashaivas there.

31. This work remains untranslated. C.V. Ramachandra Rao has published excerpts from the work's preface and chapter endings in his *Andugala Vengakavi Rāmarājīyamu lēka narapati vijayamu mariyu Dōnēru Kōnērunāthakavi Padya Bālabhāgavatamu Dvipada Bālabhāgavatamu (Aravīṭi Rājula Praśamsa)* (Nellore: Manasa Publications, 1995), and reports that an edition of the text by Panganamala Balakrishnamurti was published by the Tirumala-Tirupati Devasthanam in 1954 (p. ii). We have not been able to locate a copy of the full text.

32. *Padya-Bālabhāgavatamu* 1.10, and also in *ṣaṣṭhyantamulu*, 6 (Ramachandra Rao, *Rāmarājīyamu*, 67, 73).

33. These inscriptions inevitably trace the Aravidu genealogy through just four generations (Araviti Bukka [1], Rama Raya [2], Sriranga Raya [3], and Rama Raya and his brother Timma Raya [4]). With few exceptions, the genealogy also identifies the wives of the first three Aravidu chiefs through whom the descent was traced (Ballambika [1], Lakkambika [2], and Tirumalambika [3]). None of these inscriptions makes any claim to mythic ancestry for the Aravidus, in contrast to the Puranic lunar genealogy recorded for the ruling king, Sadashiva Raya, in the same inscriptions. Examples of such early Aravidu inscriptions include: the Mamidipundi copperplates of 1549–50; the Bevinahalli copperplates of 1551; the British Museum Plates of 1556; and the Tirupati stone inscription of Tirumala, dated 1561. See *Nellore District Inscriptions* [*NDI*] 1: no.14; *Epigraphia Indica* [*EI*] 14:16; *EI*4: no. 1; *Tirumala Tirupati Devasthanam Inscriptions* [*TTDI*] 6: no. 1.

34. *Padya Bālabhāgavatamu* 1, 27ff. (Ramachandra Rao, *Rāmarājīyamu*, 68ff.).

35. The genealogical portions of innumerable inscriptions establish that Vijayanagara's Sangama and Saluva dynasties had both claimed Lunar descent through Yadu, while the Tuluva dynasty traced its pedigree through Turvasu (Hayavadana Rao, *Mysore Gazetteer*, 1417). See, for example, *NDI* 1: no. 3 (line 8) for the descent of the Sangamas through Yadu; and *EI* 14: no. 12 (line 8) for the descent of the Tuluvas through Turvasu. For the Chalukya genealogy through Puru—and an excellent discussion of the significance of inscriptional genealogies—see Daud Ali, 'Royal Eulogy as World History: Rethinking Copper-plate Inscriptions in Cola India', in *Querying the Medieval: Texts and the History of Practices in South Asia*, eds Ronald Inden, Jonathan Walters, and Daud Ali (New York: Oxford University Press, 2000), 165–225 and figure 4.3.

36. *Epigraphia Carnatica* [*EC*] 12: Tumkur Taluk, no. 1; Hayavadana Rao, *Mysore Gazetteer*, 2119–20.

37. *Arasa* is a Kannada equivalent of *rāya*, 'king'. Hemmadi is also known as Permadi.

38. Close marital ties between the Chalukya and Kalachuri houses had been established during the reign of Vikramaditya VI, who married the Kalachuri princess Savaladevi. In turn, Vikramaditya's daughter (through his chief queen, Chandaladevi, who was not a Kalachuri) Nagaladevi was married to Kalachuri Hemmadiyarasa/Permadi, and was the mother of Bijjala. See Shrinivas Ritti and Anand Kumbhar, *Inscriptions from Solapur District* (Dharwar: Shrihari Prakashana, 1988), ix–x. We are indebted to Dr Kumud Kanitkar for bringing the Chalukya–Kalachuri marital relations to our attention.

39. Rama Raya was Krishna Raya's son-in-law.

40. *EI*4: no. 39 and *NDI* 1: no. 6, respectively.

41. *NDI* 1: no. 7.

42. *Rāmarājīyamu*, verses 166–7. The full passage reads: 'After a number of rulers in that Calukyan line had ruled the world, then there arose the king named Bijjala, like a moon rising from the ocean of that dynasty. He put down his enemies and ruled the earth. Because he ruled the city of Kalyana, which was a veritable support of the earth, he took the name of "Kalyana-Bijjala". Because he undertook to punish the wicked and protect the good, he founded a new path for the people of the world and restored *dharma* to its full-fledged, four-legged form, just like [his ancestor] Parikshit had done before him. He brought prosperity to those who were poor and thus acquired boundless fame.' (Ramachandra Rao, *Rāmarājīyamu*, 20–1. Translation ours.)

43. *Rāmarājīyamu* verse 288 (Ramachandra Rao, *Rāmarājīyamu*, 38).

44. The text refers to them not by their proper names, but by their distinctive personal titles, 'Bhuvanaikamalla' ('Sole Wrestler of the World') and 'Tribhuvanaikamalla' ('Sole Wrestler of the Three Worlds').

45. C.V. Ramachandra Rao, ed., *Ēkāmranāthuni Pratāparudra Caritramu* (Hyderabad: Andhra Pradesh Sahitya Academy, 1984), 18.

46. Someshvara II and Vikramaditya VI are presented as the grandfather and father respectively of Prola, the first historically recognizable Kakatiya ruler to appear in the text. This shows not only that the text's author was familiar with contemporary Vijayanagara claims to Chalukya descent, but also that he contested that representation by appropriating the two Chalukya emperors as Kakatiya ancestors and having Someshvara II subjugate the Vijayanagara king as a subordinate.

47. None of the reuse discussed here is precisely datable by means of foundation inscriptions or other documentary evidence. Nonetheless, given the circumstantial evidence of Aravidu involvement in the mid-century conflicts over Kalyana and their patronage of literary works asserting their Chalukya connections, we may reasonably conclude that most of the Chalukya reuse at Vijayanagara dates to this same general period, and that it resulted from Aravidu sponsorship. See the final section of this chapter for a more detailed interpretation of the chronology. For a consideration of why the Chalukya reuse cannot reasonably be ascribed to Vijayanagara's greatest ruler, Krishna Raya, see Wagoner, 'Stepped Tank', 131–2.

48. The pronounced impact on Vijayanagara architecture of building traditions from the Tamil country was first stressed by George Michell, although Leslie Orr has more recently proposed the Pandya style of the thirteenth and fourteenth centuries as the likely source. See Anna L. Dallapiccola, John M. Fritz, George Michell, and S. Rajasekhara, *The Ramachandra Temple at Vijayanagara*, Vijayanagara Research Project Monograph Series, vol. 2 (New Delhi: Manohar and AIIS, 1992), 33 and 43–5; George Michell, *Architecture and Art of Southern India: Vijayanagara and the Successor States*, New Cambridge History of India, I, 6 (Cambridge: Cambridge University Press, 1995), 25–8; idem., 'Revivalism as the Imperial Mode: Religious Architecture during the Vijayanagara Period', in *Perceptions of South Asia's Visual Past*, eds C.B. Asher and T.R. Metcalf (New Delhi: American Institute of Indian Studies and Oxford and IBH Publishing Co., 1994), 187–97; and Leslie Orr, 'Cholas, Pandyas, and "Imperial Temple Culture" in Medieval Tamilnadu', in *The Temple in South Asia*, ed. Adam Hardy (London: British Academy, 2007), 83–97.

49. The Vijayanagara site sits at the northern end of the Closepet Granite batholith, a granite formation 400 kilometres in length, to which the many picturesque tors and boulders of the site belong. In addition to this abundant granite, which was the preferred building material at the site, Vijayanagara architects also made occasional use of locally available metamorphic stone, including granulites, greenstones, and the various unclassified peninsular gneisses that form the substratum in the region. These were occasionally augmented by dolerite, a finer-grained but still very hard igneous rock that runs in isolated dikes through the surrounding granites. Dolerite was sometimes employed for doorframes and for the columns of the central bay in maṇḍapas—as in the fifteenth-century Ramachandra temple—since it could be sculpted with finer detail. See Jean-Francois Moyen et al. (2003), 'From the Roots to the Roof of a Granite: The Closepet Granite of South India', *Journal of the Geological Society of India* 62 (December): 753–68.

50. See, for example, the comments of K.T.M. Kotraiah in his 'Hampi before Founding of Vijayanagara', in *Archaeology of Hampi-Vijayanagara*, ed. K.M. Suresh (New Delhi: Bharatiya Kala Prakashan, 2008), 39–46, and especially 41.

51. There is in fact a more limited series of schist belts to the east of the Dharwar belts, centred on Sandur just south of Vijayanagara. See C. Manikyamba and S.M. Naqvi, 'Late Archaean Mantle Fertility: Constraints from Metavolcanics of the Sandur Schist Belt, India', *Gondwana Research* I/1 (1997), 69–89. However, these belts differ considerably in their lithologies from the much more extensive Dharwar belts to the west. The Sandur belts seem to be lacking in the softer chlorite and talc schists that typify the western belts, and instead consist largely of so-called greenstone—a form of metamorphosed basalt or ultra-mafic rock that is considerably harder to carve than the chlorite schist favoured in the Dharwar region. Vijayanagara sculptors sometimes used these greenstones for carving religious icons. See Newman, *The Stone Sculpture of India*, 8, 22, and 26–7.

52. For excellent documentation of temples in Raichur and Bellary districts, including many

monuments in this Ballukunde-nad style, see C.S. Patil, *Temples of Raichur and Bellary Districts* (Mysore: Directorate of Archaeology and Museums,1992).

53. Exterior elements are documented in only two instances. One is a series of plinth (*adhiṣṭhāna*) mouldings that has been recycled into a makeshift wall in the Bhuvaneshvari shrine of the Virupaksha temple. The other is the striking case of a nearly complete stepwell that has been dismantled, transported to the site, and re-constructed in the Royal Centre. See the discussion later in the chapter.

54. See John M. Fritz, George Michell, and M.S. Nagaraja Rao, *Where Kings and Gods Meet: The Royal Centre at Vijayanagara, India* (Tucson: University of Arizona Press, 1984), 9–37. In addition to following the zonal divisions proposed by Fritz, Michell, and Nagaraja Rao, we also employ their numbering system for the enclosures within the Royal Centre, and for the individual features contained therein. Thus, 'IVa/22' refers to the twenty-second feature documented within section 'a' of enclosure IV (the so-called underground chamber).

55. For the monuments of the Sacred Centre, see George Michell and Phillip B. Wagoner, *Vijayanagara: Architectural Inventory of the Sacred Centre*, 3 vols (New Delhi: American Institute of Indian Studies/ Manohar Publications, 2001).

56. We use the Vijayanagara Map Series designation to identify structures outside the Royal Centre, where there are no enclosures. See Michell and Wagoner, *Architectural Inventory*, volume 1, maps on pp. 2, 3, and 94.

57. For the Uncappa Matha, see Dhaky, *Encyclopaedia*, I/3, 189–90 and plates 548–52. For the Ranganatha temple, see Natalie Tobert, *Anegondi: Architectural Ethnography of a Royal Village*, Vijayanagara Research Project Monograph Series, vol. 7 (New Delhi: Manohar and AIIS, 2000), plate 21.

58. All of these columns are of śrīkāra type, except for the three southerly columns in the middle row, which are Dharwar-style *citrakhaṇḍa*. The southernmost column in the inner row is śrikāra, but it has an octagonally sectioned bell.

59. The lowermost capital in each case is a Chalukya cushion capital (*kumbha*), and the uppermost capitals are likewise authentic Chalukya-period bracket capitals (*potika*). Only the intervening dish capitals (*maṇḍi* and *phalaka*) are of Vijayanagara-period granite. In addition to serving to bracket off the Chalukya columns below, they also serve to accommodate—through their variations in height—the slight differences in the dimensions of the shafts, which evidently have not all been taken from the same structure.

60. G.S. Dikshit, *Local Self-Government in Mediaeval Karnataka* (Dharwar: Karnatak University, 1964), 131.

61. 'samasta-bhuvanāśraya śrī-prithvī-vallabha mahārājādhirāja paramēśvara parama-bhaṭṭāraka satyāśraya-kula-tilakam cāḷukyābharaṇam'. This is the standard series of titles with which Chalukya inscriptions generally open. Here it appears in the inscription on the ninth slab set up on the south side of the Kalleshvara temple at Bagali, dated to 1035, during the reign of Chalukya Jagadēkamalladēva-Jayasiṃha II. The tenor of these titles differed decidedly from those used by the Yadava, Kakatiya, and Hoysala successors to the Chalukyas. Even after the eclipse of their Chalukya overlords, these erstwhile feudatories generally continued to project an image of their subordinate status as loyal feudatories through the use of titles such as 'Great Tributary Lord' (*mahāmaṇḍalēśvara*). *South Indian Inscriptions* [*SII*] vol. 9, part 2: no. 89; Talbot, *Precolonial India*, 133.

62. See Phillip B. Wagoner, 'From "Pampa's Crossing" to "The Place of Lord Virupaksa": Architecture, Cult, and Patronage at Hampi before the Founding of Vijayanagara', in *Vijayanagara: Progress of Research, 1988–1991*, eds D. Devaraj and C.S. Patil (Mysore: Directorate or Archaeology and Museums, 1996), 141–74.

63. We have been unable to find any reference attesting to the presence of Bhuvaneshvari at Vijayanagara prior to the sixteenth century, whether in inscriptions or in works of literature associated with the site. She is conspicuously absent from two key epigraphs identifying major deities at the site—the 1199 Durgadevi temple inscription and the 1346 Chandragutti copper plates of Marappa—as well as from three key literary–religious texts in Kannada produced at the site during the fifteenth century, *Virūpākṣa-śataka* of c. 1410, *Pampāsthāna-varṇana* of c. 1430, and *Śivatattva-cintāmaṇi* of c. 1450, according to the detailed summaries and extracts of these texts prepared by C.T.M. Kotraiah for the Vijayanagara Research Project. The absence of pre-sixteenth-century references to Bhuvaneshvari is further confirmed by Vasundhara Filliozat, who has also made a careful study of both epigraphic and literary sources.

See Vasundhara Filliozat, 'Iconography: Religious and Civil Monuments', in *Vijayanagara—City and Empire: New Currents of Research*, eds Anna Libera Dallapiccola and Stephanie Zingel-Avé Lallement (Wiesbaden: Franz Steiner Verlag, 1985), 1:313–14. For the 1199 Durgadevi temple inscription, see *SII* 4: no. 260 and discussion in Wagoner, 'From "Pampa's Crossing"', 161ff.; for the 1346 Chandragutti copper plates, see *Annual Reports of the Mysore Archaeological Department* (ARMAD)1929, inscription no. 90, and discussion in Phillip B. Wagoner, 'Architecture and Royal Authority under the Early Sangamas', in *New Light on Hampi*, eds John M. Fritz and George Michell (Bombay: Marg Publications, 2001), 13.

Bhuvaneshvari does appear in two Sanskrit texts associated with the site, but both are difficult to date. One is Ahobala-kavi's *Virūpākṣa-vasantotsava-campū*, a poetic account of Virupaksha's spring-festival, presided over by the Vijayanagara king. In this text, Bhuvaneshvari is mentioned in passing as one of a triad of goddesses—the other two being Bhavani and Vagdevata (that is, Sarasvati)—whom the celebrants venerate as they exit the temple after worshipping Virupaksha ('paricāraka-dattāni śiva-prasāda-phala-kusumāni gṛhītvā pramuditāntaraṃgā bahir nirgatya bhavānī-bhuvaneśvarī-vāgdevatāḥ praṇamyāpi'). Throughout this text, however, Virupaksha is always represented as having a single consort, the goddess Pampa. Pancamukhi believes that the text belongs to the fourteenth century, and Anderson suggests the fifteenth century. We suspect that the text cannot date to before the early sixteenth century, owing to passing references to parts of the Virupaksha temple that were not constructed until the late fifteenth or early sixteenth centuries. See R.S. Pancamukhi, ed., *Virūpākṣa Vasantotsava Champū* (Dharwar: Kannada Research Institute, 1953), 57–8; Leona M. Anderson, *Vasantotsava: The Spring Festivals of India: Texts and Traditions* (New Delhi: D.K. Printworld, 1993), 171–97.

The other text is the *Pampāmāhātmya*, the *sthala-purāṇa* of the Hampi site, which identifies its various divinities and sacred places and recounts their associated myths. At the very end of its first section, the seven sages come to the west of the Manmukha tank, where they see the divine image of Parvati Bhuvaneshvari and ask the *kṣetra-pāla* to recount the story of her manifestation there. Although it is likely that this text embodies oral traditions going back to the Vijayanagara period and even before, it is impossible to date any given part of it in its present form. See K. Venkatarama Sastri and H. Venkatesvara Sastri, eds, *Skānda-purāṇāntargata-hemakūṭakhaṇḍātmaka Saptarṣi-yātrā-prakāśaka Pampāmāhātmyamu* (Hampi, 1933), *pūrva-bhāga, adhyāya* 98, p. 322ff.).

64. See, for example, the *Tantrasāra* of Krishnananda. Composed in Bengal around 1590, this text includes vivid iconographic descriptions of each of the ten Mahavidyas, starting with Bhuvaneshvari. In the hills of Himachal Pradesh, Bhuvaneshvari figures in the renowned 'Early Tantric Devi Series' produced in the Basohli style in the third quarter of the seventeenth century. See Pratapaditya Pal, *Hindu Religion and Iconography According to the* Tantrasāra (Los Angeles: Vichitra Press, 1981). 86; David Kinsley, *Tantric Visions of the Divine Feminine: The Ten Mahāvidyās* (Berkeley: University of California Press, 1997); Terence McInerny, 'Mysterious Origins: The Tantric Devi Series from Basohli', in *Devi—The Great Goddess: Female Divinity in South Asian Art*, ed. Vidya Dehejia (Washington DC: Arthur M. Sackler Gallery, 1999), 119–35, cat. no. 35.

65. Pal, *Hindu Religion and Iconography*, 83–6.

66. The shrine is documented in detail in Michell and Wagoner, *Vijayanagara*, 1:124–5.

67. This point is revealed by the open stone grill-work towards the outer edge of each jamb, a regular feature in the doorways of *antarāla*s but not of sancta.

68. See Anila Verghese, *Religious Traditions at Vijayanagara as Revealed through Its Monuments*, Vijayanagara Research Project Monograph Series, vol. 4. (New Delhi: Manohar and AIIS, 1995), 43–53.

69. It is also possible that these columns were taken from the periphery of an open-columned maṇḍapa, where they would have sat atop the maṇḍapa's half-wall, thus accounting for the shortness of their shanks.

70. This is a type of plinth (*adhiṣṭhāna*) in which the mouldings approximate those typically used to adorn the base or pedestal (*pīṭha*) of a cult image, with reflective symmetry around the medial knife-edged moulding.

71. This type of nine-squared arrangement of the Dikpalas would appear to be the most common. In it, the Eight Lords of the Directions are arranged in the outer squares and the central square is occupied by Shiva as Lord of the Zenith.

72. Dominic J. Davison-Jenkins, *The Irrigation and Water Supply Systems of Vijayanagara*, Vijayanagara

Research Project Monograph Series, vol. 5 (New Delhi: Manohar and AIIS, 1997), 37.

73. For the preliminary excavation report, see *Indian Archaeology 1984–85—A Review* (New Delhi: Archaeological Survey of India, 1987), 25–8.

74. The stairways take the form of stepped pyramids, each with five narrow steps leading downwards along its sides to the terrace at the top of the next level. Starting at the uppermost tier at the ground level, there are nine pyramids arranged along each side. Moving down towards the water, the number of stairway blocks on each side decreases in an odd-numbered progression, yielding seven, five, three, and then finally, in the lowermost tier, only a single stair block. In all tiers but this lowest one, the central stairway on each side is differentiated from those flanking it by being slightly wider, by projecting farther out from the baseline of the wall, and by having a more complex plan for each course, with recessed corners and projecting faces along the three sides.

75. Resonances between temple and stepwell designs are common in Chalukya architecture. For example, the stepwells at Lakkundi and Hulikere both incorporate small shrines along their sides. Unlike these monuments, however, the Vijayanagara tank does not quote the specific temple forms themselves, but, rather, the formal principles underlying their design. In particular, the greater width and projection of the central stairway block in each side of the tank presents a parallel to the similar accentuation of the central projection (*bhadra*) in the wall and superstructure of the typical Dharwar-style temple. Moreover, the projecting planes (*phalana*) on each side of the central stairways further accentuate these central forms, which parallel the accentuation of a temple's central projection by the presence of smaller ancillary projections(*upabhadras*). Ancillary projections are generally not employed on the flanking projections of the temple wall, but only on the central projections. Because of these subtle formal similarities—and also because of the stepwell's use of the same blue-green schist used in Dharwar-style temples—the stepwell exudes a decidedly Chalukya character. For the Lakkundi tank, see Dhaky, *Encyclopaedia of Indian Temple Architecture* (*EITA*), vol. I, part 3, p.102, fig. 70 and plates 273–4; for Hulikere, see idem., p. 335, fig. 180, and plates 924–5.

76. Jagdish, 'Construction Technology of the Stepped Tank in the Royal Centre (IVc/6)', in *Vijayanagara, Archaeological Exploration, 1990—2000: Papers in Memory of Channabasappa S. Patil*, eds John M. Fritz, Robert P. Brubaker, and Teresa P. Raczek, with the assistance of George Michell, Vijayanagara Research Project Monograph Series, vol. 10 (New Delhi: Manohar and American Institute of Indian Studies, 2006), part 1, 79–88.

77. There are actually two different types of locational codes used in these inscriptions. The five-part codes are used only for the stones of the projecting stairways, while a simpler, three-part code is used for the intervening sections of the walls and the terraces of each level. The three-part code includes (*a*) a directional abbreviation to indicate the side, (*b*) a number to indicate the serial position (left to right) of the stone within its course, and (*c*) a letter indicating the sequence of the masonry course moving from top to bottom.

In the five-place inscriptions, although the marks appearing in the fifth place might not seem to add any new information about locations, they would in fact have offered an efficient means of segregating all the projecting stairway stones for each side of each tier. They might therefore have been added as an aid in organizing the materials as they were being unloaded and prepared for installation at the new site.

78. Jagdish, who first deciphered the coded system of these inscriptions, suggested that these were simply mason's marks that the craftsmen responsible for designing and building the tank had incised on the blocks to guide them in placing the blocks correctly. In a footnote to his article, however, the editors of the volume suggested the possibility that the inscriptions had been carved *after* the original construction of the tank, as a guide for reassembly in moving the tank to the site from another location. A similar suggestion had earlier been made by Davison-Jenkins, in his study of the irrigation and water-supply systems at the site. See Jagdish, 'Construction Technology', 81, note 3l; Davison-Jenkins, *Irrigation* 39.

79. The only indication of the language behind the tank's abstract code is provided by the syllable *tu*—an abbreviation for the Telugu word *tūrpu*, 'east'—used as the directional indicator for the blocks belonging on the eastern side of the tank. Significantly, all the other directional indicators are abbreviations for Sanskrit loan words that are used in both Kannada and Telugu—thus, *da* for *dakṣiṇa*, 'south'; *pa* for *paścima*, 'west'; and *u* for *uttara*, 'north'. Tūrpu is the only word abbreviated in the tank's inscriptions that comes from a Dravidian root, and which is used in Telugu but not

in Kannada. This perhaps accounts for Jagdish's uncertainty about the significance of the abbreviation *tu*. He writes that 'instead of "pu," [i.e., the abbreviation for *pūrva*] the actual Kannada word for east, the letter "tu" is used to indicate the east. The meaning of "tu" is not clear'. Jagdish, 'Construction Technology', 81.

80. The first hypothesis was offered by our late colleague Balasubramanya, who suggested that using all seven tiers of the original tank might have positioned the bottom of the tank too low to be completely emptied through a pre-existing drain at the base. The second possibility has been suggested to us by John Henry Rice. Whatever the reason, the decision was made not to use the two uppermost tiers of the original tank, making these stones available for use in other contexts.

81. It also follows that the original Chalukya tank would have been both deeper and considerably wider at its top than the tank we see at Vijayanagara.

82. For a fuller and more technical account of the stepwell, and further details relating to its interpretation, see Wagoner, 'Stepped Tank'.

83. This 'occasional consecration' is called *naimittika-abhiṣeka*. For the paṭṭābhiṣeka and the naimittika-abhiṣeka, see '*Sāmrājyalakṣmī-pīṭhika* Paṭalas 47–61', in K. Vasudeva Sastri and K.S. Subrahmanya Sastri, eds, *Sāmrājya Lakshmi Pithika* (*The Emperor's Manual*), Tanjore Saraswathi Mahal Series, no. 58 (Thanjavur: Saraswathi Mahal Library, 1990). For the dating and provenance of the text, see Artatrana Sarangi, *A Treasury of Tantric Ideas: A Study of the Sāmrājyalakṣmīpīṭhika* (Calcutta: Punthi Pustak, 1993), 20–35. Sarangi follows and develops the earlier arguments of P.K. Gode, who first suggested a Vijayanagara date and provenance for the text. The inclusion of fireworks in the description of the performance of the Navaratri festival would place the text no earlier than the early sixteenth century, while certain geographical references and the use of the *amānta* system of calculating months, favoured in south India but not in the north, would locate its provenance in southern India. The text also mentions 'Vijayapuri' and 'Pampanagara' at several places, both alternate names for Vijayanagara. To these arguments of Gode and Sarangi, we would add that in the conversation between Shiva and Parvati that provides the framework for the exposition of the text, Parvati frequently addresses Shiva as 'Virupaksha', the name of his local manifestation at Vijayanagara. Since Virupaksha was also the state deity of Vijayanagara, it seems appropriate that the text's teachings should be represented as emanating directly from him. See also the discussion in Sarangi, *Treasury*, 128–51.

84. *Sāmrājyalakṣmī-pīṭhika*, Paṭalas 58–60, describing the occasional consecration (*naimittika-abhiṣeka*). The eleven rivers named are: Ganga, Yamuna, Satadru, Sarasvati, Asikni, Kaveri, Krishnaveni, Narmada, Godavari, Tapi, and Tamraparni (58.15–16). See Vasudeva Sastri and Subrahmanya Sastri, *Samrajya Lakshmi Pithika*, 187–93.

85. Thus, in prescribing the ritual for the periodic consecration (*naimittika-paṭṭābhiṣeka*), the king is to invite the officiants on the morning of the day before, 'after having bathed in a river or a tank' (*snātvā nadyāṃ taṭāke vā*, *Sāmrājyalakṣmī-pīṭhika* 57.2). See Vasudeva Sastri and Subrahmanya Sastri, *Samrajya Lakshmi Pithika*, 184.

86. *EC* 12: Tumkur Taluk, no. 44. Rev. Henry Heras, *The Aravidu Dynasty of Vijayanagara* (Madras: B.G. Paul and Co., 1927), 27–40.

87. Cesare Federici, *The Voyage and Travaile into the East India, London 1588* (Amsterdam and New York: Theatrum Orbis Terrarum and Da Capo Press, 1971), 9. For an analysis and assessment of Federici's account, see Joan Pau Rubies, *Travel and Ethnology in the Renaissance: South India through European Eyes, 1250–1625* (Cambridge: Cambridge University Press, 2000), 303–7.

88. *EI* 3: no. 34 (verses 15–16).

CHAPTER 4

# Bijapur's Revival of the Chalukya Imperium

The glorious and most bold *Daṇḍanāyaka* Nākimayya...who was a very Hanumanta to the Rāma who was the glorious [Chalukya emperor Someshvara II]...[in] the Saka year 996 [1074–75] preferred a request to Śrī-Ballavarasa at the capital of Baṅkāpura, and caused to be built a temple of the god Śrī-Svayaṃbhu-Siddheśvara of the capital of Vijayāpura [Bijapur]....

—Chalukya inscription placed in the gateway to Bijapur's citadel[1]

In the Bankapur region there is a town called Lakmir [Lakshmeshwar], the ancient capital of a great infidel ruler. Kings and nobles imitated one another in perfecting architecture and in building many exquisite and grand temples. In subsequent years, many of these have fallen into a state of ruin. But some remain standing, and four hundred temples are completely intact, having been built with the utmost of painstaking and elegant workmanship. When we saw them we were struck with awe.

—Rafi` al-Din Shirazi, who accompanied Sultan `Ali `Adil Shah on his campaign in the Chalukya heartland, 1574–75[2]

Vijayanagara was not the only sixteenth-century state to imagine, and in ways revive, the Chalukya past. To the north the Sultanate of Bijapur (1490–1686), whose sovereign territory covered much of the Chalukyas' former territory, began to display its own awareness of, and interest in, that past. Unlike Vijayanagara, which prior to the mid-sixteenth century showed at least a latent interest in the empire of Someshvara I and Vikramaditya VI, Bijapur's parent-dynasty, the Bahmani kings, had displayed no such interest. But from the 1530s on, about a decade before Rama Raya and the members of his Aravidu clan began re-fashioning themselves in Chalukya guise, the `Adil Shahi sultans of Bijapur began invoking that empire's memory. The question, then, is not just how Bijapur's rulers sought to revive the memory of the Chalukyas, but why they did so at all.

In the present chapter we examine three occasions in which `Adil Shahi rulers intervened in, or manipulated, the Chalukyas' material past, each occurring under a different sovereign—Ibrahim I (1535–58), `Ali I (1558–80), and Ibrahim II (1580–1627). The nature of those interventions or manipulations, however, differed greatly from each other, depending on the personality or ideology of the ruling sovereign, as well as the broader political context then prevailing in the `Adil Shahi state and across the plateau generally.

## BIJAPUR'S CITADEL AND THE STATE'S CONSOLIDATION

Towards the end of the fifteenth century the once-powerful Bahmani state was sliding towards disintegration. Its nobility had succumbed to poisonous internal politics, and its chief minister, endeavouring to aggrandize all power for himself, had reduced the sultan to a mere puppet. What finally doomed the state was its polarization into two mutually hostile camps. Ever since the founding of the Bahmani state in 1347, but especially after 1400, its sultans had systematically recruited military and civilian talent from the Arab, and especially the Iranian, world. Known as *gharbiān*, or 'Westerners', such men were associated with the high culture of Iran, which had acquired enormous prestige in fifteenth-century India owing to, among other things, the legacy of the great conqueror Timur (or 'Tamerlane', d. 1405). Towards the end of the fourteenth century, Timur had built up a grand empire that spanned much of the Middle East. His sack of Delhi in 1398–99 crippled the once-mighty Tughluq empire, from which it never recovered. It also stimulated a demand in India for merchants, administrators, soldiers, artists, or literati steeped in the prestigious Persian culture that Timur had so lavishly patronized, for Timur effectively personified the ideals of the Persian cosmopolis. Consequently, in the fifteenth and sixteenth centuries a steady stream of Westerners, attracted by offers of favoured status, flowed towards Indian courts, especially those of the Deccan.

Resenting the influx of these Westerner newcomers, however, was an older class that had migrated from north India in the early fourteenth century, settled in the Deccan under Tughluq patronage, overthrown the Tughluqs, and established the Bahmani Sultanate. Whereas Westerners proudly cultivated Persian language and literature, this older class, long rooted in the Deccan as sons of the soil, had adopted Indian ways and evolved their own language, Dakhni. Sometimes referred to as Dakhni Urdu, this language arose through a series of complex interactions between the local Deccani vernaculars (Marathi, Kannada, Telugu) and a Persianized dialect of Old Punjabi brought south by the north Indian settlers in the early fourteenth century.[3] By the sixteenth century the language would achieve literary status, though it lacked the trans-regional prestige of Persian. Further complicating Deccani society was the presence in several Deccan courts of black Ethiopians known as 'Habshis', recruited by state servants as military slaves. Having no natural attachment to the Persian world, and with no option of returning to Africa, Habshis tended to adopt the language and culture of their adopted home. Thus in the Bahmani Sultanate's perennial Westerner–Deccani conflicts, some of which erupted into outright civil war, Habshis tended to side with Deccanis against Westerners. It is against the backdrop of this social conflict that we can see why the Deccanis, seeking their roots in local, as opposed to Persian, culture, might turn to the Chalukya past, and even identify with it. After all, what could be more authentically indigenous, not to say prestigious, than the empire of Vikramaditya VI?

In 1490 Yusuf `Adil Khan, himself an immigrant from the Middle East and a high-ranking noble in the declining Bahmani Sultanate, gathered up a number of fellow Westerners and, retiring from Bidar to his estate in Bijapur, ordered the Friday prayers, or *khuṭba*, to be read in his own name instead of that of the Bahmani sultan. By the opening of the sixteenth century, five successor states had managed to carve independent realms out of the dying parent state. Of these, Yusuf `Adil Khan's fledgling state of Bijapur would emerge as one of the most powerful, the other principal successors being Ahmadnagar and Golconda.[4] A prominent feature of the new state under Yusuf's rule was its close identification with Iran, where a new Shi`i state was just then emerging under the Safavi dynasty of kings. In 1503, soon after the Safavi state declared its allegiance to the Shi`i sect, Yusuf followed suit in Bijapur. Yet Yusuf, mindful of the sentiments of his Sunni nobles, never went so far as to impose Shi`i rites on his subjects or banish Deccani troops from his service.[5]

But after Yusuf's death in 1510, the late king's son and successor, Isma`il, proved far more ardently devoted to foreign—that is, Persian—culture. Raised by an aunt who had immigrated straight from Iran late in Yusuf's reign, and kept from the company of Deccanis by his protective father, Isma`il grew much more fond of Turkish and Persian manners, music, and language than anything Deccani. He seldom spoke the Dakhni language, although he apparently understood it.[6] After several years of a regency in which the Deccani faction nearly managed to seize all power for itself, Isma`il, on attaining independent rule, vowed that he would never enlist Deccanis or Habshis in his service. For nearly twelve years he kept his word, maintaining no troops but Arabs, Iranians, Turks, Uzbeks, Kurds, 'and other foreigners'.[7] Eventually, he admitted into his service children of Westerners born in India, and then, by degrees, Afghans and Rajputs—but only those not born in the Deccan.[8] In 1519, he even ordered his entire army to wear scarlet caps with twelve points, imitating the followers of the monarch of Safavi Iran, and had the Friday prayers offered for Iran's Safavi family.[9] All of this despite that—or perhaps because—his own mother, Punji Khatun, was a Maratha woman, the sister of a Maratha chieftain who had served the Bahmanis.[10] Whatever his motive, Isma`il seems to have been determined to suppress the maternal half of his cultural and biological inheritance.

Throughout his reign Isma`il, like his father, was preoccupied with checking the powerful state of Vijayanagara. This was perhaps inevitable, since the `Adil Shahis had inherited from their Bahmani forbears a common border with the great southern state that lay along the rich and long-contested Raichur Doab, coveted by both Bijapur and Vijayanagara. Whereas Yusuf `Adil Khan in 1493 had successfully turned back an invasion by a Vijayanagara army,[11] Isma`il suffered utterly humiliating defeats by the southern state, the most serious being the Battle of Raichur (1520), in which his powerful adversary, Krishna Raya, nearly drove him and his entire army into a river.[12] Two years later, Krishna Raya advanced clear to Bijapur itself. A contemporary Portuguese chronicler records that the Vijayanagara king even occupied the capital for several days after the sultan had refused his outrageous demand to show his submission by kissing his foot.[13] Responding to this clear evidence of his kingdom's vulnerability, the sultan began work on a powerful stone citadel to defend his capital, replacing the mud fort that had preceded it. An inscription dated March or May 1522, built into the outside of the wall just southeast of the citadel's main gate, records that the new fortification was built specifically to repel the 'cursed' Krishna Raya.[14]

Given his strong identification with Iran and with Persian culture, it is hardly surprising that Isma`il showed no interest in a dynasty as thoroughly native as the Chalukyas. But this would change in 1535, when his son Ibrahim I (r. 1535–58) came to the throne. Reversing the policies of the father, Ibrahim brought about a top-down social revolution in the kingdom. Where Isma`il had fervently favoured Westerners, Ibrahim just as fervently favoured Deccanis; where the father had cultivated Persian, the son cultivated the indigenous languages of the Deccan; and where the former had promoted Shi`ism as a state cult, the latter abolished the practice. Ibrahim also prohibited the wearing of the Safavi-style scarlet cap with twelve points. With only a few exceptions, he dismissed all Westerners from his army, most of whom took up service in the other sultanates of the Deccan. Three thousand of them were recruited by Rama Raya, who would use them to advance his own carefully laid plans to seize power in Vijayanagara.[15] Most important, however, was the revolution that Ibrahim brought about within his civil administration. In a move that would have far-reaching consequences, he ordered that the language of all public accounts—both revenue and judicial records—be changed from Persian to either Marathi or Kannada, the two indigenous languages spoken in the `Adil Shahi state. He also placed the administration of these offices under the management of local brahmans who, Firishta writes, 'soon acquired great influence in his government'.[16]

How can one explain these dramatic changes? One clue perhaps lies in the manner in which the sultan came to power. When Isma`il died in September 1534, the late king was initially succeeded by his eldest son, Mallu, not Ibrahim. But when Mallu proved to be a worthless incompetent—he is said to have had young boys of nobles forcibly dragged to his palace 'for shameful purposes'—it was the brothers' Maratha grandmother, Punji Khatun, who intervened. This strong-willed dowager arranged that Mallu, after reigning for just six months, be blinded and that Ibrahim be enthroned.[17] It is possible that indebtedness to this woman made Ibrahim sympathetic to Maratha culture generally. It is also possible to see Ibrahim's changes in the context of his several encounters with Vijayanagara, which were of a very different sort than those of his father. Around 1536 the youthful sultan obliged a request from Salakaraja, brother-in-law of a weak successor to the Vijayanagara throne, to assist in his power struggle with the cunning and ambitious Rama Raya. In 1542, when the king died and Salakaraja tried to seize the throne for himself, he again invited Ibrahim to help shore up his cause against Rama Raya. As the sultan's army approached the southern kingdom, Rama Raya, aiming to draw away Ibrahim's forces, falsely professed loyalty to Salakaraja. Soon after Ibrahim's army had turned back to Bijapur, however, he treacherously turned on his enemy, who committed suicide, paving Rama Raya's path to de facto supremacy in Vijayanagara.[18]

Buoyed by these bloodless expeditions to Vijayanagara, and feeling less dependent than his father upon constant infusions of foreign troops in his service, Ibrahim embarked on a number of changes both to Bijapur's physical character and to its state ideology. From 1538 he boldly entitled himself 'shah', or king, and not merely 'khan' as his two predecessors at Bijapur had done. Affirming his kingdom's independence in this way ended the fiction of its subordination to a Bahmani overlord. Between 1538 and 1544, he also sponsored the construction of the great southern gateway to

Bijapur's citadel, the capital's principal entrance, thereby completing the defense of the capital's urban core that his father had begun in 1522.

Thanks to inscriptions carved at three points within the gateway, we know that construction began from the innermost doorway of the complex and proceeded outwards towards the outer door and barbican. Thus, by starting from a point outside the gateway and taking an imaginary tour through the complex towards the citadel's interior, we can see—in reverse—how the king's ideology had evolved over the course of the six years during which the complex was built. The gateway is first entered through an outer extension, or barbican, on the outside of which appears the latest inscription. Dated 1544–45 and marking the completion of the entire gateway complex, this record carries the standard Islamic credo (*kalima*), proclaiming the sultan's Sunni identity.[19] At the end of the barbican we turn right and approach the outer gate, whose lintel bears an inscription, dated 1542–43, referring to ʿAdil Shah, the world-conquering king'.[20] However, since prayers according to the Shi`i formula appear on either side of this inscription, it is clear that up to 1542 Ibrahim, like his father, had adhered to the Shi`i sect, and that sometime between 1542 and 1544—that is, soon after returning from his second expedition to Vijayanagara—the king declared himself a Sunni. This was also most likely when he adopted other measures consistent with his change of sect, namely, banishing most Westerners from his service, prohibiting the wearing of the Iranian-style cap, and changing the language of civil administration from Persian to Marathi and Kannada.

Passing through the wide outer gate and its vaulted corridor, we enter a spacious courtyard with guard-houses on either side. Looming before us on the far side of the courtyard are two massive bastions, between which is located the inner gate to the citadel. This was the earliest segment of the entire complex to have been built, and fortunately, it too can be firmly dated. To our right, high up on the gateway's inner, or northern bastion (known as the Allahi Burj), are two more inscriptions. The first of these, near where the bastion abuts the curtain wall, records the date 1538–39, when the earliest section of the complex was completed. As it was built before the sultan's conversion to Sunni Islam, this inscription gives the Islamic credo in its Shi`i form.[21] It also records the first dated instance in which Ibrahim titled himself 'shah'. To the left, or west, on this same northern bastion is another inscription, undated, invoking a Shi`i prayer, after which ʿAdil Shah' is repeated three times.[22]

Passing between the two bastions, we approach the citadel's inner gateway (Figure 4.1). Since most of this gate has been stripped away, there is no way of knowing exactly what it originally looked like. All that remains are two upright door jambs with a massive stone beam placed across the top. Each jamb is divided into two vertical bands, the outer with a simple meandering floral scroll and the inner with a complex pilaster motif, based on vertically repeating units of an octagonal shaft with vase-shaped base and capital. On stylistic grounds, these jambs appear to have been recycled from some earlier Bahmani structure.[23]

Everything else about this gate, however, evokes a Chalukya world. Built low into the southern wall by the pathway leading towards the gate is—or rather was, as it is no longer there today—a large basalt stone slab about 1 metre high and 75 centimetres wide, bearing an inscription issued by the Chalukya emperor Someshvara II in 1074–75.[24] After an opening eulogy of the emperor—'the asylum of the universe, the favourite of the world, the great king, the supreme king, the supreme lord, the

**Figure 4.1** Bijapur. Gateway to citadel, entrance to inner courtyard.

most worshipful one, the glory of the family of Satyāśraya, the ornament of the Chāḷukyas'—the inscription records the construction of a temple dedicated to Shiva (Svayambhu-Siddheshvara) in the administrative centre (*rājadhāni*) of 'Vijayapura', that is, Bijapur (see the first epigraph to this chapter). For this purpose, as well as to provide food and clothing to the ascetics studying with a particular priest at this temple, the grant authorized the local governor to set aside the income from 300 *mattar*s of a specified tract of land.[25] Directly beneath this inscription, filling up unused space on the same slab, is the opening of a second grant, this one issued by Someshvara II's younger brother and usurper, Vikramaditya VI. Undated and providing no historical information, the fragment merely endows the great emperor with the same honorifics as are found in the first grant, stating that he was 'continuing with perpetual increase at the capital of (the city of) Kalyāṇa, so as to endure as long as the moon and sun and stars might last'.[26]

What is one to make of this inscription? We might first raise the question of its intended audience. Originally, of course, it was intended for Chalukya officials at Vijayapura who would have needed to know, among other things, that the income from those 300 mattars of land should be used solely to support this Shiva temple. The audience in the time of Ibrahim `Adil Shah and his dynastic successors would have been very different. Although the inscription was recorded in Old Kannada, the script was 'in well-formed and excellently preserved Old-Canarese characters of the period',[27] meaning that it would have been legible to many educated people in the sixteenth century, who would have understood its clear references to the two most illustrious emperors of the Chalukya dynasty. Most important is the inscription's conspicuous location. Not only was this passageway used by ordinary passersby, it was also the official entry into the citadel, appropriate for ceremonial processions. Placing the inscription in such a prominent spot therefore elevated it from something merely to be read to something deserving of respect. America's Declaration of Independence and Britain's Magna Carta, enshrined in Philadelphia and London respectively, are not displayed with any expectation that the public would or should actually read them. They were placed there for the purpose of encouraging the viewing public to make the connection between their current governments, which protect and display the documents, and the political and cultural milieus that had created them. That is to say, both texts are political charters. Similarly, it is possible to see that for its `Adil Shahi patrons, the tablet at the entrance of Bijapur's gate served as a political icon, intended to display an imagined continuity between the prestigious but long-defunct Chalukyas and the current `Adil Shahi ruling class.

Given that other prominent Chalukya material (discussed later) was built into the entrance complex when Ibrahim began work on it in 1538–39, it is most likely that he would have installed this singularly Chalukya artifact at the same time. Moreover, we know that just several years after starting work on this gate complex, Ibrahim abandoned the Shi`i sect, marking a decisive break with the Westerner orientation in which he had been raised. It therefore seems possible to see the sultan's political identity as having evolved over time. Whereas his indigenizing sentiments were expressed in 1538–39 through the medium of reused Chalukya material, several years later they were expressed through the more radical step of renouncing his Shi`i faith. Along the way, he also dismissed Westerners from his service, placed brahmans in charge of public accounts, and replaced Persian with Marathi and Kannada as the languages of those accounts.

Even if one had failed to notice, or were unable to recognize, the large slab containing the Chalukya inscription immediately before the inner gate, nobody could have missed the virtual forest of reused columns—most of them Chalukya-period—that greeted the visitor immediately on passing through it (Figure 4.2). Today only fourteen columns remain standing in what had once been an ensemble of twenty-four columns divided into two groups of twelve each, separated by a passageway leading directly from the door of the gatehouse into the entrance-way's innermost courtyard. The group to the south, or the left side as one enters the citadel, still carries a network of stone beams that support the roof over what probably functioned as another guard room.[28] Six of these columns are engaged with the wall and six are free-standing. As for the group to the north, the plan included in Henry Cousens's 1916 architectural survey of the city shows twelve free-standing columns. As of 1956 there were nine; today only two remain standing.[29] But from a photograph taken in 1955–56, it is evident that all the columns on both sides of the pathway originally stood on raised plinths of the same height, thus creating a carefully balanced and dramatic entranceway to the citadel (Figure 4.3).[30] Although in modern times the northern columns have stood, as Cousens put it, 'roofless and desolate, like so many nine-pins',[31] we must imagine that this ensemble too was originally roofed, like that on the south. All of the columns remaining today are of the metropolitan Chalukya *chitrakhanda* type, except for the six in the southern group that are engaged in the inner walls of the chamber. Above all, this recycling of Chalukya material here—like that in Vijayanagara—was anything but random; the ensemble was arranged in such a way that the most visible columns greeting the visitor were the finest examples of metropolitan Chalukya art. Moreover, the two different types of columns in the two inner rows were carefully arranged for symmetry, such that they form an A-B-B-A pattern on each side of the passageway.

Clues as to where these columns had come from are found in the ten Kannada inscriptions engraved on their sides, with some columns bearing more than one inscription.[32] The earliest was recorded in 1033 and the latest in 1304, with the earliest four falling in the Chalukya period and the last six in that of their successors in this part of the Deccan, the Yadavas. All ten inscriptions record donations made to a temple in 'Vijayapura' dedicated to the god Narasimha. This was evidently an institution of considerable antiquity—older even than the city's Shiva temple (1074–75) that was mentioned in the inscription on the wall outside the gate. Its regular endowments over a span of 178 years indicate the temple's popularity, suggesting that old Bijapur may

**Figure 4.2** Bijapur. Gateway to citadel, inner courtyard, looking south.

**Figure 4.3** Gateway to citadel, inner courtyard, from inside looking southeast (in 1955–56) (From Sidney Toy, *The Strongholds of India* [London: William Heinemann Ltd., 1957]).

well have been a religious centre of some importance.

It is not likely, however, that the Narasimha temple, to which these columns originally belonged, was destroyed by `Adil Shahi rulers, or by the Bahmanis. For one thing, as Cousens noted long ago, several of these columns have cross-lined diagrams roughly scored on their sides, on which a game akin to checkers was played.[33] This means that they must have been lying prone on the ground for a considerable time, uncared for, before they were recycled in the gateway.[34] Since it continued to receive donations until as late as 1304, the Narasimha temple apparently remained in active use until it was disassembled, most likely in the context of the Khalaji conquest of the Yadava realm that began just a decade later. If so, the columns would have lain unused until Ibrahim recycled them for this entranceway.[35] Given what we otherwise know about the sultan's wish to put his kingdom on an indigenous footing, placing these stunning Chalukya columns in the citadel's most prominent location makes perfect sense. Like Someshvara II's inscription placed in the wall just a few metres away, the columns had been transformed into emblems of an earlier, illustrious time, an age with which the sultan evidently wished to associate himself and his kingdom.

## THE TEMPLE-MOSQUE OF BANKAPUR AND THE STATE'S EXPANSION

`Ali `Adil Shah (r. 1558–80) was only sixteen years old when he succeeded Ibrahim as sultan in 1558. But even before his father's death, he had been flirting with Shi`ism, to Ibrahim's great annoyance. On one occasion the prince joked that since his father had switched sects, it was incumbent upon his children to follow such a fine example. The sultan was not amused. But in the end, despite his father's efforts to shield his son from Shi`i influence, `Ali declared Bijapur an officially Shi`i state once he ascended the throne.[36]

His was not, however, the ardent or exclusive sort of Shi`ism of his grandfather, Isma`il. We hear of no dismissals of Deccani officers, no reinstating of Iranian sartorial customs. To the contrary, `Ali showed an exceptionally liberal and intellectual bent. His royal library, which was overseen by a brahman named Waman Pandit, employed nearly sixty men—calligraphers, gilders, book-binders, and illuminators. He was so devoted to reading that even while on tour or on military campaigns he would take along whole crates of books, and he would become annoyed if he were ever separated from them.[37] He was also curious about other religions. He once asked the Archbishop of Goa to send him learned priests to inform him about Christian tenets. In response, in 1561 a delegation that included a Dominican and a Jesuit priest was sent to Bijapur. According to the report filed by the Jesuit,

> This king is well conditioned, such a gentleman and very liberal and magnanimous, the most well bred prince that I have seen. He maintains a great state and courtly nobility. He goes about accompanied by many soldiers and when we go to the palace so many are the meetings with crowds of people that Lisbon's Rua Nova does not have the advantage in the matter.[38]

The sultan's liberal character was, according to these same observers, mirrored by what they saw of the countryside. On their journey between Goa and Bijapur, the delegation remarked on the atmosphere of religious tolerance in the villages, noting that non-Muslims 'have their pagodas and perform their idol-worship without anyone interfering with them'.[39]

The crowning achievement of `Ali `Adil Shah's intellectual endeavours was his authorship, in 1570, of one of the most extraordinary texts to have appeared in the pre-modern Deccan, the *Nujūm al-`ulūm*, or 'Stars of the Sciences'.[40] Written in Persian but replete with Dakhni vocabulary, the work draws on Indic, Islamic, Hellenic, and Turkic traditions to provide a comprehensive vision of medieval Deccani courtly knowledge. At one level, argues Emma Flatt, the work is a technical manual for people of Bijapur's court, covering such diverse topics as gardening, music, the power of Sufis and yogis, the qualities of elephants, or of weapons; the making of fireworks, perfumes, and sherbets; and the science of poetry, rhetoric, and medicine. But at its core it carries a deeply political message, drawing a parallel between the ability of superhuman (especially planetary) forces to control the world, and the ability of a ruler to govern his kingdom.[41] Herein lies the work's principal thesis, namely, that the key to kingship lies in the mastery of esoteric knowledge. Deborah Hutton has noted that the book's only full-page illustration depicts a ruler atop a seven-storied throne—an esoteric Islamic allusion[42]—followed by a section on the ideal design of forts, that is, practical information for an aspiring ruler. But the text also draws heavily on classical Indian ideas of kingly power—for example, the Universal Ruler's seven attributes, which include the perfect consort, minister, general, horse, and elephant—and on classical ideas of cosmology, such as the 140 *rūḥānīs*

(Hindu earth forces), which are illustrated by Tantric goddesses and their attributes.[43] Moreover, the dazzling paintings that illustrate the text defy neatly dichotomized conceptions of 'Hindu' or 'Muslim' art.[44] For example, an anthropomorphized image of Mars can be interpreted either as the legendary Persian warrior Rustam with his leopard-head helmet, or as Shiva carrying his trident. Or again, the image of the chariot that carries the sun is pulled by lions, a Perso-Islamic motif, while the sun's multiple arms carry a conch shell and a mace, which are attributes of Vishnu.[45]

\`Ali \`Adil Shah's fascination with esoteric knowledge was reflected in his actions as well as his writings. 'The sultan had an inclination for Sufism,' wrote Rafi\` al-Din Shirazi, a Westerner who joined the sultan's service in 1564.

> If he heard of an ascetic or mystic—whether Muslim or Hindu—he would certainly seek his company. He would watch them go into states of ecstasy, and at such times he would become detached from worldly matters, which he entrusted to others. Sometimes, while in the company of close associates, he would launch into [mystical] discourses lasting five or six hours. He spoke of the tranquility he had achieved. But when news of his manners reached the ears of other sultans, they took him to be mad and began contemplating seizing his territories.[46]

According to Shirazi it was just such threats, coming especially from Sultan Husain Nizam Shah of Ahmadnagar, that drove the young and insecure \`Ali to seek a defensive alliance with the powerful but treacherous ruler of Vijayanagara, Rama Raya, in order to recover the forts of Sholapur and Kalyana from Sultan Husain.

Rama Raya, technically Vijayanagara's regent but by now its de facto monarch, received this overture most warmly, since it fell squarely into his own, dark schemes. Privately, as we have seen in the previous chapter, Rama Raya had for some time coveted Kalyana, the former capital of the Chalukya empire. More recently, the city had become a bone of contention between Bijapur and Ahmadnagar. Now, through the medium of this young and as yet untested ruler from Bijapur, Rama Raya hoped to attain his goal of controlling that symbolically potent city, even if only indirectly. With \`Ali, he would wrest Kalyana from Ahmadnagar's control and then graciously allow the \`Adil Shahi ruler to govern it as his subordinate king, a classic stratagem in Indian political thought. Surely, he calculated, this inexperienced upstart would be easier to manipulate than the Nizam Shahi sultan.

Rama Raya therefore invited the Bijapur sultan to Vijayanagara for a state visit, and \`Ali accepted. What followed was a lavish affair that included days of sumptuous banquets and mutual gift-giving. Things got so convivial and so intimate that the regent's wife referred to \`Ali as her own son,[47] while members of Rama Raya's harem, to which the sultan was also admitted, kissed him on the forehead as though he were their child.[48] But as the sultan took his leave from Vijayanagara, an ominous cloud loomed on the horizon. Rama Raya failed to comply with the customary protocol of the times, which dictated that a host must escort a departing guest to the road. \`Ali was more than offended. As Firishta reports, he 'felt afflicted and considered it a duty to the dignity of his ambition to avenge him. But owing to the exigencies of the time, he didn't express his feelings. Rather, he waited for an opportunity to present itself'.[49]

Relations between the two men steadily deteriorated. When Rama Raya and his army joined \`Ali's on a campaign against Ahmadnagar in 1559, the Vijayanagara regent used the occasion to ravage Nizam Shahi land, even destroying mosques and copies of the Qur'an.[50]

Nonetheless the two allies forced Husain Nizam Shah to surrender Kalyana to `Ali, after which Rama Raya returned to Vijayanagara. But in 1562 Husain formed a pact with Golconda's Ibrahim Qutb Shah and retook the former Chalukya capital. Again `Ali solicited Rama Raya's aid to recover it, and again the latter gladly obliged by marching north with 50,000 cavalry. In the course of this campaign, during which Husain was driven clear out of his own capital, Rama Raya again desecrated mosques—by placing images in them for worship, or by using them to stable his horses.[51] In the history of the Deccan, this was one of the few recorded instances of mosques being desecrated. It did not escape `Ali's attention, nor would he forget it. Rama Raya's overbearing behaviour also extended to his treatment of `Ali's officers, who were not allowed to sit in his presence. Though thoroughly scandalized by Rama Raya's outrageous behaviour, the sultan was unable to act; he needed this powerful ally to keep Husain Nizam Shah in check and to hold onto Kalyana, for the ancient city was gradually becoming as much an obsession for `Ali as it already was for Rama Raya. Holding his bitterness to himself, the sultan continued to bide his time, pretending not to have noticed his ally's outrageous behaviour.[52]

All that changed, however, when it was learned that Rama Raya, while returning to Vijayanagara, had seized the forts of Udgir and Bagalkot from `Ali, as well as Koyilkonda and Guntur from Ibrahim Qutb Shah of Golconda. These acts of gratuitous aggression, waged with Rama Raya's customary arrogance and sense of impunity, proved the final straw. Realizing at last that Vijayanagara's regent had been viciously exploiting, sometimes even fomenting, their internecine wars over territory and forts, in 1564 the sultans of the four principal states of the northern Deccan—Bijapur, Ahmadnagar, Golconda, and Bidar—formed an offensive alliance against the great southern state. In December of that year they all met just north of the Krishna River and, after crossing it, in January 1565 waged one of the most important battles in Indian history.[53] For Vijayanagara, the Battle of Talikota was a debacle: the allies captured and beheaded Rama Raya, destroyed his army, and spent six months plundering metropolitan Vijayanagara. As we saw in Chapter 3, the great city never recovered.

If the Battle of Talikota proved a catastrophe for Vijayanagara, for Bijapur it was transformative, both ideologically and physically. Of all the allied powers, Bijapur, being immediately adjacent to Vijayanagara, reaped by far the most wealth from the defeated kingdom. `Ali `Adil Shah used this wealth to upgrade Bijapur from a provincial outpost to a major Indo-Persian capital. Two monumental projects stand out in this regard. He built a massive stone wall and moat around the city that measured nearly 11 kilometres in circumference.[54] He also constructed what remains today the largest congregational mosque in the Deccan. With its multi-bay prayer hall covered by thirty-six shallow domes, its lofty dome covering nine bays before the *miḥrāb*, its spacious courtyard with arcades on the north and south sides, and its great entranceway on the eastern end, the mosque very much followed the pattern of grand mosques in other major Indo-Persian capital cities, such as Delhi, Daulatabad, or Bidar. Henry Cousens considered that `Ali, 'as a good Muslim', had constructed the mosque to be 'a permanent memorial of the great victory of Islam over the vast infidel kingdom of the south'.[55] Evidence supporting Cousens's interpretation is found in the inscriptions in the highly contested fort of Kalyana. There, on five inscriptions stretching from 1563 to 1580—that is, both before and after Talikota—the title *ghāzī*, 'holy warrior', was added to the sultan's name.[56] At the equally contested fort of Raichur, witness to so many bitter conflicts between Bijapur and Vijayanagara, an inscription dated 1570–71 also styled `Ali ghāzī.[57] And a bastion raised in the same city in 1566 bears the chronogram (that is, *abjad* date), 'It was one year after the victory over the infidels.'[58] Clearly, at Kalyana and Raichur the contemporaries understood the Battle of Talikota, and `Ali's role in it, in a particular way: Rama Raya was an evil non-believer who had to be suppressed.

Inscriptions in Bijapur itself, on the other hand, do not reveal such triumphalist sentiments. The inscription in the city's Shahpur gate, dated 1570–71, describes `Ali as 'the just Sultan, shadow of Allah, Abu'l-Muzaffar `Ali `Adil Shah'.[59] Inscriptions on the bastions above both the Fath and the Mecca gates merely state that they had been built in 1576–77 and 1578–79 respectively by 'Baghrash Khan, a slave of `Ali `Adil Shah'.[60] Another bastion, built by a Hindu named Jagdi Rao, describes his sovereign as merely 'King `Ali `Adil Shah'.[61]

Indeed, the most interesting such inscription appears on the lintel above a postern gate in the southernmost section of the city's new wall, 60-some metres east of the Landa Qassab bastion (Figure 4.4). It, too, was patronized by a Hindu—a brahman named Baid Panditji—in

**Figure 4.4** Bijapur. Inscription and *makara-torana* in postern near the Landa Qassab Gate (in 1964) (From B.D. Verma, *The Glories of Bijapur: A History of Its Remains* [India, 1964]).

1568, just three years after Talikota. And it, too, says simply that the structure was built 'during the reign of king `Ali `Adil Shah'.[62] What is most intriguing is that immediately below the Persian inscription is a beautifully preserved and most elegant Chalukya-period *makara-toraṇa,* or ritual gate, which was probably used originally to frame the entrance to a temple vestibule (Figure 4.5). At either end of it are *makaras*, fabulous crocodiles with their snouts raised. In the middle of the *toraṇa* Shiva dances carrying a trident and drum, flanked on one side by Vishnu with a conch and a discus, and on the other by Brahma with a swan on either side of him. Although this exquisite piece of Chalukya art appears on a postern and not on a major gateway, it is perhaps significant that it was placed in the southernmost section of the city's wall, exactly homologous with Someshvara II's inscription and the Chalukya columns that Ibrahim I had positioned in the southern gateway to the citadel itself. We should therefore consider the possibility that `Ali, who would have been very familiar with the Chalukya visual references in the citadel, intentionally planned the homology. After all, Baid Panditji had been authorized to build the postern with its makara-toraṇa just two years before the sultan finished writing his *Nujūm al-`ulūm*, a text that makes constant homologies between Indic and Persian themes, whether epic, esoteric, astrological, or cosmological.

**Figure 4.5** Bijapur. Chalukya-period *makara-toraṇa* in postern near Landa Qassab gate (*Courtesy of* Yigal Bronner).

Apart from these building projects in the capital, `Ali endeavoured to conquer and annex as much as he could of Vijayanagara's former territory, filling the vacuum created when Rama Raya's brother Tirumala had survived Talikota and moved the court from metropolitan Vijayanagara to Penukonda, some 180 kilometres to the southeast. `Ali commenced his southward drive by first seizing the fort of Adoni, immediately south of the Raichur Doab along his kingdom's eastern flank. Then, in 1573, he marched from his capital directly south to Torgal, which he recovered, after a seven-month siege, from one of his own former officers who had gone over to Rama Raya's cause before Talikota. Continuing south, after a six-month siege he seized the fort of Dharwar from one of Rama Raya's former officers. Moving further south through present-day Belgaum and Dharwar districts, `Ali entered the heart of the original homeland of the Chalukya kings, as reflected in the sheer density of temples that they or their vassals had patronized in this region (see Figure 3.7, p. 91).

Sometime in 1574 the sultan moved from Dharwar to Bankapur, a formidable fortress then held by Velappa Raya, who before Talikota had been a principal attendant of Rama Raya. After his patron's death, he assumed independence and reduced a number of neighbouring chieftains to tributary status. As the `Adil Shahi army now bore down on him, Velappa Raya sent desperate appeals for assistance to Tirumala, at the new court at Penukonda. But Tirumala, revealing how quickly Vijayanagara's political system had collapsed since Talikota, lamely replied that although he would order his vassals to assist the beleaguered Bankapur fort, he could not guarantee that they would comply.[63] Velappa Raya nonetheless managed to hold out for fifteen months before surrendering to `Ali `Adil Shah's forces. When he offered to give up the fort, however, he did so on the condition that he and his family be allowed to march off with their effects. `Ali granted the request. The sultan then appointed one of his brahman officers, Bendry Pandit, to oversee the collection of revenue from the newly conquered tracts. He also sent his principal general, Mustafa Khan Ardistani, on an expedition to conquer forts still deeper to the south.[64] For the next eighteen months `Ali made Bankapur his headquarters.

During those eighteen months in 1575 and 1576, while temporarily residing in the homeland of the Chalukya emperors, `Ali substantially altered Bankapur's built landscape. Writing some thirty years after the event, the historian Firishta records that the sultan had 'ordered a superb temple within [the fort] to be destroyed, and he himself laid the first stone of a mosque, which was built on the foundation, offering up prayers for his victory'.[65]

Today a single, ruined mosque does indeed survive inside the fort, at its eastern end near the gateway.[66] But this cannot be the converted temple that Firishta mentioned, as an inscription fixed into its central *miḥrāb* dates its construction to 1538–39, which falls in the reign of `Ali's father, Ibrahim I.[67] Rather, Firishta seems to have been referring to another structure that lies opposite the gateway, so far to the west that the fort's ramparts run along its back. This had been one of the most elegant temples produced in the Chalukya age—a Shaiva temple dedicated to Nagareshvara, popularly known as the Aravattukhambada temple, or the 'Temple of Sixty Columns' (Figure 4.6). But contrary to Firishta's statement, `Ali did not exactly destroy the temple and build a mosque on its site. Instead, the archaeological record reveals that he remodelled the temple into a mosque—the only known instance of an `Adil Shahi ruler undertaking such an endeavour. Why did he do

**Figure 4.6** Bankapur. Aravattukhambada temple/Jami` mosque from the southeast. To right, the great hall, or mosque proper. To far left, the *vimāna*.

it? How did he do it? And what, if anything, might this say about how the sultan wished to position himself vis-à-vis the Chalukya past?

Inscriptions referring to the temple are dated 1093, 1112, and 1137.[68] On stylistic grounds, its *vimāna*, or shrine proper, can be dated to sometime between the 1050s and the early 1100s, that is, between the reigns of Someshvara I and Vikramaditya VI, the cultural and political high point of the Chalukya age.[69] Attached to the vimāna on the east is a four-pillared hall that originally had porches on the north, east, and southern sides, fronting the finely crafted doorframes that led into the hall. The *citrakhaṇḍa* pillars of the eastern and southern porches (the northern porch is no longer extant) are carved in the mid-sections with elaborately decorated bands (*paṭṭi*), above which are cubical blocks with two-bodied lion figures subjugating a two-bodied elephant at each corner.[70] Aligned with this hall on the east and attached by means of continuous roofing is the great hall (*raṅgamaṇḍapa*), described by Foekema as 'one of the most majestic achievements of Calukya architecture' (Figures 4.7 and 4.8).[71] Measuring nearly 20 metres across, this spacious hall of thirty-seven bays originally contained fifty-two columns—free-standing, highly polished, of dark greenish schist, and belonging to the *śrīkāra* type. The structure's east–west alignment—on axis with Mecca, the direction of prayer (*qibla*)—was not the only factor facilitating its conversion to a mosque. Equally important was the presence of this capacious open hall—the only part of a temple that could be feasibly modified to accommodate a large number of worshippers gathered for congregational Islamic worship.

**Figure 4.7** Bankapur. Aravattukhambada temple/Jami` mosque: eastern entrance to great hall.

**Figure 4.8** Bankapur. Aravattukhambada temple/Jami` mosque: central aisle, looking west.

Despite these natural advantages, `Ali still needed to make structural adjustments to effect the conversion. In the first place, the stepped plan of the hall created problems. Because of the pair of re-entrant angles at each corner, the western side of the building lacked the monumental quality of a mosque's western, or qibla wall, which customarily runs straight and unbroken for the entire length of a mosque's outer dimensions. A second and related problem stemmed from the hall's open-pillared construction, which followed the customary plan for *raṅgamaṇḍapa*s in the Chalukya style—a low half-wall bounding the *maṇḍapa* along its perimeter, and a series of smaller-scale, 'dwarf' columns resting on the top of this wall to carry the maṇḍapa's outer beams, eaves, and roofing. The spaces between these dwarf columns provided excellent seating, with comfortably angled seat-back slabs that ran around the edge of the half wall. But the outer perimeter of such a hall inevitably remains largely open, unlike a mosque's qibla wall, which had been completely enclosed almost from the very beginnings of Islam so as to minimize visual distractions and serve as a focus for prayer.[72]

To solve the first problem, `Ali's builders dismantled the re-entrant segments of the maṇḍapa at the northwest and southwest corners, taking care to provide temporary supports for the beams that had rested on the three central dwarf columns in each corner. Then, in place of these three columns, they inserted full-length columns into the structure. This extended the lines of the outer two east–west rows of columns, making them as long on the west side as the two rows of columns lining the central nave.[73] Next, his architects extended the building's foundations in order to fill out the northwestern and southwestern corners, and they reconstructed the dismantled half-walls and dwarf columns along the new foundations so that they followed the lines established by the outermost wall planes on the north, west, and south sides (Figure 4.9).

This solved the first problem, but it did not address the second one: the openness of the resulting qibla wall. A photograph of the structure taken by Henry Cousens in 1885 suggests that `Ali simply filled in with rubble masonry the space between the top of the half-wall and the superstructure (Figure 4.10). This photograph shows this plain, solid masonry above the elaborately moulded seat back course, though already by 1885 the structure appears to have been collapsing. Although the photograph shows the infill masonry only in the southwestern corner, one may presume that it originally continued across the entire expanse of the qibla wall and later either collapsed, or had been cleared away by the time Cousens had taken his photograph.

After resolving the problems of the maṇḍapa's western wall, `Ali had a miḥrāb inserted in the middle of the new qibla wall, fitting it into the space through which one had previously passed from the great hall into the eastern porch of the smaller hall (Figure 4.9).[74] This cut off the great hall from the temple proper. In addition to these structural adjustments, a good deal of figural art was chiseled off, especially the little images in the many panels and niches on the outside of the hall's seatbacks. The delicate stone screens on either side of the porch between the two halls, filled with scrollwork and images, were also badly damaged. Less damage was done to the images around the plinth of the southern porch of the temple's smaller hall.[75]

In the very few known instances of temples transformed directly into mosques in Indian history, it is instructive to note exactly what, in each case, was actually altered in the course of the change. We have seen in Chapter 2 that in 1323, when an Indian convert turned Bodhan's

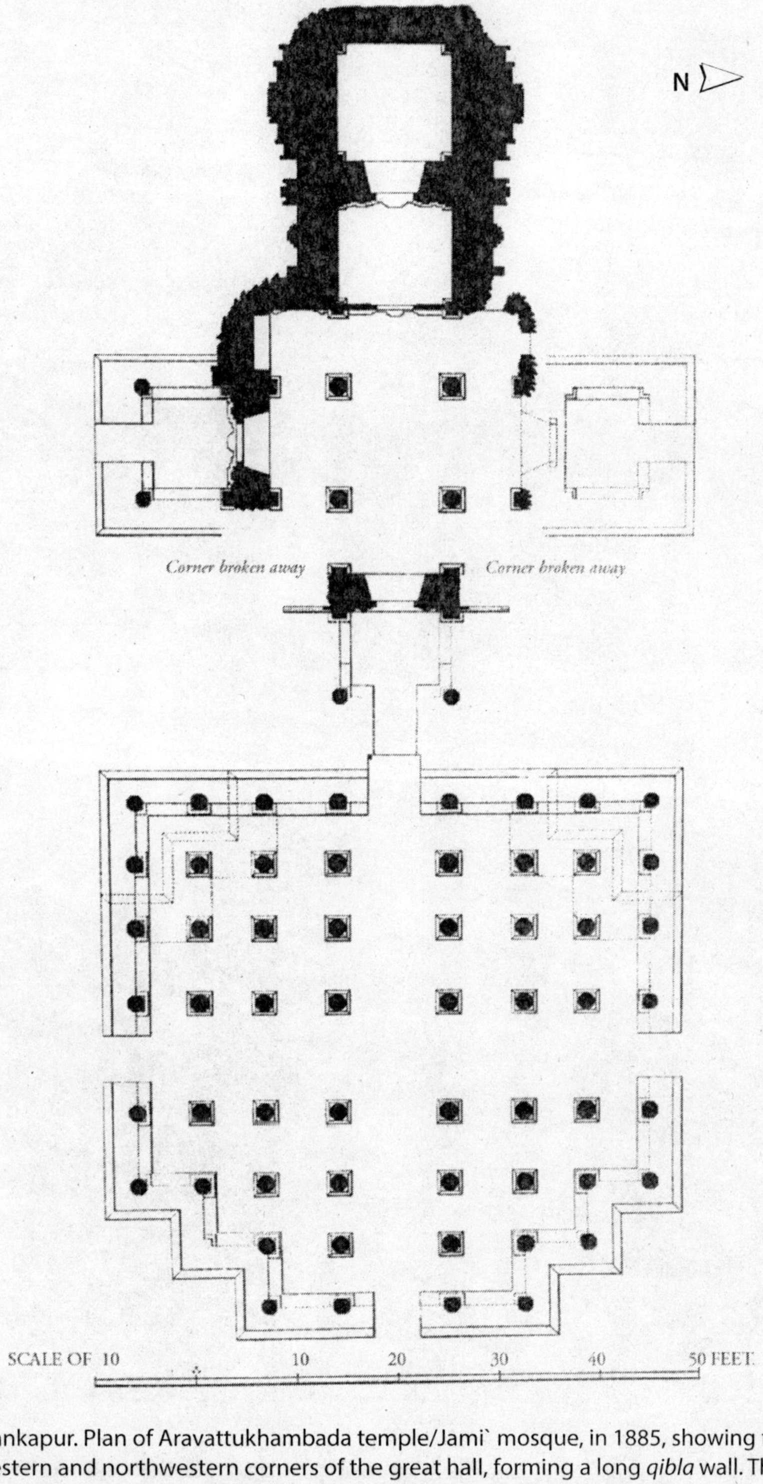


**Figure 4.9** Bankapur. Plan of Aravattukhambada temple/Jami` mosque, in 1885, showing the extensions of the southwestern and northwestern corners of the great hall, forming a long *qibla* wall. The dotted lines show the original stepped disposition of these two corners (from Henry Cousens, *Chalukyan Architecture of the Kanarese Districts* [Calcutta: Government of India, 1926]).

a

b

**Figure 4.10** Bankapur. Aravattukhambada temple/Jami` mosque: great hall from the southwest'. (a) In 1885, showing extensions of the southwest corner, where roofing is caved in (*Courtesy of the* British Library). (b) In 2010, showing modern restoration of original temple plan.

temple into a mosque, prominent semi-spheroid domes were added in the front of the structure. Although such changes were irrelevant from a ritual standpoint, they completely transformed the building's façade, suggesting that its patron did not want the temple to 'look' like a temple, preferring rather that it conform to his notion of how a proper mosque should appear. What happened at Bankapur was precisely the opposite. `Ali made no changes to the great hall that might have altered its prior character: no domes, no arches, no minarets. The most radical change that he did make—squaring off the structure's western side—was done for purely liturgical reasons. Since Muslims at prayer line up behind a qibla wall in uniform rows to accommodate rows behind the first, the qibla wall had to be extended to the full width of the prayer hall. But even this change was made in a way so as not to disrupt the overall aesthetics of the temple's great hall. By reusing the same elaborately moulded stones that had originally been used in the half-walls of the re-entrant angles, `Ali was actually preserving the great hall's Chalukya character (in its Dharwar style), suggesting the sultan's personal admiration of Chalukya aesthetics.

The sultan's respectful attitude towards the temple's aesthetic appeal would have been consistent with his authorship of a literary work as eclectic and open to Indian thought as the *Nujūm al-`ulūm*, a work he had completed just three years before embarking on his southern campaign.[76] Nor was he alone in cultivating an appreciation for Chalukya aesthetics. One officer who accompanied the sultan on this expedition, Rafi` al-Din Shirazi, recorded his awe at the beauty and elegance of the many Chalukya-era temples he witnessed in Lakshmeshwar, just 30 kilometres northeast of Bankapur (see Figure 3.7, p. 91). ``Kings and nobles', he wrote,

> imitated one another in perfecting architecture and in building many exquisite and grand temples. In subsequent years, many of these have fallen into a state of ruin. But some remain standing, and four hundred temples are completely intact, having been built with the utmost of painstaking and elegant workmanship. When we saw them we were struck with awe. Among them all, one temple measured eighty by fifty *zar*` [83.2 × 52 metres]. Both inside and outside the temple were inlaid segments carved with such precision that in the space of the palm of one's hand were carved ten human images and ten or fifteen images of grazing or flying animals, including their eyelashes and fingernails.... One can only imagine how much work went into carving the inside and outside of this temple, and how many days it took to complete it.[77]

At Bankapur, then, by preserving the specifically Chalukya character of the temple's transformed great hall, `Ali was able to indulge both his fascination with indigenous culture and his goal of asserting `Adil Shahi hegemony over a strategic fort formerly controlled by his arch-enemy, Rama Raya. He also achieved an aesthetic continuity—not rupture—between the region's Chalukya past and its `Adil Shahi present.[78]

But, one might ask, out of all the monuments that `Ali would have encountered during his southern expedition, why was the Bankapur temple the only such structure transformed in this way? A possible explanation is found in the Chalukya inscription of Someshvara II that the sultan's father had installed by the gateway to Bijapur's citadel. That inscription (see the first epigraph to this chapter) records Someshvara II's authorization of the building of Bijapur's Shiva temple in response to a request that had originated in Bankapur. The inscription thus points to a political and religious connection between these two Chalukya cities. Since `Ali was likely well aware of the contents of the inscription gracing the entrance to his own citadel, it is possible that, by establishing his headquarters in Bankapur and by transforming its great Chalukya temple into a mosque, the sultan sought to reassert a Bankapura–Vijayapura connection that would once again span both sides of the Krishna River. In that case, he would have been acting in a manner parallel to that of his great nemesis, Rama Raya, who had asserted another sort of Chalukya connection—one that also spanned the Krishna River, but which saw the Vijayanagara regent as the overlord of Kalyana, the Chalukyas' former capital.

## KALYANA FORT AND THE STATE'S MATURATION

As memories of the Deccan's Chalukya past continued to be stoked in the sixteenth century, it was perhaps inevitable that traces of those recovered memories would eventually appear in Kalyana itself. After all, whereas Vijayapura and Bankapura in Chalukya times were only provincial centres, Kalyana had been the imperial capital. Glorified in inscriptions and literature, the city's former splendour had for long been lodged in the conscious or subconscious memory of those members of élite society who were literate in Kannada or Sanskrit. And for the general population, the city's many sculptural and monumental remains stood as mute witnesses to, and reminders of, a lost but brilliant epoch.

In its heyday the ancient Chalukya capital had sprawled over an immense area, of which today's provincial town of Basavakalyan and the fort of Kalyana occupy only a small part. The principal palaces and temples of the imperial city were located several kilometres to the southeast of today's Basavakalyan, in the village presently called Narayanpur (Figure 1.2, p. 11). The fort we see today, located immediately north of Basavakalyan, consists of two circuits of concentric walls built around a small hillock, with a moat ringing the base of the fort's lower wall (Figure 4.11). The relatively high ground afforded by this hill doubtless explains its selection for the construction of the fort, which is otherwise surrounded by a wide, flat plain. The fort was built in phases, the earliest dating to the 1460s, under the authority of Bahmani rulers (1347–1510).[79] From them, the fort passed to the Barid Shahi sultans, who from the early sixteenth century ruled from nearby Bidar, the former Bahmani capital. Being the weakest of the Bahmani successor states, however, the Barid Shahi sultans had to ally themselves with one of their more powerful neighbours, which in the early sixteenth century was Bijapur. Thus, when Rama Raya offered to help Ahmadnagar seize Kalyana from its Barid Shahi overlord in 1549, the senior partner in the Bidar–Bijapur alliance, Ibrahim `Adil Shah I, was drawn into defending the fort. When he lost that struggle, Kalyana fell to the Nizam Shahi sultans of Ahmadnagar, who held it for the next ten years. By 1558, however, Rama Raya had calculated that Bijapur's young and inexperienced `Ali `Adil Shah was weaker than Ahmadnagar's Husain Nizam Shah and hence easier to manipulate. He therefore switched his support from Ahmadnagar to Bijapur. For, beyond ensuring that no single sultanate of the northern Deccan should become so powerful as to challenge Vijayanagara, Rama Raya's principal objective had consistently focussed on acquiring indirect control over Kalyana through an ally of his choosing. This explains why, during the settlement of the 1559 war between `Ali `Adil Shah and Husain Nizam Shah of Ahmadnagar—a war in which the latter was decisively defeated—the first of the three demands that Rama Raya put to Husain was that he deliver the keys of Kalyana to his new client-ally, `Ali `Adil Shah.

**Figure 4.11** Kalyana Fort. Northern side, showing moat and the two circuits of defensive walls.

Bijapur's new sultan wasted no time in putting his own stamp on the fort. Indeed, as noted earlier, `Ali's interest in Kalyana appears to have been catalysed by Rama Raya's obsession with the place. `Ali placed Kalyana under the command of a general, one Kamil Khan, whom he instructed to renovate and modernize the fortifications. While retaining most of the curtain walls on both the fort's upper and lower circuits, Kamil Khan began systematically replacing many of the older, octagonal bastions—dating to the Bahmani period—with newer, and more massive, round bastions.[80] The first of the new bastions, the so-called Keval Ram bastion, was built in 1560 to the immediate west of the fort's only gateway.[81] In 1563, another older bastion on the lower circuit was replaced with a new one. After Rama Raya's crushing defeat at Talikota, the sultan's interest in Kalyana continued to grow, reflected in his ordering the construction of nine more bastions in the fort's lower circuit and two in its upper circuit. Significantly, in all but one of the six bastions bearing foundational inscriptions, `Ali was styled ghāzī, or holy warrior, a practice not seen in the same ruler's inscriptions in the capital at Bijapur.[82] This signals not only the sultan's satisfaction in having vanquished his old enemy, it also suggests that he understood Kalyana's importance as the focus of the two sovereigns' mutual antagonism.

`Ali apparently built a total of twelve new bastions at Kalyana, ten on the fort's lower circuit, and two on its upper circuit. Six of these bear no inscriptions, but on the basis of their fabric and morphology they may be dated to the period 1573–80, when a different general, Dilawar Khan, had replaced Kamil Khan as director of construction. Whereas all twelve of them are round and very large, those built after 1573 share additional distinctive features, such as their three clearly demarcated stepped rises. More arresting is their decorative work (Figure 4.12). Built into their outer faces we find the programmatic use of recycled Chalukya temple sculpture, sometimes scattered, sometimes abundant. Much of it is non-figural in nature, as in the diamond-shaped *ratna-puṣpa* designs that were placed in symmetrically arranged rows along the bastions' outer faces. Other material is figural—gods, goddesses, *apsaras*, elephants. In the most ambitious of these bastions (number 9 of the lower circuit), an elaborate decorative frieze has been constructed, using ratna-puṣpa elements to define the upper and lower borders, and figural sculptures to fill the main field. The figural sculptures have been selectively rotated so that some preserve their proper orientation while others lie on their sides or stand completely upside-down. In many cases, these transformations appear to have had less to do with a desire to desecrate religious images than to create abstract patterns that would accentuate the sinuous rhythms enlivening some of the figures (Figure 4.13). Although the exact intent of the use of such material remains ambiguous, it is certain that the late sixteenth century witnessed a dramatic surge of interest in the

**Figure 4.12** Kalyana Fort. Large round bastion, lower circuit no. 9, built by `Ali `Adil Shah.

**Figure 4.13** Kalyana Fort. Detail of bastion no. 9 in the lower circuit.

material remnants of Kalyana's Chalukya past. This interest would intensify under the reign of `Ali's successor, Ibrahim `Adil Shah II.

Sultan Ibrahim `Adil Shah II was only nine years old in April 1580 when `Ali was assassinated by a disgruntled Habshi slave. As a result, for ten years the kingdom was governed by a series of regents while the young king was raised by `Ali's widow, Chand Bibi. Although the kingdom's ethnic tensions had been kept at bay under `Ali's judicious rule, during the ten-year regency that followed his death, the kingdom was once again plunged into bloody struggles between Deccanis, Westerners, and Habshis. The first two of those ten years saw three regents come and go, each one attempting to usurp and monopolize all power at the expense of his ethnic adversaries. The first regent, a Deccani, was the same general Kamil Khan who had overseen the first phase of Kalyana's reconstruction. He offended Chand Bibi, was dismissed, tried to flee, and was eventually captured and beheaded. The second, a Westerner, boldly imprisoned Chand Bibi herself and murdered Mustafa Khan Ardistani, the architect of the kingdom's conquest of the Karnatak. But he too overplayed his hand, fled the kingdom, and was ultimately murdered. The third, a Habshi, initially gained widespread support by freeing Chand Bibi, but was eventually ousted and blinded by another Habshi who seized the regency in 1582 and ruthlessly governed the kingdom for eight years. This last regent we have also met before—Dilawar Khan, the same officer who had completed `Ali's construction of Kalyana's bastions.

In May 1590 Ibrahim II, who had long chafed under his last regent, finally asserted his independence from the domineering Dilawar Khan, whom he outmanoeuvred and ultimately blinded.[83] But only two years later he had to confront a rebellion launched by his own younger brother, Isma`il, allied with one of the kingdom's leading nobles, `Ain al-Mulk. The sultan, however, suppressed the revolt with vigour: he captured and decapitated `Ain al-Mulk, whose head was placed on a pole outside the palace for a week before being blown from a cannon, and he had his brother executed.[84] In that same year, 1592–93, the sultan took steps to reassert his predecessor's territorial gains in the Karnatak, which had ebbed since 1580. Taking advantage of the turmoil that shook the capital during the sultan's ten-year regency, chieftains of the Karnatak had neglected to bring their annual tribute to the sultanate's regional headquarters at Bankapur. To correct this, Ibrahim II ordered a trusted general, Manjhan Khan, to proceed to Bankapur and summon the Karnatak chiefs to appear there with their tribute. This accomplished, Manjhan Khan pressed the sultanate's further conquests as far south as Mysore, which submitted to Bijapur's forces after a three-month siege.[85] Notably, Manjhan Khan's conquests of 1592–93 pushed the kingdom's southern frontier of tributary states to the upper reaches of the Kaveri River on the Mysore Plateau, which roughly coincides with the southernmost frontiers of the Chalukyas' network of tributary states.

The character of Ibrahim II's reign was famously liberal. Having witnessed savage inter-ethnic strife during his entire minority, the sultan nurtured a pragmatic attitude towards ethnic identities. At the outset of his rule many of his Sunni nobles, assuming he had been raised a Shi`i like his father, hastily arranged for the Shi`i rites to be installed in their districts. But the new sultan merely smiled at the sudden conversion of his Sunni nobles, whom he frequently chided, calling them 'political Shi`is'. In fact, he let all Muslims, Sunni and Shi`i, follow their own mode of worship.[86] Of the kingdom's two dominant political factions, however, the sultan doubtless sympathized with the Deccanis. A Mughal ambassador noted in 1603–04 that although he understood Persian, he could not speak it well, and that if he became excited or annoyed, the conversation between him and his brahman advisor, Antu Pandit, would lapse into Marathi.[87]

The sultan's sympathies toward the Deccan's indigenous culture are seen most dramatically in his passionate devotion to Indian music. Rafi` al-Din Shirazi, who had migrated from Iran to Bijapur long before the king's birth, recorded that Ibrahim II had been an avid student of music even as a child.[88] His passion for music—in particular local, Deccani music—resulted in his composition of an acclaimed work of Dakhni literature, the *Kitāb-i Nauras*, which is a collection of songs intended to be sung in different modes, or ragas, of Indian music.[89] In one of them the sultan gives us a vivid self-portrait:

> In one hand he has a musical instrument, in the other, a book which he reads and sings songs related to Nauras [the 'nine *rasa*s', or 'flavours' of Indian aesthetics]. He is robed in saffron-coloured dress, his teeth are black, the nails are painted in red and he loves all. Ibrahim, whose father is god Ganesh and the mother, pious Saraswati, has a rosary of crystal round his neck, a city like Vidyapur and an elephant as his vehicle.[90]

Vidyapur—'city of knowledge'—was the name the sultan liked to substitute for Bijapur (that is, Vijayapura, 'city of victory').[91] Most remarkable in this passage is his association with the deities Ganesh and Saraswati, whom he rhetorically identifies with his parents. He seems to have been especially attached to Saraswati, the goddess of eloquence, wisdom, and learning, the mother of poetry, the patroness of arts and of music, and the revealer of the Sanskrit language.[92] Just as extant paintings depict the sultan as he describes himself in this passage, at least one known painting, patronized by the sultan, portrays the goddess Saraswati in all her splendour.[93] Government documents of Ibrahim II's day, written in heavily Persianized Marathi, sometimes began with an invocation to Saraswati: 'aj puja shrin Sarasvati'.[94] According to one disapproving seventeenth-century Sufi tradition, the sultan even had an image of Saraswati installed in the royal palace for his personal worship.[95] The sultan's very accommodating sentiments towards Deccani and Hindu culture clearly provoked concerns among his kingdom's more scripturally oriented Muslims.

From an architectural standpoint, such accommodating sentiments were projected nowhere more clearly than in Kalyana, where a spectacular instance of `Adil Shahi manipulation of Chalukya material is witnessed in a well-preserved temple sanctum near the fort's summit (see Figure A2.1, p. 351). To reach it one first crosses a bridge over the former moat, which leads through a series of gates to the fort's lower level, defended by the lower circuit of curtain walls and twelve bastions. Advancing across a spacious court, one climbs a series of steps and through another series of gates that lead to the fort's upper level, defended by the second circuit of curtain walls and five bastions. The upper level contains private apartments, a mosque, and a series of palaces—for example, the Haidar Mahal, the Moti Mahal, the Rangin Mahal, the Taj Mahal—most of which can be dated on stylistic grounds to the seventeenth century or later. The oldest dated building presently standing in the fort is a palace known as the Raj Mahal, which consists of two facing wings opening onto an inner courtyard with a pool (Figures 4.14 and 4.15). The main wing of the palace, on the north, consists of sixteen irregularly disposed vaulted bays and is entered through three squat arches facing onto the courtyard. A Persian inscription set into this facade states that the palace was built in 1592–93, during the reign of Ibrahim II, and that its builder was Niyazmand Khan, apparently the fort's commander and regional governor.[96]

In the northwestern corner of the courtyard in front of the Raj Mahal, a single arch frames the entrance to what at first appears to be yet another set of chambers of the palace (Figure 4.16). In fact, it is the sanctum of a small Chalukya temple, stylistically datable to the late eleventh or early twelfth century.[97] Its only surviving elements are a vestibule with an elaborately carved doorway at its western end and, through the doorway, a sanctum now devoid of its divine image and pedestal. However, it still possesses its full complement of original architectural elements, including floor mouldings, corner pilasters, brackets, beams, and multi-tiered ceiling slabs, all with their sculptural decorations intact.[98] Two features of this temple are especially remarkable. First, unlike Chalukya-era monuments in Vijayanagara, which Rama Raya had dismantled from their original sites and reassembled in the heart of his capital, this temple is in situ; it still stands in the same location where it was originally constructed. Second, it surmounts the only hill in the Kalyana region, recalling the Yadava capital of Devagiri (modern Daulatabad), which was built at the base of a mountain covered with sacred sites.

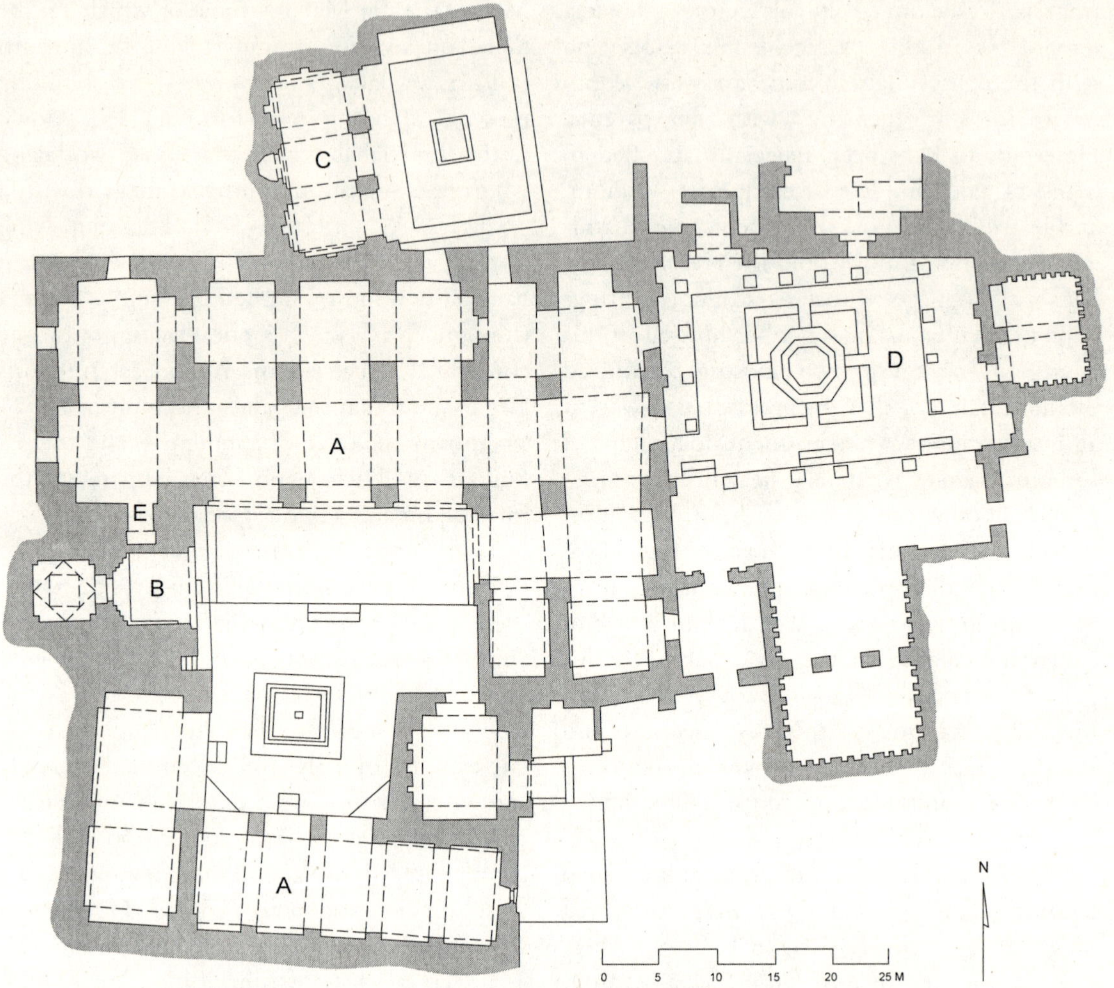


**Figure 4.14** Kalyana Fort. Plan of Raj Mahal palace and associated structures. A: Raj Mahal. B: Chalukya temple. C: Mosque. D: Rangin Mahal. E: Passageway that once connected palace with temple, now blocked.

The Ganesha image in the dedication box over the doorway suggests that the temple might have been dedicated to a form of Shiva, though this is by no means certain. But if that were the case, this might have been the same Shiva temple that Sultan Muhammad bin Tughluq had repaired and restored for public use in 1326, as was discussed in Chapter 2. We have no information on how this temple might have been used when Kalyana was ruled by the Bahmanis or their immediate successors. But when the Raj Mahal palace was built in 1592–93, the temple was encased behind an arched opening that is stylistically contemporary with those of the Raj Mahal itself, suggesting that the palace's site was purposely chosen to enable the temple's incorporation within its ambit. This conclusion is further suggested by the presence of a direct passageway—now blocked off—that served to connect the two structures

**Figure 4.15** Kalyana Fort. Raj Mahal palace. The two arched openings to the right lead to the northern wing of the Raj Mahal; that to the left leads to the Chalukya temple.

**Figure 4.16** Kalyana Fort. The arch of the Raj Mahal palace, leading to the vestibule and doorway to the sanctum of a Chalukya temple.

with each other (Figure 4.17). This passageway would have enabled one to pass directly from the interior of the palace to the doorway of the temple without entering the courtyard that both structures face. By contrast, there is no evidence that any such passageway ever connected the palace with the fort's mosque, which is located immediately behind the palace's rear, northern wall. Clearly, this Chalukya-period temple played an important role in the life of the Bijapuri governor, or of Ibrahim II himself when he visited the fort.

What sort of role might that have been? Possibly, the temple was used as a hall of private audience by the governor or the sultan. Or, perhaps it simply served to commemorate Chalukya grandeur, like a museum display, in the same manner that fragments of Chalukya art had been programmatically inserted into the outer surfaces of some of the fort's bastions a little over a decade before. A third possibility is that Ibrahim II or his governor converted the temple, whose western wall faced Mecca, into a mosque, just as `Ali had done several

**Figure 4.17** Kalyana Fort. Blocked passageway leading from the vestibule of the Raj Mahal palace to the vestibule of the Chalukya temple.

decades earlier at Bankapur. However, there is no evidence of a miḥrāb niche ever having been placed in the temple's western wall, although perhaps the entire sanctum was conceived as a miḥrāb, and the prayer hall was confined to the space of the vestibule.

A fourth possibility is that the temple served *as a temple*, complete with brahman priests. Supporting this possibility is the known charge that Ibrahim II had installed an image of Saraswati in his palace in Bijapur for his personal worship. He could easily have had similar intentions for the Kalyana temple, for it is well known that the sultan engaged with Hindu culture at many levels. Yet his own tomb shows little evidence of religious experimentation. Inscribed over its western doorway is the following verse from the Qur'an (3:60), doubtless chosen because it refers to the sultan's biblical namesake, Abraham:

No: Abraham in truth was not a Jew,
neither a Christian; but a Muslim
and one pure of faith; certainly he was never
of the idolaters.[99]

It is possible that this verse was chosen to rebut charges of religious deviation that he had faced during his lifetime.

Even if the precise purpose of the temple in Ibrahim's day remains unclear, situating the fort's principal palace around the old Chalukya temple does not appear to have been random. Rather, it seems to have been a deliberate move that was intended, at the very least, to preserve the memory of a former dynastic presence in the heart of the old Chalukya empire.

* * *

An awareness of the Chalukya past in Bijapur grew gradually over the course of the sixteenth century, facilitated in part by the abundance of surviving physical evidence of that past that lay across `Adil Shahi territory—whole sculptures or fragments thereof, structural members of temples such as *toraṇa*s or columns, or entire, still-intact temples. But since such physical evidence had been in view for several centuries before the advent of the `Adil Shahis, why did it suddenly become meaningful in the sixteenth century?

Ibrahim I's interest in the Chalukyas seems to have been related to his quest for indigenous sources of prestige, and as an alternative to things foreign, especially Iranian. It is astonishing how thoroughly this sultan repudiated the pro-Westerner policies of his father, Isma`il. His dismissal of nearly all Westerners from his army and his reliance on Deccanis and Habshis was especially radical, considering that his father had hired no Deccanis for twelve years. His replacement of Persian by Marathi or Kannada as the kingdom's official language—and the resulting influx of brahmans at all levels of the revenue and judicial bureaucracies—was equally radical. It, too, contributed to indigenizing the state's character. In the light of such sweeping measures, the sultan's placing an ensemble of metropolitan Chalukya columns and a large inscription tablet of Someshvara II into the principal gateway of the capital's new citadel is understandable, as they accorded perfectly with his pro-Deccani sentiments.

More complex was `Ali `Adil Shah's relation with the Chalukya past. If Ibrahim I was devoted mainly to consolidating the `Adil Shahi state, `Ali's reign was dominated by his titanic conflict with Rama Raya. Here was a powerful figure who could on one day take `Ali under his wing and help him acquire Kalyana, but on another desecrate mosques or ravage `Adil Shahi territory with impunity. `Ali's role in ultimately defeating his arch-nemesis at Talikota pushed this otherwise cerebral, even mystical, sultan in new directions. After Talikota he endeavoured to establish Bijapur as the Deccan's political epicentre, both in his building projects in the capital and in his efforts to expand the state's frontiers deep into the Karnatak. But just a few years before embarking on his Karnatak campaign of 1573–76, and five years after Talikota, he composed a remarkable text, the *Nujūm al-`ulūm*. Drawing equally on Indic and Persian mythology, aesthetics, religion, and political thought, the sultan aimed at forging a broad ideology for Bijapur's multicultural nobility. For, unlike his father, who had banished Westerners from his service, or his grandfather, who had banished Deccanis from it, `Ali sought to accommodate not only these two great factions, but also the many Hindu chieftains who, though formerly loyal to Rama Raya, were now part of a greater `Adil Shahi kingdom.

`Ali's liberal and tolerant personality, noted even by Portuguese visitors, did not, however, prevent him from demolishing temples patronized by such chieftains who resisted his arms. The exception was Bankapur, which was treated differently from other conquered forts in the Karnatak. Possibly recalling the Bankapura–Vijayapura connection mentioned in Someshvara II's tablet at Bijapur's citadel, `Ali made this place his headquarters, remaining there a year and a half. From an architectural standpoint, his transformation of the great hall of the Aravattukhambada temple into a mosque is remarkable in that it sought to preserve the building's original, Chalukya character even while radically altering its ritual purpose. In this sense, it may be compared with other, world-famous monuments whose original character was intentionally preserved even while their ritual function was radically changed, such as Rome's Pantheon (from pagan to Christian edifice), or Istanbul's Hagia Sophia (from church to mosque). In cases such as these, agents of change used their power not to vandalize or annihilate, but to preserve, and in this way to connect themselves with a society and a culture whose architectural achievements they manifestly admired.

Unlike his predecessors, Ibrahim II's engagement with the material culture of the Chalukyas was driven by a deep fascination not just with Indic culture in a general sense, but with Hinduism in particular. In this regard he can be fairly compared with his more famous contemporary, Akbar, who likewise engaged closely with Hindu ideas, practices, and practitioners. Like his Mughal contemporary, Ibrahim II was accused of deviating from Islam as understood by some of his subjects. Several literary sources, including his own *Kitāb-i Nauras*, mention the sultan's personal devotion to the goddess Saraswati. But there is no physical evidence that he ever installed an image of Saraswati for his personal worship in his palace in Bijapur, as his critics charged. It is only at Kalyana, the heart of the former Chalukya imperium, that we find physical evidence for the possibility of such activity. When the sultan's governor at Kalyana built the Raj Mahal palace in 1592–93, a Chalukya temple was programmatically included in the complex, connected by a passageway to the interior of the palace. Even though it is not clear precisely how the temple was used, there is no disputing that the sultan sought to integrate the temple with the most important royal palace in Kalyana, thereby connecting an `Adil Shahi present with a Chalukya past.

## NOTES

1. J.F. Fleet, 'Sanskrit and Old Canarese Inscriptions, no. XCVII', *Indian Antiquary* (May 1881), 129.

2. Rafi` al-Din Shirazi, *Tazkirat al-mulūk* (composed 1609–12), 319. Unpublished critical edition by Abu Nasr Khalidi, revised by Carl Ernst. We thank Professor Ernst for kindly sharing this with us.

3. Richard M. Eaton, *Sufis of Bijapur, 1300–1700: Social Roles of Sufis in Medieval India* (Princeton: Princeton University Press, 1978), 91–3.

4. The two lesser states were those of the `Imad Shahis of Berar, swallowed up by the Nizam Shahis in 1574, and the Barid Shahis of Bidar, whose territory was reduced to the area around Bidar by 1550, and was finally annexed to Bijapur in 1619.

5. According to Firishta, when Portuguese soldiers under Alfonso de Albuquerque seized the Bijapuri seaport of Goa in 1510, Yusuf used both Westerner and Deccani troops in an unsuccessful attempt to retake the city. John Briggs, trans., *History of the Rise of Mohamadan Power in India* (4 vols, London, 1829; repr. 3 vols, Calcutta: Editions Indian, 1966), 3:17.

6. Ibid., 3:44.

7. Ibid., 3:34.

8. Ibid., 3:27.

9. Ibid., 3:28. The twelve points on the headgear represented the twelve imams of the principal sect of Shi`ism.

10. Ibid., 3:18. Firishta, *Tārīkh* (text), 2: 13.

11. Briggs, trans., *History of the Rise*, 3: 5–7.

12. For a discussion and analysis of this battle, see Chapter 7.

13. Refusing to submit to Krishna Raya's demand, Isma`il withdrew from his capital while his adversary occupied it. Not surprisingly, this incident does not appear in any of the Bijapur chronicles. See Richard M. Eaton, '"Kiss My Foot," Said the King: Firearms, Diplomacy, and the Battle for Raichur, 1520', *Modern Asian Studies* (John F. Richards Commemorative Volume) 43, no. 1 (2009), 289–313.

14. 'The cause of inscribing the date was this that the humiliated Kishtan Rai [Krishna Raya] had been destined to be vanquished on ... March 23 [or May 21], 1522 ... because he laid siege around the above-mentioned fort. By the favour of God and the blessing of the honoured feet of the saints, the cursed Kishtan, thinking his defeat as a prizeable boon, instead of continuing the siege took to flight on the 4th day. In accordance with the order of His Majesty ... `Adil Khan, son of `Adil Khan Ghazi ... the foundation of a bastion and the citadel-wall was laid.' B.D. Verma, *The Glories of Bijapur: A History of its Remains* (India?: n.p., 1964), 82–3. The exact date of this inscription is uncertain because it is not clear whether the text reads the month as Rabi` al-Akhir or as Jumada al-Akhir.

15. Briggs, trans., *History of the Rise*, 3:47.

16. Ibid., 3:48.

17. Ibid., 3:45–6.

18. Haroon Khan Sherwani and P.M. Joshi, eds, *History of Medieval Deccan, 1295–1724* (2 vols, Hyderabad: Government of Andhra Pradesh, 1973), 1:315–17.

19. Verma, *Glories*, 83–4. The standard Sunni Muslim credo reappears two years later on the face of the so-called Karak Bijli bastion, located adjacent to the Chini Mahal some 46 metres west of the gateway, in an inscription recording that all work on the citadel had been completed on 31 May 1546. The credo here appears in letters twice as large as the others on the tablet, further underscoring the Sultan's Sunni identity. Ibrahim also grandly refers to himself in this record not by his given name but as "Abu'l Muzaffar `Adil Shah', or 'the Father of Victory, `Adil Shah'. See Verma, *Glories*, 90, 91. M. Nazim has misread this date as AH 973, corresponding to AD 1565. See M. Nazim, *Bijapur Inscriptions, Memoirs of the Archaeological Survey of India*, no. 49 (Delhi: Manager of Publications, 1936), 49.

20. Verma, *Glories*, 89–90; Nazim, *Bijapur Inscriptions*, 48.

21. Verma, *Glories*, 85–6. 'There is no God but Allah; Muhammad is the apostle of Allah, and `Ali is the friend of Allah.' See also Nazim, *Bijapur Inscriptions*, 47.

22. Verma, *Glories*, 86.

23. The pilaster type is ultimately derived from the pilaster form seen in Sultanate architecture in Delhi in the early fourteenth century, in which the shaft is framed by a vase-shaped base and capital. This form was introduced in the Deccan through the Khalaji and Tughluq conquests, but by the end of the fourteenth century it had been elaborated by subdivision into the type seen here. The specific forms seen in the gateway compare closely with forms seen in some of the Bahmani tombs at Gulbarga.

24. British officials made an estampage of the inscription in 1880, but within a year the inscription itself went missing. In 1964, B.D. Verma wrote that at that time it was in the Bijapur Museum, on the grounds of the Gol Gumbad. See Verma, *Glories*, 58n. The text of the inscription, based on the estampage, was published in Fleet, 'Sanskrit', 126–32.

25. Ibid., 129–31.

26. Ibid., 131.

27. Ibid., 127.

28. Four additional columnar supports were added to the southern group *after* Ibrahim I's construction of the gateway. One of these is a simple, rectangular-sectioned slab, while the other three are also made from recycled columns. But they differ from the original columns in several respects. They are formally simpler and of smaller dimensions, requiring vertical stacking of two shafts in each case. They lack the full sequence of capitals, and some lack any capitals at all. They also interrupt the regular intercolumniation established by the twelve primary columns, suggesting that they were subsequently inserted to alleviate concerns about the load-bearing capacity of the beams they helped support.

29. Cousens did not indicate the total number of columns that were standing at the time he made his study. But of the four 'Hindu Pillars in the Gateway of the Citadel', depicted in Plate IV of his monograph, the one on the right is not presently standing. This would suggest that all the columns indicated on his map (Plate III) were standing at the time of his survey, which is likely the case, since many more were standing in 1955 than are standing today. See Henry Cousens, *Bijapur and Its Architectural Remains: With an Historical Outline of the `Adil Shahi Dynasty* (Bombay: Government Central Press, 1916). Compare with the photograph of the columns taken in the winter of 1955–56 by Sidney Toy, and published in Sidney Toy, *The Strongholds of India* (London: William Heinemann Ltd., 1957), plate 30b.

30. Much of the plinth on the northern side has been removed, so that today the path leading to the gate from within the citadel passes between the columns of this ensemble. See the photograph of the columns taken in 1955–56 and published inToy, *Strongholds*, plate 30b.

31. Cousens, *Bijapur*, 40.

32. *South Indian Inscriptions* (*SII*) XVIII, *Bombay-Karnatak Inscriptions* 3 (1975), no. 51 (p. 38–9), no. 156 (p. 209–11), no. 158 (p. 212–13), no. 165 (p. 227–8), no. 198 (p. 278), no. 216 (p. 292–3, no. 260 (p. 343), no. 271 (p. 352–3), no. 350 (p. 442), no. 377 (p. 458). The editors have raised doubts about the authenticity of two of these, nos 51 and 165, owing to irregularities in their dates and faults in their engraving.

33. For a study of game-boards preserved at contemporary Vijayanagara, see John M. Fritz and David Gibson, 'Game Boards at Vijayanagara', in *Vijayanagara: Archaeological Explorations, 1990–2000, Papers in Memory of Channabasappa S. Patil*, eds John M. Fritz, Robert P. Brubaker, and Teresa P. Raczek (New Delhi: AIIS and Manohar, 2006), 1:65–78.

34. Cousens, *Bijapur*, 40.

35. Such was not, however, the fate of the columns of the Shiva temple mentioned in Someshvara II's inscription just outside the inner gate. Katherine Kasdorf has studied the so-called Mosque of Khwaja Jahan, located inside the citadel and stylistically contemporary with the nearby Karim al-Din mosque (1318). She reports that some of the reused pillars along the façade of this mosque bear thirteenth-century inscriptions in Old Kannada, recorded by Yadava officials and made out in favour of this same Svayambhu Shiva temple. Since some of these inscriptions indicate that additions or renovations were made to this eleventh-century temple several centuries later, we may infer that the temple was flourishing in the period immediately prior to the Khalaji invasions of the early fourteenth century. It therefore seems likely that the Khalajis disassembled this temple soon after their conquest of Vijayapura and assembled this mosque, in part, from components of the temple or its related structures. See Katherine Kasdorf, 'Translating Sacred Space in Bijapur: The Mosques of Karim al-Din and Khwaja Jahan', *Archives of Asian Art* 59 (2009), 66.

36. Briggs, trans., *History of the Rise*, 3:68–70.

37. P.M. Joshi, '`Ali `Adil Shah of Bijapur (1558–80) and His Royal Librarian: Two Ruq'as', in *The Sardhasatabdi Commemoration Volume, 1804–1954*, ed. G.C. Jhala (Bombay: Asiatic Society of Bombay, 1957), 97–8.

38. John Correia-Afonso, 'Bijapur Four Centuries Ago as Described in a Contemporary Letter', *Indica* 1 (March 1964), 87.

39. Ibid., 83.

40. `Ali's authorship of the work was not known until recently noted by Emma Flatt. As is stated on folio 43a of the Chester Beatty Library manuscript (Dublin, Ms. No. IN2), as translated by Professor Flatt, 'The writer (*rāqim*) of these traditions and the narrator (*nāqil*) of these problems and stories, the servant of the people of the house of the Prophet of Allah, is named `Ali, known as `Adil Shah.' Emma Flatt, 'The Authorship and Significance of the *Nujūm al-'ulūm*: A Sixteenth-Century Astrological Encyclopedia from Bijapur', *Journal of the American Oriental Society* 131, no. 2 (2011), 226.

41. Writes Flatt, 'By engaging with and inserting himself and his sultanate into older astrological,

cosmological, and geographical traditions, `Ali `Adil Shah firstly was aligning himself and his sultanate with powerful cosmic forces that were thought to act on daily life in the physical world; secondly he was asserting the antiquity of the geographical borders of the sultanate as a coherent entity; and thirdly he was contributing to ongoing processes of standardizing and disseminating knowledge on *jyotiḥ-śāstra* (astrology) and *`ilm al-nujūm* (science of the stars) among a broader audience. By virtue of the sustained attempt to document, explain, and translate knowledge systems through an approach that intertwined divergent beliefs into a coherent, if broad, single cosmology, `Ali `Adil Shah's *Nujūm al-`ulūm* could play an important role in the development of a courtly culture that transcended disparate ethnic, regional, or religious identities and emphasized both "local" and "cosmopolitan" aspects of knowledge.' Flatt, 'Authorship and Significance', 235.

42. The Qur'an refers to the 'Lord of the Throne' situated above the seven heavens (17:42–4). In Sufi and folk legends the Prophet Muhammad is said to have traversed these heavens during a mysterious night journey accompanied by the archangel Gabriel, in the course of which he spoke with God.

43. Deborah Hutton, *Art of the Court of Bijapur* (Bloomington: Indiana University Press, 2006), 53, 60.

44. One manuscript of the work, completed in 1570 and currently in the Chester Beatty Library in Dublin, contains remarkable illustrations, many of which appear in the distinctive palette of later Bijapur painting: bright orange, moss green, brownish red, and royal blue. See Hutton, *Art of the Court*, 59. These paintings are also discussed in Linda York Leach, *Mughal and Other Indian Paintings from the Chester Beatty Library*, 2 vols (London: Scorpion Cavendish, 1995), 2:819–89.

45. Ibid., 62–3. Emma Flatt argues that in writing this culturally hybridized work, `Ali sought to provide a common focus for his mobile and ethnically diverse nobles, for whom success was measured not in an exalted lineage, but in a refinement of courtly skills. Emma Flatt, 'Courtly Culture in the Indo-Persian States of the Medieval Deccan: 1450–1600', PhD dissertation, School of Oriental and African Studies, London, 2009, 150.

46. Shirazi, *Tazkirat al-mulūk*, 50. Our translation.

47. Briggs, trans., *History of the Rise*, 3:71.

48. Shirazi, *Tazkirat al-mulūk*, 52.

49. Firishta, *Tārīkh-i Firishta* (text), 2:36: 'Ān ḥaḍrat āzarda khāṭir gashta, intiqām-i ū-rābi raf`at-i himmat farḍ shumurda. Laik binābar taqāḍā-yi vaqt zāhir na-sākhta, intiẓār-i furṣat mīkashīd tā dar 972 A.H. kār-i khud bisākht.'

50. Briggs, trans., *History of the Rise*, 3:72.

51. Ibid., 3:73.

52. Ibid., 3:72–4. The same assessment of Rama Raya's behaviour was recorded by Rafi ` al-Din Shirazi. 'Rama Raya', he wrote, 'behaved with unimaginable pride and haughtiness. When `Ali `Adil Shah would set up camp in a place of good climate, Rama Raya's forces would follow behind and order the former's army to pick up and go elsewhere, while Rama Raya took that place. This might happen three times in one day. The issue was not so much the moving of a camp, as it was the enforcement of Rama Raya's word.' Shirazi, *Tazkirat al-mulūk*, 53.

53. See Chapter 7 for a more detailed analysis of this battle.

54. Firishta writes that the wall was completed in 1567, but this is contradicted by inscriptions on the wall's bastions, which indicate building activity lasting until at least as late as 1579. Briggs, trans., *History of the Rise*, 3: 80.

55. Cousens, *Bijapur*, 57.

56. *Epigraphia Indo-Moslemica* (*EIM*) *1935–36*, 4–8, pl. IV(a), IV(b), V(b), V(c), and VI(a).

57. *Epigraphia Indica, Arabic and Persian Supplement* (*EIAPS*) *1963*, 65, pl. XIX(b).

58. *EIM 1939–40*, 18, no. 6, pl. VII(a).

59. Nazim, *Bijapur Inscriptions*, 50.

60. Ibid., 50, 51.

61. Ibid., 49.

62. Verma, *Glories*, 90, 96–7.

63. Briggs, trans., *History of the Rise*, 3:82–3.

64. Firishta, *Tārīkh-i Firishta* (text), 2:45.

65. Briggs, trans., *History of the Rise*, 3: 84. 'Dar hamān rūz but-khāna-yi buzurg-rā shikasta `adālat-panāh va Muṣṭafa Khān barā-yi iḥrāz-i mathūbat-i ukhrawiy banā-yi masjid numūda, sang-hā ba dast-i khūd bar zamīn nihādand.' Firishta, *Tārīkh-i Firishta* (text), 2:44.

66. Henry Cousens, *Chalukyan Architecture of the Kanarese Districts* (Calcutta: Government of India Central Publication Branch, 1926), 94.

67. Evidently, Bankapur had earlier come into Bijapur's hands, either during Ibrahim's 1535–36

campaign against Vijayanagara, or during the campaign against Adoni that same year waged by his general, Asad Khan. By the end of Ibrahim I's reign (1535–58), however, the fort was again lost to Vijayanagara. See A.A. Kadiri, ''Adil Shahi Inscriptions from Bankapur', *EIAPS 1968*, 42–6.

68. M.A. Dhaky and Michael W. Meister, *Encyclopaedia of Indian Temple Architecture*, vol. 1, part 3: *South India, Upper Dravidadesa, Later Phase, 973–1376* (text) (New Delhi: AIIS, 1996), 154.

69. Dhaky argues that the *vimana*'s style belongs to the 1050s, whereas Gerard Foekema proposes that its flat shape and decorated edge would place its construction after 1100. See ibid., 154. Gerard Foekema, *Calukya Architecture: Medieval Temples of Northern Karnataka Built during the Rule of the Calukya of Kalyana and Thereafter, AD 1000–1300*, 3 vols (New Delhi: Munshiram Manoharlal, 2003), 1:133.

70. Dhaky and Meister, *Encyclopaedia*, 154.

71. Foekema, *Calukya Architecture*,1:136.

72. The Great Mosque of Kufa provides an instructive early example. When it was first built in 638, the prayer hall was open along the *qibla* side, such that, in al-Tabari's words, 'a man praying in it could see the convent known as Dayr Hind and the gate of the town known as Bab Jisr.' When the mosque was rebuilt in 670, these visual distractions were eliminated by providing the sanctuary with a solid qibla wall. See K.A.C. Creswell, *A Short Account of Early Muslim Architecture*, revised and supplemented by James W. Allan (Aldershot: Scolar Press, 1989), 7–9.

73. We deduce these alterations from the evidence provided by Henry Cousens, who documented the site in 1885 and published his observations in 1926. The mosque he saw contained fifty-eight columns, counting the six that had been introduced by `Ali `Adil Shah. Such an arrangement is also implied by the plan he published in the same volume. At some time after Cousens's book appeared in 1926, an attempt was made to 'restore' the structure to what was believed to have been its original Chalukya design, obliterating its former identity as a mosque. See Cousens, *Chalukyan Architecture,* 95, plate LXXXIX.

74. The presence of the *miḥrāb* was noted by Cousens, which implies that it was still present when he visited the site in 1885.

75. Cousens, *Chalukyan Architecture*, 94–5.

76. None of this, however, prevented `Ali from indulging in the outright destruction of temples when those were associated with enemies or rebels. Shirazi records that after defeating Vijayanagara at the Battle of Talikota, `Ali destroyed many images and temples (*Taẕkirat al-mulūk*, 319). The sultan's appreciation of Chalukya aesthetics was one thing; his tolerance for political opposition or betrayal was quite another.

77. Shirazi, *Taẕkirat al-mulūk*, 319. Our translation. The author was an Iranian merchant-turned-historian who had joined `Ali's service in 1564 and served his patron as treasurer and royal chamberlain before writing a chronicle of the dynasty's history.

78. In this respect `Ali's transformation of the Aravattukhambada temple into a mosque compares with the mid-twelfth-century Rudra-Mahalaya temple in Siddhpur, Gujarat, which Sultan Nasir al-Din Ahmad Shah I (r. 1410–44) transformed into a congregational mosque around 1414–15. The sultan of Gujarat incorporated three minor shrines of the former temple into the mosque's prayer area, two of them along the qibla wall, while much of the iconography on the jambs and lintels of the entrances to these shrines was left intact. See Alka Patel, 'Architectural Histories Entwined: The Rudra-Mahalaya/Congregational Mosque of Siddhpur, Gujarat', *Journal of the Society of Architectural Historians* 63, no. 2 (June 2004), 144–63.

79. Badayuni, *Muntakhab al-tawārīkh* (Calcutta, 1867), 3:452, cited in Haroon Khan Sherwani, *The Bahmanis of the Deccan* (New Delhi: Munshiram Manoharlal, 1985), 189. See Appendix 2 for a discussion of the chronology of the fort's construction.

80. Kamil Khan's responsibility for these new bastions is recorded in the foundation inscriptions placed on the bastions themselves. These also record that he was assisted by several different governors, styled *nā'ib ghaibat*. Whereas Kamil Khan and the succession of governors appear to have overseen the work, the sultan probably took the initiative in ordering it. For details, see Appendix 2, 'Kalyana'.

81. This is our reading of the date. Written in Old Marathi, the inscription records a gift of 50,000 silver coins [*rūkas*] to Ramana Gauda, who seems to have been the commander of a section (or the whole) of the rampart. Since the inscription does not mention Kamil Khan, work may have begun before his appointment. Our thanks to Sumit Guha for helping interpret the inscription.

82. *EIM 1935–36*, 4–8, pl. IV(a), IV(b), V(b), V(c), and VI(a).

83. Briggs, trans., *History of the Rise*, 3:87–101.

84. Ibid., 3:107–11. Harsh measures such as these suggest a need to qualify the conventional image of Ibrahim II as something of a beads-and-flowers hippie *avant le temps*. For the vicissitudes of `Ain al-Mulk's career, see Phillip B. Wagoner, 'Fortuitous Convergences and Essential Ambiguities: Transcultural Political Élites in the Medieval Deccan', in *Surprising Bedfellows: Hindus and Muslims in Medieval and Early Modern India.*, ed. Sushil Mittal (Lanham, MD: Lexington Books, 2003), 32–9.

85. Briggs, trans., *History of the Rise*, 3:106–7.

86. Ibid., 3:103.

87. P.M. Joshi, 'Asad Beg's Mission to Bijapur, 1603–04', in *Prof D.V. Potdar 61st Birthday Commemoration Volume*, ed. S. Sen (Poona, 1950), 191.

88. Shirazi, *Tazkirat al-mulūk*, 172.

89. B.G. Gayani, 'Kitab-i-Nauras', *Islamic Culture* 19, no. 2 (1945), 144; Nazir Ahmad, ed., *Kitab-i-Nauras by Ibrahim Adil Shah II* (New Delhi: Bharatiya Kala Kendra, 1956), 31.

90. Song 56 in Ahmad, *Kitab-i Nauras*, 146–7.

91. According to Shirazi, he did not officially rename the city 'Vidyapur' until 1603–04. Shirazi, *Tazkirat al-mulūk*, 170.

92. Alain Danielou, *Hindu Polytheism* (London: Routledge & Kegan Paul, 1964), 260.

93. A painting of Ibrahim by Farrukh Beg depicts the sultan dressed in saffron robes and playing a musical instrument. Even his fingernails are red, just as described in song 56 of the *Kitab-i Nauras*. See Navina Najat Haidar, 'The *Kitab-i Nauras*: Key to Bijapur's Golden Age', in *Sultans of the South: Arts of India's Deccan Courts, 1323–1687*, eds Navina Najat Haidar and Marika Sardar (New York: Metropolitan Museum of Art, 2011), 39 and figure 17. The painting of Saraswati is likewise linked with song 56, in that it is inscribed 'Ibrahim, whose father is guru Ganapati and his mother pious Saraswati'; Navina Najat Haidar, 'The *Kitab-i Nauras*', 34ff. and figure 13.

94. A.R. Kulkarni, 'Social Relations in the Marathi Country in the Medieval Period', *Indian History Congress, Proceedings*, 32nd session (Jabalpur, 1970), 234.

95. Muhyi al-Din b. Saiyid Mahmud Qadiri, *Ṣaḥīfat-i Ahl-i Hudā* (Hyderabad: National Fine Printing Press, 1966), 31. This is an Urdu translation of a Persian biography of Qadiri Sufis compiled in 1796–97, based on notes collected by Abu'l-Hasan Qadiri II in 1684–85.

96. Yazdani, 'Inscriptions from Kalyani', 10–11.

97. Specifically, the doorframe of the Kalyana temple is stylistically almost identical to that of the Mahadeva temple in Jalsingi, some 45 kilometres east of Kalyana and datable to the reign of Vikramaditya VI (1076–1127). It also compares quite closely with the doorway of the Kedareshvara temple at Dharmapuri (in Beed district, Maharashtra), dated to 1128. For the Jalsingi temple, see Foekema, *Calukya Architecture*, 1:401ff.; for the Dharmapuri temple, see Foekema, *Calukya Architecture*, 226ff.

98. The temple's exterior is nowhere visible, as the Raj Mahal palace has been built all around it.

99. Nazim, *Bijapur Inscriptions*, 38. The translation is that of A.J. Arberry, *The Koran Interpreted* (New York: Macmillan Co., 1970), 83.

# SECTION THREE

# Warangal and the Kakatiya Legacy

CHAPTER 5

# Shitab Khan and the Restoration of Kakatiya Cults and Temples

One of the *amīr*s of Humayun Shah Bahmani was Shitab Khan, who fled the court for his life. On the 27th of the month of Ramazan—which is the time for repentance—the Sultan ordered the inmates of Shitab Khan's *ḥaram* to present themselves in the courtyard of the court, where there was an assemblage of common people and soldiers. There he tortured them with various shameful and obscene acts.

—`Ali Tabataba, *Burhān-i ma'āthir*[1]

Pāncālirāya, Beloved of the Gopis, created endless quantities of pure cloth and gave it to Panchali, from his pity at seeing her so wretched with humiliation—his image, which had been removed from its place through the power of an evil disturbance, was re-established on its throne by Bhogi Chittapa Khana [that is, Shitab Khan], the lord of the earth.

—Warangal Inscription of Shitab Khan, 1504[2]

In this chapter and the next, we shall see that it was not only Chalukya antiques that were reused toward political ends in the sixteenth century. Already in 1504, some thirty years before the earliest known instance of Chalukya reuse, political figures in the eastern Deccan were creatively deploying relics of one of the Chalukyas' major successor states, the Kakatiya kingdom of the Telugu-speaking Andhra region (r. 1163–1323). As we have seen in Chapter 2, Warangal, the former Kakatiya capital, had fallen to the Tughluq sultans of Delhi in 1323 and its great Svayambhu Shiva temple demolished by Ulugh Khan, the future Sultan Muhammad bin Tughluq. But the Tughluqs proved unable to hold on to their prize, which slipped from their grasp within a decade of its conquest. Then, after a period of control by two local dynasties—the Musunuri chiefs (c. 1331–68) and the Recerla Nayakas of Rachakonda (c. 1368–1424)—in 1424 Warangal was reduced to a provincial governorship of the Bahmani sultans. In 1504, however, a fascinating but shadowy figure all but unknown in recorded history burst upon the scene and managed to wrest the city from its Bahmani governor. This was Shitab Khan, the former Bahmani *amīr* mentioned in the first epigraph to this chapter. Established now in the old Kakatiya capital, this political upstart issued a monumental inscription in which he boldly presented himself as a worthy successor to the kings of that bygone line. He also proclaimed that he had restored the cults of three deities associated with the Kakatiya state. Luckily, evidence of his patronage of two of these cults is preserved in the archaeological record. Thanks to the mutually illuminating relationship between these physical remains and textual sources, we are afforded an unusually clear and detailed view of Shitab Khan's interactions with the Kakatiya past, and thereby of the mutual relations between power, memory, and architecture.

We shall see in Chapter 6 that the Kakatiyas' urban legacy also inspired another sixteenth-century polity of the eastern Deccan, the Qutb Shahi Sultanate of Golconda. But the Qutb Shahi sultans' response to that legacy differed fundamentally from that of Shitab Khan. Whereas the latter made alterations and additions to the fabric of Warangal itself, the Qutb Shahi response was conceptual in nature. In 1592, corresponding to the advent of the second Islamic millennium of AH 1000, Qutb Shahi rulers laid out their new capital, Hyderabad, some 130 kilometres southwest of Warangal. Its prominent mosques, *`āshūr-khānas*, and other religious foundations reflect the new capital's deeply Islamic character. But in its underlying urban form and in the specific character of several of its primary urban landmarks, the city just as ineluctably reveals the impact of Warangal's Kakatiya legacy.

The cases presented in these two chapters thus add something new to our understanding of the links between architecture and historical memory in the sixteenth century. Most importantly, they highlight the continuing symbolic force of a built cityscape and the power of urban ruins to capture and hold the political imagination of sixteenth-century rulers. As we have seen in Chapter 3, knowledge of the Chalukya imperium was mediated both through individual architectural monuments and through written texts, including historical inscriptions and Chalukya-era literary works that lived on into the sixteenth century. Although comparable texts likewise preserved something of Kakatiya historical memory, the living remains of the city of Warangal itself played a more important role in structuring and transmitting that memory. Inevitably, the city had accumulated substantial changes and additions during the nearly two centuries that had elapsed since the end of the Kakatiya era. But its monumental infrastructure nonetheless remained largely intact—its walls and gateways, its road systems, and above all its central plaza defined by the four *toraṇa*s of the ruined Svayambhu Shiva temple. Saturated with memories of the Kakatiyas, these buildings, ruins, and locations provided constant reminders of the dynasty that had produced them. It is little wonder that here, in the sixteenth century, the first written accounts of Kakatiya history began to emerge.

## THE RISE OF SHITAB KHAN

According to local traditions (*kaifiyat*s) recorded in the early nineteenth century, the man who would eventually take Warangal in 1504 began life not as 'Shitab Khan' but as 'Sitapati', or 'Sitadu' for short.[3] Said to have been born in Rajapudi, a small village in coastal Andhra near the Godavari delta, Sitadu belonged to the low-ranking Boya caste, whose members traditionally followed the humble occupations of fishermen and palanquin bearers. As a boy, Sitadu worked in the house of a Niyogi brahman named Avasarala Peddiraju, tending his flocks in return for food and shelter. One day—or so the story goes—Peddiraju was going out to the fields to bring lunch to Sitadu when he was astonished to see the boy sleeping, his head shaded from the sweltering sun by the hood of a cobra. Recognizing this as a sure sign that the herd-boy would grow up to become a great and powerful man, Peddiraju relieved the boy from his herding duties and gave him a rigorous military training instead. In gratitude, Sitadu promised that whatever wealth he won would all belong to Peddiraju. The young man was given command first of 20 men, then of 200, and before long he was in charge of 500 men. He fought the Koya tribes of the nearby jungles, built a fort, and appointed the brahman Peddiraju as his minister. In short, he quickly established his credentials as a successful military commander and a rising political figure.

Much of this narrative is of course recognizable as the stuff of myth and legend, which we should not take too literally as a source for Shitab Khan's early career. But in its bare outlines—a rags-to-riches story of the humble herd-boy's transformation into a powerful military leader—it is probably not far from the mark. Certainly, nothing in the historical record contradicts the story's portrayal of Shitab Khan as an upstart, someone able to transcend his low caste origins by native talent and by pursuit of a military career.

The narratives of the kaifiyats shed little light on the circumstances of Sitadu's migration from the coast into the Deccan's interior, but he must have made this move prior to the mid-1450s, arriving at the Bahmani capital of Bidar towards the very end of the reign of Sultan Ahmad Shah II (1436–58).[4] We meet him passing in and out of the pages of both Tabataba's and Firishta's histories—although now with the new name of Shitab Khan—the first reference appearing in Tabataba's account of the calamities attending Humayun Shah's short but tumultuous reign (1458–61).[5] Like many other Telugu-speaking Hindus who entered Bahmani service in Telangana, this young warrior from the coast seems to have had little difficulty in quickly acculturating himself to the Persianate world of the court. We see this transformation in his own regular use, when referring to himself, of the name 'Shitab' (Pers. 'haste') instead of Sitapati, and of the Persianized (ultimately Mongol) title 'Khan', which Ahmad Shah presumably bestowed upon him in recognition of his talent and service. His Persianized name and title evidently became important components of his identity, as he would retain them even after his political retreat from the Persianate world later in life.[6]

Despite Shitab Khan's success as a young Bahmani officer, subsequent events conspired to set him on a different path, turning him into a confirmed enemy of the Bahmanis. According to Tabataba's chronicle *Burhān-i ma'āthir*, he was one of the many Bahmani officers who were viciously persecuted by Sultan Humayun Shah Bahmani after a series of attempted coups during his short reign. Later chroniclers would depict Humayun as an unstable ruler subject to fits of unbridled anger; Firishta even assigns him the sobriquet '*ẓālim*' 'the cruel'.[7] We are nowhere told exactly how Shitab Khan incurred Humayun's wrath, but he might well have been involved with some of those who plotted against the sultan. Whatever happened, we know from Tabataba's chronicle that around 1459–60, Shitab Khan was forced to flee for his life, leaving the women of his harem behind in Bidar, and that although it was the month of Ramadan and thus 'a time of repentance', the sultan ordered them to appear in a courtyard of the palace, where they were 'tortured with various shameful and obscene acts' before an assembly of common people and soldiers.[8]

After having his women ignominiously tortured by his own sultan, Shitab Khan disappears from the historical record for some forty-five years. Although neither Tabataba nor Firishta provides any details, it seems likely that he fled towards the coast, stopping off in eastern Telangana to disappear into the jungly hills and bide his time. In the mid-fifteenth century the eastern portions of Telangana were still very much a no-man's-land, lying between the eastern marches of the Bahmani kingdom and the even wilder zone of the Eastern Ghats, with their heavily forested mountains and tribal populations. Presumably, he would have used this time to forge alliances with various families of local chiefs and petty rajas who dominated the region. He quite likely would have been counted among the unnamed Hindu '*zamīndār*s of Telangana' repeatedly mentioned by Firishta in his account of events in the latter half of the century. Centred on the fortified towns of Warangal, Kondapalli, and Rajahmundry, these warlike chiefs are described by Firishta as perpetual thorns in the side of the Bahmanis, constantly vying with them for control of the Deccan's easternmost territories.[9]

But then in 1504, after this nearly forty-five-year hiatus, Shitab Khan suddenly reappears in the historical record, just as the Bahmani state was coming apart at the seams. This time, however, he is represented neither in Persian nor in Telugu, but in Sanskrit—as 'Sitāpa Khāna' or 'Chittāpa Khāna'—in thirty-six verses of fulsome praise composed by his brahman court poet, Madhava, and recorded for posterity on the four sides of a pink granite stele planted at the centre of Warangal (Figure 5.1).[10] Shitab Khan had this text composed to mark his conquest of the city in 1504. It is his only extant epigraphic record.

The inscription does not name the enemy from whom Shitab Khan wrested the city, but we know from other sources that Warangal was then under the governorship of Sultan Quli Qutb al-Mulk, who would soon found the Qutb Shahi kingdom but at this time was still a loyal Bahmani servant.[11] In the very first verse the poet states only that 'Sitāpa Khāna' 'captured the beautiful capital called Ekopala (i.e. Warangal), which had been taken by the Yavanas'—that is, by Persianate 'Turks'.[12] The verse identifies Shitab Khan as belonging to the Bhogi dynasty (*Bhogi-kula*), calling him 'the ornament of the kings of the earth' and 'an equal to Vikramaditya', invoking the memory of the famed Chalukya emperor Vikramatidya VI (r. 1076–1126). From the rhetoric employed both here and throughout the rest of the inscription, it is clear that Shitab Khan was boldly asserting his status as a paramount king. In doing so, moreover, he was now using Sanskritic and not Persianate terms and ideas—suggesting how actors in the sixteenth-century Deccan could draw upon, at will, the values and norms of either the Persian cosmopolis or those of the Sanskrit cosmopolis, or both simultaneously.

Later Persian historical sources corroborate the testimony of Shitab Khan's inscription and relate his growing power in the years following his capture of Warangal. By 1512, according to the anonymous *Tārīkh-i Muḥammad Shāh*, the enterprising ex-amīr had amassed an infantry force of 12,000 men and carved out a broad swathe of territory in eastern Telangana, stretching from Warangal south to Khammamet and on down to Bellamkonda, just across the Krishna River. Feeling threatened by this rising power to his east, Sultan Quli resolved to crush Shitab Khan once and for all. In his first campaign against the Telugu upstart, the sultan succeeded in taking Bellamkonda, but Shitab Khan fell back to Khammamet where he assembled a confederacy of all the neighbouring petty rajas. In a second campaign, Sultan Quli managed to rout

**Figure 5.1** Warangal Fort. Shitab Khan's inscription, now standing in the sculpture-garden on the Svayambhu Shiva site.

this huge force and take Khammamet, forcing Shitab Khan to flee to Kondapalli. There he persuaded that city's Gajapati governor that the whole of the Gajapati kingdom of Orissa would be threatened if a coalition were not assembled to defeat Sultan Quli (see Figure A2.3, p. 360). Alarmed, the Gajapati king mobilized his entire army of 300,000 infantry and 30,000 horses and sent it south to join the forces of Shitab Khan and his allies to protect the threatened coastal districts. In a pitched battle fought near the Krishna River at Palunkchipur, Sultan Quli again triumphed, despite being vastly outnumbered by Shitab Khan and his Orissan allies. Sultan Quli's armies continued to press northeastwards across the coastal tracts, taking Kondapalli, Eluru, and Rajahmundry before finally concluding a treaty with the Gajapati king and accepting the Godavari River as the boundary between their respective kingdoms.[13]

Although the Persian chronicles fail to mention the subsequent fate of Shitab Khan, we are afforded several tantalizing glimpses of his later career through two works of Telugu literature dating to the second half of the sixteenth century. According to the preface to Addanki Gangadhara-kavi's *Tapatī-Samvaraṇamu*, a work commissioned by Sultan Quli's son Ibrahim Qutb Shah (r. 1550–80), Shitab Khan was forced to flee to safety by crossing the Godavari River and taking refuge with the Gajapati king.[14] This would have been in about 1512 or 1513, following his defeat at the hands of Sultan Quli. We also hear of Shitab Khan in *Rāyavācakamu*, a retrospective account of the reign of the Vijayanagara king Krishna Raya (r. 1509–29) dating to the very end of the sixteenth century. Here, in the description of one of Krishna Raya's campaigns against the Gajapatis of Orissa dating to about 1515–16, Shitab Khan is said to have ambushed the Vijayanagara forces as they were marching through the mountain passes into the Gajapati kingdom. In this encounter, he reportedly commanded a force of 60,000 mounted archers who 'let loose a storm of arrows that fell like a monsoon cloudburst on the horsemen and foot soldiers in the passes'. Krishna Raya was able to repel Shitab Khan only by sending a small force of his best-trained cavalry to attack him from the rear. After this defeat, according to *Rāyavācakamu*, the Vijayanagara army pursued Shitab Khan all the way back to his unnamed fort. Then he vanishes forever from historical records.[15]

By 1516, Shitab Khan's career had come full circle. Starting as a young and enterprising Hindu warrior in the coastal districts, he subsequently moved into the interior Deccan where he served the Bahmani court, adjusting to its Persianate culture. Upon encountering first adversity then humiliation in the Bahmani capital of Bidar around 1459–60, he faded into the forests of eastern Telangana, only to emerge forty-five years later as a rebel and ascendant king who in 1504 presented himself in a familiar Indic style, and as a restorer of earlier glory. Meeting his undoing in the form of an even more talented and tenacious warrior—Sultan Quli—he was once again forced back to the coast and into a subordinate position, needing the protection of a more successful king. It was here, in the Godavari hills where he had spent his youth some eighty years before, that he seems to have spent his final days, a servant of the Gajapati kings of Orissa.

## SHITAB KHAN AND THE PRIZE OF WARANGAL, 1504

Viewed in hindsight, Shitab Khan ultimately failed in his attempts to attain paramount status. But from the perspective of the early years of the sixteenth century, when he controlled the major forts of eastern Telangana between the Godavari and Krishna Rivers, he must have appeared as the next rising star on the political scene. Indeed, had Sultan Quli not gained the upper hand, it might well have been Shitab Khan's descendants in the 'Bhogi Dynasty' that ended up controlling the eastern Deccan for the next century and a half, and not Sultan Quli and his Qutb Shahi successors. Clearly, Shitab Khan possessed the political skills to rally the lesser chiefs and petty rajas of Telangana under his banner, and the diplomatic skills to enlist as his ally one of the most powerful monarchs of his day, the Gajapati king of Orissa. However brief the period of his success, Shitab Khan managed to transform himself from just another local chief into a charismatic royal figure embodying considerable power and authority.

To effect this change, Shitab Khan followed a strategy well established in the Deccan for nearly a millennium. Demonstrating one's power in battle signalled only the first step in this strategy. One also had to conform to Sanskritic models of kingly behaviour, which included repairing irrigation facilities, making *agrahāram* grants to support the livelihood of brahman scholars and ritual specialists, and appointing brahmans with administrative skills to help govern one's kingdom. Crucially, these brahmans authored or commissioned works of *kāvya* poetry and *praśasti*s that helped construct a heroic image of the ruler—a project of which the poets themselves were perfectly aware.[16] One brahman poet who praised Shitab Khan was Carigonda Dharmanna, a resident of Warangal who, while patronized by Shitab Khan's minister, authored the Telugu work *Citra-bhāratamu*.[17] In praising the qualities and accomplishments of Shitab Khan—'a moon to the ocean of the Bhogi Dynasty' (I, 12)—Dharmanna compared his sovereign to legendary kings of the past:

He was
another Mandhatri
in conquering the quarters
and causing his valour to shine
another Sagara
in establishing new oceans,
in the irrigation tanks of Pakhal and other places
another Nriga
in giving, every year,
thousands of cows to the brahmans
another Rama
in granting villages
to gods and brahmans.[18]

Whereas Dharmanna praised Shitab Khan by appealing to conventional models of royal behaviour that conformed to the universalist ideals of the Sanskrit cosmopolis, Madhava—the author of the Warangal inscription that we are considering here—referred directly to the historic site his patron had just conquered: Warangal, more particularly, Kakatiya Warangal. His very first verse celebrates Shitab Khan's capture of Warangal, which is called not just a city, but a 'capital' (*rājadhāni*), implicitly invoking its earlier status under the Kakatiyas. Twenty-six verses later, our poet elaborates such associations, stating that

the great and prosperous king Shitab Khan, foremost in the family of Bhogi, captured for the worship of gods and brahmans the beautiful city of Warangal, *which was formerly ruled by a number of virtuous kings belonging to the Kakatiya family*, and which shines, even now, like the city of Kubera [the god of wealth] by possessing treasures of various kinds.[19]

By invoking the memory of the Kakatiyas and by magnifying the greatness of his patron, Madhava effectively presents Shitab Khan as having restored Warangal to its former Kakatiya greatness.

This theme of checking further decay and restoring Warangal's moral order to its original integrity is explained at the very end of the inscription. Here, Madhava recounts Shitab Khan's rescue of three Kakatiya deities in 1504 and his efforts to reinstate the worship and veneration they had lost following the Tughluq conquest of Warangal in 1323. Two of these deities were explicitly associated with the Kakatiyas. The first is 'the Goddess' (*Devi*), described as 'the mother of the world and the Lakshmi of the throne of the Kakatiya kingdom'.[20] Although her proper name is not mentioned, we can recognize her as Kakati, the Kakatiyas' own tutelary goddess, from whom the dynasty derived its name.[21] The second is Svayambhu Shiva, the Kakatiya state deity whose temple, located at the very centre of Warangal, had been demolished by the Tughluq army. Madhava describes Svayambhu Shiva as 'the wish-fulfilling jewel for the protection of the Kakatiya family, whose acts are pleasing and deep on account of the ocean of his mercy'.[22] The third deity, the only one Madhava does not explicitly connect with the Kakatiyas, is Panchaliraya, the 'Lord of Draupadi' ('Panchali' being one of Draupadi's common epithets), who we know is a form of Krishna. In all likelihood, Panchaliraya's temple had also been established in the Kakatiya period.

The inscription states that the images of 'the Goddess' and Panchaliraya had been removed from the shrines where they were first consecrated (*sthānāt calitaṃ, uccāṭitā sthānataḥ*)—Panchaliraya's 'through the power of an evil disturbance', and that of the Goddess 'by the evil Turks'.[23] Presumably, both had been uprooted from their temples during the Tughluq conquest of 1323, which we know had been the case with their companion, Svayambhu Shiva. Since Shitab Khan is further said to have 're-established' these two images (*āsthāpi punar*; *punar sthāpayat*), he evidently performed the formal rite of re-consecration, or *punaḥ pratiṣṭhā*, which Hindu ritual treatises prescribe for restoring the worship of images that for any reason had been desecrated or damaged.[24] However, whereas Warangal's new ruler claims to have restored the images of Panchaliraya and the Goddess to active ritual worship in their respective temples, there is no mention that Svayambhu Shiva's linga—the most politically charged Kakatiya icon—had been either desecrated or re-consecrated. Shitab Khan is said only to have acquired 'authority' or 'lordship' (*aiśvaryam*) by daily 'venerating' (*saṃpūjya*) the image.[25]Although the linga's severed shaft rendered it unfit for re-consecration and formal worship, it evidently could still serve as the object of informal reverence.[26]

Superficially, Shitab Khan appears to have been engaging in purely religious acts—the re-consecration and veneration of religious images. But given the inscription's larger agenda of presenting Shitab Khan as a restorer of the Kakatiya moral–political order, and the fact that two of the deities involved were intimately connected with the Kakatiya state, we must understand these restorations also as political acts, intended to bolster Shitab Khan's authority. Symbolically, re-establishing the goddess Kakati on the pedestal from which she had been uprooted was tantamount to restoring the dynasty to which she had given her name. And by positioning himself as a humble votary of Svayambhu Shiva, thereby acquiring 'authority' (aiśvaryam) from the Kakitayas' Cosmic Overlord (*rāṣṭra-devatā*), Shitab Khan effectively presented himself as a successor to the bygone dynasty, ruling over a 'restored' Kakatiya kingdom from its seat at Warangal.

This is as far as the inscription takes us in our effort to understand Shitab Khan's actions. Its testimony illuminates the difference in ritual status between the images of Panchaliraya and Kakati, both of which could be formally re-consecrated in their temples, and Svayambhu Shiva's linga, which had been too badly damaged to receive this kind of treatment. It also alerts us to Shitab Khan's use of the memory of the Kakatiyas in presenting himself as a legitimate and independent ruler. Yet the inscription remains frustratingly silent on questions relating to the tangible, physical aspects of his actions. Where were the restored temples of Panchaliraya and Kakati located? What did they look like? Were these deities housed in Kakatiya-period temples that had somehow escaped destruction at the hands of the Tughluqs, or were they built anew by Shitab Khan? If the latter were the case, did they employ Kakatiya-period building components or otherwise allude to the Kakatiya past through stylistic means? And what about the enigmatic linga of Svayambhu Shiva? If it were indeed too damaged to be re-consecrated in a temple sanctum, then where was it located and how did it relate to its larger urban environment?

Fortunately, the archaeological record can answer many of these questions for two of these three deities. Although it has not been possible to trace the temple of the restored goddess Kakati, the temple of Panchaliraya can be clearly recognized in a temple today known as the Venkateshvara-gudi, lying some 200 metres northwest of the eastern gateway in Warangal's inner stone wall. The linga of Svayambhu Shiva is also preserved; significantly, it is located not inside a temple, but in the open-air courtyard of the Shambhuni-gudi, a Shaiva shrine lying less than 100 metres south of the linga's original home in the Svayambhu Shiva temple complex. In the next two sections, we consider the material testimony provided by the Svayambhu Shiva linga, while the chapter's concluding sections turn to the Panchaliraya temple.

## FROM CULT ICON TO DYNASTIC TALISMAN: PEREGRINATIONS OF THE SVAYAMBHU SHIVA LINGA

What can be recognized as Svayambhu Shiva's linga today rests upright on the ground on the eastern side of the Shambhuni-gudi complex, where it appears as if it had sprouted organically out of the earth (Figure 5.2). It conforms to the 'four-faced linga' (*catur-mukha-linga*) type, in which four busts of Shiva in his anthropomorphic form project in high relief from the cylindrical shaft, one facing out towards each of the four quarters. Like other members of its class, this linga originally had an octagonally sectioned extension that continued downward beneath the four busts and anchored the shaft firmly in the socket of its pedestal (Figure 5.3).[27]

Only a small portion of the octagonally sectioned shaft remains intact today, however, as most of it was evidently broken off when the temple was demolished. Four-faced lingas were especially favoured for temples of the

**Figure 5.2** Warangal Fort. The 'four-faced linga' (*catur-mukha-liṅga*) of Svayambhu Shiva.

**Figure 5.3** Warangal Fort. Svayambhu Shiva linga. Several centimetres of the octagonally sectioned 'root' appear just below the busts.

*sarvatobhadra* plan, like the Svayambhu Shiva temple, in which the sanctum has not one but four doorways oriented to the cardinal directions.[28] The identification of this particular four-faced linga with that of Svayambhu Shiva is clinched by the fact that its broken octagonal shaft still lies on the surface of the excavated site, less than 12 metres from the spot it would originally have occupied in the centre of the temple (Figure 5.4).[29] The icon's shaft matches perfectly with the broken upper portion of the four-faced linga in the type of stone from which it is made (dolerite), in its slightly irregular dimensions, and even in its specific fracture patterns. In this particular four-faced linga, we certainly have the Svayambhu Shiva linga of the Kakatiyas.

Moreover, it is likely—though not absolutely certain[30]—that in Shitab Khan's day the Svayambhu Shiva linga stood where it still is today, in the courtyard of the Shambhuni-gudi. First, the stele carved with Shitab Khan's inscription itself appears to have been originally planted in this location. Although the stele has since been moved to the grounds of the ruined Svayambhu Shiva site, where it now stands as part of an open-air sculpture garden, in 1931 it was standing in the Shambhuni-gudi compound. Additional documentary evidence attests to its presence in this location as far back

**Figure 5.4** Warangal Fort. Svayambhu Shiva temple site, broken octagonal root of the *linga* (numbered '130').

as 1816.[31] Second, since epigraphic stele such as this are generally placed close to the objects whose foundations they record, and since the Svayambhu Shiva linga was the most important of his Kakatiya talismans, Shitab Khan would logically have established the rescued linga in this location.[32]

Although Shitab Khan most likely carried out his 'daily veneration' of the Svayambhu Shiva linga in the open air of the Shambhu-ni-gudi compound, this is not where he would have found it when he wrested the city from Sultan Quli in 1504. Epigraphic, material, and literary evidence all suggest that the linga would then have been located several kilometres away, in Hanamkonda—the Kakatiyas' first capital—where it had evidently been taken for safekeeping after the Tughluq conquest. There Shitab Khan would have found it prominently displayed within the so-called Thousand Pillar temple, the triple-shrined temple established by Kakatiya Rudradeva in 1163 to proclaim his independence from the Chalukyas (Figure 5.5). At the time of its founding, this temple would have played a significant part in legitimizing the nascent Kakatiya state. But by 1195 the capital had shifted to the new city of Warangal, and the new cult of Svayambhu Shiva was already eclipsing the older cult of the Tripurushas that had been celebrated in the Hanamkonda temple.[33] As a result, when the Tughluqs finally captured Warangal and demolished the politically charged Svayambhu Shiva temple in 1323, they passed over Rudradeva's earlier

**Figure 5.5** Hanamkonda, Detail of 'Thousand Pillar' temple, founded 1163.

temple, it being by then a place of little political relevance. We have seen in Chapter 2 that while marching en route to Warangal, the Tughluq army passed over another Shiva temple located in the former Chalukya capital of Kalyana, and that several years later they actually facilitated repairs to it. As former royal temples in both Hanamkonda and Kalyana were no longer politically significant in 1323, neither was subject to harm. Accordingly, Hanamkonda's 'Thousand Pillar' temple stands very well preserved even today, missing only the ephemeral brick superstructures that would originally have towered over its three shrines, and marred only by damage caused by uneven settling on its poor foundations—not by any act of desecration.[34]

Thanks to the testimony of a brief inscription preserved in the temple,[35] we know that the person responsible for taking the broken Svayambhu Shiva linga to Hanamkonda was one Gosagi Ishvara-deva, who describes himself as a warrior (*baṇṭu*) who had been in the service of the 'Kakatiya Kings'. The inscription records that Ishvara-deva had 'installed' an 'image of the Four-faced God' (*Caturmukha-devara*) in the pre-existing temple, together with several other uprooted icons that he had evidently salvaged from royal temples in Warangal, and that he had done all this 'for the strengthening of the kingdom of the illustrious Kakatiya kings'. Although the inscription is undated, the fact that its author identifies himself not as the servant of a particular, named, Kakatiya ruler, but as someone who had served the dynasty in the past, strongly suggests a date immediately after the fall of Warangal and the extinction of the Kakatiya line. Additionally, Ishvara-deva's expression of hope for the 'strengthening' of the kingdom suggests a time when the fate of the kingdom was still uncertain—after the fall of Warangal in 1323, but before the total collapse of the state was assured.

In addition to the four-faced linga of Svayambhu Shiva, Gosagi Ishvara-deva established three other images in the Hanamkonda temple. One of these was another linga, referred to in the inscription as an icon of the 'Thousand Lingas' (*vēyi liṃgālūnu*), and recognizable as what would in Sanskrit iconographic treatises be termed a *sahasra-linga* (literally, 'thousand lingas'). This was not literally a collection of a thousand lingas, but rather a single linga with the surface of its shaft carved into a thousand individual linga-like facets.[36] Epigraphic evidence from the time of the last Kakatiya monarch, Pratapa Rudra (r. 1289–1323), establishes that there was at that time a temple in Warangal that contained a Sahasra-linga, and that it had been established by Ganapati, an earlier Kakatiya king (r. 1199–1262).[37] Moreover, the fact that until as late as 1313 this temple continued to receive grants made in the presence of the Kakatiya royal preceptor (*rāca-guru-devara sannidhaṃdu*), suggests that this temple remained politically important into the early fourteenth century. As such it would have made a likely target for desecration by the Tughluq army ten years later. The shaft of this desecrated linga has survived to the present, and may be seen today in the Kasibugga temple at Warangal, where it enjoys the status of a 'guest' image (Figure 5.6).[38]

The other two icons mentioned in Gosagi Ishvara-deva's inscription were not lingas, but paired anthropomorphic depictions of Shiva and the Goddess. The first is referred to as an 'image of the God and Goddess beside Nandi', corresponding to the canonical form of Vrishabharudha-murti, in which Shiva and his consort stand next to Shiva's bull, Nandi.[39] The second is referred to as an 'image of Uma and Maheshvara', easily recognizable as the familiar Uma-Maheshvara-murti, in which the two deities are seated, with the goddess Uma to Shiva-Maheshvara's left. Although the inscription does not say so explicitly, these two images were most likely carved in stone, in the form of stele, and would originally have appeared in secondary shrines or image-niches on the outer walls of temples. We do not hear to which temple or temples they had originally belonged, but the larger context of the inscription suggests that Ishvara-deva had salvaged them from the ruins of Warangal—possibly even from the Svayambhu Shiva and/or Sahasra-linga temples, which had yielded their lingas.

Even though the inscription uses the expression 'to install' (*pratiṣṭha sēyu*)—the same phrase generally used to refer to the ritual consecration of divine images—Ishvara-deva could not possibly have performed an actual re-consecration of these icons. Having been violently uprooted from their temples and severed from their lower shafts, the two lingas would have been rendered 'effectively dead as supports for divinity', in Richard Davis's apt formulation.[40] Even if they had been completely undamaged, they could not have been installed in the 'Thousand Pillar' temple since that temple's three sancta already contained consecrated divinities. Rather than installing the images in any ritual sense, Ishvara-deva was simply installing them in a literal sense: placing them in a secure location so they could be preserved and seen by visitors to the Hanamkonda temple. Although their desecration had rendered them unfit for ritual worship, they could still serve as tokens—and

**Figure 5.6** Warangal. *Sahasra linga* from the Kasibugga Shiva temple.

reminders—of the kings who had originally established them.

Thanks to Ishvara-deva's inscription, and to the good state of preservation of the architectural space to which it refers, we can reconstruct with some certainty the environment in which the redefined Svayambhu Shiva linga would have been displayed. In the first place, the inscription states that the icon of the 'four-faced god' and its companions were installed 'in the Rudreshvara',[41] that is, in the western shrine of the temple's three shrine units. Significantly, the western shrine had been dedicated to a Shiva linga named 'Rudreshvara' after Kakatiya Rudradeva (r. 1158–95), founder of both this temple and the independent Kakatiya kingdom (Figure 5.7).[42] Ritual considerations might plausibly have dictated the placement of the rescued images in that shrine, since these are all Shaiva images, and of the temple's three shrines, only the Rudreshvara housed a Shaiva deity. Yet we believe that political considerations outweighed any others, for the temple's western shrine housed the only one of the temple's three deities whose name explicitly referenced a Kakatiya sovereign.[43] Placement of the salvaged images in the shrine founded by Rudradeva in his own name would have

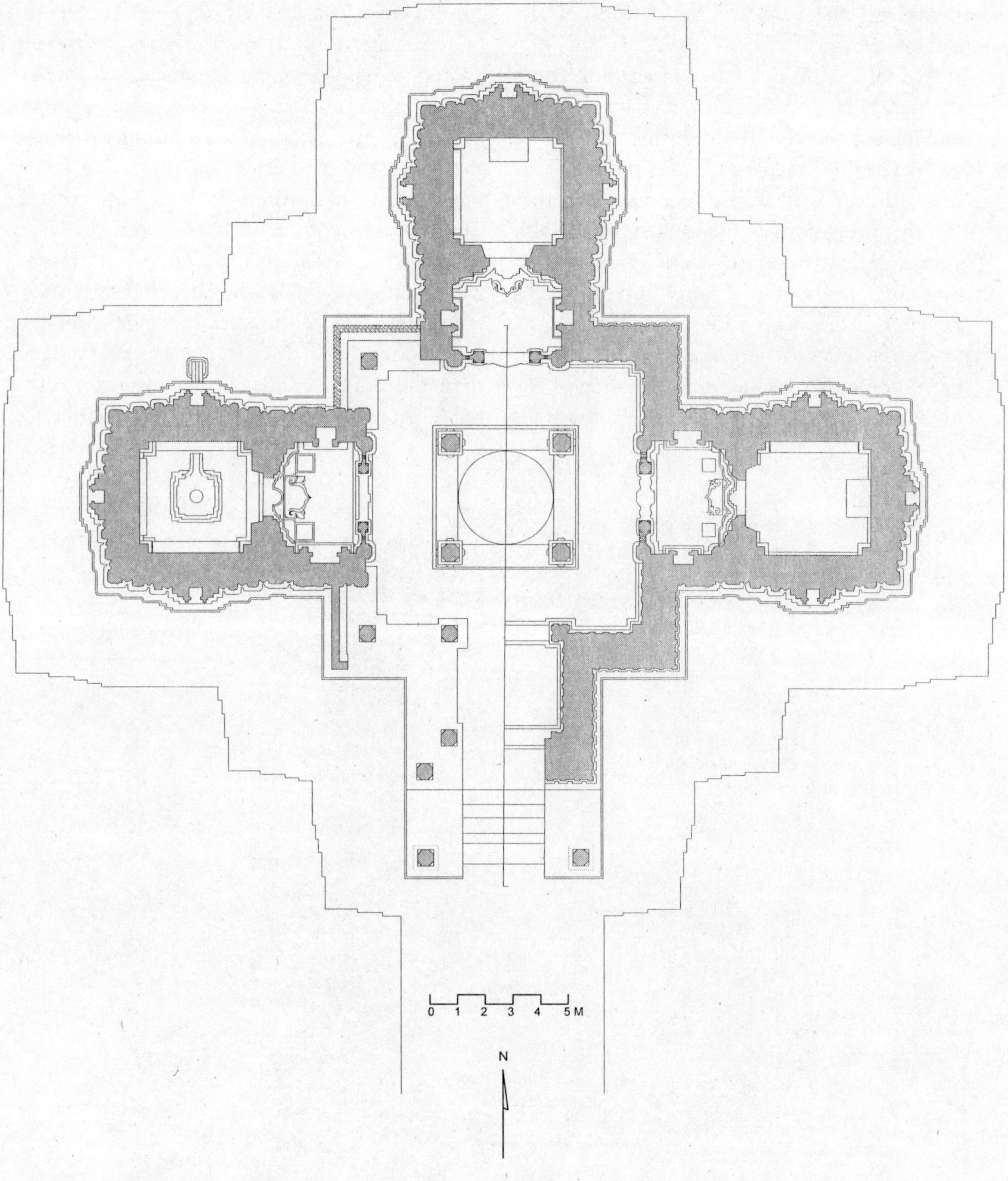


**Figure 5.7** Hanamkonda. Plan of 'Thousand Pillar' temple. The Rudreshvara shrine is the one on the left, showing a *linga* in its sanctum.

emphasized the Kakatiya associations of the relocated images.

Secondly, although the inscription does not state exactly where the rescued images were placed in the Rudreshvara shrine, we can determine their probable positions by considering the available locations together with the dimensions of the broken Svayambhu Shiva and Sahasra-lingas. Four stone shelves projecting from the shrine's interior walls provide the only appropriate location for the images (Figure 5.8). Two shelves are located in the vestibule, one in the middle of each of the side walls. Recessed niches built into the walls behind them considerably augment the depth of these shelves and form miniature shrines, complete with framing doorways, cornices, and shrine towers (Figure 5.9). Unlike these more elaborate niches of the vestibule, the two shelves in the sanctum itself, projecting from the western and northern walls respectively, are simple planks with neither recessed niches nor decorative articulation. As Figure 5.8 shows, the southern shelf-niche in the vestibule, measuring 104 centimetres in height and 93 centimetres in width, is considerably larger than the northern one, which measures only 85 centimetres by 53 centimetres. Thanks to

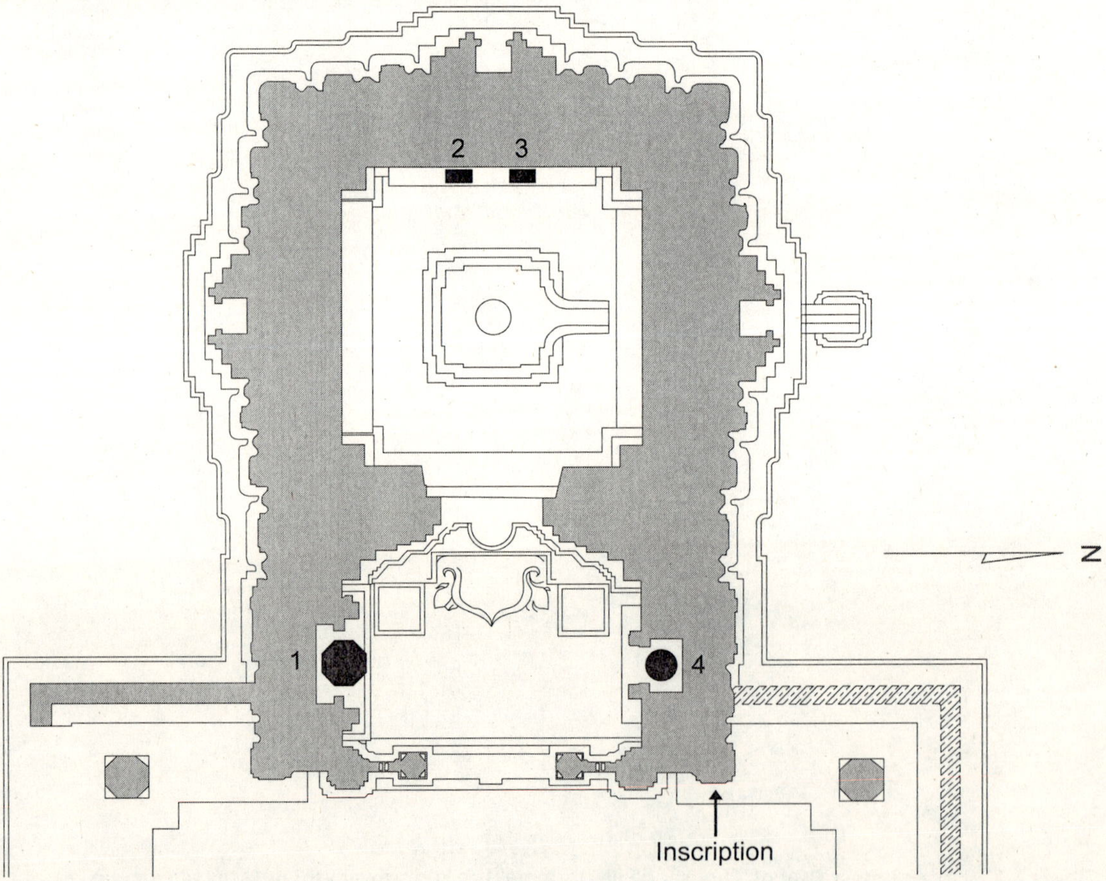


**Figure 5.8** Hanamkonda. Plan of the Rudreshvara shrine in the 'Thousand Pillar' temple, showing the probable locations of Gosagi Ishvara-deva's images.

**Figure 5.9** Hanamkonda. Miniature shrine model framing the shelf-niche on the south wall of the Rudreshvara vestibule.

its greater width, the southern niche, together with its projecting shelf, is just large enough to accommodate the broken four-faced linga of Svayambhu Shiva, while its neighbour on the north is large enough to hold the preserved portion of the Sahasra-linga.[44] This would have left the two projecting shelves within the sanctum for the Vrishabharudha-murti and Uma-Maheshvara-murti images; most likely, both would have been placed together on the rear shelf for maximum visibility from the front of the shrine.[45] This order of placement is possible, given the physical dimensions of the available shelves; it also matches the order in which the images are enumerated in the inscription, which follows the established convention of naming the deities enshrined within a multi-shrined temple by starting from the left and moving to the right.[46]

In effect, Gosagi Ishvara-deva created a striking visual monument to the recently extinguished Kakatiya state. Carefully selecting two desecrated lingas whose cults had contributed to the legitimation of the Kakatiyas, he removed them from the Kakatiyas' last capital of Warangal, recently sacked and desecrated by a Tughluq army, and brought them to the Kakatiyas' original capital of Hanamkonda.

There he installed them as 'guests' in the vestibule of the Rudreshvara shrine, where they were received by a third linga that predated them both, and which the founder of the Kakatiyas had established to mark his dynasty's status as independent monarchs.

Nearly two centuries later, when Shitab Khan entered Hanamkonda after capturing Warangal, we may infer that he would have visited this prominent dynastic shrine. There, he would have encountered three talismanic lingas, each one closely connected in some way with the Kakatiya state. Ritually intact and still occupying its proper location in the sanctum, the Rudreshvara linga would have stood out from the two lingas in the elevated alcove-shrines to either side of the vestibule. The latter clearly did not belong there, but had simply been placed in the shrine for safekeeping, as is confirmed by Gosagi Ishvara-deva's inscription. Recognizing the famous Svayambhu Shiva linga, Shitab Khan would have conceived plans to return it to its proper location at the centre of the city he had just captured. There he would reverently present himself as the custodian of the dynastic talisman, thereby strengthening his claims to authority as a latter-day successor to the Kakatiya kingdom. Accordingly, we may reasonably infer that Shitab Khan had the four-faced linga transferred back to Warangal, where it was installed in a prominent place in the courtyard of the Shambhuni-gudi, very close to its original location.

## THE MOVABLE AND THE IMMOVABLE

Before leaving Shitab Khan's interactions with the Svayambhu Shiva linga, we must briefly consider a colourful folk narrative about the linga's origin that is preserved in a mid-sixteenth-century history of the Kakatiyas, the *Pratāparudra Caritramu* of Ekamranatha. Although the episode makes no mention of Shitab Khan—and at a narrative level even *denies* that the linga had ever left Warangal—the story is full of curious details that, at a deeper, structural level, would appear to reveal the traces of a distant memory of the linga's journey to Hanamkonda and back.

The story recounts that some servants of the Kakatiya king Prolaraju had taken up a temporary job guarding an ox-cart. No mention is made either of the contents of the ox-cart or of its owner; we are only told that the royal servants had undertaken this job in order to earn some extra pay. Towards nightfall, as they were accompanying the cart at a point several miles southeast of the capital, the cart suddenly overturned for no apparent reason. Since it was rapidly getting to be too dark to repair the cart, they decided to camp at the spot of the accident until morning. Before long, a large crowd of people had collected around the cart, wondering what was going on. The next morning,

> as the king's servants were fixing the cart, they noticed that the rim of one wheel had turned to pure gold. Without even thinking of keeping that gold for themselves, they went straight to Kakatiya Prolaraju and told him what had happened. Filled with amazement, the king hurried to the spot together with his advisors, priests, and ministers, and there they discovered buried in the ground a touchstone linga of Shambhu. *The king attempted to move that golden linga full of light to Hanamkonda, but the god would not budge.*[47]

Wishing to understand the significance of the miraculous event, King Prolaraju sends for three of his most respected religious advisors—Ramaranya Shripada, Mahendra Shripada, and Tridandi Rishi—and receives them with honour at the spot. After they have worshipped the god they advise the king that he should construct a new, circular city centred on the self-manifest god. He welcomes their suggestion and appoints them to preside over the ritual establishment of the new city:

In order that the city should be invincible, Ramaranya Shripada traced out the lines for the fort in accordance with the plan called 'wheel of the wisdom of prosperity' [*śrīvidyācakrambu*], and then he had a boundary wall constructed to enclose it. They laid out a road four miles long, running from the gate of Hanamkonda right up to the temple of the touchstone linga of Shambhu, and along both sides of it they constructed temples: 250 temples to Shiva, 100 to Vishnu, 50 to the Goddess; and 40 temples dedicated to various lesser gods. After consecrating these temples, Ramaranya Shripada turned to Kakatiya Prolaraju and said, 'Everyday, immediately after you worship this linga of Shambhu, touch some iron to his linga and it will become pure gold. Distribute that gold daily to brahmans, and your kingdom will be well established indeed.' Thereafter, with the permission of the sages, Kakatiya Prolaraju every day had a 60-pound weight of iron brought and touched it to that radiant touchstone linga, whereupon it would turn into pure gold. And the king daily made a gift of that gold to the gods and brahmans for their own use.[48]

Thus was the king's pre-eminence established, and the continuation of his line assured.

One sees here compelling mythic elements, notably the miraculous manifestation of the linga out of the earth and its mysterious ability to transmute iron into gold. At one level, such elements provide a plausible rationale for why the Kakatiya capital had been shifted from Hanamkonda to the seemingly unlikely site of Warangal—a flat plain with little natural defensive potential. In this respect, the narrative can be taken as a foundation myth for Warangal, although the specific mythic terms in which it is cast—revolving around the miraculous manifestation of a linga—are more common in temple foundation myths than they are in the foundation stories for other cities in the region.[49]

More striking is the story's veiled insistence on the immovability of the miraculous linga. In fact, the tension between the movable and the immovable provides the underlying framework for the episode's whole development. Once the king has been summoned to the site of the linga's miraculous manifestation, he attempts to take the god back to his capital at Hanamkonda. But the linga refuses to budge, and accordingly it is the king, not the linga, who must shift his place of residence. While these details accord with the historical reality of the capital's shift from Hanamkonda to Warangal, on a deeper level they seem to serve as a narrative denial that the linga had ever been taken to Hanamkonda. Even more striking is how the story plays on a stock motif in south Indian narratives of temple origins. Typically, in such narratives, a wish-fulfilling cow, Kamadhenu, reveals a linga's presence by spontaneously releasing milk from her udders as she walks over the site where it is hidden.[50] In the *Pratāparudra Caritramu* episode, however, the linga is discovered not through the agency of a cow, but through the overturning of a bullock cart as it was transporting an *unnamed* cargo from the city of Hanamkonda. When the cart overturns, there is no mention of its spilled contents; in fact, the only new thing that appears on the ground after the incident is the miraculous linga.

It is difficult to avoid the conclusion that, on one level at least, the motif of the overturned ox-cart preserves a veiled memory of the linga's recent return to Warangal, even while explicitly denying that it had ever been moved.

## WARANGAL'S 'VENKATESHVARA-GUDI': THE PANCHALIRAYA TEMPLE OF SHITAB KHAN

When Shitab Khan retrieved the Svayambhu Shiva linga from its temporary home in

Hanamkonda and returned it to its original home in Warangal, he was doubtless intending to bulk up his otherwise feeble claims to legitimate rule over Telangana. His claims of having acquired 'lordship' by 'daily venerating' the Kakatiya dynasty's most politically charged icon had a similar intent. The problem, of course, was that since the icon had suffered irreversible damage, it could never be re-consecrated and restored for regular worship inside a temple.

Such was not the case, however, with respect to one of the other two images that Shitab Khan restored, namely, that of Panchaliraya. Having been spared significant damage, this image could be suitably re-consecrated and installed in a proper temple.[51] But here the problem was that as Panchaliraya's original Kakatiya-era temple was no longer standing in the early sixteenth century, Shitab Khan would therefore have to build a new temple for the god. This he did, and that temple is the one known today as the Venkateshvara-gudi, located a short distance northwest of the eastern gateway in Warangal's inner stone wall (Figures 5.10 and 5.11). For building this temple, Shitab Khan mainly used original Kakatiya-period components, which he had evidently salvaged from the collapsed remains of several different temples. One of these may well have been the deity's original residence, though there is no way to determine this with certainty.

Because of its exclusive reliance on recycled materials, Shitab Khan's Panchaliraya temple appears at first glance to be an authentic Kakatiya structure dating to the early thirteenth century, and it has in fact been accepted as such in all previous scholarship.[52] But the manner in which its constituent parts were reassembled reveals that the structure could not possibly have achieved its present form until well after

**Figure 5.10** Warangal Fort. The so-called Venkateshvara-gudi, here identified as Shitab Khan's Panchaliraya temple.

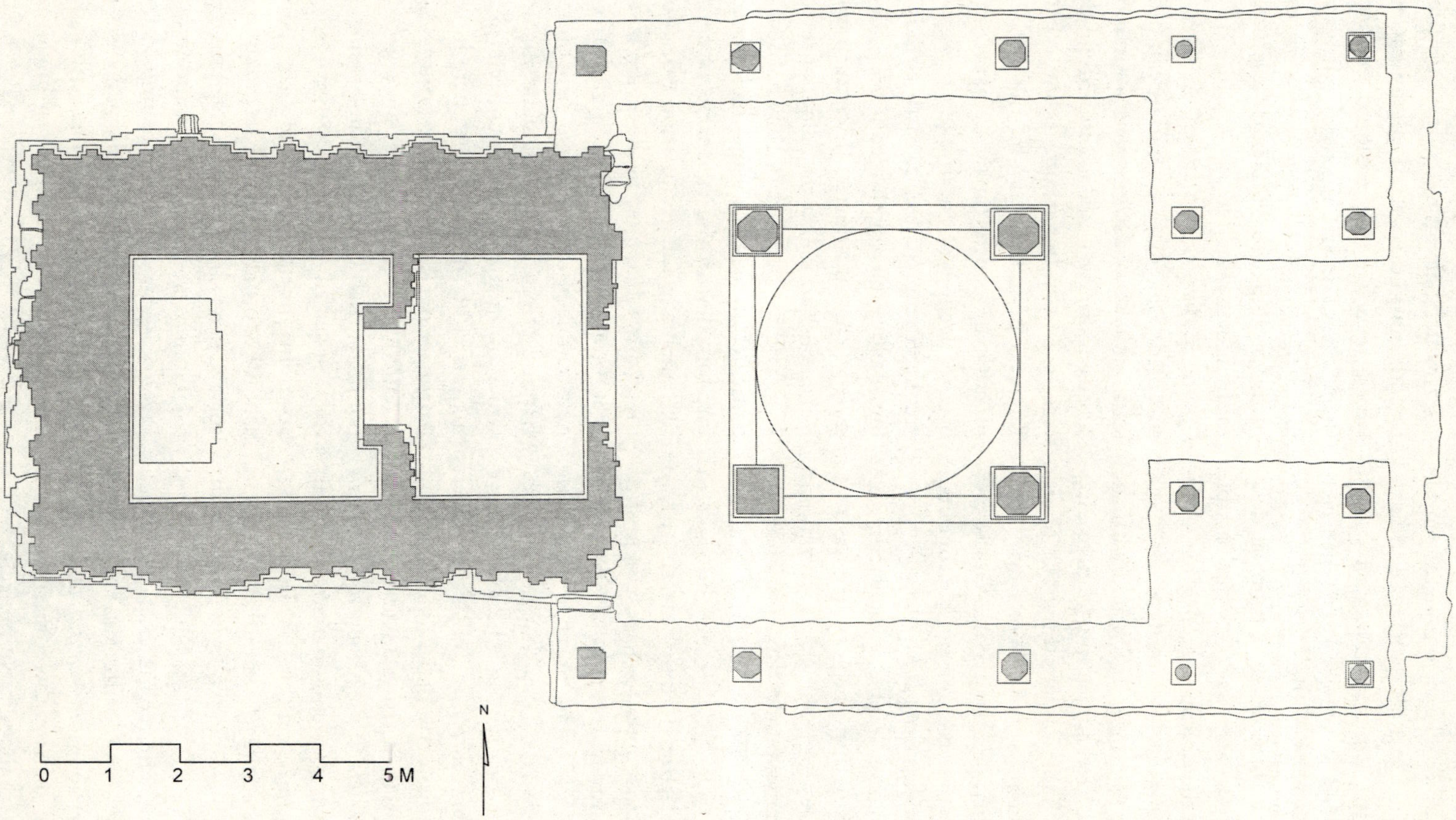


**Figure 5.11** Warangal Fort. Plan of the Panchaliraya temple, reproducing, to scale, the temple's irregularities and anomalies that had been 'corrected' in the *Encyclopaedia of Indian Temple Architecture* drawing, I/3 (Figure 267).

the Kakatiya period. The chronological implications of its structural idiosyncracies indicate that the so-called Venkateshvara-gudi was in reality reassembled in the early sixteenth century; its Vaishnava dedication—recalling that Panchaliraya is a form of the Vaishnava deity Krishna—strongly suggests that this temple must have been the one that Shitab Khan dedicated to Panchaliraya.[53]

The temple's exterior is articulated with the alternating pilastered projections and recesses typical of most Kakatiya-period temples of any pretensions—such as the 'Thousand Pillar' temple at Hanamkonda (Figure 5.5)—and these in turn are derived from the Metropolitan style of the Chalukya period. The specific forms of the Panchaliraya temple closely compare with those of early thirteenth century Kakatiya buildings, suggesting why it is commonly assigned a Kakatiya-period date. But there are serious anomalies. On the southern wall, for one thing, the pilaster shafts to the right of the central projection (*bhadra*) are so grossly misaligned that they appear to have been pushed off their bases, leaving their capitals hanging in mid-air (Figure 5.12). This misalignment arises from the use of two slabs that were not properly matched to the locations in which they have been set. The temple's vertical wall-slabs happen to come in two distinct varieties: one consists of a pilaster shaft to the left and a recessed section to the right, whereas the other reverses this order. At the two projecting units to the right of the central projection (bhadra) in question, slabs with shafts on the *left* were called for, but in assembling the building two *right*-shafted slabs were employed instead. The result is an odd and irregular rhythm, with too much space between the central projection (bhadra) and the adjacent secondary projection (*pratibhadra*), and none at all between the shaft of the corner projection (*karṇa*) and that of the adjacent projection to its right, which belongs to the vestibule (*antarāla*). In addition to this specific alignment problem, which recurs at the southern corner of the shrine's western wall, the temple displays a host of other structural anomalies not encountered in any documented temple that is securely dated to the Kakatiya period.[54]

The various irregularities observed in the so-called Venkateshvara-gudi begin to make sense only if we assume that the temple as it stands today was *not* assembled in the thirteenth century, but at some point well after the Kakatiya period. No doubt, the establishment of sultanate control in the region contributed to the decline of local traditions of temple architecture. Yet decline had already set in long before the Tughluq conquest—in fact, as early as the mid-thirteenth century, when the Kakatiyas were still at the height of their power. As Cynthia Talbot has shown, new temple construction in Telangana had been closely interlinked with the expansion of agricultural settlements in the dry interior. Accordingly, by the 1270s, when most of the region had already been brought under the plough, patronage for new temple foundations had virtually ceased.[55] Because of the reduced demand for new construction, many skilled architects and stone masons either migrated elsewhere in search of patronage or adapted their masonry skills to the production of simple, everyday objects such as boundary markers and grinding stones. Indeed, the impact of declining patronage is vividly apparent in the stark forms and simplified sculptural ornament of the few temples that do survive from this period of stagnation, such as the Gundeshvara temple at Bhutpur[56] and the Pratapa Rudra Gudi at Kolanupaka.[57] In the fourteenth century, documented cases of temple repair and reconstruction demonstrate that the gap between contemporary practice and the Kakatiya tradition had widened even further.[58]

**Figure 5.12** Warangal Fort. Panchaliraya temple: south wall, indicating the misalignment of the pilaster shafts to the right of the broad central projection (*bhadra*).

In one respect, Shitab Khan's restoration of the Panchaliraya temple presented a less challenging situation, in that an abundance of authentic Kakatiya-period components had been preserved in Warangal. These architectural elements were lying on the ground and available for the taking, waiting only to be collected and reassembled. Moreover, since thirteenth-century masons had already adorned them with sculptural ornament, Shitab Khan's masons had no need to engage in extensive sculptural carvings. On the other hand, the builders had to discern the different structural functions of each type of component in order to reassemble them in their correct syntactic order. Foraging through a pile of dilapidated materials, they had to recognize, for example, that a given block carved with a certain sequence of mouldings belonged to the building's plinth and not to its entablature, or that a given member was properly placed when it was oriented in one direction and not the other. Because of the long break in the region's architectural tradition, this type of knowledge could not be automatically assumed on the part of the masons who were constructing the building. Nonetheless, the vast majority of the components *are* in fact assembled properly. The few anomalies that do occur appear to have arisen not because of structural misunderstandings on the part of the builders, but because certain components needed to complete the structure were unavailable. In the case of the misaligned pilaster shafts, for example, the masons evidently realized that the slabs they were using were of the wrong variety, but they utilized them anyway since by that point in the construction, slabs of the proper variety had been exhausted and these presented the best available options.[59] If anything, we should see substitutions of this nature *not* as shortcomings, but as inventive solutions to the problems posed by inadequate supplies of materials. In any case, the building appears authentic enough that even the most competent modern authorities have long mistaken it for a thirteenth-century structure.

In the temple's vestibule doorway we see a particularly remarkable solution to this problem of supply (Figure 5.13). M.A. Dhaky has noted that the doorframe here is 'of a strange sort', referring presumably to its failure to conform to any of the standard designs for doorways attested in the Kakatiya tradition.[60] As in typical Kakatiya doorways, the doorjambs here are divided into a number of projecting sculptural bands (*śākhas*), but the specific ornamental motifs used in these bands are quite different. Moreover, they cover the entirety of

**Figure 5.13** Warangal Fort. Panchaliraya temple: doorway to vestibule. The support pier inside the doorway opening dates to the twentieth century.

**Figure 5.14** Warangal Fort. Panchaliraya temple: detail of right jamb as actually oriented, showing gravity-defying festoons to right and to left.

the jamb, instead of just the upper two-thirds as in typical doorframes. On closer inspection, we see that these were not originally doorjambs at all, but sections of ceiling beams that were rotated from their proper horizontal orientation to serve as vertical members instead. As a result, the many small festooned bands included in their decoration no longer fall naturally downward. Instead, they appear to defy gravity by projecting sideways, in toward the doorway's opening (Figure 5.14). Unable to locate a surviving Kakatiya period doorframe for the vestibule, Shitab Khan's masons responded by modifying ceiling beams to make them seem closely comparable.

Careful inspection of the doorway's masonry fabric reveals further insights. First, each jamb is actually composed of two differently decorated beams standing side-by-side, so as to produce a doorframe that approximates both the proportions and the decorative patterning of a Kakatiya doorway (Figure 5.15). Second, viewed from inside the vestibule, the rear faces of the doorjambs appear completely devoid of sculptural ornamentation, unlike Kakatiya ceiling beams, which are inevitably ornamented on both of their faces (Figure 5.16).

Evidently, Shitab Khan's builders took two separate ceiling beams and, making the most of scarce resources, split each one lengthwise, using

**Figure 5.15** Warangal Fort. Panchaliraya temple: left jamb of doorway, showing joint between the inner and outer beam blocks.

one set of decorated faces for the left jamb and the other set for the right. This interpretation is confirmed by the relative thinness of the stones, the presence of splitting marks along the edges of their inside faces,[61] and by the three rougher and lighter-coloured rectangular areas along the inner edges of the doorjambs. These marks are the remnants of the projecting lotus-bosses that typically adorn the undersides of Kakatiya ceiling beams (Figures 5.17 and 5.18). But Shitab Khan's masons evidently chiselled them off. Why? Because Kakatiya precedent did not permit such lotus-bosses along the edges of doorway openings.[62]

All told, the degree of informed improvisation in assembling this doorway is truly impressive. Shitab Khan's builders showed not only creativity, but a deep commitment to reusing actual physical relics of the Kakatiya past. In part this reflected their poorly developed skills in sculptural carving. It was far easier to reuse Kakatiya components that were already sculpted—even if beams had to serve as doorjambs—than to fabricate a completely new doorway in the Kakatiya style, for which they lacked the requisite sculptural skills.

But there was another reason Shitab Khan relied on prefabricated Kakatiya building

**Figure 5.16** Warangal Fort. Panchaliraya temple: inside face of right doorjamb, showing seam and three rectangular splitting marks in the block to the left.

components. As we have seen, Madhava's inscription interprets Shitab Khan as having restored the Kakatiya moral–political universe after nearly two centuries of disorder. To this end, his re-consecration of Kakatiya deities made one sort of statement about this revival, while his restoration of Panchaliraya's temple made another, more visually powerful statement of the same political achievement. What is more, Shitab Khan's subjects would have understood perfectly well that their sovereign was deliberately reassembling architectural components of known Kakatiya origin. By reassembling some of these components into an edifice that closely approximated their original order, Shitab Khan was doing much more than merely restoring collapsed buildings. Metaphorically, he accomplished what 'all the king's men' could not do for Humpty Dumpty: he reassembled the broken fragments of the Kakatiya kingdom, placing himself in the position of its heir, its reassembler, and its king.

## THE HUMILIATION OF DRAUPADI, AND OF SHITAB KHAN'S WIVES

Although the stylistic qualities of the Panchaliraya temple leave little doubt about the foundation's political significance, the characterization

**Figure 5.17** Warangal Fort. Panchaliraya temple: left doorjamb, showing lighter areas where the lotus bosses were chiselled away from the underside of the beam.

of the god Panchaliraya found in Shitab Khan's inscription calls attention to yet other dimensions of meaning that must have resonated deeply within the walls of this shrine. We may recall that Panchaliraya was the only one of the three deities mentioned in the inscription not explicitly connected with the Kakatiyas. This suggests that however much the components of the restored temple might have referenced the Kakatiyas, other factors ultimately attracted Shitab Khan to this particular deity.

The name 'Panchaliraya' does not seem to be attested in any context other than that of early sixteenth-century Warangal. Yet the god's epithet 'Beloved of the Gopis' (*gōpikā-vallabhaḥ*) indicates that he was understood to be a form of Krishna. The name 'Pāncālirāya' literally means 'King (or Lord) of Pāncāli'—Panchali being one of the most common epithets of the epic heroine Draupadi, who was the daughter of the king of Panchala and the common wife of the five Pandava heroes in India's great epic, the Mahābhārata. The 'Lord of Panchali' must thus be understood as the particular form of Krishna who was once worshipped by Draupadi—much as the deity Rameshvara is the form of Shiva once worshipped by the epic hero Rama.[63]

**Figure 5.18** Warangal Fort. Beam fragment from the Svayambhu Shiva site, showing lotus boss carved on its underside (here, the upper surface).

This interpretation is further confirmed by the inscription's statement that 'Panchaliraya'—that is, Krishna—had once 'created endless quantities of pure cloth and given it to Panchali out of pity at seeing her so wretched with humiliation'.[64] This passage refers to the moving episode in the Mahābhārata in which Draupadi is publicly humiliated in the assembly hall of the capital through the perfidy of Duhshasana, who strips her garment from her even as she is menstruating. When Draupadi calls out to Krishna to protect her, he intervenes by making the garment endless.[65] Panchalishvara is thus conceived as Krishna, manifesting his ultimate divine form as Vishnu, and miraculously intervening to protect the innocent and helpless Draupadi. He is the deity who protects her from the supreme humiliation a woman can face at the hands of a man—being disrobed and subjected to attempted rape in public.

This, as we saw earlier in this chapter, was precisely the humiliation that Shitab Khan's wives had faced some forty-five years earlier, around 1459–60, when they were 'tortured with various shameful and obscene acts' in the most public space of the Bahmani court in Bidar, surrounded by mere commoners—and that, too, during the holy month of Ramadan. Although the historian Tabataba is too concerned with decorum to say anything further about this 'shameful and obscene' torture that had taken place at the orders of Sultan Humayun Bahmani, it must have been unspeakably cruel. Moreover, it seems doubtful that any of the unfortunate victims would have managed to escape with their lives. For Shitab Khan, it must have been particularly bitter to bear the knowledge that it was his own decision to flee Bidar that had left his women vulnerable and without protection. We will never know for sure, but circumstantial evidence suggests that, during his lost years in hiding, he found solace in the Mahābhārata's story of Krishna's divine intervention to protect Draupadi when her own husbands were helpless to save her. In this light, the Panchaliraya temple not only made a public statement about Shitab Khan's restoration of the Kakatiya moral–political order, but also served on a more personal level as a memorial to his wives, and as an attempt to overcome his own sense of guilt and moral failure.

* * *

The stormy and tragic career of Shitab Khan illustrates several themes that resonate throughout this study. One is how memory and architecture, working in mutual engagement, can mediate relations between a sixteenth-century 'present' and a deeper, Chalukya or Kakatiya past. Some 180 years after the collapse of the Kakatiya dynasty, local memory of the late dynasty informed how Shitab Khan asserted his claims to rule Warangal once he had seized the former Kakatiya capital from its Qutb Shahi overlords. One way he did this was by building the Panchaliraya temple from Kakatiya-period structural elements. But he was unable to re-establish the Kakatiyas' principal dynastic cult, that of their state-deity, Svayambhu Shiva, owing to the severity of the Tughluqs' destruction of that deity's image and the enormous temple complex that had housed it. So as an alternative, having located the god's icon in Hanamkonda where it had been taken for safe keeping following the Tughluq conquest, he had it returned to Warangal where he could 'venerate' it near its original site in the heart of the Kakatiyas' ancient stone fort.

Shitab Khan's career also illustrates the power of narrative traditions—whether local or trans-regional—to mediate the present and the past, or even the present and the mythic past. Sixteenth-century residents of Warangal preserved the memory of the journey of Svayambhu Shiva's linga from Hanamkonda back to Warangal by linking local memory of that event to south Indian folk traditions respecting the origins of important political or religious centres. At the same time, pan-Indian narratives—namely, the episode in the epic Mahābhārata concerning the humiliation of the heroine, Draupadi—could mediate the present with a mythic past. Arguably, the defining moment in Shitab Khan's career occurred when, as a young officer in Bahmani service, he was forced to flee that service, whereupon his own wives were publicly humiliated at the court of Bidar. Following those events he spent nearly forty-five years in the eastern Deccan's jungles before rising to regional power in Warangal. During all that time, though, he seems to have been haunted by the shame of having abandoned his wives and subjecting them to public humiliation. Unable fully to atone for that act, he did the next best thing once he possessed sufficient resources: he patronized the cult of a deity who, in an episode from the Mahābhārata that paralleled his own experience, actually did rescue a woman from such humiliation.

In the last analysis, Shitab Khan's career should be placed in its larger, geo-political context. Having snuffed out the Kakatiya dynasty in 1323, the Tughluqs themselves lost control over the Telugu country only nine years later, after which the region soon disintegrated politically. Of the new states that emerged to dominate the peninsula, not one was centred in the Telugu country. By the mid-fourteenth century the

Bahmani sultans controlled the northwestern and central Deccan down to the Krishna River, while the kings of Vijayanagara ruled the southern plateau. In 1434 the Gajapati dynasty of kings rose to power in coastal Orissa and soon dominated the eastern coastal strip down to the Krishna delta. From this point on, these three major powers—the Bahmanis, Vijayanagara, and the Gajapatis—became increasingly drawn into mutual conflict as they strove to stake their claims to newly annexed Telugu districts.[66]

This three-way division of the Deccan left vast portions of the Telugu country in a political vacuum, distant enough from the cores of the three major powers to present opportunities for enterprising warriors and local chiefs bent on carving out their own territories. From as early as 1332, the region produced a steady succession of such chiefs, some of which—notably the Recherla chieftains[67]—managed to establish small but stable kingdoms lasting several generations. One such chieftain, Rao Dharmanayaka, briefly acquired effective control of Warangal in the 1460s, anticipating Shitab Khan's own career there by some four decades. Highlighting the city's status as a political vacuum, albeit one with deep memories of Kakatiya glory, in 1464 Rao Dharmanayaka made a public donation in which he styled himself 'Master in stabilizing the Kakatiya kingdom' (*kākata-rājya-sthāpanācārya*), the same title that Kakatiya kings had once bestowed on their own loyal subordinates.[68] Using this archaic title made the chieftain appear independent from both of the powers then contending for control of the region, the Bahmanis and the Gajapatis. It was a natural strategy for someone of local origins attempting to carve out a place for himself in the marchland between major regional powers.

Shitab Khan's career therefore followed a familiar pattern in a region distinguished by two prominent features: first, it was a political vacuum, or shatter zone, but second, a region saturated with memories of a glorious past. This particular combination ensured not only that local upstarts would periodically appear claiming to control the region, but that they would bolster such claims by connecting themselves with its illustrious past. What distinguished Shitab Khan from previous such actors, however, was his ability to alter the city's architectural and religious landscape through the iconic reuse of earlier sculptural or structural components. In this respect, his architectural manipulations can be justly compared with those of Rama Raya at Vijayanagara, those of Ibrahim I at Bijapur, or with those of Ibrahim `Adil Shah II at Kalyana.

But the memory of past glory could be invoked in ways more subtle than simply reassembling physical artifacts left behind by departed dynasties. In the next chapter, we explore the distinctive ways in which the Qutb Shahi sultans of Golconda used memories of the Kakatiyas in establishing their new capital of Hyderabad.

## NOTES

1. `Ali Tabataba, *Burhān-i ma'āthir* (Delhi: Majlis-i Makhtutat-i Farsiya, 1936), 95. Our translation.

2. *Inscriptions of Andhra Pradesh* (*IAP*)—*Warangal District*, no. 111.

3. This summary is based on the account of the *Kimmūru Kaifiyat* in the Mackenzie collection, as summarized in Hirananda Sastri, *Shitab Khan of Warangal*, Hyderabad Archaeological Series, no. 9 (Hyderabad: Nizam's Government, 1932), 6–7. Rajapudi is located in the Jaggampeta *taluk* of the present-day East Godavari district in Andhra Pradesh. Kimmuru lies some 12 kilometres to the east, in the adjoining Yeleshvaram taluk. In addition to Hirananda Sastri's short monograph, other works dealing with Shitab Khan include H.K. Sherwani, *History of the Qutb Shahi Dynasty* (New Delhi: Munshiram Manoharlal, 1974), 25–7 and 63–4, note 62; idem., 'The Identity

of Shitab Khan of Warangal', *The Journal of the Pakistan Historical Society* 5 (October, 1957), 220–5; Adiraju Virabhadraravu, *Ṣitābukhānu anu Sītāpatirāju* (Haidrābādu: Lakṣmaṇarāya Pariśodhaka Maṇḍali, 1961) [in Telugu; unfortunately this volume was not available to us]; and Cynthia Talbot, *Precolonial India in Practice: Society, Region, and Identity in Medieval Andhra* (New York: Oxford University Press, 2001), 182.

4. If we assume that Sitapati/Shitab Khan was twenty-five years old when forced from the capital in about 1460, he might have arrived at Bidar several years before, in his early twenties. That would have made him sixty-four when he conquered Warangal in 1504, and seventy-six when he ambushed Krishna Raya in 1516 (see later). A number of the most prominent military figures of the sixteenth century—including both Rama Raya and Sultan Quli—lived into their eighties, and remained active on the battlefield until the very end.

5. In addition to the Shitab Khan considered here, whose documented activities span the period c.1450–1520, another Shitab Khan figures in the account of events during the reign of Ibrahim Qutb Shah (1550–80) given in the anonymous *Tārīkh-i Muḥammad Shāh*. Given the great time gap between their respective periods of activity, it is clear that the later Shitab Khan must have been a different person. See the discussion by H.K. Sherwani, *Qutb Shahi Dynasty*, 63–4, note 62.

6. In sixteenth-century Sanskrit and Telugu sources, Shitab Khan is not called 'Sītāpati' but rather 'Chittāpa', Sittāpa, or some other variant representing a transliteration of the Persianized form of Sitapati back into the Indic languages. The various forms used include, in Sanskrit, 'Chittāpa/Sitāpa/Sittāpa Khāna' (in Shitab Khan's Warangal inscription, discussed later), and in Telugu, 'Citāṃbu Khāna' (the *Citrabhāratamu* of Carigoṇḍa Dharmanna, *pīṭhika*, pp. 10–14), 'Citāpa Khānuṃḍu' (in the *Tapatī-Samvaraṇamu* of Addanki Gangadhara-kavi, I, 25), and 'Chitāpu Khānuṃḍu' (in the anonymous *Rāyavācakamu*, C.V. Ramachandra Rao edition, 65). Only in the much later Telugu kaifiyats is his name given as 'Sītapati' or, in shortened form, 'Sītaḍu'.

7. The historian H.K. Sherwani is mystified by the fierce propaganda campaign launched against Humayun by Persian chroniclers more than a century after the sultan's reign. Refuting allegations of Humayun's tyranny, Sherwani cites the testimony of the contemporary Bahmani official Mahmud Gawan, who was no sycophant and who had only the highest praise for Humayun's character and generosity. See Haroon Khan Sherwani, *The Bahmanis of the Deccan* (New Delhi: Munshiram Manoharlal, 1985), 180–6, 322.

8. Tabataba, *Burhān-i ma'āthir*, 95, J.S. King, trans., 'History of the Bahmani Dynasty', *Indian Antiquary* 28 (1899), 246–7.

9. Briggs, trans., *History of the Rise*, 2:305–7.

10. The inscription was first published, together with a translation and a learned historical study based on an unpublished paper by K.V. Lakshmana Rao, in Hirananda Sastri, *Shitab Khan*, 15–20. The inscription has since been republished; see *IAP—Warangal*, no. 111.

11. According to Tabataba, in 1497 Sultan Quli 'obtained sovereignty over all the feudatory chiefs of Telingana', and 'added to his former possessions the towns of Warangal and Kovilakonda with their dependencies'. *Burhān-i ma'āthir*, J.S. King, trans., 'History of the Bahmani Dynasty', *Indian Antiquary* 28 (1899), 315.

12. Hirananda Sastri, *Shitab Khan*, 20.

13. Briggs, trans., *History of the Rise*, 3:216–19.

14. 'kampam-andi citāpa-khānuṃḍu gautamī taṭini laṃghiṃci pōbuṭamu veṭṭe', I, 25. See Patibanda Madhavasarma, ed., *Tapatī Samvaraṇamu, Addanki Gangādharakavi Praṇītamu* (Hyderabad: Sri Parameshvara Publications, 1972), 6.

15. Phillip B. Wagoner, *Tidings of the King: A Translation and Ethnohistorical Analysis of the* Rayavacakamu (Honolulu: University of Hawaii Press, 1993), 145–6.

16. As an anonymous Telugu poem from the fourteenth century put it,

The world encircled by oceans
would not know
whether a king lifted Mount Meru itself,
if he did not have a poet
to write about him. (*Sakala-nīti-sammatamu*, trans. V. Narayana Rao, 1987, 142).

17. Oleti Venkatarama Sastri, ed., *Citra-bhāratamu, Carikoṇḍa Dharmanna praṇītamu*, (Madras: Vavilla Ramaswamy Shastrulu and Sons, 1934). This text has not been translated.

18. *Citra-bhāratamu* I, 13. Our translation.

19. *IAP—Warangal*, no. 111 (lines 108–11) 'Pūrvvaṃ Kākati-vamśya-rāja-nivahair=yā=pālitā dharmātmabhir=yyā nānā-[nidhi]bhiḥ Kubera-nagar=īv=ādhyāsitā dyotate | ramyāṃ Ekaśilāpurīṃ savibhavaś Cittāpa Khāno nṛpo=gṛhṇād Bhogi-kulāgranīḥ sura-dharā-dev=ārccanāy=ādhikaḥ ||' Translation adapted from Hirananda Sastri, *Shitab Khan*, 23. Emphasis ours.

20. *IAP—Warangal*, no. 111, 'Kākati-rājya-pīṭha-kamal=ānādir jagan-mātṛkā', line 133

21. Although there are no known references to this goddess during the Kakatiya period itself, there are a number of references to her dating to the fifteenth and sixteenth centuries. Kumarasvami-Somapithin, the fifteenth-century commentator on the *Pratāparudrīya* of Vidyanatha, states that the form of Durga known as Kakati was the tutelary deity (*kula-devatā*) of the rulers of the city of Warangal, and that because they were devoted to this goddess they were called Kakatiyas. Also in the fifteenth century, Vinukonda Vallabharaya refers in his *Krīḍābhirāmamu* to another goddess of Warangal, Ekavira, as being a companion of the goddess Kakatamma. See V. Raghavan, ed., *Pratāparudrīyam* (Madras: Sanskrit Education Society of Madras, 1970), 7; Velcheru Narayana Rao and David Shulman, trans., *A Lover's Guide to Warangal: The* Krīḍābhirāmamu *by Vinukonda Vallabharaya* (Delhi: Permanent Black, 2002), 53–4; P.V. Parabrahma Sastry, *The Kakatiyas of Warangal* (Hyderabad: Government of Andhra Pradesh, 1978), 22–3.

22. *IAP—Warangal*, no. 111, 'Kākati-vaṃśya-rakṣaṇa-vidhau cintāmaṇiṃ sat-kṛpā-pārāvāra-gabhīra-cāru-caritaṃ devaṃ', lines 136–7.

23. *IAP—Warangal*, no. 111, 'Dur-īti-vibhavāt' (line 130); 'Turuṣka-kujanair', line 134.

24. The Āgamas and other ritual texts enumerate and describe various ways that images can become ritually compromised. These include physical damage (breakage, cracking, burning, general wear and decay caused by regular use, willful destruction, and natural phenomena such as lightning, fire, and flood), as well as ritual pollution (through contact with Candalas, outcastes, menstruating women, corpses, or animals), and ritual problems (worship with the wrong mantras, accidental damage done by priests in the course of worship, or failure to perform regular worship). The texts also distinguish between minor forms of damage and damage so severe that the image must be ritually discarded and replaced with another. Images subject to minor forms of damage may be repaired and re-consecrated. For example, 'Once broken limbs have been rejoined to the body, consecration is to be performed again, but without performing the rites of either the immersion in water [*jalādhivāsam*], or the opening of the eyes [*netronmīlana*].' *Nirṇaya-Sindhu*, 2: 1250, quoting a Pancarātra text. But severely damaged images must be replaced. For example, 'A linga which is incomplete [*hīnaṃ*], which has been licked by flames [*jvalan=ālīḍhaṃ*], that is worn out [*jīrṇaṃ*], that is cracked [*sa-sphoṭakaṃ*], or is broken [*bhagnaṃ*]—such a linga, even if it has never been subjected to a break in worship, should be abandoned [*tyaktvā*] and replaced [*punas-tat-sthāpayet*] with a new linga [*navaṃ lingaṃ*]', *Mayamata* XXXV, 25. See Bruno Dagens, *Mayamata: Traité Sanskrit d'Architecture* (Pondicherry: Institut Français d'Indologie, 1976), 2:356–7. Different texts, however, disagree over what constitutes severe or minor damage, and most texts record differences of opinion even within their own ritual communities. For an informative discussion of textual prescriptions relating to re-consecration, see Richard Davis, *Lives of Indian Images* (Princeton: Princeton University Press, 1997), 252–6.

25. While the word *saṃpūjya* (and its related nominal form, *pūjā*) is often used to refer to the formal worship offered to consecrated images within their temple sancta, it can also be used in a more general sense, to refer to the honour or veneration offered to a revered person, or to unconsecrated secondary images, such as those carved in the niches of a temple's outer walls. Because the inscription says nothing about a *punaḥ pratiṣṭhā* rite having been performed for Svayambhu Shiva, saṃpūjya here probably means informal veneration.

26. Strictly speaking, Shitab Khan's continued veneration of the broken Svayambhu Shiva linga would appear to have violated most ritual texts, which stipulate that damaged images that cannot be re-consecrated should be discarded. But this prescription is often ignored even today, and damaged images are sometimes set up in temple *maṇḍapa*s where visitors may honour them before proceeding to the consecrated icon in the sanctum. For example, in the late 1990s, when the temple at Kudavelli Sangam was being relocated to Alampur to escape submersion from the construction of the Srisailam Hydro-Electric Project, a broken crystal linga was discovered beneath the foundations. When the temple was being re-consecrated after the

move to its new site, a debate arose as to whether the broken linga could be consecrated. Priests ultimately determined that the linga could be re-installed, according to their reading of a ritual text, the *Nirṇaya Sindhu.* See I.K. Sarma, 'Transplant of Kūḍali Saṅgameśvara Temple and Some Āgamic Principles', in *Deccan Heritage*, eds Harsh K. Gupta, Aloka Prasher-Sen, and D. Balasubramanian (Hyderabad: Universities Press India Limited, 2000), 186. Sarma cites a 1986 edition of the text published in Madras, which we have not been able to locate. The purported passage in the *Nirṇaya Sindhu* does not appear in the Chowkhamba Sanskrit Series edition that we have consulted.

27. In ordinary lingas, which lack sculpted faces, the shaft is divided into three vertical portions distinguished by the geometric form of their sections: the upper cylindrical portion (*rudra-bhāga*) rising above the base, the octagonal portion (*viṣṇu-bhāga*) within the base, and a square portion (*brahma-bhāga*) extending beneath the base and into the floor of the sanctum. See V. Ganapati Sthapati, *Indian Sculpture and Iconography: Forms and Measurements* (Pondicherry: Sri Aurobindo Society, 2002), 36 and illustration. In the case of four-faced lingas, however, the lower two portions of the shaft generally share the same geometric form, whether square, as prescribed in several iconographic texts, or octagonal, as depicted in a drawing by Ganapati Sthapati, *Indian Sculpture*, 41.

28. See, for example, the prescriptions of the *Īśānaśivagurudeva-paddhati*, Kriyāpāda, paṭala 40, v. 12: 'A four-faced linga is to be established in a four-doored shrine' ('catur-dvāre tu bhavano kuryālingam caturmukham'). T. Ganapati Sastri, ed., *Īśānaśivagurudeva-paddhati* of *Īśānaśivagurudeva*, 2 vols (Delhi: Oriental Book Centre, 2006), 2:848.

29. The lower end of this shaft is smoothly polished, and there is no trace of breakage, establishing that this linga had no square-sectioned *brahma-bhāga*.

30. In recent years there has been considerable movement of sculptures and architectural fragments from one part of the Warangal site to another, as the Archaeological Survey of India has carried out its various programmes of excavation and conservation. Svayambhu Shiva's four-faced linga has itself been moved at least once—from a spot under a tree in the Shambhuni-gudi courtyard, where it stood in 1999, to a spot right up against the northeast corner of the temple's maṇḍapa where we found it in 2005. If such movement is possible within the span of just a few years, we should be cautious before concluding that a given monument has been immobile over the course of a full five centuries or more.

31. According to the Hyderabad Government's 'Resolution' of 1931, published as a foreword to Hirananda Sastri's 1932 publication, the inscription was located 'in front of Śambhuni Gudi in the Warangal Fort'. More than a century earlier, in 1816, the inscription was standing in this same spot when it was transcribed by Narrain Row, one of Colin Mackenzie's assistants. In his report for April–August 1816, he wrote that 'in front of the Pagoda of Parisavady Sambhodoo [that is, the Shambhuni-gudi] is a very highly finished stone pillar [recording that] Sitapakhan [conquered Warangal]'. See Hirananda Sastri, *Shitab Khan*, v; British Library, Asian, Pacific, and African Collections, European Manuscripts, Mackenzie Translations, Class XII, no. 47, folio 59r.

32. Considerable circumstantial evidence supports this conclusion. A photograph of the Shambhuni-gudi courtyard published by S. Gopalakrishna Murthy in 1964 shows the linga, as well as the muzzle of one of the Nandi images and part of the temple's maṇḍapa. That the linga stood here as early as the sixteenth century is implied in the *Pratāparudra Caritramu*, a popular history of the Kakatiyas written in about 1550. According to this text, the city of Warangal was laid out around a Shiva linga that had miraculously sprouted from the ground—a mythologized reference, we believe, to Svayambhu Shiva, literally 'the self manifest Shiva', whose four-faced linga indeed appears as if it had arisen from the earth. The fact that this linga is referred to in the text as the 'touchstone linga of Sambhu' (*sparśavēdiyagu śambhu-lingaṃbu*) further suggests that it had been located in the Sambhulinga compound in the sixteenth century, for as late as the early nineteenth century this temple was still being called the 'Pagoda of Parisavedi Sambhudu'. This is also how Narrain Row referred to the Shambhuni-gudi in 1816. See S. Gopalakrishyna Murthy, *The Sculpture of the Kakatiyas* (Hyderabad: Government of Andhra Pradesh, 1964), figure 31; C.V. Ramachandra Rao, ed., *Ēkāmranāthuni Pratāparudra Caritramu* (Hyderabad: Andhra Pradesh Sahitya Academy, 1984), 23–4; Mackenzie Translations, folio 59r.

33. The Tripurusha or Traipurusha cult, dedicated to the conjoined worship of Shiva, Visnu, and Brahma, was relatively widespread between the ninth and eleventh centuries, especially in the areas of the

Dharwar, Gulbarga, Raichur, and Bijapur districts. In Telangana, Brahma is usually replaced by Surya, but the type is still termed *tripuruṣa* in inscriptions. See A. Sundara, 'Traipuruṣa Dēvālayas in Inscriptions and Related Temples in Dharwad-Bijapur Region', in *Indian Epigraphy: Its Bearing on the History of Art*, eds Frederick M. Asher and G.S. Gai (New Delhi: Oxford and IBH, 1985), 203–8; Phillip B. Wagoner, 'Modal Marking of Temple Types in Kakatiya Andhra: Towards a Theory of Decorum for Indian Temple Architecture', in *Syllables of Sky: Studies in South Indian Civilization in Honour of Velcheru Narayana Rao*, ed. David Shulman (New Delhi: Oxford University Press, 1995), 452ff.

34. In order to reduce their total load, the towers over the sancta of Kakatiya temples were generally made of brick, rather than stone. Although the Ramappa temple at Palampet is the only Kakatiya monument that retained its brick superstructure into modern times (it has since been restored, using new bricks), loose courses of brick can still be found atop a number of other buildings, including the 'Thousand Pillar' temple at Hanamkonda. The original Ramappa bricks were extremely porous, thus further reducing their density. As for the foundations, the exemplary work of M. Pandu Ranga Rao and his collaborators has established the use of the so-called confined sand-box method, in which an excavated pit was lined with dry masonry stone walls and then filled with sand to provide the foundation. Even load-bearing members were supported on sand rather than being taken to solid strata. As a result, when the sand gradually percolated out of the retaining box due to ground water circulation, the structure often failed. See D. Someshvar Rao, 'Floating Bricks of Ramappa Temple, Palampet: A Technological Innovation in Brick Making during Kakatiya Period', in *Engineering and Technological Achievements during the Kakatiya Period*, ed. M. Pandu Ranga Rao (Warangal: INTACH, 1996), 73–5; L.D.P. Vittal, 'Architectural Glory and Method of Construction of the Kakatiyas', in *Engineering and Technological Achievements during the Kakatiya Period*, ed. Ranga Rao, 77–82; M. Pandu Ranga Rao and Deva Pratap, 'Geotechnical Evaluation of Construction Materials of Kakatiya Structures', in *Engineering and Technological Achievements during the Kakatiya Period*, ed. Ranga Rao, 103–12. See also M. Pandu Ranga Rao, S. Raghavachari, N. Babu Shanker, and A.U.R. Somayajulu, *Geotechnical Appraisal and Evaluation of Kakatiya Monuments, Warangal, A.P.* (Warangal: Department of Civil Engineering, Regional Engineering College, 1987).

35. See *Corpus of Inscriptions in the Telangana Districts* (*CITD*) 2: no. 4; *IAP—Warangal*, no. 94.

36. See T.A. Gopinatha Rao, *Elements of Hindu Iconography* (Varanasi: Indological Book House, 1971), vol. 2, part 1, p. 96.

37. The deity is identified as 'Sahasra-linga Gaṇapatīsvara-dēvara'. See *CITD* 2: no. 16, and *IAP—Warangal*, no. 89.

38. This is the only known *sahasra-linga* from the Kakatiya territories. It stands today not in a sanctum, but on a pedestal in the *maṇḍapa* of the temple, suggesting its 'guest' status, and its shaft shows signs of flaking and fractures. Its stylistically post-Kakatiya base further indicates its later installation here as a non-consecrated, secondary image. The ring of cement around the linga where it joins the base suggests that the lower portion of its shaft is largely missing. Its identification with the 'Sahasra-linga Ganapatisvara' linga was first proposed by S. Gopalakrishna Murthy, *Sculpture of the Kakatiyas*, 35 and figure 52.

39. *Mayamata* XXXVI, 62b–64. This form is also known as 'Vṛṣavāhana-mūrti'. See Dagens, *Mayamata* 2: 388–9.

40. Davis, *Lives of Indian Images*, 253.

41. In fact, this verbal testimony is visually underscored by the location of the inscription, which is incised on the pilaster to the right of this shrine's outer doorway.

42. *Rudrēśvara*, lit. '[Shiva who is the] lord of Rudra[-deva]'.

43. The shrine's founder is named in neither the shrine to the north, which is dedicated to Visnu as 'Śrī-Vāsudevara', nor in the shrine to the east, which is dedicated to Surya as 'Śrī-Sūrya-dēvara'.

44. The icon would have been positioned so that the bust appearing frontally in Figure 5.2 faced the viewer. This is because the image situated directly behind it is almost completely effaced, while the two images that flank it are both relatively well preserved, especially on the sides that face outwards towards the front. The dimensions of the linga's octagonal shaft (65.5 centimetres wide between opposite faces) would have enabled it to fit perfectly between the back wall of the niche and the front edge of the projecting shelf, had there been no busts attached to it. But since the decorative doorway that frames the niche is not quite wide enough fully to accommodate the two lateral busts within its

space, the linga would have been displaced slightly forward, so that several centimetres of its shaft and the entirety of the forward bust would have projected beyond the edge of the shelf. But this would not have displaced its centre of gravity so far forward as to make it unstable. As for the northern niche, the opening of its doorframe is 53 centimetres, just wide enough to allow the Sahasra-linga—measuring 50 centimetres in diameter—to fit comfortably through the doorway and rest within its interior, measuring 75 centimetres wide, 85 centimetres deep, and 85 centimetres high.

45. Although neither of these two images is identifiable today, the 27-centimetre projection of the two shelves in the sanctum is adequate to accommodate most stele-type images, which rarely exceed 25 centimetres in depth.

46. A good example of this convention is provided by the foundation inscription of the Thousand Pillared Temple at Hanamkonda, which records that Kakatiya Rudradeva 'established Rudresvara, Śrī-Vāsudēvara, and Śrī-Sūrya-dēvara' (*Rudrēśvaramunu Śrī Vāsudēvara Śrī Sūryya-dēvarānu pratiṣṭha sēyiṃce*), which accords with these deities' locations respectively in the western, northern, and eastern shrines. Small images of these same three deities have been sculpted in relief on the top of the inscription slab, in the same order, on the slab's western, northern, and eastern faces. *CITD* 2:2 (lines 7–8).

47. Ramachandra Rao, ed., *Pratāparudra Caritramu*, 23. Our translation. Emphasis ours.

48. Ibid., 23–4. Our translation.

49. For a discussion of the foundation myth of the city of Vijayanagara, see Wagoner, *Tidings*, 33–50.

50. See the discussion of this motif in David D. Shulman, *Tamil Temple Myths: Sacrifice and Divine Marriage in the South Indian Śaiva Tradition* (Princeton: Princeton University Press, 1980), 96–8, 107, 232–3.

51. Although the image must have been intact when Shitab Khan re-consecrated it in the temple, only fragments of its feet survive in the temple today.

52. A Kakatiya date is explicitly assumed by S. Gopalakrishna Murthy, who mistakenly believed that the Venkateshvara-gudi was the Sahasralinga Ganapatishvara temple of Ganapati's age. More recently, M.A. Dhaky has suggested a date in the thirteenth century, but he vacillates somewhat, noting correctly that 'the building as it stands seems in part re-erected'. A Kakatiya date appears implicitly assumed by M. Radhakrishna Sarma. See Gopalakrishna Murthy, *Sculpture of the Kakatiyas*, 35; B. Rajendra Prasad, *The Art of South India: Andhra Pradesh* (Delhi: Sundeep Prakashan, 1980), 185; M.A. Dhaky, *Encyclopaedia of Indian Temple Architecture*, vol. I, part 3: *South India, Upper Dravidadesa, Later Phase* (New Delhi: American Institute for Indian Studies, 1996), 504; and M. Radhakrishna Sarma, *Temples of Telingana: The Architecture, Iconography, and Sculpture of the Calukya and Kakatiya Temples* (Hyderabad: Booklinks, 1972), 109.

53. Although the temple was subsequently desecrated at some point after Shitab Khan's re-consecration, its Vaishnava dedication is clear from preserved iconographic indicators. As for the image itself, only its base and feet survive in the sanctum today, but its Vaishnava identity is unequivocally revealed by the small image of Garuḍa (Visnu's bird-vehicle), carved in low relief on the front of the base just below the feet. That the feet are in *samapada* stance suggests that the image would perhaps have taken the form of one of the twenty-four forms of Vishnu (*catur-vimśati-mūrti*). Additionally, the *dvārapāla*s standing guard at the vestibule doorway hold Vaishnava attributes (discus and conch). These crudely carved figures do not belong to the Kakatiya period, but clearly date from the time of Shitab Khan's restoration. Finally, in the courtyard to the east of the temple's maṇḍapa there is a *dhvaja-stambha* carved with Vaishnava emblems, including figures of the Kurma-avatara, Hanuman, and the Shrivaishnava sectarian mark (*nāmam*), and also a large stele carved with an image of Hanuman in the heroic stance (*Vīrāñjaneya*).

54. In addition to the misaligned pilaster shafts, the anomalies include: (1) the presence of masons' marks on these vertical slabs, apparently consisting of a slab-to-slab matching code represented by individual Telugu letters and bracket-shaped alignment indicators; (2) a mismatch in the number of wall divisions (*anga*s) between the west wall, which has four (*caturanga*), and the north and south walls, which have three (*tryanga*); (3) an odd rhythm in the wall articulation of the vestibule (*antarāla*), which has a multi-faceted *bhadra* projection abutting the corner projection (*karṇa*) of the shrine, and then two additional projections before the corner projection where it joins the pillared hall; (4) the use of an inverted block properly belonging to the uppermost course of a plinth (*adhiṣṭhāna*) in place of a block carved with the mouldings of the pilaster-base course (*pāduka*), towards the east end of the south

wall of the vestibule; (5) the use of modified ceiling beams instead of proper doorjambs in the doorframe of the vestibule (discussed in greater detail later); (6) the re-cutting of the lower blocks (*jaṅghā*) of the pilasters on either side of the vestibule doorway, so as to provide crudely carved, sunken relief images of Vaishnava doorway guardians (*dvārapālas*); (7) the cutting-off of the outer bands of the sanctum doorway, so as to remove the Shaiva doorway guardians that originally stood in front of them (but neglecting to remove their upper hands, which are still visible holding the Shaiva attributes of *ḍamaru* and trident); (8) the crude, tripartite articulation of the half-walls of the maṇḍapa, which lack entirely any mouldings; and (9) the use of at least nine distinct morphological/stylistic varieties of *citrakhaṇḍa* columns in the maṇḍapa, which have most likely been reused from as many as five or six different temples of varying age.

55. For the links between new temple construction and agrarian expansion, see Cynthia Talbot, *Precolonial India in Practice: Society, Region, and Identity in Medieval Andhra* (New York: Oxford University Press, 2001), 93–9. Although significant numbers of inscriptions in the late twelfth and early thirteenth centuries record the foundation of new temples, very few foundation inscriptions date to the latter half of the thirteenth century.

56. This is one of the last epigraphically datable Kakatiya temples (1276; *CITD* 2: 50). For plan, section, and elevation, as well as detailed drawings of columns and doorway, see P. Sreenivasachar, *The Archaeological Bulletin No. II* (Hyderabad: Government of Andhra Pradesh, 1963), figures 20 and 21.

57. This temple has no foundation inscription but is stylistically datable to the late thirteenth century. See Dhaky, *Encyclopaedia* I/3, p. 512 and plates 1557–9. Kolanupaka is also known as Kulpak.

58. For example, an inscription dated 1357 records the re-consecration of the Erakeshvara temple at Pillalamarri under the patronage of Era Potu Lenka, a subordinate of the Musunuri chief Kapaya Nayaka who had seized Warangal from the Tughluqs in the early 1330s. For the nature and circumstances of the damage inflicted on the temple, see the discussion in Chapter 2, pp. 41–2. The Erakeshvara temple was originally founded in 1208. Although the nature of these repairs is not described in the inscription, they are immediately obvious due to their drastic difference from the temple's original fabric. We can thus see that Era Potu Lenka arranged for new doorframes to be carved and inserted into the openings at the side entrances of the temple's hall in order to shore up fractured roof beams and to provide a more secure perimeter for the temple. Comparing one of these later doorframes of 1357 with a doorway dating from the time of the temple's original construction in 1208, we see that the fourteenth-century mason did not even attempt to reproduce the characteristic forms of the Kakatiya style. Whereas the original Kakatiya-period doorway is painstakingly sculpted into multiple decorative bands, the later door is but a vague and distant paraphrase. It accurately follows the structural logic of the earlier doorway, in that it is articulated into the same set of five slabs—threshold, a pair of jambs, and a lintel in two courses—but the vestigial ornament applied to these slabs is reduced to the barest minimum of plain bands and projecting bosses. *CITD* 2:40, 42.

59. Similarly, a little further to the right on the temple's southern wall, a block with the wrong sequence of mouldings has been used to fill out the pilaster-base course, which elsewhere consists of two projecting horizontal mouldings separated by a recess. But here again, Shitab Khan's men apparently ran out of the appropriate types of block; so they used, after inverting it, an extra block that properly belonged to the uppermost course of the plinth.

60. Dhaky, *Encyclopaedia of Indian Temple Architecture* (*EITA*) I/3, 504. The 'peculiar' quality of this doorway has also been signalled by M. Radhakrishna Sarma, who writes that 'the doorway of the antarāla [vestibule] of the Venkatesa-gudi is peculiar in that the sides of the frame are divided into continuous vertical bands … the carvings on them being uninterrupted by the horizontal divisions'. Radhakrishna Sarma, *Temples of Telingana*, 191.

61. Shitab Khan's stone masons split beams in the same way that blocks of granitic stone are quarried today. A series of small rectangular sockets was chiselled into the surface of the stone, in a line along the face that was to be split. Blunt rectangular chisels were then inserted into the sockets and struck until the stone split. For a detailed discussion of the method, see Carla M. Sinopoli, *The Political Economy of Craft Production: Crafting Empire in South India, c. 1350–1650* (Cambridge: Cambridge University Press, 2003), 213–18.

62. As the stones were split in half, the remaining scars are rectangular in shape, rather than square. The

beam shown in Figure 5.18 shows only a single lotus boss, but beams with three or more are not uncommon; see, for example, the ceiling beams in the Nagulapadu *trikuta* temple. *EITA* I, part 3 (1996), plates 1573, 1574, and 1575.

63. Although the Telugu 'rāya' is generally used to refer to human kings, in 'Panchaliraya' it is used in the sense of 'īśvara', a common term for a divine lord. This is confirmed by the *Citrabhāratamu* of Carigonda Dharmanna—the earlier-mentioned Telugu version of the Mahābhārata composed under the patronage of Shitab Khan's minister—which refers twice to this deity and his temple in the city of Warangal but uses the more expected forms 'Pāñcālīśvara' and 'Pāncāli-vibhuḍu', both meaning 'Lord of Panchali'. See Venkatarama Sastri, ed., *Citra-bhāratamu, pīṭhika* (verses) 11 and 65.

64. *IAP-Warangal*, no. 111, 'Pāṃcālyai paribhūta-dainya-bahuḷa-prodyat-kṛpāveśataḥ prādād akṣaya-vastra-jātam-amalaṃ', lines 128–9.

65. See P.C. Roy [K.M.Ganguli], trans. *The Mahābhārata of Krishna-Dwaipayana Vyasa*, second edition (Calcutta: Oriental Publishing, n.d.), vol. 2: 144–5. This translation is based on the vulgate text (II, 68, 41–8), in which Draupadi's connection with Krishna is explicitly drawn:

> 'When the attire of Draupadi was being thus dragged, she thought of Hari (And she herself cried aloud, saying), 'O Govinda, O thou who dwellest in Dwaraka, O Krishna, O thou who art fond of cow-herdesses (of Vrindavana). O Kesava, seest thou not that the Kauravas are humiliating me. O Lord, O husband of Lakshmi, O Lord of Vraja (Vrindavana), O destroyer of all afflictions, O Janarddana, rescue me who am sinking in the Kaurava Ocean. O Krishna, O Krishna, O thou great yogin, thou soul of the universe, Thou creator of all things, O Govinda, save me who am distressed,—who am losing my senses in the midst of the Kurus.' Thus did that afflicted lady resplendent still in her beauty, O king covering her face cried aloud, thinking of Krishna, of Hari, of the lord of the three worlds. Hearing the words of Draupadi, Krishna was deeply moved. And leaving his seat, the benevolent one from compassion, arrived there on foot. And while Yajnaseni was crying aloud to Krishna, also called Vishnu and Hari and Nara for protection, the illustrious Dharma, remaining unseen, covered her with excellent clothes of many hues. And, O monarch as the attire of Draupadi was being dragged, after one was taken off, another of the same kind, appeared covering her. And thus did it continue till many clothes were seen. And, O exalted one, owing to the protection of Dharma, hundreds upon hundreds of robes of many hues came off Draupadi's person.

For the original text, see *Śrīman Mahābhāratam—mūla-mātram* (Gorakhpur: Gita Press, 1955), vol. I: 389. In the Poona critical edition, there is no reference to Krishna being responsible for the miracle. Instead, it is merely noted that 'when her skirt was being stripped off, another skirt appeared everytime'. J.A.B. Van Buitenen, trans., *The Mahābhārata: 2. The Book of the Assembly Hall, 3. The Book of the Forest* (Chicago: University of Chicago Press, 1975), 146.

66. In 1423 the Bahmanis made the first move by shifting their capital from Gulbarga to Bidar, placing them somewhat closer to eastern Telangana than Gulbarga had been. By 1435 their forces had taken control first of Warangal and then of most of the other key forts in eastern Telangana. But their rule over Warangal did not go unchallenged. By 1448 the first Gajapati king, Kapileshvara, had extended his sway southward clear to Rajahmundry, which he made the seat of a new administrative province in the Godavari delta. Six years later his nephew marched down to gain control of principal forts in the Krishna delta, Kondavidu, Addanki, and Vinukonda. From this coastal position, the Gajapatis in 1458 expanded their influence westward into southeastern Telangana after a local Recherla chieftain based in the fort of Devarakonda had supported a failed attempt to usurp the Bahmani throne from Sultan Humayun Shah (r. 1458–61). When the sultan retaliated by attacking Devarakonda, the chieftain sought aid from Kapileshvara, the Gajapati king. The latter obliged by sending in a vast force that not only defeated the Bahmani army at Devarakonda but, in February 1460, went on to seize Warangal. Although the former Kakatiya capital was now theoretically in the hands of the Gajapatis, actual control of the new territories was left to their Recherla allies.

67. These chiefs, also known as the 'Recherla Nayakas', ruled from Rachakonda and Devarakonda. But they should not be confused with the earlier line of (unrelated) chiefs known as the 'Recherla Reddis', who were prominent Kakatiya feudatories in the thirteenth century.

68. *IAP—Warangal*, no. 110, line 12.

CHAPTER 6

# Qutb Shahi Warangal and the Foundation of Hyderabad

He has climbed the seven mountains, crossed the seven seas, and circled the seven continents—
His fame fills the fourteen worlds!
Our king Malkibha Ramachandra [Ibrahim Qutb Shah]
is truly a seventh *cakravartin* and a seventeenth king!

—from a Telugu panegyric verse dedicated to Sultan Ibrahim Qutb Shah[1]

When the moon was in the constellation of Leo and Jupiter was in his own mansion, the sultan [Muhammad Quli Qutb Shah] ordered architects and masons to prepare the plans of a city which would be unequalled the world over and would be a replica of paradise itself.

— *Tārīkh-i Muḥammad Quṭb Shāh*[2]

The history of the Qutb Shahi Sultanate of Golconda, as seen in the last chapter, was intimately intertwined with the city of Warangal. The dynasty's founder, Sultan Quli, had held the city as part of his appanage from as early as 1495, and it was he who took back the city from Shitab Khan after defeating that upstart around 1512. From that point until the Mughal conquest in the seventeenth century, Warangal appears to have remained under the firm control of the Qutb Shahis, although we hear next to nothing about the city in written historical sources.[3] Nonetheless, the evidence of Qutb Shahi presence is written into the cityscape, mostly in the form of modest updates to the city's fortifications and in decorative modifications to buildings that betray elements of the Qutb Shahi style.

Like Shitab Khan, various Qutb Shahi sultans—especially Muhammad Quli—were apparently impressed by the city's Kakatiya remains, although unlike Shitab Khan, they do not appear to have registered this fascination in written form. Instead, Qutb Shahi interest in the city is revealed in the plan of the new capital that Muhammad Quli laid out in 1591—Hyderabad. In this chapter, we argue that the Kakatiya capital of Warangal served as the principal conceptual model for Sultan Muhammad Quli's new capital. Previous scholarship, however, has not properly recognized Hyderabad's debt to its Kakatiya predecessor. By over-emphasizing the 'foreignness' and Persianate character of the Qutb Shahi Sultanate, scholars have dismissed the contributions of the local, Telugu-speaking majority as irrelevant to the definition of Qutb Shahi culture. As a result, Qutb Shahi Hyderabad continues to be perceived as an essentially 'Islamic' space, cordoned off in a separate conceptual universe that remains socially isolated and categorically distinct from the 'Hindu' space of Warangal.

To understand the Kakatiya origins of the new Qutb Shahi capital, this chapter first reviews the early history of the Qutb Shahi Sultanate, focussing on the rulers of the first three generations—Sultan Quli (1496–1543), Ibrahim (1550–80), and Muhammad Quli (1580–1612).[4] Here we examine how a succession dispute following Sultan Quli's death ended up transforming the Qutb Shahi house from a family of Iranian immigrants to an Indianized family with strong connections to the Telugu language and the Telangana region. The second section explores how the complex social make-up of Golconda's ruling élite nurtured a composite culture in which the forms and practices of the Persian and Sanskrit cosmopolises became inextricably interwoven. The third section examines the built form of Qutb Shahi Warangal as it existed in the sixteenth century, and how the city's plan served as a monumental expression of imperial aspirations. The final section considers how the form and meaning of Hyderabad's layout responded to those of the earlier city of Warangal.[5]

## THE INDIANIZATION OF AN IMMIGRANT PERSIAN FAMILY

The story of Sultan Quli, the founder of the Qutb Shahi Sultanate, encapsulates the dynamic interrelations between Central Asia, Iran, and the Deccan in the fifteenth and sixteenth centuries, as well as the expansive nature of the Persian cosmopolis in that period.[6] Born around 1470 near Hamadan in western Iran, Sultan Quli belonged to the Qara Qoyunlu ('Black Sheep') Turkmen, a confederation of tribal Turks that the Mongols had pushed westward out of Central Asia some three centuries earlier. By the late fourteenth century, these Turks had become fully Persianized and, under the rule of their sultan, Jahan Shah (1434–67), had emerged as the dominant force in most of western Iran and northern Iraq. Just a few years before Sultan Quli's birth, however, Sultan Jahan Shah died and a rival group of Turkmens, the Aq Qoyunlu ('White Sheep'), encroached on Qara Qoyunlu territories. Tensions came to a head when the Aq Qoyunlu sultan vowed to crush the Qara Qoyunlu.[7] Accordingly, Sultan Quli's family decided to send the eight-year-old boy to India, accompanied by his uncle. The two refugees eventually reached the Deccan, where they entered the service of the Bahmani sultan Mahmud Shah (r. 1482–1518) at his capital of Bidar. In 1490 Sultan Quli's uncle returned to Iran, but Sultan Quli, now in his twentieth year, chose to remain in the Deccan, reportedly believing that in that land 'bravery and prowess were regarded as passports for favors'.[8]

In the final decade of the fifteenth century, Telangana, the easternmost province of the Bahmani kingdom, was slipping from Bahmani control as local chieftains rebelled. When Mahmud Shah decided to send a commander and troops to bring these districts back into line, Sultan Quli volunteered for the assignment and quickly accomplished the task.[9] On another occasion, he and a small group of Westerners managed to save Mahmud Shah's life when some disgruntled Deccani officers attempted to assassinate him. In reward for such services, the sultan made the young foreigner the second-ranking minister of state and bestowed on him the title 'Qutb al-Mulk'. Shortly thereafter, in 1496, Mahmud Shah honoured him with the title 'commander of the commanders' (*amīr al-umarā'*) and appointed him governor of the province of Telangana.[10]

Despite Sultan Quli's earlier successes in the region, by 1496 the territorial extent of the Telangana province had greatly shrunk from what it had been several decades earlier, when Bahmani power was at its greatest. Then, thanks largely to the able leadership of the minister Mahmud Gawan (fl. 1458–81), the Bahmanis' Telangana holdings had extended all the way to Masulipatnam and other shipping ports on the eastern coast. But now, the province extended only from Golconda to Warangal; all the forts of eastern Telangana and the coastal districts had fallen to local Hindu chieftains. Worse, Sultan Quli faced the threat of annexation of his territories by various competitors. After 1528, when the last Bahmani sultan died, these included former Bahmani *amīr*s who were attempting to establish themselves as independent sultans in their own right. As a result, from 1496 until about 1534, Sultan Quli had to wage war almost constantly. Most of his campaigns ended in success, and by his death in 1543 he ruled as the undisputed lord of all Telangana east of Bidar and between the Godavari and Krishna Rivers. He even controlled the major forts south of the Krishna in the present day Guntur district. Although he never assumed the title of 'sulṭān', he had effectively established a sultanate, which under his successors would be known as 'Qutb Shahi', after his title 'Qutb al-Mulk'. Together with the `Adil Shahis of Bijapur and the Nizam Shahis of Ahmadnagar, the Qutb Shahi kingdom centred on Golconda would emerge as one of the three most important Bahmani successor states. It would last until the Mughal conquest in 1687.

Although Sultan Quli had intended that his son Qutb al-Din succeed him as ruler of Telangana, on his death in 1543 his next-born son, Jamshid, entertained his own ideas and ordered his older brother blinded, thereby clearing his way to the throne. The usurper then summoned to the capital his two younger brothers, Daulat and Ibrahim, whom he evidently aimed to eliminate. They, however, ignored his orders and instead took refuge in neighbouring kingdoms. For his part, Ibrahim, just thirteen years of age at this time, found his way to Vijayanagara, where Rama Raya had seized effective power a year earlier, in 1542, There, the powerful autocrat received the Qutb Shahi prince, assigned him an estate for his maintenance, and, we are told, 'treated him with the utmost respect and attention'.[11]

Ibrahim's life thus seemed to recapitulate that of his father, who had also been forced at a young age to flee his native land in order to escape certain assassination. Although Sultan Quli had fled from Iran all the way to distant India, he found refuge in the familiar Persianate surroundings of the Bahmani court. Ibrahim, in contrast, had fled a much shorter geographic distance, but he traversed a far greater one culturally, notwithstanding that the Indic culture of the Vijayanagara court had by the mid-sixteenth century been tempered by the adoption of many Persianate customs and practices. During the seven years of his residence at Vijayanagara, which happened to coincide with the most impressionable years of his youth, Ibrahim quickly became acculturated to the norms and practices of the Indic courtly world. By the end of his stay he—like Shitab Khan before him, but for very different reasons—could function with equal ease in both Persianate and Indic courtly cultures.

In 1550 Sultan Jamshid Qutb Shah died, whereupon a small faction of nobles placed the former sultan's two-year-old son on the throne as a puppet. But soon a larger and more influential section of the nobility dominated by local Telugu chiefs known as *nāyakwāṛis* rallied around Ibrahim's cause and wrote secretly to him at Vijayanagara, inviting him to return to Golconda to take the throne.[12] The prince agreed to the proposition. As soon as he had crossed the Krishna River and entered into Golconda territory, Ibrahim was met by a group of Qutb Shahi nobles at the head of 3,000 horses and 5,000 foot soldiers. With ever more nobles flocking to his cause as he marched to Golconda, on 25 July 1550 Ibrahim finally reached the capital, where the nāyakwāṛi commander Jagadeva Rao presented him with the keys to the fort and the citadel. The next day he was crowned as Ibrahim Qutb Shah.

Despite continuous conflict with his neighbours, Ibrahim's thirty-year reign saw little cumulative change in the kingdom's territorial extent. In the early 1560s, however, Golconda's relations with Vijayanagara soured when, as we have seen in Chapter 4, Rama Raya aggressively manipulated interstate relations to his advantage. By this time Rama Raya had begun shrewdly entering into alliances first with one sultanate and then with another, always with a view to obtaining indirect control over the former Chalukya capital of Kalyana. This policy inevitably pitted his northern neighbours both with and against one another in a seemingly endless series of shifting alliances. Rama Raya also fomented rebellions among the Qutb Shahi nāyakwāṛis along his northern border, which further strained Ibrahim's friendship with his former protector. At the same time, Vijayanagara's powerful ruler repeatedly failed to honour agreements he had made with his allies, while imposing humiliating conditions on defeated adversaries. Finally, in 1565, Rama Raya's many affronts and insults induced the four northern sultanates to form a grand coalition for launching a joint expedition against their southern neighbour, which resulted in one of the great watersheds of Indian history—the Battle of Talikota. This battle saw the southerners' army annihilated, Rama Raya himself beheaded, and the Vijayanagara kingdom reduced to a mere shadow of its former self (for details, see Chapter 7, pp. 268–71).

Upon Ibrahim's death in 1580, the throne passed to Muhammad Quli, the third of Ibrahim's six sons.[13] Although Muhammad Quli took part in a number of military campaigns, he is remembered more for his literary accomplishments than for his exploits on the battlefield. He wrote a *dīwān* in Dakhni—the first such work to have survived in this language—that provides fascinating insights into his sensibilities. In some of these collected poems, Muhammad Quli celebrates beautiful women and splendid palaces and gardens, while in others he recounts with enthusiasm his participation in local festivals, both Muslim and Hindu.[14] The work also reveals how inextricably interwoven Persianate and Indic literary cultures had become at Golconda by the early 1600s, just as they had at Bijapur a generation earlier. Although the dīwān form itself and many of its specific poetic conventions stem from the Persian poetic tradition, others, like that of speaking through an assumed female voice in the language of *viraha*, or love in separation, are ultimately Indic in origin, as Carla Petievitch has argued.[15] In addition to writing this Dakhni dīwān, Muhammad Quli also composed Persian verse and patronized poets writing in Dakhni, Persian, and Telugu. One of these was the poet Wajhi, who based his Dakhni work *Quṭb-Mushtarī* on an imagined romance between the sultan and a fictional Bengali princess known as Mushtari.[16] In this work, the hero, Qutb (literally, the pole-star), is the sultan himself, while all the other characters are given the names of planets, as if to suggest that they literally revolve around the imperial hero.[17]

Apart from authoring, inspiring, or patronizing Dakhni, Persian, and Telugu literature, Muhammad Quli left as his principal legacy the founding of Hyderabad, marking the advent of the second Islamic millennium in AH 1000 (AD 1591). But the naming of his new capital has a curious history. It seems that a salacious rumour concerning Muhammad Quli's supposed affair with a Hindu prostitute named Bhagmati had been circulating at this time, owing possibly to the sultan's actual amorous proclivities, or to his representation as the romantic hero in Wajhi's *Quṭb Mushtarī*. In any event, it was rumoured that Muhammad Quli had fallen in love with Bhagmati and even named his new city after her, initially calling it Bhagnagar. 'The Sultan', wrote Firishta,

> was greatly fascinated by a prostitute (*fāḥisha*) named Bhagmati. He ordered that whenever she came to court she should be attended by a thousand horsemen so that she should not look one whit inferior to any of the big nobles. About this time, the climate of Golconda had become so bad that it had been telling on the health of its inhabitants, and it was for this reason that Muhammad Quli Qutb Shah founded and populated a city four *kuroh* [ca. 13 kilometres] away which became unequalled throughout the length and breadth of India for its planning as well as for its cleanliness. He called it Bhagnagar at first, but later he was sorry for what he had done and changed the name to Hyderabad.[18]

H.K. Sherwani has shown that this story has little factual basis, since official Qutb Shahi sources of Muhammad Quli's time make no references either to Bhagmati or to Bhagnagar.[19] Moreover, the earliest known coins struck in the new city, which date to this sultan's reign, give the mint-name simply as 'Dar al-Saltanat Hyderabad', not Bhagnagar.[20] The anonymous *Tārīkh-i Muḥammad Quṭb Shāh,* which is the closest thing to an official Qutb Shahi history that survives, consistently refers to the new city as Hyderabad, never Bhagnagar; nor does it mention the Bhagmati story. Sherwani suggests that 'Bhagnagar' probably represents a corrupted pronunciation of 'Baghnagar', or 'City of Gardens', the name commonly used for the city in both Dakhni and Telugu.[21] Once the name had been corrupted in this way, he writes, the 'romantic among the litterateurs' would have been responsible for the rise and spread of the popular story. The sultan's reputation as an aesthete probably added to its popular appeal.

Sherwani fails, however, to address some of the most striking and consistent details in the various tellings of the story. These include Bhagmati's identification as a prostitute (fāḥisha) and Muhammad Quli's assigning her a cavalry force of 1,000 horses 'so that she should not look one whit inferior to any of the big nobles'. In effect, the story presents her as an equal to the sultan's proper amīrs, despite her inferior status as a woman. For Persian élites of the Westerner class, the figure of Bhagmati, as a Hindu and commander of horse troops, could have called to mind the class of Hindu nāyakwāṛis, who were also favoured by the Qutb Shahi house. If this were the case, and there is no direct evidence that it was, then her identity as a woman would have implied that the nāyakwāṛis were effeminate—a gross insult from the perspective of Telugu martial culture[22]—while her status as a prostitute would suggest that the nāyakwāṛis were effectively selling themselves to the Qutb Shahis, calling into question the sincerity of their commitment to the Qutb Shahi cause. In this case, the story would likely not have emerged from 'romantically-minded litterateurs', as Sherwani argues, but from recently arrived 'Westerners' who felt uneasy about the high degree of Indic-Persianate cultural accommodation that had marked the Qutb Shahi court by this time.[23] For despite their Iranian origins, the Qutb Shahis and many of the Westerners who served them had become significantly Indianized, were literate in Telugu, and were regularly involved in complex interactions with their local Indian counterparts. Let us examine more closely the socio-cultural make-up of Golconda's ruling élite.

## GOLCONDA'S MULTI-ETHNIC ÉLITE: WESTERNERS, DECCANIS, NAYAKWARIS, AND NIYOGIS

As we saw in Chapter 4, the Bahmani Sultanate and its successor states were characterized by considerable ethnic diversity, which often led to political factionalism. Among Muslims, the principal division was between Westerners and Deccanis. The former included immigrants from the Arab and Persian worlds who tended to identify closely with the Persian language and were generally Shi`i Muslims. By contrast, the more locally rooted Deccanis, distantly descended from north Indian migrants, identified with the Dakhni language and followed Sunni Islam. Sultan Quli had begun his rise at the Bahmani court in the context of Westerner–Deccani antagonism, and throughout the first half of the sixteenth century the Qutb Shahi court witnessed intermittent conflicts between these two factions.

By the second half of the century additional social forces unique to the eastern Deccan had come into play, resulting in a more complex articulation of the Golconda élite. Individuals from two other groups now joined Westerners and Deccanis in the competition for power and influence. These were the nāyakwāṛis, Telugu-speaking Hindu warriors whose political prominence dates back to the Kakatiya period; and the Niyogis, worldly oriented Telugu brahmans who took up service in the state's administrative apparatus. The presence of these four groups, all vying for royal favour and political influence, made factions and alliances at Golconda's court more complex than was the case at the other Deccani courts.

In Persian sources relating to Golconda, the term 'nāyakwāṛi' refers to a Telugu-speaking Hindu military commander and is derived from the Telugu 'nāyakavāḍi' or 'nāyakavāḍa', which Telugu inscriptions in the region used in the same sense. As such, it is simply a variant form of 'nāyakuḍu' or Nayaka, a term more commonly used to refer to these same commanders in the Vijayanagara territories.[24] There is no essential difference between nāyakwāṛis and *nāyaka*s, as members of this class under either name often migrated back and forth between Golconda and Vijayanagara.[25] Like nāyakas, nāyakwāṛis belonged to different families and lineages that often competed with one another for dominance in a given region. Although nāyakwāṛi families tended to maintain strong ties to particular ancestral locales, the more successful among them enjoyed a high degree of mobility, as they moved with relative ease from one place to the next in search of military service under rulers who would grant them estates for maintaining their troops. As a class, they had adopted Persianate forms of military and administrative technology and were thoroughly familiar with Persianate courtly practices. Some of the highest ranking Qutb Shahi officers were nāyakwāṛis, such as Jagadeva Rao, who governed the Kaulas district during Jamshid's reign and was described as 'the most trustworthy of all the sardars [commanders]'.[26] Although he played a crucial part in facilitating Ibrahim's succession and was appointed prime minister, Jagadeva Rao moved on soon thereafter, first to Berar in the northern Deccan to take up service with the

Imad Shahis, and then to Vijayanagara, where he became a prominent commander under Rama Raya.[27] Indeed, Rama Raya himself had begun his career as a nāyakwāṛi commander in the service of Sultan Quli before falling from favour and fleeing to Vijayanagara to take up service under Krishna Raya.[28]

The fourth group, the Niyogis, encompassed brahmans who had given up their caste's traditional priestly roles to assume salaried political and administrative appointments in the state bureaucracy.[29] They by no means constituted a unified group, being internally divided both along sectarian religious lines and by the levels and types of appointments they held.[30] Most Niyogis served at lower administrative levels, typically as accountants (*karaṇams*) who maintained tax ledgers and other records of use to the state.[31] Most karaṇams worked at the village level and hence remain anonymous to us. But we can identify others, such as the *sthala-karaṇams*, who maintained the records of an entire district,[32] or the *nagara-karaṇams*, who maintained those of a town or city.[33] Niyogis also served as diplomatic representatives (*nēbati*, *sthānāpati*) posted to the courts of neighbouring states, as governors of towns and cities (*paṭṭanādhyakṣa*), or even as ministerial advisors (*pradhāni*) to the sultan. One prominent Niyogi family provides examples of all three such posts, as we can see from the introduction to a Telugu literary work written by one of its members, Nebati Krishnayamatya.[34] In the mid-fifteenth century the author's great-great-great grandfather, Nagaraju, had served as a nēbati, or diplomatic representative, under the Bahmanis; because Nagaraju's immediate descendants continued to serve the Bahmanis in this capacity, they assumed the family name of Nebati.[35] Krishnayamatya's father, Kamalanabhamatya, had so impressed Ibrahim Qutb Shah with his qualities that the sultan appointed him governor of the town of Pangal.[36] Krishnayamatya himself served as an advisor in Muhammad Quli's ministerial council.[37]

The Qutb Shahis' political viability critically depended on their ability to recruit and enlist talented individuals from all four of these social groups. As a result, members of these groups necessarily interacted closely and regularly with individuals who differed from them in significant ways. Such regularly recurring interactions and alliances led to the deeply composite character of Golconda's culture, ensuring the mutual intelligibility of Indic and Persianate cultural forms and leading to the emergence of shared forms of expression.

Two cases can illustrate how this composite culture operated. The first involves an historic alliance that was forged at the fort of Koyilkonda in 1550 amidst the succession dispute following Jamshid's death. Although the anonymous Qutb Shahi historian refers to the episode in passing, its fuller details are known only from a commemorative Telugu inscription that was set up at the fort's entrance the following year (Figure 6.1).[38] Here we learn that eleven of the fort's nāyakwāṛi commanders and two of their Westerner counterparts—Pir Miyan and Saiyid `Ali Miyan[39]—had sworn a mutual pact to support Ibrahim in his claim to the throne, and that all the lower-ranking military personnel at the fort supported the action. After making the pact, the group sent Saiyid `Ali Miyan to Vijayanagara to invite Ibrahim back to his ancestral kingdom and to pledge the support of their strategic fort. When Ibrahim reached Koyilkonda, he 'sat himself upon the sofa of the master'[40] and addressed the assembled men in chaste Telugu, saying, 'Although I was at Vijayanagara, you have brought me here; am I to trust you?'[41] In response, they swore their absolute allegiance to the prince, sealed with imprecations that would bring a range of

**Figure 6.1** Koyilkonda. Stone inscription, 1551.

calamities upon themselves should any among them violate their agreement.

This fascinating text reveals several important things. First, it documents the forging of a working relationship between a group of nāyakwāṛis and two Westerners based on a shared political agenda. Even before the succession dispute emerged, the men of the two groups would already have shared much in common, collectively garrisoning and defending the strategic fort at Koyilkonda. But with the throne now in dispute, both groups recognized in Ibrahim a candidate who reflected their own situations, effectively transcending their differences. Westerners could readily identify with the son of a Westerner, while the nāyakwāṛis would naturally relate to someone who had just returned from the Telugu milieu of Rama Raya's Vijayanagara, and with whom they could converse in their native language.

Second, in the richly variegated texture of its language, the inscription reveals the extent to which Telugu and Persian had already become intertwined in Golconda's composite cultural milieu. Golconda's inscriptions were often issued bilingually, with the Persian text at the top and a Telugu version below, reflecting Persian's status as the court's official language, and Telugu's as the language of the countryside. In contrast, the present inscription is recorded only in Telugu, since it was issued not by a central state authority, but by the garrison's local commanders, who were predominantly nāyakwāṛis. Nonetheless, its Telugu is replete with Persian loanwords, suggesting the extent of bilingualism among the garrison's different speech communities.[42] Whereas the brief statement of (the ostensibly Westerner) Ibrahim appears in pure Telugu, the speech of the (ostensibly sons-of-the soil) nāyakwāṛis is liberally peppered with Arabo-Persian vocabulary, from the strings of titles used to introduce Ibrahim[43] to the names of occupational groups among Koyilkonda's garrison[44] and various other expressions, including the words for 'retainers', 'gateway', 'corruption', and even 'men'.[45] Not only in its content, but even in its language, the inscription reveals the mutual acculturation of Telugu and Persian speech communities in Qutb Shahi Andhra.

Finally, the inscription suggests how religion and religious culture were understood by the Qutb Shahi political élite at mid-century. Consider the variety of imprecations invoked upon those who might break the pact. In some cases, breaking the pact is considered the 'same sin'[46] as violating a religious taboo.[47] Three distinct taboos are invoked, however, since it was recognized that the pact might potentially be violated by Hindus, Sunnis, or Shi`is. Hindus who reneged on their word would 'incur the sin of slaughtering cows and brahmans in Varanasi',[48] while 'Turks' who did so would incur the sin of 'slaughtering pigs in Mecca' or that of 'killing Imam Husain on the battlefield [of Karbala]'.[49] On the one hand, this threefold imprecation recognized that significant ritual differences distinguished the groups to which they belonged. But on the other hand, the three different acts were understood to share an underlying functional equivalence, implying that the three religious traditions shared a common ethical basis.[50] They all shared common notions respecting the power of vows, the moral darkness of 'sin', and the inviolable sacredness of pilgrimage sites. By recognizing these shared underlying values, the Hindu, Sunni, and Shi`i commanders at Koyilkonda could identify a common ground for concerted action.

The second case reveals the complex web of relationships binding a Deccani noble to the brahmans living in his domain—both Niyogis and the more traditionally minded Vedic brahmans. The noble `Abd al-Qadir Amin Khan (fl. 1568–83) was a prominent amīr during Ibrahim's reign who hailed from a locally established Deccani family. Since at least his grandfather's generation, Amin Khan's family had been administering the region around Patancheru, some 30 kilometres northwest of modern Hyderabad.[51] More clearly than Shitab Khan or even Ibrahim Qutb Shah, Amin Khan simultaneously inhabited two cultural universes—the one Persianate and Islamic, the other Indic and Hindu—that converged in the town of Patancheru. There, Amin Khan patronized the construction of a number of characteristically Islamic structures, including an impressive tomb to serve as his final resting place, and a mosque located nearby (Figure 6.2). The former was completed in 1568, the latter in 1583. He also issued two Persian inscriptions in fine *thuluth* script on one of the walls of his tomb (Figure 6.3).[52] In these inscriptions, he presents himself as a pious Muslim—a 'humble, lowly, and insignificant servant'—and a devoted disciple of a Sufi saint of the Qadiri order, Shah Muhammad al-Qadiri al-Multani, and as a grand-disciple of the latter's master, Shaikh Ibrahim Makhdum Shah-ji Muhammad Qadiri (d. 1564) of Bidar.[53] Amin Khan states that completion of the tomb was accomplished not by himself but 'by the grace of God, Almighty', and with the spiritual help of the twelfth-century founder of the Qadiri order, Shaikh Muhyi al-Din `Abd al-Qadir (d. 1166).

**Figure 6.2** Patancheru. Tomb of Amin Khan.

At the same time, Amin Khan enthusiastically patronized Telugu literature, commissioning the poet Ponnikanti Telaganarya to compose his *Yayāti Caritramu*, a Telugu adaptation of the story of Yayati from the Mahābhārata.[54] As the first known example of a work written in so-called pure Telugu (*acca-tĕlugu*), this work holds considerable significance for Telugu literary history. In attempting to account for this new convention of artificially 'purifying' Telugu of all direct Sanskrit loan-words (*tatsamas*), V. Narayana Rao has suggested that Telaganarya and his followers were influenced by the conventions of Persian poetry.[55] In particular, Firdausi's *Shāh-nāma* (AD 980) provided the classical model by deliberately using Persian wherever possible, thereby attempting to turn back the tide of Arabicization and recapture something of the purity of pre-Islamic Persian culture. The creation of acca-tĕlugu may therefore represent a form of stylistic accommodation in which certain values and practices of the classical Persian poetic tradition were transferred to Telugu for the benefit of the Persianate patron.[56]

Telaganarya's preface to his *Yayāti Caritramu* also provides valuable information about Amin Khan himself. Here we learn that he employed as his personal secretary (*rāyasam*) a prominent Niyogi brahman named Maringanti Appana, through whom he persuaded Telaganarya to accept the commission.[57] Apart from his deep

**Figure 6.3** Patancheru. The two inscriptions of Amin Khan's tomb. Upper panel dated 1568; lower panel dated 1583.

commitment to the prosperity of his district and the welfare of its inhabitants, Amin Khan also patronized traditional Vedic brahmans by establishing a tax-free brahman village (*agrahāram*) named 'Aminpuram' and relinquished his claim to its taxes so that the residents could use them for their own support.[58] Aminpuram's brahmans would not have been niyogis, but traditional *vaidiki* brahmans, who through Amin Khan's endeavours were able to devote themselves full-time to Vedic study and teaching.[59] His support of the region's brahmans even extended to helping them defray the costs of their marriage ceremonies.[60] In addition, he built in Aminpuram a large irrigation tank (*ceruvu*) to ensure the productivity of the village's lands, and a charitable garden planted with fruit trees and medicinal plants that were made available to the public. Located some 6 kilometres to the southeast of Patancheru, Aminpuram and its tank still exist today, suggesting that Telaganarya did not exaggerate about his patron's benefactions.

Taken together, these two cases indicate something of the cultural complexity of Golconda's élite society. Not only did Indic and Persianate cultural universes exist side by side in Qutb Shahi Andhra, but individuals regularly moved back and forth between these two worlds as they interacted with élite counterparts from other classes. Given this socio-cultural fluidity, Qutb Shahi architecture could hardly have drawn inspiration exclusively from Persianate or Islamic models. To the contrary, patrons, builders, and craftsmen, being familiar with pre-Sultanate Indic models and paradigms, freely took inspiration from their region's earlier monuments as they drafted designs for their own buildings. Looming especially large in the Qutb Shahi architectural imagination was the monumental complex at the heart of Warangal, the central plaza that the Kakatiyas had built around the former site of the great Svayambhu Shiva temple.

## QUTB SHAHI WARANGAL: FORM AND MEANING

Although Warangal is commonly thought of today as a 'Hindu' city, by the time Muhammad Quli began laying out his new capital of Hyderabad this 'Hindu' city had already been a sultanate town for nearly as long as it was held by Indic polities.[61] To be sure, the city did retain unusual remnants from its Kakatiya past, but these were complemented everywhere by newer structures of types and styles that would have been familiar from Golconda and other Qutb Shahi urban centres. On the one hand, Qutb Shahi rulers updated the city's defences in response to the introduction of gunpowder weapons by building new parapets atop the battlements of the city's inner wall (Figure 6.4),[62] by adding semicircular barbicans in front of the eastern and western gates of this wall,[63] and by building a massive octagonal gun platform and an adjacent powder magazine at the city's highest point.[64] All of these additions are securely datable to the Qutb Shahi period on

**Figure 6.4** Warangal Fort. Portion of the inner wall, showing original Kakatiya merlons (foreground) and merlons rebuilt in the Qutb Shahi period (background).

both typological and stylistic grounds. On the other hand, they provided certain pre-existing structures in the city with new decorative veneers in carved stucco, effectively 'updating' them by applying motifs commonly used for the ornamentation of later sixteenth-century Qutb Shahi buildings. Only two fragmentary patches of this stucco veneer survive today, one on an arch in one of the city's Bahmani-period gateways (Figure 6.5), and the other on the main façade of the Khush Mahal audience hall constructed by the Tughluqs (Figure 6.6). Qutb Shahi–style stucco motifs were likely much more widespread, but have largely vanished because of the impermanence of the stucco medium.[65]

Given the extent of these renovations of the city's urban fabric, it is telling that so much of the city's antique character was deliberately maintained. In particular, the monumental plaza at the heart of Warangal was preserved as it had been at the end of the city's Tughluq occupation (1323–31)—a largely open square marked on each side by a Kakatiya-period

**Figure 6.5** Warangal Fort: Western gateway of outer wall, constructed in the Bahmani period with small patch of decorative stucco of the Qutb Shahi period.

**Figure 6.6** Warangal Fort. Khush Mahal: detail of Qutb Shahi decorative stucco on entrance façade.

*toraṇa*. Towering over 9 metres high and 12 metres wide, these structures possess a monumentality that can be sensed only vaguely through photographs (Figure 1.6, p. 18). With respect to their distinctive forms, Warangal's toraṇas have often been viewed as somewhat distant and austere echoes of the better-known toraṇas from such ancient Buddhist sites as Sanchi and Bharhut.[66] While these earlier toraṇas generally had but two columns, and often as many as three curving crossbars, their Kakatiya descendants consist of a pair of columns at either side, supporting a single straight crossbar with projecting ends. As in the ancient toraṇas, the cantilevered ends of the crossbars at Warangal are supported by brackets, although here they take the form not of figural tree spirits but of sinuous, double-curved struts with linear architectural mouldings at either end. Although not nearly as rich in figural sculpture as the ancient Sanchi toraṇas, with their ambitious narrative panels and elaborate programmes of symbolic ornament, the Warangal toraṇas do still carry some figural sculpture in addition to their carved architectural ornament. Most important iconographically is the motif of the secondary decorative 'arch' above the crossbar proper (Figure 6.7). This element is a *makara-toraṇa* like those we have seen in previous chapters, here consisting of a flattened arch of undulating lotus rhizomes with pendant buds, issuing from the mouths of two florid makara-crocodiles that are barely visible behind the small pavilion-like structures atop each column. Also notable are the lions frolicking along the upper and lower surfaces of the brackets, the geese above the projecting ends of the crossbars, and a number of male caryatid figures and lotus-bearing goddesses contained within small shrine-like niches along the crossbar's face. There is no sign that stucco decoration was ever added to these portals to obscure their imagery; nor has any damage ever been inflicted upon the figural sculptures adorning them. To the contrary, as Marika Sardar has recently suggested, they may well have provided the models for several sculptural motifs that frequently appear on the lintels of Bahmani-period gateways in the Telangana region, including lions, geese, and lotuses.[67]

Contextual evidence suggests that these toraṇas were understood as products of the city's Kakatiya past; in fact, it was in Qutb Shahi Warangal that a tradition of Telugu historiography relating to the Kakatiyas first appeared. Ekamranatha composed his *Pratāparudra*

**Figure 6.7** Warangal Fort. Detail of Kakatiya-period *toraṇa* crossbar, showing scuptural motifs of *makara-toraṇa,* lions, and goddesses (*Courtesy of* John Henry Rice).

*Caritramu* in Warangal about 1550, and some fifty years later Kase Sarvappa wrote the *Śrī-Siddheśvara Caritramu* in the nearby suburb of Hanamkonda.[68] The face of the southern toraṇa itself bears an inscription referring to a fourteenth-century Sanskrit historical *kāvya* on the Kakatiyas (*Kākatīya Carita*), an excerpt of which was inscribed on the face of a boulder in Hanamkonda.[69] With Warangal so saturated with historical awareness of the Kakatiya past, and with Kakatiya historical texts literally inscribed into the landscape, the city's Qutb Shahi occupants surely understood the toraṇas as relics from the city's Kakatiya past.

They must also have understood the original significance of these portals. We know that the Kakatiyas had planned their capital in the form of a cosmogram, the city's form replicating that of the larger world as understood in traditional Indian cosmography.[70] According to this conception, as elaborated in various Purāṇa texts, the world consists of a great circular continent surrounded by a ring-shaped ocean of saltwater, which is in turn encircled by a series of six more ring-shaped continents separated by their respective seas of sugar-cane juice, wine, ghee, curds, milk, and fresh water. The central circular continent, called Jambudvipa, measures 100,000 *yojana*s in diameter (approximately 1.5 million kilometres) with the cosmic mountain Meru at its centre. At the top of Mt Meru, and thus in the centre of the entire cosmos, dwells Shiva in his form of Lord of the Universe. Surrounding Mt Meru, Jambudvipa is divided into four subcontinents, of which the southern one—Bharatavarsha—represents the known world of ancient India. This cosmos is permeated by a four-quartered structure so that, for example, four smaller mountains stand on Meru's flanks, one in each of the cardinal directions, while the celestial river Ganga, after it has fallen from heaven to the top of Mt Meru, divides into four mighty rivers that flow out to the salt sea—again, one in each of the cardinal directions.[71]

The plan of Warangal and its four toraṇas must be understood in terms of this cosmogrammatic structure (see Figure A2.3, p. 360). The city by no means precisely replicates this structure, its circular form being somewhat irregular and its central node displaced slightly to the northeast of its actual geometric centre. Yet the cosmogrammatic *intention* behind the plan is clear enough. The area within the city's inner wall replicates the central continent of Jambudvipa, the moat beyond this wall corresponding to the surrounding salt sea. The area between this moat and the city's outer wall corresponds to the first ring-shaped continent, Plaksha, and the second moat answers to the sea of wine surrounding that continent. At the conceptual centre of the city, the mountain-like temple of Svayambhu Shiva would have replicated the form of Mt Meru and contained the *rāṣṭra-devatā*, or state-deity, of the Kakatiya kingdom, just as the Lord of the Universe dwells atop Mt Meru in the Puranic cosmography. The toraṇas beyond the walls of this temple are in positions corresponding to the sources of the four rivers, which similarly begin their course at the base of Mt Meru and flow out to the salt sea, just as the city's four axial avenues radiated out from the central temple square to the four gateways in the stone wall and then crossed over the moat beyond. A conceptual association between the toraṇas and these four rivers is further supported by their iconography, which is restricted almost entirely to 'watery' themes such as the crocodiles-and-lotus meanders (makara-toraṇa) running along the top of the crossbar, the lotus-goddesses carved along its lower face, and the geese sitting atop the projecting ends. Through the geometry of its main morphological features, then, the city replicated the structural features of the larger cosmos over which the Kakatiyas aspired to rule. The city would have functioned as a symbolic tool for the expression of their imperium: by exercising their dominion within this microcosmic realm, the city's rulers could hope to dominate ritually the larger world whose form it reflected.

Even with the Svayambhu Shiva temple dismantled and gone, Warangal's Qutb Shahi occupants could not have missed the intentions behind the city's cosmographic plan. We have seen that many members of the Qutb Shahi élite were steeped in Telugu literature, and they would have had access to texts such as Marana's Telugu adaptation of the *Mārkaṇḍeya Purāṇamu*, written in Warangal during the reign of Pratapa Rudra (1289–1323). This text includes a detailed account of the traditional Puranic cosmography as outlined earlier, resonating closely with the form of Warangal.[72] Moreover, a number of Telugu panegyric verses dedicated to Ibrahim Qutb Shah confirm that he was well acquainted with traditional Indic cosmographic conceptions.[73] These verses address Ibrahim as 'Malk Ibharama', or even as 'Malkibha Ramachandra', playfully suggesting an equivalence between Ibrahim and Rama, the paragon of royal virtue in the Indic tradition. One such verse begins by celebrating Ibharama's boundless generosity in supporting musicians, poets, and other men of learning, but then moves on to a more iconic image of the king in the traditional Indic guise of a universal emperor or *cakravartin*:

If he so much as smiles, he'll give you hundreds when you know the subtleties of music and song.

If he is moved to say, 'Come,' he'll give thousands when you're a bold poet who can shine in his court.

If he says, 'Here, sit with me,' he'll give you hundreds of thousands when you know the rules and the art of poetry.

If he says 'Shahbash!' ['well done!'] he'll give you millions when you're one of his favourite scholars.

Oh Emperor Ibharama! Your resplendent form
puts to shame even the pearls of your parasol—
they only glow from the light
of the fame you have won
protecting the wheel of this earth surrounded by four oceans.[74]

Here the verse invokes the idea of the parasol or *chattra*, an ancient symbol of cosmic kingship in both the Indic and Persianate traditions, and one of the seven symbols of a conquering king, or cakravartin. Significantly, the verse also credits 'Ibharama' with protecting the entire earth, which is envisioned as a wheel (*dhātri-cakra*) girt by the four oceans, one in each of the cardinal directions, calling to mind the image of Jambudvipa surrounded by the ring of its salt sea. Another such verse is even more explicit in its cosmographic imagery:

He has climbed the seven mountains
crossed the seven seas
and circled the seven continents—
his fame fills the fourteen worlds.
Malkibha Ramachandra
is truly a seventh *cakravartin*
and a seventeenth king![75]

Ibrahim is said to have climbed the seven great mountain ranges that run across Jambudvipa, circumambulated all seven of the continents, and crossed all seven of the cosmic oceans, justifying his status as a *seventh* cakravartin, and a *seventeenth* king—even though tradition recognizes only *six* legendary cakravartins and *sixteen* exemplary kings.

For the Qutb Shahi élite, then, this unique, open plaza bounded by Warangal's four toraṇas possessed a powerful symbolic valence, rich in memories of the Kakatiya past and redolent with ideas of imperial dominion. The presence of the Khush Mahal audience hall just west of the plaza, associated with the imperial power of the Delhi Sultanate, would only have enhanced the attraction of this space for Qutb Shahi rulers. The fragmentary remains of Qutb Shahi stucco decoration along the Khush Mahal's entrance façade confirms its relevance for the Qutb Shahis, suggesting that it continued in use as an audience hall for the city's governor. Moreover, the hall was visually and conceptually linked with the plaza to its east because of the perfect alignment of the niche at the northern end of its eastern wall with the western and eastern toraṇas of the plaza. As an urban space, Warangal's central plaza was unique in the Qutb Shahi realm—until, that is, the early 1590s, when Muhammad Quli built his new capital of Hyderabad.

## THE FOUNDING OF HYDERABAD: FORM AND MEANING OF THE MILLENNIAL CITY

In 1591, Sultan Muhammad Quli marked the beginning of the second Islamic millennium by founding a new city, Hyderabad, as the Qutb Shahi capital.[76] Laid out on a level plain southeast of the Musi River, just a few kilometres from the old capital at Golconda, Hyderabad follows a plan that, we argue, was inspired in fundamental respects by the earlier imperial model of Warangal. It is true that Hyderabad, unlike Warangal, was not walled, although walls would later be constructed between 1724 and 1740.[77] And Hyderabad's buildings could not be farther in style from the Kakatiya monuments of Warangal. But in its underlying urban conception, Muhammad Quli's new capital reveals itself as an unmistakable response to the earlier city. Both Hyderabad and Warangal were established as new foundations, intended to replace older capitals centred on hill forts that offered little room for expansion for their growing populations. Both cities were laid out on open ground to the southeast of the hill forts that they had superseded—Warangal 6.5 kilometres southeast of Hanamkonda, and Hyderabad 7.5 kilometres east-southeast of Golconda. Most importantly, both cities were laid out according to a four-quartered imperial plan produced by four axial avenues running out in the cardinal directions from a central point. Both cities designated that central point with a distinctive structure indicating the crossing of these four axial avenues. In both cities, a broad open plaza defined by four lofty gateways was placed immediately to the north of the central crossing point. And in both cities a palace complex axially aligned with the plaza was placed to its immediate west. In Warangal, the complex we presently see, the Khush Mahal, was built by the Tughluqs shortly after they conquered the Kakatiyas in 1323, possibly on the site of the Kakatiya palace.

Warangal's underlying urban conception was realized in Hyderabad by building a new, north–south road to intersect with a pre-existing east–west highway that had run between Golconda and Masulipatnam, the state's chief port on the Bay of Bengal. This central crossing was marked by the new city's first building to be completed: the Charminar (1591), justly characterized by George Michell as 'the most original architectural conception of the Qutb Shahis, and indeed of any of the Deccani Sultans'[78] (Figure 6.8). Just 100 metres to the north of the Charminar, a vast open plaza was laid out, straddling the city's northern avenue and measuring nearly 220 metres on each side.[79]

Like Warangal's central plaza, Hyderabad's was defined by four lofty gateways completed in 1592 and collectively known as the Char Kaman, or the 'four bows', a reference to their imposing arches (Figures 6.9 and 6.10). Like Warangal's toraṇas, these gateways were free-standing and had no surrounding enclosure

**Figure 6.8** Hyderabad. The Charminar (1591).

wall, although the square plaza lying within them may have been visually demarcated by pavements or trees along the perimeter. These portals marked out an open forecourt for Muhammad Quli's expansive palace complex, which began just beyond the western Kaman and ran westward all the way to the bank of the river. Apart from a square reservoir at the centre of the plaza—the *chār-sū-kā ḥauẓ*—the remaining area within the square was preserved as open space. The lofty arches of the Char Kaman can still be seen today, although the open plaza they once defined was long ago swallowed up by the city's dense urban fabric. Nothing at all remains of the palace complex that once stood to their west, as these buildings were destroyed following the Mughal conquest of Golconda in 1687.[80]

Being massive pylons pierced in the middle by lofty pointed arches, the Char Kaman could hardly be more different in physical, structural terms from their trabeate models at Warangal. They are nonetheless identical in their spatial conception and larger contextual situation. Moreover, both plazas replicate the larger four-quartered structure of the cities that surround them, even though neither plaza lies at its city's actual geometric centre, but a short distance to the north. Both plazas likely served as places of assembly before their

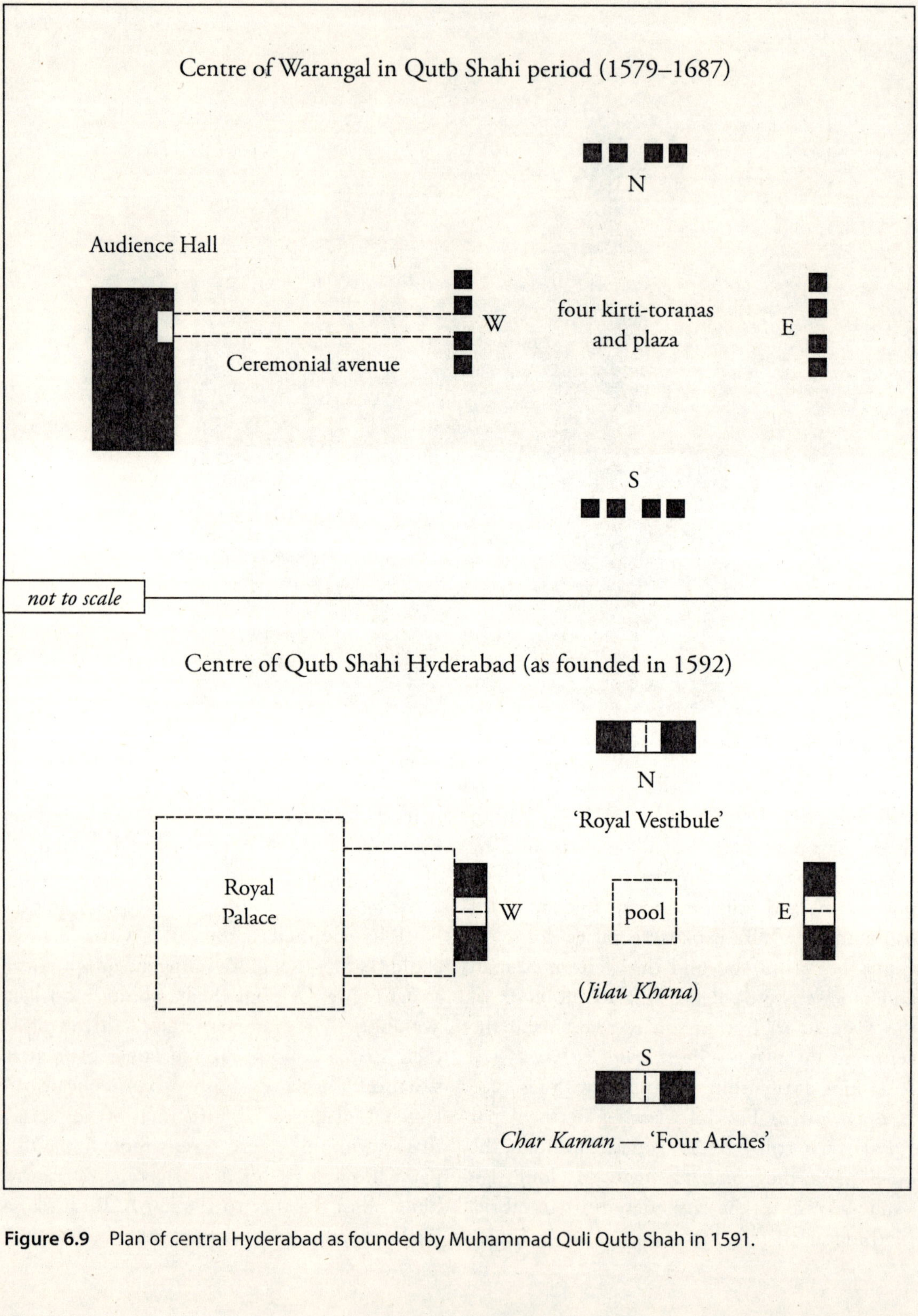


**Figure 6.9** Plan of central Hyderabad as founded by Muhammad Quli Qutb Shah in 1591.

respective palace complexes,[81] but on a deeper, symbolic level, they also served as microcosmic representations of the larger cities around them. Given the many striking similarities between the two plazas, as well as what we know about Qutb Shahi interest in Warangal, it is difficult to avoid the conclusion that Muhammad Quli and his planners were responding to the earlier city as they designed Hyderabad.

Oddly, however, this local genealogy of Hyderabad's plan has been totally overlooked. Most authorities have stressed the Islamic antecedents of Hyderabad—in particular, by viewing it as a replica of the Qur'anic paradise, as the author of the anonymous *Tārīkh-i Muḥammad Quṭb Shāh* suggests in the second epigraph that opens this chapter.[82] Others have sought to locate its inspiration in the urban planning traditions of Timurid Central Asia or Safavid Iran. That is to say, they have tended to view the city within the context of the larger history of Perso-Islamic, and not Indian, urban design. Those scholars who argue that Hyderabad's layout was inspired by Safavid Isfahan note that the latter city also revolved around a vast open plaza, the Maidan-i Shah.[83] Robert McChesney has shown that this plaza was laid out between 1590 and 1595, during Shah Abbas's first campaign of construction in the new capital.[84] At Isfahan too, the palace complex adjoined the *maidān* on its western side, and the gateway that linked the two—the

**Figure 6.10** Hyderabad. Southern portal of the Char Kaman ensemble (1592), seen from the Charminar.

Ali Qapu—served not merely as a gateway, but also as a place of reception linking the public maidān with the more restricted zone of the palace to its west. Much has also been made of the supposed role in Hyderabad's planning played by Muhammad Quli's famed minister Mir Momin Astarabadi, who was not only a Westerner, but a native of Isfahan.

But there are difficulties in identifying Isfahan as the source of Hyderabad's plan. First, Isfahan's maidān is a long, rectangular space measuring 510 metres north to south and only 158 metres running east to west, which was originally a polo ground and space for military exercises. Second, Isfahan's maidān, unlike Hyderabad's central plaza, was enclosed along its perimeter even in its earliest phase of construction.[85] Finally, Hyderabad's Char Kaman plaza was completed by 1592, or several years before Isfahan's Maidan-i Shah and Ali Qapu had been completed, and a decade before the associated structures on the other three sides had been built.[86] Without these buildings providing entrance gates to respond to that of the Ali Qapu on the west, the space of the maidān would have looked very unlike Hyderabad's plaza.

A second possible source for Hyderabad's plan has been proposed by George Michell who, noting the close resemblance of the Char Kaman to the Registan in Samarqand, concludes that the former owes much to the Timurids of Central Asia.[87] But here the difficulty is that Samarqand's Registan did not assume its present form until the seventeenth century, when the construction of the Tilakari Madrasa (1646–60) closed off the northern side of the space, which had until then been bounded only on its east and west sides.[88] But even then, the plaza remained unbounded on its southern side, as it still is today. A further problem is that the two plazas differ conceptually, since the Registan is bounded entirely by religious structures and does not include a palatial zone adjoining it as Hyderabad does.

Hyderabad is further linked to Warangal through its most famous monument—the Charminar. Notwithstanding its iconic status, this structure does not fit readily into any established building category known from the medieval Islamic world.[89] Although its wide central arches and flanking *mīnār* towers call to mind the forms of a gateway, this 'gateway' is not articulated with any wall, and it leads nowhere except into its own enigmatic interior, centred on a fountain. Although it contains a small, exquisite mosque in its uppermost storey, the building as a whole is clearly neither a mosque, nor simply a grand platform for a mosque. Its functional identity being by no means readily apparent, the building has been understood in various ways in the centuries since its construction.[90]

Viewed from within the context of the local Deccani architectural tradition, however, the monument's function quickly becomes clear. The Charminar appears to belong to a well-defined type of Deccani monument, the *chaubārā* or 'four-fold house', which is often found at the centre of medieval Deccani cities marking the intersection of four cardinal avenues.[91] These chaubārās vary significantly in their design, even while they are identical with respect to their situation and the idea of 'quartering' referenced through their names. At Bidar, the capital of the Bahmani Sultanate from the mid-fifteenth century on, the lower town is structured by two main avenues that run roughly east–west and north–south, and the point of their intersection is occupied by a chaubārā in the form of a tapering, circular tower (Figure 6.11).[92] This tower rises some 21 metres above the ground, thus providing an excellent platform for surveillance, but its form

**Figure 6.11** Bidar. The Bahmani *chaubārā*.

does not accentuate the four-quartered conception revealed by its name. Another Bahmani chaubārā is preserved at Udgir, a major Bahmani stronghold in eastern Maharashtra, where the building similarly serves to anchor the crossing of the cardinal avenues in the lower town (Figure 6.12). Though not as lofty as Bidar's, being only two storeys high, this chaubārā is octagonally planned and articulated by arches so as to specify its connection with the four quarters—and for that matter, with the four intermediate directions as well. Another Bahmani town in eastern Maharashtra, Kandhar, has a chaubārā of modern construction standing at its centre; it is at least conceivable that this might have replaced an original of the Bahmani period.

These examples of chaubārās all happen to be from sultanate centres, but it is clear that the type goes back to an even earlier era. The plaza defined by Warangal's *kirti-toraṇa*s lies some distance northeast of the actual crossing of the city's four main avenues, which in the Kakatiya period would have intersected at a point some 60 metres southwest of the southern toraṇa. At that point an enigmatic, two-storeyed pavilion still stands (Figure 6.13). This building seems to have puzzled M.A. Dhaky, who speculated that it might have played some kind of secular function.[93] In form, it is the height of simplicity: a single-bayed, open pillared maṇḍapa carrying its roof on four *citrakhaṇḍa* columns, and above this, a second identical

**Figure 6.12** Udgir. Bahmani-period *chaubārā*.

storey of slightly reduced proportions. Since it stands at the centre of the city and its sides are oriented in the directions of the city's four gateways, it would seem to represent the earliest known example of a chaubārā known from the Deccan, and perhaps the ultimate inspiration behind Hyderabad's Charminar.

The Charminar, however, represents an infinitely more complex and sophisticated rendition of the chaubārā type; in fact, it represents the very pinnacle of the form's development. As experienced from outside at ground level, the Charminar is an essentially cubic structure that presents an alternating rhythm of interlocking voids and solids (Figure 6.8). Its four cardinal sides are relieved by spacious arches, great open spaces physically inviting movement inside, towards the centre of the building's domed chamber, while the intervening corners present the contrast of the four mīnārs that rise up over the core of the building and give it its name. These powerful solid forms pull the eye upward and afford access to the building's two upper storeys through spiral stairways contained within. The first of the building's two upper storeys is essentially a mezzanine, with an arcade providing views outward from each side, and a continuous circular line of arches inside, affording views down into the central space from a level just below the springing of the flattened dome (Figure 6.14). The uppermost storey is occupied by a small but sumptuously decorated

**Figure 6.13** Warangal. Proto-*chaubārā* (*courtesy of* AIIS photo-archive).

mosque, tucked neatly into the square space between the mīnārs, and all but invisible from the ground (Figure 6.15).

As a latter-day chaubārā, marking the centre of its city and by extension of the fourfold universe, the Charminar fits squarely within the Indic tradition of cosmographic architecture. Yet its form and conception reveal the impact of Islamic and Persianate ideas to a degree not seen in any earlier chaubārā. In the first place, the Charminar is not oriented precisely to the cardinal directions, but exhibits a declination of 10 degrees, so that the four sides of the monument are oriented at 10, 100, 190, and 280 degrees. This departure from perfect cardinality resulted from a concern that the mosque on the building's upper floor should be properly oriented towards the *qibla* of Mecca, which was interpreted as lying 10 degrees north of due west—that is, at 280 degrees.[94] Owing to the Charminar's orientation, the entire urban grid of the city, which is projected from the central point of the Charminar, comes to be oriented to the qibla, a suitable orientation for a city designed to commemorate the beginning of the second Islamic millennium.

Strictly Islamic concerns, however, were not the only ones to motivate the designers of this edifice. Equally important was the pre-Islamic Iranian idea of the *chahār-ṭāq*—literally the

**Figure 6.14** Hyderabad. The Charminar: interior view of mezzanine storey.

**Figure 6.15** Hyderabad. The Charminar: prayer hall of mosque on uppermost storey (photograph by Marie Martin; *courtesy of* Art, Architecture, and Engineering Library, University of Michigan, and the American Council for Southern Asian Art).

'four arches'—which served as a widespread symbolic image of the cosmos in medieval Persian poetry. This literary symbol envisioned the universe as a domed quadrangular building of vast proportions, carried on four arches and illuminated at its apex by the sun as the light of heaven and earth. Such a conception inspired physical manifestations in diverse media, from small ceramic bowls and lamps to full-scale architectural monuments like throne rooms and tombs that literally replicated the chahār-ṭāq's four arches and celestial dome.[95] In casting Hyderabad's chaubārā not as a simple post-and-lintel maṇḍapa as at Warangal, nor as a circular or octagonal tower as at Bidar and Udgir, but as an expansive four-arched structure vaulted inside by a dome with a solar lotus at its apex (Figure 6.14), the designers of the Charminar seized on the underlying similarities between Indic and Persianate conceptions of the cosmos. By creating a monument that was at once Indic, Persianate, and Islamic, the Charminar's designers and patron have affirmed the fundamental commensurability of these diverse cultural traditions that flowed together with such vitality in the Qutb Shahi kingdom.

* * *

That Muhammad Quli drew on the model of Warangal in planning his new capital of Hyderabad should not be surprising. Telugu-speaking Hindus formed the vast majority of the population of his kingdom.[96] Members of the sultanate's high-ranking immigrant nobility and the Qutb Shahi family itself cultivated Telugu language, literature, and courtly culture.[97] By the second half of the sixteenth century, the kingdom depended almost entirely on brahmans and members of local warrior families to fill all but the very highest-level administrative positions.[98] By then Westerners, Deccanis, Niyogi brahmans, and nāyakwāṛi warriors had all acquired significant stakes in the kingdom's power structure. Above all, members of each group understood that they all shared a common political destiny, as we saw revealed in the pacts made by the various ethnic groups garrisoned in Koyilkonda Fort in 1550, or in the extravagant benefactions made in Patancheru by Amin Khan. An awareness of that common destiny seems to have fostered among Golconda's ruling class the growth of a composite culture that combined elements of both the Persian and the Sanskrit cosmopolises.

But these were mainly contributing, or enabling, factors. What proved decisive was the Qutb Shahis' prolonged rule over Warangal, a city saturated with the Kakatiyas' rich architectural legacy, where visual reminders of that kingdom's former presence lay everywhere to be seen. Even Ulugh Khan—who had directed the Tughluq conquest of the Kakatiyas in 1323 and had demolished Warangal's great Svayambhu Shiva temple—seems to have understood the cosmographic significance of the city's central plaza. Crucially, he realized that the plaza's symbolism was not specific to the Kakatiya king he had just defeated, but was generic, and hence capable of being reused. This much we know from what he chose to destroy and what he chose to preserve. Whereas he demolished the Svayambhu Shiva temple, which contained the dynasty's *raṣṭra-devatā*, or state-deity—an image specific to the Kakatiyas' authority, and to their authority alone—he chose to preserve the four majestic toraṇas that served as gateways to that temple. For those toraṇas not only lent spatial definition to the plaza; they defined, symbolically, the four quarters of the universe. Although classical Hindu cosmography had informed their original design and placement, conveniently enough, these same toraṇas could also serve the old Iranian idea of the chahār-ṭāq, the 'four arches' that supported a cosmos divided into four quarters. Fitting within the cosmographic symbolism of both the Sanskrit and Persian cosmopolises, the toraṇas could be understood as generic. Moreover, by situating his own newly built Tughluq palace—the 'Khush Mahal'—in axial alignment with the plaza's eastern and western toraṇas, Ulugh Khan signalled his awareness of the toraṇas' symbolic potency, and of course, his intention of building upon that potency.

In this sense Muhammad Quli, by responding to Warangal's cosmographic symbolism in designing his new capital of Hyderabad, was following in the footsteps of his Tughluq predecessor, for both he and Ulugh Khan drew upon that part of the Kakatiya architectural legacy that was most abstract, most cosmographic, and most generically imperial in both Persian and Indian classical traditions. By contrast, Shitab Khan, endeavouring to project himself as something of a latter-day Kakatiya maharaja, restored the specifically Kakatiya dynastic elements of that legacy. As we have seen, he did this by patronizing the actual images identified with the Kakatiyas' former rule, the same images that Ulugh Khan had been determined to uproot.

In the final analysis, modern scholarship's failure to see Hyderabad's plan as echoing that of the former Kakatiya capital lies in an abiding tendency to see South Asian art and history through civilizational lenses, together with their accompanying civilizational blinders. Because Hyderabad was founded by a Muslim sultan, so the reasoning seems to go, the city must have adhered to 'Islamic' conceptions and models of urban space. Conversely Warangal, having been founded by Hindu maharajas, is conventionally pigeon-holed as occupying 'Hindu' space, conceptually walled off from 'Muslim' space. But such reasoning is fraught with problems: among other things, it assimilates an enormous span of culture into two homogenized and mutually exclusive essences, and then it projects these essences backwards in time, on the assumption that they are as unchanging through time as they are through space. By refuting such crude and ahistorical reasoning, however, the case of Hyderabad's conceptual origins can open us up to different ways of thinking about South Asia's past.

## NOTES

1. Veturi Prabhakara Sastry, ed.,*Cāṭu-padya-maṇi-mañjari* (Hyderabad: Maṇi Manjari Pracuraṇalu, 1988), I: 210. Translation ours.

2. *Tārīkh-i Muḥammad Quṭb Shāh*, 348, as quoted by H.K. Sherwani, *History of the Qutb Shahi Dynasty* (New Delhi: Munshiram Manoharlal, 1974), 301.

3. There is a single inscription of Qutb Shahi date, although as a funerary inscription it does not refer to the reigning sultan. This inscription is carved on a sarcophagus and records the demise of one Sultan Quli, son of Mirza `Alī Khāwar, in either AD 1557 or 1564 (both dates are given). Yazdani cautions that this figure is not to be mistaken with the founder of the Qutb Shahi dynasty, whose father was Uwais Qulī. Warangal is also the location of the *dargāh* of the Sufi saint Shah Jamal al-Din Baghdadi, who arrived in the Deccan from Medina during the reign of Muhammad Quli and died in 1591, the year of Hyderabad's founding. If the location of his dargāh is any indication, he would most likely have lived in Warangal during the 1580s. See G. Yazdani, 'Two Inscriptions from the Warangal Fort', in *Epigraphia Indo-Moslemica* (*EIM*) *1931–32*, 31–2, pl. XXI (a); Sadiq Naqvi, *Muslim Religious Institutions and Their Role under the Qutb Shahis* (Hyderabad: Bab-ul-ilm Society, 1993), 117. For Sultan Quli's ancestry and descent, see V. Minorsky, 'The Qara-Qoyunlu and the Quṭb Shāhs (Turkmenica 10)', *Bulletin of the School of Oriental and African Studies* 17 no. 1 (1955), 70–1.

4. Two other sultans, Jamshid (1543–50) and Subhan (1550), ruled during the seven years between the end of Sultan Quli's reign and Ibrahim's accession.

5. Parts of this chapter draw on Phillip B. Wagoner, 'The Place of Warangal's *Kīrti Toraṇas* in the History of Indian Islamic Architecture', *Religion and the Arts* 8/1 (2004): 25–9; idem., 'The Charminar as *Chaubara*: Cosmological Symbolism in the Urban Architecture of the Deccan', in *The Architecture of the*

*Indian Sultanates*, eds Abha Narain Lambah and Alka Patel (Mumbai: Marg Publications, 2006), 104–13; idem., 'The Multiple Worlds of Amin Khan: Crossing Persianate and Indic Cultural Boundaries in the Qutb Shahi Kingdom', in *Sultans of the South: Arts of India's Deccan Courts, 1323–1687*, eds Navina Najat Haidar and Marika Sardar (New York: Metropolitan Museum of Art, 2011), 90–101.

6. This section is based primarily on the *Tārīkh-i guzīda-yi Sulṭān Muḥammad Quṭb Shāhī* (anonymous) translated by V. Minorsky, 'The Qara-Qoyonlu and the Qutb-Shāhs (Turkmenica, 10)', *Bulletin of the School of Oriental and African Studies* 17, no. 1 (1955), and also by John Briggs, trans., *History of the Rise of the Mahomedan Power in India* (Calcutta: Editions Indian, 1966), 3:202–92.

7. Minorsky, 'Qara-Qoyonlu', 70.

8. Cited in H.K. Sherwani and P.M., eds, *History of Medieval Deccan, 1295–1724* (Hyderabad: Government of Andhra Pradesh, 1973), 1:413.

9. Briggs, trans., *History of the Rise*, 3:194.

10. Ibid., 3:205–6.

11. Ibid., 3:229.

12. Ibrahim's mastery of the Telugu language and his acculturation to Indic courtly practices during his stay at Vijayanagara possibly influenced the *nāyakwāṛis*' preference for him over other contenders for the throne.

13. According to the *Tārīkh-i Muḥammad Quṭb Shāh*, Ibrahim's first son `Abd al-Qadir was confined in the fort at Devarakonda where he died at the age of twenty-one. The second son, Mirza Husain Quli, drowned while swimming at the age of twenty-six. Briggs, trans., *History of the Rise*, 3:268.

14. See Carla Petievich's important study and translations of selected verses in *When Men Speak as Women: Vocal Masquerade in Indo-Muslim Poetry* (New Delhi: Oxford University Press, 2007), 133–63; see also Laura Weinstein's study of Muhammad Quli's *Diwan*, 'Variations on a Persian Theme: Adaptation and Incorporation of Persian Painting at the 16th Century Court of Golconda', forthcoming in *The Visual World of Muslim India: The Art, Culture, and Society of the Deccan in the Early Modern Era*, ed. Laura Parodi (London: I.B. Tauris).

15. Petievitch, *When Men Speak*, 6–9.

16. See H.K. Sherwani, *History of the Qutb Shahi Dynasty* (New Delhi: Munshiram Manoharlal, 1974), 327–30.

17. Qutb dreams one night of a beautiful young woman and, still obsessed with her upon awaking, sets off with his painter-companion, Utarad (Mercury), to find her. The two eventually reach Bengal and discover her identity as the princess Mushtari (Jupiter). Utarad volunteers his services to the king of Bengal and introduces Qutb's portrait into the murals he paints in the princess's apartments. Seeing the painting, Mushtari falls in love with Qutb, who persuades her to accompany him back to Hyderabad, where the two are married. See the summary of the poem's story in Sherwani, *Qutb Shahi Dynasty*, 328–9.

18. This translation is a composite, based on the translations of Briggs, trans., *History of the Rise*, 3:201, and of Sherwani, in *Qutb Shahi Dynasty*, 340.

19. Sherwani, *Qutb Shahi Dynasty*, 339–48.

20. Stan Goron and J.P. Goenka, *The Coins of the Indian Sultanates* (New Delhi: Munshiram Manoharlal, 2001), 339.

21. Although Sherwani elsewhere says that there appear to be no references to the city as Bhagnagar or Baghnagar in contemporary Telugu sources, there is in fact a reference to the city as 'Bāgānagaram' in *Rāyavācakamu*, written in Madurai c. 1595–1602, less than a decade after the city's founding (see Wagoner, *Tidings of the King*,127, and discussion on 18). Sherwani does quote the jewel merchant Jean-Baptiste Tavernier, who wrote in 1652 that 'Bagnagar was founded by the grandfather of the present king (`Abdullah)' and adds that 'here the king had very fair gardens'. He also quotes Rafi` al-Din Shirazi, who wrote in the 1590s that 'the whole city is just one large garden'. Sherwani, *Qutb Shahi Dynasty*, 347–8, citing *Tazkirat al-mulūk*, fol. 61b.

22. The importance of virility among the nāyakwāṛis is captured in a colourful imprecation that occurs in the Koyilkonda inscription of 1551, discussed later: 'Further, if any among us who wears a moustache on the face violates this promise, his moustache is as good as a prostitute's pubic hair.'

23. Given that the two earliest references to the story appear in Mughal texts written from an outsider's disapproving perspective, such an interpretation seems credible. The first reference appears in a letter written to the Mughal emperor Akbar by Faizi, who was then serving as imperial resident in the northern Deccani cities of Burhanpur and Ahmadnagar; the second is in Nizam al-Din Ahmad's historical text, *Ṭabaqāt-i Akbarī*. Both references were written at the very

outset of Mughal expansion into the Deccan. Since neither author recorded the Qutb Shahi ruler's name correctly—Faizi calls Muhammad Quli 'Ahmad Quli', and Nizam al-Din calls him 'Muhammad `Ali Qutb al-Mulk'—one suspects that the Mughal authors were not inventing the story themselves, but were simply passing on, with both amusement and disdain, what they had learned as hearsay from people they had met in the Deccan. See Sherwani, *Qutb Shahi Dynasty*, 339–40.

24. See *Śrī Sūryarāyāndhra Nighaṇṭuvu* (Hyderabad: Telugu University, 1988), 4:115, column 2.

25. The difference in terminology might simply reflect differences in dialect between the Telangana region and those districts lying south of the Krishna River.

26. *Tārīkh-i Muḥammad Quṭb Shāh*, folio 116, cited in Sherwani, *Qutb Shahi Dynasty*, 97.

27. For Jagadeva Rao, see Sherwani, *Qutb Shahi Dynasty*, 86, 88–91, 97, 99–104, and 125–7. Other notable nāyakwāṛis included Asva Rao, who was one of Muhammad Quli's able commanders, and Surya Rao, a commander under Ibrahim, who is remembered more for his role in fomenting a rebellion among all the nāyakwāṛi fort commanders.

28. The details are recounted in *Tārīkh-i Muḥammad Quṭb Shāh*, in Briggs, trans., *History of the Rise*, 3:228–9.

29. The term Niyogi literally means 'appointee' and is derived from the Telugu word for an appointment or office, *niyōgamu*. We use the term strictly for the sake of convenience, as it did not come into regular use until long after the sixteenth century. It is not likely that these sixteenth-century 'niyogis' constituted a single brahman caste in the sixteenth century, as Niyogis do today. Rather, they constituted a loose occupational class, made up of a number of different lineages and sectarian groups. In the nineteenth and early twentieth centuries, brahmans who followed *niyogi* occupations came to be defined as a distinct caste-community in opposition to *vaidiki* brahmans, who followed traditional brahman occupations as priests and astrologers, and with whom they were often in conflict. Today, niyogis comprise a number of distinct groups, of which the Aruvela and Nandavarikalu are the most important. The Aruvela community can be traced back with confidence at least to the sixteenth century, when its members included some of the most prominent Telugu court poets of the day, such as Mukku Timmanna and Madayagari Mallana. See K.S. Singh, *India's Communities, N–Z. People of India National Series* (Delhi: Anthropological Survey of India and Oxford University Press, 1998), 6:2644–8; K.V. Lakshmana Rao, 'Āndhra Brāhmaṇulalōni Niyōgi-Vaidika Bhēda Kāla-nirṇayamu', in his *Lakṣmaṇarāya Vyāsāvaḷi* (Vijayawada: Adarsha Granthamandali, 1965 [1923]), 1–17.

30. Interestingly, many of the most prominent Qutb Shahi Niyogis happened to belong to Shrivaishnava families, although Shaiva Niyogis are also revealed in the sources.

31. For a useful discussion of the institution of *karaṇam* and its importance for the development of new modes of history-writing in the sixteenth century, see V. Narayana Rao, David Shulman, and Sanjay Subrahmanyam, *Textures of Time: Writing History in South India, 1600–1800* (Delhi: Permanent Black, 2001), 19–23 and 93–139.

32. One such was Goparaju Mahapatra, who was responsible for the six *sthalas* (micro-regions) of the Kondapalli district in the 1520s. He appears in Sultan Quli's Kondapalli inscription of 1528 as the *sthala-karaṇam* responsible for maintaining land and tax records for the six sthalas of the Kondapalli district. See Z.A. Desai, 'Qutb Shahi Inscriptions from Andhra State. I, II: Inscriptions from Kondapalli', in *Epigraphia Indica, Arabic and Persian Supplement* (*EIAPS*) *1953 and 1954*, 23–9.

33. One such was Sarangu Tammayya, a brahman poet who states in the preface to his *Vaijayanti Vilāsamu* that he served in the capacity of karaṇam of Golconda during the reign of Muhammad Quli Qutb Shah ('mahammadu śāhi yēlun ī yenubadi nālgu durgamulan ēlina yēlika gōlakoṇḍa dad-ghana-nagarasthalin garaṇikamb onarinceḍu damma mantra ...' I, 30). Given the size and complexity of the city's economy, Tammayya was probably one of a number of revenue officers for the city. But he was hardly a minor functionary, as he was accustomed to being summoned by the sultan on a regular basis ('yā janapati rammu pommana brajaljayaveṭṭa gṛhasthulaunanan', I, 30). For the text, see *Vaijayantī Vilāsamu anu nāmāntara-mugala Vipranārāyaṇa Caritramu, Sārangu Tammaya praṇītamu* (Madras: Vavilla Ramaswamy Shastrulu and Sons, 1966); for a discussion of the text and its author, see Arudra, *Samagra Āndhra Sāhityam—ārava sampuṭam: Navābula Aravīṭi-rājula yugālu* (Vijayawada: Praja-shakti Book House, 1990), 79–85.

34. This work is the *Ocean of Royal Policy* (*Rājanīti-ratnākaram*), known from a single palm-leaf manuscript (MS. no. 616) in the Sanskrit Academy Collection of Osmania University. Although the work unfortunately still remains unpublished, some 27 stanzas from its 100-verse preface have been excerpted and printed in an important Telugu study by B. Rama Raju: 'Nebati Kṛṣṇayāmātyuḍu', in *Khutub Ṣāhī Sultānulu—Āndhra Saṃskṛti*, ed. B. Rāmarāju (Haidrābādu: Idāra Adbiyāte Urdū, 1962), 97–112.

35. 'Because Nagaraju and his descendants took up the work of *nebati* serving in the presence of the sultans and shahs of Bidar, the family has since been known by the name of "Nebati" and achieved great renown.' ('Nāgarāju santatamu Bĕḍanda-koṭa Sulutānu-śahā samukhambunandu nebati pani yuddharinci bahubabhangula jeyaga nāṭinunḍi "Nebati"yanan iṇṭi pera kaḍu brastutik ĕkkĕ jagaddhitambugan'), *Rājanīti-ratnākaramu* I, 59, quoted in Rama Raju, 'Nebati', 107.

36. The text reads 'Malik Ibharāma kṣamānātha-candrumḍu mĕccagā sat-kīrti hĕccināḍu Pānugaṇṭi-vara-paṭṭaṇ=ādhyakṣuḍai…' (Ibid., I, 80, quoted in Rama Raju, 'Nebati', 109). From the description of Pangal as a 'major town' (*vara-paṭṭaṇa*, lit. 'choice town'), this should be identified as the Pangal in Mahbubnagar district that was a major fortified stronghold in the region. There is another Pangal in Nalgonda district, but this seems to have been a smaller and less strategic place during the Qutb Shahi period. It did, however, receive some irrigation improvements by a (Muslim) officer under Ibrahim. See G. Yazdani, 'Inscription of Ibrahim Qutb Shah from the Pangal Tank, Nalgonda District,' *EIM 1925–26*, 23–5, pl. XI(a).

37. The post of 'minister' is variously referred to in Telugu as *pradhāni*, *mantri*, or *āmātya*. A glance at Krishnayamatya's family tree shows that most of his ancestors were accorded one or another of these titles, starting in the third generation with Ananta-pradhāni. However, we know from other sources that these 'titles' were often little more than honorifics and were frequently used by brahmans from Niyogi families whether or not they held a ministerial position in any state. In his own case, however, Krishnayamatya states that he occupies the post of a minister and confidant of Muhammad Quli Qutb Shah. Thus, when Krishnayamatya's precepter, Rangacharya, exhorts him to compose the *Ocean of Royal Policy*, he supports the suggestion by underscoring Krishnayamatya's literary accomplishments and his political standing and experience: 'Muhammad [Quli Qutb] Shah Sultan is the ruler of eighty-four forts, and you are his minister, his confidant, and a fine poet' ('sarasa caurāsi durga rakṣādhurīṇuḍaina mahammadu śāhu sultānuk=īvu gala pradhānivi hituḍavu kavivaruḍavu', *Rājanīti Ratnākaram* I, 36, quoted in Rama Raju, 'Nebati', 103). This verse suggests that Krishnayamatya did not use the title 'āmātya' simply as an honorific, as some of his ancestors may have done, but was actually appointed to a ministerial post at the capital where he enjoyed regular access to Muhammad Quli and the other members of his court.

Krishnayamatya's brother Narasamantri is described in the preface as having been publicly honoured by the court in the presence of the sultan in recognition of his skill in promulgating not only the science of politics (*nīti-śāstra*) but also those of poetics (*kāvya-śāstra*), drama (*nāṭaka-śāstra*), and grammar (*śabda-śāstra*); *Rājanīti Ratnākaram* I, 93, quoted in Rama Raju, 'Nebati', 111.

38. The inscription has been published by N. Lakshmi Narayan Rao as 'Appendix A' to the *Annual Report of the Archaeological Department of His Exalted Highness the Nizam's Dominions for 1928–29* (Calcutta: Baptist Mission Press, 1931), 21–4 (hereafter 'Koyilkonda Inscription'). It is discussed in Sherwani, *Qutb Shahi Dynasty*, 103–4, and 118, no. 64. See also John F. Richards, *Mughal Administration in Golconda* (Oxford: Clarendon Press, 1975), 11–12.

39. The inscription does not identify these two figures as Westerners, but given Saiyid `Ali Miyan's name, and the circumstantial evidence of the imprecations, discussed later, the identification seems probable.

40. 'ḍevaravāri sopā-lonu kurcumḍi', Koyilkonda Inscription, lines 36–7.

41. 'nenu vijayanagarāna vumḍagānu toḍuka-vastiri nammudunā?' Ibid., lines 38–40.

42. Extensive lexical borrowing such as this only occurs in situations where, in Franklin Southworth's words, 'there was social contact between two groups of a sufficient extent to produce individuals who were (to some extent) bilingual, who thus served as the agents of diffusion'. Southworth further notes that 'evidence of … borrowing of words from one language to another leads not only to an inference of … contact and acculturation between groups, but often provides explicit clues about the cultural areas of contact…'

This is borne out by the present case, where most of the loanwords relate to the political and military spheres. See Franklin C. Southworth, *Linguistic Archaeology of South Asia* (London and New York: Routledge, 2005), 16, 21.

43. These titles are transliterated in Telugu script as *Hajarati Khājāyĕvamda Mĕsanada-Āli Manasaba Mŏali Vulugu Ājam Malika Yiburāhimu-Śaha Kutubuna-Maluka Vŏḍayalu-gāru*, in which only the last term is Telugu, the rest being corruptions of Arabo-Persian titles. These titles differ somewhat from those accorded to Ibrahim in official Persian inscriptions.

44. The occupational groups mentioned include clerks (*kārukūnālumnnu*, from *kārkūn*), officers (*hudārlumnnu,* probably from *huzur*), soldiers (*laskarilumnnu*, from *lashkar*), and artillerymen (*tupākilumnnu*, from *tup*).

45. 'Retainers' = *haśĕm*, from *ḥashamat*; 'gateway' = *darvāja*, from *darwāza*; 'corruption'= *harāmukhŏrigi*, from *ḥarām-khwārī*; and 'men' = *marrdamānālumnnu*, from *mardumān*.

46. *Aṃta doṣāna podumu*, after naming the religious taboo in question.

47. The text contains other types of imprecations as well. One of them would have appealed to the values of virility and sexual purity shared by the warrior nāyakwāṛis: 'Further, if any among us who wears a moustache on the face violates this promise, his moustache is as good as a prostitute's pubic hair. If they still violate it, they will be considered to have given their wives to low class people, and if they still violate it they will be considered to have given their wives to asses.' Two further imprecations appealed to acts that would apparently have been deemed especially terrifying or repulsive by all present, regardless of religious or cultural affiliation: 'Moreover, if any among us commits treachery, he should be thrown into a giant frying vat.... Further, those of us who violate this vow will incur the sin of eating the flesh of dogs and crows, cooked in wine in a human skull, while riding westward on the back of a donkey.'

48. 'govu-brāmhmani Vāraṇāsi-lonu caṃpinaṃta-doṣāna bodumu', Koyilkonda Inscription, lines 50–3.

49. paṃdini Makkā-lonu campinaṃta doṣāna podumu ... musāphu-lona [emending from 'musāphuāna'] Yimāmu Husaini caṃpina-doṣāna podumu', ibid., lines 65–8. One might think that fear of the sin of 'slaughtering pigs in Mecca' would have covered both Sunni and Shi`i Muslims. Adding a second act that would specifically address Shi`i religious sensibilities most likely acknowledged the factional differences separating Westerners from Deccanis. The slaying of Husain at Karbala provided the fundamental reference point for Shi`i sectarian identity, not only historically, but also ritually, given the importance of the annual Muharram festival, with its collective outpouring of grief for the martyred Husain.

50. This recognition of functional equivalence is underscored by the identical verbal formulation of the three sins, since each is expressed as an act of killing that is performed at a specific, sacred location.

51. Amin Khan has been discussed with characteristic insight by Sherwani, in *Qutb Shahi Dynasty*, 183–5. For a fuller consideration, see Phillip B. Wagoner, 'The Multiple Worlds of Amin Khan: Crossing Persianate and Indic Cultural Boundaries in Qutb Shahi Andhra', in *Sultans of the South: Arts of India's Deccan Courts, 1323–1687*, eds Navina Haidar and Marika Sardar (New York and New Haven: Metropolitan Museum of Art and Yale University Press, 2011), 90–101, and idem., 'Amin Khan's Garden: Charitable Gardens in the Qutb Shahi Kingdom', in *Garden and Landscape Practices in Precolonial India: Histories from the Deccan*, eds Daud Ali and Emma Flatt (New Delhi: Routledge, 2011), 98–126.

52. The inscription of Amin Khan published by Yazdani is actually two distinct inscriptions engraved on two separate slabs of stone but fitted together within the same arched niche on the east side of the tomb. The upper slab consists of an invocation and six lines of text arranged in three registers; the lower slab consists of two lines in a single register. Although the joint between the two slabs is not visible in the estampage published by Yazdani, it can be seen quite clearly in the field. The two inscriptions record two distinct acts that are separated by fifteen years. The upper inscription records the completion of the tomb in AD 1568 (not 1558, as erroneously appears in Yazdani's translation); the lower inscription records the construction of the mosque in 1583. See Ghulam Yazdani, 'A Quṭb Shāhī Inscription from Patancheru, Medak District, Hyderabad State', in *EIM 1935–36*, 60–2, XXXIX. See also M.A. Nayeem, *The Heritage of the Qutb Shahis of Golconda and Hyderabad* (Hyderabad: Hyderabad Publishers, 2006), 206–7, 209, 218, 229.

53. Shaikh Ibrahim Makhdum Shah-ji Muhammad Qadiri died in 1564 and was entombed in Bidar. See `Abd al-Jabbar Mulkapuri's *Tazkira-yi Auliyā-yi Dakan*

(Urdu lithograph, 2 vols, Hyderabad: Hasan Press, 1912–13), 842. The tomb is situated outside the city on the old Chidri road and is described in Ghulam Yazdani, *Bidar: Its History and Monuments* (London: Oxford University Press, 1947), 200–2.

54. Ponnikaṇṭi Telaganārya, *Yayāti Caritramu*, ed., M. Rangakṛṣṇamācāryulu (Haidrābādu: Kākati Pablikēṣans, 1977). See in particular Rangakrishnamacharyulu's introduction to the text, and also Niḍudavōlu Śivasundarēśvara Rāvu, 'Acca Tenugu Pāduṣā—Amīnu Khānu', in *Khutub Ṣāhī Sultānulu—Āndhra Saṃskṛti*, ed. B. Rāmarāju (Haidrābādu: Idāra Adbiyāte Urdū, 1962), 128–33 [all in Telugu].

55. V. Narayana Rao, 'Multiple Literary Cultures in Telugu: Court, Temple, and Public', in *Literary Cultures in History: Reconstructions from South Asia*, ed. Sheldon Pollock (Berkeley: University of California Press, 2003), 384n1.

56. Since ordinary Telugu literary language of the sixteenth century typically relies so heavily on Sanskrit-derived vocabulary, the effect is a striking one, and the language often becomes both arcane and exotic-sounding. The effect is like purging all French and Latin loanwords from English and replacing them with Anglo-Saxon derivatives. A vivid example is provided by Joseph M. Williams, who 'tongueturned' one of his own naturally written sentences to make the point: 'Together working with the outcome of the Norman Greatwin was the Newbirth' (that is, 'Conspiring with the influence of the Norman Conquest was the Renaissance'), Joseph M. Williams, *Style: Toward Clarity and Grace* (Chicago: University of Chicago Press, 1990), 4. Many Telugu poets after Telaganarya seem to have appreciated this effect as they followed suit by writing *acca-tĕlugu* literary works of their own.

57. On the Mariṅgaṇṭi brothers, see Wagoner, 'Multiple Worlds', and in Telugu, Ārudra, *Samagra Āndhra Sāhityam*, 143–8. The family originally hailed from the Devarakonda region.

58. *Yayāti Caritramu* I, 30.

59. There are other documented cases in the Deccan of Muslims patronizing *vaidiki* brahmans by establishing *agrahāram* villages. A Sanskrit copper plate inscription from Bevinahalli records the establishment of an agrahāram grant by one 'Ainanamalukka' (= `Ain al-Mulk) and individually lists the names, clans, and schools of Vedic recitation of the eighty brahman beneficiaries. Ainanamalukka may be identified with the *amīr* `Ain al-Mulk Gīlāni, a Persian 'Westerner' whose peripatetic career took him from the service of Bijapur to Vijayanagara and then back again to Bijapur. For a discussion of `Ain al-Mulk and his agrahāram grant, see Phillip B. Wagoner, 'Fortuitous Convergences and Essential Ambiguities: Transcultural Political Élites in the Medieval Deccan', in *Surprising Bedfellows: Hindus and Muslims in Medieval and Early Modern India*, ed. Sushil Mittal (Lanham, MD: Lexington Books, 2003), 32–4.

60. *Yayāti Caritramu* I, 33, 36–8.

61. Since the earliest reference to Warangal dates to 1195, the city would have existed for 396 years by the time Muhammad Quli founded Hyderabad in 1591. Of this total, it had been ruled by Indic polities for 229 years, and by Persianate polities for 167 years. The former included the Kakatiyas (1195–1323, or 128 years), the Musunuri chiefs (1331–68, or 37 years), the Recharla Nayakas (1368–1424, or 56 years), and Shitab Khan (1504–12, or 8 years). Persianate polities included the Delhi Sultanate (1323–31, or 8 years), the Bahmani Sultanate (1424–1504, or 80 years), and the Qutb Shahis (1512–91, or 79 years). See N. Venkataramanayya, *Inscriptions of Andhra Pradesh: Warangal District* (Hyderabad: Government of Andhra Pradesh, 1974), no. 42.

62. Atop the inner stone wall of the Kakatiya city, the diminutive and essentially decorative crenellations belonging to the Kakatiya period were removed from the parapets, although small portions still remain above the interior courtyards of the gateways to the fort. These small crenellations were replaced by massive spade-shaped merlons that provided ample cover and afforded an assortment of differently angled loopholes through which matchlocks could be fired. In their form and proportions, they belong to the sixteenth century; stylistically, they closely resemble those used at Golconda and other fortified Qutb Shahi centres.

63. These barbicans provide an extra layer of defensive protection to the gates they front. Similar curving barbicans are known only from sixteenth-century Golconda, where they appear before some of the gateways in the outer walls (erected c. 1560, early in the reign of Ibrahim), including the Patancheru Darwaza, the Banjara Darwaza, and the Palace Area Gate. The *Tārīkh-i Muḥammad Quṭb Shāhī* briefly mentions this building campaign at Hyderabad (Briggs, trans., *History of the Rise*, 3:245). See also Ghulam Yazdani, 'Inscriptions in Golconda Fort', *EIM*

*1913–14*, 48–9, pl. XIX (a), and the discussion in Marika Sardar, *Golconda Through Time: A Mirror of the Evolving Deccan* (New York University Institute of Fine Arts, doctoral dissertation, May 2007), 125ff.

64. Despite the platform's unusual octagonal plan, it compares with cavaliers or gun platforms known from many other fortified centres in the sixteenth-century Deccan, including Golconda. On the upper level of its platform, which is circular, the cavalier would have borne a single large cannon capable of rotating a full 360 degrees. Though placed considerably closer to the southeastern section of the city's inner wall, its commanding elevation atop the rocky outcropping would have extended its range, making it possible for gunners to reach even the plain beyond the stone wall on the opposite, northwestern side of the fort, a kilometre away. A few metres from the cavalier is a small cubical chamber with a shallow vaulted ceiling, recognizable as a powder magazine.

65. See Appendix 2, 'Warangal', note 43.

66. George Michell notes that 'while the decoration of these portals is typical of the Kakatiya style, with sharply cut tower-like motifs, looped garlands and birds, the form of the portals is familiar from the gateways of early Buddhist architecture (such as those at Sanchi)'. Similarly, M.A. Dhaky notes that 'the toraṇa, despite some ornamentation in its upper section, seems somewhat austerely designed and in concept distantly recalls the Sanci toraṇas of the Sungan-Satavahana periods'. See G. Michell, *Penguin Guide to the Monuments of India* (London: Penguin, 1989), 1: 39; M.A. Dhaky, *Encyclopedia of Indian Temple Architecture* (New Delhi: American Institute of Indian Studies, 1996), vol. 1, part 3: 507.

67. Sardar, *Golconda through Time*, 50, 53ff.

68. For further discussion of the rise of Kakatiya historiography, and of the *Pratāparudra Caritramu* in particular, see Cynthia Talbot, *Precolonial India in Practice* (New York: Oxford University Press, 2001), 180–202. For a discussion of the manuscript history of the *Siddheśvara Caritramu* and related texts, see Phillip B. Wagoner, 'From Manuscript to Archive to Print: The Mackenzie Collection and Later Telugu Literary Historiography', in *The Madras School of Orientalism: Producing Knowledge in Colonial South India*, ed. Thomas R. Trautmann (New Delhi: Oxford University Press, 2009), 183–205.

69. This *Kākatīya Carita* is no longer extant, save for the thirty-six verse excerpt carved into the rock at Hanamkonda. An inscription on the temple site's southern toraṇa mentions the work's author as Nrisimha-kavi, a court poet during the reign of Pratapa Rudra. Other inscriptions of this poet are incised into the *kirti-toraṇas* of the eastern and northern toraṇas, while a single verse praising 'Virarudra' (that is, Pratapa Rudra) is carved on the rock face of the Ekasila hill, on which the Qutb Shahi gun emplacement is now located. See *IAP-Warangal* nos 95, 97, 98, 101 and 106. See also P.V. Parabrahma Sastry, [*Siddhōdvāha*] *of Nṛsiṃha* (Andhra Pradesh Government Epigraphy Series no. 2, Hyderabad: Government of Andhra Pradesh, 1968), 2.

70. See George Michell, 'City as Cosmogram: The Circular Plan of Warangal', *South Asian Studies* 8 (1992): 15–16, and Phillip B. Wagoner, 'A Dense Epitome of the World: The Image of Warangal in the *Krīḍābhirāmamu*', afterword to *A Lover's Guide to Warangal: The* Krīḍābhirāmamu by Vinukoṇḍa Vallabharāya, trans. Velcheru Narayana Rao and David Shulman (New Delhi: Permanent Black, 2002), 99–100.

71. See, for example, the excerpts from the Sanskrit *Kūrma Purāṇa* translated by Cornelia Dimmitt and J.A.B. Van Buitenen, *Classical Hindu Mythology: A Reader in the Sanskrit Purāṇas* (Philadelphia: Temple University Press, 1978), 52–5, and the account in the Sanskrit *Mārkaṇḍeya Purana*, trans. F.E. Pargiter (Delhi: Indological Book House, 1969), 275–83.

72. See G.V. Subrahmanyam, ed., *Śrī Mārana Mārkaṇḍeya Purāṇamu* (Hyderabad: Andhra Pradesh Sahitya Akademi, 1984), 239–54, canto 4, verses 131–210.

73. These panegyrics appear in extemporaneous verses, or *cāṭu*, that have been preserved in oral circulation and collected in the early twentieth century. Cāṭus, according to Rao and Shulman, are 'remembered and used in social communication among a community of people who constitute themselves as a group by sharing a certain body of knowledge and ideology. The cāṭu defines, expresses, and communicates such knowledge and ideology among specific communities'. See Velcheru Narayana Rao and David Shulman, *A Poem at the Right Moment: Remembered Verses from Premodern South India* (Berkeley and Los Angeles: University of California Press, 1998), 6–7.

74. Veturi Prabhakara Sastri, ed., *Cāṭu-padya-maṇi-mañjari* (Hyderabad: Mani Manjari Publishers, 1988), I:205. Translation ours.

75. Ibid., I:210. Translation ours.

76. The circumstances of the city's foundation are narrated by the anonymous author of the *Tārīkh-i Muḥammad Quṭb Shāh*; see Briggs, trans., *History of the Rise*, 3:271–2. It appears, however, that Briggs has embellished his text by referring to the Bhagmati story, which according to Sherwani is altogether absent in this text. For the most detailed consideration of the city's founding, see Sherwani, *Qutb Shahi Dynasty*, 300–16, 343.

77. S.P. Shorey, 'Eighteenth-Century Hyderabad: Anatomy of an Old Map', *Environmental Design: Journal of the Islamic Environmental Design Research Centre* 1–2 (1993), 180–5. Significantly, the city was not walled when first constructed, most likely owing to the Deccan's relative geopolitical stability in the late sixteenth century, and a concomitant sense that fortifications were unnecessary. In any case, nearby Golconda continued to serve as the strategic fortress for the city.

78. George Michell and Mark Zebrowski, *Art and Architecture of the Deccan Sultanates* (Cambridge: Cambridge University Press, 1999), 51.

79. At 220 metres squared, the Char Kaman plaza is both larger and more regular than the Warangal plaza, which measures 152 metres north to south and 134 metres east to west.

80. Three other public structures were completed as part of the city's first phase of construction. These were the Badshahi `Ashur-khana (1592–96), a sacred structure for housing the *`alams* used in Muharram processions, a hospital and medical school known as the Dar al-Shifa (1595), and a Jami` Masjid (1597).

81. Although this is likely the case at Warangal, it was certainly the case of Hyderabad. We know that the space within the Char Kaman was formerly known as the 'royal vestibule' (*jilau khāna*), and that its western gateway, or 'lofty gate of the royal residence' (*daulat khāna-i `ālī*), led directly into the Qutb Shahi palace compound. The opposite archway on the east side of the plaza was known as the 'gate of drums' (*naqār khāna*) and provided the platform from which the royal drums were sounded at the entrance to the palatial zone. The entire plaza was thus marked out as a forecourt or place of assembly before the palace proper. Accordingly, there were no other structures within this vast open space apart from a 'four-cornered reservoir' (*chār-sū-kā ḥauẓ*) situated at its centre. Syed Ali Asgar Bilgrami, *Landmarks of the Deccan: A Comprehensive Guide to the Archaeological Remains of the City and Suburbs of Hyderabad* (Hyderabad: Government Press, 1927), 19–21.

82. For an interpretation of Hyderabad's plan as a replica of paradise, see Jan Pieper, 'Hyderabad: A Qur'anic Paradise in Architectural Metaphors', *Environmental Design: Journal of the Islamic Environmental Design Research Centre* 0 (1984), 46–51.

83. See V.K. Bawa, 'The Politics of Architecture in Qutb Shahi Hyderabad: A Preliminary Analysis', in *Studies in the History of the Deccan, Medieval and Modern: Professor A. R. Kulkarni Felicitation Volume*, eds M.A. Nayeem, Aniruddha Ray, and K.S. Mathew (Delhi: Pragati Publications, 2002), 333; Sadiq Naqvi, *The Iranian Afaquies Contribution to the Qutb Shahi and Adil Shahi Kingdoms* (Hyderabad: Dr. Sadiq Naqvi, 2003), 95–6; and M.A. Nayeem, *The Heritage of the Qutb Shahis of Golconda and Hyderabad* (Hyderabad: Hyderabad Publishers, 2006), 10.

84. R.D. McChesney, 'Four Sources on Shah 'Abbas's Building of Isfahan', *Muqarnas* 5 (1988), 115.

85. Ibid., 114–15.

86. Ibid., 117–24. The building complexes on these other three sides are, on the north, the *qaiṣarīya,* a market; on the east, the Shaikh Lutfullah mosque and madrasa; and on the south, the Masjid-i Shah (known today as the Masjid-i Imam). The sources suggest that construction of the latter began only in 1611. Although the *qaiṣarīya* was being developed as early as about 1591, one source suggests that its elaborate entrance was built *after* the completion of the Masjid-i Shah on the south, and that it was constructed in order to create a direct formal balance with the entrance to the mosque. The Shaikh Lutfullah mosque and madrasa, completed in 1618, was the last complex to be constructed.

87. Michell and Zebrowski, *Art and Architecture*, 53.

88. On the west was Ulugh Beg's madrasa, constructed between 1417 and 1421, and responding to it on the east was Ulugh Beg's *khānaqāh,* which was subsequently replaced by the Shirdar Madrasa (1616–36). See Sheila Blair and Jonathan Bloom, *The Art and Architecture of Islam, 1250–1800* (New Haven: Yale University Press, 1994), 45, 204–6.

89. Another building known as the Char Minar, a domed square with four arches and four minarets marking its corners, is found in Bukhara, Uzbekistan. But it was not constructed until 1807, more than two

centuries after the Charminar of Hyderabad. See Edgar Knobloch, *Monuments of Central Asia: A Guide to the Archaeology, Art, and Architecture of Turkestan* (London: I.B. Tauris, 2001), 128 and colour plate 67. A second structure in Bukhara that shares the Char Minar's conception is the small pavilion in the courtyard of the mausoleum of Hazrat Baha' al-Din Naqshbandi (d. 1389). While the mausoleum itself dates from the fourteenth century, the age of this small pavilion is not known. See Knobloch, *Monuments,* 130 and plate 40. Both of these buildings differ from the Charminar of Hyderabad in being single-storeyed, with the dome exposed on the exterior.

90. It has been described as a madrasa or khānaqāh, a gateway to the Qutb Shahi palace, a water reservoir, a replica of a *ta`ziya* commemorating the end of an outbreak of cholera, and a replica of the shrine of Imam `Ali al-Riza at Mashhad, intended as a surrogate for those who could not complete the physical pilgrimage to Iran. For a thorough review of these interpretations, see Sherwani, *Qutb Shahi Dynasty*, 304–5.

91. A connection between the Charminar and the *chaubārā* at Bidar was first noted by H.K. Sherwani, who saw both buildings as examples of a worldwide class of monuments that functioned to mark city centres. He did not, however, cite any other examples of chaubārās from the Deccan, focussing instead on more general comparisons between the Charminar and such monuments as the Arc de Triomphe in Paris and the classical '*tetrapylae* of the old Greek towns'. See Sherwani, *Qutb Shahi Dynasty*, 305; idem., *Muhammad Quli Qutb Shah: Founder of Hyderabad* (London: Asia Publishing House, 1967), 20.

92. Although local tradition avers that this chaubārā dates to Bidar's pre-Islamic period, most of its present form likely dates to the time of Bidar's rebuilding as the Bahmani capital, at the beginning of the reign of Sultan Ahmad Shah I al-Wali (r. 1422–36). See Ghulam Yazdani, *Bidar: Its History and Monuments* (London: Oxford University Press, 1947), 90–1.

93. Dhaky, *Encyclopaedia,* vol. 1, part 3, 507, and plate 1537.

94. As David King has pointed out, local understandings of *qibla* orientation often changed significantly from one period to the next. The Charminar mosque's qibla of 280 degrees had been used in this part of the eastern Deccan since the Tughluq era, as is evident from the remains of the ruined Tughluq Jami` Masjid of Warangal-Sultanpur, which was likewise oriented to a qibla of 280 degrees. But just a few years later, in Hyderabad itself, the Jami` Masjid built by Sultan Muhammad Quli in 1597 conformed not to the qibla grid established by the Charminar, but to a qibla of approximately 270 degrees. The history of qibla orientations in the Deccan, or in any part of India, has yet to be written. See David A. King, *World-Maps for Finding the Direction and Distance to Mecca: Innovation and Tradition in Islamic Science* (Leiden: Brill, 1999), 124–7; S.P. Shorey, 'Hyderabad: Garden to a City', in *Golconda and Hyderabad*, ed. Shehbaz H. Safrani (Bombay: Marg, 1992), 20.

95. Assadullah Souren Melikian-Chirvani, 'The Light of Heaven and Earth: From the *Chahār-ṭāq* to the *Miḥrāb*', *Bulletin of the Asia Institute* (Detroit), new series, 4 (1990), 95–131.

96. The author of the anonymous Dutch *Relation* of 1614 notes that 'the real inhabitants of the country are Gentus or heathens', Gentu being one of the more common words used by seventeenth-century Europeans to designate Hindus. He also makes several references suggesting that there were many places in the country where no Muslims lived, or where there were at best 'perhaps a thousand' Hindus to one Muslim. See W.F. Moreland, *Relations of Golconda in the Early Seventeenth Century* (London: Hakluyt Society, 1931), 69 and 71. Similarly, William Methwold, who was present as a trader in Masulipatam from 1618 to 1622, notes that the Qutb Shahi king 'is a Mahometan, descended from Persian ancestors'. He further notes that 'the King's religion is predominant in the authority and the quality of the professors, not in the number of soules; for the ancient naturals of the countrey, commonly called Gentiles [that is, Hindus], or Heathens, exceed them in a very great proportion'. Moreland, *Relations of Golconda,*12.

97. Benjamin B. Cohen has similarly stressed the composite nature of culture, religion, and politics in nineteenth-century Hyderabad State, focussing on the importance of the *samsthans* (local Hindu kingdoms) in the negotiation of power within the state. See his *Kingship and Colonialism in India's Deccan, 1850–1948* (New York: Palgrave Macmillan, 2007), 2.

98. See, for example, Richards, *Mughal Administration*, chapter 1, 'Brahmins and Nayaks', 17–19.

SECTION FOUR

# The Raichur Doab in the Age of Gunpowder

CHAPTER 7

# The Military Revolution in the Deccan

I also send your highness a Goan master gunsmith; they make guns as good as the Bohemians and also equipped with screwed in breech plugs. There he will work for you. I am sending you some samples of their work with Pero Masquarenhas.

—Afonso de Albuquerque, viceroy of the *Estado da India*, writing from Goa to King Manuel I of Portugal (1513)[1]

Aflatun Khan laid the foundation of a very strong fortification in this fort. In it, he constructed a stone bastion, the like of which had not been seen by the eyes of the world. It was higher than the heavenly sphere; hence its date has come to be 'the heavenly sphere.' O Kind One! Year 974 (1566–67AD).

—Inscription on a bastion of Galna Fort, 1566–67[2]

Up to this point in our study of power, memory, and architecture, we have focussed mainly on the latter two categories—more particularly, how memory influenced architecture in Vijayanagara, Bijapur, Kalyana, Warangal, or Hyderabad. Of course, power was never absent in these cases. Questions of *whose* memory might achieve architectural expression, and in what form, always involved patronage, and networks of patronage necessarily involved persons or institutions capable of mobilizing human and capital resources, which is a matter of power. In most of the cases we have seen, the patrons were powerful political players, if not sovereigns, while the structures they patronized—temples, mosques, gateways, palaces—were all monuments intended to make particular statements of how such patrons wished, among other things, to position themselves vis-à-vis the past as well as the present.

The present chapter considers another kind of power, namely, the kind that derived from the introduction and diffusion of firearms, a new technology that revolutionized warfare in the sixteenth-century Deccan, as it did in most of the world. Several questions guide our inquiry. Why did cannons appear in the Deccan before anywhere else in India's interior? Why did military advances occur in some parts of the plateau, but not in others? What effects did new military technologies have on the Deccan's architectural landscape, and on society at large? And how might changes wrought by these new technologies relate to the much-discussed notion of an early modern 'military revolution'?[3]

## THE RAICHUR DOAB AS A CONTESTED ZONE, 1294–1520

The best answers to these questions are found in the Raichur Doab, the fertile tract of land lying between, and on either side of, the Krishna and Tungabhadra Rivers, which run west to east through the heart of the plateau (Figure 7.1). In this region one can trace the evolution of military technology and architecture from the thirteenth century onwards, culminating in two remarkable and decisive battles—that of Raichur in 1520 and of Talikota in 1565. The Battle of Talikota, which permanently altered the political map of the plateau, is widely recognized as a turning point in Indian history, signalling as it did a crushing defeat for Vijayanagara and the virtual destruction of its great metropolitan capital. But the somewhat earlier Battle of Raichur is hardly mentioned in standard histories of South Asia—if it is mentioned at all—even though it established several milestones in the military history of India. It also planted the political seeds that forty-five years later would ripen as the Battle of Talikota.

Raichur's pivotal role in the evolution of military technology and architecture in the Deccan derives in large part from its location. The fort lay in the heart of a coveted zone exceptionally rich in agriculture and minerals. In the twelfth and thirteenth centuries, the tract also lay at the juncture of the three most powerful successor states to the Chalukyas—the Hoysalas of Dwarasamudra, the Yadavas Devagiri, and the Kakatiyas of Warangal. In 1294 Vithalanatha, a subordinate of the last Kakatiya monarch, seized the Raichur Doab from Yadava control and built an imposing complex of walls and gates that enclose Raichur's urban core.[4] With their massive slabs of finely dressed ashlar granite measuring up to 6 metres long and a metre high, joined without mortar, these walls were in their own day considered an engineering marvel. They are certainly the most impressive of any Kakatiya fortifications still standing in the Deccan, apart from those in Warangal, the dynasty's capital (Figure 7.2).

In the fourteenth century, following invasions by armies of the Delhi Sultanate, the Raichur Doab got swept into a new political order dictated ultimately by Turks from north India. After the collapse of the Kakatiya state in 1323, Sultan Muhammad bin Tughluq (r. 1325–51) subcontracted governance of much of the central and southern Deccan to local client-chiefs, whom he integrated into his imperial service as *amīr*s ('commanders'). The Raichur Doab appears to have been among the regions assigned to Harihara Sangama, a chieftain formerly loyal to the Hoysalas.[5] But by 1339 Harihara had already asserted his independence from his Tughluq overlords,[6] and when Delhi lost all of its Deccan possessions to anti-Tughluq forces in 1347, he and his brothers carved out a new state centred on a local pilgrimage site on the southern banks of the Tungabhadra River directly south of the Raichur Doab. Thus was born the city and kingdom of Vijayanagara.

Amidst the confusion surrounding the expulsion of Tughluq imperial forces from the plateau, the Bahmani sultans claimed the entire Raichur Doab clear down to the Tungabhadra River. Vijayanagara, however, bitterly contested this claim, based evidently on its *prior* control of the Doab in the days of Harihara. Accordingly, for a century and a half Vijayanagara's kings launched repeated, but mainly unsuccessful, invasions of the Doab, for throughout this period the region remained mainly under Bahmani control.[7] For most of the first half of

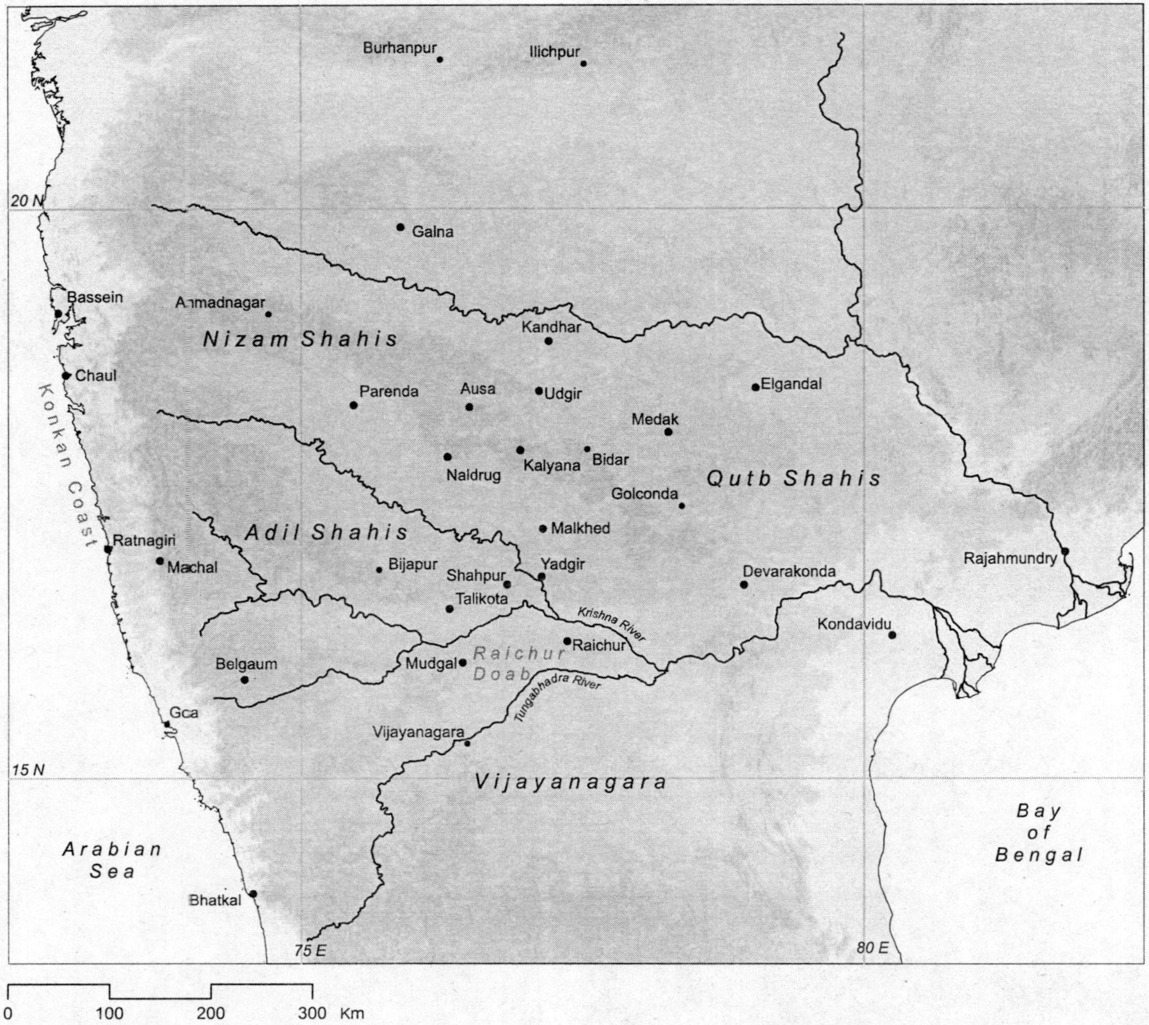


Figure 7.1 Map of the Deccan, first half of the sixteenth century.

**Figure 7.2** Raichur. Section of the Kakatiya wall (1294).

the fifteenth century, the southern state even had to make annual tributary payments to the Bahmani treasury.[8] In 1468–69, recognizing the Doab's strategic importance to its security, Bahmani authorities built a new wall around Raichur Fort, altogether encircling the old Kakatiya wall (Figure 7.3; also see Figure A2.2, p. 355).[9]

However, around the turn of the sixteenth century there appeared three new players whose actions would govern subsequent struggles over the Doab. First, in 1490, amidst the Bahmani kingdom's growing internal decay, the governor of that kingdom's important provincial centre of Bijapur, Yusuf `Adil Khan, declared his de facto independence, at the same time claiming the Raichur Doab as part of his domain.[10] Second, in the years after 1498 the Portuguese *Estado da India*, determined to monopolize control over Arabian Sea commerce, emerged as a powerful naval and land power in western India. Its commercial and political influence would soon extend from their coastal enclaves to the Deccan's interior. And third, in 1505 there appeared in Vijayanagara a vigorous new dynasty of kings under whose rise the balance of power in the Doab would tilt towards the south for the first time in a century and a half. In 1509 there rose to the throne the renowned Krishna Raya (r. 1509–29), whose twenty years of rule are widely acclaimed as the acme of Vijayanagara's power and glory. As

**Figure 7.3** Raichur. Section of the Bahmani wall (1468–69).

heir to Vijayanagara's long-standing quest to possess the Raichur Doab, Krishna Raya would find support for his cause in the Portuguese, whose general hostility towards Muslim states had already been shaped by the anti-Muslim *reconquista* movement in Spain and Portugal. Thus, in 1510 the Estado's viceroy and master-strategist Afonso de Albuquerque (1509–15), assisted by a coastal warlord loyal to Vijayanagara, seized the port of Goa from Yusuf `Adil Khan's fledging kingdom of Bijapur. The Raichur Doab now became the object of a three-cornered struggle involving Bijapur, Vijayanagara, and, supporting the latter from their base in Goa, the Portuguese Estado da India.

## GUNPOWDER TECHNOLOGY IN THE DECCAN, 1450–1520

Apart from the considerable political influence that the Portuguese brought to the Deccan, they also introduced new forms of gunpowder technology to the region. The extent of their influence in this regard, however, is hotly debated. Much depends on how one evaluates the state of India's firearm technology *prior* to the Europeans' arrival. In an important monograph, Iqtidar Alam Khan has argued that in the second half of the fifteenth century Indians were using cannons cast in brass or bronze, as well as handguns.[11] But the matter is complicated. The nomenclature of weapons changed over time; few Indian sources are contemporary with the battles they describe; and later sources often use words anachronistically, projecting terms of their own day backwards to earlier periods. In view of such considerations, Jos Gommans has questioned Iqtidar Alam Khan's assertions respecting a fifteenth-century horizon for the earliest appearance of firearms in India.[12]

Notwithstanding Gommans's reservations, however, there is considerable evidence, both literary and archaeological, that firearms were indeed being used in peninsular India prior to the rise of Portuguese power in the region. The most conclusive archaeological evidence of this is the gun ports that Bahmani rulers built into the walls at Bidar, Kalyana, and Raichur—circular or arched at Bidar and Kalyana, square at Raichur (Figures 7.4, 7.5, and 7.6).[13] At Kalyana the construction of walls bearing such ports appears to date to 1461–63,[14] those of Raichur to 1468–70,[15] and those of Bidar to the reign of Muhammad III (1463–82).[16] These nearly simultaneous construction activities thus point to the 1460s as the earliest horizon for the use of cannons in the Deccan—indeed, in India.

Literary evidence for the advent of gunpowder technology in the region appears at about the same time. The famous Bahmani *vazīr* Mahmud Gawan (fl. 1453–81) wrote that in January 1471 troops under his command besieged and demolished the fort of Machal (in the Sahyadri range inland from the Arabian

**Figure 7.4** Bidar. Citadel wall and two-storeyed polygonal bastion (c. 1463–82). The bastion shows three arched openings for cannons, above each of which are four smaller loopholes for shooting arrows or matchlocks.

**Figure 7.5** Raichur. Outer curtain wall, showing square gun-ports.

**Figure 7.6** Raichur. Square gun-port, looking out from inside parapet walls.

Sea port of Ratnagiri) by deploying 'roaring thunder [*ra`d*], which having the effect of a thunderbolt, showered [on the fort] like rain'—a passage that suggests the use of siege cannon.[17] This report would seem to support Firishta's statement that in the very next year, Bahmani forces used cannons (*top* and *ḍarbuzan*) during their siege of Belgaum, an ally of Vijayanagara.[18] Firishta adds that on that occasion engineers under Gawan's command called *ātish-bāzān* ('fire-workers') deployed explosive mines that peoples of the Deccan had never seen before.[19]

European sources recorded shortly after the advent of the Portuguese also refer to the use of firearms among local powers in the region. Gaspar Correia, Albuquerque's secretary and an early chronicler of the Estado da India, records that in 1502 Portuguese naval squadrons were bombarded from the hilltop overlooking the port of Bhatkal.[20] Several years later the Italian traveller Ludovico di Varthema recorded seeing artillery at the port of Chaul, then controlled by Sultan Ahmad Nizam Shah of Ahmadnagar.[21] Albuquerque's own son recalled that when his father took Goa in 1510, Bijapuri defenders greeted the invaders with artillery fire.[22] Later that same year, after first losing and then recapturing the city, Albuquerque seized from Bijapur's defenders 100 large guns (*bombardas*) and a 'large quantity' of smaller artillery.[23]

The presence of cannon technology in the Deccan prior to European maritime contact, then, seems beyond dispute. More challenging is reconstructing the vectors by which such technology reached the Deccan in the late fifteenth and early sixteenth centuries. It is theoretically possible that the ordnance used at Bhatkal in 1502, or seen at Chaul several years later, had been captured from the Portuguese in some naval engagement and then subsequently turned against the same Europeans. But this is unlikely, given the very short time that had elapsed since Vasco da Gama's 1498 voyage to Calicut—the dawn of Portuguese presence in the Indian Ocean—and especially given the Bahmanis' known offensive and defensive use of cannons in the Deccan interior since the 1460s. In our view, the most likely source of this technology was the Mamluk sultans of Egypt, who possessed both cannon technology (Figure 7.7) and a vested interest in the lucrative spice trade from India to Europe during the latter half of the fifteenth century.[24] We know that the Bahmani vazīr Mahmud Gawan, the same figure who wrote of besieging the fort of Machal in 1471 with 'roaring thunder [ra`d]', also maintained close commercial and diplomatic relations with both Mamluk Egypt and the Ottomans.[25] Having captured the strategic seaport of Goa (then a protectorate of Vijayanagara) in 1472,[26] Gawan for the next ten years sent Bahmani agents through Mamluk Egypt to Bursa, in western Anatolia, and from there into the Ottoman Balkans for marketing Indian textiles.[27]

It is thus very likely that the Mamluks furnished the Bahmanis with ordnance in exchange for textiles, spices, and other commodities destined for western markets. The best material evidence for this inference is the crude forged-iron tube cannons that still lie on the bastions of former Bahmani forts at Bidar, Medak, Yadgir, and Devarakonda. These early cannons appear typologically identical to those that the Ottomans reportedly captured from the Mamluks in the late fifteenth or early sixteenth century, and which are preserved in Istanbul's Military Museum (Figure 7.7).[28] Inasmuch as walls with gun ports were being built in at least three major Bahmani forts in or soon after the 1460s, as noted earlier, we may infer that the tube cannons presently standing on the four

**Figure 7.7** Mamluk tube gun captured by the Ottomans (Military Museum, Istanbul).

mentioned forts were either introduced to the Deccan from across the Arabian Sea, or still more likely, were produced in the Deccan from Mamluk prototypes.

A second vector of technology transfer came somewhat later via the Portuguese, some of whose own weapons appear to have been quickly assimilated into an ongoing, indigenous tradition of firearms manufacture in the western Deccan. For, when they conquered Goa in 1510, the Portuguese found that the Bijapuris had already established a formidable munitions plant in that city. According to an important document transcribed by Gaspar Correia, at the time of the Portuguese conquest there were in Goa

large houses with storage space which the Turks [*os rumes*] had filled with all the materials necessary for shipbuilding, and lots of iron and mortar artillery, large and small, and also two of our camel cannons and eight cradles [*berços*] and mortars which the Turks had brought from the defeat of Dom Lourenco at Chaul [in January 1508], and other metal pieces in their fashion and a great number of metal guns, and a large quantity of gunpowder, saltpetre and utensils used in the making of these, and an enormous quantity of all kinds of weapons.[29]

Correia's reference to *our* camel cannons, cradles, and mortars clearly points to this second, European vector of technology transfer to India. In the Battle of Chaul of 1508, mentioned here, a group of warships belonging to Mamluk Egypt and the sultan of Gujarat had engaged and defeated a Portuguese naval squadron off the Konkan coast. This was the first military reversal the Portuguese had suffered in the Indian Ocean since their arrival there a decade earlier.[30] As the extract relates, one consequence of the engagement was that Turks ('Rumis'), who were evidently mercenaries in the victorious coalition, captured firearms from the Portuguese and took them to Goa where they were integrated into the existing stock of that city's arsenal.[31] Further information on this pattern of technology transfer is furnished by the historian Duarte Barbosa, who was in India from about 1500 to about 1516. He writes that the same parties that fought off Chaul in 1508 engaged in a second maritime battle the following year off the Gujarat coast near Diu. In this engagement, which the Portuguese won, a group of Turks escaped to Goa and were promptly received and employed by Bijapuri authorities in the Goa arsenal. Local Muslim merchants, continues Barbosa, helped resettle these men in Goa; they also financed the building of shipyards and plants for the manufacture of both iron and bronze ordnance.[32]

Following the two naval engagements of 1508 and 1509, then, guns captured from the Portuguese found their way to Goa, followed by Mamluk or Ottoman gunners and gunsmiths.[33] Numerous Venetian and Genoese renegades also inhabited Goa at that time of the Portuguese conquest of 1510, and these, too, were likely employed in the arsenal.[34] All of these influences considerably enriched and expanded Goa's existing firearms industry. Building on these several vectors of technology transfer—the Mamluk, the European, and the Ottoman—gunsmiths of Goa working under Bijapuri authority seem to have made very high quality firearms, both cannons and matchlocks. Indeed, after taking possession of the city in 1510, the Portuguese viceroy, Albuquerque, was so impressed with the gun-making skills he encountered in Goa that he sent to the king of Portugal samples of the heavy cannons made by local Muslims.[35] Nor was the high quality of locally manufactured firearms confined to cannon-making. In early December 1513, the viceroy reported that matchlocks made by Goa's master gunsmiths were as good as those made in Bohemia; he even sent one of those gunsmiths to Lisbon to work for the Portuguese crown, presumably with a view to sharing with Portuguese military engineers the techniques in gun manufacture currently being used in western India.[36] One expert on guns of the period, Rainer Daehnhardt, speaks of an 'Indo-Portuguese' tradition of matchlocks that were produced after 1510 in the arsenal of Portuguese Goa, the so-called Casa das Dez Mil Espingardas ('House of the Ten Thousand Guns').[37] This style of firearms would soon spread not only into the Deccan interior but, by the mid-sixteenth century, throughout Portuguese Asia as far as Japan.[38]

In another letter sent to the king in December 1513, Albuquerque praised the abilities of Muslim gunsmiths in Goa who had formerly served the Bijapur Sultanate, had fled after the Portuguese took that city, but who were induced to return to Goa and continue their work for the Portuguese Crown. The viceroy even acknowledged—quite remarkably—that these gunsmiths had become 'our masters in artillery and the making of cannons and guns, which they make of iron here in Goa and are better than the German ones'.[39] Given that the Portuguese at this time considered guns made in Germany and Bohemia to be the finest anywhere,[40] Albuquerque's statement should serve as a corrective to the conventional image, tirelessly repeated in history textbooks, of Europe as the undisputed font of military technology in the early modern era, and of the rest of the world as passive recipients of Europe's technology. To the contrary, what we see here are gunsmiths in the western Deccan who had already assimilated earlier firearm technologies from Turkish and Portuguese sources, had amalgamated these traditions with their own, and who were now transferring technologies in precisely the opposite direction, from India to western Europe.

## THE BATTLE OF RAICHUR, 1520

With Muslim gunsmiths of the western Deccan having achieved such remarkable competence in gunpowder technology by the early sixteenth century, what were the consequences of this achievement? An answer to this question may be found in a single, decisive battle—actually a pair of battles—waged at and near the fort of Raichur in May and June, 1520. Having passed from Bahmani to Bijapur's control in the late fifteenth century, Raichur had been an early player in military modernization under both Bahmani and `Adil Shahi administrations. The contemporary Portuguese horse merchant and chronicler Fernão Nunes reported that by the time of the battle we are considering, Raichur's `Adil Shahi defenders had placed 200 heavy cannons and many smaller cannons along the curtain walls between the fort's bastions, and that they had mounted 30 stone-hurling catapults (*trabuco*) on those bastions.[41] Nunes, who seems to have been an eyewitness to the battle of 1520,[42] was evidently referring here to cannons that were placed in the square gun ports that had been built into the fort's curtain walls when the walls were constructed in 1468–70 (Figure 7.6). In any event, Nunes's report is the earliest known European reference to the use of cannons anywhere in India's interior.

The Battle of Raichur followed a dispute between Vijayanagara and Bijapur over the purchase of war-horses, which both states had been importing from overseas through Portuguese Goa. Sometime in 1519 Krishna Raya entrusted a Muslim merchant with the sum of 40,000 *pardaos* to purchase war-horses from that port. But the merchant absconded to Bijapur, and when Krishna Raya demanded that Isma`il `Adil Khan return both the merchant and the money, Isma`il refused to oblige. Enraged at the sultan's impudent behaviour, Krishna Raya used the dispute to justify a full-scale invasion of Bijapuri territory, targeting Raichur evidently on the grounds that that fort had once belonged to Vijayanagara. In early 1520 the king moved north with a force of 27,600 cavalry and an immense infantry. In all, writes Nunes, the army included archers, cavalry using a variety of weapons, matchlock-men (*espimgardeiros*), swordsmen with shields, war-elephants, and 'several cannon' (*allgũs tiros de fogo*).[43]

Upon reaching Raichur, Krishna Raya concentrated his main attack on the fort's eastern side, near the present Kati Gate. Although the defenders fired on Vijayanagara's forces with cannons and matchlocks, together with arrows, Krishna Raya's besiegers used no artillery against Raichur's walls. Instead, his commanders offered their men monetary inducements to approach the walls and dismantle them with crowbars and pick-axes, paying them in sums proportionate to the size of the stones dislodged. In this dreary manner the siege dragged on for three months.[44] Then in early May 1520, while the siege was still in progress, Krishna Raya learned that Isma`il `Adil Khan had marched down from Bijapur to relieve the embattled fort, and that the sultan had camped on the northern side of the Krishna River with 18,000 cavalry, 150 war-elephants, and considerable infantry. He also brought along a substantial amount of field artillery. Suspending his siege at Raichur, Krishna Raya moved his entire army up to the Krishna River to prevent Bijapur's forces from entering the Doab. A pitched battle between the two armies began several hours after dawn on 19 May 1520 when the sultan, having moved his forces to the southern side of the river, ill-advisedly fired all his artillery at once into Vijayanagara's massed front lines. When those lines broke, Krishna Raya mounted his horse and moved forward with his remaining divisions of heavy cavalry. Not having sufficient time to reload their cannons, the Bijapuri artillery corps was evidently encircled by Vijayanagara's cavalry, which forced the Bijapuris to abandon their ordnance and take flight. The main part of Bijapur's army was driven back towards, and finally into, the Krishna River. This was followed by horrific slaughter. Many `Adil Shahi forces drowned attempting to re-cross the river; others were picked off by Vijayanagara's archers while in the water or while scrambling ashore. In the midst of the chaos, Isma`il `Adil Khan managed to jump on an elephant, barely escaping with his life.[45]

Having soundly defeated the Bijapuris on the battlefield, Vijayanagara's army now returned to Raichur to resume its siege of the fort. At this point a new factor enters Nunes's narrative—the arrival of twenty Portuguese mercenaries who, led by one Cristovão de Figueiredo, had just joined Krishna Raya's forces at Raichur as matchlock-men (*espimgardeyros*).[46] Noticing how fearlessly Bijapuri defenders roamed about the fort's walls, fully exposed to the view of the besiegers, de Figueiredo and his comrades began picking them off with their guns, allowing Krishna Raya's men to resume dismantling the walls relatively unhindered. This operation proved so successful that the defenders were forced to abandon their first line of fortification and place their women and children in the city's hill-top citadel.[47] A turning point in the siege was reached on 14 June when the governor of the city, seeking a better view of exactly where the Portuguese snipers were positioned, leaned out in front of one of the merlons and was instantly killed by a matchlock shot that struck his forehead. This so snapped the morale of Raichur's defenders that they promptly abandoned the wall. The next day the Bijapuris opened the city gate and filed out, begging for mercy, and the day after that, Krishna Raya formally took possession of the city.[48]

What can this battle tell us about the state of gunpowder weaponry in the early sixteenth-century Deccan? The first thing to notice is its counter-intuitive outcome, which probably explains its absence in historical literature. On the one hand, the battle's winners, Vijayanagara, are said to have left their capital with only 'several' cannons, and they used little if any artillery either at Raichur Fort or in the pitched battle by the river. On the other hand, the losing side, Bijapur, possessed and used considerable artillery both offensively by the Krishna River and defensively at Raichur Fort—a consequence of the rapid development of firearms technology in the arsenal at Goa when that city was under first Bahmani and then `Adil Shahi control (1472–1510). Unlike Krishna Raya, Isma`il `Adil Khan brought a great deal of ordnance to the battlefield. Nunes reports that his retreating army was forced to abandon 400 heavy cannons and 900 gun-carriages, in addition to 4,000 war-horses and 100 elephants.[49] In fact, writes Nunes, Isma`il had boldly entered the Raichur Doab because he was confident that the great strength of his artillery (*a gramde artelharya*) would give him a quick victory. Indeed, the sultan's opening barrage did give him temporary field advantage. And yet he lost.

Second, it is clear that Bijapur's deployment of cannons proved fatally ineffective both offensively, when deployed in the pitched battle by the river, and defensively, when mounted along the fort's curtain walls. In the pitched battle, Bijapur's gunners evidently made the tactical mistake of firing all their cannons at once, instead of staggering their volleys. As a result, they could not reload and fire successive rounds of shot quickly enough before being overwhelmed by Vijayanagara's swift and powerful cavalry. Things went no better at Raichur's fort. There, as Nunes makes clear, Bijapur's gunners were unable to manoeuvre their cannons so as to screen the walls with flanking fire.[50] Being fixed in their gun ports along the fort's curtain walls, the cannons were virtually immobile and hence of little value against besiegers who managed to approach the wall beneath them.

Finally, and perhaps most importantly, the antagonists in this battle appear to have drawn directly opposite conclusions from its outcome. The losing Bijapuris understood that, despite the advances in cannon technology already made at their Goa arsenal, they had much to learn about the deployment of field cannons. They would need considerable practice before this new technology could become truly lethal to opponents who had mastered the tactics and techniques of cavalry warfare. Similarly, at Raichur, the military engineers' conservative approach to mounting cannons on the fort's ramparts proved their own undoing. Owing to the arrangement of the fort's defences—with thirty stone-hurling catapults placed on the bastions and several hundred heavy and light cannons fixed along the curtain walls in immobile positions—each shot fired from those cannons would tend to land in nearly the same, predictable spot in front of the fort. As a result, Krishna Raya's men were able to dismantle a portion of the city's walls without suffering prohibitively high casualty rates. In short, Bijapur's forces at Raichur Fort deployed the new gunpowder technology in a manner that proved just as disastrous there as did their deployment of cannons in the pitched battle by the Krishna River. Yet crucially, Bijapur's political leaders chose not to abandon the new technology that had so decisively failed them at Raichur. To the contrary, they and their engineers would mount an accelerated drive to master the use of cannons both defensively and offensively. It is often the case that states assimilate new technologies by a gradual process of trial and error, in respect of which failures can be as important as successes. Such, we shall presently see, is what happened at Bijapur.

Meanwhile Krishna Raya, though evidently impressed with the effectiveness of the matchlocks used by his Portuguese mercenaries, failed to see cannon warfare as the wave of the future. Prevailing against Bijapur's artillery both in pitched battle and at the fort seems to have reconfirmed the king's confidence in the efficacy of the day's conventional warfare. Accordingly, we find no evidence that he followed up his victories by establishing an arsenal or matchlock foundry in his kingdom. Nor did he or his successors ever mount cannons on the walls of their capital or their provincial forts, or in other ways adapt their defensive systems so as to accommodate gunpowder technology, a point established with respect to metropolitan Vijayanagara in a recent study by Robert Brubaker.[51] For the rest of its existence, the Vijayanagara state simply failed to take gunpowder technology very seriously. Whereas defeat at Raichur would catalyse Bijapur to embark on a remarkable drive for military modernization, victory lulled Krishna Raya and his successors into a state of relative complacency—a mistake for which they would later pay a very heavy price.

## THE EVOLUTION OF GUNPOWDER WEAPONRY AND FORTIFICATIONS, 1520–1600

Bijapur's military engineers appear to have closely studied the reasons for their devastating defeat at Raichur, for in the course of the next forty years they formulated a series of technological solutions that were both creative and far-reaching.[52] Although contemporary accounts are largely silent on this development, our examination of a considerable body of material evidence—more than a hundred specimens of early modern cannons surviving at sixteen Deccani forts—speaks to the matter with clarity.

To appreciate the strides made by Bijapur's engineers in the decades following the Battle of Raichur, it is important to recognize the level of military technology available to them in 1520. The guns used to defend Raichur were almost certainly wrought-iron breech-loaders, similar to those used in contemporary western Eurasia.[53] These guns were made from a series of long iron staves that formed the inner barrel and were bound together by tightly fitted iron hoops and reinforcing rings that were forge-welded together (Figure 7.8).[54] As breech-loaders, they had two detachable parts—a barrel open at both ends and a separate powder chamber, closed at the breech, with a narrower flange at the front end made to fit into the bore of the barrel (Figure 7.9). The advantage of the removable chambers was that the powder could be loaded into them directly and quickly,

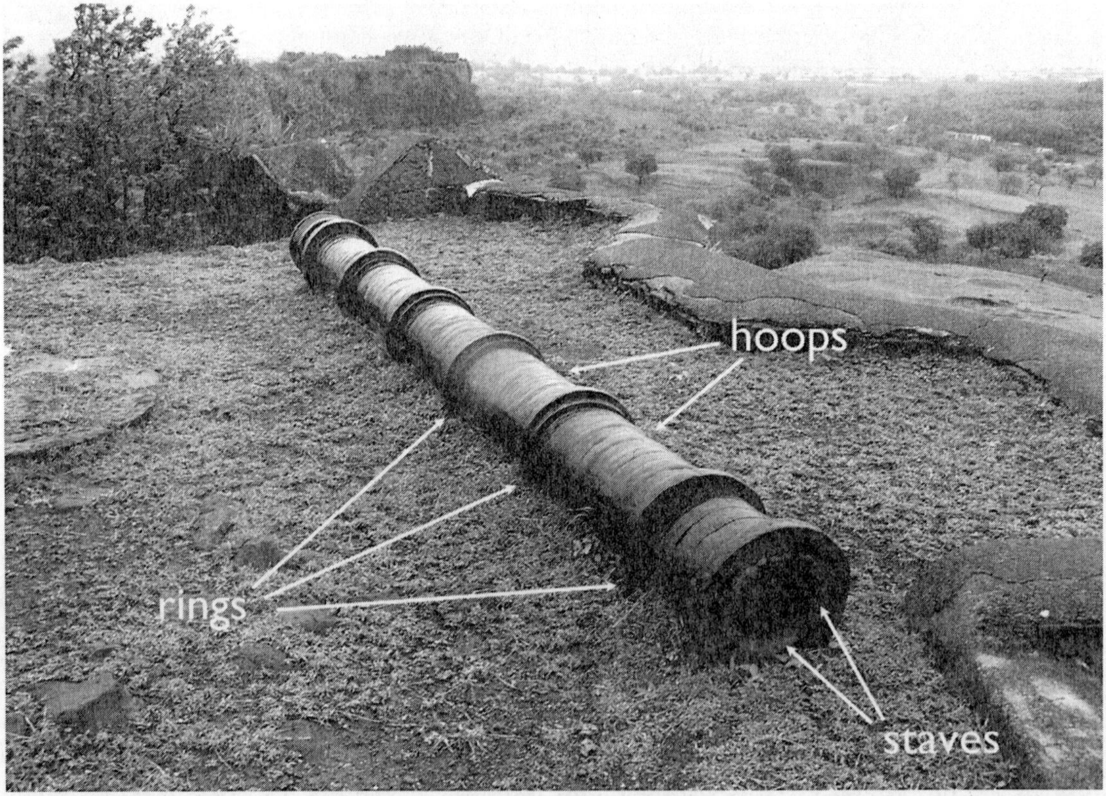


**Figure 7.8** Bidar Fort. Cannon no. 3.

**Figure 7.9** Devarakonda Fort. Powder chamber for cannon no. 1.

without having to ram it down a barrel still hot from the previous firing. But their two-part construction also meant that they had to be immobilized on heavy wooden carriages designed to keep the powder chamber tightly fitted into the barrel (Figure 7.10).[55] Such a mounting system, combined with the small, square gun ports built into Raichur's parapets, seriously restricted the guns' manoeuvrability, especially their vertical movement.

Building on technical features borrowed from western Eurasia, in the decades following the Battle of Raichur, Deccani gun-makers pioneered technological breakthroughs that were without precedent anywhere. Strategically, their goal was to build a new generation of guns that could control a wide swathe of territory lying before a fort in order to prevent attackers from approaching its walls with siege equipment, or even with pickaxes, as Vijayanagara's soldiers had done at Raichur Fort. To do this, they aimed to replace the earlier technology of stone-flinging catapults, which had theretofore been used on bastions, with large, wrought-iron or cast bronze muzzle-loaders that could be rotated both laterally and vertically. In the course of our field research, we personally examined a total of 107 cannons at Bidar, Bijapur, Devarakonda, Elgandal, Golconda, Kalyana, Kandhar, Malkhed, Medak, Mudgal, Naldurg, Parenda, Raichur, Shahapur, Udgir, and Yadgir. Only about a dozen of those that are dated were

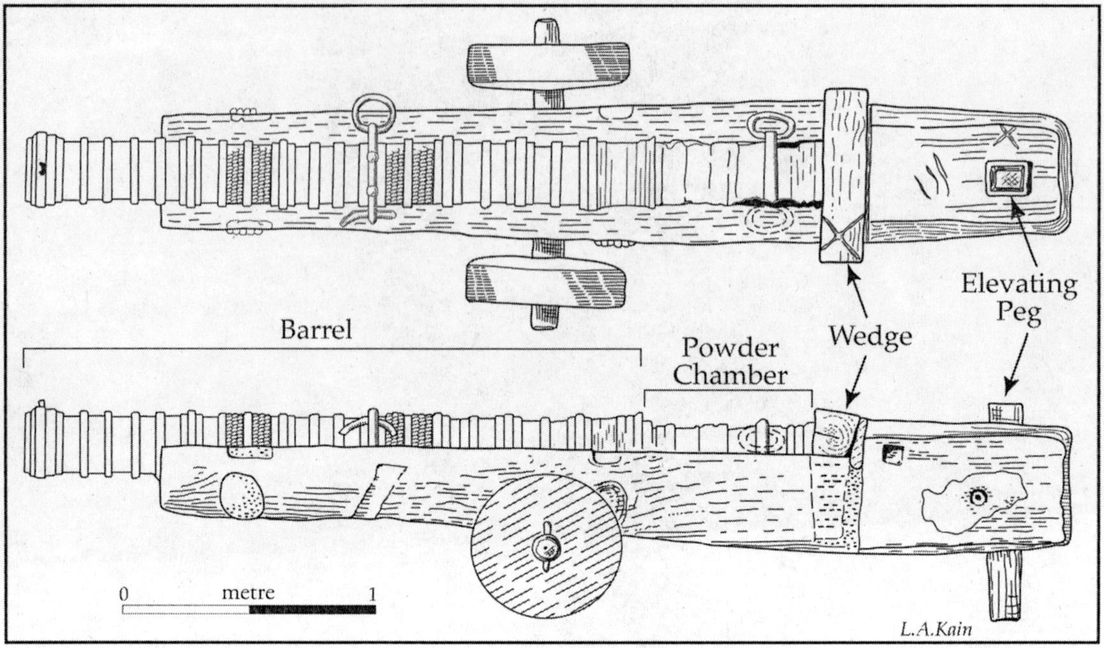


**Figure 7.10** Gun-carriage for *Mary Rose* breech-loader, 1545. Deccani breach-loaders would have required use of comparable gun carriages (after Peter Marsden, *Sealed by Time: The Loss and Recovery of the* Mary Rose [Portsmouth: The Mary Rose Trust, 2003]).

made in the sixteenth or seventeenth centuries (see Table 7.1). Yet the information they contain, combined with an analysis of the more numerous undated cannons we examined, suggest trends in early modern metallurgy in the Deccan.

The guns themselves varied widely in size, typically ranging from 2 to 5 metres in length, with the longest exceeding 9 metres; their bores typically ranged from 15 to 40 centimetres in diameter, with the largest exceeding 70 centimetres. Guns associated with the various sultanates also bore distinctive characteristics. For example, the Nizam Shahi sultans of Ahmadnagar led the other sultanates in the art of casting high-quality bronze cannons, a skill evidently acquired from immigrant Ottoman Turkish master gunsmiths who had been recruited by the Nizam Shahi rulers of Ahmadnagar.[56] Taking advantage of their proximity to Arabian Sea shipping lanes, these sultans also acquired arms made in Europe.[57] For their part, the `Adil Shahi sultans of Bijapur manufactured a great many wrought-iron cannons that, while certainly serviceable, were hardly the highly polished works of art produced by either of their neighbours. As we will see, their energies were mainly devoted to pioneering innovations in mounting systems and bastion design. Further to the east, the Barid Shahi sultans of Bidar made forge-welded iron cannons of exceptionally high quality, polished to such a degree as to be nearly undistinguishable from cast bronze. Many of them are also beautifully decorated with floral or animal designs in metal inlay, with cartouches containing lines of Persian verse or passages from the Qur'an.[58] By contrast the Qutb Shahi

**Table 7.1** Dated cannons on Deccan forts, 1543–1663

| Date | Site | Location | Sovereign | Name | Material | Length | Bore | Source |
|---|---|---|---|---|---|---|---|---|
| 1543 | Ausa | NE bastion | Burhan Nizam Shah I | – | Cast bronze | 239 | 24 | |
| 1549 | Ahmadnagar, Parenda, Bijapur | Sharza Burj (Bijapur) | Burhan Nizam Shah I | Malik-i Maidan | Cast bronze | 436 | 71 | |
| 1557 | Yadgir | Bastion east of gate 7 | Ibrahim `Adil Shah I | – | Wrought iron | 412 | 20 | |
| 1569 | Bidar | Mandu gate | `Ali Barid Shah | Top-i Ilahi | Wrought iron | 450 | 48 | |
| 1569 | Bidar | Kala Burj | `Ali Barid Shah | Top-i Ilahi | Wrought iron | 562 | 48 | |
| 1580 | Bidar | North end of Purana Qil`a | Ibrahim Barid Shah | Fath-i Lashkar | Wrought iron | 346 | 37 | |
| 1583 | Bijapur | Haidari Burj | Ibrahim `Adil Shahi | Lambacharri | Wrought iron | 932 | 30 | |
| 1587 | Bidar | Lal Burj | Qasim Barid Shah II | Top-i Haidari | Wrought iron | 371 | 37 | |
| 1591 | Bidar | Mandu Burj | Qasim Barid Shah II | Top-i Mahmud Shahi | – | – | – | Deloche, 'Gunpowder', 584 |
| 1598–1621 | Ausa | Northwest bastion | A Nizam Shahi king [bought from Philip III of Spain] | – | Cast bronze | 324 | 13 | |
| 1627 | Parenda | West bastion | Burhan Nizam Shah III | – | Cast bronze | 308 | 16 | |
| 1644 | Golkonda | Bada Burj | `Abd Allah Qutb Shah | – | Wrought iron | 509 | 31 | Balasubramaniam 133 |
| 1646 | Bijapur | City's south wall | Muhammad `Adil Shah | Landa Kesab | Wrought iron | 657 | 50 | Deloche, 'Gunpowder', 584 |
| 1660 | Parenda | Southwest bastion | `Ali `Adil Shah II | Azdaha paikar | Cast bronze | 486 | 17 | |
| 1663 | Parenda | Northeast bastion | `Ali `Adil Shah II | Malik-i maidan | Cast bronze | 395 | 23 | |

sultans of Golconda, the easternmost sultanate, lagged far behind the others in terms of either bastion design or cannon manufacture.[59]

To accomplish the goal of mounting these huge cannons atop the bastions of Deccani forts, several engineering breakthroughs were needed. In particular, two technological innovations proved crucial, both of them pioneered by engineers in Bijapur's service. In order to give their cannons vertical movement, engineers borrowed the western Eurasian idea of the trunnion, that is, the cylindrical pivot projecting from the sides of a cannon's barrel, permitting it to be raised or lowered independent of the carriage on which it was mounted. Both European and Ottoman engineers had been building cannons with trunnions in the early sixteenth century, and we have clear evidence that this technology diffused to the Deccan at that time. On the northeastern bastion at Ausa lies a bronze Ottoman-style muzzle-loader with trunnions (Figure 7.11). An inscription on its barrel indicates that it had been made for Sultan Burhan Nizam Shah I of Ahmadnagar in 1543 by an immigrant Ottoman gunfounder named Ustad Muhammad bin Husain Rumi.[60] Likely used as a field cannon before being fixed on a bastion, this gun suggests the pathway by which the trunnion concept reached the Deccan.

**Figure 7.11** Ausa fort. Nizam Shahi cannon (cannon no. 2), made by an Ottoman gunfounder in 1543.

To give a cannon lateral movement, Deccani engineers took from the Portuguese the idea of mounting a gun on a swivel-fork attached to the gun's trunnions. The Portuguese had been using such a mounting device on small cast bronze or wrought-iron breech-loaders called berços, or 'cradles'—so called because of the open space behind their barrels to accommodate a removable powder chamber. The swivel-fork beneath the barrel mounted on the gun's trunnions gave the gun both vertical and lateral movement (Figure 7.12). Measuring only a metre or so in length, berços were commonly mounted on the gunnels of sixteenth-century Portuguese ships.[61]

We have seen that when the Portuguese were defeated off the port of Chaul in 1508, guns of this particular type were among the weapons that the victors plundered from Portuguese vessels and took to Goa, then a Bijapuri

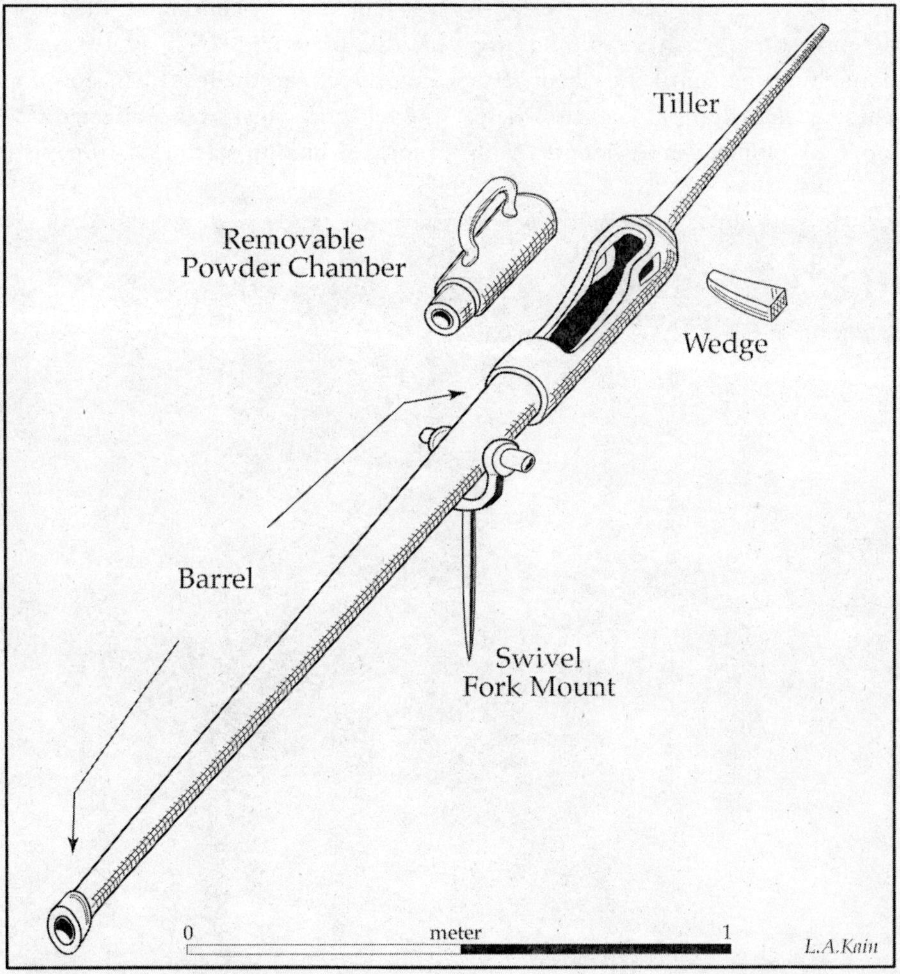


**Figure 7.12** Portuguese berço gun, showing the 'cradle' for the powder chamber and the swivel-fork mount (After John Francis Guilmartin Jr, *Gunpowder and Galleys: Changing Technology and Mediterranean Warfare at Sea in the Sixteenth Century* [Cambridge: Cambridge University Press, 1974]).

possession. Once brought ashore, they were swiftly integrated into Goa's gun foundry and arsenal, for locally made wrought-iron copies of these European models soon appeared in the interior (Figure 7.13).[62] These are the guns referred to in Indian sources as 'firangi'—literally 'Frankish'—with reference to their Portuguese inspiration.[63]

In the 1550s, engineers at Bijapur's hill fort at Yadgir, not far north of Raichur, appear to have taken the lead in creatively adapting the principle of trunnions and swivel-forks for directly mounting massive cannons atop bastions, something that until then had never been attempted in Europe or elsewhere. Four of Yadgir's cannons were evidently built sequentially, as each gun introduced different degrees of improvements or refinements not found in its predecessors. Since an inscription on the third cannon in this sequence records that it was made in 1557 by one Muhammad Aqa, we may infer that the late 1550s saw the active phase of this experimentation, and that this unsung engineer was the creative force behind it (Figure 7.14).[64] Muhammad Aqa's technological innovation consisted of several interlinked components that together allowed a single gun to command an unusually wide swathe of terrain. First, it involved fixing the gun directly to the fort by means of a modified swivel fork, which was fabricated from a cubic block of granite set on an iron pin to enable

**Figure 7.13** Ausa Fort. Indian adaptation of Portuguese *berço*.

**Figure 7.14** Yadgir Fort. Cannon no. 3: 'Under the superintendence of Muhammad Aqa, AH 965 [AD 1557]'.

the gun to swivel from side to side. Second, it necessitated affixing trunnions to the gun's barrel, and cutting channels into the surface of the block to accommodate both the trunnions and the body of the barrel as it was raised and lowered. Third, to take full advantage of the flexibility of aiming that this mounting system provided, the gun was mounted not on the wall of the fort, but either on a semi-circular bastion projecting from it—where it could cover an arc of nearly 180 degrees—or on a separate circular gun platform at the very top of the fort, allowing a full 360 degrees of coverage (Figure 7.15). In effect, the gun was being treated as a massive, oversized berço, with the result that a single gun could cover a much broader area in front of the fort.

A final innovation seen at Yadgir was the construction of a deep, circular channel near the edge of the platform. By positioning a heavy wooden post into this channel at the point directly behind the cannon's breech, and driving a wooden wedge between the breech and the post's inner surface, some of the recoil force would have been absorbed and transmitted to the heavy, stone construction of the gun platform.[65] This last innovation, however, evidently proved inadequate for the task, as is witnessed by the fractured state of two of Yadgir's four stone mounting blocks, and our discovery

**Figure 7.15** Yadgir Fort. Cannon no. 4 (late 1550s).

of an extra mounting block that was being held in reserve near the base of the cavalier of Yadgir cannon 4. Since such stone mounting systems are extremely rare in the Deccan,[66] it seems that this aspect of Muhammad Aqa's experiment represented something of a developmental dead end.

By about 1560, however, solutions to this problem were worked out at several other hill forts—for example, Kalyana, Naldurg, Parenda, and Kandhar—along Bijapur's northern border with the Nizam Shahi Sultanate of Ahmadnagar. These solutions required engineers to go beyond experimenting with the guns and their mounting system, and to make fundamental changes in the architecture of the fort itself. `Ali `Adil Shah's remodelling of Kalyana in the 1560s illustrates the process.[67] Existing bastions, apparently dating to the Bahmani period, were completely rebuilt as massive, solid platforms and provided with a distinctive, new type of crowning cavalier rising above the top of the bastion. At most of these bastions, the guns were mounted on heavy wrought-iron swivel forks, while the rear portion of the cavalier was carried up to provide a continuous, solid recoil wall (Figures 7.16 and 7.17). Driving a wooden wedge between the breech of the cannon and the recoil wall would have absorbed the force of the gun when fired, taking the strain off the iron swivel far more effectively than had the system earlier attempted at Yadgir.

The earlier bastions of these remodelled forts were apparently filled in with earth, with some of their masonry recycled in the outer facing of the new bastions. The end result was a massive platform of solid earth, encased within strong stone masonry, and girded about the top with a continuous parapet of alternating merlons and embrasures (Figure 7.18). Atop this massive platform, the cavalier rises up to yet another level. This two-tiered disposition permitted an effective spatial differentiation between the higher level occupied by the cannon and its firing crew, and the battlement below with its loop-holed merlons and embrasures for small arms fire. The platform on the higher level was protected by a two-part masonry wall, articulated along the outer edge as a series of merlons and embrasures, and at the rear as the solid recoil wall described earlier. Pairs of sockets near the tops of the sides of the merlons were intended to hold small wooden beams for affixing wooden shutters, which would have been kept closed on all sides except the one through which the gun was being fired, thus sheltering the gun crew from incoming small arms fire.[68]

If building high cavaliers on existing bastions gave a fort's big guns greater range, a further innovation—perhaps the ultimate step in this direction—was the introduction of immense, free-standing stone cavaliers that towered far above all the bastions, and sometimes above

**Figure 7.16** Kalyaṇa Fort. Cannon on bastion no. 6 in the upper circuit.

**Figure 7.17** Kalyana Fort. Cavalier atop bastion no. 10, from inside.

**Figure 7.18** Kalyana Fort. Bastion no. 8 in lower circuit, showing cavalier on top. Note the difference in masonry fabric between the fifteenth-century wall (to right) and the sixteenth-century bastion.

the entire fort. On the top of such cylindrically shaped platforms, cannons mounted on swivel forks commanded a 360 degree sweep of the fort's surrounding countryside. One of the earliest of these to appear was at Yadgir, where Muhammad Aqa had experimented with mounting large cannons on swivel mounts in the late 1550s. In the following several decades, gigantic cavaliers with great guns began appearing at other strategic `Adil Shahi forts. At Naldurg sometime after 1560, engineers placed two large cannons on a massive cavalier 27 metres high and 20 metres in diameter at the top, accessible by a long staircase of 77 steps (Figure 7.19).[69] Almost as high is Bijapur's Haidari Burj, a cavalier which, built in 1583, rises to a height of about 24 metres and carries one of the longest cannons in India, the 'Lambacharri' gun, measuring 9.32 metres.[70] One of the most spectacular such structures is found in Mudgal, where an enormous cylindrical tower was raised 9 metres high and 28 metres in diameter. Since the cavalier was built at the peak of a hill in the middle of the fort's enclosure, the gun that was once mounted on its platform—it is not there today—would have had a commanding 360 degree sweep over the whole of the surrounding countryside.[71]

In short, the mid-sixteenth century saw fundamental changes in the Deccan's architectural landscape as fortifications built in the pre-gunpowder age were rebuilt to accommodate the new style of mounting cannons. Table 7.2, which documents the construction of new bastions in the Deccan, shows the chronology and the geography of the new system's diffusion across the plateau. Nearly half of the seventy-four dated bastions built between 1500 and the Mughal conquest of the Deccan in 1686–87 were built during the thirty years

**Figure 7.19** Naldurg Fort. Cavalier (1560), with powder magazine to right.

**Table 7.2** Dated bastions of the Deccan, 1500–1600

| Date | Site | District | Name of Bastion | Sovereign | Builder | Source |
|---|---|---|---|---|---|---|
| 1512 | Panhala | Kolhapur | — | — | Sikandar | *EIAPS* (1971), 67, pl. XVII(b) |
| 1515 | Raichur | Raichur | 'Burj al-Fath' | Mahmud Bahmani | — | *EIM* (1939–40), 16, pl. VI(a) |
| 1539 | Panhala | Kolhapur | — | Ibrahim `Adil Shah I | Yusuf the Abdar | *EIAPS* (1971), 68, pl. XVIII(b) |
| 1546 | Raichur | Raichur | — | Ibrahim `Adil Shah I | Ahmad Haji Gunabadi | *EIAPS* (1963), 62, pl. XIX(a) |
| 1548 | Raichur | Raichur | — | Ibrahim `Adil Shah I | — | *EIAPS* (1963), 63, pl. XX(a) |
| 1558 | Gulbarga | Gulbarga | 'Burj-i Daulat' | `Ali `Adil Shah I | `Arab Khan[1] | *EIM* (1907–08), 2 [no plate]; see also Desai, *South India*, no. 573 |
| 1558 | Gulbarga | Gulbarga | Putli Burj | `Ali `Adil Shah I | `Arab Khan | Desai, *South India*, no. 574[2] |
| 1560 | Kalyana | Bidar | Lower bastion no. 1 | `Ali `Adil Shah I | — | Unpublished Marathi inscription; located on inside upper face of bastion |
| 1560 | Naldurg | Osmanabad | 'completed the fort' | `Ali `Adil Shah I | Nimatullah, son of Khwaja Isma'il Kurd Khiraji of Nihawand | *EIM (*1917–18), 2, pl. I(b) |
| 1561 | Bijapur | Bijapur | Tabut Burj | `Ali `Adil Shah I | — | Nazim, *Bijapur Inscriptions,* 49, pl. VI |
| 1563 | Kalyana | Bidar | Lower bastion no. 5 | `Ali `Adil Shah I | Kamil Khan | *EIM* (1935–36), 5, pl. IV(a) |
| 1564 | Gulbarga | Gulbarga | — | `Ali `Adil Shah I | Khan-i `A`zam Hamid Khan Bahmani | *EIM* (1907–08), 3[3] See also Desai *South India*, no. 577 |
| 1564 | Gulbarga | " | [2 bastions constructed, acc. to previous inscription] | " | " | " |
| 1565 | Raichur | Raichur | 'Shah-i Burj' | `Ali `Adil Shah I | Ikhlas Khan | *EIM* (1939–40), 17, pl. VII(a) |
| 1565–89 | Kandhar | Nanded | — | Murtaza Nizam Shah I | Ghori Khan | *EIM* (1919–20), 22, pl X(b) |
| 1566 | Kandhar | Nanded | — | Murtaza Nizam Shah I | Pulad Khan | *EIM* (1919–20), 22, pl. X(a) |
| 1566 | Galna | Nasik | — | Murtaza Nizam Shah I (?) | Aflatun Khan | *EIAPS* (1967), 45, pl. XI(b) |
| 1567 | Kalyana | Bidar | Lower bastion no. 6 | `Ali `Adil Shah I | Kamil Khan | *EIM* (1935–36), 5 pl. IV(b) |
| 1568 | Kalyana | Bidar | Lower bastion no. 10 | `Ali `Adil Shah I | Kamil Khan | *EIM* (1935–36), 6 pl. V(b) |
| 1569 | Dharur | Bhir | 'Burj-i `Ali' | `Ali `Adil Shah I | Kishwar Ghazi | *ARIE* 1965–66), D, 190; See also Desai, *Western India*, no. 829[4] |
| 1569 | Galna | Nasik | 'Fathi Burj' | Murtaza Nizam Shah I | Aflatun Khan | *EIAPS* (1957–58), 13, pl. IV(b) |
| 1570 | Raichur | Raichur | — | `Ali `Adil Shah I | Tahir Khan | *EIAPS* (1963), 65, pl. XIX(b) |
| 1573 | Kalyana | Bidar | Lower bastion no. 8 | `Ali `Adil Shah I | Kamil Khan | *EIM* (1935–36), 7, pl. V(c) |
| 1574 | Mudgal | Raichur | `Ali Burj | `Ali `Adil Shah I | — | *EIM* (1935–36), 16, pl. X(a) |
| 1574 | Gulbarga | Gulbarga | — | `Ali `Adil Shah I | Babaji Dabit Khan | *EIM* (1907–08), 3 [no plate]; see also Desai, *South India*, no. 581 |
| 1576 | Bijapur | Bijapur | Firingi Burj | `Ali `Adil Shah I | — | Nazim, 50 |
| 1576 | Janjira | Kolaba | 'constructed the fort and bastions' | Murtaza Nizam Shah I | Fahim Khan | *ARIE* (1959–60), D, 140; See also Desai, *Western India*, no. 1110 |

| | | | | | | |
|---|---|---|---|---|---|---|
| 1577 | Dharur | Bhir | 'Burj-i Hazrat-i Diwan-i A`la Murtazashahi' (Hathi Burj) | Murtaza Nizam Shah I | Ahmad Aqa | *ARIE* (1965–66), B, 353; See also Desai, *Western India*, no. 831 |
| 1577 | Gawilgarh | Amravati | 'Burj-i Bahram' | Murtaza Nizam Shah I | Bahram | *EIM* (1907–08), 11 [no plate] |
| 1577 | Panhala | Kolhapur | 'Burj-i Qudrat' | `Ali `Adil Shah I | Shams al-Din | *EIAPS* (1971), 73, pl. XIX(a) |
| 1579 | Dharur | Bhir | Twelve Imams Burj | Murtaza Nizam Shah I | Turk Khan | *ARIE* (1965–66), D, 189; See also Desai, *Western India*, no. 832 |
| 1579 | Galna | Nasik | Murad Burj | Murtaza Nizam Shah I | — | *EIAPS* (1967), 49, pl. XII(b) |
| 1579 | Panhala | Kolhapur | — | `Ali `Adil Shah I | Ahmad `Ali[5] | *EIAPS* (1971), 74–75, pl. XX(a) |
| 1580 | Galna | Nasik | — | Murtaza Nizam Shah I | Pulad Khan | *EIAPS* (1967), 54, pl. XIII(b) |
| 1580–1627 | Mudgal | Raichur | —[6] | Ibrahim `Adil Shah II | Dilawar Khan | *EIM* (1935–36), 18, pl. XI(a) |
| 1583 | Galna | Nasik | — | Murtaza Nizam Shah I | Pulad Khan | *EIAPS* (1967), 55–56, pl. XIV(b) |
| 1583 | Bijapur | Bijapur | Haidari Burj | Ibrahim `Adil Shah II | — | Nazim, 51 |
| 1583 | Vishalgarh | Kolhapur | Daulat Burj | Ibrahim `Adil Shah II | Dilawar Khan | ARIE (1963–64), D, 211; See also Desai, *Western India*, no. 2149 |
| 1586 | Gulbarga | Gulbarga | Fath Burj | Ibrahim `Adil Shah II | Muhammad Haidar | *EIM* (1907–08), 6 [no plate]; See also Desai, *South India*, no. 584 |
| 1588 | Mudgal | Raichur | 'Burj-i Fath-i Jang' | Ibrahim `Adil Shah II (but begun in reign of `Ali) | | Diyanat Khan *EIM* (1935–36), 15, IX(a) |
| 1589 | Kandhar | Nanded | 'Burj-i Ibrahimi' | ? | Ibrahim Khan | *EIM* (1919–20), 22, pl. XI(a) |
| 1589 | Kandhar | Nanded | 'Shahi Burj' | ? | Ibrahim Khan | *EIM* (1919–20), 23, pl. XI(b) |
| 1590 | Bankapur | Dharwar | 'Burj-i Khan-i Najafi' | Ibrahim `Adil Shah II | Najafi Khan | *EIAPS* (1968), 46, pl. VI(b) |
| 1591 | Raichur | Raichur | 'Burj-i `Ali bin Abi Talib' | Ibrahim `Adil Shah II | Khawas Khan | *EIM* (1939–40), 18, pl. VII(b) |
| 1597 | Bankapur | Dharwar | — | Ibrahim `Adil Shah II | Khurshid Khan | *EIAPS* (1968), 47, pl. VII(a) |

*Source*: Authors.

*Notes*: [1] The reading given in *EIM* (1907–08) is `Izzat Khan, but Desai reads it as `Arab Khan.

[2] Desai cites *EIM* (1907–08), p. 2, but it does not appear to give any text of a second *burj* foundation by `Arab Khan.

[3] *EIM* (1907–08) gives the date as AH 986/AD 1578–79, but Desai reads it as 972 Hijri (=1564–65).

[4] Desai is uncertain as to whether or not the `Adil Shahis held Dharur at this point, since the name of the ruler is evidently not mentioned. However, see Firishta (Briggs III: 80–81) who notes that Kamal Kishwar Khan was sent by `Ali `Adil Shah to harrass the Nizam Shahis along the border, and that he took some territory and built a new fort, called Dharur. He remains in control of the fort until Murtaza Nizam Shah comes and takes it back (slaying him in the process). So any bastion he built must have been constructed during a period of Adil Shahi control.

[5] Kadiri notes that this Ahmad `Ali is said to be the son of Raun `Ali and to bear the title Shamshir al-Mulk. He goes on to suggest that Raun `Ali is the Shamshir al-Mulk of the Mudgal and Raichur inscriptions, and that Ahmad `Ali would have inherited the title from his father. See *EIAPS* (1971), 74.

[6] Although the first hemistitch of line five is completely effaced, and accordingly there is no reference to the foundation of a burj, the inscription is on a burj and the second half of the hemistitch reads 'the like of which is not to be found in Iraq or Tabriz'. Desai, *South India*, no. 1241 infers it must have referred to the bastion.

between 1560 and 1590—clearly the period when rulers and governors most feverishly raced to remodel their forts. Moreover, 62 per cent of those seventy-four bastions were built by rulers of Bijapur, whose lead in this activity may be attributed to several factors. First, the `Adil Shahis' location in the western portion of the plateau gave them direct access to new ideas arriving from across the Arabian Sea, such as the trunnion and the swivel-fork. Second, Isma`il `Adil Khan's stunning defeat at Raichur in 1520 seems to have inspired his successors to compensate for his humiliating loss by mastering the techniques of cannon warfare. Isma`il's immediate successor, Ibrahim I (r. 1535–58), oversaw the innovative experiments at Yadgir that launched the Deccan's military transformation. But it was in `Ali's reign (r. 1558–80) that that transformation truly took off. No Deccan ruler played a more active role in modernizing the military profile of the Deccan's forts.

The third reason Bijapur was such a military pioneer was that that state emerged as by far the greatest beneficiary of Vijayanagara's catastrophic defeat in the 1565 Battle of Talikota. Loot plundered from their fabulously rich rival to the south enabled `Ali to embark on massive investments in military modernization throughout his domain.

## THE BATTLE OF TALIKOTA, 1565

If the battlefield is the ultimate test for any weapon system, the Battle of Talikota, waged in 1565, revealed the wide gap in military technology that had opened between the northern and southern Deccan since the Battle of Raichur, fought forty-five years earlier. Indeed, the two battles appear to have been linked in a curious way. In 1520, having crushed Isma`il `Adil Khan both at Raichur Fort and in the nearby pitched battle, Krishna Raya chose to adopt a posture of contemptuous arrogance towards his defeated foe. First, the Vijayanagara king promised to return the spoils of his victory to Isma`il on the sole condition that the latter come down to his court and show his submission by kissing his foot.[72] When the Bijapur sultan refused, Krishna Raya humiliated his adversary further by marching to Isma`il's own capital—which, still lacking a fortified citadel, Isma`il had prudently vacated—and occupying it for several days. Participating in these audacious manoeuvres was Vijayanagara's ambitious courtier Rama Raya, who had married one of Krishna Raya's daughters. Soon after the king's death in 1529, Rama Raya began laying the groundwork for his own takeover of the Vijayanagara state, which came to fruition in 1550 when he placed its de jure sovereign, Sadashiva Raya, under effective house arrest and began governing the kingdom as an autocrat. At the same time, he continued his father-in-law's arrogant policies toward Bijapur and the other northern sultanates by playing them off against each other, all the while pursuing—as we have seen in Chapter 4—his objective of indirectly controlling the old Chalukya capital of Kalyana. But in his haughty policies vis-à-vis his alleged 'allies' to the north, which included the desecration of mosques,[73] Rama Raya overplayed his hand, ultimately driving the northern sultanates to abandon their mutual rivalries and join in a grand coalition to confront Vijayanagara and its high-handed autocrat. Although no direct evidence proves the point, Rama Raya quite possibly picked up his arrogant posture vis-à-vis the northern sultanates from the example of his own father-in-law, Krishna Raya, following the Battle of Raichur.

The great battle took place in early January 1565 some 12 miles south of the Krishna River. Upon reconnoitring at the town of Talikota, located to the north of that river, the combined forces of Bijapur, Ahmadnagar, Bidar, and

Golconda marched due west, crossed the river, and engaged the immense army of Rama Raya and his brothers near the town of Banahatti in present-day Bagalkot district.[74] According to the historian Firishta, our best chronicler of the battle, Rama Raya's haughty arrogance did not slacken even when confronted with the formidable coalition arrayed before him. He ordered his commanders to bring him the severed head of Husain Nizam Shah and to capture alive both Ibrahim Qutb Shah and `Ali `Adil Shah so that they could spend the rest of their days confined in iron cages.

Events, however, went otherwise. At battle's end it was Rama Raya who was taken alive from the battlefield, snatched by the trunk of one of the Ahmadnagar elephants and delivered straightaway to Husain Nizam Shah. Given the several occasions on which the Vijayanagara ruler had humiliated the Nizam Shahi sultan,[75] it was altogether fitting that he was brought before Husain, who clearly savoured this moment of supreme revenge. The chronicler Rafi` al-Din Shirazi, who was in Bijapur's service at the time, relates that Husain, having first seen to it that his 'guest' was comfortably seated before him, politely asked Rama Raya about his health. Saying nothing, the octogenarian merely pointed to his head, indicating that he had reached his destiny. At this point a Nizam Shahi noble who happened to be present, incredulous at these mock pleasantries, grew uncontrollably agitated. Referring to the Vijayanagara ruler's one-time friendship with Bijapur's `Ali `Adil Shah, on whom Rama Raya had warmly conferred fictive kinship, the noble exclaimed,

> Rama Raya's army has just now been crushed by his 'son' `Ali `Adil Shah! This accursed, arrogant infidel should not be left here before you. There is no time for delay![76]

With that outburst, and with Husain's evident approval, the noble severed Rama Raya's head, placed it on the tip of a spear, and proudly displayed it before the allied troops as a sign of victory. Some forty years later the allies, in commemoration of this historic victory, continued publicly to display Rama Raya's severed head as a trophy.[77] In 1829 a sculptured representation of it served as the opening of one of the sewers in Bijapur's citadel.[78] This is possibly the same sculpture that is currently housed in the city's Archaeological Museum, and which effectively captures the sculptor's attempt to portray what he took to be Rama Raya's thoroughly demonic character (Figure 7.20).

What role did firearms play in this battle? To be sure, Rama Raya brought considerable firepower with him. Firishta records that he fielded 70,000 cavalry and 90,000 infantry, the latter being mainly matchlock-men and archers, although we do not know in what proportion these were distributed.[79] In his front line he interspersed 1,000 cannons with 2,000 war-elephants. Indeed, the battle was initiated with his firing nearly 50,000 rockets (*bān*), matchlocks (*tufang*), and cannons (*top va ḍarbuzan*) at the allies.[80] But the battle was decided by far more effective use of firepower by the allies. Husain Nizam Shah, who commanded the centre of the allies' battle formation, brought up 600 cannons of different calibres, arranged in three rows and fastened together with strong chains and ropes so as to prevent Rama Raya's cavalry from breaking through the allies' lines.[81] In the first row were placed 200 heavy cannons (*top-hāyi kalān*), in the second were intermediate cannons (*ḍarbuzan*), and in the third row were the swivel cannons (*zaṃbūrak*)—smaller than the intermediate cannons but larger than matchlocks. All the artillery were under the command of Chalabi Rumi Khan, a Turk who, Firishta notes, had earlier served in Europe with

**Figure 7.20** Stone sculpture of Rama Raya. Archaeological Museum, Bijapur (*Courtesy of* Archaeological Survey of India).

distinction, evidently as an Ottoman officer.[82] Masking the artillery stood several thousand archers who showered arrows on Rama Raya's advancing infantry. When the latter got to within range of the allies' cannons, the archers suddenly fell back while the cannons opened fire. The Vijayanagara infantry initially gave way but charged the guns a second time, and in response Chalabi Rumi Khan ordered the gunners to load their ordnance with copper coins and fire at the enemy from close range, a procedure that instantly killed some 5,000 attackers.[83] Although that figure comprised only a fraction of the total of Vijayanagara's casualties on that day, estimated at 100,000,[84] Firishta notes that it was the repulse of this charge by the allies' cannons that decided the battle's outcome.[85]

Just as the Battle of Raichur had been fought both on an open field and at the fort of Raichur itself, the Battle of Talikota really had two sites. The first was the battlefield near the village of Bannihatti where Raya Rama's army was routed. This was followed by the allies' march down to the sprawling metropolis of Vijayanagara itself. Here, the wide gap that had opened up between Vijayanagara's defence system and that of its northern rivals proved fatal. Not only had engineers at the great capital failed to mount cannons on their bastions, or even on curtain walls; the city never incorporated any of the defensive features that had become standard in the northern Deccan, such as semicircular bastions, high and thick merlons, wide walkways on ramparts, box machicolations (projecting turrets), broad moats, cavaliers, complex gateways flanked by stout, round towers, or barbicans (built-up extensions in front of outer walls).[86] Vijayanagara's defences had essentially remained what they were in the days of the Battle of Raichur: stone walls built without mortar, separated by square bastions. When, therefore, the victorious coalition of armies from the northern sultanates marched down to loot the city following Rama Raya's defeat in the pitched battle, the great capital lay helpless before the advancing allies. No attempt was made to repel the onslaught; indeed, given the state of the city's defences, no viable attempt could have been made to defend it.

## A 'MILITARY REVOLUTION' IN THE DECCAN?

Even though changes in cannon design in the mid-sixteenth-century Deccan had been inspired by technology borrowed from Ottoman and European sources, the nature of those changes, the architectural innovations they spawned, and their political consequences differed radically from developments in contemporary Europe. This invites an attempt to situate military changes in the sixteenth-century Deccan in relation to an early modern 'military revolution', a theory that has been hotly debated among historians of early modern Europe since the 1960s and, more recently, in world history circles.[87] First proposed by Michael Roberts in 1955, the theory found an ardent advocate in Geoffrey Parker, who from the mid-1970s on refined, elaborated, and stoutly defended it.[88] In 1995 Parker characterized early modern Europe's 'military revolution' in terms of a series of critical innovations, namely: (1) the advent, in the fifteenth century, of large siege cannons capable of destroying the vertical walls of medieval forts, which led in the early sixteenth century to (2) a new design of forts that could resist artillery siege, the so-called *trace italienne* style. This in turn produced protracted sieges of the new forts, the capture of which diminished the utility of cavalries but did require (3) large infantries. Raising such armies, however, required (4) expanded administrative structures and more efficient taxation systems, that is, modern states. Finally, (5) the ability to mount cannons aboard ships, combined with the planting of the new forts in coastal enclaves overseas, enabled Europeans to project their power on a global stage, leading ultimately to the 'rise of the West'.[89]

Such a sweeping formulation naturally provoked considerable academic discussion, and not a little opposition, on both empirical and conceptual grounds—for example, that the theory was technologically deterministic, chronologically misplaced, or burdened with a marked teleological trajectory.[90] More recently, Parker and Sanjay Subrahmanyam in a joint essay globalized the discussion—and also dodged the theory's teleological tendencies—by considering the different ways that firearms were received by a number of Asian societies in the early modern period. They found that local responses to the introduction of firearms in India, China, Japan, and mainland Southeast Asia varied widely, running the gamut from enthusiastic acceptance accompanied by innovation to more-or-less outright rejection. 'A bald contrast between dynamic and forward-looking European military systems and static non-European ones', they conclude, 'will not work.'[91] Our study of the early modern Deccan would support that position. Indeed, respecting the question of a unidirectional flow of military technology from Europe overseas, implicit in conventional understandings of the 'military revolution',[92] we have seen that as early as 1513 some technology moved in precisely the opposite direction, from Muslim gunsmiths in Goa formerly employed by the Bijapur state, to Lisbon.

In other respects, too, the early modern Deccani experience with military technology veered sharply from the contemporary European pattern. Consider fort design. Sixteenth-century Europeans and Deccanis responded very differently to the threat of siege cannons capable of battering down stone walls. In Europe, as the advent of such cannons tipped the balance in favour of the attackers, defenders of cities or forts sought to neutralize that advantage by radically reconfiguring the defence of strongholds and urban centres. Using the so-called trace italienne design, walls were lowered and thickened to give incoming projectiles less target to hit, wide ditches were added to keep siege guns at a greater distance, and angled bastions were added to cover blind spots along the walls. The last feature gave the new forts their characteristic arrow-shaped bastions and overall star-shaped pattern.[93] By building slanting, low-profile walls that denied prominent targets to besieging cannons, the trace italienne system adopted an essentially defensive posture, the general idea being not so much to eliminate the besiegers as to minimize the destructive force of their attack, a strategy that led to protracted siege campaigns and wars that could last for many years.[94]

Such a strategy seems also to have inhibited significant change between the sixteenth and nineteenth centuries in how defensive cannons were deployed in Euro-American forts. The practice of mounting guns on wheeled, wooden carriages and placing them behind curtain walls with their muzzles poking through gun ports is seen in strongholds built as late as Fort Ticonderoga (1755) in upstate New York, or Fort Sumter (1860) in coastal South Carolina. Such forts reveal essentially the same mode of deploying defensive cannon as that used by Henry VIII in strongholds built along the English Channel in 1539, some two or three centuries earlier.[95] Such a response hardly suggests 'revolution', but rather something closer to stagnation.

But in the Deccan, as Jean Deloche has noted, architectural response to the advent of siege cannons took a path very different from that in Europe, or anywhere else.[96] It was not as though Deccani engineers were unaware of the Europeans' new style of fortification. As early as 1535 the Portuguese built a fortress in the classic trace italienne style at Bassein, a seaport some 70 kilometres north of modern Mumbai; and in 1612 they built another such stronghold at Aguada, just west of Old Goa on the coast of the Arabian Sea. Deccani engineers simply chose to pioneer a very different strategy. Instead of building low with a view to denying besieging cannons a prominent target, engineers in Bijapur and in the neighbouring sultanates built bastions with even higher profiles than those they had replaced, complete with cavaliers and gun platforms on which huge cannons could be mounted and rotated both vertically and up to a full 360 degrees of range laterally. Deccani officials were very much aware of this engineering breakthrough, for in their foundational inscriptions they repeatedly drew attention to the towering height of these new bastions. For example, the governor of the fort of Galna, one Aflatun Khan, trumpeted that the likes of one of his bastions 'had not been seen by the eyes of the world. It was higher than the heavenly sphere'.[97]

By building such commanding heights and mounting huge swivel guns on them, the idea was not so much to protect the fort from enemy fire as it was to prevent besiegers from approaching close enough to fire effectively at all. Planting big guns on high platforms necessarily increased the range of those guns, permitting a fort's defenders to target an attacking force *before* it could threaten a fort's defensive perimeter.

In short, we find here a strategy of defending a fort by taking the offensive, as opposed to the more purely defensive posture of Europe's trace italienne. Essentially, whereas Europeans radically altered their fort design without significantly changing how they mounted their cannons, Deccanis first built larger and more manoeuvrable cannons and then adapted their fort design to accommodate them.

Indeed, patrons of the Deccani system seem to have grasped the military significance of both the big swivel guns they introduced and the newly designed bastions on which those guns rested. This is seen in the foundation inscriptions, recorded in Persian, found on the new guns and, especially, the remodelled bastions. In the sixteenth-century Deccan, such inscriptions were normally reserved for recording only what patrons regarded as the most important of public acts—for example, the construction of mosques, gateways, irrigation tanks, public wells, tombs of prominent personages, or the promulgation of tax codes. What is more, many of these guns and bastions were given personal names, suggesting a nearly affective relationship between patron and object—for example, the cannons 'Fath-i Lashkar' ('Victory of the Army') and 'Top-i Illahi' ('the Divine Gun') at Bidar, or the bastions 'Fath Burj' ('Victory Bastion') and 'Shah Burj' ('King's Bastion') at Raichur. No pre-sixteenth-century bastions were honoured with foundation inscriptions, much less personal names.

What were the political consequences of these military innovations? Significantly, the period of intensive bastion rebuilding in the northern Deccan correlates with an overall stabilization of frontiers between all the leading sultanates of the Deccan Plateau—Ahmadnagar, Bijapur, Golconda, and Bidar. By conferring a defensive advantage on holders of forts, and by making it increasingly difficult for an attacker to carry out a successful siege, the new advances in military technology seem to have frozen interstate political boundaries where they had existed during the 1560s. The sequence of Figures A1.3–A1.10 document the changing interstate frontiers between 1510 and 1580, while Figure 7.21 summarizes the information presented in those eight maps by indicating the number of times forts of the Deccan are known to have changed hands during those years.

Two inferences emerge from an inspection of these maps—one spatial, one temporal. First, by knowing which of the Deccan's forts changed hands most often during the sixteenth century, we can accurately identify which of the plateau's various frontiers were stable and which were not. As seen in Figure 7.21, it is clear that two frontiers witnessed considerable instability in the sixteenth century: in the south, the Raichur Doab separating Vijayanagara from Bijapur; and, to the north, the long arc running west to east through the forts of Parenda, Sholapur, Naldurg, Kalyana, and Bidar. Along this arc Sholapur, Naldurg, and Kalyana had been seized by neighbouring sovereigns as many as three times each in the sixteenth century. The second point to be inferred from these maps is temporal. We can see from the sequence of Figures A1.3–A1.10 and Table 7.3 that the most intense period of interstate conflict occurred in the single decade of 1549 to 1559, when Parenda, Naldurg, and Kalyana all changed hands twice, and Sholapur once. But from the 1560s on, sieges, if attempted at all, were apparently no longer successful.[98] The Deccan's interstate frontiers had become stable. As we see in Table 7.3, this stability can be dated from the time that rulers had begun building the new, high-profile bastions and gun mounts on their forts.

Moreover, as the northern Deccan's borders stabilized, states exhibited more distinctive

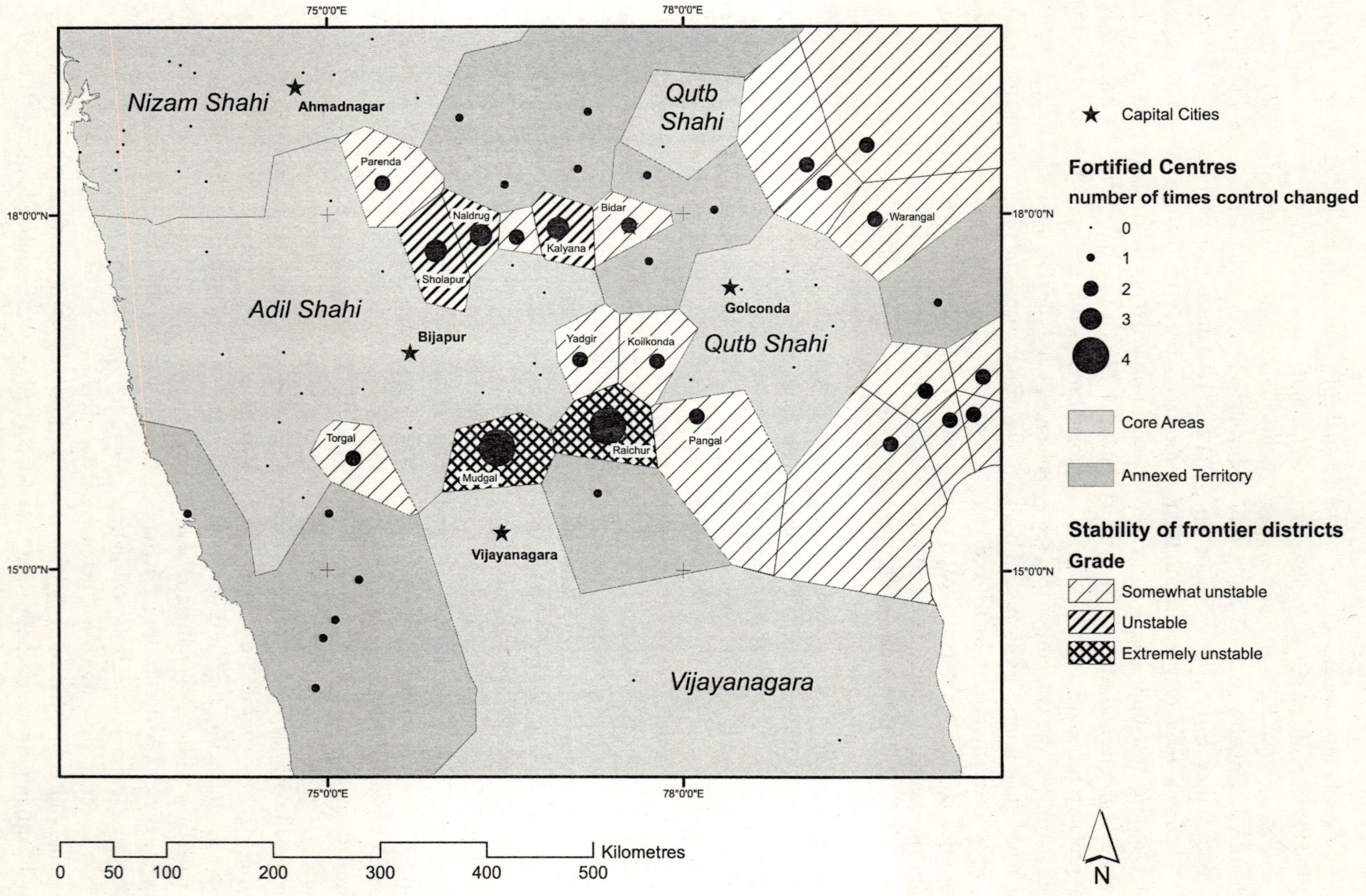


**Figure 7.21** Unstable frontier zones in the Deccan, sixteenth century.

**Table 7.3** Number of documented bastions built in the Deccan by decade, and changing control of forts in the northern contested zone, 1500–1600

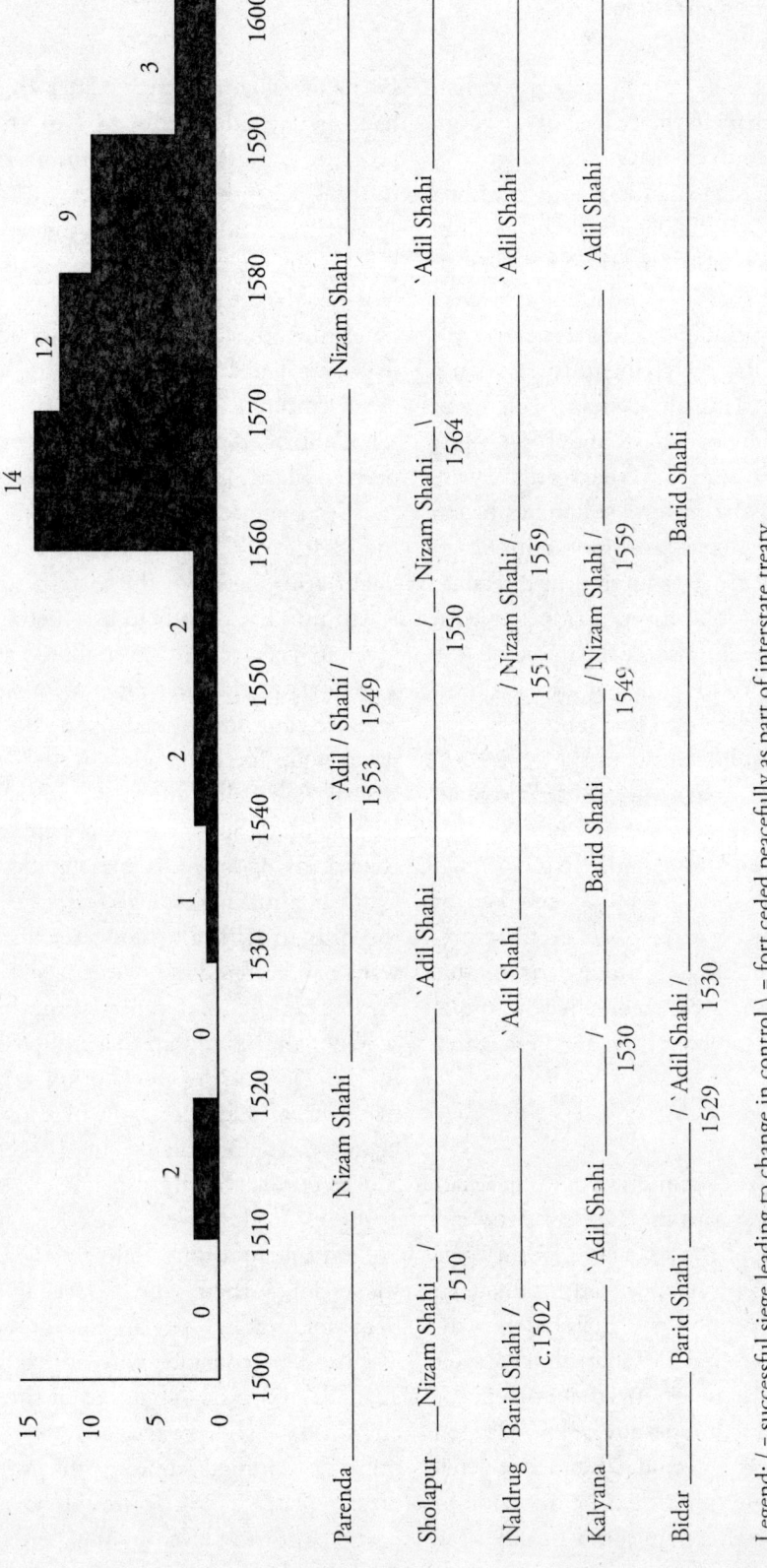

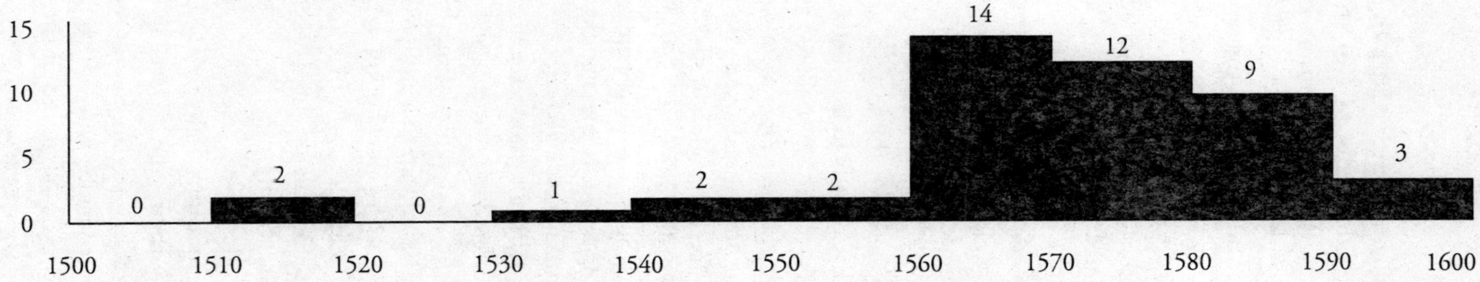


Parenda ____ Nizam Shahi ____ `Adil / Shahi / ____ Nizam Shahi ____
1553 1549

Sholapur __Nizam Shahi__ / ____ `Adil Shahi ____ / __ Nizam Shahi __\ ____ `Adil Shahi ____
1510 1550 1564

Naldrug Barid Shahi / ____ `Adil Shahi ____ / Nizam Shahi / ____ `Adil Shahi ____
c.1502 1551 1559

Kalyana ____ `Adil Shahi ____ / ____ Barid Shahi ____ / Nizam Shahi / ____ `Adil Shahi ____
1530 1549 1559

Bidar ____ Barid Shahi ____ / `Adil Shahi / ____ Barid Shahi ____
1529 1530

Legend: / = successful siege leading to change in control \ = fort ceded peacefully as part of interstate treaty

*Source*: Authors.

identities than at any time since they had emerged as successors to the Bahmani kingdom in the early sixteenth century. We see this in coinage. Although the issuance of coins stamped with its own dynastic name signalled a Muslim state's legal independence, for the first seven or eight decades of their independent existence the Deccan's four principal sultanates chose not to issue such coins, preferring instead to use existing stocks of Bahmani coinage. But then, rather abruptly, between 1578 and 1584—just as the northern Deccan's internal borders were stabilizing—all of the region's sultanates began issuing their own coins as common currency.[99] The sharp, mid-century reduction in interstate violence, and the stabilization of frontiers with which it is associated, also correlates with the surge of cultural production that characterized the Deccan in the late sixteenth and early seventeenth centuries. For it was in the post-1560 period that Ahmadnagar's Murtaza Nizam Shah I (r. 1565–88), Bijapur's Ibrahim `Adil Shah II (r. 1580–1618), and Golconda's Muhammad Quli Qutb Shah (r. 1580–1612) emerged as famously generous patrons of architecture, music, art, and literature, and it was in this period that we witness the emergence of unique styles in art and architecture at these three kingdoms.[100]

* * *

Deccanis had been acquainted with gunpowder and firearms from at least the 1460s. By the end of the first decade of the sixteenth century, the `Adil Shahi rulers of Bijapur had attained an advanced level of cannon and matchlock manufacture at their arsenal in Goa. Shortly after capturing that city in 1510, the Portuguese viceroy, Alfonso de Albuquerque, acknowledged that the firearms he found in Goa's arsenal were superior to anything then being made in Europe. But up to this point, and through the Battle of Raichur ten years later, Bijapur's rulers had merely added firearms to their military repertoire. Nothing like a 'military revolution' in the Deccan had occurred yet.

But by mid-century, firearms were playing an increasingly important role both on battlefields and in sieges. Now they could determine the outcome of pitched battles, as happened in 1565 at the Battle of Talikota. Siege cannons also played a decisive role in seizing forts, especially those that had formerly been under Vijayanagara's authority and had *not* been modernized. Just several years after the Battle of Talikota, for example, a Qutb Shahi army besieged the eastern stronghold of Rajahmundry, then held by chieftains formerly loyal to the recently annihilated Rama Raya. The fort quickly fell after a four-month barrage by cannon fire had opened a breach fifty paces wide in the citadel's walls.[101] In 1579 a similar fate befell another eastern stronghold, Kondavidu, then held by a nephew of Rama Raya. Having failed to take the fort by storm, a Qutb Shahi army dragged its siege cannon up the hills to within a moderate distance of the walls and battered down one face of the citadel, facilitating the fort's capitulation.[102]

Does all this add up to a 'military revolution' in the Deccan? If this notion is understood in terms of a single chain of cause-and-effect changes, as formulated by Parker in 1995, the Deccan certainly did not experience such a thing. If, however, one were to speak of 'military adaptation', following Jeremy Black's suggestion, then the Deccani experience becomes more readily comprehensible.[103] We need to consider why and how Deccanis adapted new technologies to fit their particular circumstances. One factor was the frequent military conflicts among the various states of the plateau, which would have motivated participants to develop more efficient means of prosecuting war. Using the frequency with which forts changed hands as an index of a region's relative stability, the map in Figure 7.21 reveals two principal military frontier zones in the sixteenth-century Deccan: Bijapur's northern border with Ahmadnagar (Kalyana, Naldurg, Sholapur, Parenda, Ganjoti), and Bijapur's southern border with Vijayanagara (Raichur, Mudgal, Torgal). Tellingly, forts along these two frontier zones were among the first to be modernized with renovated bastions and cannon-mounting systems, suggesting a correlation between the intensity of conflict and the likelihood of modernization.

Further, the Deccan's unique topography, with its many hilltops spiking up from an otherwise flat plateau, seems to have pushed technological experimentation and adaptation in a certain direction. For centuries prior to the advent of gunpowder, Deccanis had taken advantage of the plateau's naturally hilly terrain by building forts on its many promontories (Figure 7.22). Being easier to defend than plains forts, hill forts enabled chieftains to control surrounding countrysides and their rural populations by using both the stick of coercion, that is, a fort's garrisoned cavalry, and the carrot of holding (or withholding) grain stored in their granaries. In this way, power itself was conceived in terms of the ability to use prominent heights in order to dominate the people below. When firearms reached the Deccan, it seemed natural to adapt new gunpowder technologies to serve that same conception. So they built upwards, placing larger cannons on higher positions, and mounting them on swivels so as to control more ground below. After all, it was on hill forts—namely Yadgir, followed by Kalyana and Naldurg—that Bijapuri authorities from the 1550s on first experimented with

**Figure 7.22** Shahapur Fort.

mounting large cannons high on bastions and cavaliers.

Although interstate warfare and a hilly topography were found throughout the Deccan Plateau, it is notable that extensive technological experimentation occurred only in the plateau's northern sector among the successor states to the Bahmani kingdom, and not in the southern kingdom of Vijayanagara. Here the Battle of Raichur (1520), and more precisely the opposing responses to that battle's outcome, appears to have been critical in triggering the chain of important technological innovations that occurred in one part of the plateau but not in the other. In Vijayanagara, victory at Raichur without a significant use of firearms had lulled its leaders into a state of complacency, with the result that their military system stagnated until their own catastrophic defeat and political collapse in 1565. In Bijapur, by contrast, crushing defeats both at Raichur Fort and on a nearby battlefield stimulated the kingdom's rulers to overcome their earlier, faulty use of firearms by embarking on a crash programme of experimentation and adaptation.

To the visitor who surveys the many hill forts that dot the Deccan plateau today, two features stand out most prominently: their imposing bastions bearing enormous guns, and their large granary facilities (Figure 7.23).

**Figure 7.23** Devarakonda Fort. Three granaries, seen below, in the middle, and at top.

Each feature symbolizes a very different sort of power. The former projects a stark image of brute force, whereas the latter more subtly signals a commander's ability either to feed or to withhold. Today these vast, empty granaries contain only cavernous, dead space. Yet the sight of such structures lying so close to fearsome engines of destruction reminds one that if the technologies pioneered by Deccani engineers introduced tactical innovations in the ways of war, strategically, they ended up accommodating entrenched conceptions of power and social relations.

## NOTES

1. Rainer Daehnhardt, *The Bewitched Gun: the Introduction of the Firearm in the Far East by the Portuguese* (Lisbon: Texto Editora, 1994), 39.

2. *Epigraphia Indica, Arabic and Persian Supplement* (*EIAPS*) *1967*, 45, pl. XI(b).

3. Parts of this chapter draw on Richard M. Eaton, '"Kiss My Foot," Said the King: Firearms, Diplomacy, and the Battle for Raichur, 1520', *Modern Asian Studies* (John F. Richards Commemorative Volume) 43, no. 1 (2009), 289–313, and idem., 'India's Military Revolution: The View from the Early Sixteenth-Century Deccan', in *Warfare, Religion, and Society in Indian History*, eds Raziuddin Aquil and Kaushik Roy (New Delhi: Manohar, 2012), 85–108.

4. For Vithalanatha's inscription, see P. Sreenivasachar, 'Note on the Raichur Inscription of Vithala-natha, dated Śaka 1216 (c. 1294 A.D.)', *Annual Reports of the Archaeological Department of Hyderabad* (*ARADH*) *1935–36*, Appendix E, 32–5.

5. Ibn Battuta, *The Rehla of Ibn Battuta*, trans. Mahdi Husain (Baroda: Oriental Institute, 1953), 96; Zia al-Din Barani, 'Tārīkh-i Fīrūz Shāhī', in *The History of India as Told by Its Own Historians*, eds and trans H.M. Elliot and John Dowson (Allahabad: Kitab Mahal, 1964), 3:245; `Abd al-Malik `Isami, *Futūḥu's Salāṭīn*, ed. and trans. Agha Mahdi Husain (Bombay: Asia Publishing House, 1967), 3: 902.

6. In 1339 Harihara was ruling independently over widely dispersed regions and had adopted the grandiose title 'Lord of the Oceans of East and West'. In 1342 Ibn Battuta identified him as the sovereign over the Muslim ruler of the port of Honavar in northern Malabar, without mentioning any connection he might have had with the Tughluqs. Vasundhara Filliozat, *l'Épipgraphie de Vijayanagara du début à 1377* (Paris: École Francaise de l'Extrême-Orient, 1973), 2–4. Ibn Battuta, *Rehla*, 118.

7. Vijayanagara launched major invasions in 1362, 1378, 1398, and 1443, and they did achieve a few successes in the disputed region. In 1362, 1436, and 1443 their forces briefly seized Mudgal, located in the Doab some 60 miles west of Raichur city. On each occasion, however, the fort was soon recovered by Bahmani authorities. A.A. Kadiri, 'Bahmani Inscriptions from Raichur District', *EIAPS 1962*, 54–5.

8. In 1407, Firuz Bahmani concluded a treaty with Deva Raya I stipulating that the Vijayanagara king remit an annual payment of 100,000 *hūns* in coin. In both 1417 and 1436 the Bahmanis launched wars with Vijayanagara over non-payment of the tribute. A 1444 Sanskrit inscription at Bidar confirms that as of that date Deva Raya II was still paying his state's annual tribute to the Bahmani treasury. See Haroon Khan Sherwani, *Bahmanis of the Deccan* (New Delhi: Munshiram Manoharlal, 1985), 113, 115, 159, 164–5; Kadiri, 'Bahmani Inscriptions', 54–5.

9. See Chapter 8 for a discussion of this wall and its gateways.

10. Isma`il was nonetheless careful to acknowledge the Bahmanis' legal sovereignty. Two inscriptions in Raichur dated 1515 record the names of both Sultan Mahmud Bahmani and Isma`il `Adil Khan, Bijapur's effective sultan. It was not until 1538, after the last nominal Bahmani sovereign had sailed off on a pilgrimage to Mecca from which he never returned, that the fourth of Bijapur's rulers, Ibrahim, styled himself 'sultan'. *Epigraphia Indo-Moslemica* (*EIM*) *1939–40*, 14–16, pl. V(b), and 16, pl. VI(a).

11. Iqtidar Alam Khan, *Gunpowder and Firearms: Warfare in Medieval India* (Delhi: Oxford University Press, 2004), 42–4.

12. Jos Gommans, *Mughal Warfare: Indian Frontiers and High Roads to Empire, 1500–1700* (New York: Routledge, 2002), 146 and footnote 52.

13. As these gun ports are too large for muskets, and too close to the floor level of the battlement to facilitate shooting arrows, they could only have been built to accommodate cannons. At Raichur the square

gun ports were positioned at the pavement of the battlement, while loopholes were placed at a higher elevation that would enable firing by either bows or matchlock firearms.

14. The period of the construction of Kalyana's walls is mentioned in Abd al-Qadir Badayuni, *Muntakhab al-tawārīkh* (Calcutta, 1867), 3:452, cited in Sherwani, *Bahmanis of the Deccan*, 189.

15. The dating of Raichur's walls is inferred from the dates of the construction of the two gates that pierced them, the Kamani gate and the Mecca gate, built in 1468–69 and 1469–70 respectively. The areas on the western wall where the square gun ports are found appear to be completely continuous with the rest of the masonry and with the gate itself, which is dated 1469–70. Kadiri, 'Bahmani Inscriptions from Raichur District', 58–60.

16. Firishta writes that Sultan Muhammad III (r. 1463–82), while campaigning in the eastern Deccan, ordered Mahmud Gawan to repair an old fort originally built during the Tughluq occupation, and that while doing so, Gawan equipped the fort with cannons (*top*) and light cannons (*ḍarbuzan*). Firishta, *Tārīkh-i Firishta* (text), 1:355. Yazdani reasons that if the sultan were willing to equip even minor forts with cannons, he would surely have done the same at his capital. See G. Yazdani, *Bidar, Its History and Monuments* (London: Oxford University Press, 1947), 29.

17. Mahmud Gawan, *Riyādh al-inshā'* (Hyderabad: Government Press, 1948), 72. 'ra`d-i chakāchak ṣā`iqa tā'thīr chunān bārān gardānīd.' Iqtidar Alam Khan has argued that the terms *ra`d* or *kamān-i ra`d* were the generic terms used in contemporary Persian texts for the primitive firearms in vogue in India, Central Asia, and Iran during the fifteenth century. Iqtidar Alam Khan, *Gunpowder and Firearms*, 10.

18. Firishta, *Tārīkh-i Firishta* (Lucknow: Nawal Kishor, 1864–65), 1:352.

19. 'Bi sākhtan-i sarkūb va naqb ki tā ān zamān dar Dakan shā'i` nabūd.' Ibid., 1:352. Cf. John Briggs, trans., *History of the Rise of the Mahomedan Power in India* (1829; repr. Calcutta: Editions Indian, 1966), 2:303.

20. Gaspar Correia, *Lendas da India* (Lisbon: Typ. da Academia Real das Sciencias, 1860), 1:289–90. Cited in Sanjay Subrahmanyam, *The Political Economy of Commerce: Southern India, 1500–1650* (Cambridge: Cambridge University Press, 1990), 124.

21. John Winter Jones, trans., *The Travels of Ludovico di Varthema* (1863; repr. New York: Burt Franklin, n.d.), 114.

22. Afonso de Albuquerque, *The Commentaries of the Great Afonso Dalbuquerque, Second Viceroy of India*, trans., Walter de Gray Birch (4 vols, 1875–84; repr. New York: B. Franklin, 1970), 2:89.

23. Ibid., 3:16.

24. An inscribed powder chamber from a wrought-iron cannon made in the reign of Sultan Qayit Bay (r. 1468–96) is preserved in the Military Museum in Istanbul, inventory no. 102. We also know that the Ottoman sultan Bayazid II (r. 1481–1512) lent the Mamluks artillery and copper for casting cannons for the latter's Indian Ocean fleet. Giancarlo Casale, *The Ottoman Age of Exploration* (Oxford: Oxford University Press, 2010), 32n79.

25. In the published collection of Gawan's correspondence, letter 134 is addressed to the Mamluk sultan, and letters 5, 56, 143, and 144 are addressed to Ottoman sultans. Thanks to Gawan's exertions, the Bahmanis were the only Indian state to exchange ambassadors with the Ottoman court. In 1481, a Bahmani deputation bearing elephants, giraffes, spices, ornaments, and other precious gifts was sent to congratulate Bayazid (r. 1481–1512) on his accession to the Ottoman throne. See Gawan, *Riyāḍ.* See also Shai Har-El, *Struggle for Domination in the Middle East: The Ottoman-Mamluk War, 1485–91* (Leiden: Brill, 1995), 113, 130.

26. Sherwani, *Bahmanis*, 218–19.

27. See Halil Inalcik, 'Bursa and the Commerce of the Levant', *Journal of the Economic and Social History of the Orient* 3, no. 2 (1960), 141.

28. We thank Mark Wyers for measuring the two Mamluk guns preserved in Istanbul's Military Museum. The following table compares the dimensions of these two guns with six wrought-iron tube guns discovered at Deccani forts. The notation for the pattern of hoops follows the system proposed by Robert D. Smith, according to which '1' refers to the band, '2' refers to the hoop over the band, and '3' refers to a hoop of greater diameter than a '2' hoop. See R.D. Smith, 'Towards a New Typology for Wrought Iron Ordnance', *International Journal of Nautical Archaeology and Underwater Exploration* 17, no. 1 (1988), 11.

| *Gun* | *Length of barrel in cm* | *Bore in cm* | *Pattern of hoops* |
|---|---|---|---|
| Mamluk 1 (Istanbul) | 172.5 | 18 | 9 hoops in 12 pattern |
| Mamluk 2 (Istanbul) | 152.5 | 17.5 | 8 hoops in 12 pattern |
| Bidar 3 | 426 | 17 | 6 sets in 1232 pattern |
| Medak 2 | 328 | 15 | 3 sets in 12 pattern |
| Yadgir 1 | ? [gun mostly buried] | ? | 3 sets (visible) in 12 pattern |
| Medak 1 | 227 | 16 | 2 sets of lug hoops in 123 pattern |
| Devarakonda 1 | 210 | 23.5 | 3 sets of lug hoops in 123 pattern |
| Bidar 9 | 265 | 35 | no hoops |

29. Correia, *Lendas da India*, 2:60. Cited and translated in Daehnhardt, *Bewitched Gun*, 37.

30. This conflict had been precipitated by Mamluk and Ottoman concerns over the Portuguese disruption of trade in the region. See Casale, *Ottoman Age*, 25–9; Palmira Brummett, *Ottoman Seapower and Levantine Diplomacy in the Age of Discovery* (Albany: SUNY Press, 1994), 111–15; M. Longworth Dames, 'The Portuguese and Turks in the Indian Ocean in the Sixteenth Century', *Journal of the Royal Asiatic Society* 53, no. 1 (1921), 1–11; E. Denison Ross, 'The Portuguese in India and Arabia between 1507 and 1517', *Journal of the Royal Asiatic Society* 53, no. 1 (1921), 547.

31. As Casale notes, most Portuguese sources of this period 'use the notoriously vague terms "Turk" and "Rumi" with reference to both Ottomans and Mamluks'. Casale, *Ottoman Age*, 213n77.

32. Mansel L. Dames, trans., *The Book of Duarte Barbosa* (1918; repr. Nendeln/Liechtenstein: Kraus Reprint, 1967), 1:175–7.

33. For the state of Ottoman gun technology in the sixteenth century, see Gabor Agoston, *Guns for the Sultan: Military Power and the Weapons Industry in the Ottoman Empire* (Cambridge: Cambridge University Press, 2005). For a discussion of the diffusion of Ottoman firearms technology in sixteenth-century Asia, see Salih Ozbaran, 'The Ottomans' Role in the Diffusion of Fire-arms and Military Technology in Asia and Africa in the Sixteenth Century', in his *The Ottoman Response to European Expansion* (Istanbul: Isis Press, 1994), 61–6.

34. A Florentine merchant who participated in the Portuguese conquest of Goa mentioned that the defenders of its citadel 'were almost all Turks, and renegade Christians of every sort; among whom were Venetians and Genoese in the largest numbers'. Subrahmanyam, *Political Economy of Commerce*, 255.

35. Albuquerque, Affonso de, *Cartasde Affonso de Albuquerque*, eds Raymundo Antonia de Bulhão Pato and Henrique Lopes de Mendonca (Lisbon: Typ. da Academia real das sciencias de Lisboa, 1884), 1:28. Cited in Daehnhardt, *Bewitched Gun*, 38.

36. Albuquerque, *Cartas*, 1:174; cited in Daehnhardt, *Bewitched Gun*, 39.

37. Writes Daehnhardt, 'The knowledge of Luso-German gunmaking, coming from Lisbon, was fused with the Goan and Arab knowledge which already existed in Goa, creating a completely new particular form, the Indo-Portuguese gunmaking [tradition].' Daehnhardt, *Bewitched Gun*, 41.

38. Ibid., 39–41. 'The Portuguese', writes Daehnhardt, 'received arquebuses, muskets and guns from Bohemia with this matchlock ignition system and used them in Portugal and in overseas explorations. Having arrived in Goa, these arms suffered technical evolution for more than thirty years (a human generation), finally finding their way, again through Portuguese hands, to the Far East and becoming the "fathers" of Japanese, Javanese and Cingalese [*sic*] arms.' Ibid., 53–4.

39. '... easy se tornaram todolos oficiaees d artelharia, de bombardas e espimgardas, as quaees se fazem de ferro em goa milhores que has d alemanha.' Albuquerque, *Cartas* 1:203; cited in Daehnhardt, *Bewitched Gun*, 38–9.

40. Ibid., 39.

41. 'Chronicle of Fernão Nuniz', in *A Forgotten Empire, Vijayanagara: a Contribution to the History of India*, trans., Robert Sewell (1900; repr. New Delhi: Publications Division, 1962), 316.

42. There is evidence that Nunes, who resided in metropolitan Vijayanagara for three years, had been living in coastal India since 1512. Joan-Pau Rubiés writes that the Portuguese chronicler can 'perhaps be identified with the Fernão Nunes who in 1512 was

*escrivão de feitor* of Calicut, and who in 1526 appears as *escrivão de fazenda* in Cochin'. Joan-Pau Rubiés, *Travel and Ethnology in the Renaissance: South India through European Eyes, 1250–1625* (Cambridge: Cambridge University Press, 2000), 204. In this case, Nunes, who compiled his chronicle around 1531, would have heard first-hand reports of the battle shortly after its conclusion. It is also possible that he recorded remembered traditions some eight years later, most likely from participants. But it is most probable that he witnessed the battle himself. Robert Sewell, who translated Nunes's account and also wrote the first modern history of Vijayanagara, notes that throughout Nunes's account of the battle, 'there is much that impels the belief that either himself or his informant was present at the Hindu camp while these events were taking place. The narrative of the campaign, in complete contrast to that of the remainder of the history, reads like the account of an eye-witness; especially in the passages describing the fortress of Raichur and the camp—where the supplies were so great that "you could find everything that you wanted," where "you saw" the goldsmiths and artisans at work as if in a city, where "you will find" all kinds of precious stones offered for sale...."' Sewell, *Forgotten Empire*, 148.

43. 'Chronicle of Fernão Nuniz', 311–13; David Lopes, *Chronica dos Reis de Bisnaga: Manuscripto Inedito do Seculo XVI* (Lisbon: Impr. Nac., 1897), 28. We may compare the numbers of combatants mentioned by Nunes with those mentioned by Muhammad Qasim Firishta, the Iran-born historian of the Deccan who wrote in Bijapur some ninety years after the battle. Firishta writes that Krishna Raya had 'at least 50,000 cavalry, besides a vast host of foot'. Nunes, by contrast, carefully broke down the forces in the service of Vijayanagara's major nobles, their combined total being 573,000 infantry, 27,600 cavalry, and 725 elephants. See Briggs, trans., *History of the Rise*, 3:29. 'Chronicle of Fernão Nuniz', 311–12.

44. Ibid., 315.

45. Ibid., 323–4.

46. Although European mercenaries and renegades had begun appearing in the service of Indian coastal powers as early as 1502, this was the first major conflict in the Indian interior in which Europeans are known to have participated. But as Maria Augusta Lima Cruz notes, in European accounts only those who served armies under Muslim control were understood as renegades. Thus Cristovão de Figueiredo, otherwise a horse-merchant, is depicted by Nunes not as a renegade but as a courageous *fidalgo* who boasted to Krishna Raya that 'the whole business of the Portuguese was war' and that the greatest favour the king could grant would be to allow him to accompany the Vijayanagara army to Raichur. A contingent of fifty other Portuguese mercenaries fought and died for Isma`il `Adil Khan at the battle by the Krishna River. Although Nunes called these men renegades (*arrenegados*), he could not refrain from admiring their 'great deeds' in killing 'so many men that they left a broad road behind them which no one dared enter'. Maria Augusta Lima Cruz, 'Exiles and Renegades in Early Sixteenth Century Portuguese India', *Indian Economic and Social History Review* 23, no. 3 (1986), 258, 260. Sewell, trans., *Forgotten Empire*, 325, 326. Sewell mistakenly gives the number of Portuguese mercenaries fighting for Bijapur as 500, instead of 50. Cf. Lopes, *Chronica*, 39.

47. 'Chronicle of Fernão Nuniz', 326–7.

48. Ibid., 328–30. Nunes writes that the captain leaned his body out in front of a merlon (*deitamdo o corpo amte húas ameyas*), even though the parapet of Raichur's wall was continuous, and not divided into merlons and embrasures. Since Nunes was writing some ten years after the battle, and this is a very unusual disposition for a parapet, he is probably misremembering this detail of the fortifications at the site. We are grateful to Javier Castro-Ibaseta for his help in interpreting this passage in the original Portuguese text.

49. 'quoatro centos tiros grossos d artelharia, afora meuda, forão o numero das carretas d ellas novecentas....' Cannons and gun-carriages are often enumerated separately in sixteenth-century sources, and the number of carriages is generally at least double that of the cannons, so as to provide replacements when existing carriages were damaged. Lopes, *Chronica*, 39; 'Chronicle of Fernão Nuniz', 326.

50. Writes Nunes, 'The King's people came without fear to the wall, where already it was damaged in many places, because the city had its cannons so high up that these could do no injury to the men who were at the foot of the wall.' 'Chronicle of Fernão Nuniz', 327.

51. Concludes Brubaker, 'Vijayanagara's defenses were [n]ever modified in any way to either take advantage of, or compensate for, respectively, the new possibilities or new threats posed by gunpowder weaponry.' Or again: 'With respect to measures that could have been taken to strengthen the defenses in

the face of assaults conducted using artillery, evidence is wholly lacking. Thus, for example, later walls were not constructed within wide ditches in order to make these less vulnerable to artillery fire while at the same time retaining their value as barriers to the advance of infantry.... Similarly, although each of Vijayanagara's defensive circuits itself varies in thickness, the later defences are not any thicker than the earlier walls, nor is there evidence to suggest that the thickness of any was augmented in order to increase its ability to withstand assault by artillery. Finally, although the walls everywhere appear to have been similar in height to the bastions, and although the parapet walkways were clearly wide enough along some stretches to facilitate the movement of artillery pieces, other stretches are clearly narrow enough that this task could likely have been performed only with some difficulty.' See Robert Brubaker, 'Cornerstones of Control: the Infrastructure of Imperial Security at Vijayanagara, South India', PhD dissertation, Department of Anthropology, University of Michigan, 2004, 452, 453.

52. Whereas most of the technological initiative appears to have been taken by engineers serving the `Adil Shah sultans of Bijapur, the neighbouring kingdoms of Ahmadnagar and Bidar were also active in assimilating the new military innovations, together with their architectural implications. By contrast Golconda, the easternmost sultanate of the sixteenth-century Deccan, lagged behind its neighbours to the west in modernizing its military profile, while Vijayanagara assimilated none of these innovations.

53. We know from Afonso de Albuquerque's 1513 correspondence with the king of Portugal that Bijapur's gun foundry in Goa was then manufacturing cannons made of iron (see note 39). There is no evidence that cast bronze cannons appeared in the Deccan before 1543, the date that a Turkish smith made such a gun now located on the northeastern bastion of the fort of Ausa. Throughout the sixteenth century, the number of forged-iron cannons continued to dominate over cast bronze, owing mainly to the much greater expense of copper, the chief alloy used in cast bronze ordnance.

54. See Robert D. Smith, 'The Technology of Wrought-Iron Artillery', *Royal Armouries Yearbook* 5 (2000), 68–79; idem., 'Towards a New Typology for Wrought Iron Ordnance', *The International Journal of Nautical Archaeology and Underwater Exploration* 17, no. 1 (1988), 5–16. For the history of wrought-iron cannons made in the eastern Deccan, see S. Jai Kishan, 'Forge-welded Cannons in the Forts of Karimnagar District in Andhra Pradesh', *Indian Journal of History of Science* 40, no. 4 (2005), 487–501.

55. Carriages have not been preserved in any of the Deccani examples we have documented, but in all likelihood they would have been similar in general design to those used contemporaneously in the Middle East and Europe. These carriages are best represented by a number of well-preserved specimens recovered from the wreck of the *Mary Rose*, an English warship that sank in Portsmouth harbour in 1545. See Peter Marsden, *Sealed by Time: The Loss and Recovery of the Mary Rose* (Portsmouth: The Mary Rose Trust, 2003), figure 12.21. In these examples, the hollowed-out channel that held the barrel extended some distance behind it so as to accommodate the powder chamber. Once the chamber was loaded and fitted in place, it was driven firmly against the barrel by means of a wooden wedge, hammered into the gap between the chamber's end and the rear wall of the channel. Most of the *Mary Rose* carriages were provided with a single pair of wooden wheels, which would have permitted side-to-side adjustment by turning the back of the carriage. The wheels additionally served the purpose of elevating the front of the gun, thus permitting a higher angle of fire. When a more level angle of fire was required, a wooden elevating peg at the rear of the carriage provided a means of partially lowering the gun's muzzle. All in all, however, the vertical angle of fire could have been adjusted only to a limited degree, and not at all in the downward direction. Moreover, the thin wooden elevating peg would have been subjected to shearing stress from the recoil every time the gun was fired.

56. The three earliest datable cast bronze guns—Ausa 1 (950/1543), Bijapur's 'Malik-i Maidan' (956/1549), and Udgir 1 (undated)—were all made by a single gunfounder. This was a certain Muhammad bin Husain Rumi, whose *nisbah* indicates that he had migrated from Ottoman Turkey, where bronze gunfounding had already achieved a high level of perfection by the late fifteenth century. All three guns were made for the Nizam Shahi sultan. Of the total of thirteen cannons found at the fort of Parenda, a Nizam Shahi stronghold, nearly all were made of cast bronze.

57. One of the bronze guns at their fort at Parenda had been manufactured in 1627 by Everhard Splinter at Enkhuizen in Holland for the Dutch East India Company. Two other guns by this founder are in

museums in London (1629) and Stockholm (1640). See A.N. Kennard, *Gunfounding and Gunfounders: A Directory of Cannon Founders from Earliest Times to 1850* (London: Arms and Armour Press, 1986), 141. A third (1638) was salvaged from a shipwreck in the Wadden Sea. We identified another imported gun, located on the northwestern bastion of the Nizam Shahi fort at Ausa, that was originally made for King Philip III of Spain (1598–1621). When this gun was made, Portugal was part of the Spanish Hapsburg empire and Philip III was using the title 'King of the East and West Indies' (Rey de las Indias Orientales y Occidentales). Typologically, this gun is identical to the bronze 50-pounder curtow (weight 5,429 lb) made by master Remigy de Halut, Fondeur Royale at the Malines Royal Gunfoundry near Antwerp, dated 1556 and recovered from the wreck of *La Trinidad Valencera.* See Colin Martin, *Full Fathom Five: Wrecks of the Spanish Armada* (New York: Viking, 1975), pl. IIb (rear), IIIa, IIIb, and IVa; figure 15, top for line drawing. Whether the Nizam Shahis purchased these guns or seized them as battle spoils is unknown.

58. Bidar's tradition of high-quality metal working in cannon production is consonant with that city's renown for the production of fine inlaid metal ware for domestic use, the so-called Bidri ware, which also emerged in the Barid Shahi period. See Susan Stronge, *Bidri Ware: Inlaid Metalwork from India* (London: Victoria and Albert Museum, 1985).

59. The cannons we found on Qutb Shahi forts—all of them wrought-iron and some of them breech-loaders—were the crudest of the lot. The only record of a remodelled bastion constructed in the Qutb Shahi domain appears as late as 1602, at Medak. Moreover, the gun on this bastion is a breech-loading tube gun—a type that had been common in Europe in the mid-fifteenth century. At the Qutb Shahi capital itself, the Mughals replaced many of Golconda's wrought-iron cannons with the same cast bronze guns they had used to reduce the fort in 1687. Jean Deloche, 'Gunpowder Artillery and Military Architecture in South India (15–18th Century)', *Indian Journal of History of Science* 40, no. 4 (2005), 584.

60. The date's third digit on the gun is indistinct, but it is most likely a '0', which would yield the manufacture date as AH 950, or 1543–44.

61. This can be inferred both from excavated shipwrecks of this period and from a 1525 gun list from Portuguese India. See Robert Douglas Smith, 'Bronze Breech-loading Swivel Guns: A Preliminary Survey', in *A Farewell to Arms, Studies on the History of Arms and Armour*, eds Gert Groenendijk, Piet de Gryse, Dirk Staat, and Heleen Bronder (Delft: Legermuseum, 2004), 167–9; Joe J. Simmons III, 'Wrought-iron Ordnance: Revealing Discoveries from the New World', *The International Journal of Nautical Archaeology and Underwater Exploration* 17, no. 1 (1988), 25–34; Donald H. Keith, 'Shipwrecks of the Explorers', chapter 3 of *Ships and Shipwrecks of the Americas*, ed. George F. Bass (New York: Thames and Hudson, 1996), 45–68; Richard Barker, 'A Gun-List from Portuguese India, 1525', *Journal of the Ordnance Society* 8 (1996), 53–6.

62. Such guns can be found in various forts in the western Deccan, such as at Ausa, Naldurg, and Parenda.

63. Interestingly, Portuguese *berços* were also introduced to China in the early sixteenth century, where they were also copied and referred to as 'Frankish' (*fo-lang-chi* in Chinese). See Joseph Needham, Ho Ping-Yü, Lu Gwei-Djen, and Wang Ling, *Science and Civilisation in China*, Vol.5: *Chemistry and Chemical Technology*, Part 7: *Military Technology, the Gunpowder Epic* (Cambridge: Cambridge University Press, 1986), 367–76.

64. An inscription on the cannon's muzzle records that it was made 'under the superintendence of Muhammad Aqa, 965 [AD 1557]' [*dar kārkard-i Muḥammad Āqā, tis`a mi'a sittīn khams*]. *EIM 1929–30*, 3, pl. II(a).

65. We owe this insight to our colleague John Friedrich, who accompanied us on our visit to Yadgir.

66. At least one other such mounting device is reported from the nearby fort of Shahapur. Personal communication with Klaus Rotzer, 25 October 2008.

67. Because many of Kalyana's remodelled bastions are dated, we are in an especially good position to reconstruct the sequence of that fort's modernization. See Table 7.2.

68. There is an apparent limitation to the design of the new-style bastion-cavalier, namely, that the provision of only three or four embrasures along the outer edge of the cavalier would significantly limit the area of coverage of its gun, even while the alternating merlons provided an element of protection for the gun crew. We suspect that this problem may have been addressed by the planners of these features through carefully controlled placement and orientation of the cavaliers on adjacent bastions. If the embrasures of adjacent

cavaliers provided different, complementary areas of coverage, then each bastion-cavalier would have become an integral part of the fort's larger defensive system.

69. Jean Deloche, *Studies on Fortification in India* (Pondicherry: École Française d'Extrême-Orient, 2007), 107. An inscription on the Jami` mosque in Naldurg states that the mosque and the fort were both built in 1560. This date could refer either to the date that the entire fort, including the cavalier, was completed, or the date that its construction was begun. *EIM 1917–18*, 2, pl. I(b).

70. Deloche, *Studies*, 109.

71. Jean Deloche, *Four Forts of the Deccan* (Pondicherry: École Française d'Extrême-Orient, 2009), 60. Apart from Naldurg and Mudgal, similar such structures can be found at Elgandal, Malkhed, and Raichur.

72. Sewell, trans., *Forgotten Empire*, 335. For a more detailed discussion see Chapter 8.

73. Briggs, trans., *History of the Rise*, 3:73, 74.

74. There has been much scholarly dispute over the appropriate name for the battle. The doyen of Deccan history, H.K. Sherwani insisted on calling it the Battle of Banahatti on the reasonable grounds that the battle was actually fought near the village of that name. Nilkanta Sastri, N. Venkataramanayya, and R. Subrahmanyam preferred to call it the Battle of Rakkasi-Tangadi on the grounds that Rama Raya's army had been encamped between two villages of those names. However, it has been nearly universally recognized as the Battle of Talikota, after the place where the allies combined forces before crossing the Krishna River to confront Rama Raya. See H.K. Sherwani and P.M. Joshi, eds, *History of Medieval Deccan*, 1295–1724 (Hyderabad: Government of Andhra Pradesh, 1973), 1:128 and note 179.

75. In 1561, Rama Raya had driven Husain from his capital at Ahmadnagar and forced the desperate sultan to sue for peace. Rama Raya agreed to this only if the sultan would meet three humiliating conditions: that he cede Kalyana to Bijapur, then allied with Vijayanagara, that he execute one of his finest generals for having interfered with the siege of Ahmadnagar, and that he personally come to Rama Raya's headquarters and eat *pan* (betel leaf) from his hand. Briggs, trans., *History of the Rise*, 3:147.

76. Rafi` al-Din Shirazi, *Tazkirāt al-mulūk* (composed 1609–12), 75–6. Unpublished critical edition by Abu Nasr Khalidi, revised by Carl Ernst. We thank Professor Ernst for kindly sharing this with us.

77. Ibid., 76. In 1829, John Briggs noted that 'the real head, annually covered with oil and red pigment, has been exhibited to the pious Mahomedans of Ahmudnuggur, on the anniversary of the battle, for the last two hundred and fifty-four years, by the descendants of the executioner, in whose hands it has remained till the present period'. Briggs, trans., *History of the Rise*, 3:79, note.

78. Briggs, trans., *History of the Rise*, 3:79, note.

79. Ibid., 3:150. Cf. Firishta, *Tārīkh*, 2:128; 'haftād hazār savār va nuh lak piyāda-yi jangī ki akthar topchī va tīr-andāz būdand.'

80. Briggs, trans., *History of the Rise*, 3:78; Firishta, *Tārīkh*, 2:40. 'piyādagān-i Bījānagar pīsh-i ṣaf-hāīstāda … qarīb panjāh hazār bān va tufang va top va ḍarbuzan har daf`a sar mīdādand.'

81. Briggs, trans., *History of the Rise*, 3:78.

82. Ibid., 3:151; Firishta, *Tārīkh*, 2:128.

83. Briggs, trans., *History of the Rise*, 3:151–2. According to Rafi` al-Din Shirazi, small coins were discharged from two huge cannons of Husain Nizam Shah. One of these was the famous 'Malik-i Maidan', an immense bronze cannon that Ustad Muhammad bin Husain Rumi had made for the Nizam Shahi sultan in 1549, and which now stands in Bijapur. The other one was likely another massive cast bronze cannon, known as 'Karak Bijli', which was also cast by Rumi. Unfortunately, it sank in the Krishna River while being brought back north after the battle. Shirazi, *Tazkirāt al-mulūk*, 75. See also R. Balasubramaniam, *The Saga of Indian Cannons* (New Delhi: Aryan Books International, 2008), 24–5.

84. Briggs, trans., *History of the Rise*, 3:79.

85. Ibid., 3:152. 'Chuleby Roomy Khan had provided bags of copper money to load [the cannon] with, should the enemy close; and these proved so destructive, that upwards of five thousand Hindoos were left dead close to the muzzles of the guns, before they retreated. The repulse of this charge seems to have decided the fate of the day….'

86. See Brubaker, 'Cornerstones of Control', 106, 451–53. On the failure of Vijayanagara and other South Indian forts to adopt the sort of military modernization that took place in the northern Deccan, see Jean Deloche, 'Survival of the Hindu System of Fortification in South India (15th—18th Century)', in his *Studies on Fortification in India*, 153–86. South Indian capitals,

such as Penukonda, Chandragiri, Tiruchchirappalli, Tanjavur, Madurai, and Palaiyamkottai adhered to the pre-gunpowder system of defences until the late eighteenth century. A likely reason for this conservative tradition was that, notwithstanding Vijayanagara's destruction in 1565, the *nayaka*s (petty rulers) of the south regarded themselves as successors to that kingdom and consequently continued to venerate its metropolitan capital in the condition it had been in prior to 1565. See Phillip B. Wagoner, *Tidings of the King: A Translation and Ethnohistorical Analysis of the* Rayavacakamu (Honolulu: University of Hawaii Press, 1993).

87. A good entrée into the voluminous literature on the Military Revolution debate is Clifford J. Rogers, ed., *The Military Revolution Debate: Readings on the Military Transformation of Early Modern Europe* (Boulder: Westview, 1995). See also David Eltis, *The Military Revolution in Sixteenth-Century Europe* (London: Tauris Academic Studies, 1995); Andrew Ayton and J.L. Price, *The Medieval Military Revolution: State, Society and Military Change in Medieval and Early Modern Europe* (London: Tauris Academic Studies, 1995); Bert S. Hall, *Weapons and Warfare in Renaissance Europe: Gunpowder, Technology, and Tactics* (Baltimore: Johns Hopkins University Press, 1997), 201–35; Jeremy Black, *War and the World: Military Power and the Fate of Continents, 1450–2000* (New Haven: Yale University Press, 1998); Kelly DeVries and Robert D. Smith, *Medieval Weapons: An Illustrated History of Their Impact* (Santa Barbara: ABC-CLIO, 2007); Frank Tallett and D.J.B. Trim, eds, *European Warfare, 1350–1750* (Cambridge: Cambridge University Press, 2010).

88. Roberts presented his thesis as an inaugural lecture before The Queen's University of Belfast in 1955; it was subsequently published as 'The Military Revolution, 1560–1660', in Michael Roberts, *Essays in Swedish History* (Minneapolis: University of Minnesota Press, 1967), 195–25. Geoffrey Parker's principle elaboration of the theory is found in his *The Military Revolution: Military Innovation and the Rise of the West* (Cambridge: Cambridge University Press, 1988).

89. Geoffrey Parker, 'In Defense of the Military Revolution', in *Military Revolution Debate*, ed. Rogers, 338.

90. Such arguments are most trenchantly advanced by Jeremy Black. See his *Beyond the Military Revolution: War in the Seventeenth-Century World* (New York: Palgrave Macmillan, 2011).

91. Geoffrey Parker and Sanjay Subrahmanyam, 'Arms and the Asian: Revisiting European Firearms and Their Place in Early Modern Asia', *Revista de Cultura* (Macau), 26: (2008), 32. Indeed, their analysis suggests that in Japan during the 1560s and 1570s two features of Europe's 'military revolution'—the construction of geometrically designed forts to provide flanking fire, and the rotational firing of musket volleys—evolved independently of European influence, and that the latter actually appeared in Japan twenty years *before* it did in Europe. Parker and Subrahmanyam, 'Arms and the Asian', 30–2.

92. This view is most explicit in David B. Ralston, *Importing the European Army: The Introduction of European Military Techniques and Institutions into the Extra-European World, 1600–1914* (Chicago: University of Chicago Press, 1990).

93. Parker, *Military Revolution*, 6–24. See also Simon Pepper and Nicholas Adams, *Firearms & Fortifications: Military Architecture and Siege Warfare in Sixteenth-Century Siena* (Chicago: University of Chicago Press, 1986); Christopher Duffy, *Siege Warfare: The Fortress in the Early Modern World, 1494–1660* (London: Routledge & Kegan Paul, 1979); idem., *Fire & Stone: the Science of Fortress Warfare, 1660–1860* (London: Greenhill Books, 1996).

94. Parker, *Military Revolution*, 43.

95. For Henry VIII's castle, see the manuscript illustration reproduced in Parker, *Military Revolution*, 27.

96. See Deloche, 'Gunpowder Artillery', 373–7; idem., *Studies on Fortification in India*, 141–2.

97. *EIAPS 1967*, 45, pl. XI(b).

98. The only fort to have changed hands after 1559 was Sholapur, but that was not seized militarily, but transferred as a dowry gift from Husain Nizam Shah to `Ali `Adil Shah when `Ali married Husain's daughter in the early 1560s.

99. The first was `Ali `Adil Shah I (r. 1558–89), who issued silver 'larin' coins from the port of Dabul in 1578. He also issued two varieties of copper coins, one with *ṭughrā* characters on both sides and the other with ordinary, but crude lettering. In Ahmadnagar, the first coins minted by the Nizam Shahi sultans appeared in 1581. Although the Qutb Shahi sultans of Golconda minted a few coins rather early, these

appear to have been curiosities and did not circulate as coinage. It was not until the reign of Muhammad Quli Qutb Shah (r. 1580–1611), whose first coins appeared in 1580 or 1581, that their coins achieved widespread circulation as currency. Similarly, the Barid Shahi sultans of Bidar did not start issuing their own coinage until the reign of Ibrahim Barid Shah (1580–87). See Dilip Rajgor, *Standard Catalogue of Sultanate Coins of India* (Bombay: Amrapali Publications, 1990), 625; Stan Goron and J.P. Goenka, *The Coins of the Indian Sultanates* (New Delhi Munshiram Manoharlal, 2001), 315, 321, 326, 336. One might argue that such an affirmation of a kingdom's independent identity arose in defensive reaction to growing Mughal pressures on Deccan states. But Mughal expansion in the Deccan did not begin until the 1590s, or at the earliest, the late 1580s with the succession struggle that followed the death of Ahmadnagar's Sultan Murtaza Nizam Shah. See Muzaffar Alam and Sanjay Subrahmanyam, 'The Deccan Frontier and Mughal Expansion, ca. 1600: Contemporary Perspectives', *Journal of the Economic and Social History of the Orient* 47, no. 3 (2004), 357–89.

100. See George Michell and Mark Zebrowski, *Art and Architecture of the Deccan Sultanates* (Cambridge: Cambridge University Press, 1999), 115–225.

101. 'Anonymous History of the Qutb Shahis', in Briggs, trans., *History of the Rise*, 253.

102. Ibid., 3:263.

103. Black, *Beyond the Military Revolution*, 5.

CHAPTER 8

# The Political Functions of City Gates

What I have done to [Isma`il `Adil Khan] and taken from him he has richly deserved; as regards returning it to him that does not seem to me reasonable, nor am I going to do it. And as for your further statement that ye will all turn against me in aid of him if I do not do as ye ask, I pray you do not take the trouble to come hither, for I will myself go to seek ye if ye dare to await me in your lands.

—Krishna Raya's letter to the rulers of the northern Deccan, 1520[1]

Next day the King [Krishna Raya] sent to call the ambassador [of Isma`il `Adil Khan], and after other things had been spoken of between them, the King said that he would be content to restore everything to the Ydallcão [`Adil Khan] according to his wish … provided the Ydallcão would come and kiss his foot.

—Account of the merchant and chronicler Fernão Nunes, ca. 1531[2]

The spread of gunpowder technology was only one means by which Deccani states projected power. Another, far more subtle, form of state power and authority appeared in the words, images, and symbols that were projected visually in grand and imposing gateway complexes. The sixteenth century witnessed the construction of many such gateways in Deccani towns and cities—some of which we have already examined, such as the neo-Chalukya entrance to Bijapur's citadel completed by Ibrahim `Adil Shah I in 1544. To be sure, gateways had always been important features of cities and fortified centres, but in the turbulent sixteenth century new gateways appeared with increasing frequency and in ever more elaborate designs.[3] Defensive concerns account in part for the profusion of new gateways, but not entirely, for they were also heavily laden with symbolic significance and served important ritual functions. In fact, in many ways gateways represented the quintessential symbols of power and authority in the sixteenth-century Deccan. It is therefore puzzling that they have received such scant scholarly attention, whether from historians or architectural historians.[4]

In this chapter, we attempt to redress this imbalance by examining several key symbolic–ritual functions of gateways as they are manifest in the city gates of Raichur. First, focussing on the city's primary, eastern gate known today as the Kati Darwaza, we consider the practice of rebuilding gateways as a means of proclaiming a change in the control of a town. Standing out in the otherwise undifferentiated expanse of a city's outer wall, and subjected to constant use as primary points of access into their cities, prominent and elaborately designed gateways naturally came to serve synecdochically as recognizable insignia of these cities. Consequently, rulers who had just taken control of a provincial town, and who sought visual confirmation of their political presence, were intent on replacing some of that town's old gateways with new ones built in the style of their own metropolitan centres. Raichur's Kati Darwaza presents a particularly rich case in point—actually, an architectural palimpsest, as its fabric reveals three separate rebuildings, at least two of which clearly correlate with shifts in the political control of the city.

Second, we will see that city gates could function not just as zones of passage, but also as destinations in their own right. Many contained components that were palatial in function, providing ancillary sites for the enactment of royal ceremonies of reception and appearance. Such functions were enabled by a productive spatial juxtaposition between an elevated upper storey where the ruler could appear from a projecting pavilion (*jharokhā*), and a succession of open courtyards below, through which those seeking audience would be ushered. Though hardly unique in incorporating such features for the performance of rituals of appearance, the well-preserved Naurangi Darwaza in Raichur's northern wall offers an unusually vivid example of the gateway-palace as an architectural type. Indeed, such gateways could even serve as the physical stage on which interstate diplomacy unfolded. Constructed by Krishna Raya immediately after he captured Raichur from Isma`il `Adil Khan of Bijapur in 1520, the Naurangi Darwaza, so the evidence suggests, was planned as a means of defiantly provoking Isma`il and the other chiefs of the northern Deccan, and of communicating Krishna Raya's expansionist intentions.

## GATEWAYS AND THE 'SYMBOLIC APPROPRIATION OF THE LAND': RAICHUR'S KATI DARWAZA

In his landmark study on the formation of Islamic art, Oleg Grabar draws attention to an important type of early Islamic artwork related to the classical *tropaion*, or 'victory monument'.[5] Whether taking the form of a painting, sculpture, or building, these tropaia functioned to express 'the rule of a land or an area by a culture, or even the simple presence in a land of an alien or new element, through some visually perceptible form'.[6]

In the Deccan, a vivid example of this process is provided by a small mosque inside the fort at Adoni, a key Vijayanagara stronghold located some 60 kilometres south of Raichur.[7] Originally founded sometime in the first half of the sixteenth century when Adoni was still under Vijayanagara's control, the mosque was evidently intended to serve the religious needs of the Muslims among the soldiers who manned the garrison. As such, it conformed to a local interpretation of the style used for small temples and mosques at the Vijayanagara capital, with a post-and-lintel construction employing *citrakhaṇḍa* columns, flat ceilings, and plain masonic walls carried on a moulded plinth (Figure 8.1).[8] In about 1568, several years after the Battle of Talikota, the army of `Ali `Adil Shah successfully besieged the fort and marked its annexation by constructing a new façade for this mosque.[9] Just as the original style of the mosque had emulated the style of metropolitan Vijayanagara, `Ali's addition exhibited a local version of the style of metropolitan `Adil Shahi Bijapur, based on that dynasty's signature vocabulary of piers and arches, bracketed eaves, and carved stucco (Figure 8.2). Through the design and placement of this façade, as well as through several modifications to the Vijayanagara-style interior—such as plastering over the outer circuit of Vijayanagara-style citrakhaṇḍa columns (Figure 8.3)—`Ali's builders were able partially to obscure the original Vijayanagara fabric of the mosque, thus erasing a conspicuous trace of the fort's earlier political affiliation and asserting its new position within the `Adil Shahi state.

In much the same way, the two early sixteenth-century reconstructions of Raichur's main gateway can be understood in terms of their successive patrons' desires to effect a 'symbolic appropriation of the land'. Just as the Adoni mosque's most prominent and visible outer face—its façade—served as the primary focus for `Ali's intervention, so too at Raichur, the Kati Darwaza served as the focus of attempts to mark the city's shifting political affiliation. Considerable evidence indicates that the Kati Darwaza was indeed the city's most prominent outer face and its primary entrance.

First, it conforms typologically to the design of a 'major gate', as opposed to an entrance of only secondary importance. Contemporary inscriptions made this distinction themselves, employing one set of terms to refer to major gates—*agusĕ* in Kannada, *gavini* in Telugu, and *darwāza* in Persian—and another term to refer to secondary gates, called *diḍḍi* in all three languages.[10] Major gates were not only considerably larger than secondary entrances, they also took a distinctive form enabling them

**Figure 8.1** Adoni Fort mosque. Seen from southwest, showing Vijayanagara-style fabric of original building (first half of sixteenth century).

**Figure 8.2** Adoni Fort mosque. Seen from east, showing Bijapuri-style façade added to Vijayanagara style core (c. 1568).

**Figure 8.3** Adoni Fort mosque. View of interior wall, showing Bijapuri plastering of Vijayanagara period *citrakhaṇḍa* columns.

to serve two apparently conflicting ends. As the primary access points into their cities, these gates had to be readily accessible to wheeled vehicular traffic and elephants, the royal vehicles of their day, which dictated both their placement on level ground and their grand dimensions.[11] But major gates also had to be defensible, with provisions for both permitting and prohibiting access into their cities. This accounts for their multiple gatehouses with massive door-leaves that could be firmly closed and bolted against stone jambs to secure the city when under attack.[12] It also accounts for the succession of bounded courtyards separating these gatehouses and for the battlements atop their walls, which provided a continuous platform from which projectiles could be unleashed on any attacking force that had managed to breach an outer gatehouse. Most importantly, the 'bent-axis' layout of these courtyards and doorways dictated that the outer and inner gatehouses of each courtyard were never aligned along a single axis, but were always placed in adjacent walls, necessitating a 90-degree turn to the right or left. As a result, a continuous battlement always faced any doorway, enabling defenders to shoot attackers attempting to force their entry into an inner gatehouse. By contrast, secondary service entrances, or posterns—the 'diḍḍi' of inscriptions—are small doorways consisting of little more than a simple straight-through passageway in the city wall, with a single set of door-leaves closing off its outer side.[13]

Second, although the Kati Darwaza was one of four major bent-axis gates in Raichur's outer wall, the layout of the city's primary roadways and the location of its major fifteenth- and sixteenth-century structures identify it as the city's primary entrance and 'urban façade' (see Figure A2.2, p. 355). As we saw in the preceding chapter, early modern Raichur was bounded by two concentric circuits of walls: an inner circuit that had been constructed at the end of the thirteenth century,[14] and a later, outer circuit constructed between 1468 and 1470 by the Bahmani governor Mallu Khan.[15] The Kakatiya design of a wall with only two gateways—on its eastern and western sides respectively—was maintained by Mallu Khan, who likewise built a single pair of gates in his wall, on the eastern and western sides. But the eastern gate, the Kati Darwaza, evidently served as the city's preferred entrance in his time.[16] Lying in direct east–west alignment with the earlier Kakatiya gate, this gate created a formal axial avenue, in contrast to the situation on the western side, where the new gate was displaced some 100 metres to the south. Mallu Khan also left twice as much space between the Kati Darwaza and the old Kakatiya gate than he did between the corresponding gates on the city's western side, establishing a centre of gravity that was clearly weighted towards the east. Accordingly, it was the eastern half of the main road that became the favoured site for new construction, as is attested by the presence here of five mosques built between 1500 and 1669.[17] In contrast, no mosques or other monumental buildings appear to have been built along the western half of the same road. Similarly, although two new gates were added in the outer wall during the sixteenth century—the Naurangi Darwaza on the north in 1520 and the Khandaq Darwaza on the south in 1551—the lack of historic structures along the road running between them suggests that these northern and southern gates never acquired the same degree of importance as did the Kati Darwaza.[18]

The Kati Darwaza's continuous importance is further suggested by the three reconstructions it underwent after its initial construction in 1458, two of which took place in the sixteenth century.[19] Little is left of the complex today, owing to the intense urban development that has swallowed up much of the gate and adjacent segments of the wall. But thankfully, one gatehouse is well preserved, together with a few tantalizing parts of the courtyard behind it. Of Mallu Khan's original gate there is no discernable trace save the foundation inscription, which at some point was retrieved and fixed into the inner eastern wall of the partially preserved courtyard. Most of what we do see today is the product of the gate's first reconstruction, undertaken by Krishna Raya in 1520 immediately following his stunning victory over Isma`il `Adil Khan of Bijapur at the Battle of Raichur (Figures 8.4 and 8.5).[20]

Traces of the gate's second rebuilding are visible primarily in the tympanum of the outer arch of Krishna Raya's gatehouse, where a Persian inscription has been inserted, as well as in the inner façade of the partially preserved courtyard, where a new eave supported on Bijapur-style brackets was added above the arcade. This work—really more a remodelling

**Figure 8.4** Raichur. Kati Darwaza: gatehouse of gateway, as reconstructed by Krishna Raya c.1520, viewed from outside.

**Figure 8.5** Raichur. Kati Darwaza: gatehouse of Krishna Raya, viewed from inside.

than an entire reconstruction—was undertaken in 1550 under the patronage of the Bijapuri governor, Shamshir al-Mulk.[21] The third campaign of reconstruction, dated to 1622–23 during the time of the Bijapuri governor `Abd al-Muhammad, does not appear to have greatly altered the gate at ground level, but it did see the construction of a palace above the gate.[22]

Krishna Raya's reconstruction of the gateway appears to conform perfectly to the process described by Grabar as 'the symbolic appropriation of the land'. We know from Nunes's account of the siege of Raichur that the king had focussed his efforts along the city's eastern side, directing his men to dismantle the wall with crowbars and pickaxes.[23] Although Nunes suggests that the eastern side was chosen because the ground was flat there, the decision was more likely dictated by the primacy of Raichur's eastern gate and the symbolic effect of attacking the city frontally, right at its main entrance. Nunes also implies that the wall was dismantled solely for the purpose of enabling the attacking army to pour in and seize the city. While no doubt the immediate goal, this dismantling of the walls would also have erased some of the most prominent visual traces of the city's long occupation by the Bahmanis and their `Adil Shahi successors, especially if it extended to include the gateway running through those walls.[24] It would also have generated an ample store of ready-to-use stone building material, so that immediately after the siege engineers could begin work on the construction of a new gate, the forms of which would unequivocally announce that Raichur had returned to Vijayanagara's control.[25] Although Nunes never states that a new gate was constructed for the city, he does record that 'the King stayed for some days' after the fort's surrender in order to repair the walls and 'to make all the arrangements' necessary for bringing the city under Vijayanagara's governance.[26] All available evidence suggests that one of the 'necessary arrangements' overseen by the king was the construction of a new, Vijayanagara-style gateway, so as to mark clearly the change in the city's control.

Crucially, the contrast effected through the change in gateways was not one based on a supposed opposition between 'Islamic' and 'Hindu' architectural styles, however those might be conceived. Rather, the contrast was between two distinct metropolitan variants within a single overarching Deccani tradition of urban architecture. As much as the Persianate and Sanskritic worlds may have differed in their interpretation of the forms appropriate for religious architecture—as witnessed in the changing fortunes of the Adoni mosque discussed earlier—they nonetheless shared very similar understandings of what was appropriate in the secular realm of urban, courtly architecture. More precisely, by the sixteenth century, the Persian and Sanskrit cosmopolises had penetrated one another so thoroughly in the Deccan that it had become possible—even normal—to combine their architectural components in the same monuments. Thus, from at least the fifteenth century, constructional material such as mortared rubble masonry and carved stucco were shared in common by architects both at Vijayanagara and at Bidar or Bijapur, as was also a common formal vocabulary of piers, arches, and domes.[27] But at the same time, these common forms would be differently interpreted and decorated at the various metropolitan centres, thereby giving rise to distinctive and easily recognizable metropolitan styles.

When Krishna Raya replaced Mallu Khan's gateway, then, he did not reject either its bent-axis layout or its vocabulary of arches and domes. What he rejected was a certain fifteenth-century decorative vocabulary that was inescapably associated with the Bahmani sultans during their greatest period of ascendancy. Although the Bahmani gate is now gone without a trace, we can still gain some sense of its likely appearance from Mallu Khan's other gateway, the Mecca Darwaza, which still stands in the city's western wall. This gateway has itself been greatly altered, yet its original Bahmani character may still be discerned through its heavily restored forms (Figure 8.6).[28] Typical of the fifteenth-century Bahmani style is the pyramidally profiled dome over its outermost preserved gatehouse and the chaste articulation of the gate's wall surfaces, unrelieved save by the pairs of nested arches framing the openings. Also typical of the Bahmani style is the frieze near the top of the outer gatehouse's upper storey.[29] Consisting of a continuous series of recessed bricks forming a diamond pattern, this motif was probably inspired by fifteenth-century Persian architectural tile work.[30]

In place of such restrained and geometric forms as those found in the Mecca Darwaza, Krishna Raya's gatehouse at the Kati Darwaza displays a more exuberant and sculptural aesthetic that immediately calls to mind the world of metropolitan Vijayanagara (Figure 8.7a). Whether they were instructed verbally by their patron, or visually through a showing of simple sketches and drawings, the local stonemasons and sculptors interpreted such decorative forms as the familiar Indic *makara-toraṇa*, one of which they introduced as a lintel within the gatehouse's arched opening. Although the makara figures of this toraṇa appear stiff and rigid when compared to contemporary decorative sculptures from the Vijayanagara

**Figure 8.6** Raichur. Mecca Darwaza (1469/70): outermost preserved gatehouse, viewed from inside.

capital, their forms are still far more organic in conception than those of the otherwise comparable animal motifs figuring on Bahmani or `Adil Shahi gateways.[31] Other local interpretations of forms associated with metropolitan Vijayanagara include the bracketed capitals (*potika*) supporting the makara-toraṇa lintel, and the pair of Vijayanagara-style citrakhaṇḍa pilasters framing its entrance (Figure 8.8). Even though the style of all these decorative elements is decidedly archaic and behind the times in comparison to what was happening in the capital in the 1520s, there is no confusing the Vijayanagara stylistic affinity of this gatehouse and its decorative forms.

The Vijayanagara identity of the gatehouse would have been still more pronounced before 1550, when one key element of its decoration was removed in connection with the subsequent renovation of Shamshir al-Mulk. This was a stone slab originally fitted into the tympanum of the arch above the makara-toraṇa, which would likely have been carved with a sculptural frieze in three or four registers. Although this slab has disappeared without a trace, its nature may yet be inferred from a similar element employed in the better-preserved Naurangi Darwaza, built by Krishna Raya at the same time (Figure 8.7b).[32] Since the two gateways appear to have been identical in almost every respect, we may

a

b

**Figure 8.7** (a) Raichur. Kati Darwaza, view of upper portion of Krishna Raya's gatehouse from the outside (the calligraphic panel is a later addition; *courtesy of* John Henry Rice). (b) Raichur. Naurangi Darwaza, view of tympanum of second gatehouse.

**Figure 8.8** Raichur. Kati Darwaza: Krishna Raya's gatehouse, showing detail of *citrakhaṇḍa* pilaster and *potika* brackets.

conclude that the Kati Darwaza gatehouse would likewise have featured such a sculptured tympanum panel. It, too, would most likely have presented characters and scenes from the Rāmāyaṇa, just as in the Naurangi Darwaza panel (see later), where, in the central register, a divine triad of Rama, Lakshmana, and Sita stands at the centre flanked on either side by their monkey allies, while various characters and scenes from the Rāmāyaṇa occupy the remainder of the three registers.

The narrative sculptures in the tympanum of Krishna Raya's Kati Darwaza would have contributed to the viewer's overall understanding of the gateway. In relying upon iconography rather than epigraphy—literally, a 'writing in images' as opposed to a 'writing on' of text—Vijayanagara's architects made a choice that underlines one of the fundamental stylistic differences between the Vijayanagara courtly style and that of the Bahmanis and their successors. Whereas Mallu Khan had affixed a monumental inscription to the façade of his gateway, Krishna Raya used in its place narrative sculptures and other established iconographic forms. Ironically, the underlying content of the two messages can be recognized as essentially the same, as each begins by invoking the divine and then proceeds to summon the presence of the king into the gateway, expressing hopes for his prosperity and for the defeat of his enemies.[33] Yet, from the broader perspective of a gateway's ability to signal the political identity of its city, it is not the message's content but its medium that is important—the latter being as much a signature element of a given architectural style as its characteristic forms and motifs. To sixteenth-century residents or visitors passing through Raichur's primary eastern gate, the shift from monumental epigraphy to a new form of 'writing in images' would have served as one of the clearest indications that the city was now part of Vijayanagara's territory.

By the mid-sixteenth century, however, the wheel of political fortune had once again turned, and again the city's Kati Darwaza would be rebuilt. Owing to a succession dispute and attendant political instability in Vijayanagara following Krishna Raya's death in 1529, the southern kingdom lost the entire Raichur Doab to Bijapur in 1536.[34] However, the reconstruction of Raichur's Kati Darwaza did not take place until 1550, by which time relations between Bijapur and Vijayanagara had grown exceptionally hostile. In about 1544 Rama Raya had sent his brother Venkatadri to recapture Raichur, and although he seems to have failed in this mission, he is credited with having defeated Ibrahim `Adil Shah I in a field campaign on the banks of the Bhima River.[35] Then, in about 1549, Burhan Nizam Shah of Ahmadnagar and Rama Raya concluded a new alliance that Ibrahim `Adil Shah perceived as dangerously threatening. Firishta writes that the Bijapur sultan treated Vijayanagara's ambassadors with 'such marked neglect, that they became alarmed, and retired abruptly, without taking leave, to Vijayanagara'.[36] This diplomatic affront enraged Rama Raya and served as a pretext for renewed invasions of `Adil Shahi territory. In 1549 Burhan Nizam Shah, instigated by Rama Raya, successfully besieged Bijapur's fort of Kalyana, and then in 1550 the two allies began plans for a siege of Raichur the following year.[37] It was precisely at this point, amidst a rising threat from Vijayanagara and at a moment when an attack by Rama Raya appeared immanent, that Raichur's governor, Shamshir al-Mulk, recorded his 'construction' (*banā'*) of a new gate on the site of Krishna Raya's Kati Darwaza.[38] The governor evidently sought to mask, and thereby to deny, the Vijayanagara character of Krishna Raya's earlier gate.

The minimal extent of Shamshir al-Mulk's architectural intervention further supports such an interpretation. Clearly preoccupied with the rising threat from Rama Raya, the governor would have been hard pressed to undertake a wholesale rebuilding of the complex, as Krishna Raya had done some thirty years before. Instead, he concentrated his efforts on appropriating Krishna Raya's gatehouse, which he did by simply removing its carved, iconographic tympanum slab and replacing it with a new slab bearing a monumental Persian inscription. Dated AD 1550, this inscription records that 'it'—implicitly, the gateway or gatehouse—was constructed during the reign of Sultan Ibrahim `Adil Shah I by Shamshir al-Mulk. On the face of it, the text of this inscription seems to imply that the gateway was built in 1550, and not in 1520 as we have argued here. But the irregular and disturbed fabric of the outer arch's masonry—together with the stylistic discordance between the Persian calligraphy and the sculptured makara-toraṇa below it—belies the truth of the inscription's claim, revealing that the panel had in fact been inserted into the façade in place of the original tympanum. In effect, the inscription serves to appropriate Krishna Raya's gateway by presenting Shamshir al-Mulk as its builder. Moreover, by introducing an epigraphic mode of communication in place of the iconographic one that had earlier been present, and by invoking God and the Shi`i Imams as well as the ruling `Adil Shahi sultan and his governor, the inscription strove to effect another 'symbolic appropriation of the land'—this time, marking Raichur as part of the `Adil Shahi realm, and doing so in a remarkably economical way.

Shamshir al-Mulk was not being completely misleading, however, in claiming to have 'constructed' (*binā' karda*) the gateway, for he did engage in some remodelling of the façade of the inner courtyard. There, along the northern wall, now largely obscured by small shops and trees, runs a partially preserved arcade that is roughly comparable to the one preserved in the analogous courtyard of the Naurangi Darwaza. However, subtle stylistic features distinguish this arcade from that of the other gate. Not only are there lotus rosettes in the spandrels of the arches, but the arcade is shaded by a projecting eave carried on a type of bracketing that is distinctive of mid-sixteenth-century Bijapuri architecture (Figure 8.9).[39] It appears likely, then, that Shamshir al-Mulk also rebuilt the inner façade of the courtyard, which further extended the `Adil Shahi stylistic idiom projected through his foundation inscription.

## GATEWAY AS PALACE: KRISHNA RAYA'S NAURANGI DARWAZA

In considering the complex history of the Kati Darwaza and its rebuildings, we have had to

**Figure 8.9** Raichur. Kati Darwaza: detail of eave brackets in Shamshir al-Mulk's addition.

tread carefully to disentangle the multiple layers that, sedimented into the gate's built fabric, reveal the efforts of successive rulers to stake their claims to newly acquired territory. By contrast, our second theme—the palatial functions that gateways could serve—is much more straightforward, since our principal example of the 'gateway palace', Raichur's Naurangi Darwaza, shows no evidence of subsequent rebuildings. Located towards the eastern end of Raichur's northern wall, this structure is in fact one of the best-preserved gateway complexes in the entire Deccan. Thanks to the limited period of its active use, it provides a vivid and nearly complete picture of the layout and functioning of such a gate in the prime of its life.

Though lacking a surviving foundation inscription, the Naurangi Darwaza can be confidently ascribed to Krishna Raya's patronage on the basis of its elaborate sculptural programme, which includes friezes narrating stories from the Rāmāyaṇa. Syed Yusuf, who submitted an official report on Raichur to the Nizam of Hyderabad's Archaeological Department in 1929, believed that a Bahmani or `Adil Shahi patron had built the gateway using sculptural material from previous Hindu structures.[40] But this is not possible, as these sculptures comprise an integral part of the gateway's overall design and iconographic programme. This extensive use of Hindu iconography, together with an absence of Persian inscriptions, suggests that it was built when the city was under Vijayanagara's control. In fact, the mythological narratives are punctuated by scenes of contemporary courtly life that feature men and women wearing the distinctive dress styles of the Vijayanagara élite. In the most striking and finely executed of these, a Vijayanagara king is depicted seated in royal ease on his throne, wearing his tall conical *kuḷḷāyi* and conversing with several women who stand before him (Figure 8.10).[41] Taken together, the iconography and style of the Naurangi Darwaza indicate a date during the period of Krishna Raya's occupation of Raichur (1520–9), as opposed to either of the other two periods when the city was under Vijayanagara's control.[42] We would further argue that the gate was constructed contemporaneously with Krishna Raya's rebuilding of the Kati Darwaza, which, when intact, would have closely resembled the Naurangi Darwaza, and that both gates were likely constructed immediately following that king's capture of Raichur in June 1520. It would therefore follow that the Vijayanagara king depicted in the gateway's reliefs was not likely the image of a generic ruler, but rather, a portrait of the ruling king himself—Krishna Raya.

As experienced at the ground level, the Naurangi Darwaza presents a particularly elaborate example of the bent-axis gateway type, consisting of a series of three linked courtyards bounded by four gates (Figure 8.11). The outermost courtyard, lying to the north, is conceived as a simple rectangular forecourt, informal and unpaved, but well protected by a substantial barbican wall. Its largely dilapidated gatehouse is situated at the northernmost end of its eastern wall, so that immediately upon entering it one has little choice but to turn left and proceed to the south. At the southern end of the courtyard, one confronts a pair of massive bastions with an imposing gatehouse in between (Figure 8.12). This gatehouse perfectly illustrates what George Michell has dubbed the 'Vijayanagara courtly style', in which the Persianate forms of the Tughluq and Bahmani styles are inventively combined with sculptures, mouldings, and other Indic elements better known from the Vijayanagara style of temple architecture.[43] Thus, the opening of this gatehouse is defined by a post-and-lintel element—a familiar Indic makara-toraṇa that is the twin of that in the

**Figure 8.10** Raichur. Naurangi Darwaza: detail of frieze in first inner courtyard, showing the Vijayanagara king Krishna Raya and female attendants.

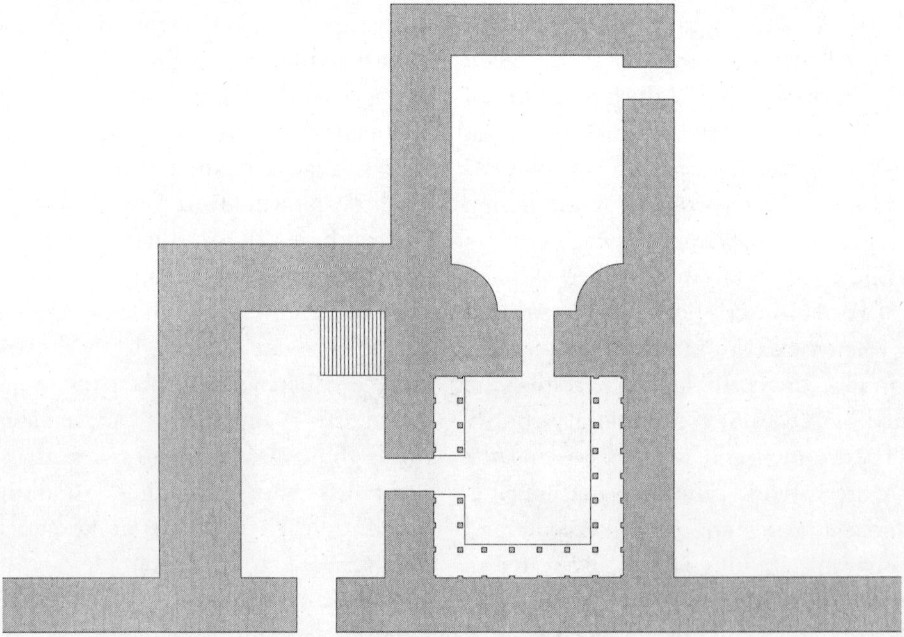

**Figure 8.11** Raichur. Naurangi Darwaza: schematic plan (not to scale).

Kati Darwaza—but this is in turn framed by a pair of nesting arches inscribed within a rectangular frame, in typical Persianate fashion.[44] Between the top of the makara-toraṇa and the lower surface of the inner arch, the tympanum is carved with the three registers of narrative relief sculpture to which we have previously alluded (Figure 8.7b). In the shortest register at the top, a Shri Vaishnava sectarian marking—the Y-shaped nāmam of the Tengalai sect—occupies the centre, and is flanked by two of Vishnu's divine attributes, the discus on the left and the conch on the right. In the second register, a divine triad of Lakshmana, Rama, and Sita stands at the centre, flanked on either side by their monkey allies, while in the lowest register, Vishnu's loyal servants Hanuman and Garuda stand immediately left and right of the central axis, while the two sides of the register are filled with generic scenes of women and a scene of the monkey-kings Vali and Sugriva fighting.

This commingling of Indic and Persianate elements continues unabated in the gatehouse's interior, which both spatially and structurally exhibits a strongly Persianate character (Figure 8.13). Although its particular composition has close analogues in the architecture of the Vijayanagara capital, its vocabulary of heavy masonry piers, arches, and central dome can be traced back to models in the earlier architecture of the Deccani sultanates. In particular, the zone

**Figure 8.12** Raichur. Naurangi Darwaza: gatehouse at southern end of first courtyard, leading to second courtyard. The inner arched opening is the result of conservation work carried out in the twentieth century.

of transition between the arches and the dome features the same types of kite-shaped pendentives that are familiar from early sixteenth-century architecture at Bijapur, but which is also seen at the Vijayanagara capital (Figure 8.14).[45] At the same time, an assortment of relief sculptures of various Hindu deities and Indic motifs—Krishna stealing the cow-girls' clothes, and a crouching man-lion, to name but two—have been sculpted along the bases of the piers in this gatehouse, facing in at eye-level towards the central passageway (Figure 8.13).

Leaving the gatehouse, one emerges into the light of the second courtyard at the very heart of the Naurangi Darwaza (Figure 8.15). Aesthetically, this is the most highly charged space within the entire complex. In contrast to the first courtyard, this one is paved, approximately square, and defined by arcades running around the four sides in front of a shallow gallery two bays deep. Just above the arcades, a continuous sculpted frieze runs across the wall, containing narrative scenes familiar from the Rāmāyaṇa, interspersed with assorted mythic scenes and vignettes of contemporary Vijayanagara courtly life. In the middle of the western side, the gallery arcade turns 90 degrees and extends several metres

**Figure 8.13** Raichur. Naurangi Darwaza: interior of second gatehouse.

**Figure 8.14** Raichur. Naurangi Darwaza: interior of second gatehouse, showing dome and zone of transition above central passageway.

**Figure 8.15** Raichur. Naurangi Darwaza: second courtyard, looking to the south.

to the west, creating a deeper space so as to frame and accentuate the imposing façade of the next gatehouse, which is the obvious focal point of the entire composition (Figure 8.16). We will return to the significance of this façade momentarily.

Proceeding through this third gatehouse, we arrive at the innermost courtyard of the complex, which is laid out as a rectangle with its long axis running north to south. Like the previous courtyard, it too is paved, but unlike it, there is little sculptural embellishment here. Certainly, neither of the gatehouse façades fronting this courtyard is as complex and ornamented as those providing entrance into the preceding courtyards, which were clearly designed to address the beholder with complex iconographic messages. At the southern end of the courtyard is the fourth and final barrier on the way into the city; passing through this relatively plain and unornamented gatehouse, one finally emerges into the open urban space of Raichur.

Whereas the Naurangi Darwaza was normally experienced as a succession of spaces affording a controlled means of passage into or out of the city, the elevation of the walls of the middle courtyard reveals another, more specialized,

**Figure 8.16** Raichur. Naurangi Darwaza: view of third gatehouse as seen from the second courtyard.

way of experiencing the gateway—namely, as a space with palatial functions. Surviving architectural elements show that the walls of this courtyard were originally surmounted by a set of continuous, second-storey palatial pavilions (*jharokhās*), focussed inwards and down towards the courtyard below.[46] Fortunately, a portion of this second storey is preserved on the western side of the courtyard, where it affords a clear sense of the character of this space (Figure 8.16).[47] Here, a pavilion (jharokhā), carried on brackets and axially aligned over the lofty arch of the gatehouse below, projects outwards enough to afford vistas through its arched openings down into the courtyard below. A pair of arches flank the structure on each side. This scheme evidently would have continued around all four sides of the courtyard, albeit with differences in the numbers and disposition of the pavilions; this is indicated by the existence of clustered sets of brackets supporting projections of the cornice level, which only make sense if they had served as supports for pavilions in the now-vanished upper storey (Figure 8.15). It is conceivable that only the inner façade of this upper storey was executed in stone, while the rooms behind it were constructed with timber or brick to lessen the load carried by the ground storey.[48] In its overall appearance, this central courtyard recalls the so-called Queen's Bath at metropolitan Vijayanagara, which likewise featured open arcades rhythmically interrupted by projecting pavilions that afford vistas down into the sunken water basin below.[49]

Significantly, many of the royal structures in metropolitan Vijayanagara share the Naurangi Darwaza's spatial configuration of an elevated pavilion looking down into a courtyard, although in most of these cases the relationship is along a linear axis, as opposed to being centrally focussed as in our gateway. This is true of the residential palaces excavated in the 'Noblemen's Quarters', where raised floor areas in a U-shaped formation define a lower courtyard that is on axis with a forward-facing chamber on the highest level.[50] In an even more pronounced way, it is also the case with the so-called Hundred Columned Hall with its upper storey carried on pillars and overlooking the open courtyard to its north.[51] All this suggests the palatial conception of the Naurangi Darwaza's upper storey, which provided an elevated pavilion from which the king or his governor could appear to those assembled in the courtyard below.

How might this gateway-palace have been used for rituals of royal audience? Although textual descriptions of such ceremonies are not available, their general spatial pattern can be inferred through a careful reading of the architectural record itself. First, whereas entering or exiting the gateway involved continuous movement in a single direction—either into or out of the city—rituals of royal appearance inevitably necessitated two opposing paths of movement that would have converged on the central courtyard. On such occasions, those approaching the royal presence would have entered the central courtyard from the outermost court, once the doors of the second gatehouse had been opened. Filing into the court of reception, they would have assembled by rank before the lofty gatehouse on the western side of the court, waiting for the ruler to appear. The ground-level doors of this gatehouse would presumably have been closed and bolted to prohibit further movement through this gate and into the royal zone of the innermost courtyard. Meanwhile, the ruler would have made his way into this innermost court from the other direction, coming from his place of residence inside the city. He would have proceeded across the rectangular court, going all the way to its northern end, where a monumental stone staircase provided him with access to the pavilion of appearance overlooking the central court.[52] Making his entrance accompanied by the beating of drums and the intoning of musical instruments, he would have taken his seat in the gatehouse's central pavilion and gazed down upon the assembled crowd from above.

The layout of the courtyard and the details of its sculptural programme also suggest how the ruler would have been perceived on these occasions. Obviously, the ruler's elevated position in the upper storey spatially asserted his superior status. His political centrality was also affirmed by his position on the median axis of the courtyard's western façade. Unlike the other three sides, where the pavilions are arranged in pairs,[53] the western side has three, and since the central one is located over the gatehouse—which rises still higher than the cornice level of the flanking walls—it is still further elevated with respect to the two flanking pavilions, thus establishing a pyramidal composition with the ruler appearing at top and centre. Simply by situating himself within the central arch of this pavilion with a pair of attendants or guards symmetrically disposed in the arches on either side, the king would have projected a powerful image of himself, leaving no doubt as to his pivotal importance within the state.[54]

The composition of the façade further conveyed a number of subtle visual statements that suggested the king's quasi-divine status, effectively equating him with Vishnu in the form of Rama. In large measure, this derives from the similarities between this façade and that of the previous gatehouse, through which participants would have just passed on their way into the central courtyard. Just as the ideal king Rama had appeared near the top of the tympanum of that gatehouse, flanked by Lakshmana and Sita, so too did the flesh-and-blood king appear in the pavilion's central arch, flanked by his subordinates. And just as Rama's triad had stood over the images of Hanuman and Garuda in the register below, so too did the king appear above two flanking images of these same exemplary divine servants of Vishnu. Both are accompanied by Vishnu's attributes of conch and discus, sculpted in short extensions of the sculptural frieze carrying across the face of the gatehouse before it is interrupted by the arched opening. Hanuman and Garuda also face inwards, just as they do in the tympanum of the previous gate, further implying that the figure appearing above them—that is, the person seated in the pavilion—was himself a partial manifestation of Vishnu (Figures 8.17 and 8.18).

This deliberate conflation of the roles of Rama/Vishnu and the king occurs at other places in the gateway's sculptural programme as well, most notably in the two central panels of the frieze on the southern wall directly opposite the point of entrance into the court. There, on the panel above the third arch, are the two culminating scenes in a sequence of reliefs narrating the Rāmāyaṇa, while to its immediate right, over the fourth arch, is a court scene showing the Vijayanagara king seated in conversation with a group of women. Both Rama and Krishna Raya are presented in nearly identical poses, seated on a throne facing right, in a posture of 'royal ease' with left leg crossed over right (Figure 8.19). In fact, the only thing distinguishing the two images is that Rama wears the metallic *kirīṭa* crown worn by Vishnu and his avatars, whereas the earthly king wears the conical cloth *kuḷḷāyi* of the Vijayanagara court. The iconographic programme of the gateway thus visually blurs the boundaries between god and king, much as occurs in contemporary courtly panegyrics, such as the

**Figure 8.17** Raichur. Naurangi Darwaza: tympanum of outer façade of second gatehouse (left) and outer façade of third gatehouse (right), showing relative positions of Rama, Hanuman, and Garuda (left) and the king, Garuda, and Hanuman (right).

**Figure 8.18** Raichur. Naurangi Darwaza: images of Garuda (left) and Hanuman (right), just below the *jharokhā* pavilion of the third gate.

following panegyric verse that describes one of Krishna Raya's military victories by identifying him with Narasimha and Kariraja-varada, two forms of Vishnu:

Krishna Raya the Man-Lion [that is, Narasimha]!

You slew the Turks from afar by the mere power of your great name.

O Lord of the elephant king [that is, Kariraja-varada]!

At the mere sight of you the great host of elephants hurried away in fear.[55]

**Figure 8.19** Raichur. Naurangi Darwaza: narrative reliefs of Rama and of Krishna Raya in the second courtyard of the gateway.

The Naurangi Darwaza thus functioned as a pivotal node for articulating royal authority in Krishna Raya's Raichur. By serving as a location for receptions and royal appearances at the threshold between city and countryside, it made the ruler visible at the outermost boundary of his fortress and projected his claims to power out into the surrounding territory. In the first instance, it did this by periodically serving as a stage for royal receptions, such as the welcoming of ambassadors from neighbouring kingdoms or of the king's own military commanders returning from their campaigns. Even if visiting ambassadors were invited up into the palatial pavilion to sit together with the king, the architecture itself affirmed that the king, not the visitor, was bestowing the honour. Additionally, the gateway's entire design, especially the sculptural frieze in the central courtyard, deliberately blurred the boundaries between royalty and divinity, so that even in the ruler's absence, the empty pavilion could recall his quasi-divine status.

## GATEWAY DIPLOMACY AFTER THE SIEGE OF RAICHUR[56]

Why did Krishna Raya build the Naurangi Darwaza where he did, in the city's northern wall where no gate had previously existed? Since nothing suggests that the city's northern quarter was undergoing development in the early sixteenth century, it would not appear likely that the gateway was primarily intended to facilitate access through the city's northern wall. The actual reasons behind the gate's northern siting emerge only when we consider its construction against the background of Vijayanagara's crushing victory over Bijapur at the Battle of Raichur, and the diplomacy between Krishna Raya and the defeated Isma`il `Adil Khan that followed that battle. In this light, the construction of the gate emerges as merely one among several aggressive and threatening gestures that Krishna Raya made towards all the rulers of the northern Deccan—especially Bijapur's Isma`il `Adil Khan.

According to Nunes, after entering the conquered city on 15 June 1520, Krishna Raya treated the inhabitants with clemency, generously inviting those who wished to stay to remain in the city, and allowing those who wished to leave to take all of their property with them.[57] Before long, the news of his victory had reached the capitals of the Deccan's other rulers, who in turn dispatched envoys to Raichur, where the king was still in residence. Nunes notes that the envoys were 'astonished ... to see that the King had captured so strong a city [but] they were much more surprised to see how great was his power and how numerous his troops'. Nunes continues:

> Having arrived where he was they gave him the letters they had brought, and these were forthwith read. In these, the chiefs told the King that he ought to content himself with having defeated the Ydallcao [Isma`il ` Adil Khan] as he had done, and ought not to wage further war; they begged him of his goodness to return to the Ydallcao that which he had taken from him, and that if they did so they would always obey whatever he commanded; but if he was not of a mind to do this, then he must know for certain that they would be compelled to turn against him and forthwith join the Ydallcao, for whom they would speedily recover that which he had now lost.[58]

In response, the king wrote a single letter to them all, giving copies to the envoys. Although the letter began in the most courteous of terms, its tone quickly grew defiant and aggressive:

> As regards the Ydallcao, what I have done to him and taken from him he has richly deserved; as regards returning it to him, that does not seem to me reasonable, nor am I going to do it; and as for your further statement that ye will all turn against me in aid of him if I do not do as ye ask, I pray you do not take the trouble to come hither, for I will myself go to seek ye if ye dare to await me in your lands;—and this I send you for answer.[59]

Having dismissed the envoys with this answer, and 'after having made all the arrangements that were necessary for the government of the city',[60] Krishna Raya continued to stay in the city for 'some days'. Finally, 'after repairing the walls' and leaving a garrison of troops behind to guard the place, he departed for his capital.

Following Krishna Raya's return to Vijayanagara and the round of festivities that celebrated the king's victories at Raichur, the other principal player in this drama—the defeated Isma`il `Adil Khan of Bijapur—sent an envoy to the capital to negotiate a final settlement between the two adversaries. After keeping him waiting for an entire month, the king finally admitted the ambassador for a private audience. The latter conveyed a bold request from Isma`il `Adil Khan, namely, that should Krishna Raya restore to Bijapur the city of Raichur—together with the artillery, tents, horses, and elephants that the `Adil Shahis had lost in the recent battle—Isma`il would remain the king's enduring and loyal friend. In response, Krishna Raya agreed to grant all these requests, and even to release Bijapur's highest-ranking officer, Salabat Khan, who had been captured after the battle, on the sole condition that Isma`il first come down to Vijayanagara and kiss his foot (*contanto que ho ydallcão lhe viesse beijar o pee*).

When this response was conveyed to Isma`il, the latter replied through his ambassador that, whereas he was 'of full mind joyfully to do that which the King wished', it was unfortunately not possible for him to comply since he could not legally enter another king's sovereign territory. In response, Krishna Raya offered to accommodate the sultan's concerns for diplomatic correctness by meeting the sultan at their common border near the fort of Mudgal, where, presumably, Isma`il could kiss the king's foot. But without even waiting for the sultan's response, Krishna Raya proceeded north to Mudgal, accompanied by a formidable army doubtless intended to focus the sultan's mind. But Isma`il, who had no intention of journeying to Mudgal or of ever enduring the humiliation of kissing the king's foot, stalled and prevaricated while his messengers notified the king that he was on the way and would reach Mudgal very soon.[61]

When it became clear, however, that Isma`il was not going to present himself at the border, Krishna Raya opted for a more brazenly aggressive course of action, namely, of bringing his foot to the sultan, so that the latter could kiss it in his own domain without having to travel anywhere. The king and his army then entered `Adil Shahi territory, moving as far north as Isma`il's capital of Bijapur, which the sultan prudently vacated before the king's arrival. With Isma`il absent, Krishna Raya's men proceeded to damage several of the city's prominent houses, on the feeble excuse that they needed firewood. When Isma`il, through envoys, protested this reckless behaviour, Krishna Raya lamely replied that he had been unable to restrain his men from their destructive activities. Meanwhile the sultan, preferring to suffer the humiliation of his capital's desecration than to kiss Krishna Raya's foot, simply avoided his capital as long as the king was in the city. Eventually Krishna Raya, having made his point, returned to his own capital.[62]

Nunes's account of these varied events that followed the Battle of Raichur is crucially important for interpreting the larger intentions that lay behind the conception and design of the Naurangi Darwaza. First, we may contrast the attitude of respect and generosity that Krishna Raya showed towards the residents of the town, with the contempt and defiance he showed towards the envoys of the northern sultanates who had come to lobby on Isma`il's behalf. Scoffing at the latter's insinuations, he threatened to launch invasions into their own lands. It was precisely at this point, we suggest, that Krishna Raya undertook to construct a new gate in the northern wall of the city, that is to say, the part of the wall that faced and directly confronted his adversaries. Conceived as a monument that would complement his written reply to the northern sultans, the Naurangi Darwaza would serve as a constant reminder to them of the imminent threat posed by the southern kingdom. By opening up a symbolic node on the city's northern wall—one that was marked stylistically with Vijayanagara's identity, confronted his northern adversaries, and provided a stage on which the king could enact his superior status to visiting envoys—the new gate would serve as an architectural corollary to the defiant message contained in his letter.

Second, the unfolding of the almost farcical foot-kissing drama sheds suggestive light on the choice and placement of certain themes in the narrative frieze of the gateway's innermost court. In the context of royal etiquette and ceremonials, Krishna Raya's eagerness to have Isma`il kiss his foot can be understood as a gesture indicating political superiority and subordination.[63] But in view of the king's crushing defeat of Isma`il on the battlefield and at Raichur Fort, and in view of his belligerent behaviour towards the envoys of other sultans of the Deccan, his demand that the sultan of Bijapur kiss his foot can also be seen as an act of deliberate humiliation, which Isma`il would have no part of. In any event, it is difficult to miss the homology between Nunes's report of the king's behaviour and several key sculptures in the Naurangi Darwaza. We refer here to the deliberate side-by-side juxtaposition of Rama and Krishna Raya in the sculptural frieze of the central courtyard (Figure 8.19). Together occupying the midpoint of the frieze on the courtyard's southern wall, the two kings—one belonging to the mythic past, the other to the immediate present—appear together in the very first section of relief that one would see on entering the courtyard from the gatehouse on the north. We may recall that one of the features blurring the distinction between the two royal figures is their common representation in the seated posture of royal ease, with the left leg crossed over the right knee, so that its foot dangles comfortably in mid-air. Here, it would seem that Krishna Raya was still engaged in diplomacy with his defeated foe, generously proffering his foot and suggesting that he was still ready to return the fort in exchange for a single, subordinating kiss from Isma`il.

* * *

A major theme of this chapter is the use of architecture to proclaim a new dynasty's claim over territory—what Oleg Grabar calls the 'symbolic appropriation of the land'. In introducing how new rulers built new gateways or gave existing gateways politically charged 'face-lifts', we discussed `Ali `Adil Shah's remodelling of the fort mosque at Adoni around 1568, after Bijapur had seized that stronghold from Vijayanagara (Figures 8.1, 8.2, and 8.3). At some point in the early sixteenth century Vijayanagara's rulers had built the mosque using the architectural vocabulary of the Vijayanagara capital: post-and-lintel construction, flat ceilings, *citrakhaṇḍa* columns, and plain masonic walls carried on a moulded plinth. In his remodelling of the structure, `Ali plastered over the mosque's outer circuit of citrakhaṇḍa columns and adorned its façade with arches, bracketed eaves, and carved stucco work typical of the metropolitan Bijapuri style. Ironically, though, the original mosque had conformed so closely to the style of Vijayanagara's temples that in modern times militant Hindu youths tore down the minarets that `Ali `Adil Shah had added to its façade, acting in the mistaken belief that the sultan had destroyed a Hindu temple before building a mosque in its place.[64]

But this was not a case of temple desecration, even though some modern-day commentators have claimed as much.[65] The structure's religious identity as a mosque had not changed; what had been a mosque under Vijayanagara's rule remained a mosque under Bijapur's rule. All that changed was its dynastic affiliation. Modifying its façade with just enough visual cues to align the mosque stylistically with metropolitan Bijapur instead of with metropolitan Vijayanagara, the sultan gave public and visual notice of the presence of a new ruling power in the region.

Contrasting `Ali's treatment of the Adoni mosque with the same ruler's treatment of the temple in Bankapur some six years later, as discussed in Chapter 4, reveals much about how power, memory, and architecture interacted in the sixteenth century. Whereas at Adoni the sultan retained the mosque's identity as a mosque but radically altered its style from that of metropolitan Vijayanagara to that of metropolitan Bijapur, in Bankapur he did just the opposite.

What he encountered in Bankapur was not a structure associated with Vijayanagara, but a spectacular twelfth-century Shiva temple built in the Dharwar style of the imperial Kalyana Chalukyas. While transforming the great temple into a mosque, `Ali scrupulously maintained its earlier stylistic signature. Since the Bankapur temple was so clearly identified visually with the long-defunct but still-remembered Chalukya imperium, and not at all with the recently defeated rulers of Vijayanagara, there was no need to alter its façade or in any way disguise its obvious Chalukya identity. To the contrary, desiring to establish his own dynasty's continuity with the Kalyana Chalukyas, still fresh in popular memory after more than four centuries, `Ali sought to preserve the ancient temple's aesthetic character even while altering its ritual function.

Unlike Bankapur, however, Raichur had no surviving structures associated with the Chalukyas of Kalyana. Instead, the city straddled a hotly contested frontier zone that lay between two bitter rivals, each harbouring ancient claims to its territory. In this situation, both Vijayanagara and its `Adil Shahi rivals to the north endeavoured to obliterate, or at least upstage, signs of their enemy's prior presence, while visually proclaiming their own presence. Thus, in the aftermath of the Battle of Raichur of 1520, Krishna Raya modified the city's Kati Darwaza in ways that publicly announced Vijayanagara's triumph over the city's `Adil Shahi and Bahmani predecessors. At the same time, he built his elaborate Naurangi Darwaza, provocatively facing Bijapur and saturated with public art in the metropolitan Vijayanagara style.

Two years later, in the midst of Krishna Raya's efforts to force Isma`il `Adil Khan to submit to him by kissing his foot, the Vijayanagara king invaded Bijapur, briefly occupying the `Adil Shahi capital. Immediately after this episode Isma`il built a stone citadel, replacing the mud fort that had preceded it, for the specific purpose of repelling the 'cursed' Krishna Raya.[66] We have seen in Chapter 4 that between 1538 and 1544 Isma`il's successor, Ibrahim `Adil Shah, built the principal gateway to that citadel. And yet, although this gateway faced south, the material introduced into it indicates that Ibrahim was concerned not so much with confronting Bijapur's southern enemy as with appropriating the Chalukya legacy that had spanned the territories of both states. It was only after re-conquering Raichur, the principal bone of contention between the two states, that Bijapur resorted to the sort of 'gateway politics' in which Krishna Raya had engaged in 1520. In 1550, at the height of hostilities between Bijapur and Vijayanagara, the governor of Raichur reasserted Bijapur's sovereignty over the city by simply stating as much in a Perso-Arabic inscription over the city's principal gateway, the Kati Darwaza, replacing the iconography that Krishna Raya had installed in that very spot.[67]

There is a larger point to make respecting the sort of rhetorical or visual projections of power discussed in this chapter, and that is that a 'symbolic appropriation of the land' is merely that—symbolic. Every visual expression of power presupposed a prior acquisition of control of territory, typically by force. The Battle of Raichur, which delivered the Raichur Doab to Vijayanagara in 1520, was won not by symbols or rhetoric, but by the superiority of disciplined infantry and heavy cavalry over ineptly handled cannon. And forty-five years later at the Battle of Talikota, Vijayanagara was defeated principally by the superior use of firepower, the result of decades of military modernization on the part of the northern sultanates, especially the `Adil Shahis of Bijapur. As we saw in the preceding chapter, from at least 1508 Bijapur's ruling class had wholeheartedly embraced technological newness in the military domain, steadily developing newer, bigger guns, while designing and building taller bastions or cavaliers on which to mount them. Although Bijapur's Shamshir al-Mulk did indulge in a display of political rhetoric in remodelling Raichur's Kati Darwaza, for the most part, sixteenth-century Bijapuri rulers focussed on acquiring the sort of raw power that is delivered at the end of a muzzle.

We do not find this in Vijayanagara. We have seen in the preceding chapter how Krishna Raya's crushing defeat of Isma`il `Adil Khan in 1520 had lulled Vijayanagara's king and his successors into a state of complacency respecting the need to develop gunpowder technology. What this chapter has shown is that, accompanying Vijayanagara's neglect of firepower was its embrace of an earlier, aesthetically oriented mode of warfare, one based more on displaying the symbols of power—iconography, rhetoric, pageantry, elaborately designed palatial gateways, diplomatic belligerence—than on power itself, that is, its material substance. This choice, for which Krishna Raya was mainly responsible, proved fatal for Vijayanagara's ultimate destiny.

## NOTES

1. Quoted by Fernão Nunes, in *A Forgotten Empire, Vijayanagara: A Contribution to the History of India*, trans. Robert Sewell (1900; repr. New Delhi: Publications Division, 1962), 331.

2. Ibid., 335.

3. At Raichur, for example, gateways were constructed between 1294 and 1673 at nine different locations in the city's two circuits of walls, and at two of these locations they were subjected to subsequent renovations and reconstructions, bringing the total number of distinct gateway foundations to thirteen. Of these, seven were made in the sixteenth century.

4. The most important study remains that of Coomaraswamy, which appeared as long ago as 1930 and was confined to the early historic period. Scattered reports and documentation of ancient and early medieval city gates have occasionally appeared in specialized archaeological reports, some of which have been summarized and synthesized by Jean Deloche. But the building type still awaits a comprehensive and synthetic study addressing its broader cultural functions. For classical and medieval Europe and the Islamic Middle East, on the other hand, there are a number of important studies, starting with E. Baldwin Smith, to whose work we are much indebted for its conceptual framework. See Ananda K. Coomaraswamy, 'Early Indian Architecture, I: Cities and City Gates, etc.', *Eastern Art* 2 (1930), 208–25; Jean Deloche, *Studies on Fortification in India* (Pondicherry: Institut Francais de Pondichery and Ecole Francaise d'Extreme Orient, 2007); E. Baldwin Smith, *Architectural Symbolism of Imperial Rome and the Middle Ages* (Princeton: Princeton University Press, 1956). See also Slobodan Ćurčić, 'Late Antique Palaces: The Meaning of Urban Context', *Ars Orientalis* 23 (1993):67–90; Julian Gardner, 'An Introduction to the Iconography of the Medieval Italian City Gate', *Dumbarton Oaks Papers* 41(1987),199–213; Felicity Ratté, 'Architectural Invitations: Images of City Gates in Medieval Italian Painting', *Gesta* 38, no. 2 (1999), 142–53; K.A.C. Creswell, 'Bāb', *Encyclopaedia of Islam*, 2nd edn, eds H.A.R. Gibb, J.H. Kramers, E. Lévi-Provençal, J. Schacht, B. Lewis, and C. Pellat (Leiden: Brill, 1960–), I:830–2; Jamel Akbar, 'Gates as Signs of Autonomy in Muslim Towns', *Muqarnas* 10 (1993), 141–7; Yasser Tabbaa, *Constructions of Power and Piety in Medieval Aleppo* (University Park, PA: Pennsylvania State University Press, 1997), especially chapter 1, 'The City: Aleppo under the Ayyubids'.

5. Oleg Grabar, *The Formation of Islamic Art*, revised and enlarged edition (New Haven: Yale University Press, 1987), chapter 3, 'The Symbolic Appropriation of the Land'

6. Ibid., 43. For a broader discussion of various categories of *tropaia* in Islamic art, see Thomas Leisten, 'Mashhad al-Nasr: Monuments of War and Victory in Medieval Islamic Art', *Muqarnas* 13 (1996), 7–26.

7. Not to be confused with the Mosque of Mas`ud Khan (1683) in Adoni town, this smaller mosque is located on the lowest level of the fort and remains undocumented. For Mas`ud Khan's mosque, see George Michell and Mark Zebrowski, *Architecture and Art of the Deccan Sultanates* (Cambridge: Cambridge University Press, 1999), figure 65.

8. The mosque therefore compares with, for example, Ahmad Khan's 'dharmasala' in Vijayanagara's Muslim quarter. See George Michell, 'Architecture of the Muslim Quarters of Vijayanagara', in *Vijayanagara, Progress of Research, 1983–84*, ed. M.S. Nagaraja Rao (Mysore: Directorate of Archaeology and Museums, 1985), 101–18; Phillip B. Wagoner, 'Fortuitous Convergences and Essential Ambiguities: Transcultural Political Élites in the Medieval Deccan', in *Surprising Bedfellows: Hindus and Muslims in Medieval and Early Modern India*, ed. Sushil Mittal (Lanham, MD: Lexington Books, 2003), 31–54.

9. For the shift to `Adil Shahi control, see John Briggs, trans., *History of the Rise of Mahomedan Power in India* (3 vols, Calcutta: Editions Indian, 1966), 3:81–2. There are no inscriptions, and Firishta makes no mention of the updating of this mosque or of other architectural undertakings, but stylistic evidence suggests that it would have occurred soon after 1568.

10. Kannada inscriptions at Mudgal systematically distinguish the major, bent-axis gates termed *agusĕ*, from the smaller, secondary service entrances termed *diḍḍi*. At Vijayanagara itself, however, bent-axis gateways are rare, and most of the city's main gates take a different, straight-through form that had been common in India since at least the third century BC. These are termed *bāgilu* to distinguish them from the bent-axis agusĕ. In contemporary sixteenth-century Telugu literary sources, a three-way distinction is drawn between the bent-axis main gate called *gavini* (equivalent to the Kannada agusĕ), the old-fashioned straight-through gate called *vākili* (equivalent to Kannada bāgilu), and the secondary diḍḍi. See the description of the gateways of Warangal in C.V Ramachandra Rao, ed., *Ekāmranāthuni Pratāparudra Caritramu* (Hyderabad: Andhra Pradesh Sahitya Akademi, 1984), 34. See also C.S. Patil, 'Mudugal Fort and Its Bearing on the Defense System at Vijayanagara', in *Vijayanagara: Progress of Research, 1988–91*, eds D.V. Devaraj, Channabasappa S. Patil, and John M. Fritz (Mysore: Directorate of Archaeology and Museums, 1996), 197–209; M.S. Nagaraaja Rao and C.S. Patil, 'Epigraphical References to the City Gates and Watch Towers of Vijayanagara', in *Vijayanagara, Progress of Research, 1983–84*, eds M.S. Nagaraja Rao and George Michell (Mysore: Directorate of Archaeology and Museums, 1985), 96–100. Regarding secondary gates, called diḍḍi, at Vijayanagara, see John M. Fritz, 'Sally Ports and Other Small Entries in the Fortifications of the Urban Core (NPj, NPu, etc.)', in *Vijayanagara: Archaeological Exploration, 1999–2000. Papers in Memory of Channabasappa S. Patil*, eds John M. Fritz, Robert P. Brubaker, and Teresa P. Raczek (New Delhi: Manohar and AIIS, 2006), 1:157–80.

Persian inscriptions indiscriminately use *darwāza*, the related terms *dar* or *dargāh*, or the Arabic equivalent *bāb*, for both bent-axis and straight-through types of main city gates. For secondary entrances, however, the term 'diddi' is used, borrowing from the equivalent Kannada and Telugu term. An example is the 'Trust in God Postern' (*tawakkul diḍḍi*) in Raichur's south-western wall. *Epigraphia Indica, Arabic and Persian Supplement* (*EIAPS*) *1963*, 69, pl. XXII[a].

Whereas the straight-through design for city gates in India dates back at least to the third century BC, the bent-axis design represents a much newer form that was first perfected in Syria and Egypt during the first half of the thirteenth century. The bent-axis design (Arabic *bāshūra*) represents a response to the widespread diffusion of the counterweight trebuchet (*manjanīq*), a powerful new form of siege engine. The four bent-axis gateways in Warangal's stone wall, rebuilt under the initiative of Rudramadevi (r. 1262–89), represent the first documented appearance of the type in the Deccan.

11. In contrast to secondary gates, primary city gates of the bent-axis type never incorporate stairs, raised thresholds, or other changes of level within their passageways. At Raichur, the fort's primary road still runs through the eastern Kati Darwaza, and municipal buses can still ply the route and negotiate the gateway with little difficulty.

12. None of the door-leaves survives from the gates at Raichur, but teak door-leaves do survive at many sixteenth- and seventeenth-century fortified sites, including a well-preserved pair at Mudgal bearing a foundation inscription dated to 1560.

13. Not intended to function as major thoroughfares, diḍḍīs allowed pedestrians to pass through the city walls far from a main gateway complex. These entrances were less likely targets for attack by a besieging force since they were located at points where the city walls crossed elevated and rocky ground. Nor could they be used by wheeled vehicles. They often incorporated steps and changes of level within their passageways; in rare cases, they were flanked by the raised guards' platforms seen in the gatehouses of primary city gates.

14. The inner wall was constructed in 1294 by the Kakatiya chief Gona Vithalanatha, who commemorated the act with a Telugu inscription carved into the outer surface of the wall just south of its western gate. Vithalanatha notes that he had constructed a 'stone fort' (*śilā-durggamu*) for the city, which stands as the earliest documented instance of stone fortification in this part of the Deccan. See P. Sreenivasachar, 'Note on the Raichur Inscription of Vithala-natha, dated Śaka 1216 (c. 1294 A.D.)', *Annual Reports of the Archaeological Department of Hyderabad* (*ARADH*) *1935–36*, Appendix E, 32–5.

15. Mallu Khan is represented as the builder of the eastern (1468–99) and western (1469–70) gates in the outer wall, which suggests that he was most likely also responsible for constructing the wall through which they open. See *EIAPS 1962*, 58–9, pl. XVI(b); and 59–60, pl. XVII(a).

16. A comparison of the contents of Mallu Khan's two foundation inscriptions also suggests the primacy of the eastern gateway (see previous note for references). It was the first of the two gateways to be completed (1468–69), and its inscription is longer and more detailed than its counterpart in the Mecca Darwaza. Both inscriptions begin with the profession of faith, record the date of construction, and identify Muhammad Shah III as the reigning Bahmani sultan and Mallu Khan as the patron responsible for the undertaking. The inscription in the eastern gate, however, additionally names Muhammad Shah's two predecessors on the Bahmani throne—Humayun Shah and 'Sultan `Ala `al-Din' (that is, Ahmad Shah II)—and contains a verse invoking auspiciousness and security on the gate and upon the city's governor:

May this gate be always open to the whole world! May the enemy be under the dust in this gate!
O Lord! May this gate be never bereft of such a Khan! May he always be prosperous, honourable, fortunate, and happy!

The first line nicely sums up the dual purpose of a primary city gate: namely, to allow open access to the city even while protecting it from its enemies.

17. These are the Daftar Masjid, built c.1500–10; the Ek Minar ki Masjid, built 1513; the Fort Jami` Masjid, built 1577–8; the Jami` Masjid in the Saraf Bazaar, built 1628–9; and the Sikandari Masjid, built 1669–70. For the Daftar Masjid, see Elizabeth Schotten Merklinger, *Indian Islamic Architecture: The Deccan, 1347–1686* (Warminster, England: Aris and Phillips Ltd., 1981), 116; for the Ek Minar ki Masjid, see *EIAPS 1962*, 65–6, pl. XX(a); for the Fort Jami` Masjid, see *EIAPS 1963*, 66, pl. XXI(b); for the Jami` Masjid in the Saraf Bazaar, see *EIAPS 1963*, 76–7, pl. XXIV(a); the date of the Sikandari Masjid is based on local tradition. For a study of Raichur's mosques as a whole, see Elizabeth Schotten Merklinger, 'The Mosques of Rāičūr: A Preliminary Classification', *Kunst des Orients* XII 1/2 (n.d.), 79–94.

18. Furthermore, the main road that today links Raichur to points north and south runs on the eastern side of the fort, immediately adjacent to the Kati Darwaza. In all likelihood, this modern road follows the general course of a transportation route that had already been established by the Bahmani period. The pre-eminence of this road has diminished somewhat since the end of the nineteenth century, when a major Bombay–Madras rail line was constructed along the western side of the city, creating a new commercial node around the railway station. As a result, there is now a second centre of gravity outside the western wall of the city, where the Mecca Darwaza overshadows the Kati Darwaza as the 'urban façade' of the walled city. See Joseph E. Schwartzberg, *A Historical Atlas of South Asia*, second impression (New York: Oxford University Press, 1992), plate XI.D.2.

19. The Kati Darwaza is one of only two gates at Raichur for which there is evidence of reconstruction. The other is the 'Sikandari Darwaza', as the eastern gateway through the Kakatiya wall is called. The original Kakatiya gate was renovated in 1673 by Aqa Khusrau, governor of the fort during the reign of Sultan Sikandar Qadiri (that is, `Adil Shah). *EIAPS 1963*, 77–8, pl. XXIV(b).

20. Krishna Raya's patronage of the reconstruction of this gate is not documented either epigraphically or in contemporary historical texts. However, both the stylistic evidence and the contextual evidence of Raichur's changing political affiliation overwhelmingly indicate that the reconstruction was undertaken during his occupation, apparently after his capture of Raichur in 1520. The elements belonging to this phase of the Kati Darwaza are the structural fabric of the sole surviving gatehouse and most of its decorative detail, as well as the general bent-axis layout of the partly preserved courtyard behind it.

21. *EIAPS 1963*, 63–4, pl. XX(b).

22. *EIAPS 1963*, 70–1, pl. XXIII(b), and 71–2, pl. XXIII(c). See note 42 for a discussion of this palace.

23. Sewell, *Forgotten Empire*, 315, 316, and 328.

24. Because Raichur had been within Vijayanagara's territory at the time of the state's origins, Vijayanagara's rulers viewed the Bahmani occupation of Raichur as a wrongful appropriation of territory that had rightfully been theirs. This explains the state's persistent attempts to retake the city throughout the fifteenth century. Nunes even relates an anecdote about Krishna Raya's discovery of the testament of the earlier ruler Saluva Narasimha, enjoining upon his successors that they should devote themselves to the goal of capturing 'three fortresses that at his death remained in revolt against him'—Raichur, Mudgal, and Udayagiri. Ibid., 302.

25. Indeed, Nunes remarks that the king ensured that the men were paid for each stone they brought, according to its size, suggesting that building a new gateway was part of Krishna Raya's intention even at the outset of the siege. Ibid., 315.

26. Nunes, in ibid., 332.

27. The close stylistic kinship between the courtly, non-religious structures constructed at the Vijayanagara capital and contemporary architecture of the Bahmanis and their successor states was first stressed by George Michell. In the Vijayanagara 'courtly style', as Michell terms it, the Persianate forms of the Tughluq and Bahmani styles are inventively combined with sculptures, mouldings, and other Indic elements better known from the Vijayanagara style of temple architecture. George Michell, *The Vijayanagara Courtly Style: Incorporation and Synthesis in the Royal Architecture of Southern India, 15th–17th Centuries* (Delhi: Manohar and AIIS, 1992).

28. Since the gateway is now bisected by a modern roadway and the outermost preserved courtyard has been turned into a performance space by the construction of bleachers, it is difficult to discern its spatial layout. In the two preserved gatehouses, the masonry joints have been freshly mortared, and the decorative detail seems to belong entirely to recent times, even though it appears faithfully to follow a fifteenth-century Bahmani vocabulary.

29. The uppermost ornamental band, a course of brick-shaped stones set on angle so as to create a zipper-like frieze, is another characteristic early Bahmani decorative device, but it is one that was also used in the Vijayanagara courtly style, at least at provincial centres like Raichur.

30. For comparable examples of this sort of ornament, see the small fifteenth-century pavilion at Gogi, the domed gateway to the mosque in the Dargah of Khalifat al-Rahman in Firuzabad, or the so-called Kali mosque at Malkhed. Merklinger dates this latter structure to the late fourteenth century, but this date is probably too early, as elements of its style—such as the so-called beam and brick pendentives employed in its zone of transition—continue well on into the fifteenth century, as seen, for example, in the Tomb of Humayun Shah (d. 1461) at the Bahmani necropolis at Ashtur. See George Michell and Richard Maxwell Eaton, *Firuzabad: Palace City of the Deccan* (London: Oxford University Press, 1992), figure 50; Merklinger, *Indian Islamic Architecture*, 75 (figure 122), 111 (catalogue no. 24).

31. See, for example, Hermann Goetz, 'Indo-Islamic Figural Sculpture', *Ars Orientalis* 5 (1963), 235–41, figure 6 (heraldic lion figure from the Takht-i Kirmani at Bidar), figure 7 (heraldic lion figure from the Sharza Darwaza at Bidar), figure 8 (relief on the entrance of Bijapur palace), and figure 16 (heraldic lion reliefs from the Sharza Burj, Bijapur).

32. See the section, 'Gateway as Palace: Krishna Raya's Naurangi Darwaza'.

33. The invocation of the divine is literal and verbal in the case of Mallu Khan's inscription, opening as it does with the Islamic profession of faith. In the case of Krishna Raya's sculptured gatehouse façade, the invocation was iconographic, as the very top of the panel (assuming parallelism with its preserved counterpart in the Naurangi Darwaza) would likely have begun with three divine symbols serving as a visual invocation of the god Vishnu—the *nāmam* or Shrivaishnava sectarian mark, flanked by Vishnu's conch and discus. The body of both messages revolves around themes of kingship, prosperity, and the vanquishing of enemies. Thus Mallu Khan's inscription lauds its patron as 'the supreme lord (*khān-i a`ẓam*) Mallu Khan Hafiz' and expresses the hope that 'this gate may be never bereft of such a Khan', while at the same time invoking prosperity upon him and curses upon his enemies ('May he always be prosperous, honourable, fortunate, and happy!'; and 'may the enemy be under the dust in this gate'). Although Krishna Raya's tympanum speaks in images, and therefore in a more indirect and figurative way, we can still see its preoccupation with essentially the same set of themes. Thus, its focal point is the ideal king Rama, standing at the centre of the median

register and surrounded by auspicious motifs, including the figures of women as the human embodiment of happiness and prosperity (*śrī*) and the makara-toraṇa evoking the waters of life and thus the ideas of abundance and fortune. But interspersed among these figures are scenes of the monkey princes Vali and Sugriva fighting, destined to end in the slaying of Vali and the elevation of Sugriva as Rama's chief ally, who will in turn enable Rama to slay his own enemy, Ravana.

34. We know that by 1536 Bijapur controlled Mudgal, the other major city of the Raichur Doab, since the `Adil Shahi governor of that city, Shamshir al-Mulk, issued an inscription from there in that year. Although the inscription remains unpublished, a summary can be found in *Annual Reports on Indian Epigraphy* (*ARIE*) *1958*, D125. Firishta puts Bijapur's conquest of Raichur 'after the death of Hemraj [= Krishna Raya]' without specifying a date, but he does say that it was after the city had been 'in possession of the infidels for seventeen years'. As the chronicler was using the shorter, lunar calendar, that would work out to sixteen solar years from 1520, or 1536. See Briggs, trans., *History of the Rise*, 3:40.

35. C. Hayavadana Rao, *Mysore Gazetteer, Compiled for Government*, vol. 2 *Historical*, part 3 *Medieval: From the Foundation of the Vijayanagara Kingdom to the Destruction of Vijayanagara by Tipū Sultān in 1776* (Bangalore: Government Press, 1930), 2048–9.

36. Briggs, trans., *History of the Rise*, 3:62.

37. Ibid., 3:63–4.

38. *EIAPS 1963*, 63–4, pl. XX (b). Shamshir al-Mulk appears to be the same official who had governed Mudgal in 1536. A.A. Kadiri believes that he is the same Shamshir al-Mulk who is mentioned as the father of one Ahmad `Ali in an inscription from Panhala dated 1579–80. He is not known from Firishta or any other sources. *ARIE 1958*, D125; *EIAPS 1971*, 73–5, pl. XX(a)

39. Comparable examples of this Bijapuri-style bracketing system may be seen in the mosque constructed in Naldurg (1560) and in the façade addition to the Adoni fort mosque (c.1568), discussed earlier. In its simplest form, this system consists of a series of brackets projecting perpendicularly from the wall, carrying transverse brackets parallel to the wall, which in turn support the mid-points of the rafters carrying the eave slabs. In some examples, including Shamshir al-Mulk's gateway, the rafters are eliminated and the eave slabs are carried directly on the cross-brackets. The underside of each bracket typically adopts an S-shaped curving profile and is ornamented with one or more pendant lotus buds. In the later sixteenth and early seventeenth centuries, the perpendicular brackets become further subdivided, and the number of pendant lotus buds further increases, until the overall effect is like a frieze of ornate stalactites. See, for example, the bracketing of the Ibrahim Rauza at Bijapur (1626).

40. *ARADH 1929–30*, 17. Although Ghulam Yazdani was the head of the Nizam's Archaeological Department, in 1929 he was out of the country on official business. In his absence Syed Yusuf served as acting assistant director, toured Raichur, and submitted the report for the 1929–30 volume. Syed Yusuf's opinion about the sculptures having been reused has been echoed by Suguna Sarma in her monograph on Raichur. See V. Suguna Sarma, *History and Antiquities of Raichur Fort* (Delhi: Bharat Kala Prakashan, 1998), 92.

41. For the *kuḷḷāyi* and the system of Vijayanagara court dress, see Phillip B. Wagoner, '"Sultan among Hindu Kings": Dress, Titles, and the Islamicization of Hindu Culture at Vijayanagara', *Journal of Asian Studies* 55, no. 4 (November 1996), 851–80.

42. Raichur was under Vijayanagara control also in the early Sangama period, from about 1327 until 1347, and again between 1552 and 1565 during the heyday of Rama Raya. The best evidence that the Naurangi Darwaza was built in the 1520s is the prevalence of Shrivaishnava sectarian imagery in its iconographic programme, for Shrivaishnavism had become a major cultural force at the Vijayanagara court only in the late fifteenth and early sixteenth centuries. Moreover, the sculptural frieze of the main courtyard includes an image of Ranganatha, the presiding deity at Srirangam in the Tamil country, which is the most sacred among the three main Shrivaishnava pilgrimage centres. According to donative inscriptions, Krishna Raya went on a pilgrimage to Srirangam and made donations there in 1516 and 1517, and again in 1524. Also significant is the Tengalai *nāmam* (sectarian mark) at the apex of the tympanum above the outer arch of the gatehouse to the main courtyard, flanked by Vishnu's discus (*cakra*) and conch (*śankha*). The positioning of this sectarian mark at the top of the gateway's façade announces the Shrivaishnava identity of the space within, just as the nāmam worn on the forehead serves to identify the religious affiliation of its wearer. Shrivaishnavism remained ascendant during the reign of Rama Raya.

By that time, though, the architectural conception of gateways had changed markedly—even in the peripheral zone of the Raichur Doab—as is evidenced by the eastern gateway erected at nearby Mudgal, under the patronage of Vengalappa Nayaka in 1560. See A.A. Kadiri, 'Bahmani Inscriptions from Raichur District', *EIAPS 1962*, 53–6; Anila Verghese, *Religious Traditions at Vijayanagara as Revealed through Its Monuments.* Vijayanagara Research Project Monograph Series, vol. 4 (New Delhi: Manohar and American Institute of Indian Studies, 1995), 75.

43. Michell, *Vijayanagara Courtly Style*, 67–8.

44. The smaller arched opening within the space of the makara-toraṇa is the product of conservation work carried out in the early twentieth century.

45. See, for example, Yusuf `Adil Khan's Old Jami` Masjid, dated to 1512. By the time the Naurangi Darwaza was built, however, these forms had long been appropriated and 'naturalized' as part of the formal idiom of the Vijayanagara 'Courtly Style'. They can be seen in such monuments as the nine-domed pavilion (structure VI/3) in the Royal Centre. See Merklinger, *Indian Islamic Architecture: The Deccan*, figure 130; John Fritz, George Michell, and M.S. Nagaraja Rao, *Where Kings and Gods Meet: The Royal Centre at Vijayanagara, India* (Tucson: University of Arizona Press, 1984), figure 7.7; Michell, *The Vijayanagara Courtly Style*, 11–12 and figure 11.

46. There was nothing unusual about this juxtaposition of palace and gate, even at Raichur. From epigraphic evidence we know that the Kati Darwaza, as rebuilt by `Abd al-Muhammad in 1622, also had a palatial function. An inscription records that the `Adil Shahi governor, `Abd al-Muhammad, built a 'lofty and strong palace' (*qaṣr-i `ālī mashīd*) above the gateway. Another inscription of his, dated the same year, seems to describe this same palace, referring to its 'nine arches [which] were completely decorated', and mentioning a 'pavilion on its top'. Unlike the Naurangi Darwaza, this gateway had been built and rebuilt a number of times and is now largely dismantled to allow for bus traffic into the old city. Today only tantalizing traces of the palace remain. *EIAPS 1963*, 70–2, pl. XXIII (b) and XXIII(c).

Important examples of the gateway-palace type survive elsewhere in the Deccan, in both Persianate and Indic contexts. At least two are known from the Bahmani period in the fifteenth century. One is the so-called Shah Darwaza at the early Bahmani stronghold of Sagar, in which substantial portions of a mezzanine level and an upper storey are well-enough preserved to permit reconstruction. Interpreting the level of the guards' platforms as a separate storey, Helen Philon sees this structure as a four-storeyed gateway. The other example is the Gumbad Darwaza at the entrance to the citadel of Bidar, which has an upper gallery storey with two small chambers opening north and south off the central dome, and on the east, a small chamber with a window opening outwards on to the east façade. Klaus Rotzer suggests that the latter 'could have been used by a ruler to appear to an audience assembled in the open square in front'. See Helen Philon, 'Daulatabad, Gulbarga, Firuzabad, and Sagar under the Early Bahmanis, 1347–1422', in *Silent Splendour: Palaces of the Deccan, 14th–19th centuries*, ed. Helen Philon (Mumbai: Marg Publications, 2010), 38–41, figures 3–5, and plan 10; Klaus Rotzer, 'Fortifications', in *Silent Splendour*, ed. Philon, 30, figure 8, and plan 17.

In the Indic context there survives a well-preserved example from Chitradurga, an important Vijayanagara stronghold under the early Sangamas. Built in 1338–39, this gateway was neither an actual city gate nor a gate to a citadel, but an analogously functioning entrance to a sacred complex centred upon a temple. Referred to in the inscriptions variously as a 'palace' (*upparigĕ*), 'stone palace' (*kalla upparigĕ*), or 'three-storeyed palace' (*muṟu-nĕlĕya upparigĕ*), this small and self-contained structure is a single gatehouse with a passageway flanked by raised guards' platforms at ground level and two functional and accessible upper storeys. The latter served as the 'palace' to which the deity's portable image, having been brought from its temple, would appear to worshippers below. In addition to the epigraphically documented 'stone palace' at Chitradurga, five other examples of the type are preserved—one more at Chitradurga and four at Vijayanagara itself—attesting to the currency of the form in the early Vijayanagara era. See Phillip B. Wagoner, 'Kannada *kalla upparige* "Stone Palace": Multi-storeyed Entrance Pavilions in Pre- and Early-Vijayanagara Architecture', *Ars Orientalis* 31 (2001), 167–83.

47. This upper storey appears in the earliest available photograph of the gate, dating to 1929 when Syed Yusuf of the Archaeological Department of Hyderabad

State visited the site and published a description of the fort and its monuments. The masonry of this upper storey has since been mortared and repaired, but it is still close to its original appearance. See *ARADH 1929–30*, 6–19, and figure 7 (unnumbered) for the photograph.

48. Timber construction was the norm for palaces and other royal structures at the Vijayanagara capital throughout its history. There, in the Royal Centre of the site, all that generally remains both of residential palaces and of more public places of royal appearance are their stone basement platforms, the wooden walls and superstructures having long since vanished. Charred remnants of the wooden structures have been found amid thick depositions of ash in most of the residential palaces excavated in the so-called Noblemen's Quarters (NMQ) sector of the site. See C.S. Patil, 'Palace Architecture at Vijayanagara', in *Vijayanagara, Progress of Research, 1983–84*, eds M.S. Nagaraja Rao and George Michell (Mysore: Directorate of Archaeology and Museums, 1985), 119–32. An important exception to this general pattern is seen in the baths, pavilions, and other buildings constructed in the 'Vijayanagara Courtly Style', which typically used stone masonry throughout.

49. See Fritz, Michell, and Nagaraja Rao, *Where Kings and Gods Meet*, 124ff., and figure 7.2. This square water pavilion (XX/1) is the dominant structure in enclosure XX of the Royal Centre. Based on the style of its carved stucco ornament, Helen Philon has suggested a date of c. 1500 for this structure. See Helen Philon, 'Plaster Decoration on Sultanate-styled Courtly Buildings', in *New Light on Hampi*, eds John M. Fritz and George Michell, photographs by Clare Arni (Mumbai: Marg Publications, 2001), 85–7.

50. See Patil, 'Palace Architecture at Vijayanagara'.

51. For the 'Hundred-Columned Hall' and its relationship to the courtyard to its north (IIIa), see Fritz, Michell, and Nagaraja Rao, *Where Kings and Gods Meet*, 20–3 and 102–3.

52. This monumental stone staircase recalls the one leading to the (now vanished) upper storey of the 'Hundred-Columned Hall' at Vijayanagara; see previous note for references.

53. In fact the northern side also had three pavilions—a pair over the gatehouse, located off-centre to the east, and a third over the short arcade segment of two bays extending to the west. But because of the asymmetrical arrangement of this façade, there is no axially marked 'central' pavilion on this side.

54. Only the central pavilion above this gatehouse has three arches. All the other pavilions would have had only two arches, as is clearly implied by their having been supported on three brackets, instead of four as in the central western pavilion.

55. In the first half of this passage, Krishna Raya is equated with Vishnu in his man-lion incarnation (Narasimha avatar); in the second, he is equated with Vishnu in the form he took to liberate an elephant king (Kariraja-varada). The verse is quoted in the *Rāyavācakamu*, where it is ascribed to the celebrated poet Mukku Timmayya. See Wagoner, *Tidings of the King*, 141.

56. Parts of this section draw on Richard M. Eaton, '"Kiss My Foot," Said the King: Firearms, Diplomacy, and the Battle for Raichur', *Modern Asian Studies* 42, no. 1 (2009), 289–313.

57. Sewell, *Forgotten Empire*, 330.

58. Ibid., 331.

59. Ibid.

60. Ibid., 332.

61. Ibid., 332–5.

62. Ibid., 336.

63. In both Persianate and Sanskritic courtly culture, a political subordinate was expected to define himself by bringing his head in contact with his superior's foot, demonstrating that even the highest and purest part of the subordinate's body is still beneath the lowest and least pure part of his lord's. In the Sanskritic tradition, this act was often ritually performed by the servant prostrating himself and placing his lord's foot on his head, an act vividly described by poets. In Kalidasa's *Raghuvamsa*, for example, Prince Aja is said to have placed his left foot on the heads of other kings (VII, 70); King Dasaratha's feet were touched by the heads of hundreds of kings, and the rays emitted by the diamonds in their crowns were brightened by the red lustre of the king's red toenails (IX, 13); Rama, when he is about to be banished to the forest, agrees to his brother Bharata's request to leave behind a pair of his wooden slippers—in essence, surrogate feet—which his brother can continue to honour in his absence as the 'presiding-deity' (*rājyādhidevata*) of the kingdom (XII, 17). Such poetic conceits remained common even into the medieval and early modern periods. As we saw in Chapter 3, Vijnaneshvara described the feet

of his patron Chalukya Vikramaditya VI as 'aglow with rays of light from gems on the crowns of bowing kings' (*Mitākṣarā* colophon, verse 6; translation ours). In the mid-sixteenth century, the Telugu poet Bhattu Murti credited Rama Raya's brother Venkatadri with defeating the `Adil Shahi sultan and making him sue for peace by prostrating himself and touching Venkatadri's feet with his head (*tala-dat-pādamu dālce*). See *The Raghuvamsa of Kalidasa, with the Commentary of Mallinatha*, ed. Gopal Raghunath Nandargikar (5th edn, Delhi: Motilal Banarsidass, 1982); and *Narasabhūpālīyamu*, excerpted in S. Krishnaswami Ayyangar, *Sources of Vijayanagar History* (Madras: University of Madras,1919), no. 69, 224–7.

64. This is the testimony of local residents. Broken pieces of the minarets can still be found lying on the ground. Tombs in the mosque's courtyard were also desecrated.

65. In their 1990 book *Hindu Temples: What Happened to Them?* Arun Shourie and Sita Ram Goel mistakenly included the Adoni mosque as an instance of temple destruction by Muslims. Arun Shourie and Sita Ram Goel, *Hindu Temples: What Happened to Them?* (New Delhi: Voice of India, 1990), 85.

66. B.D. Verma, *The Glories of Bijapur: A History of Its Remains* (India[?], 1964), 82–3.

67. A year later, in 1551, `Adil Shahi authorities in Raichur built the city's fourth city gate, the Khandaq Darwaza, which pierced the city's southern wall. However, although this gate faced the Vijayanagara capital and may well have made a political statement, as had the Kati Darwaza, we know nothing of its iconographic or epigraphic programme since it is at present mostly submerged under water. *EIAPS 1963*, 64–5, pl. XIX(c).

# Conclusion

Central to this book's analytical framework is its distinction between the Deccan's secondary and primary centres. Metaphorically speaking, these two kinds of sites are the study's sheep and wolves—the former being the prizes so fiercely contested by the latter. Indeed, a good deal of Deccani history in our period was driven by struggles over the control of secondary centres.

This study makes three principal claims regarding the roles played by these centres. The first has to do with the *nature* of the contestations over them. These break down into two analytically distinct types: (1) struggles over their physical possession, and (2) attempts to appropriate their remembered legacies. The map in Figure 7.21 (p. 274) shows that many secondary centres, especially those lying along the plateau's volatile internal political frontiers, were successfully besieged and transferred to the sovereign control of a rival primary centre. Here the goal was simply territorial gain. In other cases, however, it was control over the *legacy* of certain centres that mattered, and not necessarily physical control of the site itself. We have seen that the ancient Chalukya capital of Kalyana, still saturated with memories of former splendour five centuries after its eclipse, became an enduring preoccupation for members of Vijayanagara's Aravidu dynasty. It was a special obsession for Rama Raya, owing to that ruler's tenuous claims to legitimate authority at Vijayanagara and his consequent desire to associate himself and his family with the Chalukya imperial legacy. Other cases in this study illustrate both types of control simultaneously. Around 1504 Shitab Khan seized physical control of Warangal from Bahmani authorities and promptly established himself as a petty 'king' over a good deal of the eastern plateau. To this end he took unusual measures to associate himself with the legacy of the Kakatiya dynasty of kings who had ruled from Warangal nearly two centuries earlier.

A primary centre might appropriate the legacy of a former dynasty in any of several ways. One of these was to build its own monument around an existing iconic structure, as when Sultan Ibrahim `Adil Shah II incorporated an in situ Chalukya temple into his royal palace at Kalyana. Another was to reproduce the conceptual design of a former capital in a new city of one's own. In 1591 Golconda's Sultan Muhammad Quli Qutb Shah did this when he mapped the plan of the former Kakatiya capital of Warangal onto Hyderabad, his own new capital. Most typically, however, iconic fragments of sites associated with a former ruling dynasty were simply relocated to one of the Deccan's great primary centres. This occurred when sovereigns at both Vijayanagara and Bijapur systematically recovered building components from Chalukya architectural monuments and reassembled them in the hearts of their respective capitals. Columns of the Chalukya period, whether carved in the Dharwar or the metropolitan style, were especially favoured for this purpose. Being iconic tokens of former imperial power that were standardized in form, numerous in quantity, and nearly ubiquitous throughout the plateau, such columns were immediately recognizable as belonging to the Chalukya period, and hence capable of conveying a broad constellation of meanings associated with that dynasty's remembered grandeur. The repositioning of these columns some five centuries after the Chalukya collapse compares with the actions of emperor Charlemagne (r. 800–14) who, with a view to associating himself and his kingdom with ancient Rome five centuries after that empire's demise, removed Roman columns from Italy to his capital in Aix-la-Chapelle (or Aachen), in northern Europe.

A second major finding of this study pertains to the *outcomes* of contestations over secondary centres. As various primary centres jockeyed for position on the plateau's political chessboard, the territorial outcomes of their struggles usually proved to be of only temporary significance. Even when a primary centre succeeded in wresting control of a secondary centre from the grip of another primary centre, the advantage seldom tipped the Deccan's overall balance of power. However, one outcome of these conflicts that did make a difference, and a very significant one, was in the area of munitions technology and military architecture. In 1520 Bijapur's Isma`il `Adil Khan was defeated both on the battlefield and at Raichur fort, temporarily resolving the balance of power in the long-contested Raichur Doab. Vijayanagara and its famous king Krishna Raya had triumphed in these engagements by using the conventional military technologies of the day: heavy cavalry on the field and infantry sappers in siege. By contrast, Isma`il deployed some 400 heavy cannons on the field, but he lost the pitched battle. He also used several hundred heavy and light cannons defending Raichur fort, which his commanders nonetheless surrendered. Krishna Raya evidently concluded from these decisive victories that firearms were of little practical use. His successors did the same, and for the next half century Vijayanagara's rulers smugly continued to rely on conventional military technologies, to their own ultimate cost.

By contrast, Bijapur's rulers responded to their defeat at Raichur by expanding and improving the gunpowder technology that both they and their predecessors, the Bahmani sultans, had already pioneered at Goa. The result was a phenomenal spurt in munitions innovation, both in the evolution of cannons and their mounting systems, and in the design and construction of new bastions and gun platforms. These developments had far-reaching consequences. First, while military innovation in Vijayanagara stagnated, sultanates of the northern Deccan recruited Ottoman technological expertise and developed a new generation of field cannons, leading to the decisive Battle of Talikota in which Vijayanagara's army was routed and its great capital plundered. Second, from the mid-sixteenth century onwards, the development of higher and stronger bastions with improved gun-mounts rendered the capture of secondary centres in the northern Deccan increasingly difficult, and hence uncommon, which significantly stabilized the Deccan's internal political frontiers.

The third major finding of this study pertains to the insignificant role played by religion in struggles over secondary centres, or even between primary centres. This would challenge conventional characterizations of pre-modern Indian history as largely a narrative of two religious communities, Hindus and Muslims, construed as timeless, monolithic, and more often than not, mutually opposed. This also requires us to rethink conventional understandings of the Deccan's religious geography. Writing in the early 1600s, the Bijapur-based historian Firishta conceived of the Deccan not in religious terms, but as that part of the Indian peninsula that embraced native speakers of Marathi, Telugu, and Kannada—that is, a region corresponding roughly to modern Maharashtra, Andhra Pradesh, and Karnataka.[1] Yet in modern scholarship this region is conventionally understood to have been sharply divided in the pre-modern era between a 'Muslim' zone north of the Krishna River, and a 'Hindu' zone to its south, with that river serving as a kind of civilizational 'Maginot Line'. In part, this image is a legacy of the historian Robert Sewell who, writing in 1900, first brought the history of Vijayanagara to the attention of the reading public, and who described that state as a 'Hindu bulwark against Muhammadan conquests'.[2] Additionally, when UNESCO designated metropolitan Vijayanagara a World Heritage site in 1986, much scholarly attention (and funding) became focussed on that city's rich archaeological record. This, in turn, inclined scholars to view the kingdom of Vijayanagara—whose northern border ran along the Krishna River—in isolation from the plateau's northern half. Our own preference is for Firishta's more inclusive notion of the Deccan, a region this study has shown to have been an intercommunicating, multicultural zone that was hardly frozen along religious lines.

We first encountered evidence challenging notions of a religiously polarized plateau in the treatment of pre-existing Hindu temples during or shortly after the Delhi Sultanate's conquest of the region. Crucially, commanders or administrators in Delhi's imperial service did not position themselves in opposition to local religious institutions. Indeed, the hundreds of apolitical Hindu temples that lay in the path of advancing armies—whether large or small—were generally ignored, or even actively patronized. Sultan Muhammad bin Tughluq's repair of a Shiva temple in Kalyana in 1326, with a view to restoring that institution for normal worship, suggests that the Tughluqs' provincial government quickly assumed a position of proprietary responsibility for those already-existing temples that lay within its sovereign jurisdiction. What that government did oppose, however, and oppose vehemently, was resistance to its rule. Any temple patronized by an active opponent of the regime was either desecrated so as to render it ritually unusable, or it was demolished, its structural components often recycled in new edifices. But such practices did not mark any fundamental or permanent 'Hindu–Muslim divide'. In fact, they reflected traditional Indian practice. The *Mānosollāsa*, a twelfth-century Chalukya text attributed to Maharaja Someshvara III himself, plainly recommended that a conquering king should destroy his enemy's royal temple.[3]

In the mid-fourteenth century, the Delhi Sultanate's colonial rule in the Deccan was overthrown and followed by two successor states, Vijayanagara and the Bahmani Sultanate. But we would reject 'textbook' and popular perceptions of the Deccan that depict these states as exclusively Hindu and Muslim entities. To be sure, the two states grew from very different religious origins. Vijayanagara, having grafted itself onto a popular Shiva cult by the banks of the Tungabhadra River, adopted a form of Shiva as its cosmic overlord, while the Bahmani state availed itself of spiritually powerful Sufi shaikhs who acted as the state's spiritual midwives and guarantors. But by the sixteenth century such religious differences had become significantly attenuated, as is reflected in, among other things, the two states' patronage of public architecture. Rather than making public statements about religion, state-sponsored building projects placed in strategic locations in both Vijayanagara and Bijapur betrayed efforts on both sides of the Krishna River to claim an association with the long-defunct but still-remembered Chalukya empire.

Something of this sort was also happening in the sixteenth-century eastern Deccan. When he seized Warangal from its Bahmani overlords around 1504, Shitab Khan directed most of his propagandistic efforts toward evoking the memory of that city's former ruling dynasty, the Kakatiyas. Two of the three cults he revived were specifically identified with that kingdom—the goddess Kakati, from whom the Kakatiyas took their name, and Svayambhu Shiva, the kingdom's cosmic overlord. To house the icon of the third deity, Panchaliraya, Shitab Khan built a new temple confected entirely from material belonging to the Kakatiya period. Although the icons and temples that Shitab Khan patronized were all Hindu, their specific association with the Kakatiya kings endowed his actions with an overtly political aim, namely, of appealing to the memory of a locally revered ruling dynasty. Similarly, in 1591 when Sultan Muhammad Quli Qutb Shah of Golconda patterned his new city of Hyderabad on the plan of Warangal, he was hardly appealing to religious sentiments. Rather, applying Warangal's conceptual layout to that of Hyderabad would have seemed perfectly natural to a culturally mixed governing class that, by the end of the sixteenth century, had become thoroughly steeped in the language, poetry, and aesthetics of the Telugu-speaking eastern plateau. Modern characterizations of Hyderabad as an originally 'Muslim city', whatever that might mean, are simply misplaced.

The attenuation of religion in the Deccan Plateau was actually one dimension of a deeper trend in the region's cultural history, which saw a gradual merging of the Sanskrit and Persian cosmopolises—a process that grew increasingly apparent between the fourteenth and sixteenth centuries. Before they first encountered one another in the Deccan in the fourteenth century, the two cosmopolises had remained distinct, stemming as they did from different literary traditions. But by the sixteenth century their mutual intermingling had proceeded to a remarkable degree, especially in courtly contexts. The image of Krishna Raya in the frieze that runs along the cornice of Raichur's Naurangi Darwaza reveals precisely this process. Even while a contextual reading of that frieze identifies the king with the divine hero of the *Rāmāyaṇa*, Krishna Raya is also depicted wearing a tall, conical headgear made of brocaded fabric known as a *kuḷḷāyi* in Telugu. That term had been assimilated into the Telugu language from the Persian *kulāh*, which denoted a type of prestigious headgear that had already diffused throughout the Persian-speaking world in the early modern period. In this single image, then, a sixteenth-century Deccani monarch can be understood as drawing simultaneously from two discourses of power and civilization. Other individuals also drew on one or the other discourse, or both simultaneously, depending on the context. In the eastern Deccan, the ambitious chieftain who had begun life as Sitapati adopted the Persianized title Shitab Khan when in service of the Bahmani court at Bidar. When in rebellion against his overlords, rather than reclaiming his original name, he Sanskritized his

Persian title to Sitapa Khana. By the sixteenth century, such hybridization took many forms across the plateau. In Vijayanagara, Persianate domes and vaulted arches were built into many of the principal buildings of the capital city's Royal Centre. In Bijapur, Sultan Ibrahim `Adil Shah incorporated a forest of Chalukya-period columns into the primary gateway of his citadel, while his successor, Sultan `Ali `Adil Shah, drew equally from Indic and Persianate notions of astrology, cosmology, and mythology in his esoteric literary composition, the *Nujūm al-`ulūm*.

Finally, throughout this study we have seen how political figures manipulated the built environment, which then took on new functions or projected new meanings in accordance with changing political circumstances. We have seen, for example, how a Hindu chieftain of Bodhan responded to the Tughluq conquest by converting to Islam and transforming a former Kakatiya temple into a mosque. Through such means as placing a profusion of domes over its front hall, he not only redefined the building's ritual space but also affirmed his allegiance to the Tughluqs. In similar fashion, but two centuries later, we saw how Sultan Ibrahim `Adil Shah, seeking to identify his reign with local history, installed in the principal gateway to Bijapur's citadel an antique Chalukya inscription that had authorized the construction of a temple in the same city some four and a half centuries before. Or again, we saw how the ambitious strongman Rama Raya, having usurped power from the legitimate king of Vijayanagara, endeavoured to compensate for his lack of legitimacy by claiming ties to the Chalukya house. Architecturally, he did this by constructing a neo-Chalukya Bhuvaneshvari shrine in the heart of the capital's Sacred Centre and by importing a Chalukya stepped tank into the heart of the city's Royal Centre. In a similar idiom, but for different reasons, Sultan Ibrahim `Adil Shah II incorporated the sanctum of a Chalukya temple into the palace complex that he had built atop Kalyana fort in 1592–93. Further examples could be adduced, as when Krishna Raya seized Raichur in 1520 and stamped his authority over the city by remodelling its principal gateway and erasing its original Bahmani features; or conversely, when `Ali `Adil Shah marked his conquest of Adoni fort by obscuring the original Vijayanagara features of a small mosque in the fort and stamping it instead with the distinctive signature of metropolitan Bijapur.

Although such manipulations of the Deccan's built landscape were especially evident in the turbulent sixteenth century, they hardly ceased with the close of that century. The Mughal and British dispensations, in turn, saw their own interventions, which were in many respects comparable to those of the sixteenth century. It is only in recent decades that one sees a new and very different pattern in the interplay of power, memory, and architecture. The liberalization of India's economy since the 1990s not only opened the country to increased foreign capital and tourism, it also increased the disposable income of the country's growing middle class, enlarging domestic tourism as well. Seizing on new opportunities afforded by this growing industry, government agencies charged with preserving archaeological sites increasingly partnered with those responsible for promoting tourism. As a result, prominent archaeological sites were increasingly presented in ways designed to attract more visitors, thereby accommodating India's growing consumer economy.

Warangal fort provides a poignant illustration of this trend. To attract tourists to the site of the former Kakatiya capital, the Hyderabad Circle of the Archaeological Survey of India has re-arranged surviving fragments of the fort's demolished temple in ways that it imagines might be pleasing to tourists (Figure C.1). Elaborately sculpted triangular slabs, originally intended to span the corners of square ceiling bays, have been reoriented vertically and set atop pairs of columns to show off their figural sculptures. Now appearing as friezes composed within a triangular pediment, these reinterpreted slabs suggest the 'classical' status of Kakatiya sculptures.

Meanwhile, the Kakatiya Urban Development Authority, or KUDA, as Warangal's primary urban development agency is known, has constructed a small children's park nearby, which includes among other attractions a children's train with coaches in the form of geese (Figure C.2).[4] Directly visible from this park is one of the four magnificent ceremonial gateways (*toraṇa)* that had once led to the great temple dedicated to Svayambhu Shiva, the Kakatiyas' state-deity. Although Tughluq invaders had demolished the temple in 1323, they had spared the four gateways, using them to frame the mosque and palace that formed the centre of their provincial government. Being the most widely recognized emblem of the Kakatiya dynasty, the gateways now serve as the centrepieces of what has become, in effect, a Kakatiya theme park.

By a remarkable coincidence, however, the goose carriages in the adjacent amusement park resonate playfully with the forms of the geese (*hamsa*) atop the arms of the nearby Kakatiya gateways, one of which can be seen silhouetted against the horizon in Figure C.2.[5] To the Kakatiyas, the geese on the toraṇas had symbolized water, fertility, and an agrarian-based prosperity. To the site's new government patrons, however, and to the promoters of a more globalized and commercialized India, the geese of the children's train—with their uncanny resemblance to Walt Disney's Donald Duck—symbolize a more profit-oriented sort of prosperity, something quite distant from what the Kakatiyas could possibly have imagined. The juxtaposition of these two versions of the same waterfowl, coming from such distant worlds of meaning, suggests that we are now witnessing a new and very different pattern in the interplay of power, memory, and architecture. That, however, is another story.

## NOTES

1. Firishta, *Tārīkh-i Firishta*, 2 vols (Lucknow, 1864–65), I:10.
2. Robert Sewell, *A Forgotten Empire, Vijayanagara: A Contribution to the History of India* (1900; repr. New Delhi: Publications Division, 1962), 1.
3. P. Arundhati, *Royal Life in Manosollasa* (Delhi: Sundeep Prakashan, 1994), 66.
4. See 'KUDA plans mega projects', *The Hindu*, Thursday, 12 October 2006, online edition. Available at http://www.hindu.com/2006/10/12/stories/2006101201530200.htm.
5. The gateway's right arm had originally borne the sculpture of a second *hamsa*, but it is now missing. Vegetal scrollwork adorns both groups of geese. In the Kakatiya *toraṇa*, such scrollwork sprouts from the tail of the hamsa; in the train carriages it is confined to the surface of the breast and the wings.

**Figure C.1** Warangal Fort. Svayambhu Shiva temple site: the ASI's sculpture garden.

**Figure C.2** Warangal Fort. Train with goose carriages in the KUDA children's park.

APPENDIX 1

# Notes on Method

## PRELIMINARY CONSIDERATIONS AND SPATIAL RESEARCH METHODS

Three immediate tasks were required before we could pursue our larger goal of elucidating the political roles played by the Deccan's secondary centres. First, in order to gain a clearer understanding of how secondary urban centres functioned in the sixteenth-century Deccan, we wanted to discern the specific political and economic roles they played, and learn how they were connected with both higher-order cities and lower-level towns and villages. Second, to situate our three main study sites in a larger perspective, we recognized the value of identifying and examining as many other secondary centres as possible. Third, given our interest in frontiers, we needed to develop a typology of inter-state boundaries, both to distinguish between more fixed 'borders' and less sharply defined frontier zones, and to determine where exactly the different kinds of boundaries lay. We address each of these points in turn.

*Secondary centres and their functions*: We understand secondary centres as sites that are intermediate, both in size and in number, between the handful of densely populated primary cities and the innumerable small agricultural villages and hamlets that dot the countryside. Secondary centres mediated economically, socially, and politically between the villages within their hinterlands and the capital cities to which they were subordinate. According to an important study by Hiroshi Fukazawa, the `Adil Shahi Sultanate was divided into three different types of administrative divisions: *mu`āmala*, *qal`a*, and *pargana*.[1] Fukazawa saw the first two as variants of 'crown lands' entrusted to Persian-speaking administrators—called *ḥavāldārs*—who were directly appointed by the sultan. Parganas, by contrast, were administered by a largely hereditary class of Marathi- and Kannada-speaking officers—*desāīs*, *deshmukhs*, *kulkarnīs*, and so on—who represented a pre-sultanate tradition of revenue administration. Fukazawa based his analysis on some 360 administrative documents that had survived from the `Adil Shahi period, the vast majority of which date from the seventeenth century. Since only twenty-four of those records date to the latter half of the sixteenth century, and none earlier, Fukazawa himself realized that there was insufficient evidence for reconstructing administrative institutions and arrangements in their formative phase.[2]

Although few paper records from the sixteenth century survive, there does exist another body of contemporary evidence that can shed considerable light on the sultanates' administrative structure in the earlier periods. This is the rich corpus of historical inscriptions, mostly in Persian, that were carved into stone stelae and fitted into various urban buildings. A systematic review of this epigraphic corpus—greatly aided by the two well-indexed topographic lists of inscriptions prepared by Z.A. Desai[3]—yields a number of suggestive findings. First, sixteenth-century inscriptions refer to only one local administrative unit, the mu`āmala, roughly equivalent to 'district'.[4] With one or two minor exceptions, most mu`āmalas appear to have consisted of a fortified secondary urban centre and the villages within its surrounding territory. Accordingly, the mu`āmala is generally named after the city or fort at its heart. Examples from the sixteenth century include the mu`āmala of Raichur (first mentioned in 1498), and the mu`āmalas of Kondapalli (1524–25), Bijapur (1550), Nusratabad (that is, Sagar, 1561–62), Velha Goa (1570–71), Sholapur (1578–79), and Kalyana (1580).

Second, in sixteenth-century inscriptions the officer in charge of a mu`āmala was never referred to by the term 'ḥavāldār' (literally, 'holder of a position of trust');[5] rather, the term for such an officer is generally nā'ib-i ghaibat, literally, a 'deputy in [the sultan's] absence'. This difference in terminology suggests a more patrimonial quality to the administrative arrangements than was the case in the seventeenth century, by which time the bureaucratic element had become more pronounced. The term nā'ib-i ghaibat is associated with mu`āmala in Bijapur, Velha Goa, Sholapur, and Kalyana.[6] The fact that one inscription names a certain Dabit Khan as the nā'ib-i ghaibat at Sholapur[7] while two others identify him as nā'ib-i ghaibat of the mu`āmala of Sholapur[8] suggests that a nā'ib-i ghaibat was the governor of both the city and the district it controlled. Other inscriptions speak of the nā'ib-i ghaibat of the city of Gulbarga[9] and of the forts of Yadgir[10] and Mudgal.[11]

Third, many inscriptions mention that their cities were fortified, referring to the 'citadel' (*ḥiṣār*) or 'fort' (*qal`a*), or recording the construction of bastions (*burj*) and other elements of fortification. These indicate the strategic importance of a mu`āmala as a military centre, something amply confirmed by the archaeological record. One apparent exception that proves the rule is the '*mu`āmala* of Nusratabad town (*qaṣba*)', as Sagar was then known. Though fortified with a mud wall in the early Bahmani period, the wall had apparently become breached and ineffective by the sixteenth century. Accordingly, in 1561–62 the governor Mir Muhammad constructed 'a fort (qal`a) and an auspicous town (*qaṣba-i mubārak*)' at the nearby site of Shahapur, evidently to serve the older town's defensive functions.[12]

Finally, mu`āmala centres were more than fortified strongholds. Inscriptions at two of them, Kalyana and Shahapur, distinguish between the ḥiṣār or qal`a—that is, the elevated citadel or fort—and the larger town below, designated as qaṣba. In both towns nā'ib-i ghaibats had constructed marketplaces (*peth, peint*) to promote the commercial livelihood of the town. It therefore seems likely that most secondary cities would have included a sizeable 'lower town', or qaṣba, to serve as the primary commercial centre for the surrounding district.

Occupants of the post of nā'ib-i ghaibat evidently held their districts as *iqṭā`*s, or military service tenures. Such districts were distributed to officers who collected their revenues, using a portion of them to maintain a stipulated number of troops that were available to the sultan on demand. Such officers were also expected to ensure the prosperity of their districts, maintain law and order, and uphold justice. Although the term iqṭā` is not found in sixteenth-century inscriptions, the iqṭā` system appears to have been in use in the Deccan at this time. For we know that fourteenth-century Tughluq officers in the Deccan referred to a holder of an iqṭā` as a *mālik al-sharq*,[13] and also that in the sixteenth-century Deccan the latter term was used interchangeably with nā'ib-i ghaibat.[14] It would therefore follow that a mu`āmala, the district that a nā'ib-i ghaibat governed, was understood in the sense of an iqṭā`, that is, a military service tenure. Moreover, sixteenth-century Deccani inscriptions represent the mālik al-sharq as carrying out certain actions that would not be possible unless he held iqṭā` rights. At Bijapur in 1320, and at Raichur in 1498, we find him alienating land revenue or commercial taxes within his district for charitable purposes.[15] And at Malliabad in 1513, and at Velha Goa in 1570–71, we find the mālik al-sharq introducing new economic policies that are decidedly to the advantage of their districts' inhabitants.[16]

We may conclude that secondary centres provided the key economic, social, and political links between the world of the agricultural village and that of the courtly élite in the capital. In effect, secondary urban centres functioned as administrative instruments for converting the productive surplus of the land into political and military power, both for the city's governor and for the crown, which explains their fortified nature. Not only did they have to provide secure storage for reserves of grain—granaries being one of the most common building types represented in their citadels—but they also had to serve as fortified garrisons for the troops maintained and fed by their governors. These garrisoned troops had two primary functions: to enforce the regular collection of revenue from the surrounding countryside, and to protect the centre from predatory rivals. Despite such precautions, contests for the control of productive secondary centres were very common, especially along the frontiers between neighbouring states. But even centres well within the territory of a given state were open to such contests when that state's central power was on the wane. This is how Yusuf `Adil Khan, the founder of the `Adil Shahi Sultanate, came to power at the end of the fifteenth century as the Bahmani state was collapsing. As Firishta notes, 'he wrested many forts from the governors of [the Bahmani Sultan] Mahmud Shah, and subdued all the country from the river Bhima to Bijapur, the inhabitants of which territory submitted to his authority…'[17] The implication is clear: the capture of secondary centres enabled control of the surrounding district, and control of the district enabled the submission of its inhabitants.

*Identifying and locating the secondary centres*: Given the importance of the plateau's secondary centres, it seemed worthwhile to compile a database of as many of them as possible. Firishta's comprehensive and detailed *Gulshan-i Ibrāhīmī* (or *Tārīkh-i Firishta*) appeared to be the ideal source for the construction of this database. Since neither the Persian text of Firishta nor Briggs's translation is indexed, we produced our own alphabetical toponym index listing all such places mentioned in the text. Under the name of each site, our annotations listed the page numbers of each reference to it, as well as a summary of the information conveyed and the date of the events described. Firishta's remarks generally relate to the details of sieges and battles relating to the control of the site in question. In this way, we produced a preliminary list of the names of over 100 fortified secondary cities that figured in Firishta's text.

A second step in this analysis was to determine the geographic locations of the various sites in order to incorporate them into a spatial database using Geographic Information Systems software (ArcGIS). This we did with the aid of a pre-existing GIS shapefile for populated places in contemporary South Asia.[18] As most of the places recorded in Firishta still preserve their sixteenth-century names, they were readily located by searching on these gazetteer shapefiles. In some instances, even though parts of the names had changed—for example, 'Ramgir' is today 'Ramgarh'—the resulting names were close enough to permit ready identification, especially when references to nearby sites offered further corroboration. For a handful of places, the names were completely different (for example, Firishta's 'Shahdurg' is today's 'Panhala'), requiring additional research to determine their location. Finally, there was a residuum of sites that still eluded our attempts to locate them with certainty—approximately 15 per cent of all the places mentioned in Firishta. Even so, we managed to identify and locate a total of ninety-six sites, enabling us to create a new GIS shapefile plotting each of the sites and providing associated data in the attribute table (see map in Figure A1.1). The latter included: site category (primary centre, secondary centre, seaport, and so on), the number of times Firishta mentioned the site, the number of times it was besieged, the number of times it changed hands; and the identity of the state that controlled it at even, ten-year intervals (1500, 1510, 1520, … 1600).

*Plotting interstate borders and analysing the nature of frontiers*: Using our data from Firishta, we next undertook to produce a new set of maps for our study area, with three particular aims. The first was to represent political boundaries more systematically than conventional maps, which tend to be impressionistic in rendering political boundaries and seldom indicate their sources. Second, in order to show the shifting nature of political boundaries, our maps are plotted at regular ten-year intervals throughout the course of the sixteenth century.[19] And third, our maps aim to distinguish between stable and unstable boundaries.

Having constructed a spatial database and developed an understanding of how fortified secondary centres functioned, we could then prepare our maps. First, using the GIS shapefile constructed from our toponym index, we generated a network of Thiessen polygons around the various fortified sites with a view to projecting visually the approximate area of influence that each site commanded—in other words, the area of the mu`āmala (see map in Figure A1.2). Thiessen polygons offer a generalized hypothetical model for predicting areas of political/military influence around each centre in a non-hierarchical network of sites. Since the sides of each polygon are equidistant from adjacent centres, the borders around any given site effectively define that area to which an army could march from its own centre and arrive before a force marching from an adjacent centre. As the Thiessen model assumes flat, even terrain and the absence of a hierarchy among sites—neither of which holds true for our case—the resulting polygons remain only an approximate model of a mu`āmala's actual area of control. In theory, we could have modified the polygons to take into account those geographic factors that might affect an army's speed of movement. But that would have required much more data than was at our disposal.

We made a series of eight separate maps, drawn at ten-year intervals, each showing the approximate territorial extent of each state at that moment (see maps in Figures A1.3–A1.10). Recalling Firishta's remark that control of a fort leads to control of its territory, we assumed that the territorial extent of each state would comprise the combined territories of all the forts under its control. Accordingly, we first displayed each map so that the marker symbols for the secondary centres varied by colour to indicate the particular states that controlled them at that moment. We then drew a subset of the Thiessen polygon lines to distinguish adjacent arrays of differently coloured markers from one another. Once connected, these lines indicated the approximate interstate boundaries separating the various states at that moment. The resulting maps are only approximations, of course, but as models of territorial extent, we believe that they are nonetheless far more accurate and objectively grounded than any offered in previous maps.[20] This is because our maps assume that a state's effective territorial control depends on its control of secondary urban centres. Our maps also attempt to capture the variability of boundaries over time by offering a series of momentary 'snapshots' taken at regular intervals.

Finally, we compiled the data from all eight of these maps to produce a composite map revealing three distinct types of territory in the sixteenth-century Deccan (Figure 7.21, p. 274). The light grey areas indicate stable cores that a given state consistently controlled throughout the sixteenth century. The darker grey areas indicate 'annexed territories'. In other words, having originally belonged to one state, they were at some point annexed by another and remained part of it for the duration of the period. Finally, the variously hatched areas indicate three different grades of 'unstable frontier zones'. These districts—together with the forts that dominated them—changed hands between states two, three, or even four times over the course of the sixteenth century.

An analysis of this final map revealed several important patterns. First, two qualitatively different kinds of boundaries appeared: the stable, and essentially linear borders that separated contiguous core areas, and the unstable, relatively broad zones that lay between highly contested secondary centres. Second, it revealed that two of our key study sites, Raichur and Kalyana, were contested not in isolation or solely for their own sake, but in the context of broader networks of contested sites in unstable or extremely unstable frontier zones. For example, the fate of Raichur was inextricably linked with that of

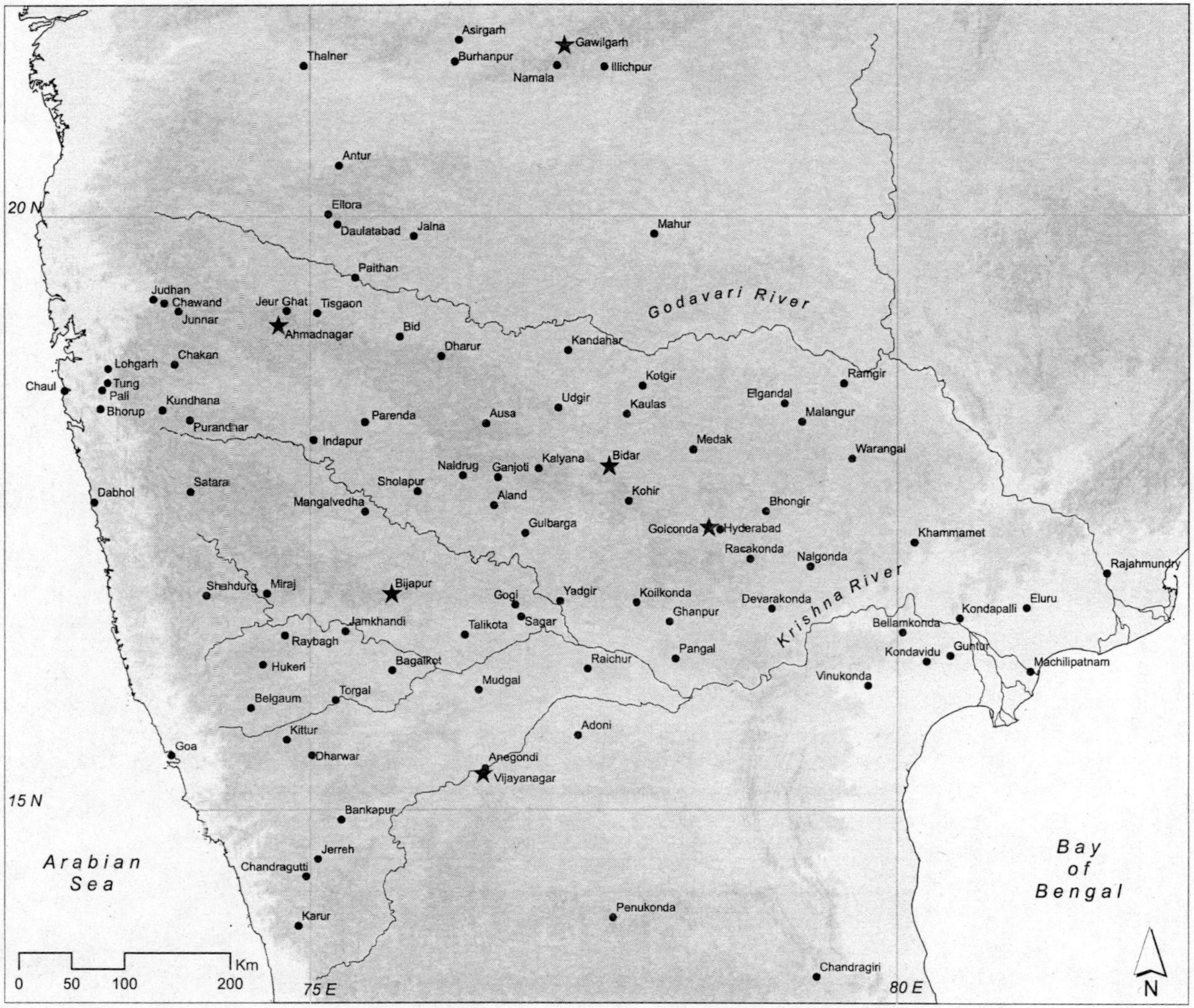


**Figure A1.1** Primary and secondary centres mentioned in Firishta.

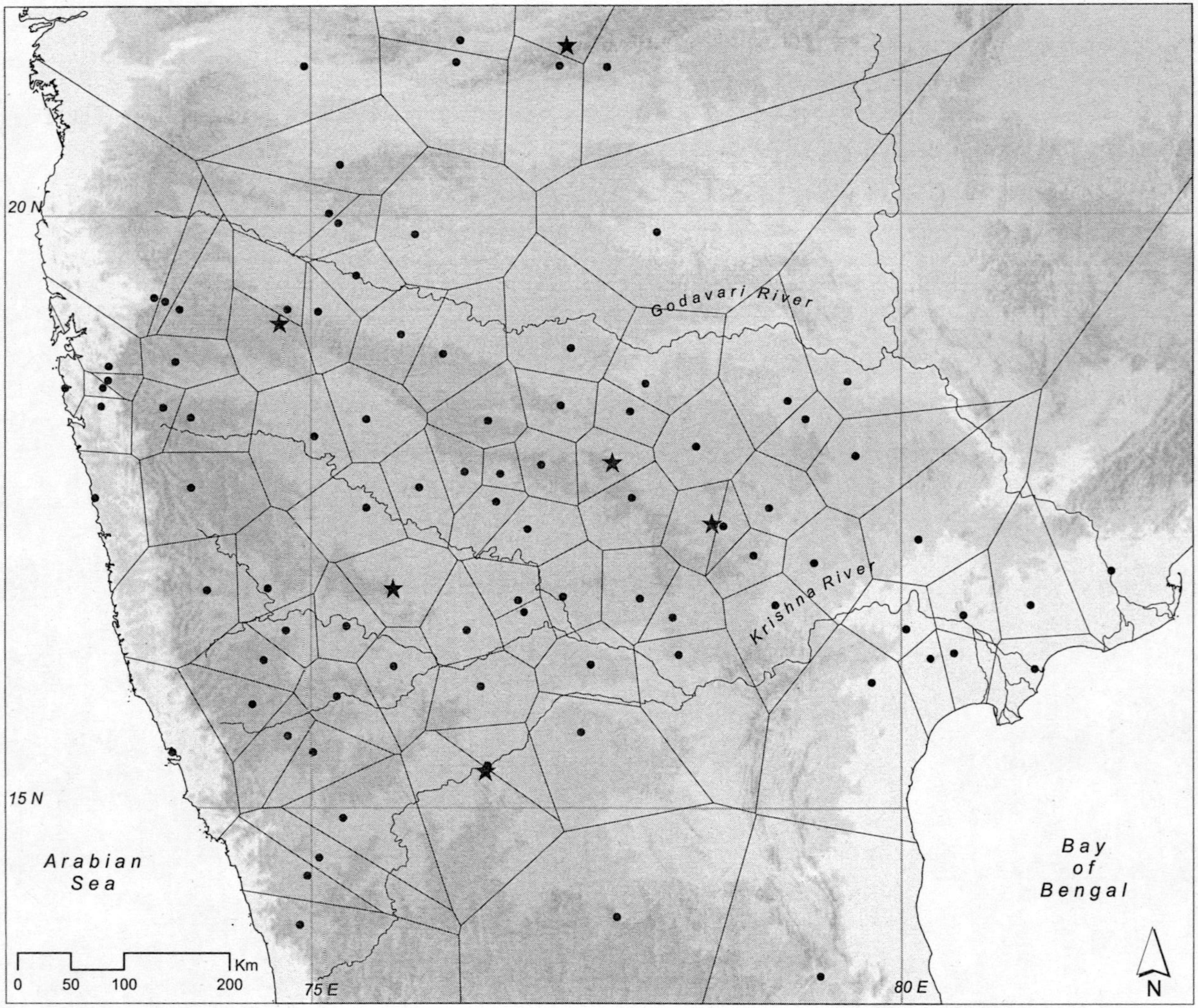


Figure A1.2 Thiessen polygons based on primary and secondary centres.

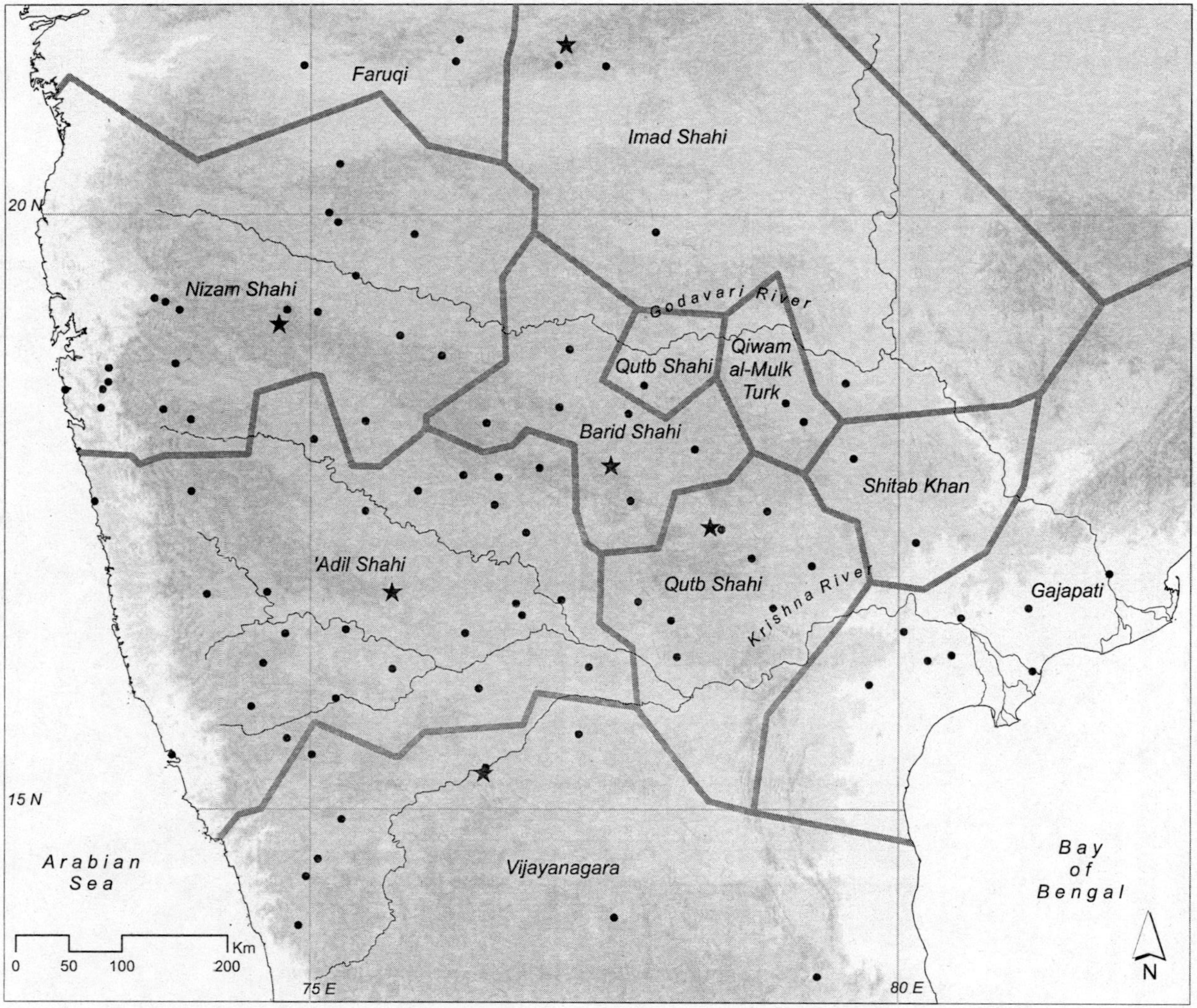


**Figure A1.3** Territorial boundaries of Deccan states: 1510.

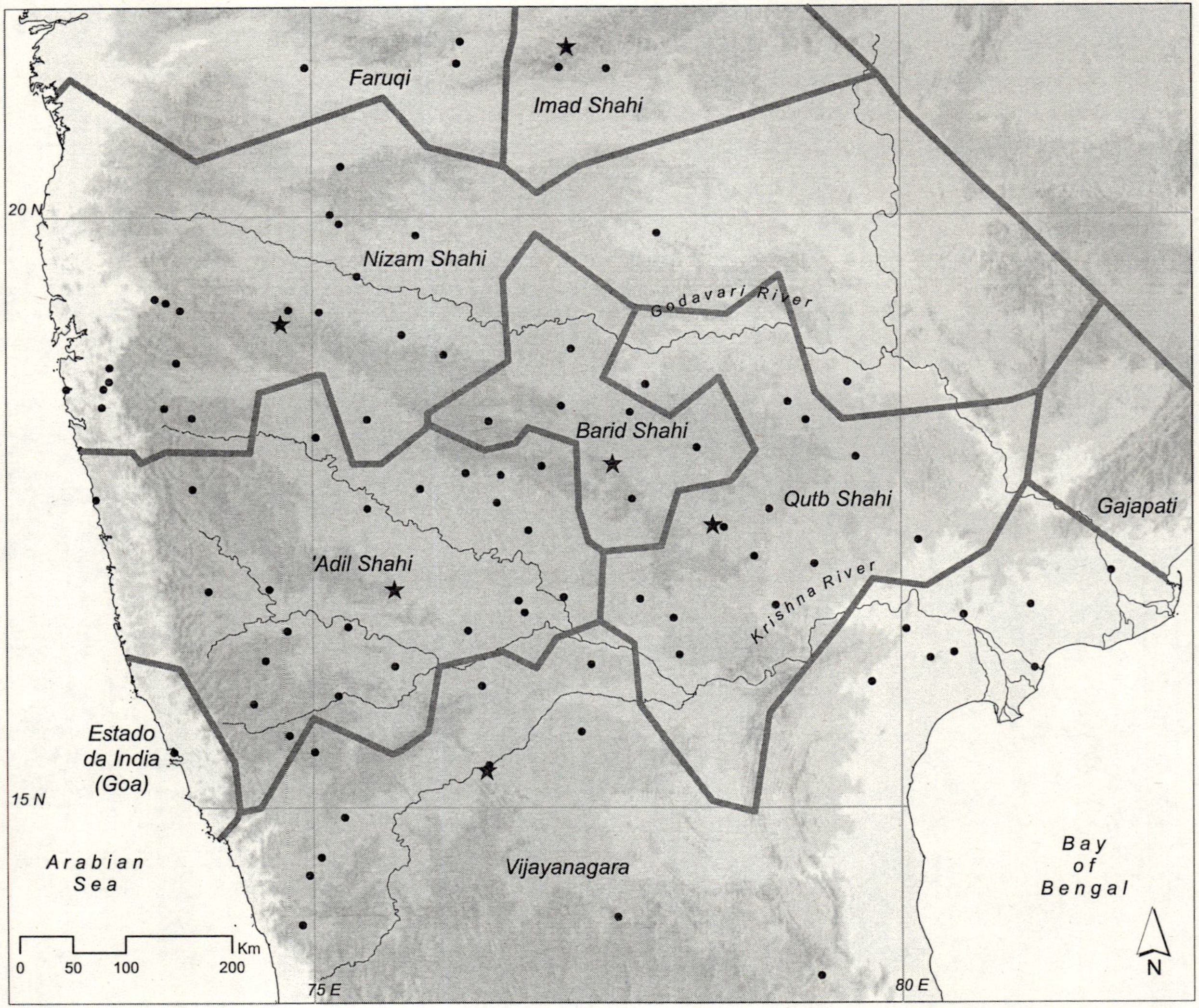


**Figure A1.4** Territorial boundaries of Deccan states: 1520.

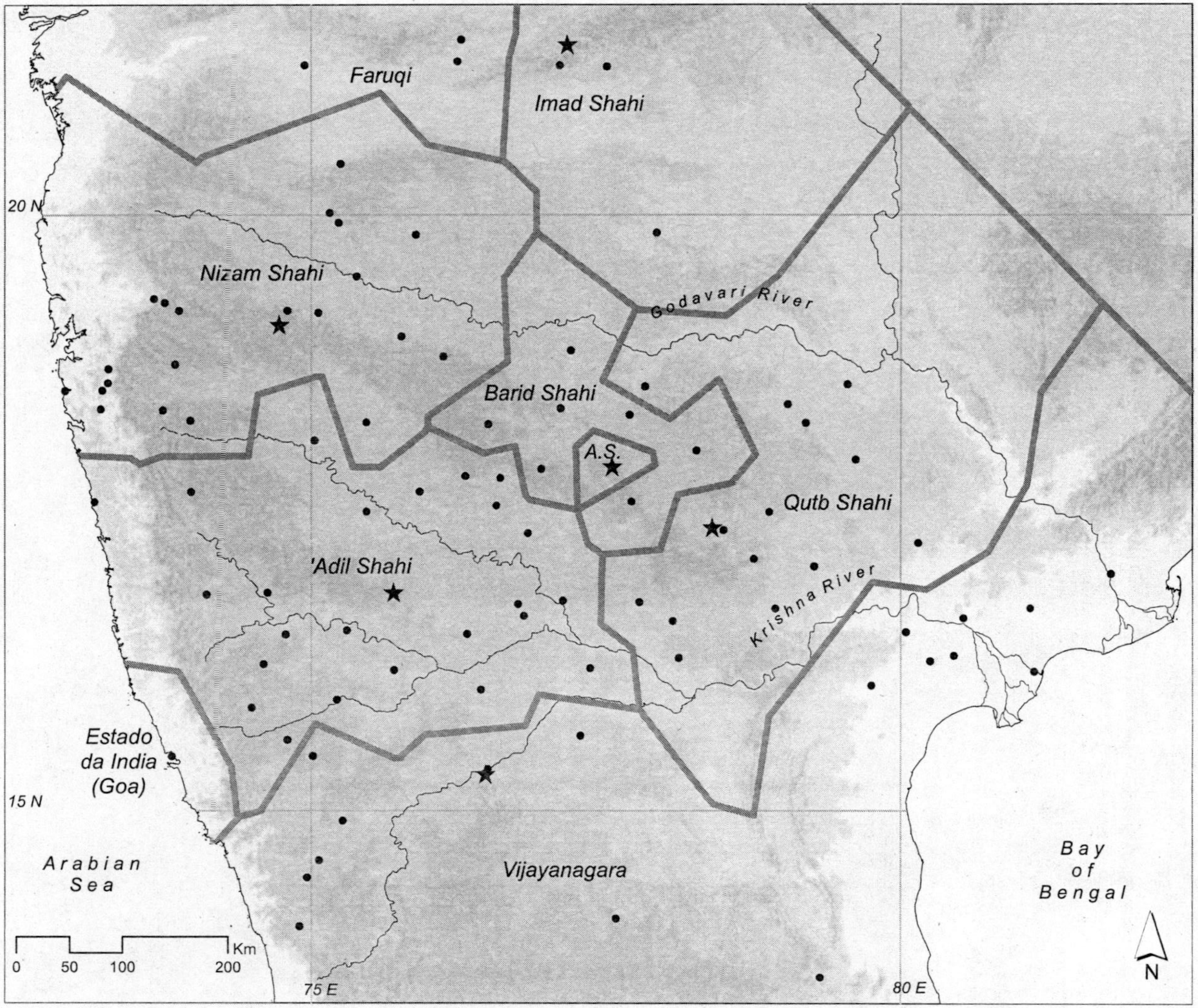


**Figure A1.5** Territo·ial boundaries of Deccan states: 1530.

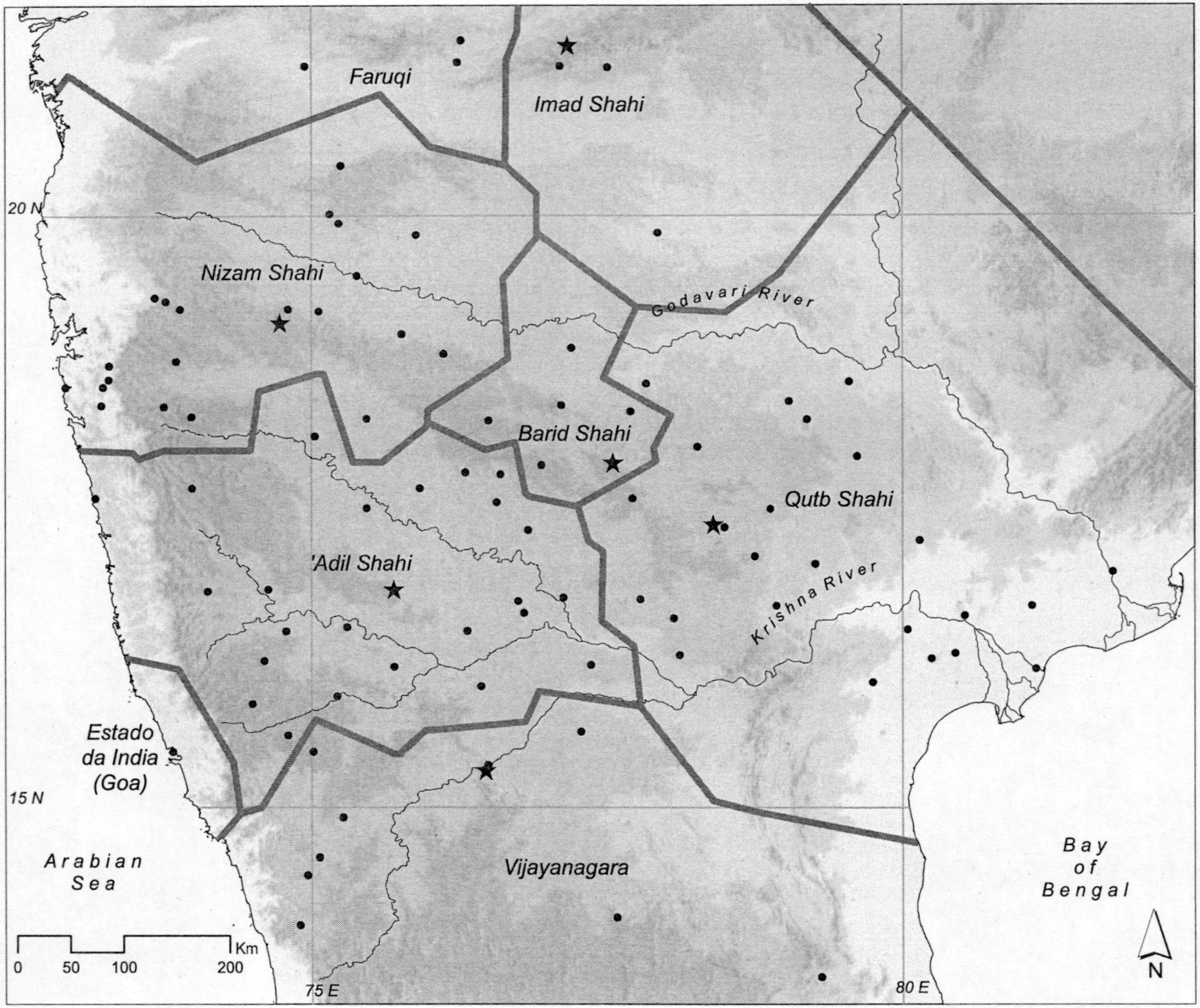


**Figure A1.6** Territorial boundaries of Deccan states: 1540.

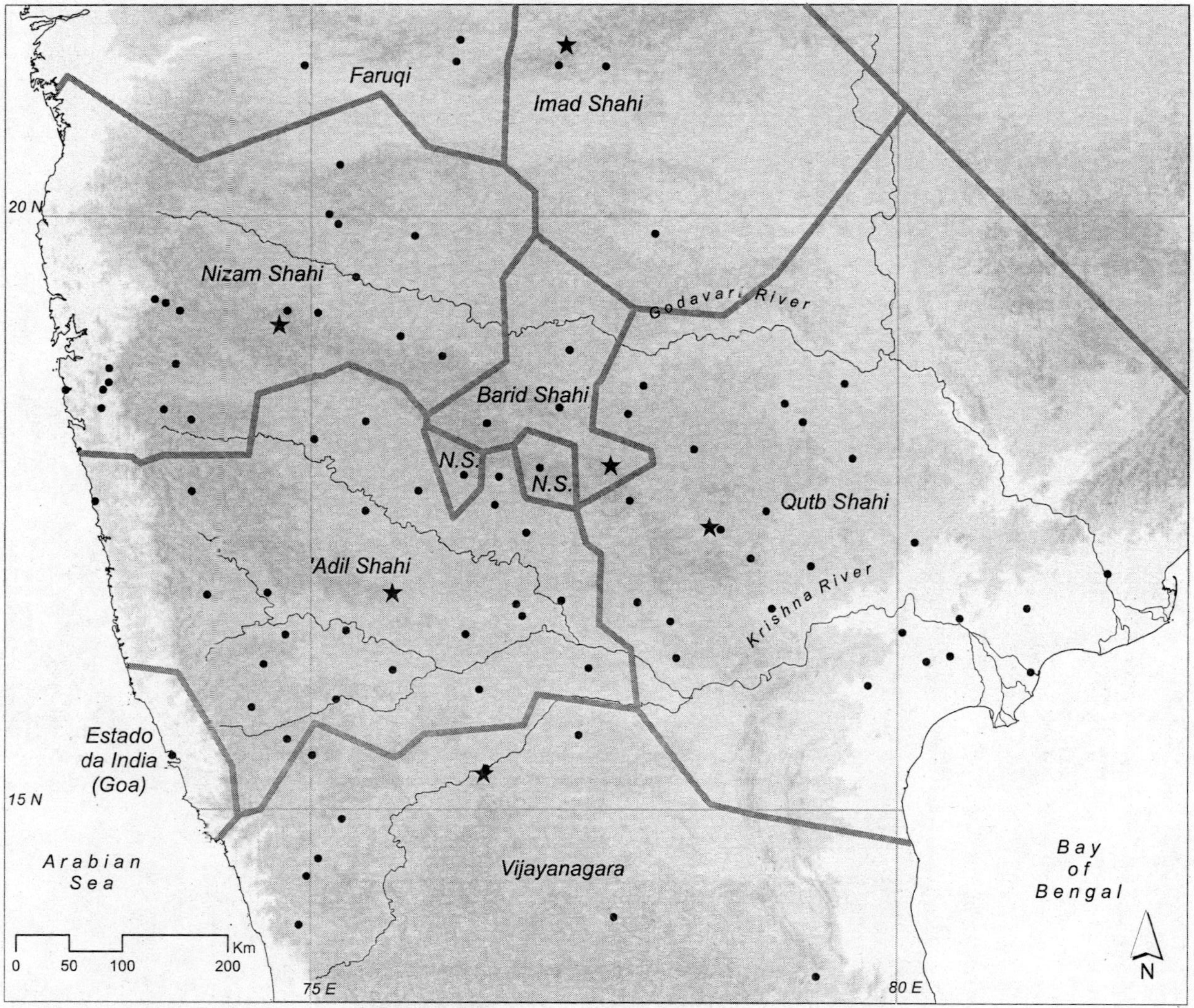


**Figure A1.7** Territorial boundaries of Deccan states: 1550.

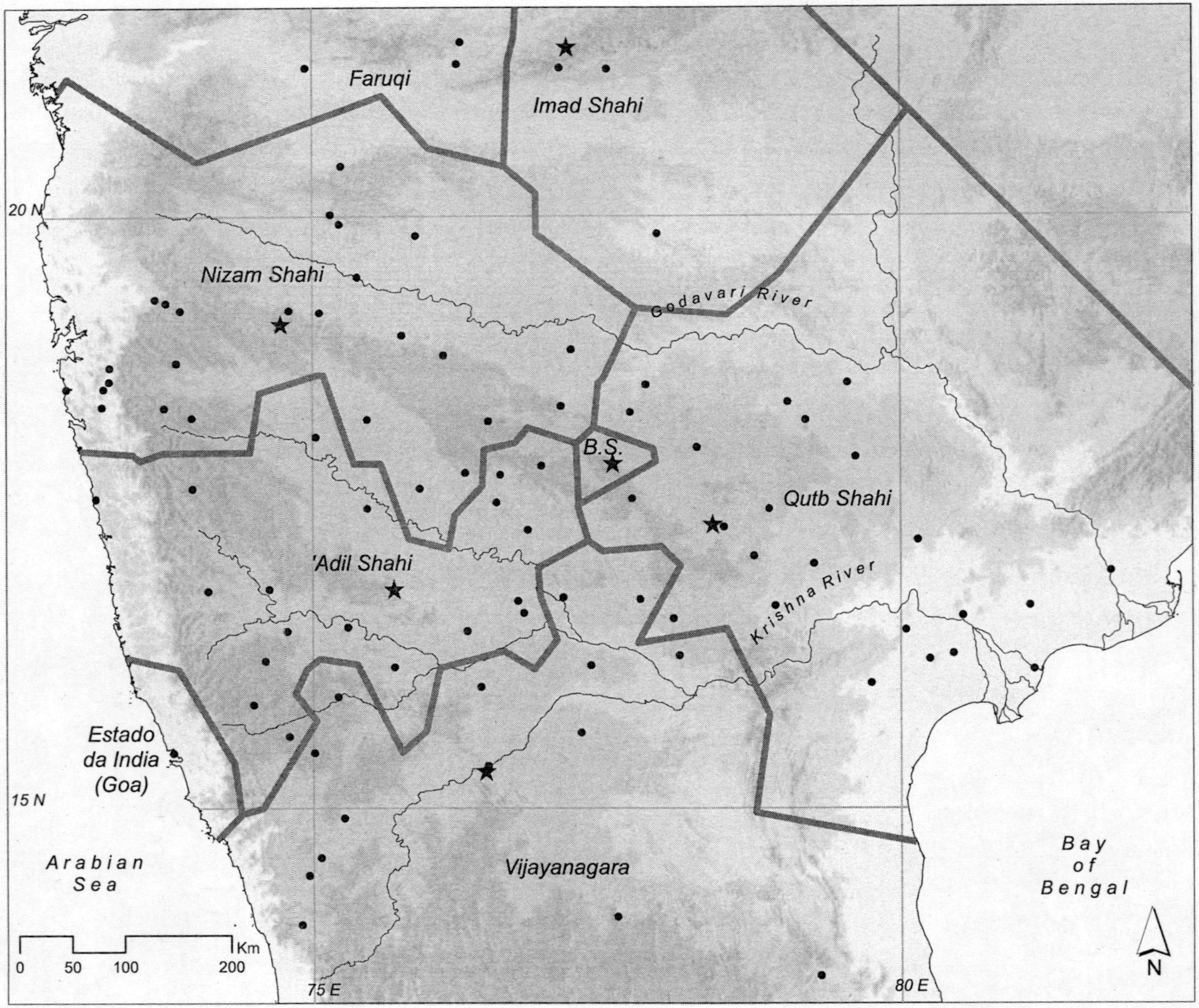


**Figure A1.8** Territorial boundaries of Deccan states: 1560.

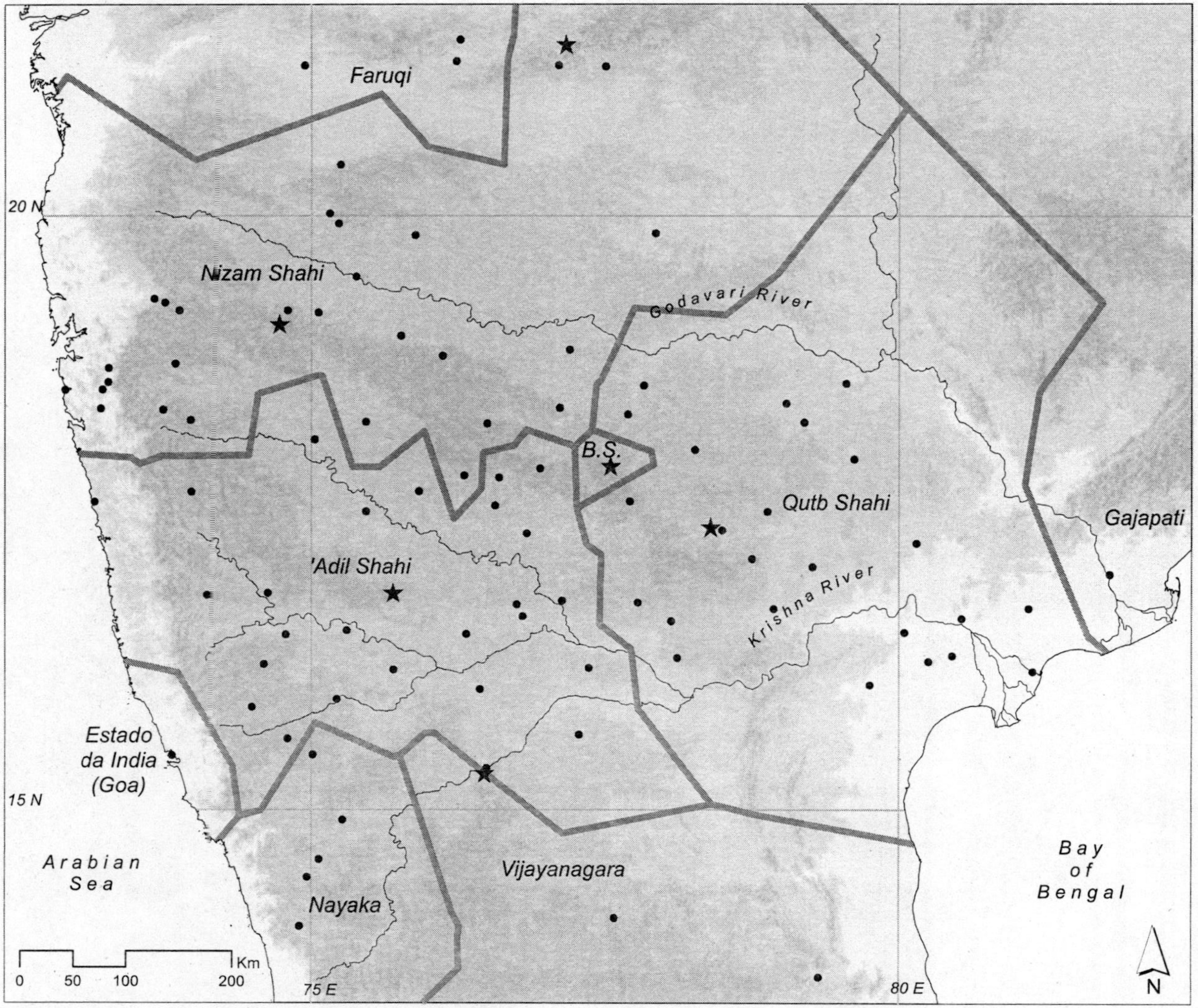


**Figure A1.9** Territo-ial boundaries of Deccan states: 1570.

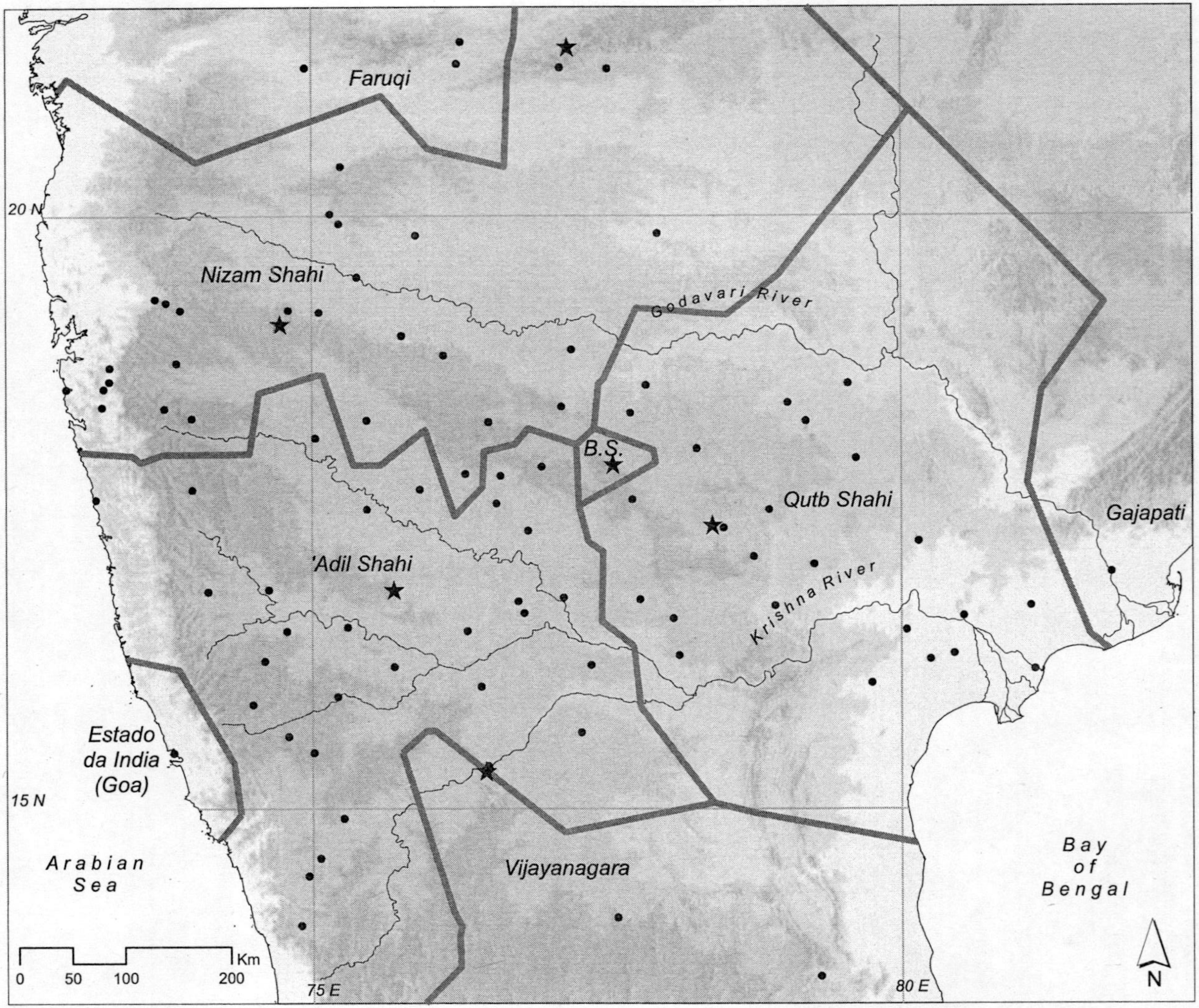


**Figure A1.10** Territorial boundaries of Deccan states: 1580.

Mudgal, which lay immediately to its west. These were the only forts that changed hands four times during the sixteenth century, and neither fell without the other also falling or surrendering. Third, the map suggested that the nature of the unstable frontier zone around Raichur differed from that around Kalyana. For its part, the Raichur frontier zone lies in the highly fertile tract between the Krishna and Tungabhadra Rivers and straddles a broad political frontier separating the Vijayanagara kingdom from the sultanates of Bijapur and Golconda. In contrast, the Kalyana frontier zone lies at a higher elevation and away from a riverine plain, along the southern flank of a low range of hills running northwest to southeast. It runs between the cores of four states—Bijapur, Ahmadnagar, Golconda, and Bidar—riven by mutual rivalries over territory. Consequently, this frontier zone was not as tightly integrated as the southern one, as the two most contested sites in this zone, Kalyana and Sholapur, were often controlled by different primary centres.

## FIELDWORK METHODS

While helping elucidate sixteenth-century geopolitics, the spatial analysis outlined provided only part of the picture, the other being the archaeological record of the sites themselves. Accordingly, we planned two seasons of fieldwork in order to visit as many sites as possible and to survey and document their urban and architectural remains. We began by selecting forty-eight sites, namely, (1) the three main study sites of Raichur, Kalyana, and Warangal; (2) five primary centres (Bidar, Bijapur, Golconda, Hyderabad, and Vijayanagara); (3) thirty-one secondary centres across the plateau, and (4) nine sites with well-preserved examples of Chalukya temple architecture (see list given later).

We carried out our fieldwork in two seasons of six weeks each in June and July of both 2005 and 2006. Our specific activities at any given site varied depending on the category of the site and the amount and availability of prior documentation. At Warangal, for example, considerable prior documentation enabled us to focus on the buildings and cults patronized by Shitab Khan. On the other hand, neither Kalyana nor Raichur had been thoroughly studied, obliging us to locate and identify as many architectural and archaeological features as possible and to make a detailed photographic record of each one. In addition to the building types that architectural historians have customarily favoured—mosques, temples, tombs, and palaces—we also recorded a wide range of more neglected features, such as moats, fortifications, armories, city gates, tanks, stepwells, roads, pathways, and granaries. For two structures at Kalyana—the main gateway complex and the Raj Mahal palace complex—we commissioned and oversaw the production of measured architectural drawings by a team of Indian architects led by Gunjan Srivastava. We also located and recorded historical inscriptions in Persian, Telugu, and Kannada. Although most of these had already been published in epigraphic publications, being able to record their exact locations proved useful for interpreting them.

Lacking adequate maps for Kalyana and Raichur, we carried out GPS-surveys of both sites, using a Thales Mobile-Mapper and ArcGIS software. Satellite data for the two sites was purchased from Digital Globe and imported into ArcGIS to create a base-map that could be uploaded to the Mobile-Mapper unit. By walking each site and following the circuits of fortifications and other features, we logged and mapped all the primary features to within sub-metre accuracy. This method proved especially efficacious at Raichur, today a bustling district headquarters where much of the town's innermost stone wall had been dismantled to provide building material for modern structures. By combining the evidence of the satellite imagery, GPS readings, and ground-level photographs, we reconstructed the outlines of the city's main sixteenth-century features in an ArcGIS mapfile. Since Warangal was already represented by useful site maps published by Michell (1992),[21] our map for this site is simply a compilation based on our Digital Globe data and the cultural features shown on his maps.

We carried out more limited exploration and more selective documentation at the other forty-five sites we visited. At the Chalukya temple sites, we aimed to refine our understanding of the two regionally distinct variants of the Chalukya style and to gather data relating to sixteenth-century reuse. Fortunately, the five primary centres were well covered in scholarly literature, enabling us to focus our attention on specific buildings and features relevant to our study of the sixteenth-century revival of Chalukya and Kakatiya memory. In contrast, at most of the thirty-one secondary centres that we visited—many of them remote hill forts—we were entering largely uncharted territory. Although occasionally guided by Ghulam Yazdani's brief but helpful notes in the *Annual Reports of the Archaeological Department of Hyderabad*, more often than not we were on our own.[22] Here we were often torn between two conflicting goals—wanting to document as much as possible, but needing to become familiar with as many sites as possible in the region. In the end, breadth won out over depth, forcing us to be very selective in what we studied at each site. In general, we focussed on (1) gauging the size and overall layout of the fortifications; (2) recording specimens of early modern cannons lying in situ; (3) recording historical inscriptions; and (4) documenting key buildings and features relevant to our primary theme of the interactions between power, memory, and architecture. Despite time constraints, we managed to complete enough GPS surveys at eleven of these secondary fortified centres to map at least their primary circuits of fortifications. This valuable data clarified where our study sites fit within the larger regional site hierarchy. It also enabled us to understand different approaches to designing fortifications in the various regions of the Deccan.

Both before and after each of our field seasons, we carried out text-based research in order to reconstruct the histories of our study sites and to determine the chronology and the motivating factors of the various contestations over them. The primary sources for this analysis included published inscriptions in Persian, Telugu, Kannada, and Sanskrit; roughly contemporary Persian historical works (especially the *Gulshan-i Ibrāhīmī* [or *Tārīkh-i Firishta*] of Firishta, the anonymous *Tārīkh-i Muḥammad Quṭb Shāh*, the *Burhān-i ma'āthir* of Tabataba, and the *Tazkirat al-mulūk* of Rafi` al-Din Shirazi), and the historical prefaces to an assortment of contemporary literary works in Telugu.[23]

## ARCHITECTURAL HISTORY AND BUILDINGS ARCHAEOLOGY

Our concern in this project lies not only in the initial circumstances in which buildings have been constructed, but also in the changes that those buildings have undergone during their lifetimes. Methodologically, this approach aligns us with the archaeological sub-field known as buildings archaeology. Mainstream architectural history, at least among those specializing in South Asia, has tended to privilege those chains of historical causation that lead up to and culminate in the moment of a building's creation. The study of a building's patronage, its intended uses and meanings, the conditions of its production, its impact on the formation of distinct stylistic traditions, or its relationship with past tradition—such themes have dominated the study of South Asia's architectural history. By contrast, buildings archaeology focusses more on those causal chains that unfold *after* the moment of initial creation. The buildings archaeologist will typically investigate how the physical fabric of the building has changed over its lifetime, and how these changes can point to new patterns of use, new modes of understanding the building, and even new communities that have used it. This does not mean that, as academic approaches to the study of built landscapes, architectural history and buildings archaeology are mutually incompatible. Nor does it imply that architectural history is somehow irrelevant to the buildings archaeologist. To the contrary, a sound knowledge of architectural history is a pre-requisite for success in any buildings archaeology investigation, for the two disciplinary approaches are closely related and often complement one another in their respective findings.

In practical terms, buildings archaeology relies heavily on the analysis of discontinuities in materials, constructional techniques, and style to reveal a structure's different 'stratigraphic units'.[24] A buildings archaeologist understands that term somewhat differently from how an excavation-based archaeologist understands it. To the former, a 'stratigraphic unit' refers to a part of the building that has resulted from a single 'building action' and therefore represents a discrete period of construction.[25] Stratigraphic units are thus distinguished from different stages or phases of work within an otherwise single, continuous programme of construction.[26] One should also distinguish between 'positive' stratigraphic units—that is, those that represent additions to a building—and 'negative' ones, which represent deletions of certain parts. Analysing the nature of the points of contact between adjacent stratigraphic units (abutments, alignments, misalignments, overlays, insertions, and so on) can disclose the relative sequence of the stratigraphic units, and by extension, of the different periods of construction. Placing the changing character of the building within its proper chronological context allows one to pose higher order questions relating to changes in a building's use, understanding, and social context.

Unfortunately, buildings archaeology remains little developed in the South Asian context. As a result, the kinds of resources that are often available in other parts of the world are lacking here, for example, reference databases for the dating of samples of mortar (based on chemical composition), wood (based on established dendrochronological sequences), and other materials. Our own application of the methods of buildings archaeology has sometimes been beset with challenges, but the results have nonetheless been encouraging. We believe they have led to many findings that would not otherwise have been attainable.

## LIST OF SITES VISITED, 2005–06

(all sites are fortified except Gogi, Patancheru, and the Chalukya temples sites)

1. **Main study sites**
   Kalyana
   Raichur
   Warangal/Hanamkonda

2. **Primary centres/capital cities**
   Bidar
   Bijapur
   Golconda
   Hyderabad
   Vijayanagara

3. **Secondary centres**
   Adoni
   Ausa
   Balkonda
   Bankapur
   Bhongir
   Bodhan
   Devarakonda
   Elgandal
   Ganjoti (not located)
   Gogi (`Adil Shahi necropolis)
   Gulbarga
   Kandhar
   Kaulas
   Kohir (not located)
   Koyilkonda
   Medak
   Mudgal
   Malkhed
   Malliabad
   Manvi
   Naldurg
   Parenda
   Patancheru (suburb of Golconda-Hyderabad)
   Racakonda
   Sagar
   Shahpur (Andhra Pradesh)
   Shahapur (Karnataka)
   Sholapur
   Talikota
   Udgir
   Yadgir

4. **Chalukya temple sites**
   Arisibidu
   Bagali
   Chaudadampura

Harpanahalli
Hirehadagali
Jalsingi
Kuruvatti
Narayanpur
Umapur

Additional sites figuring in the study, visited by one or the other of the authors independently:
Ahmadnagar (E 2001)
Bankapur (E 2010)
Delhi/Tughluqabad (E 2001; W 1999)
Devagiri/Daulatabad (E 2001; W 2000)
Firuzabad (E 2001; W 2000)
Istanbul (E 2011)
Pillalamarri (W 1983)
Rajahmundry (W 2000)

## NOTES

1. Hiroshi Fukazawa, 'The Local Administration of the Adilshahi Sultanate (1489–1686)', in his *The Medieval Deccan: Peasants, Social Systems, and States, Sixteenth to Eighteenth Centuries* (Delhi: Oxford University Press, 1991), 1–48.

2. Ibid., 6.

3. Ziyaud-Din A. Desai, *A Topographical List of Arabic, Persian, and Urdu Inscriptions of South India* (New Delhi: Indian Council of Historical Research, 1989); and idem., *Arabic, Persian, and Urdu Inscriptions of West India: A Topographical List* (New Delhi: Sundeep Prakashan, 1999). We used the indices of these two indispensible works to identify all occurrences of the relevant administrative terms such as *mu`āmala*, *qal`a*, *pargana*, *ḥavāldār*, *nā'ib-i ghaibat*, *mālik al-sharq*, and their variant forms. We then consulted the original inscriptions, for the most part published in the series *Epigraphia Indo-Moslemica* (1907–50) and its successor, *Epigraphia Indica: Arabic and Persian Supplement* (1951–76). In the notes that follow, we refer to the inscriptions by their serial number in Desai's two *Topographical Lists* (prefixing the number with 'S' for the South India volume and 'W' for the West India volume).

4. Parganas are mentioned in only two inscriptions dating from the sixteenth century. One refers to pargana Raibag, in the present-day Dharwar district, Karnataka (W1346, dated 1555), and the other to pargana Potwaram, in the present-day Medak district, Andhra Pradesh (S1283, dating to the sixteenth century). Similarly, the officers associated with the parganas in seventeenth-century sources rarely appear in the sixteenth-century epigraphic corpus. Thus, *desāī* appears only in two inscriptions. In one, the context suggests that the desāīs were officers in a mu`āmala who were subordinate to the nā'ib-i ghaibat (W2136, dated 1570–1); in the other, the desāīs appear to have been the officers in charge of a pargana (W1346; dated 1555).

5. The earliest firm epigraphic occurrence of the title ḥavāldār appears in an inscription from Siruguppa dated 1627 (S1521). In fact, it refers not to an ordinary ḥavāldār, but to a *sar-ḥavāldār* ('head-havaldar') of four distinct administrative units, each of which happens to be a distinct kind, namely, the mu`āmala of Raichur, the qal`a of Adoni, the *mukhāṣa* of Siruguppa, and the *qaṣba* of Muhammadnur (that is, Kurnool). An even earlier inscription from Raichur dated 1609 (S1377) refers to the root term *ḥavāla* ('custody'), from which ḥavāldār is derived. By the 1640s, the term ḥavāldār had gained widespread usage in place of nā'ib-i ghaibat.

6. Bijapur: S250 (1559); Velha Goa: W2136 (1570–71); Sholapur: W1984 and W1987 (1578–79 and 1580–81); Kalyana: S942 (1580).

7. W1986 (c.1580).

8. W1984 (1578–79) and W1987 (1580–81).

9. S581 (1574–75) and S582 (1586), both reading *nā'ib-i ghaibat-i shahr-i Aḥsanābād* (that is, Gulbarga).

10. S1634 (1546), recording the construction of a tank 'under the supervision (*kār-kard*) of Amrit Khan, the *nā'ib-i ghaibat*'; and S1635 (1556), recording the completion of a well 'under the supervision (*kār-kard*) of Malik `Ali Beg, entitled `Ali Khan, the *nā'ib-i ghaibat*'.

11. S1240 (1548).

12. S1490 (1561–62).

13. An inscription from Kalyana records the construction of a mosque during the reign of the sultan of Delhi, Muhammad bin Tughluq, 'at a time when the iqta` was held by Malik ash-Sharq Qiwam al-Daulat wa'l-Din, Vazir of the province (*iqlīm*) of Deogir' (S934, dated 1326).

14. The Bahmanis used only the title *mālik al-sharq* to refer to a governor of a mu`āmalas. The term 'nā'ib-i ghaibat' did not appear until 1512, when the Bahmani Sultanate was devolving into independent successor states. The last documented instance of the title mālik

al-sharq being used independently is the following year, in 1513. After that, it was never again employed by itself, although it continued to be used in conjunction with the newer title nā'ib-i ghaibat throughout the rest of the sixteenth century. For mālik al-sharq as an independent title, see W525 (1271), S230 (1320–21), S934 (1326), W801 (1332–33), S563 (1380), S1076 (1470–71), S1214 (fifteenth century), S1352 (1498–99), and S1213 (1513). For mālik al-sharq used together with nā'ib-i ghaibat, see S940 (1568), W2136 (1570–71), and S942 (1580).

15. At Bijapur in 1320–21, the *mālik al-mulūk al-sharq* Karim al-Daulat wa'l-Din, patron of the Karim al-Din mosque, gave a grant of the revenue from 24 *nitān*s of land to the builder of his mosque (S230). At Raichur in 1498–99, the mālik al-sharq Malik `Ambar endowed a mosque by granting it the revenue from 9 *chāwar*s of land in the village of Gabur within his mu`āmala, as well as the taxes collected from forty shops in Raichur itself (S1352).

16. At Malliabad in 1513, mālik al-sharq Malik `Ambar issued a *qaul-nāma* setting lower rates of taxation both on agricultural produce and on commercial taxes (S1213). At Velha Goa in 1570–71, mālik al-sharq Malik Zahid Baig, who was the nā'ib-i ghaibat of the mu`āmala, promulgated an order prohibiting the practice of *niputrik*, whereby the state assumed a deceased person's personal property if he had no male issue to inherit it (W2136).

17. Briggs, trans., *History of the Rise*, 3: 4–5.

18. A 'shapefile' is a simple GIS file type that displays geographic features as points, lines, or polygons according to their spatial coordinates, and which links these features to attribute tables recording various kinds of data associated with them.

19. Even the best maps have not always dealt adequately with the dimension of time in delineating territorial boundaries. Joseph Schwartzberg's *A Historical Atlas of South Asia* (New York: Oxford University Press, 1992) moves in this direction, but even this authoritative source tends to represent territorial boundaries over periods of as long as a century or more. See, for example, Schwartzberg, *Atlas*, map Plates V.4.d and e, 'Major states of South India 1390–1485' and 'Major States of South India 1485–1605'.

20. These maps have two particular limitations. First, because Firishta resided in the court of Bijapur, he refers mostly to places located in the core region of the Deccan, between the Godavari and Krishna–Tungabhadra Rivers. Beyond these rivers, the number of sites he mentions falls off rapidly. Second, there is the problem of edge effects, that is, 'the tendency for spatial operations to return incorrect values near the edge of a map, often because the neighbourhood used to calculate them has been artificially truncated'. This is most noticeable along the northeastern and southern edges of the map. Because there are no outlying points to limit the outer boundaries of the Thiessen polygons along these edges, the polygons generated there do not accurately represent the sites' zones of control or mu`āmalas. See James Conolly and Mark Lake, *Geographical Information Systems in Archaeology* (Cambridge: Cambridge University Press, 2006), 292.

21. George Michell, 'The City as Cosmogram', with an appendix by Phillip B. Wagoner, *South Asian Studies* 8, no. 1 (1992): 1–18.

22. At two of the secondary sites we visited—Ganjoti and Kohir—we were unable to locate any traces of a late-medieval/early modern settlement, despite searching the area and making inquiries with the local residents.

23. These included the *Padya-Bāla-Bhāgavatamu* of Doneru Konerunatha-kavi, the *Vasucaritramu* of Bhattu Murti, the *Rāmarājīyamu* of Andugula Vengakavi, the *Yayāti Caritramu* of Ponnikanti Telaganarya, and the *Tapati Samvaraṇamu* of Addanki Gangadhara-kavi, among others.

24. This formulation is based on Iain Stuart, 'The Analysis of Bricks from Archaeological Sites in Australia', *Australasian Historical Archaeology* 23 (2005), 81.

25. For a thoughtful discussion of building stratigraphy, see Anna Boatto and Daniela Pittaluga, 'Building Archaeology: A Non-Destructive Archaeology', available online at http://www.ndt.net/article/wcndt00/papers/idn365/idn365.htm (accessed 15 July 2013).

26. Warwick Rodwell, *The Archaeology of the English Church* (London: B.T. Batsford, 1981), 68 and 126–7.

APPENDIX 2

# Overview of the Three Primary Study Sites

This appendix provides historical overviews of each of the primary study sites, focussing on urban form and its development. It is not intended as a comprehensive account of every significant monument or feature at each site, but rather as a convenient summary focussing on their overall nature and historical development. We focus mainly on the city walls and gateways that delimit each site, as well as on other monumental features—roadways, palaces, mosques, temples, tanks, and so on—that contribute substantially to each site's urban character.

The site accounts are divided into broad chronological phases, corresponding sometimes to different occupational periods, and sometimes to distinct campaigns of construction within a given period of occupation. In working out the chronologies of development for Kalyana and Raichur, published inscriptions were very helpful, especially when still in situ in the gateways, bastions, and other structures whose foundations they record. On the other hand, we relied entirely on stylistic, typological, and contextual evidence to work out the dating for Warangal, which has only one preserved foundation inscription for the entire 500-year period under consideration.

## A. KALYANA

(Basavakalyan Taluk, Bidar District, Karnataka)
*17°52'12"N76°57'00"E*

Presently known as Basavakalyan in honour of Basava, the twelfth-century Virashaiva reformer, the city of Kalyana served as the capital of the Chalukya empire from the outset of the eleventh century. Judging from the density of architectural debris, the capital's centre must then have been at Narayanpur, which lies some 3 kilometres southeast of the present town. After the empire's collapse in the last quarter of the twelfth century, several successor states struggled to control the site, but none was able to revive it as an imperial centre since it was located too far away from their respective power bases. By the early fourteenth century, though still a prosperous market town, Kalyana had lost its imperial afterglow.[1] During their brief occupation of the Deccan, officials of the Delhi Sultanate built a congregational mosque for the town's Muslim residents (in 1323).[2] Kalyana continued to thrive as a market centre in the Bahmani period, but it was politically overshadowed by Bahmani capitals, first at Gulbarga, and from 1424, at Bidar.

In the 1460s, evidently, Bahmani rulers built the site's first stone fortifications, which the `Adil Shahis extensively renovated between 1560 and 1580, and again in 1646. Located on a small hillock on the north side of the present town, the fort features two concentric enclosures roughly circular in plan, the perimeter of its outer wall measuring 990 metres and enclosing a total area of 5.92 hectares. Twelve bastions project from the outer wall to overlook a moat contained by a counterscarp and a broad, sloping glacis. One enters the fort only from the southeast, through a series of four successive gateways and

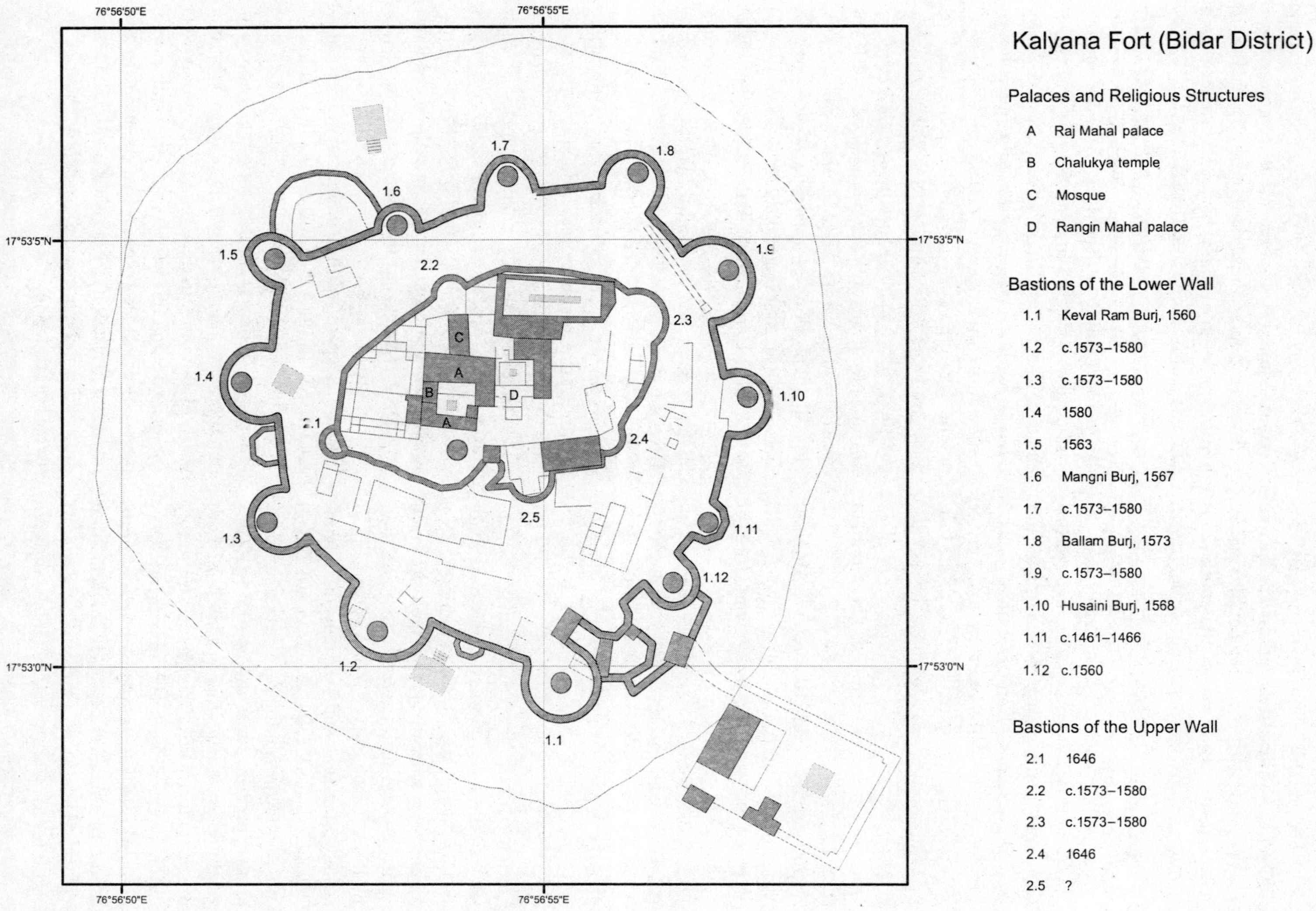

76°56'50"E
76°56'55"E
17°53'5"N
17°53'0"N
1.1
1.2
1.3
1.4
1.5
1.6
1.7
1.8
1.9
1.10
1.11
1.12
2.1
2.2
2.3
2.4
2.5
A
B
C
D
Kalyana Fort (Bidar District)
Palaces and Religious Structures
A Raj Mahal palace
B Chalukya temple
C Mosque
D Rangin Mahal palace
Bastions of the Lower Wall
1.1 Keval Ram Burj, 1560
1.2 c.1573–1580
1.3 c.1573–1580
1.4 1580
1.5 1563
1.6 Mangni Burj, 1567
1.7 c.1573–1580
1.8 Ballam Burj, 1573
1.9 c.1573–1580
1.10 Husaini Burj, 1568
1.11 c.1461–1466
1.12 c.1560
Bastions of the Upper Wall
2.1 1646
2.2 c.1573–1580
2.3 c.1573–1580
2.4 1646
2.5 ?

**Figure A2.1** Site map of Kalyana Fort.

courtyards.[3] The roughly elliptical inner wall runs on a southwest to northeast axis with five projecting bastions, one at each narrow end, one in the middle of the northern side, and two on the south. This upper enclosure, dense with palatial structures in varying states of preservation, lies closer to the northern segment of the lower wall, thereby creating a broader area between the two enclosures on the south. Within this intermediate zone, exposed foundations and partially preserved segments of walls reveal the outlines of an assortment of rectilinear buildings—possibly barracks and service buildings—that once occupied this zone of the fort.

Construction of the fortifications can be assigned to three distinct phases:

Phase 1c.1460–64: Construction of the Bahmani fort

Phase 2 1560–80: Modernization under `Ali `Adil Shah

1560–73: under superintendence of Kamil Khan

1573–80: under superintendence of Dilavar Khan

Phase 3 c.1646: Strengthening of the upper wall during the reign of Muhammad `Adil Shah

#### Phase 1: c.1460–64

The sixteenth-century Mughal historian Badauni reportedly stated that Kalyana's walls were built between 1461 and 1466.[4] This is supported by stylistic comparisons between the earliest preserved portions of Kalyana's fortifications and those built at nearby Bidar during the reign of Muhammad III (r.1463–82), coinciding with the advent of gunpowder warfare in the Deccan. There, the Bahmani capital was provided with double-galleried ramparts with enclosed battlements at the ground level surmounted by open-air battlements above—in both the curtain walls and the polygonal projecting bastions. The walls at both the upper and lower levels are pierced by large port holes to accommodate cannon and smaller loopholes for the firing of matchlocks. These openings are located at two heights within each level, with the larger portholes (generally circular) located just above the inner floor level, as required by cannons mounted on carriages, and the loopholes above at shoulder level. Two to five loopholes for smaller arms lie between each adjacent pair of cannon portholes.

Since many surviving sections of Kalyana's walls share an identical morphology and a strikingly similar masonry fabric with this late fifteenth-century work at Bidar, the two must be roughly contemporaneous. The entire curtain wall of the fort's outer rampart (with the sole exception of segment I/5–6) conforms to this type, as do also the polygonal bastion I/11, the two polygonal bastions flanking the second gate ('Bichchu Darwaza') in the entrance complex, and the polygonal breastworks standing in front of curtain wall segments I/1–2 and I/3–4 (see site plan in Figure A2.1). At the top of the fort, only small portions of this type of wall survive, including just two incomplete sections of curtain wall at II/3–4 and II/4–5. Presumably, the rest of the curtain walls here were originally constructed in this fashion but were subsequently replaced by newer work in Phases 2 and 3.

In terms of fabric, work of this phase generally employs smoothly dressed ashlar, occasionally mixed with blocks of rougher finish. Much of the dressed ashlar appears to have been reused from dismantled Chalukya-period temple material; many of these blocks reveal disjointed portions of decorative ornament, only rarely displaying larger-scale figural sculptures. Headers generally appear after every two or three stretchers, and the courses tend to be relatively narrow and even, compared to later fabrics. The entire expanse of the wall is built in one continuous rise, without stepped back levelling courses.[5] The joints between blocks often contain gaps where little mortar is preserved, at least on the surface. The one surviving junction between an original curtain wall and bastion (curtain I/10–11 and bastion I/11) shows a bonding of the two structures, with several blocks 'bent' and carrying across the joint. In this phase, no projecting string course divides the top of the wall from the parapet above, whose merlons are invariably spade shaped.

**Phase 2: 1560–80**

In contrast to Phase 1, we can securely date this second phase thanks to a series of six foundation inscriptions—the first in Old Marathi (1560) and the rest in Persian—recording the construction of new bastions for the fort's outer wall.[6] Each of the five Persian inscriptions refers to `Ali `Adil Shah I as the reigning sultan and identifies the city's governor, of whom there were four during this brief period. The inscriptions also record the names of the two military engineers who successively superintended the construction: Kamil Khan from 1560 to 1573, and Dilawar Khan from 1573 to 1580. Both men later served as regents during the early years of Ibrahim `Adil Shah II's reign, suggesting the prominence of military engineers at this time.

Each of Kamil Khan's four inscriptions records the completion of the bastion on which it is located: bastions I/5 (1563), I/6 (1567), I/10 (1568), and I/8 (1573) (see Table A2.1). He also appears to have rebuilt a section of curtain wall I/5–6 and to have built the broad semicircular breastwork in front of it, judging by their identical fabric with that of his bastions (see later). By contrast, Dilawar Khan's single inscription records that 'this edifice was completed (*shud tamām īn `imārat*)', referring to bastion I/4, on which it is located. But then it continues, 'the citadel of the town of Kalyan was finished (*murattab shud hiṣār-i qaṣbat-i Kalyān*) by the Khan of high rank, Dilavar Khan—may he live forever!' and adds that 'during the regime of Malik al-Sharq Malik Isma`il Na'ib Ghaibat of the said district, a sum of 6,000 huns was spent on the work'.[7] This apparently refers to the completion of both the bastion on which the inscription is located and all the remaining work that Dilawar Khan had undertaken. This unspecified work evidently refers to the four bastions in the lower wall (I/2, I/3, I/7, and I/9) and the two in the upper wall (II/2 and II/3) that lack foundation inscriptions but otherwise compare in fabric with Dilawar Khan's dated bastion.

The bastions constructed by Kamil Khan and Dilawar Khan represent modernized upgrades of the original Phase 1 bastions, which must have existed at the same locations as their Phase 2 replacements. In fact, these earlier Bahmani bastions probably remain encased within the Phase 2 bastions seen today. The upgrading aimed at creating suitable platforms for large cannons, which were mounted on cavaliers atop the bastions. To this end, engineers filled in the lower galleries of the Phase 1 bastions with earth and rubble and clad the earlier bastions with the stone that is visible today. These bastions all abut the Phase 1 curtain wall, rather than being

**Table A2.1** Bastions constructed at Kalyana during Phase 2

| Date | Bastion number | Engineer | Governor (*nā'ib-i ghaibat*) | Ruler |
|---|---|---|---|---|
| 1560 | I/1 | Ramana Gauda? | – | – |
| 1563 | I/5 | Kamil Khan | Rustam Khan | `Ali `Adil Shah |
| 1567 | I/6 | Kamil Khan | Sayyid Muhammad | `Ali `Adil Shah |
| 1568 | I/10 | Kamil Khan | Malik Sadr al-Din | `Ali `Adil Shah |
| 1573 | I/8 | Kamil Khan | Sayyid Muhammad | `Ali `Adil Shah |
| 1573–80 | I/2 | Dilawar Khan | Malik Isma`il? | `Ali `Adil Shah |
| 1573–80 | I/3 | Dilawar Khan | Malik Isma`il? | `Ali `Adil Shah |
| 1573–80 | I/7 | Dilawar Khan | Malik Isma`il? | `Ali `Adil Shah |
| 1573–80 | I/9 | Dilawar Khan | Malik Isma`il? | `Ali `Adil Shah |
| 1573–80 | II/2 | Dilawar Khan | Malik Isma`il? | `Ali `Adil Shah |
| 1573–80 | II/3 | Dilawar Khan | Malik Isma`il? | `Ali `Adil Shah |
| 1580 | I/4 | Dilawar Khan | Malik Isma`il | `Ali `Adil Shah |

bonded together with it as in the case of the sole surviving Phase 1 bastion (I/11), thus providing clear structural evidence for the priority of Phase 1. All the Phase 2 bastions are round, as opposed to the polygonal bastions of Phase 1, and with only one exception (I/6) they are extremely large, measuring twice or even three times the diameter of the preserved Phase 1 bastion. Unlike the latter bastion with its internal gallery, Phase 2 bastions are solid platforms with no openings in their outer stone faces below the parapet. In all but two cases, their battlements are protected by 'box type' merlons with bevelled tops.[8] In five of the twelve Phase 2 bastions a projecting string course demarcates the bastion from the parapet above. All of them carry a circular cavalier that rises above the level of the battlement and is approached by a pair of stairways winding up its back.

The stone blocks of the dated bastions of Kamil Khan and Dilawar Khan tend to be larger than those used in Phase 1, and most are more roughly hewn, showing irregular, flint-like fracture patterns on their surfaces. The masonry courses are frequently more irregular than in Phase 1, with little concern for the regular alternation of stretchers and headers that characterized the earlier phase. In places, square-shaped blocks appear in continuous sequences, while in others, three or four courses of larger blocks follow several courses of smaller ones, creating a pattern resembling alligator skin (for example, bastion I/5). Mortar is also much more prominent and better preserved than in the earlier phase.

Two features distinguish the dated bastion of Dilawar Khan (I/4) from the slightly earlier ones of Kamil Khan, despite their similarities in fabric. First, the masonry coursing is more irregular in Dilawar Khan's bastion, where a single course of relatively taller blocks abruptly becomes two courses of smaller blocks. Second, Dilawar Khan's bastion makes much more programmatic use of Chalukya decorative sculpture, even involving figural sculptures of Hindu deities. Since one or both of these characteristics may also be seen in the undated bastions I/2, I/3, I/7, I/9, II/2, and II/3, it seems reasonable to ascribe them to Dilawar Khan, datable to the period between 1573 and 1580. Moreover, whereas Phase 1 bastions were built in a single continuous rise of masonry, those of Kamil Khan show a gradual increase in the number of rises from two to four. The dated bastion of Dilawar Khan, as well as the other four here ascribed to him, are all built in three rises.

### Phase 3: c.1646

A final phase of construction strengthened the defences of Kalyana's upper wall through the building of two distinctive bastions, II/1 and II/4, and several adjoining sections of curtain wall of identical fabric. Thanks to an inscription on the eastern outer wall of the Raj Mahal palace, we can date this work to 1646, under the initiative of the fort's commander, Sidi Dilavar, during the reign of Muhammad `Adil Shah. The inscription states that 'at the top of the citadel he [Sidi Dilawar] built fine towers and placed guns on them to repel the enemy', further adding that 'he constructed mountain-like ramparts at three points and made them a monument for a long period'. The 'fine towers' evidently refer to bastions II/1 and II/4, while most of the upper curtain walls, being of the same fabric as these two bastions, were probably built by Sidi Dilavar, or perhaps by an immediate successor. Additionally, the stones in the walls adjacent to his bastions are bonded together with the masonry of the bastions themselves, underscoring their contemporaneity.[9]

Sidi Dilavar's bastions are round in plan, but quite small—just under 10 metres in diameter. They end in integral cavaliers that are continuous in size and fabric with the bastions themselves, in contrast to the smaller cavaliers atop the massive bastions of Phase 2. The stone blocks used in building these integral bastion-cavaliers tend to be smaller in dimensions, reverting more or less to the sizes and proportions that had been used in Phase 1, although they continue to be only roughly dressed, with flint-like fracture patterns, as in Phase 2. Similarly, their masonry courses are fairly regular and narrow, as in Phase 1, and they generally consist of alternating longer and shorter blocks. One finds in this phase the

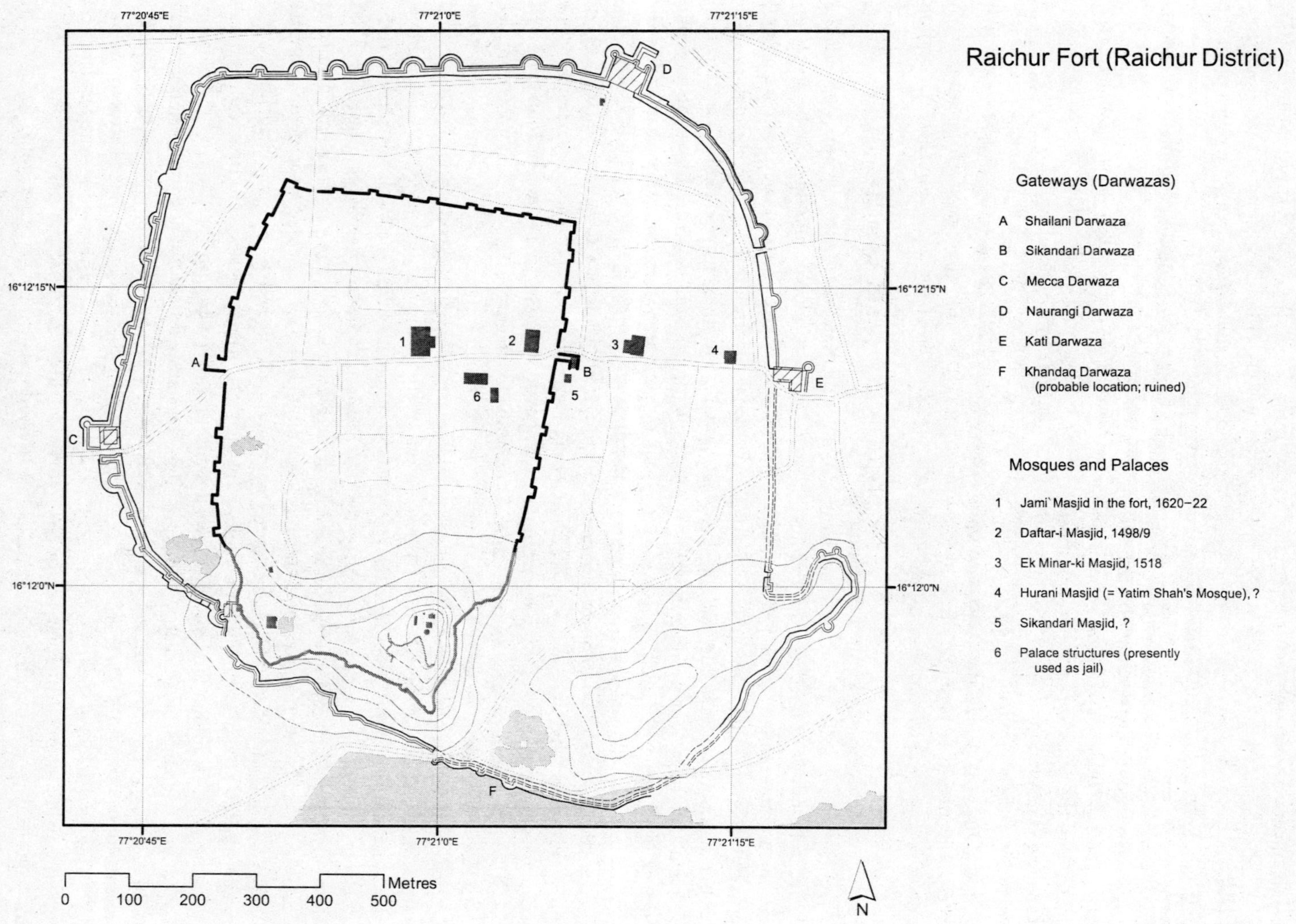
Raichur Fort (Raichur District)
Gateways (Darwazas)
A Shailani Darwaza
B Sikandari Darwaza
C Mecca Darwaza
D Naurangi Darwaza
E Kati Darwaza
F Khandaq Darwaza (probable location; ruined)
Mosques and Palaces
1 Jami` Masjid in the fort, 1620–22
2 Daftar-i Masjid, 1498/9
3 Ek Minar-ki Masjid, 1518
4 Hurani Masjid (= Yatim Shah's Mosque), ?
5 Sikandari Masjid, ?
6 Palace structures (presently used as jail)
77°20'45"E
77°21'0"E
77°21'15"E
16°12'15"N
16°12'0"N
0 100 200 300 400 500 Metres
N

**Figure A2.2** Site map of Raichur Fort.

most minimal appearance of reused architectural-sculptural fragments, mostly architectural friezes.

## B. RAICHUR

(Raichur Taluk, Raichur District, Karnataka)
*16°12'25"N77°21'15"E*

Raichur is today a thriving district headquarters and commercial centre. Unlike at Kalyana, where the fort is located on the outskirts of the town's most populated area, Raichur's fort lies at the heart of the town and is densely populated. As a result, the forces of development endanger the preservation of the fort, as builders utilize the city's old walls and other structures as convenient sources of building material.

Though much harder to discern than at Kalyana, enough vestiges of the medieval and early modern town survive to permit us to trace its main features. These include a double ring of stone fortifications: an inner rectangular enclosure measuring approximately half a kilometre on each side, and an outer wall, irregular in outline but tending towards a more circular plan. The outer wall measures 4.29 kilometres along its perimeter, enclosing an area of just under 100 hectares (99.87). Since the inner enclosure is displaced slightly to the west, the outer wall encloses more space along the east and southeast. Nine city gates survive—two in the inner circuit of walls, and seven in the outer—and some of these reveal multiple periods of construction and modification. Just as it does today, the main artery of the fort in its earlier period ran from east to west, traversing the four gateways known today as Kati Darwaza (in the outer eastern wall), Sikandari Darwaza (inner eastern wall), Shailani Darwaza (inner western wall), and Mecca Darwaza (outer western wall). Most of the town's historic buildings front this road, including five mosques, two shrines, and the remnants of a palatial complex, now occupied by the municipal jail. A rocky outcrop rises steeply in the site's southern end and serves as a citadel (*bālā ḥiṣār*), with several small buildings—a pavilion, a small mosque, and a gun platform—clustered together at its highest point. Several tanks dot the cityscape, mostly concentrated in the southwestern sector. Projecting to the northeast from the southeastern part of the outer wall is a narrow spur, evidently a barbican that protected a large postern gate (*diḍḍi*) located at the root of the wall's projection.

The fort's construction may be divided into five main phases:

Phase 1 c.1296–1313: Kakatiya occupation
Phase 2 c.1313–1410: Tughluq, Vijayanagara, and early Bahmani occupations
Phase 3 c.1465–1520: Later Bahmani and early `Adil Shahi occupations
Phase 4 c.1520–30: Vijayanagara occupation
Phase 5 c.1530–1670: Later `Adil Shahi occupation

#### Phase 1: c.1296–1313: Kakatiya Period

In 1296, the Kakatiya feudatory Gona Vithalanatha issued an inscription recording that he had conquered a number of forts in the Doab region and occupied Raichur, already a thriving market town (*paṭṭaṇa*).[10] He added that he had built a 'stone fort' (*silā-durggamu*), doubtless referring to the imposing wall of cyclopean stone masonry that carries his inscription.

Today, Vithalanatha's 'stone fort' is best preserved along its western side, but enough partial segments of its northern and eastern sides remain to permit its mapping (see Figure A2.2). The wall traces out three sides of a rough rectangle, each measuring about half a kilometre in length and consisting of a curtain wall from which square bastions project at variable intervals. No fourth wall on the south was needed, as the fort's eastern and western walls abut the lower flanks of the high, rocky outcrop to the south. The latter not only closed off the fortified space on the fort's southern side, it also served as a citadel and place of refuge in times of siege. Today, the inner wall continues irregularly up the flanks of the outcrop, but the starkly different fabric of this southern wall identifies it as a later addition belonging to Phase 5 (see later). Two gateways provided access to the fort on the western and eastern sides—the Shailani and Sikandari Darwazas, respectively. Though poorly preserved today, these gateways clearly followed the same bent-axis design seen in Warangal's gateways.

Vithalanatha modelled Raichur's fort, a combination of earth and stone, on that of Kakatiya Warangal, which had been completed just a generation earlier. At both forts massive slabs of hewn granite averaging about 1 × 1 × 3 metres in size and carefully fitted together without mortar serve as a protective casing for an inner earthen core. At Raichur, granite slabs typically alternate, with one block laid as a 'stretcher' running parallel to the wall's surface, and the next laid as a perpendicular 'header' projecting into the core of the wall to help bond the structure together. These courses tend to be staggered, so that the headers in one course are overlain by the stretchers in the next. Although the walls are not fully preserved, we assume that they approximated their better-preserved counterparts at Warangal, where a diminutive and essentially decorative parapet with crenellations would have provided limited cover to defenders.

### Phase 2: c.1313–1410: Tughluq and Early Bahmani Periods

Just nineteen years after Vithalanatha fortified Raichur, the city encountered the superior military force of the Delhi Sultanate. According to Firishta, during the course of Delhi's fifth invasion of the Deccan in 1313, the general Malik Kafur penetrated as far south as Raichur and Mudgal, laying the country to waste. The general appears to have brought Raichur under sultanate control on this occasion, for the towering minaret of the Ek Minar ki Masjid, which presently stands as an integral part of the mosque, appears originally to have been a free-standing tower, built some two centuries before 1513, when the mosque itself was built. Since the style and fabric of this minaret relate more closely to monuments of the early fourteenth century,[11] one might ascribe it to Malik Kafur, who would have constructed the tower as a monument commemorating his victory and conquest of Raichur in the same way that Delhi's Qutb Minar originally commemorated a military victory.[12]

From about 1339 for nearly a decade the city seems to have been held by Harihara Sangama, one of the founders of the future state of Vijayanagara, but it then passed into Bahmani control with the founding of that sultanate in 1347. Although the earliest surviving Bahmani inscriptions from Raichur date only from the middle of the fifteenth century, architectural evidence from the latter half of the fourteenth century and the beginning of the fifteenth points to an emerging shrine complex and ritual centre inside the old Kakatiya Fort. This was located on the site of what would later become the so-called Fort Jami` Masjid on the north side of the main east–west road defined by the gateways of the Kakatiya Fort.[13] Before the construction of the mosque, however, this site appears to have served as a small shrine complex, with a domed gateway providing access to the enclosure on the east, a small domed tomb within the courtyard, and an unpretentious `*īdgāh*-like structure along the west to mark the *qibla* for prayer.[14]

### Phase 3: c.1465–1520: Later Bahmani and Early `Adil Shahi Periods

Although little monumental architecture was constructed in Raichur during its first century of Bahmani control, in 1468 and 1469 its governor, Khan-I A`zam Mallu Khan Hafiz, built a new and much larger stone wall around the old Kakatiya city and added gateways on its western and eastern ends.[15] The wall is best viewed along its western side, north from Mallu Khan's western gate, today's Mecca Darwaza. It is built of smaller blocks—and more nearly square, though quite irregular—than those of the Kakatiya wall. No mortar is evident, and in places gaps are filled with chinking stones. Square bastions project from the curtain at regular intervals. Although the parapet is missing in much of the wall, well-preserved segments can be seen at various places along its western side. Here the wall is continuous—as opposed to being divided into merlons and embrasures—and features an evenly spaced row of vertical loopholes interrupted at regular intervals by larger square openings that served as cannon ports. The lower half-wall (or *fausse braye*) before the Bahmani wall appears to belong to a later period of construction in the sixteenth century.

The new Bahmani wall completely enclosed the Kakatiya city and nearly doubled its size. On the western and northern sides, the builders closely followed the rectangular layout of the older city, while on the east and south, the new wall sweeps outwards to incorporate a second rocky outcrop. On the south the wall runs along the elevated ground at the southern flank of the hillock that had defined the fourth side of the Kakatiya city. Mallu Khan also followed the earlier fort's plan by placing his two gateways along the eastern and western portions of his walls, in effect extending the original east–west avenue of the Kakatiya city outwards to the two new gates. But in two respects, Mallu Khan gave precedence to the eastern gate of his expanded city, just as Malik Kafur had a century and a half earlier, when he erected his victory minaret outside the old city's eastern gate. First, along the western side, he ran the new wall closer to the old one and, by positioning his western gate some 100 metres south of the east–west axis, he avoided direct alignment with Vithalanatha's western gate. Second, by having his eastern wall sweep outwards, he enclosed Malik Kafur's minaret within the city and provided a longer and more formal extension of the main thoroughfare on that side of the city. Most of Raichur's subsequent architectural development would take place along this eastern half of the main avenue, from the shrine complex lying at the heart of the inner city out through Mallu Khan's eastern gate and even beyond. By 1628, six mosques and a palace complex had appeared along this formal avenue. This surely formed the heart of the city's commercial life, for an inscription dated 1498–99 records the endowment of forty shops adjacent to one of these mosques, the Daftar Masjid, which was to be maintained by the income of these shops.[16]

Nothing of the Bahmani eastern gateway is visible today, but it must have stood on the site of the present Kati Darwaza, since Mallu Khan's 1468 inscription is set into the wall of this gateway's inner courtyard.[17] The governor's second gateway inscription, dated 1469, lies on a slab built into the wall of the city's western gateway, or Mecca Darwaza. Despite clear signs of modern rebuilding, much of this gateway's original character is preserved. Although it follows the bent-axis plan of the city's earlier Kakatiya gateways, the Mecca Darwaza presents a very different, Persianate interpretation of the type. Only a single courtyard remains, entered on the west through a vaulted gatehouse surmounted by a pyramidal dome and exhibiting several other fifteenth-century Bahmani stylistic features. Inside the courtyard and turning to the right, one faces a second vaulted gatehouse, the inner courtyard of which has now vanished. The main road into the fortified part of the city traverses this open space.

In the opening decades of the sixteenth century, as the `Adil Shahis were asserting their independence from the Bahmanis, we have the first evidence that improvements were made to the bastions of Raichur's outer wall. An inscription dated 1515 records the 'construction' (that is, renovation) of a bastion under the supervision of the local `Adil Shahi governor, Nizam al-Din Ahmad al-Kirmani. Unfortunately, by the early twentieth century, this inscription and some ten others like it had become dissociated from the bastions on which they were originally located, thus compromising their utility in tracing the fort's architectural development.[18]

### Phase 4: c.1520–30: Vijayanagara Occupation

Modernization of the fort continued during Vijayanagara's decade-long occupation after the Battle of Raichur. Although neither Krishna Raya nor his subordinates left inscriptions recording their construction projects, their patronage is unmistakable from the style of the work carried out, which combines the Bahmani-derived arches and vaults of the 'Vijayanagara Courtly Style' with characteristic Indic forms such as *potika* bracket capitals, *makara-toraṇa*s, lotus petal mouldings, and an array of animated figure sculptures portraying deities, warriors, and narrative reliefs.[19]

The eastern gateway in the Bahmani wall appears to have been dismantled during Krishna Raya's siege and subsequently rebuilt in the metropolitan Vijayanagara style, although only the southern gatehouse in the present Kati Darwaza survives from this rebuilding. Krishna Raya built another new gate in the outer northern wall, the well-preserved Naurangi Darwaza, where there is no evidence of a gate having previously stood (see detailed discussion in Chapter 8). Also exhibiting a Vijayanagara stylistic character are the three bastions standing just west of the Naurangi Darwaza, with their lively figure sculptures and projecting machicolations supported on brackets of potikas and rampant leogryphs (*vyāla*).

Several Hindu temples in Raichur might have been established or expanded during Vijayanagara's occupation, most of them located on secondary streets in residential neighbourhoods, not on the main east–west avenue. One such temple is known only from an inscription, dated 1521, located in Vijayawada in coastal Andhra. It states that Kanthamaraju Singaraju, an officer of Krishna Raya, had established a temple to Sriranganatha of Raichur, together with a well (*bāvi*), a watering-shed (*calivandri*) and a garden (*toṇṭā*).[20] However, it has not been possible to identify the actual temple to which this record refers.

**Phase 5: c.1530–1670: Later `Adil Shahi Period**

After Krishna Raya's death in 1529, Isma`il`Adil Khan took advantage of the ensuing confusion to retake Raichur and Mudgal. By the mid-1540s, `Adil Shahi engineers were busily working to expand and update the fort's bastions to serve as platforms for heavy cannons, just as they were doing at Yadgir, Kalyana, and other strongholds. According to surviving inscriptions, new bastions were completed in 1546, 1548, 1565, 1570, 1591, 1609, 1629, and 1670.[21] Two inscriptions dated 1609 but no longer in situ record the construction of a bastion by one Malik Raihan, when Malik Yaqut was Raichur's governor.[22] Their nearly identical size, decoration, and content suggest that they both refer to the same structure. One of them states that the bastion faces west, which evidently refers to the third bastion north of the Mecca Darwaza. This structure not only faces west, but its two empty recesses—in the inner wall on either side of the stairway leading up from the battlement to the top of the cavalier—could have accommodated the inscription slabs. The bastion features a high cavalier, with a central swivel hole in its stone floor for mounting a heavy cannon, and bevel-topped merlons alternating with broad embrasures through which the gun could be fired. The sculptural decoration of this bastion is confined to animal and vegetal figures—elephants, lions, *hamsa*s, and lotus blooms—unlike the site's Vijayanagara bastions, which feature human and divine figures.

The `Adil Shahis also extended the Bahmani walls of the inner fort, so that they continue over the rough terrain of the Bala Hisar hill, thus completing their circuit. They also built some important gateways. As discussed in Chapter 8, in 1550 the governor Shamshir al-Mulk modified Krishna Raya's eastern gateway,[23] but his work was mostly confined to removing some of the most prominent Vijayanagara stylistic features and replacing them with elements stamped with the style of metropolitan Bijapur. An inscription records that the following year another gateway was built, presumably by the same governor.[24] This seems to refer to the gateway identified in a 1929–30 report as the Khandaq Darwaza ('Gate of the Moat'), located immediately adjacent to the large tank known as the Khas Baoli.[25] Two enigmatic structures, now partially submerged in the Khas Baoli into which they project on the southern and western sides, are evidently the gatehouses of this complex, as they feature arched openings on their narrow ends and a perpendicular arrangement of their longitudinal axes. The southern structure is in fact joined to what remains of the adjacent Bahmani wall, which is very poorly preserved in this sector of the site.[26] If this interpretation is correct, then the courtyard of the Khandaq Darwaza must be submerged beneath the waters of the Khas Baoli, a later feature.

In the opening years of Ibrahim `Adil Shah II's reign, the officer Yusuf `Ali Khan completed some important work in the southwestern quadrant of the fort's outer wall. Here he excavated the moat, built a well, and, adjacent to it, added a postern gate (diḍḍi), completing the work in 1582.[27] The following year, he removed a massive boulder that had blocked the narrow and rocky corridor running between the

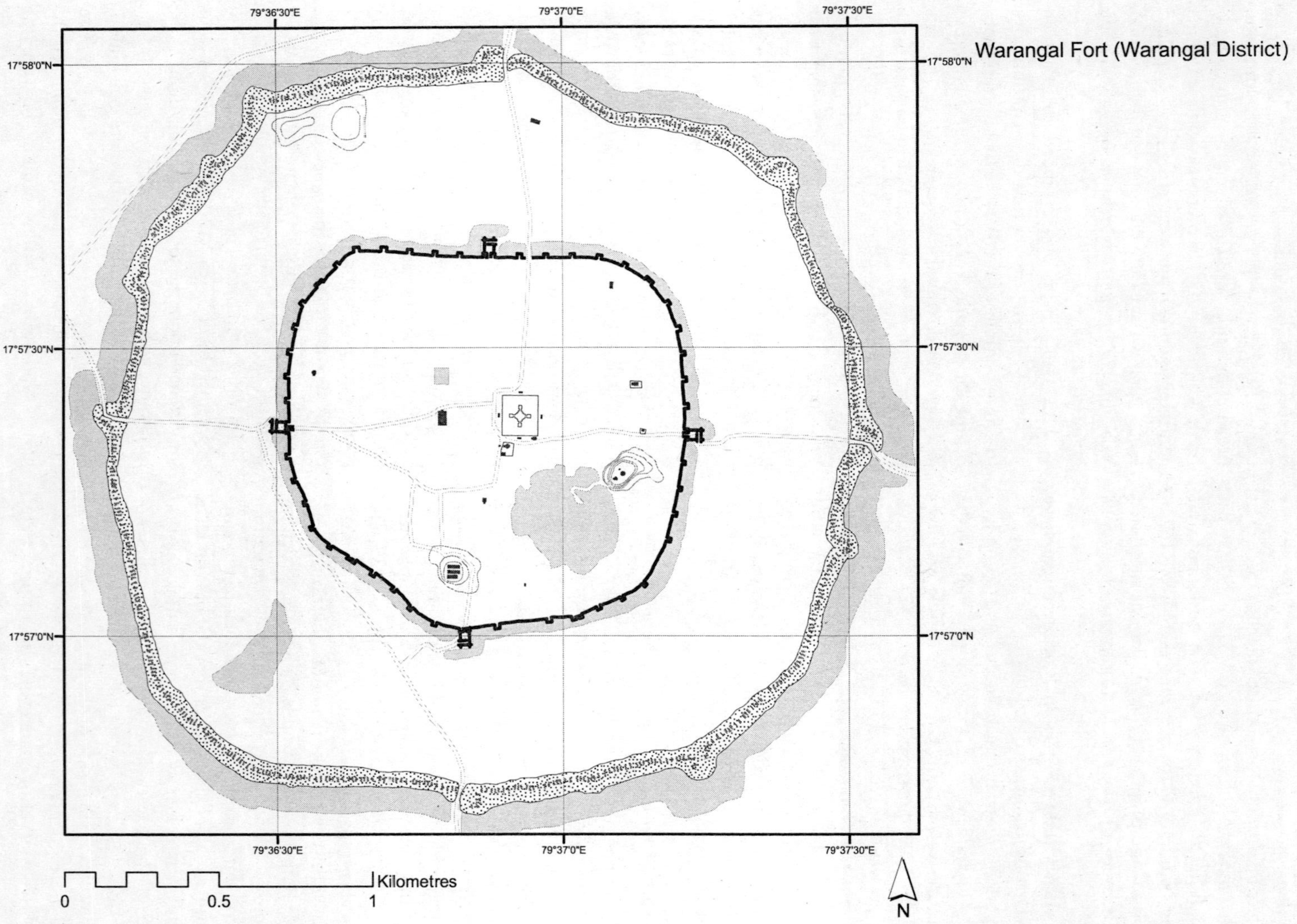


**Figure A2.3** Site map of Warangal Fort.

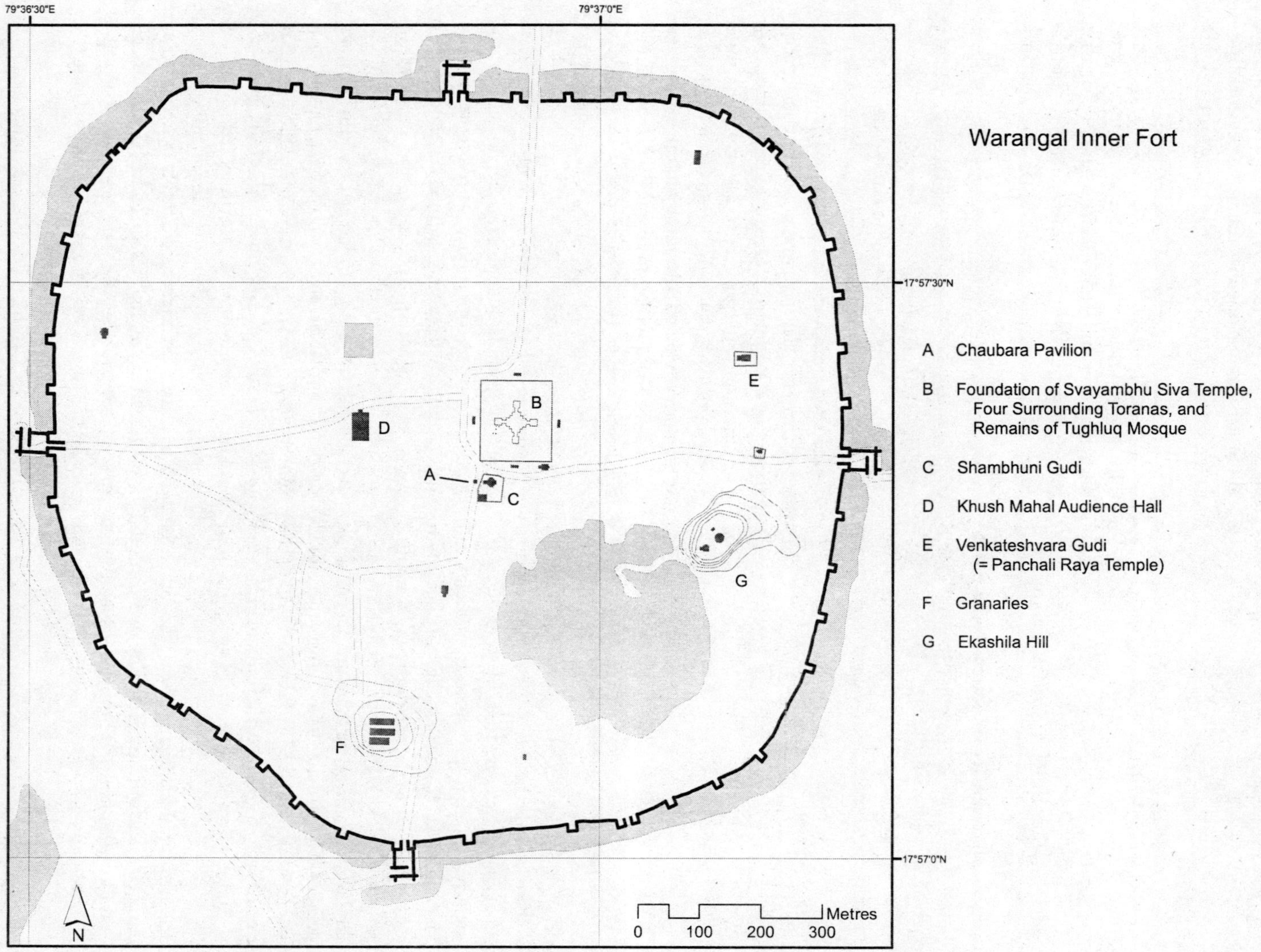


**Figure A2.4** Site map of Warangal Inner Fort.

inner and outer walls, and he 'constructed a *diddi* in its place', which he named the 'Tawakkul Diddi'. Both the postern and remnants of the massive boulder are still visible.

## C. WARANGAL

(Warangal Taluk, Warangal District, Andhra Pradesh)
*17°57'23"N79°36'55"E*

Warangal is another thriving district headquarters, its population more than twice that of Raichur's.[28] But its main urban district is located to the northwest of the old Kakatiya capital, thereby minimizing development pressures on the city's historic sector. Unlike Raichur or Kalyana, Warangal has few foundation inscriptions, making it necessary to rely on broad stylistic indicators to distinguish the city's building phases. Here we identify five such phases:
Phase 1: c.1190–1323 Kakatiya period
Phase 2: c.1323–1331 Tughluq occupation
Phase 3: c.1424–1504 Bahmani occupation
Phase 4: c.1504–1512 Shitab Khan's occupation
Phase 5: c.1512–1687 Qutb Shahi occupation

### Phase 1: c.1190–1323: Kakatiya Period

Indirect epigraphic evidence suggests that Warangal was founded towards the end of the twelfth century, during the reign of Kakatiya Rudradeva. Prior to this time, the Kakatiya kings had ruled from their capital at Hanamkonda, a much smaller fortified town that is now a northwestern suburb of Warangal. An inscription dated 1195 states that Rudradeva was ruling from Warangal at that time,[29] and some three decades later his successor Ganapati credited Rudradeva with having founded the city.[30]All of the last three Kakatiyas—Ganapati, Rudramadevi, and Pratapa Rudra—identify themselves as ruling from Warangal.[31]

Thirteenth-century Warangal was laid out in a very nearly circular form, protected by two concentric rings of fortifications.[32] The outer wall consisted of a massive rampart of packed earth averaging about 60 metres wide at the base, and up to a height of 10 metres where it is not badly eroded. This rampart is approximately 2.4 kilometres in diameter and contains an area of about 485 hectares (1,200 acres). Before it stands a broad moat averaging about 70 metres in width. Eight ground-level passageways cut through the wall at approximately the cardinal and intermediate points, but it is unclear whether these passageways could have been closed. The two on the east and west are today lined with masonry and controlled by gateways at their inner ends, but these are clearly rebuildings of the fifteenth century, when the Bahmanis occupied the fort (see later).

The inner wall measures just over 1 kilometre in diameter and contains an area of about 78 hectares (193 acres). It averages about 15 metres in thickness at its base, and about 5 to 8 metres in height from the ground to the walkway of the battlement. It was constructed from a combination of earth and stone, using massive slabs of dressed granite (averaging about 1 × 1 × 3 metres), carefully fitted without any mortar, as an outer protective casing for the inner earthen core. Although the fabric of the wall varies from place to place, the most typical pattern features a regular alternation in courses: in one course the blocks are laid parallel to the wall's surface, in another they are laid as perpendicular stringers projecting into the core of the wall to help bond the structure together. The inner face of the rampart is graded at an angle of approximately 30 degrees, and here the earthen core is lined with long rectangular slabs arranged stepwise, creating a continuous stairway providing access to the top of the rampart from any point within the fort. The battlement walkway averages about 5 to 7 metres in width and was originally protected by a low parapet topped with diminutive crenellations, traces of which are now preserved only atop the inner walls of the gateways.

Like the outer wall, the inner stone wall is preceded by a moat, likely produced from excavating the earth for the wall's core. It is irregular but averages about 40 metres in width and is usually dry except during the rainy season. Forty-five rectangular bastions project outwards from the wall, typically measuring about 12 × 16 metres and separated by 60 to 100 metre intervals. Four monumental gateway complexes pierce the wall, all essentially identical and approximately aligned with the cardinal directions. Each is defined by barbican walls projecting outward from the main curtain wall to a distance of about 55 metres and separated by about 37 metres. A cross wall further subdivides the enclosed space into two open courtyards—a narrow outer rectangle measuring 8.5 by 26 metres, and an inner, approximately square courtyard measuring 25 × 26 metres. Although the road goes straight to the gateway, it turns sharply to the left just before leading to the gateway's outermost doorway, which stands at the left end of the outer rectangular court. The roadway passes through the outer doorway, between a pair of raised guards' platforms, and through the open courtyard. It then turns left through a second doorway and traverses the inner courtyard before passing through a third and final doorway into the fort itself. Battlements running along the tops of the barbican walls provided an extra measure of active defence.

Today, roads run in from the four gateways to meet at the centre of the city. Although they presently wind considerably to avoid the protected archaeological zone at the centre of the site, they were probably much straighter when originally built. Most likely, they would have intersected at the small two-storeyed *chaubārā* that stands just a few metres west of the present-day Shambhuni-gudi. To the northeast of this intersection lay the precinct of the great Svayambhu Shiva temple that housed the four-faced linga of the Kakatiyas' state deity. Now lying in ruins, this temple was a centrally planned *sarvatobhadra* shrine, with doors facing the cardinal directions so that Shiva could look out from his sanctum to survey the four quarters over which he ruled. The four celebrated toraṇas standing just outside the temple compound further expressed this idea of universal dominion. It has been suggested that the Kakatiya palace complex stood to the west of the Svayambhu Shiva precinct, although little definitive evidence supports this possibility.[33] Several smaller temples dot the cityscape, but more work is needed to determine whether they are of Kakatiya date, or whether, like the 'Venkateshvara-gudi' discussed under Phase 4, they represent later reconstructions from twelfth- and thirteenth-century Kakatiya components.

### Phase 2: c.1323–31: Tughluq Occupation

After his final defeat of Kakatiya Pratapa Rudra, the Tughluq prince Ulugh Khan occupied Warangal and initiated an architectural makeover of the city's central zone, recasting Warangal into 'Sultanpur', a provincial capital of the Delhi Sultanate. In order to undermine the Kakatiya king's authority, he broke in two the linga of Svayambhu Shiva and razed the temple complex, sparing only its four toraṇas. In its place he built a vast congregational mosque, prominently employing columns, ceiling panels, and other components retrieved from the earlier temple. Finally, to commemorate the conquest Ulugh Khan built an audience hall in the style of metropolitan Delhi—the so-called Khush Mahal—a short distance to the west of the newly constructed mosque. Like the temple before it, the Tughluq mosque is no longer standing, owing either to structural failure or to human intervention. It is possible that Kapaya Nayaka dismantled it when he wrested Warangal from the Tughluqs in the early 1330s.[34]

### Phase 3: c.1424–1504: Bahmani Occupation

As mentioned earlier, the style of the two stone gateways on the eastern and western sides of the outer 'mud' wall suggests that these monumental entrances were constructed at some point in the fifteenth century, during the period of Bahmani rule. Each consists of a long, stone-lined passageway with an angled bend leading through the projection in the earthen embankment. They continue into a gatehouse with an arched doorway at its outer end, followed by flanking guards' platforms on either side and ending in a triple-arched facade on the inner side. The fifteenth-century style of these two gates is suggested by several features linking them to gateways at Bidar. These include the gently bent angle of the passageway (cf. the passageway leading from the Sharza Darwaza to the Gumbad Darwaza at the entrance to Bidar's citadel), the configuration of the doubled, receding pointed arches within a sunken square frame, the bold quality of the simple stonework, and the general lack of ornamentation.

Given the construction of these two monumental gateways, and the neglect of the passageways on the other sides of the outer wall, it is tempting to conclude that Bahmani-period Warangal was becoming organized around a dominant east–west axis, focussing on the avenue running through the fort's two walls, much as at contemporary Raichur. The primacy of this east–west orientation is further underscored by the placement of two pairs of reused leogryph (vyāla) balustrades—likely retrieved from among the fragments of the Svayambhu Shiva temple—in the eastern and western gateways of the inner stone wall. If this interpretation is correct, then the present-day habitation pattern within Warangal Fort, with residences and shops clustered primarily along the two sides of the east–west thoroughfare, may well represent the continuing legacy of the Bahmani period settlement.[35]

Two other monuments in the inner fort possibly date to the Bahmani period—an unidentified vaulted hall consisting of two rows of five bays each, located in the northeastern sector,[36] and a complex of three rectangular halls in the southwestern quadrant.[37] These latter structures most likely served as granaries, considering their overall form and their location atop an elevated, sheetrock outcropping. This position would have promoted drainage away from the base of the structures, while the open sheetrock area would have provided ample workspace for threshing and winnowing the grain before taking it inside. In fact, hundreds of grinding slicks are worn into the sheetrock around the structures, such as would have been produced by hulling and polishing grain. Structurally, the buildings combine rubble masonry and timber construction,[38] a type of construction one occasionally finds in Bahmani-period buildings, but apparently not later.[39] This, too, would support the dating proposed here. Other examples of granaries of this type are preserved at Bhongir and Golconda, both of them occupied by the Bahmanis in the fifteenth century.

### Phase 4: c.1504–12: Shitab Khan's Occupation

In keeping with the relatively short period of his rule of Warangal, Shitab Khan, for reasons explored in Chapter 5, made few contributions to the city's built form beyond repairing and re-consecrating Kakatiya period temples. We find only one new building showing his involvement: the so-called Venkateshvara-gudi temple, located some 350 metres east-northeast of the Svayambhu Shiva complex. As explained in Chapter 5, Shitab Khan constructed this temple reusing authentic components from several distinct Kakatiya-period temples, and within its sanctum he re-consecrated a form of Krishna known as Panchaliraya.

### Phase 5: c.1512–1687: Qutb Shahi Occupation

Warangal's Qutb Shahi rulers carried out several projects to improve the city's defences, largely in response to the introduction of gunpowder weapons in the sixteenth century. Most importantly, they rebuilt the parapets atop the battlements of the city's inner wall, replacing the diminutive and essentially decorative Kakatiya crenellations with massive spade-shaped merlons with differently angled loopholes through which matchlocks could be fired. They also built semicircular barbicans in front of the eastern and western gates of the city's inner wall, providing an extra layer of defensive protection to these most actively used gates.[40] Finally, they built a massive octagonal gun platform at the city's highest point—Ekasila Hill—together with an adjacent powder magazine.[41] On both typological and stylistic grounds, we may attribute all of these additions to the Qutb Shahi period.

Apart from these utilitarian projects, the Qutb Shahis also decorated certain pre-existing structures with veneers in carved stucco. Since this ornamentation featured motifs commonly used on late sixteenth-century Qutb Shahi buildings, Warangal's rulers were, in effect, symbolically appropriating those earlier structures on which they appeared. Only two fragmentary patches of this stucco veneer survive today, one on an arch in one of the city's Bahmani-period gateways (see Figure 6.5, p. 215), and the other on the main façade of the

Tughluqs' 'Khush Mahal' audience hall (see Figure 6.6, p. 216).[42] Though likely much more widespread formerly, Qutb Shahi-style stucco motifs have largely vanished because of the impermanence of the medium.

## NOTES

1. An inscription dated 1323 refers to Kalyana as a 'great' or 'honoured' town (*al-qaṣbat-i mu`aẓzamat-i Kalyān*). See *Epigraphia Indo-Moslemica* (*EIM*) *1935–36*, 1–3, pl. I.

2. Ibid.

3. Fronting this gateway complex on the other side of the moat is an enclosed court with a lofty entrance gate constructed in 1883 by the Nawab of Kalyana, Sayyid Muhammad Mehdi Husain Khan (r. 1871–94). Several impressive buildings of the Nawabi period lie within the courtyard, including the well-preserved Husaini Bargah on the west, which Yazdani reports was used for the administration of justice and for social and religious functions. G. Yazdani, 'Appendix A: Note on the Antiquities of Kalyani', in *Annual Reports of the Archaeological Department of Hyderabad* (*ARADH*) *1933–34*, 17–23.

4. H.K. Sherwani states that the walls and bastions of the fort at Kalyana were built during the minority of Ahmad Shah III (1461–63) and Muhammad Shah III (1463–66), when the Bahmani state was ruled by a council of regents. Although Sherwani cites Badauni's *Muntakhab al-tawārīkh* (Calcutta: 1867), 3:452 as the basis for this statement, we have not been able to obtain a copy of the Persian text to corroborate Sherwani's statement. Haroon Khan Sherwani, *Bahmanis of the Deccan* (New Delhi: Munshiram Manoharlal, 1985), 189.

5. A wall can be constructed either in a single continuous rise of masonry or in two or more stepped rises, in which a leveling course is introduced and the masonry of the new rise is slightly stepped back from the face of the lower rise.

6. The Marathi inscription is apparently unpublished. For the others, see G. Yazdani, 'Inscriptions from Kalyani', *EIM 1935–36*, 1–14.

7. *EIM 1935–36*, 8 and pl. VI(a).

8. It is not clear whether this is the original form of the merlons, or whether it might be the product of alterations made in Phase 3.

9. That is, curtain segments II/5–1 and II/1–2 bond with bastion II/1, and curtain segments II/3–4 and II/4–5 bond with bastion II/4. By contrast, the masonry of curtain sections adjacent to pre-existing bastions abuts the masonry of those earlier bastions (that is, curtain segments II/1–2 and II/2–3 abut bastion II/2; segments II/2–3 and II/3–4 abut bastion II/3).

10. For the inscription, see P. Sreenivasachar, 'A Note on the Raichur Inscription of Vithala-natha, dated Saka 1216 (c.1294 AD)', *ARADH 1935–36,* Appendix E, 32–5.

11. Elizabeth Schotten Merklinger, 'The Mosques of Rāičūr: A Preliminary Classification', *Kunst des Orients* XII, nos 1 and 2 (1979):80–2.

12. See Finbarr B. Flood, 'Pillars, Palimpsests, and Princely Practices: Translating the Past in Sultanate Delhi', *RES: Anthropology and Aesthetics* 43 (Spring 2003), 103. As Flood notes, the Qutb Minar was called a *jaya-stambha* or 'victory pillar' in contemporary Sanskrit inscriptions. Delhi Sultanate rulers were fascinated with the ancient Indic *jaya-stambha*s of the pre-sultanate past, which they often incorporated into their mosques, calling them *manār*s, suggesting the semantic convergence between the two types of sultanate period monuments. The idea of a victory tower certainly persisted through Malik Kafur's day. His own master, Sultan `Ala al-Din Khalaji, left unfinished the base of another such monument in the Qutb mosque complex when he died in 1318.

13. Merklinger mistakenly writes that the Fort Jami` Masjid was founded in 1577, citing an inscription of that year located in the mosque's northern *miḥrāb*. Although this inscription does not record the foundation of any mosque, another inscription located in the southern miḥrāb, which is clearly a foundation inscription, states that the mosque was begun in 1620 and completed in 1622.

14. Merklinger, 'Mosques', 82–3.

15. Two inscriptions record the construction of gateways in the new wall. Although neither inscription explicitly mentions a wall, Mallu Khan must have been responsible for it as well, since its physical character is in keeping with mid-fifteenth century Bahmani work from this part of the Deccan, and there is no point in building a defensive gateway where there is no wall. See *Epigraphia Indica, Arabic and Persian Supplement* (*EIAPS*) 1962, 58–60, plates XVI(b) and XVII(a)

16. *EIAPS 1962*, 61–2, and plate XVIII. Of the city's nine gateways, the only two that experienced documented rebuildings lie at the avenue's eastern end—those of Vithalanatha and Mallu Khan.

17. This gateway was reconstructed three times after Mallu Khan's original foundation—in c. 1520, in 1550, and again in 1622. Local tradition holds that there was an earlier gateway, called the Kamani Darwaza, located on the site of the present Kati Darwaza. This may refer to the original gateway constructed by Mallu Khan. Meaning 'the Arched Gateway', the Kamani Darwaza would have been the first arcuate gateway constructed at Raichur, the earlier Kakatiya gateways having been of trabeate construction.

18. They are today housed in the Andhra Pradesh State Museum in Hyderabad. See K.M. Ahmad, 'Inscriptions of Raichur in the Hyderabad Museum', *EIM 1939–40*, 10–23.

19. For the characteristics of this important style, see George Michell, *The Vijayanagara Courtly Style: Incorporation and Synthesis in the Royal Architecture of Southern India, 15th–17th Centuries*, Vijayanagara Research Project Monograph Series, vol. 3 (New Delhi: Manohar and AIIS, 1992).

20. *South Indian Inscriptions* (*SII*) 4: no. 789 (lines 147–51).

21. *EIAPS 1963*, 62–5, plates XIX(a), XIX(b), and XX(a); *EIM 1939–40*, 17–23, plates VI, VII(b), VIII, VIII(b), IX, X(a).

22. *EIM 1939–40*, 19–21 and plates VIII(a) & VIII(b). Ahmad miscalculated the *abjad* date for the inscription shown in plate VIII(b) yielding a date, he writes, of AH1028/AD1619. The correct calculation yields AH1018/AD1609, the same date as the other inscription of this pair.

23. *EIAPS1963*, 63–4 and pl. XX(b).

24. Ibid., 64 and pl. XIX(c). Kadiri reports that this inscription was located 'on the inner side of the gate of the lake near Andheri Baoli'. The 'lake' in question must certainly be the so-called Khas Baoli, the large body of water within the Bahmani wall on the south side of the fort. We were unable to locate this inscription in the field.

25. *ARADH 1929–30*, 'Sketch Map of Raichur Fort' following plate XIII.

26. Making matters even more difficult, the southern face of the wall here is lapped by the waters of the large reservoir immediately to its south, which made it impossible to access during our field seasons in 2005 and 2006.

27. *EIAPS 1963*, 67–9, plates XXII(a–c). Three inscriptions document various aspects of this work.

28. According to preliminary reports from India's 2011 census, Raichur's urban population is 232,456 while the population of Warangal city is 620,116. (Figures from http://www.census2011.co.in/ [accessed 15 July 2013].)

29. *IAP-Warangal*, no. 42, (p. 118, lines 5–7): 'Orugaṃṭinĕlavīṭa … rājyambusĕyucuṃḍagānu'.

30. *EI* 3: no. 15 (verse 9).

31. See, for example, *CITD* 2: nos 50, 52, 53, and 55.

32. Today a third, outermost wall of rammed earth rings the city. Measuring 12.5 kilometres in diameter, it is detectable on topographic maps and satellite photographs, although only certain segments can be traced on the ground. Literary evidence suggests that this third wall was not built in the Kakatiya period, but some centuries later, as through the middle of the sixteenth century both Persian and Telugu literary and historical texts speak only of two walls—an inner stone wall, and an outer, earthen wall.

33. George Michell, 'City as Cosmogram: The Circular Plan of Warangal', *South Asian Studies* 8 (1992), 12–14.

34. For details of the Tughluq monuments, see Phillip B. Wagoner and John Henry Rice, 'From Delhi to the Deccan: Newly Discovered Tughluq Monuments at Warangal-Sultanpur and the Beginnings of Indo-Islamic Architecture in Southern India', *Artibus Asiae* LXI/1(2001), 77–117.

35. This pattern is clearly evident on the oldest known map of Warangal, surveyed in 1767 by the sub-engineer Henry Montresor, and published in 1808. See *Oriental Repertory, Published at the Charge of the East-India Company, by [Alexander] Dalrymple*, 2 vols (London: Printed by William Ballantine, Duke Street, Adelphi, Strand, 1808). See Volume 2, fifth plate at the end (following page 600) (British Library, G13655 and G13656).

36. See Michell, 'City as Cosmogram',12 and figure 19. Michell suggests that this building may have served as a stable.

37. See ibid., 12 and figure 18 for an illustration and brief discussion of these structures.

38. None of the timber elements survives, but the 'ghosts' of timber posts can be seen at regular intervals along the inside face of the stone walls, where the stone recedes slightly to make room for the now non-existent posts.

39. Bahmani examples include the eastern gateway to the fort at Sagar, constructed by Firuz Shah in 1407–08, which has substantial amounts of its timber structure still preserved, and the Bahmani palace at Daulatabad (early fifteenth century?), which also has a substantial amount of its timber intact. See George Michell and Mark Zebrowski, *Architecture and Art of the Deccan Sultanates* (Cambridge: Cambridge University Press, 1999), 26–7 and figure 6; and S.K. Aruni, 'Sagar: Provincial Headquarters of the Islamic Deccan', *Bulletin of the Deccan College* 56–7 (1996–97), 220–3.

40. Similar curving barbicans are known only from sixteenth-century Golconda, where they appear before some of the gateways in the outer walls (erected c.1560, early in the reign of Ibrahim), including the Patancheru Darwaza, the Banjara Darwaza, and the Palace Area Gate. The *Tārīkh-i Muḥammad Quṭb Shāhī* briefly mentions this building campaign at Hyderabad (Briggs, trans., *History of the Rise*, 3:245). See also Ghulam Yazdani, 'Inscriptions in Golconda Fort', *EIM 1913–14*, 48–9, pl. XIX(a), and the discussion in Marika Sardar, 'Golconda through Time: A Mirror of the Evolving Deccan', New York University Institute of Fine Arts, PhD dissertation, May 2007, 125ff.

41. Despite the platform's unusual octagonal plan, it compares with cavaliers or gun platforms known from many other fortified centres in the sixteenth-century Deccan, including Golconda itself. On the upper level of its platform, which is circular, the cavalier would have borne a single large cannon mounted to rotate a full 360 degrees. Though placed considerably closer to the southeastern section of the city's inner wall, its commanding elevation atop the rocky outcropping would have extended its range, enabling gunners to reach even the plain beyond the stone wall on the opposite, northwestern side of the fort, a kilometre away. A few metres from the cavalier is a small cubical chamber with a shallow vaulted ceiling. From its solid rubble masonry construction and lack of openings other than the doorway, this is recognizable as a powder magazine.

42. Traces of stucco decorative impost blocks in the characteristic Qutb Shahi style are visible on the inner archway of the Bahmani-period gateway that pierces the city's western, outer walls. With their distinctive horizontal mouldings derived from the earlier vocabulary of Kakatiya *citrakhaṇḍa* columns, these impost blocks were clearly applied to a plain fifteenth-century Bahmani-style arch that had lacked imposts. Traces of sixteenth-century stucco also remain on the northern façade of the Khush Mahal, built by the Tughluqs in the early fourteenth century. This stucco work includes Qutb Shahi standards topped with 'pineapple' motifs that were applied to the projecting angles of the wall on either side of the entrance.

# Select Bibliography


## PRIMARY SOURCES

### Epigraphic and Numismatic Sources

*ARADH*. *Annual Reports of the Archaeological Department of His Exalted Highness the Nizam's Dominions, 1914–1941*. Calcutta: Baptist Mission Press, 1916–c.1943.

*ARIE*. *Annual Reports on Indian Epigraphy, 1905–1978*. Delhi: Manager of Publications, c.1905–c.1978.

*ARMAD*. *Annual Reports of the Mysore Archaeological Department, 1916–1964*. Mysore: Government of Mysore, c.1916–c.1964.

*CITD*. *Corpus of Inscriptions in the Telangana Districts*. Parts 1–3, ed. P. Sreenivasachar; part 4, ed. Mallampalli Somasekhara Sarma. Hyderabad: Nizam's Government (1–3), Government of Andhra Pradesh (4), 1940–1973.

Desai, Ziyaud-Din A. *Arabic, Persian, and Urdu Inscriptions of West India: A Topographical List*. New Delhi: Sundeep Prakashan, 1999.

———. *A Topographical List of Arabic, Persian, and Urdu Inscriptions of South India*. New Delhi: Indian Council of Historical Research, 1989.

*EC*. *Epigraphia Carnatica*, vols 1–16. Edited by B. Lewis Rice. Bangalore, Mangalore, Mysore: Government Press, 1889–1955.

*EI*. *Epigraphia Indica*, vols 1–43. Calcutta/Delhi: Archaeological Survey of India, 1892–2012.

*EIAPS*. *Epigraphia Indica, Arabic and Persian Supplement, 1951/52–1977*. Delhi: Manager of Publications, c.1951/52–1977.

*EIM*. *Epigraphia Indo-Moslemica, 1907/08–1949/50*. Delhi: Manager of Publications, c.1907–1954.

Filliozat, Vasundhara. *l'Épigraphie de Vijayanagara du début à 1377*. Paris: École française d'extrême-orient, 1973.

Fleet, J.F. 'Sanskrit and Old-Canarese Inscriptions. No. XCVII', *Indian Antiquary* 10 (May, 1881): 126–31.

Goron, Stan and J.P. Goenka. *The Coins of the Indian Sultanates*. New Delhi: Munshiram Manoharlal, 2001.

*IAP—Warangal*. *Inscriptions of Andhra Pradesh—Warangal District*. Edited by N. Venkataramanayya. Epigraphical Series no. 6. Hyderabad: Government of Andhra Pradesh, 1974.

Naik, A.V. 'Inscriptions of the Deccan: An Epigraphical Survey (*circa* 300 B.C.–1300 A.D.),' *Bulletin of the Deccan College Research Institute* 9, nos 1–2 (1948): 1–160.

Nazim, Muhammad. *Bijapur Inscriptions*. Memoirs of the Archeological Survey of India, no. 49. Delhi: Manager of Publications, 1936.

*NDI*. *Nellore District Inscriptions*. A Collection of the Copper-Plate and Stone Inscriptions in the Nellore District, eds Alan Butterworth and V. Venugopal Chetty, vols 1–3. Madras: Government Press, 1905.

Ritti, Shrinivas and Anand Kumbhar. *Inscriptions from Solapur District*. Dharwar: Shrihari Prakashana, 1988.

*SII*. *South Indian Inscriptions*, vols 1–27. Madras: Government Press, 1890–2001.

*TTDI*. *Tirumala Tirupati Devasthanam Inscriptions*. Edited by S. Subrahmanya Sastry and V. Vijayaraghavacharya, vols 1–7. Tirupati: Tirumala Tirupati Devasthanam, 1930–38.

### Historical and Literary Works

#### *Arabic*

*Rehla* of Ibn Battuta. Translated by Mahdi Husain. Baroda: Oriental Institute, 1953.

#### *Persian*

*Burhān-i ma'āthir* of `Ali Tabataba. Delhi: Majlis-i Makhtutat-i Farsiya, 1936.

———. Extracts translated by J.S. King, 'History of the Bahmani Dynasty', *Indian Antiquary* 28 (1899); and by T.W. Haig, 'History of the Nizam Shahi Kings of Ahmadnagar', *Indian Antiquary* 49 (1920), 50 (1921), 51 (1922), 52 (1923).

*Futūḥus-salāṭīn* of `Abd al-Malik `Isami. Edited by A.S. Usha. Madras: University of Madras, 1948.

———. Edited and translated as *Futūḥu's Salāṭīn* by Agha Mahdi Husain. 3 vols. London: Asia Publishing House, 1967.

*Riyāḍ al-inshā'* of Mahmud Gawan. Hyderabad: Government Press, 1948.

*Tārīkh-i Firishta* of Muhammad Qasim Firishta. 2 vols. Lucknow: Nawal Kishor, 1864–65.

———. Translated by John Briggs as *History of the Rise of the Mahomedan Power in India*. 4 vols. London, 1829. Reprint in 4 vols. Calcutta: Editions Indian, 1966.

*Tārīkh-i Fīrūz Shāhī* of Zia al-Din Barani. Extracts in *The History of India as Told by Its Own Historians*, translated and edited by H.M. Elliott and John Dowson, 3: 93–268. 8 vols. Allahabad: Kitab Mahal, 1964.

*Tārīkh-i Muḥammad Quṭb Shāh* (also called *Tārīkh-i guzīda-yi Sulṭān Muḥammad Quṭb Shāhī*). Translated by John Briggs in *History of the Rise of the Mahomedan Power in India*, 3: 202–92. 4 vols. London, 1829. Reprint in 4 vols. Calcutta: Editions Indian, 1966.

———. Excerpts translated by V. Minorsky, 'The Qara-Qoyonlu and the Qutb-Shāhs (Turkmenica, 10)', *Bulletin of the School of Oriental and African Studies* 17, no. 1 (1955): 50–73.

*Tazkirat al-mulūk* of Rafi` al-Din Shirazi. Composed 1609–12. Unpublished critical edition by Abu Nasr Khalidi, revised by Carl W. Ernst. Personal possession of Professor Ernst.

#### *Dakhni or Urdu*

*Kitāb-i-Nauras* of Ibrahim Adil Shah II. Edited by Nazir Ahmad. New Delhi: Bharatiya Kala Kendra, 1956.

*Ṣaḥīfat-i Ahl-i Hudā* of Muhyi al-Din b. Saiyid Mahmud Qadiri. Hyderabad: National Fine Printing Press, 1966.

#### *Sanskrit*

Mahābhārata of Vyāsa. *Śrīman Mahābhāratam (mūla-mātram)*. Vol. 1, Ādi, Sabhā, and Vana Parvans. Gorakhpur: Gita Press, 2013 V.S. [1956].

———. *The Mahābhārata of Krishna-Dwaipayana Vyasa*. Translated by P.C. Roy [K.M. Ganguli]. Second edition. Calcutta: Oriental Publishing, n.d.

———. *The Mahābhārata: 2. The Book of the Assembly Hall, 3. The Book of the Forest*. Translated by J.A.B. van Buitenen. Chicago: University of Chicago Press, 1975.

*Mānasollāsa* of Someśvara. *Royal Life in Mānosollāsa*. Translated by P. Arundhati. Delhi: Sundeep Prakashan, 1994.

*Mayamata*. Edited and translated as *Mayamata: Traité Sanskrit d'Architecture* by Bruno Dagens. 2 vols. Pondicherry: Institut Français d'Indologie, 1970 and 1976.

*Mitākṣarā* of Vijñāneśvara. *The Yajñavālkya Smṛti with Vīramitrodaya, the Commentary of Mitra Miśra, and Mitākṣarā, the Commentary of Vijñāneśvara*, eds Narayana Sastri, Khiste Sahityacharya, and Jagannatha Sastri Hosinga Sahityopadhyaya. Benares: Chowkhamba Sanskrit Series Office, 1930.

———. *Yajnavalkya Smriti with the Commentary of Vijnaneśvara called the Mitākṣarā and Notes from the Gloss of Bālambhaṭṭa*. Book 1, *The Āchāra Adhyāya*. Translated by Srisa Chandra Vidyārṇava. Allahabad: The Panini Office, 1918.

———. *The Sacred Laws of the Aryas as Taught in the School of Yajnavalkya and Explained by Vijnanesvara in his Well-known Commentary Named the Mitākṣarā*. Vol. 3, *The Prāyaścitta Adhyāya*. Translated by S.N. Naraharayya. Allahabad: Sudhindranatha Vasu, 1913.

*Nirṇayasindhu* of Kamalākara Bhaṭṭa. *The Nirṇayasindhu by Kamalākara Bhaṭṭa, with a commentary by Kṛṣṇam Bhaṭṭa.* Edited by Gopal Sastri Nene. 2 vols. Benares: Chowkhamba Sanskrit Series Office, 1930.

*Pampāmāhātmyamu. Skānda-purāṇāntargatahema-kūṭa-khaṇḍātmaka saptarṣi-yātrā prakāśa-ka Pampāmāhātmyamu*. Edited by K. Venkatarama Sastri and H. Venkatesvara Sastri. Hampi, 1933.

*Pratāparudrīyam* of Vidyānātha. With the *Ratnāpaṇa* commentary of Kumaraswami Somapithin. Edited by V. Raghavan. Madras: Sanskrit Education Society of Madras, 1970.

———. *Le Pratāparudrīya de Vidyānātha avec le commentaire Ratnāpaṇa de Kumārasvāmin*. Translated by Pierre-Sylvain Filliozat. Pondicherry: Institut Francais d'Indologie, 1963.

*Sāmrājya Lakṣmīpīṭhikā*. Edited by K. Vasudeva Sastri and K.S. Subrahmanya Sastri. Tanjore Saraswati Mahal Series no. 58. Thanjavur: Saraswati Mahal Library, 1990.

*Vikramāṅkadevacaritam* of Bilhaṇa. *The Vikramānka-devacharita, a Life of King Vikramāditya—Tribuvanamalla of Kalyāṇa*. Edited by Georg Bühler. Bombay: Government Central Book Depot, 1875.

*Vikramāṅkadevacaritam* of Bilhaṇa. *Bilhaṇa's Vikramāṅkadevacaritam: Glimpses of the History of the Cālukyas of Kalyāṇa*. Translated by Sures Chandra Banerji and Amal Kumar Gupta. Calcutta: Sambodhi Publications, 1965.

*Virūpākṣa Vasantotsava Champū* of Ahobala-kavi. Edited by R.S. Pancamukhi. Dharwar: Kannada Research Institute, 1953.

### *Kannada*

Kotraiah, C.T.M. and Anna L. Dallapiccola, *King, Court, and Capital: An Anthology of Kannada Literary Sources from the Vijayanagara Period*. Vijayanagara Research Project Monograph Series, Vol. 9. New Delhi: Manohar and American Institute of Indian Studies, 2003.

Ramanujan, A.K. trans. *Speaking of Śiva.* London: Penguin Books, 1973.

### *Telugu*

*Cāṭu-padya-maṇi-mañjari.* Edited by Veturi Prabhakara Sastri. Hyderabad: Mani Manjari Prachuranalu, 1988.

*Citrabhāratamu* of Carigoṇḍa Dharmanna. Edited by Oleti Venkataraya Sastri. Madras: Vavilla Ramaswamy Sastrulu and Sons, 1934.

*Mārkaṇḍeya Purāṇamu* of Mārana. Edited by G.V. Subrahmanyam. Hyderabad: Andhra Pradesh Sahitya Academy, 1984.

*Padya-Bālabhāgavatamu* of Doneru Konerunatha-kavi. *Andugala Vengakavi Rāmarājīyamu lēka narapati vijayamu mariyu Dōnēru Kōnērunāthakavi Padya Bālabhāgavatamu Dvipada Bālabhāgavatamu (Aravīṭi Rājula Praśamsa)*. Edited by C.V. Ramachandra Rao. Nellore: Manasa Publications, 1995.

*Pratāparudra-caritramu* of Ekāmranātha. *Ekāmranāthuni Pratāparudra Caritramu*. Edited by C.V. Ramachandra Rao. Hyderabad: Andhra Pradesh Sahitya Academy, 1984.

*Rājanīti-ratnākaramu* of Nebati Kṛṣṇaya. Unpublished MS. (no. 616) in the Sanskrit

Academy Collection of Osmania University. Excerpts from the preface in B. Rama Raju, 'Nebati Kṛṣṇayāmātyuḍu', in *Khutub Ṣāhī Sultānulu—Āndhra Saṃskṛti*, ed. B. Rama Raju, 97–112. Hyderabad: Idara-i Adabiyat-i Urdu, 1962.

*Rāmarājīyamu* of Vengakavi. *Andugala Vengakavi Rāmarājīyamu lēka narapati vijayamu mariyu Dōnēru Kōnērunāthakavi Padya Bālabhāgavatamu Dvipada Bālabhāgavatamu (Aravīṭi Rājula Praśamsa)*. Edited by C.V. Ramachandra Rao. Nellore: Manasa Publications, 1995.

*Rāyavācakamu*. Edited by C.V. Ramachandra Rao. Hyderabad: Andhra Pradesh Sahitya Academy, 1982.

———. Translated as *Tidings of the King: A Translation and Ethnohistorical Analysis of the Rāyavācakamu* by Phillip B. Wagoner. Honolulu: University of Hawai'i Press, 1993.

*Tapatī-Samvaraṇamu* of Addanki Gangadhara-kavi. Edited by Patibanda Madhavasarma. Hyderabad: Parameshvara Publications, 1972.

*Vaijayantī Vilāsamu* of Sārangu Tammaya. *Vaijayantī Vilāsamu anu nāmāntaramugala Vipranārāyaṇa Caritramu, Sārangu Tammaya praṇītamu*. Madras: Vavilla Ramaswamy Shastrulu and Sons, 1966.

*Vasucaritramu* of Bhaṭṭumūrti. *Rāmarājabhūṣaṇuni Vasucaritramu: Āndhra Pancakāvyamulalo Reṇḍavadi*. Edited by Ravuri Dorasami Sharma. Vijayawada: Emesco Books, 1997.

*Yayāti Caritramu* of Ponnikanti Telaganarya. Edited by M. Rangakrishnamacharyulu. Hyderabad: Kakati Publications, 1977.

*European*

Albuquerque, Afonso de. *The Commentaries of the Great Afonso Dalbuquerque, Second Viceroy of India*, trans. Walter de Gray Birch. 1875–84; repr. 4 vols. New York: B. Franklin, 1970.

Barbosa, Duarte. *The Book of Duarte Barbosa*, trans. Mansel L. Dames. 1918; repr. 2 vols. Nendeln/Liechtenstein: Kraus Reprint, 1967.

'Chronicle of Fernão Nuniz'. In *A Forgotten Empire, Vijayanagara: a Contribution to the History of India*, trans. Robert Sewell. 1900; repr. New Delhi: Publications Division, 1962.

Correia-Afonso, John. 'Bijapur Four Centuries Ago as Described in a Contemporary Letter', *Indica* 1 (March, 1964): 81–8.

Correia, Gaspar. *Lendas da India*. Lisbon: Typ. da Academia Real das Sciencias, 1860.

Federici, Cesare. *The Voyage and Travaile into the East India, London 1588*, trans. Thomas Hickock. Amsterdam and New York: Theatrum Orbis Terrarum and Da Capo Press, 1971 (facsimile edition of 1588).

Lopes, David, trans. *Chronica dos Reis de Bisnaga: Manuscripto Inedito do Seculo XVI*. Lisbon: Impr. Nac., 1897.

'Report of Narrain Row from April to August 1816', Mackenzie Translations, Class XII, no. 47. Asian, Pacific, and African Collections, European Manuscripts. London, British Library.

Moreland, W.F. *Relations of Golconda in the Early Seventeenth Century*. London: Hakluyt Society, 1931.

Varthema, Ludovico di. *The Travels of Ludovico di Varthema*, trans. John Winter Jones. 1863; repr. New York: Burt Franklin, n.d.

*Various Languages*

Krishnaswami Ayyangar, S. *Sources of Vijayanagar History*. Madras: University of Madras, 1919.

## SECONDARY SOURCES

Alam, Muzaffar. *The Languages of Political Islam: India, 1200–1800*. Chicago: University of Chicago Press, 2004.

Alam, Muzaffar and Sanjay Subrahmanyam. 'The Deccan Frontier and Mughal Expansion, ca. 1600: Contemporary Perspectives', *Journal of the Economic and Social History of the Orient* 47 no. 3 (2004): 357–89.

Ali, Daud and Emma Flatt, eds. *Garden and Landscape Practices in Precolonial India:*

*Histories from the Deccan.* New Delhi: Routledge, 2011.

Anderson, Leona M. *Vasantotsava: The Spring Festivals of India, Texts and Traditions.* New Delhi: D.K. Printworld, 1993.

Arjomand, Said Amir. 'Evolution of the Persianate Polity and its Transmission to India', *Journal of Persianate Studies* 2 (2009): 116–36.

Aruni, S.K. 'Sagar: Provincial Headquarters of the Islamic Deccan', *Bulletin of the Deccan College* 56–7 (1996–7): 219–29.

Bhandarkar, R.G. *Early History of the Deccan and Miscellaneous Historical Essays.* 1933. Reprint, Poona: Bhandarkar Oriental Research Institute, 1983.

Bilgrami, Syed Ali Asgar. *Landmarks of the Deccan: A Comprehensive Guide to the Archaeological Remains of the City and Suburbs of Hyderabad.* Hyderabad: Government Press, 1927.

Black, Jeremy. *Beyond the Military Revolution: War in the Seventeenth-Century World.* New York: Palgrave Macmillan, 2011.

Blair, Sheila and Jonathan Bloom. *The Art and Architecture of Islam, 1250–1800.* New Haven: Yale University Press, 1994.

Bronner, Yigal. 'The Poetics of Ambivalence: Imagining and Unimagining the Political in Bilhana's *Vikramankadevacarita*', *Journal of Indian Philosophy* 38, no. 5 (2010): 457–83.

Brubaker, Robert. *Cornerstones of Control: the Infrastructure of Imperial Security at Vijayanagara, South India.* PhD dissertation, Department of Anthropology, University of Michigan, 2004.

Bulliet, Richard W. *Cotton, Climate, and Camels in Early Islamic Iran: A Moment in World History.* New York: Columbia University Press, 2009.

Burgess, James. *Report on the Antiquities of the Bidar and Aurangabad Districts.* London: Wm. H. Allen, 1878.

Casale, Giancarlo. *The Ottoman Age of Exploration.* Oxford: Oxford University Press, 2010.

Chattopadhyaya, B.D. *Representing the Other? Sanskrit Sources and the Muslims.* New Delhi, 1998.

Coomaraswamy, Ananda K. 'Early Indian Architecture, I: Cities and City Gates, etc.', *Eastern Art* 2 (1930): 208–25.

Cousens, Henry. *The Chalukyan Architecture of the Kanarese Districts*, Archaeological Survey of India, New Imperial Series. Vol. 42. Calcutta: Government of India, 1926.

———. *Mediaeval Temples of the Dakhan.* Archaeological Survey of India Reports, New Imperial Series. Vol. 48. Calcutta: Government of India, 1931.

Cox, Whitney M. 'Law, Literature, and the Problem of Politics in Medieval India', in *Law and Hinduism: an Introduction*, eds Timothy Lubin, Donald R. Davis, Jr, and Jayanth K. Krishnan, 167–82. Cambridge: Cambridge University Press, 2010.

———. 'Scribe and Script in the Calukya West Deccan', *Indian Economic and Social History Review* 47, no. 1 (2010): 1–28.

Cruz, Maria Augusta Lima. 'Exiles and Renegades in Early Sixteenth Century Portuguese India', *Indian Economic and Social History Review* 23, no. 3 (1986): 249–62.

Daehnhardt, Rainer. *The Bewitched Gun: the Introduction of the Firearm in the Far East by the Portuguese.* Lisbon: Texto Editora, 1994.

Daniel, Elton L. *The Political and Social History of Khurasan under Abbasid Rule.* Minneapolis: Blblioteca Islamica, 1979.

Darling, Linda T. '"Do Justice, Do Justice, for that is Paradise": Middle Eastern Advice for Indian Muslim Rulers', *Comparative Studies of South Asia, Africa and the Middle East* 22, nos 1 and 2 (2002): 3–19.

Davis, Richard. 'Indian Art Objects as Loot', *Journal of Asian Studies* 52, no. 1 (Feb. 1993): 22–48.

———. *Lives of Indian Images.* Princeton: Princeton University Press, 1997.

Davison-Jenkins, Dominic J. *The Irrigation and Water Supply Systems of Vijayanagara*, Vijayanagara Research Project Monograph Series, Vol. 5. New Delhi: Manohar and American Institute of Indian Studies, 1997.

Deloche, Jean. *Four Forts of the Deccan.* Pondicherry: École Française d'Extrême-Orient, 2009.

———. 'Gunpowder Artillery and Military Architecture in South India (15–18th Century)', *Indian Journal of History of Science* 40 no. 4 (2005): 573–96.

———. *Studies on Fortification in India.* Pondicherry: École Française d'Extrême-Orient, 2007.

Desai, P.B. *Jainism in South India and Some Jain Epigraphs.* Sholapur: Jaina Samskrti Samrakshaka Sangha, 1957.

Dhaky, M.A. *Encyclopaedia of Indian Temple Architecture.* Vol. 1, part 3: *South India, Upper Dravidadesa, Later Phase, A.D. 973–1326.* New Delhi: American Institute for Indian Studies, 1996.

———. *The Indian Temple Forms in Karnata Inscriptions and Architecture.* New Delhi: Abhinav Publications, 1977.

Eaton, Richard M. 'India's Military Revolution: The View from the Early Sixteenth-Century Deccan', in *Warfare, Religion, and Society in Indian History,* eds Raziuddin Aquil and Kaushik Roy, 85–108. New Delhi: Manohar, 2012.

———. '"Kiss My Foot," Said the King: Firearms, Diplomacy, and the Battle for Raichur, 1520', *Modern Asian Studies* (John F. Richards Commemorative Volume) 43, no. 1 (2009): 289–313.

———. 'Muhammad bin Tughluq and Temples of the Deccan, 1321–26', in *Sultans of the South: Arts of India's Deccan Courts, 1323–1687,* eds Navina Najat Haidar and Marika Sardar, 178–87. New York and New Haven: Metropolitan Museum of Art and Yale University Press, 2011.

———. *A Social History of the Deccan, 1300–1761: Eight Indian Lives.* Cambridge: Cambridge University Press, 2005.

———. *Sufis of Bijapur, 1300–1700: Social Roles of Sufis in Medieval India.* Princeton: Princeton University Press, 1978.

———. 'Temple Desecration and Indo-Muslim States', in *Beyond Turk and Hindu: Rethinking Religious Identities in Islamicate South Asia,* eds David Gilmartin and Bruce B. Lawrence, 246–81. Gainesville: University Press of Florida, 2000.

*Encyclopaedia of Indian Temple Architecture.* Edited by Michael W. Meister, M.A. Dhaky, and Krishna Deva. 2 Vols, multiple parts. New Delhi: American Institute of Indian Studies; Philadelphia: University of Pennsylvania Press, 1983.

Fergusson, James, James Burgess, and Richard Phené Spiers, *History of Indian and Eastern Architecture.* 2 Vols. Delhi: Munshiram Manoharlal, 1967 (revised edition of 1876).

Filliozat, Vasundhara. 'Iconography: Religious and Civil Monuments', in *Vijayanagara—City and Empire: New Currents of Research,* eds Anna Libera Dallapiccola and Stephanie Zingel-Avé Lallement, I: 308–16. Wiesbaden: Franz Steiner Verlag, 1985.

Flatt, Emma. 'The Authorship and Significance of the *Nujūm al-`ulūm*: A Sixteenth-Century Astrological Encyclopedia from Bijapur', *Journal of the American Oriental Society* 131, no. 2 (2011): 223–44.

———. 'Courtly Culture in the Indo-Persian States of the Medieval Deccan: 1450–1600'. PhD dissertation, London, School of Oriental and African Studies, 2009.

Fleet, J.F. *The Dynasties of the Kanarese Districts of the Bombay Presidency from the Earliest Historical Times to the Muhammadan Conquest of A.D. 1318.* Bombay: Govt. Central Press, 1882.

Flood, Finbarr B. 'Appropriation as Inscription: Making History in the First Friday Mosque of Delhi', in *Reuse Value:* Spolia *and Appropriation in Art and Architecture from Constantine to Sherrie Levine,* eds Richard Brilliant and Dale Kinney, 121–47. Burlington, VT: Ashgate, 2011.

———. *Objects of Translation: Material Culture and Medieval 'Hindu-Muslim' Encounter.* Princeton: Princeton University Press, 2009.

———. 'Pillars, Palimpsests, and Princely Practices: Translating the Past in Sultanate Delhi', *RES:*

*Anthropology and Aesthetics* 43 (Spring 2003): 95–116.

Foekema, Gerard. *Calukya Architecture: Medieval Temples of Northern Karnataka Built during the Rule of the Calukya of Kalyana and Thereafter, AD 1000–1300.* 3 Vols. New Delhi: Munshiram Manoharlal, 2003.

Fritz, John M., George Michell, and M.S. Nagaraja Rao. *Where Kings and Gods Meet: The Royal Centre at Vijayanagara, India.* Tucson: University of Arizona Press, 1984.

Fukazawa, Hiroshi. 'The Local Administration of the Adilshahi Sultanate (1489–1686)', in Hiroshi Fukazawa, *The Medieval Deccan: Peasants, Social Systems, and States, Sixteenth to Eighteenth Centuries*: 1–48. Delhi: Oxford University Press, 1991.

Gayani, B.G. 'Kitab-i-Nauras', *Islamic Culture* 19, no. 2 (1945): 140–52.

Goetz, Hermann. 'Indo-Islamic Figural Sculpture', *Ars Orientalis* 5 (1963): 235–41.

Gommans, Jos. *Mughal Warfare: Indian Frontiers and High Roads to Empire, 1500–1700.* New York: Routledge, 2002.

Gopal, B.R. *The Chalukyas of Kalyana and the Kalachuris.* Dharwad: Karnatak University, 1981.

Gopalakrishna Murthy, S. *The Sculpture of the Kakatiyas.* Hyderabad: Government of Andhra Pradesh, 1964.

Gould, Rebecca K. 'How Newness Enters the World: the Methodology of Sheldon Pollock', *Comparative Studies of South Asia, Africa, and the Middle East* 28, no. 3 (2008): 186–203.

Grabar, Oleg. *The Formation of Islamic Art.* Revised and enlarged edition: New Haven: Yale University Press, 1987.

Haidar, Navina Najat. 'The *Kitab-i Nauras*: Key to Bijapur's Golden Age', in *Sultans of the South: Arts of India's Deccan Courts, 1323–1687*, eds Navina Najat Haidar and Marika Sardar, 26–43. New York: Metropolitan Museum of Art, 2011.

Hardy, Adam. *Indian Temple Architecture: Form and Transformation—The Karnata Dravida Tradition, Seventh to Thirteenth Centuries.* New Delhi: Indira Gandhi National Centre for the Arts and Abhinav Publications, 1995.

Heras, Henry. *The Aravidu Dynasty of Vijayanagara.* Madras: B.G. Paul and Co., 1927.

Hirananda Sastri. *Shitab Khan of Warangal.* Hyderabad Archaeological Series, no. 9. Hyderabad: Nizam's Government, 1932.

Hutton, Deborah. *Art of the Court of Bijapur.* Bloomington: Indiana University Press, 2006.

Inalcik, Halil. 'Bursa and the Commerce of the Levant', *Journal of the Economic and Social History of the Orient* 3, no. 2 (1960): 131–47.

Iqtidar Alam Khan. *Gunpowder and Firearms: Warfare in Medieval India.* Delhi: Oxford University Press, 2004.

Ishwaran, K., *Religion and Society among the Lingayats of South India.* Leiden: E.J. Brill, 1983.

Jagdish. 'Construction Technology of the Stepped Tank in the Royal Centre (IVc/6)', in *Vijayanagara, Archaeological Exploration, 1990–2000: Papers in Memory of Channabasappa S. Patil*, eds John M. Fritz, Robert P. Brubaker, and Teresa P. Raczek, with the assistance of George Michell. I: 79–88. Vijayanagara Research Project Monograph Series. Vol. 10. New Delhi: Manohar and American Institute of Indian Studies, 2006.

Joshi, P.M. "Ali `Adil Shah of Bijapur (1558–80) and his Royal Librarian: Two Ruq'as', in *The Sardhasatabdi Commemoration Volume, 1804–1954*, ed. G.C. Jhala, 97–107. Bombay: Asiatic Society of Bombay, 1957.

———. 'Asad Beg's Mission to Bijapur, 1603–04', in *Prof D.V. Potdar 61st Birthday Commemoration Volume*, ed. S. Sen, 181–96. Poona, 1950.

Kadiri, A.A. 'Bahmani Inscriptions from Raichur District'. *EIAPS 1962*, 53–66.

Kasdorf, Katherine E. 'Translating Sacred Space in Bijapur: the Mosques of Karim al-Din and Khwaja Jahan', *Archives of Asian Art* 59 (2009): 57–80.

Kulkarni, A.R. 'Social Relations in the Marathi Country in the Medieval Period', *Indian*

*History Congress, Proceedings*, 32nd session (Jabalpur), 1970: 231–69.

Kramrisch, Stella. *The Hindu Temple.* 2 Vols Calcutta: University of Calcutta, 1946.

Krishna Sastri, H. 'The Second Vijayanagara Dynasty: Its Viceroys and Ministers', in *Archaeological Survey of India, Annual Report for the Years 1908–9*, 164–201. Calcutta: Office of the Superintendent of Government Printing, 1912.

Lambourn, Elizabeth. 'India from Aden: *Khuṭba* and Muslim Urban Networks in Late Thirteenth-Century India', in *Secondary Cities and Urban Networking in the Indian Ocean Realm, c. 1400–1800*, ed. Kenneth R. Hall, 55–97. Lanham: Lexington Books, 2008.

Lambton, Ann K.S. 'Justice in the Medieval Persian Theory of Kingship', *Studia Islamica* 17 (1962): 91–119.

———. '*Quis custodiet custodies*: Some Reflections on the Persian Theory of Government', *Studia Islamica* 5 (1956): 125–48.

Mate, M.S. and T.V. Pathy, eds. *Daulatabad (A Report on the Archaeological Investigations).* Pune: Deccan College Post Graduate & Research Institute, 1992.

Meisami, Julie Scott. *Persian Historiography to the End of the Twelfth Century.* Edinburgh: Edinburgh University Press, 1999.

Meister, Michael W. 'Mountain Temples and Temple-Mountains: Masrur', *Journal of the Society of Architectural Historians* 65 (2006): 26–49.

———. 'The "Two-and-a-Half-Day" Mosque', *Oriental Art* 18, no. 1 (1972): 57–63.

Merklinger, Elizabeth Schotten. *Indian Islamic Architecture: The Deccan, 1347–1686.* Warminster, England: Aris and Phillips Ltd., 1981.

———. 'The Mosques of Rāičūr: A Preliminary Classification', *Kunst des Orients* XII 1/2 (n.d.): 79–94.

Michell, George. *Architecture and Art of Southern India: Vijayanagara and the Successor States*, New Cambridge History of India, I, 6. Cam-bridge: Cambridge University Press, 1995.

Michell, George. 'City as Cosmogram: The Circular Plan of Warangal', *South Asian Studies* 8 (1992): 1–18.

———. *The Vijayanagara Courtly Style: Incorporation and Synthesis in the Royal Architecture of Southern India, 15th–17th Centuries.* Delhi: Manohar and American Institute of Indian Studies, 1992.

Michell, George and Mark Zebrowski. *Architecture and Art of the Deccan Sultanates.* Cambridge: Cambridge University Press, 1999.

Michell, George and Phillip B. Wagoner. *Vijayanagara: Architectural Inventory of the Sacred Centre.* 3 Vols. New Delhi: American Institute of Indian Studies/Manohar Publications, 2001.

Michell, George and Richard Maxwell Eaton. *Firuzabad: Palace City of the Deccan.* London: Oxford University Press, 1992.

Minorsky, V. 'The Qara-Qoyunlu and the Quṭb Shāhs (Turkmenica 10)', *Bulletin of the School of Oriental and African Studies* 17, no. 1 (1955): 50–73.

Misra, B.N. *Studies on Bilhana and His Vikramankadevacarita.* New Delhi: K.B. Publications, 1976.

Mulkapuri, `Abd al-Jabbar. *Taẕkīra-yi Auliyā-yi Dakan.* Urdu lithograph, 2 Vols. Hyderabad: Hasan Press, 1912–13.

Murthy, N.S. Ramachandra. *Forts of Andhra Pradesh (from the earliest times up to 16th c. A.D.).* Delhi: Bharatiya Kala Prakashan, 1996.

Nagaraja Rao, M.S., ed. *The Chalukyas of Kalyana (Seminar Papers).* Bangalore: The Mythic Society, 1983.

Naqvi, Sadiq. *The Iranian Afaquies Contribution to the Qutb Shahi and Adil Shahi Kingdoms.* Hyderabad: Dr. Sadiq Naqvi, 2003.

———. *Muslim Religious Institutions and Their Role under the Qutb Shahis.* Hyderabad: Bab-ul-ilm Society, 1993.

Narayana Rao, V. David Shulman, and Sanjay Subrahmanyam. *Textures of Time: Writing History in South India, 1600–1800*. Delhi: Permanent Black, 2001.

Naravane, M.S. *Forts of Maharashtra*. New Delhi: APH Publishing Corporation. 1995.

Nayeem, M.A. *The Heritage of the Qutb Shahis of Golconda and Hyderabad.* Hyderabad: Hyderabad Publishers, 2006.

Nayeem, M.A., Aniruddha Ray, and K.S. Mathew, eds, *Studies in the History of the Deccan, Medieval and Modern: Professor A.R. Kulkarni Felicitation Volume.* Delhi: Pragati Publications, 2002.

Nazim, Muhammad. *Bijapur Inscriptions, Memoirs of the Archeological Survey of India*, no. 49. Delhi: Manager of Publications, 1936.

Newman, Richard. *The Stone Sculpture of India: A Study of the Materials Used by Indian Sculptors from ca. 2nd century B.C. to the 16th century.* Cambridge: Harvard University Art Museums, 1984.

Nilakanta Sastri, K.A. 'The Chāḷukyas of Kalyāṇi, Appendix C: The Kalachuris of Kalyāṇi', in *Early History of the Deccan*, ed. G. Yazdani, I: 456–68. London: Oxford University Press, 1960.

Orr, Leslie. 'Cholas, Pandyas, and "Imperial Temple Culture" in Medieval Tamilnadu', in *The Temple in South Asia*, ed. Adam Hardy, 83–97. London: British Academy, 2007.

Paddayya, K. 'Towards the Archaeology of the Medieval Shorapur Doab, Deccan', *Islamic Culture* 64, nos 2–3 (1990): 75–112.

Pal, Pratapaditya. *Hindu Religion and Iconography according to the* Tantrasāra. Los Angeles: Vichitra Press, 1981.

Pandu Ranga Rao, M. ed. *Engineering and Technological Achievements during the Kakatiya Period.* Warangal: INTACH, 1996.

M. Pandu Ranga Rao, S. Raghavachari, N. Babu Shanker, and A.U.R. Somayajulu. *Geotechnical Appraisal and Evaluation of Kakatiya Monuments, Warangal, A.P.* Warangal: Department of Civil Engineering, Regional Engineering College, 1987.

Parabrahma Sastry, P.V. *The Kakatiyas of Warangal.* Hyderabad: Government of Andhra Pradesh, 1978.

Parker, Geoffrey. *The Military Revolution: Military Innovation and the Rise of the West.* Cambridge: Cambridge University Press, 1988.

Parker, Geoffrey and Sanjay Subrahmanyam. 'Arms and the Asian: Revisiting European Firearms and their Place in Early Modern Asia', *Revista de Cultura* (Macau) 26 (2008): 12–42.

Patel, Alka. 'Architectural Histories Entwined: The Rudra-Mahalaya/Congregational Mosque of Siddhpur, Gujarat', *The Journal of the Society of Architectural Historians* 63, no. 2 (June 2004): 144–63.

———. *Building Communities in Gujarat: Architecture and Society during the Twelfth through Fourteenth Centuries.* Leiden: Brill, 2004.

———. 'Expanding the Ghurid Architectural Corpus East of the Indus: The Jāgeśvara Temple at Sādaḍi, Rajasthan', *Archives of Asian Art* 59 (2009): 33–56.

Pathak, Vishwambhar Sharan. *Ancient Historians of India: A Study in Historical Biographies.* Bombay: Asia Publishing House, 1966.

Patil, C.S. 'Mudugal Fort and Its Bearing on the Defense System at Vijayanagara', in *Vijayanagara, Progress of Research, 1988–1991*, eds D.V. Devaraj, Channabasappa S. Patil, and John M. Fritz, 197–209. Mysore: Directorate of Archaeology and Museums, 1996.

———. 'Palace Architecture at Vijayanagara', in *Vijayanagara, Progress of Research, 1983–84*, eds M.S. Nagaraja Rao and George Michell, 119–32. Mysore: Directorate of Archaeology and Museums, 1985.

Petievich, Carla. *When Men Speak as Women: Vocal Masquerade in Indo-Muslim Poetry.* New Delhi: Oxford University Press, 2007.

Philon, Helen, ed. *Silent Splendour: Palaces of the Deccan, 14th–19th Centuries*. Mumbai: Marg Publications, 2010.

Pollock, Sheldon. 'The Cosmopolitan Vernacular', *Journal of Asian Studies* 57, no. 1 (1998): 6–37.

Pollock, Sheldon. *The Language of the Gods in the World of Men: Sanskrit, Culture, and Power in Premodern India.* Berkeley: University of California Press, 2006.

———. 'The Sanskrit Cosmopolis, A.D. 300–1300: Transculturation, Vernacularization, and the Question of Ideology', in *Ideology and Status of Sanskrit: Contributions to the History of the Sanskrit Language*, ed. J.E.M. Houben, 197–248. Leiden: Brill, 1996.

Radhakrishna Sarma, M. *Temples of Telingana: The Architecture, Iconography, and Sculpture of the Calukya and Kakatiya Temples.* Hyderabad: Booklinks, 1972.

Rama Raju, B. 'Nebati Kṛṣṇayāmātyuḍu', in *Khutub Ṣāhī Sultānulu—Āndhra Saṃskṛti,* ed. B. Rama Raju, 97–112. Hyderabad: Idara-i Adabiyat-i Urdu, 1962.

Rea, Alexander. *Chalukyan Architecture: Including Examples from Bellary District, Madras Presidency.* Archaeological Survey of India, New Imperial Series, Vol. 21. Madras: Government Press, 1896.

Rice, John Henry. 'Image, Text, Monument: A Reexamination of the Philadelphia Brahma and "Later Cālukyan" Sculpture', *Artibus Asiae* 68, no. 2 (2008): 169–214.

Richards, John F. *Mughal Administration in Golconda.* Oxford: Clarendon Press, 1975.

Rogers, Clifford J., ed. *The Military Revolution Debate: Readings on the Military Transformation of Early Modern Europe.* Boulder: Westview, 1995.

Ross, E. Denison. 'The Portuguese in India and Arabia between 1507 and 1517', *Journal of the Royal Asiatic Society* 53, no. 1 (1921): 545–62.

Rubies, Joan Pau. *Travel and Ethnology in the Renaissance: South India through European Eyes, 1250–1625.* Cambridge: Cambridge University Press, 2000.

Sardar, Marika. *Golconda through Time: A Mirror of the Evolving Deccan.* PhD dissertation, New York University Institute of Fine Arts, 2007.

Schwartzberg, Joseph E. 'Cosmographical Mapping', in *The History of Cartography,* vol. 2, part 1: *Cartography in the Traditional Islamic and South Asian Societies*, eds J.B. Harley and David Woodward, 332–8. Chicago: University of Chicago Press, 1987.

Sears, Tamara I. 'Fortified Mathas and Fortress Mosques: The Transformation and Reuse of Hindu Monastic Sites in the Thirteenth and Fourteenth Centuries', *Archives of Asian Art* 59 (2009): 7–31.

Sewell, Robert. *A Forgotten Empire, Vijayanagara: A Contribution to the History of India.* 1900. Reprint, New Delhi: Publications Division, 1962.

Sharma, Sunil. *Persian Poetry at the Indian Frontier: Mas`ud Sa`d Salman of Lahore.* New Delhi: Permanent Black, 2000.

Sherwani, Haroon Khan. *The Bahmanis of the Deccan.* New Delhi: Munshiram Manoharlal, 1985.

———. *History of the Qutb Shahi Dynasty.* New Delhi: Munshiram Manoharlal, 1974.

———. 'The Identity of Shitab Khan of Warangal', *The Journal of the Pakistan Historical Society* 5 (October, 1957): 220–5.

———. *Muhammad Quli Qutb Shah: Founder of Hyderabad.* London: Asia Publishing House, 1967.

Sherwani, Haroon Khan and P.M. Joshi, eds. *History of Medieval Deccan, 1295–1724.* 2 vols. Hyderabad: Government of Andhra Pradesh, 1973.

Shokoohy, Mehrdad. *Muslim Architecture of South India: The Sultanate of Ma`bar and the Traditions of Maritime Settlers on the Malabar and Coromandel Coasts (Tamil Nadu, Kerala, and Goa).* London: Routledge Curzon, 2003.

Shokoohy, Mehrdad and Natalie H. Shokoohy, *Tughluqabad: A Paradigm for Indo-Islamic Urban Planning and Its Architectural Components.* London: Araxus Books, 2007.

Shorey, S.P. 'Hyderabad: Garden to a City', in *Golconda and Hyderabad*, ed. Shehbaz H. Safrani. Bombay: Marg, 1992.

Sinha, Ajay. *Imagining Architects: Creativity in the Religious Monuments of India.* Newark, DE: University of Delaware Press, 2000.

Sinopoli, Carla M. *The Political Economy of Craft Production: Crafting Empire in South India, c. 1350–1650*. Cambridge: Cambridge University Press, 2003.

Śivasundarēśvara Rāvu, Niḍudavōlu. 'Acca Tenugu Pāduṣā—Amīnu Khānu', in *Khutub Ṣāhī Sultānulu—Āndhra Saṃskṛti*, ed. B. Rama Raju, 128–33. Hyderabad: Idara-i Adabiyt-i Urdu, 1962.

Smith, Robert Douglas. 'Bronze Breech-loading Swivel Guns: a Preliminary Survey', in *A Farewell to Arms, Studies on the History of Arms and Armour*, eds Gert Groenendijk, Piet de Gryse, Dirk Staat, and Heleen Bronder, 166–81. Delft: Legermuseum, 2004.

———. 'The Technology of Wrought-Iron Artillery', *Royal Armouries Yearbook* 5 (2000): 68–79.

———. 'Towards a New Typology for Wrought Iron Ordnance', *International Journal of Nautical Archaeology and Underwater Exploration* 17, no. 1 (1988): 5–16.

Sridhara Babu, D. *Kingship, State, and Religion in South India According to South Indian Historical Biographies of Kings (Madhurāvijaya, Acyutarāyābhyudaya, and Vemabhūpālacarita*. Inaugural Dissertation, Georg-August-Universitat, Gottingen, 1975.

Subrahmanyam, Sanjay. *The Political Economy of Commerce: Southern India, 1500–1650*. Cambridge: Cambridge University Press, 1990.

Suguna Sarma, V. *History and Antiquities of Raichur Fort*. Delhi: Bharat Kala Prakashan, 1998.

Sundara, A. 'Traipuruṣa Dēvālayas in Inscriptions and Related Temples in Dharwad-Bijapur Region', in *Indian Epigraphy: Its Bearing on the History of Art*, eds Frederick M. Asher and G.S. Gai, 203–8. New Delhi: Oxford and IBH, 1985.

Talbot, Cynthia. *Precolonial India in Practice: Society, Region, and Identity in Medieval Andhra*. New York: Columbia University Press, 2001.

Tobert, Natalie. *Anegondi: Architectural Ethnography of a Royal Village*. Vijayanagara Research Project Monograph Series, Vol. 7. New Delhi: Manohar and AIIS, 2000.

Toy, Sidney. *The Strongholds of India*. London: William Heinemann Ltd., 1957.

Verghese, Anila. *Religious Traditions at Vijayanagara as Revealed through Its Monuments*. Vijayanagara Research Project Monograph Series, Vol. 4. New Delhi: Manohar and American Institute of Indian Studies, 1995.

Verma, B.D. *The Glories of Bijapur: A History of Its Remains*. India(?), 1964.

Wagoner, Phillip B. 'The Charminar as *Chaubara*: Cosmological Symbolism in the Urban Architecture of the Deccan', in *The Architecture of the Indian Sultanates*, eds Abha Narain Lambah and Alka Patel, 104–13. Mumbai: Marg Publications, 2006.

———. '"A Dense Epitome of the World": The Image of Warangal in the *Krīḍābhirāmamu*', afterword to Velcheru Narayana Rao and David Shulman, trans., *A Lover's Guide to Warangal: The* Krīḍābhirāmamu *by Vinukoṇḍa Vallabharāya*, 85–103. New Delhi: Permanent Black, 2002.

———. 'Fortuitous Convergences and Essential Ambiguities: Transcultural Political Elites in the Medieval Deccan', in *Surprising Bedfellows: Hindus and Muslims in Medieval and Early Modern India*, ed. Sushil Mittal, 31–54. Lanham, MD: Lexington Books, 2003.

———. 'From "Pampa's Crossing" to "The Place of Lord Virupaksa": Architecture, Cult, and Patronage at Hampi before the Founding of Vijayanagara', in *Vijayanagara: Progress of Research, 1988–1991*, eds D. Devaraj and C.S. Patil, 141–74. Mysore: Directorate of Archaeology and Museums, 1996.

———. 'Kannada *kalla upparige* "Stone Palace": Multi-storeyed Entrance Pavilions in Pre- and Early-Vijayanagara Architecture', *Ars Orientalis* 31(2001): 167–83.

———. 'The Multiple Worlds of Amin Khan: Crossing Persianate and Indic Cultural Boundaries in Qutb Shahi Andhra', in *Sultans of the South: Arts of India's Deccan Courts,*

*1323–1687*, eds Navina Haidar and Marika Sardar, 90–101. New York and New Haven: Metropolitan Museum of Art and Yale University Press, 2011.

Wagoner, Phillip B. 'Retrieving the Chalukyan Past: The Politics of Architectural Reuse in Sixteenth-Century Deccan', *South Asian Studies* 23 (2007): 1–29.

———. 'Retrieving the Chalukyan Past: The Stepped Tank in the Royal Centre', in *South India under Vijayanagara: Art and Archaeology*, eds Anila Verghese and Anna Dallapiccola, 118–35. New Delhi: Oxford University Press, 2011.

———. '"Sultan among Hindu Kings": Dress, Titles, and the Islamicization of Hindu Culture at Vijayanagara', *Journal of Asian Studies* 55, no. 4 (November 1996): 851–80.

———. *Tidings of the King: A Translation and Ethnohistorical Analysis of the* Rayavacakamu. Honolulu: University of Hawaii Press, 1993.

Wagoner, Phillip B. and John Henry Rice, 'From Delhi to the Deccan: Newly Discovered Tughluq Monuments at Warangal-Sultanpur and the Beginnings of Indo-Islamic Architecture in the Deccan', *Artibus Asiae* LXI, no. 1(2001): 84–106.

Warder, A.K. *An Introduction to Indian Historiography.* Bombay: Popular Prakashan, 1972.

Weinstein, Laura. 'Variations on a Persian Theme: Adaptation and Incorporation of Persian Painting at the 16th Century Court of Golconda', in *The Visual World of Muslim India: The Art, Culture, and Society of the Deccan in the Early Modern Era*, ed. Laura Parodi. London: I.B. Tauris, forthcoming.

Welch, Anthony and Howard Crane. 'The Tughluqs: Master Builders of the Delhi Sultanate', *Muqarnas* 1 (1983): 123–66.

Yazdani, Ghulam. *Bidar: Its History and Monuments.* London: Oxford University Press, 1947.

———, ed. *The Early History of the Deccan*, Parts VII–XI. London: Oxford University Press, 1960.

# Index

# About the Authors

**Richard M. Eaton** is professor of history at the University of Arizona, Tucson. His research focusses on the social and cultural history of pre-modern India (1000–1800), especially on the range of historical interactions between Iran and India, and on Islam in South Asia. He has published several books on the social roles of Sufis (Muslim mystics) in the Indian sultanate of Bijapur (1300–1700), the growth of Islam in Bengal (1204–1760), and the social history of the Deccan from 1300 to 1761. His publications include *Social History of the Deccan, 1300–1761: Eight Indian Lives* (2005); *The Rise of Islam and the Bengal Frontier, 1204–1760* (1993); *India's Islamic Traditions, 711–1750* (ed., 2002); *Essays on Islam and Indian History* (2000); *Sufis of Bijapur, 1300–1700: Social Roles of Sufis in Medieval India* (1978).

**Phillip B. Wagoner** is professor of art history and professor in the archaeology programme at Wesleyan University in Connecticut. His research focusses on the cultural history of the Deccan region of southern India, primarily in the late medieval and early modern periods (1200–1600). He is particularly interested in the historical interactions between the region's established Indic culture and the Persianate culture that arrived with the Delhi Sultanate in the early fourteenth century. He is the author of *Tidings of the King: A Translation and Ethnohistorical Analysis of the Rayavacakamu* (1993) and, with George Michell, of *Vijayanagara: Architectural Inventory of the Sacred Centre* (2001). He has also published numerous articles relating to architecture, urbanism, and elite culture at the courts of Vijayanagara and Deccan Sultanates.